Brazilian Cinema

Brazilian Cinema

Expanded Edition

Randal Johnson and Robert Stam,
Editors

Columbia University Press

New York

Morningside Edition

Chapter 36 originally appeared in *Iris: A Journal of Theory of Image and Sound* 13 (Summer 1991).

Library of Congress Cataloging-in-Publication Data
Main entry under title:

Brazilian cinema / Randal Johnson and Robert Stam.—Expanded ed.,
   Morningside ed.
     p. cm.
   Includes bibliographical references and index.
   ISBN 978-0-231-10267-4 (pbk. : alk. paper)
    1. Motion pictures—Brazil. I. Johnson, Randal, 1948– .
II. Stam, Robert, 1941– .
PN1993.5.B6B7   1995
791.43′0981—dc20   95–18447

Printed in the United States of America

Contents

Dedicated to **PAULO EMILIO SALLES GOMES** (1916–1977)
for all he has done to preserve the Brazilian cinematic memory.

Preface

Despite appearances, this book—the first to appear in English on Brazilian cinema—is not an anthology. We have made no attempt to "anthologize" the best that has been written on the subject; there is no mention, for example, of the important work of U.S. critics such as Ernest Callenbach, Joan Dassin, Thomas Kavanaugh, and Bill Van Wert, or French critics René Gardies, Michel Esteve, Louis Marcorelles, and Marie-Claire Ropars-Wuilleumier. Rather, the book was conceived and developed as a collective project by Brazilian and American scholars. With the exception of the documents section (Part II), most of the material was written expressly for this volume. The contributors share, within the limits of ideological nuance and personality differences, a common view of Brazilian cinema. The book constitutes, in this sense, a mosaic, where each contribution helps to complete the whole.

Our title, *Brazilian Cinema*, is, in one sense, misleading. We have not spoken, and could not possibly speak, of Brazilian cinema in its entirety. We focus, rather, on a certain critical Brazilian cinema, and especially on that cinema made after 1960. Even in this period, however, the book omits major trends and figures. To name only a few: Walter Hugo Khoury, a prolific *cineaste* often described as the "Brazilian Bergman"; Amâncio Mazzaropi, undoubtedly the most popular (in box office terms) figure in Brazilian cinema; José Mojica Marins (Zé do Caixão), Brazil's answer to George Romero, a specialist in a kind of cannibalistic sub-genre of the horror film; and the entire *pornochanchada* genre, erotic comedies that make up a substantial share of Brazilian cinema today.

This book is also not impartial for we are enthusiastic about Brazilian cinema and passionately concerned about its future. Furthermore, we find the "neutrality" of most film histories and anthologies to be highly suspect. A typical "neutral" film history published in the United States, for example, frequently ignores or pays mere lip service to Brazilian or other Third World cinemas. At the same time, it is not our intention to idealize Brazilian cinema, which is not immune to class conflict and personal quarrel. For this reason, many of the articles form part of a debate concerning the direction of that cinema.

We have attempted to avoid unnecessary repetitions. In order to complete the mosaic, we collaborated as much as possible with the writers of the articles. In the case of translations, we often worked with the authors so as not to lose the nuances of their language or the fine points of their arguments. All translations, by the way, were done by ourselves except when otherwise indicated.

After first reference, titles are given in English for films in distribution in the United States, except those, like *Macunaíma*, *São Bernardo*, and *Vidas Secas*, which are known by their original titles.

Acknowledgments

We would like to thank all of the contributors for their enthusiastic participation in this project. Special thanks are due as well to Fabiano Canosa, who has been involved in the book from its conception and who provided us not only with stills and written material, but also set up invaluable contacts. We would also like to thank the following persons and institutions for their suggestions and assistance (in alphabetical order): Bertrand Augst, Luis Carlos Barreto, Julianne Burton, Elenice de Castro, Luiz Antonio Coelho, Suzanne Fedak, Jairo Ferreira, Maria José Castro Ferreira, Luis Fernando Goulart, Aparecida de Godoy Johnson, Sérgio Cláudio Lima, Sérgio Muniz, Gilda Penteado, Nelson Penteado, Jair Leal Piantino, José Antônio Pinheiro, Francisco Ramalho Jr., Carlos Roberto Rodrigues de Souza, João Carlos Rodrigues, João Silvério Trevisan, Embrafilme, Escola de Comunicações e Artes da Universidade de São Paulo, Cinemateca do Museu de Arte Moderna (Rio de Janeiro), Museu de Imagem e Som (São Paulo), the Museu Lasar Segall (São Paulo), and the editors of *Jump Cut*. All previously published material used by permission. Marsha Kinder's *Tent of Miracles*, published originally in *Film Quarterly* 31, no. 4 (Summer 1978), copyright Board of Regents, University of California. For photographs, we are indebted to New Yorker Films, New Line Cinema, Embrafilme, Unifilm, the Cinemateca de São Paulo, and the Cinemateca do Museu de Arte Moderna (Rio de Janeiro). Finally, we would like to thank Terrence M. Donovan and Anne Hebenstreit, our editors, for their many helpful suggestions.

Brazilian Cinema

Part I

The Shape of Brazilian Film History

Looking at Brazilian cinema for an American is like looking into a distorting mirror. The image is familiar enough to reassure but alien enough to fascinate. Brazil seems familiar because it is the New World country that most strikingly resembles the United States in both its historical formation and its ethnic composition. Both countries began as colonies of European states—Great Britain and Portugal. In both countries there ensued a conquest of vast territories that involved the near-genocidal subjugation of Amerindian peoples. Both countries massively imported slaves from Africa, and both abolished the institution of slavery in the latter half of the nineteenth century. Both received waves of immigration from all over the world, ultimately forming pluri-ethnic societies with substantial Indian, black, Japanese, German, Italian, Slavic, and Jewish communities.

Brazilian cultural history is marked by the same struggle for independence from Europe that characterizes the American experience. Ralph Waldo Emerson's "American Scholar" address, which Oliver Wendell Holmes called our "intellectual Declaration of Independence," came only a year after a similar declaration by Brazilian poet Gonçalves de Magalhães. Both countries witnessed a literary struggle between what Marcus Cunliffe calls "palefaces," European-oriented writers like Henry James in the United States and Machado de Assis in Brazil, and "redskins," aggressively native artists like Mark Twain and Walt Whitman in the United States and Mário de Andrade in Brazil.

The crucial difference between the American and Brazilian historical experience derives from the fact that in the United States formal political independence led to real economic independence, while in Brazil formal independence from Portugal led only to British free-trade imperialism in the nineteenth century and to American domination in the twentieth. No intelligent discussion of Brazil's cultural production can ignore the central fact of its economic dependency. The specific forms of this dependency are inevitably shaped by the characteristics of the international economic system and by Brazil's function within it. Brazil's "underdevelopment" is structurally linked to the development of the nations that have successively dominated it. At the international level, na-

Poster for *Paz e Amor* (1910)

tions have become stratified in a global economy whose basic characteristic is the penetration of underdeveloped economies by developed countries through the extractive, manufacturing, commercial, and financial sectors. Within this international system, Brazil has always been economically vulnerable, dependent on decisions made in metropolitan centers of power. Brazilian economic history has been marked by periodic booms — sugar, gold, rubber, cacao, coffee — that have enriched foreigners (Robinson Crusoe, we might recall, makes his fortune from a sugar *engenho* in Brazil) and a native elite, but have not, by and large, benefitted the mass of the Brazilian people. More recent tendencies, especially the emergence of the multinational corporations, have served only to deepen this historical deformation of the Brazilian economy.

The political and economic realities of dependency inevitably condition the nature of Brazilian cultural production. The existing global distribution of power makes the First World nations of the West cultural "transmitters" while it reduces Brazil and other Third World countries to "receivers." The flow of sounds and images tends to be unidirectional. Thus while Brazil is inundated with North American cultural products — from television series and Hollywood films to best-sellers — Americans receive precious little of the vast Brazilian cultural production. While American films are seen daily throughout Brazil,

Brazilian films do not reach their potential audience in the United States or even within Brazil itself.

This non-reciprocity applies equally to television programming. For the hundreds of American films shown on Brazilian television, only a handful of Brazilian films are shown. This disproportion does not derive, as one might naively assume, from a lack of quality Brazilian films—national films could supply all channels for years on end. The problem is rather an economic one; it is more profitable for Brazilian programmers to screen American films and television series in which American media stars speak fluent dubbed Portuguese than to produce their own programs. American films, having already covered their costs on the domestic market, are profitably "dumped" on Brazil at very low prices. Foreign films, as a result, literally prevent Brazilian films from reaching the television screen.

Given this one-way flow of sounds, images, and information, many Americans conclude, not irrationally, that those cultures of which the media seldom speak must be without merit or interest. This conclusion strikes us as unfortunate. It deprives Americans of the rich experience of one of the most culturally vital and formally innovative cinemas in the world. Our purpose, therefore, is to provide some of the cultural and cinematic background necessary for appreciating Brazilian cinema in depth and in its context. To do that, it is necessary to know where Brazilian cinema comes from. What is its history?

The Early Years

Every cinematic tradition has its own intertext. Every film is part of a text larger than itself; each film is a discourse responding to other discourses; each film answers and echoes those that have preceded it. To appreciate current Brazilian films, it is important to know the tradition from which they spring. Since Brazilian cinema became internationally famous through Cinema Novo, it is especially important to know that much came *before* Cinema Novo and that much has come *since* Cinema Novo.

Brazilian cinema did not begin with *O Pagador de Promessas* ("The Given Word," 1962), the film that won First Prize at Cannes, nor with *Black Orpheus* (1958)—that film is French—or *O Cangaceiro* (1953), double prize-winner at Cannes and distributed in twenty-two countries, nor with the films of Carmen Miranda in the thirties. Cinema reached Brazil only six months after Lumière revealed his *cinématographe* in Paris in late 1895. The first screening of what was called the "omnigraph" was held in Rio de Janeiro on 8 July 1896. Italo-Brazilian Affonso Segreto introduced the first filmmaking equipment in 1898. During the next few years he filmed public ceremonies, festivals, Presidential outings, and other local scenes and events. Although initially greeted with fascination and amazement, cinematic spectacle did not become a

O Guarani (1916)

widespread and stable form of entertainment until several years later. The delay, as Paulo Emílio Salles Gomes points out, was due to underdevelopment in electricity, even in the national capital. When energy was industrialized in Rio de Janeiro, exhibition halls "proliferated like mushrooms."[1] Brazilian exhibitors resolved to make their own films on national topics to supply these halls.

From 1900 to 1912, Brazilian films dominated the internal market, reaching an annual production of over one hundred films. Documentaries and newsreels, made with amazing rapidity and dealing with current events of local interest, fostered a public habit of frequent movie going. Segreto himself strengthened such domination by producing, toward the middle of the decade, filmic re-creations of notorious local crimes, rather like our own *The Great Train Robbery* (Edwin S. Porter, 1903). The first widely popular Brazilian film was Antônio Leal's 1908 reconstruction of just such a criminal incident, entitled *Os Estranguladores* ("The Stranglers"). 1908 was, in fact, a year of intense filmmaking activity in Brazil and marks the beginning of what has since been called the *Bela Época*, or Golden Age, of Brazilian cinema. [2] During that year, Leal made another crime film—*A Mala Sinistra* ("The Sinister Suitcase")—about a murderer who dispatched the corpse of his victim to Europe in a suitcase. The year also saw the release of the first Brazilian comedy, *Nhô Anastácio Chegou de Viagem* ("Mr. Anastácio Arrived From a Trip"), starring the well-known comedian Leonardo, as well as the first film about Brazil's national obsession, soccer. During the final years of the decade, filmmakers, under a vertically integrated system of production, distribution, and exhibition, produced a wide variety of genres. Sung films (performed by singers from behind the screen, much as in *Singin' in the Rain*) drew on both the Brazilian and the international repertoire. An adaptation of Carlos Gomes's opera *O Guarani* was filmed in four parts, and numerous versions of the immensely popular *The Merry Widow* appeared, one of which, apparently, was somewhat risqué. Carnival films like *O Cordão* ("Carnival Merrymakers") and *Pela Vitória dos Clubes Carnavalescos* ("For the Victory of the Carnival Clubs") had a wide following, as did historical dramas (*Inês de Castro*) and adaptations of national and international literary classics (*Uncle Tom's Cabin*). But by far the most popular film of the *Bela Época* was the satirical musical review *Paz de Amor* ("Peace and Love"; Alberto Botelho, 1910). The film was a light-hearted critique of national politics and social mores of Rio de Janeiro. It deals with the life of a fantasy king, Olin I, a barely disguised anagram of the name of Brazi''s new president, Nilo Peçanha, who, in his inaugural address, declared that he would rule with peace and love (whence the title). Based on a story by Patrocínio Filho, the film easily surpassed all other films, both foreign and national, in popularity. The

Lia Jardim in *Morfina* (1927)

success of this film and others, interestingly, was initially limited to the Brazilian upper-classes, unlike the situation in Europe and the United States where cinema immediately became a lower-class diversion. Maintained and subsidized by wealthy and well-traveled members of Brazil's urban elite, cinema was first seen as a sign of status and class. Only later, with increased urbanization and industrialization, did it become a form of mass entertainment.

In 1911 a group of North American businessmen, received with open arms by Rio de Janeiro dignitaries, went to investigate the exploitability of the Brazilian market. By that time North American cinema had organized itself as an international industry, and the takeover of the Brazilian market was easily achieved. No one, it seems, had thought of rendering the importation of foreign films difficult in order to protect the budding national industry. The *Bela Época* ended as Brazilian films were forced off the screens by North American and European products. The foreign film became the standard by which all films were to be judged, thus rendering problematic the exhibition of the less technically polished Brazilian product. Since local distributors lacked the infrastructural organization possessed by foreign distributors, the internal market began to function for the benefit of the industrial products from abroad. From that point on, when forced to choose between the guaranteed profit of inexpensive foreign films that covered costs easily in their home market, and the risks involved in dealing with the national product, exhibitors tended to opt for the foreign film. The Brazilian market became a tropical appendage of the North American market. The bulk of local production came to consist of documentaries and newsreels, a form of production that, as Jean-Claude Bernardet pointed out, has been neglected by Brazilian film historians due to a questionable and highly ideological privileging of the feature fiction film.

There were, of course, individual filmmakers who produced fiction films in the face of foreign domination. In Rio de Janeiro, Luis de Barros adapted classic works of Brazilian literature, specifically a series of Romantic novels: *A Viuvinha* ("The Little Widow," 1914), *Iracema* (1917), and *Ubirajara* (1919), all based on works by the romantic writer José de Alencar. In the Italian working-class districts of São Paulo, meanwhile, Gilberto Rossi and other immigrants were creating an embryonic infrastructure for the production of features by making newsreels, documentaries, and commercial and political propaganda films. From this group arose the *Escola de Artes Cinematográficas Azzurri* ("The Azzurri School of Cinematic Arts"), the first of a number of such schools that spread throughout Brazil. After thus training filmmakers and technicians, Rossi and his partners began making fiction films of great vitality and interest. Together with José Medina, Rossi made a social drama, *Exemplo Regenerador* ("Redeeming Example," 1919), a commercial success that led them to make other films of the same kind, including the "photo-drama" *Perversidade* ("Perversity," 1921), an "amus-

22

Mário Peixoto's *Limite* (1930)

ing São Paulo comedy," *Carlitinhos* (1921), and *A Culpa dos Outros* ("The Fault of Others," 1922), a "cine-drama which shows how far a man can be degraded by alcohol." But the real triumph of Rossi and Medina was *Fragmentos da Vida* ("Fragments of Life," 1929), based on an O. Henry short story and their only studio production. Erich von Stroheim reportedly praised the film when he saw it at the Fourth Centennial Celebration of the City of São Paulo. Largely blocked, however, in its in-dustrial development, stifled by foreign commercial and cultural domination, Brazilian cinema in the twenties evolved primarily in regional cycles, often far removed from the busy urban capitals. Film cycles developed in Rio Grande do Sul (in the extreme south), Recife (northeast), Manaus (on the Amazon), Cataguases (Minas Gerais), and Campinas (interior of the state of São Paulo).

The Brazilian films of the twenties and early thirties betrayed a wide range of foreign influences. Eugênio Centenaro, an Italo-Brazilian, renamed himself E. C. Kerrigan and made ersatz westerns whose characters bore names like Bill and Tom. Often the influence took the form of parody, a mode that expressed the ambivalence Brazilians felt toward foreign films. Luis de Barros parodied Ramon Novarro's *The Pagan* (in Portuguese, *O Pagão*, 1929) in *O Babão* ("The Idiot," 1930). Parody articulated the mingled affection and resentment with which Brazilians regarded the success of foreign films. Through parody, Brazilian filmmakers could make fun of foreign films, laugh at their own inability to emulate their glossy production values, and indirectly capitalize on their success. After the Carlos Manga spoofs of *High Noon* and *Samson and Delilah* in the fifties, more recent films have parodied *King Kong* and *Jaws* (see article by João Luiz Vieira in this volume).

The influence of the European avant-garde also made itself felt in a number of Brazilian films. Adalberto Kemeny and Rodolfo Lustig made *São Paulo: Sinfonia de uma Metrópole* ("São Paulo: Symphony of a Metropolis," 1929) in transparent homage to European city-symphony films like Walter Ruttmann's *Berlin, Die Symphonie Einer Grossstadt* ("Berlin: Symphony of a Great City," 1927) and Alberto Cavalcânti's *Rien que les Heures* (1926). One avant-garde film, Mário Peixoto's *Limite* ("Limit," 1930), although initially seen by very few people, acquired the status of a myth as *the* Brazilian experimental film. Only eighteen when he made the film, Peixoto was widely conversant with European avant-garde cinema. His film, which Eisenstein called a "work of genius," developed a technique of multiple narration and experimented with duration and montage as well as with subjective camera movement. (See Robert Stam's article on Brazilian avant-garde cinema in this volume.)

The most important filmmaker to emerge in this period was undoubtedly Humberto Mauro. French film historian Georges Sadoul calls Mauro "a great cinéaste," a "pioneer of Latin American film art," who will one day "impose himself internationally as a master of cinema."[3] Glauber Rocha cites Mauro as the most important precursor of Cinema Novo, while underground filmmaker Rogério Sganzerla finds in his "in-

São Paulo: Symphony of a Metropolis (1929)

expensive, direct, and ludic" films an antecedent for the low-budget avant-garde films of the late sixties.[4] Although influenced by foreign films, Mauro was felicitously unsuccessful in his attempts at imitation, thanks to what Salles Gomes calls the Brazilian "creative incapacity for copying." At the same time, Mauro was aware of the need for a specifically Brazilian cinema:

> Cinema here in Brazil will have to emerge from our Brazilian milieu, with all its qualities and defects. . . .If American cinema already accustomed us to the luxuriousness and the variety of its productions, it has not yet robbed us of our natural enthusiasm for the faithful representation of everything we are or that we wish to be.[5]

Mauro's first film, *Valadião, O Cratera* (1925), was inspired by the Pearl White serials and by Thomas Ince westerns. Mauro's camera follows a band of desperadoes through the mountains of Minas Gerais. After kidnapping a young girl, the thieves are brought to justice and the girl is saved. His next film, *Na Primavera da Vida* ("In the Spring of Life," 1926) reportedly shows traces of American avant-garde films from the teens and twenties, and treats the social problems connected with bootleg rum. Mauro was extremely impressed by Griffith's *Broken Blossoms* (1919) and Henry King's *Tol'able David* (1921), and the influence of both directors is obvious in *Tesouro Perdido* ("Lost Treasure," 1927). After seeing Ruttmann's *Berlin, Die Symphonie Einer Grossstadt* (1927) Mauro made a similar film about his native Cataguases. *Sangue Mineiro* ("Minas Blood," 1930) represents a transition between Mauro's work in Minas Gerais and his subsequent work in Rio de Janeiro since it includes sequences filmed in both places. *Ganga Bruta* ("Brutal Gang," 1933),

Humberto Mauro's *Sangue Mineiro* (1929)

Mauro's masterpiece, deeply impressed the future Cinema Novo directors who saw it at a 1961 Retrospective. The film creatively melds the cinematic styles of expressionism and Soviet montage in a story about a man who kills his bride on the honeymoon and then attempts to rebuild his life. In *Favela dos Meus Amores* ("Favela of My Loves," 1934), Mauro went into the favelas of Rio de Janeiro to record the everyday life and songs of the people there. He said of the film: "I simply grabbed life in the favelas as it was. I documented it." When asked if he saw himself as a precursor of Neo-Realism, Mauro replied: "What is Neo-Realism? Isn't it simply realism?"[6]

A wave of optimism swept Brazilian film circles with the advent of sound. Foreign cinema, no longer understood by Brazilian audiences, would, it was thought, simply self-destruct. Impelled by such naive optimism, producer-director Adhemar Gonzaga founded the Cinédia Studios and invited Mauro to direct its first production, *Lábios sem Beijos* ("Lips without Kisses," 1930). It was the American, Wallace Downey, ironically, who made the first commercially successful sound film, *Coisas Nossas* ("Our Things," 1931). The thirties also witnessed the birth of a very Brazilian genre: the *chanchada*. Partially modelled on American musicals (and particularly on the "radio-broadcast" musicals) of the same

Aurora and Carmen Miranda in *Alô, Alô Carnaval* (1936)

period, but with roots as well in the Brazilian comic theater and in the "sung films" about carnival, the *chanchada* typically features musical and dance numbers often woven around a backstage plot. *Chanchada* as such begins with sound and especially with Adhemar Gonzaga's *Alô, Alô, Brasil* (1935) and *Alô, Alô, Carnaval* (1936), both of which featured Carmen Miranda, already quite popular from radio performances and records. Shortly thereafter, Carmen Miranda went to Hollywood, where her energy was exploited by the Fox machine. "Once again," Brazilian historian Carlos Roberto de Sousa wryly remarks, "we furnished raw material for North American industry."[7] Carmen Miranda was enlisted in Hollywood's campaign to attract the Latin American audience, the only strong foreign market left after the closure of Europe. Musical after musical was set in Brazil or Argentina to provide the proper setting for the Brazilian Bombshell. (See the article by Sérgio Augusto in this volume.)

Hundreds of *chanchadas* dominated Brazilian film production throughout the late thirties, forties, and fifties. Although they fostered an idealized and inconsequential image of Brazilians, crystallized in a perpetually playful Rio de Janeiro, the *chanchadas* had the virtue of establishing an authentic link between Brazilians and their cinema. With the crescent popularity of television in the late fifties, the *chanchadas* lost their broad popular appeal, although there are traces of the genre in Andrade's *Macunaíma* (1969) and Diegues's *Quando O Carnaval Chegar* ("When Carnival Comes," 1971), not to mention the *chanchada*'s debased offspring, the *pornochanchada*.

Women have made an extremely important contribution to Brazilian cinema, not only as actresses but also as directors and producers. Carmen Santos, for example, began as an actress in *Urutau* (1919) but already in the twenties was producing her own films. In the early thirties she founded her own studio — Brasil Vita Filme — under the technical direction of Humberto Mauro. In 1948 she produced, scripted, and directed *Inconfidência Mineira* ("Conspiracy in Minas"), in which she was also the principal actress. During the same period, Gilda de Abreu contributed her astonishingly diverse talents — songwriter, popular and operatic singer, actress, scriptwriter, director and producer. In 1946 she scripted, directed, and co-produced *O Ébrio* ("The Drunkard"), an immensely popular melodrama of which 500 copies — a Brazilian record — were made. (See article by Elice Munerato and Maria Helena Darcy de Oliveira in this volume.)

In the late nineteen-forties, a group linked to São Paulo's industrial bourgeoisie and led by Francisco Matarazzo Sobrinho, inspired by the commercial success of the *chanchada*, but scorning what they saw as that genre's "vulgarity," founded the Vera Cruz film company. Its studios were modelled on the Metro-Goldwyn-Mayer Studios at a time when the studio system in Hollywood itself was beginning to decline. Brazilian-born Alberto Cavalcânti came to direct the organization, but left before it went bankrupt in 1954. Vera Cruz produced eighteen feature films, the

Gilda de Abreu's *O Ébrio*

most famous of which was Lima Barreto's *O Cangaceiro* (1953), double prize winner at Cannes and a world-wide success that was distributed in some twenty-two countries.

The films of Vera Cruz realized, in a sense, a long cherished goal of many Brazilian filmmakers: a level of artistic quality equal to that of Europe or the United States. Through their themes, genres, and production values they achieved the "look" of First World dominant cinema. They adopted the full panoply of conventional devices: sophisticated sets, classical framing, elaborate lighting, fluid cutting and camera movement, dissolves for passage of time and so on. In many films, the physiognomies of the actors, the decor, the costumes, and the music were calculated to evoke an European ambiance. Blond actresses like Eliane Lage crystalized this ideal. The "period" biography of composer Zequinha de Abreu, *Tico-Tico no Fubá*, for example, recalls the atmosphere of *fin de sièle* Europe more than it evokes rural Brazil in the twenties. *Sinhá Moça*, although it adopts a novel by Maria Dezzone Pacheco Fernandes, resembles the psychological dramas of an Ibsen, in accord with the elitist choice of texts by the Brazilian Comedy Theatre, the theatrical counterpart to the Vera Cruz studios.

Although Vera Cruz improved the technical level of Brazilian cinema, it made many serious errors. Too ambitious, it aimed at conquering the world market before consolidating the Brazilian market. In order to reach the international market, it naively left distribution in the hands of Columbia Pictures, an organization more interested in promoting its own films than in fostering a vital Brazilian industry. Most important, Vera Cruz was flawed in its very conception, an attempt to create First World cinema in a Third World country. A tropical Hollywood, it set up an expensive and luxurious system with contract stars and directors, but

Ângela (1952): a Vera Cruz production

without the economic infrastructure on which to base such a system. It imitated Hollywood in everything except its financial success. Finally, in its attempt to create a "classy" cinema with glossy production values, it completely ignored the tastes, interests, and real situation of the Brazilian people. The elitist class values of Vera Cruz would be subsequently swept away by Cinema Novo.

Even after the death of Vera Cruz, however, São Paulo continued to produce films of value. Alberto Cavalcânti, for example, made three films in Brazil after leaving the directorship of Vera Cruz: *Simão O Caolho* ("One-Eyed Simon," 1952), *Canto do Mar* ("Song of the Sea," 1954), a remake of his French-made *En Rade* (1927), and *Mulher de Verdade* ("A True Woman," 1954). The production company Brasil Filmes took over Vera Cruz's defunct studios and made several films of various genres: comedies such as *O Gato de Madame* ("The Madame's Cat," 1956), starring Mazzaropi, and *Osso, Amor e Papagaios* ("Bones, Love and Parrots," 1957), based on Lima Barreto's short story "A Nova Califórnia"; psychological dramas (Walter Hugo Khoury's *Estranho Encontro* — "Strange Encounter" — 1958, and Rubem Biáfora's *Ravina*, 1958); and literary adaptations of works by such authors as Érico Veríssimo and José de Alencar. Known for its "serious" films (in contrast to the frivolity of Rio's *chanchadas*), São Paulo production of the period also included films that dealt, at least indirectly, with social problems, such as Osvaldo Sampaio's *A Estrada* ("The Highway," 1957), which deals with the lives of truckdrivers in the interior of the state, and Galileu Garcia's *Cara de Fogo* ("Face of Fire," 1958), about the violence and prejudice faced by a family as it attempts to build a new life in a rural community.

Cinema Novo

Cinema Novo (and similar movements in theater and popular music) grew out of a process of cultural renovation that began in the early fifties and was strengthened with the election of Juscelino Kubitschek as president in 1955. The period of his presidency was somewhat atypical in terms of the general tendencies of Brazilian political life since the Revolution of 1930 when Getúlio Vargas took power, atypical, especially, in its relative stability. Kubitschek was the only civilian president in the 1930–1964 period to remain legally in office throughout his designated term. His administration, characterized by economic expansion and industrialization, was stable for several reasons but primarily because he managed to unite the Brazilian people behind a common ideology: developmentalism.

Developmentalist ideology was, by its nature, riddled with contradictions. A powerful catalyst for popular mobilization, it was also an effective way of controlling and defusing social and political conflict. The government fanned nationalist sentiment, but at the same time based its economic policy on foreign investment. The administration's open-handed generosity to foreign investors increasingly alienated the left, and the end of Kubitschek's presidency was marked by vocal opposition from many sectors. By 1959, virtually all governmental crises revolved around economic questions such as inflation — one result of developmentalist policies — and the role of foreign capital in the nation's economy. The middle class became increasingly politicized, and power became consolidated in the hands of the industrial bourgeoisie. In the northeast, Peasant Leagues led by Francisco Julião pressed for agrarian reform.[8]

We are dealing, then, with a period of apparent economic expansion based on foreign investment, a period of political militancy, strong nationalist sentiments, and increasing social polarization. The Kubitschek years and the early sixties were essentially optimistic; Brazil, it was felt, was on the verge of escaping underdevelopment. The ultra-modern architecture of Brasília symbolizes the euphoric mentality of the period. The optimism and nationalism of the period continued through the 1960 election of Jânio Quadros, his resignation after less than seven months in office, and the presidency of João Goulart until the 1964 military coup that brutally unmasked an already existing structural crisis.

For the purposes of this general overview, we will break down the Cinema Novo movement into several phases, each corresponding to a specific period of Brazilian political life. After a preparatory period running roughly from 1954 to 1960, we see three main phases: a first phase going from 1960 to 1964, the date of the first *coup d'état*; from 1964 to

30

Nelson Pereira dos Santos's *Rio Quarenta Graus* (1955)

Anselmo Duarte's *The Given Word* (1962)

1968, the date of the second *coup*-within-the-*coup*; and from 1968 to 1972. After 1972, it becomes increasingly difficult to speak of Cinema Novo; one must speak, rather, of Brazilian Cinema. The period leading up to the present is marked by esthetic pluralism under the auspices of the state organ Embrafilme. While such *a posteriori* divisions are artificial and problematic, they are also broadly useful, because they illustrate the inseparable connection between political struggle and cultural production. While on one level Cinema Novo remained faithful to its initial project — to present a progressive and critical vision of Brazilian society — on another, its political strategies and esthetic options were profoundly inflected by political events.

The first signs of a new awakening in Brazilian cinema occurred several years before the official beginnings of the movement, coinciding, ironically, with the bankruptcy of the Vera Cruz Studios. Although Brazilian cinema, out of economic necessity, had always been predominantly nonindustrial in its form of production, in the post–Vera Cruz period filmmakers began opting for independent, artisan forms as a matter of esthetic and political choice. Alex Viany's *Agulha no Palheiro* ("Needle in the Haystack," 1953) attempted for the first time to put the lessons of Italian Neo-Realism into practice in Brazil: films made in natural settings with non-professional actors, popular themes, and a simple, straightforward cinematic language. Even more important was Nelson Pereira dos Santos's *Rio 40 Graus* ("Rio 40 Degrees"). By its independent production and critical stance toward established social structures, this film marked a decisive step toward a new kind of cinema. It is difficult to overestimate the contribution of Nelson Pereira dos Santos to Brazilian cinema. His practical contribution to the formation of Cinema Novo includes, besides *Rio 40 Graus*, the film *Rio Zona Norte* ("Rio Northern Zone," 1957), the production of Roberto Santos's *O Grande Momento* ("The Great Moment," 1958) and the editing of several early Cinema Novo films like Rocha's *Barravento* (1962) and Leon Hirszman's *Pedreira de São Diogo* ("São Diogo Quarry," 1961), which was incorporated into the feature length *Cinco Vezes Favela* ("Favela Five Times," 1961), an early landmark of Cinema Novo produced by the leftist Popular Center of Culture of the National Students' Union. More important, dos Santos became a kind of generous presiding spirit, the "conscience," in Glauber Rocha's words, of Cinema Novo.

The initial phase of Cinema Novo extends from 1960 to 1964, including films completed or near completion when the military overthrew João Goulart on 1 April 1964. It is in this period that Cinema Novo cohered as a movement, that it made its first feature films and formulated its political and esthetic ideas. The journal *Metropolitano* of the Metropolitan Students' Union became a forum for critics like David Neves and Sérgio Augusto and for filmmakers like Rocha and Diegues. The directors shared their opposition to commercial Brazilian cinema, to Hollywood films and Hollywood esthetics, and to Brazilian cinema's col-

Glauber Rocha's *Barravento* (1962)

onization by Hollywood distribution chains. In their desire to make independent non-industrial films, they drew on two foreign models: Italian Neo-Realism, for its use of non-actors and location shooting, and the French New Wave, not so much for its thematics or esthetics, but rather as a production strategy. While scornful of the politics of the New Wave—"We were making political films when the New Wave was still talking about unrequited love," Carlos Diegues once said—they borrowed its strategy of low-budget indepedently produced films based on the talent of specific *auteurs*. Most important, these directors saw filmmaking as political praxis, a contribution to the struggle against neo-colonialism. Rather than exploit the tropical paradise conviviality of *chanchada*, or the just-like-Europe classiness of Vera Cruz, the Cinema Novo directors searched out the dark corners of Brazilian life—its *favelas* and its *sertão*—the places where Brazil's social contradictions appeared most dramatically.

The most important films of the first phase of Cinema Novo include *Cinco Vezes Favela*; the short *Arraial do Cabo* (1960) and the feature *Porto das Caixas* (1962) by Paulo César Saraceni; *Barravento* (1962) and *Deus e o Diabo na Terra do Sol* ("Black God, White Devil," 1964), by Glauber Rocha; *Os Cafajestes* ("The Hustlers," 1962) and *Os Fuzis* ("The Guns," 1964), by Mozambican-born Rui Guerra; *Ganga Zumba* (1963), by Carlos Diegues; and *Vidas Secas* ("Barren Lives," 1963), by Nelson Pereira dos Santos. The films of this phase deal typically, although not exclusively, with the problems confronting the urban and rural lumpen-proletariat: starvation, violence, religious alienation, and economic ex-

Vidas Secas (1963)

ploitation. The films share a certain political optimism, characteristic of the developmentalist years, but due as well to the youth of the directors, a kind of faith that merely showing these problems would be a first step toward their solution. *Barravento* exposed the alienating role of religion in a fishing community. *The Guns* and *Barren Lives* dealt with the oppression of peasants by landowners, while *Black God, White Devil* demystified the twin alienations of millennial cults (the black god) and of apolitical *cangaceiro* violence (the white devil). *Ganga Zumba* memorialized the seventeenth-century slave republic of Palmares and called, by historical analogy, for a revolt of the oppressed against their oppressors. Made *for* the people by an educated middle-class radical elite, these films occasionally transmitted a paternalistic vision of the Brazilian masses. In *Barravento*, as critic Jean-Claude Bernardet points out, political salvation comes from the city; it is not generated by the community. Esthetically, these "sad, ugly, desperate films" showed a commitment to what Rocha's manifesto called "An Esthetic of Hunger," combining slow, reflexive rhythms with uncompromising, often harsh, images and sounds.

The second phase of Cinema Novo extends from 1964, the year of the first *coup d'état*, through 1968, the year of the *coup*-within-the-*coup* that handed power to even more reactionary sectors of the army. These two events, taken together, constituted an historical cataclysm that left democratic institutions and a political style—populism—in ruins.

34

Saraceni's *O Desafio* (1966)

Democratic forms were replaced by authoritarian military rule; the social gains of the previous era were reversed; laws were signed assuring foreign corporations high profits; and North American capital flowed into Brazil. Many filmmakers, not surprisingly, poked around the smouldering ruins of democratic populism in an attempt to disentangle the causes of a disaster of such magnitude. If the films of the first phase were optimistic, those of the second phase are anguished cries of perplexity; they are analyses of *failure* — of populism, of developmentalism, and of leftist intellectuals. Paulo César Saraceni's *O Desafio* ("The Challenge," 1966), Rocha's *Terra em Transe* ("Land in Anguish," 1967), Gustavo Dahl's *O Bravo Guerreiro* ("The Brave Warrior," 1968), and dos Santos's *Fome de Amor* ("Hunger for Love," 1968) all dissect the failures of the left. Gustavo Dahl, writing of his own *Bravo Guerreiro*, sums it up:

> In *O Desafio*, in *Land in Anguish*, and in *The Brave Warrior*, there wanders the same personage — a petit-bourgeois intellectual, tangled up in doubts, a wretch in crisis. He may be a journalist, a poet, a legislator, in any case he's always perplexed, hesitating, a weak person who would like to tragically transcend his condition.[9]

Although the left, unprepared for armed struggle, was politically and militarily defeated in 1964, its cultural presence, paradoxically, remained strong even after the *coup d'état*, exercising a kind of hegemony despite the dictatorship. Marxist books proliferated in the bookstores, anti-imperialist plays drew large audiences, and many filmmakers went from left reformism to radical critique. One senses in these films an angry

35

Land in Anguish (1967)

disillusionment with what Roberto Schwarz calls "the populist deformation of Marxism," a Marxism that was strong on anti-imperialism but
weak on class struggle. The contradictory class-alliances of left populism
are satirized in Rocha's *Land in Anguish*, where pompous senators and
progressive priests, party intellectuals and military leaders, samba
together in what Rocha calls the "tragic carnival of Brazilian politics."

If the films of the first phase displayed—Glauber Rocha being the obvious exception—a commitment to realism as a style, the films of the second phase tend toward self-referentiality and anti-illusionism. While the
films of the first phase tended to be rural in their setting, films of the second phase were predominantly urban. Luiz Sérgio Person's *São Paulo
S.A.* (1965), with its punning title—S.A. means both "Incorporated" and
"Anonymous Society"—deals with alienated labor and alienated love in
São Paulo; Leon Hirszman's *A Falecida* ("The Deceased," 1965), explores
the spiritual torments of the urban middle class; and Carlos Diegues's *A
Grande Cidade* ("The Big City," 1966) treats the fate of impoverished
northeasterners in Rio de Janeiro. At the same time, many films were
drawn from Brazilian literary classics, notably: Andrade's *O Padre e a
Moça* ("The Priest and the Girl," 1966), based on a poem by Carlos
Drummond de Andrade; Walter Lima Jr.'s *Menino de Engenho* ("Plantation Boy," 1966), based on a novel by José Lins do Rego; and Roberto
Santos's *A Hora e Vez de Augusto Matraga* (Matraga, 1966), based on a
short story by Guimarães Rosa.

During the second phase of Cinema Novo, filmmakers realized that
although their cinema was "popular" in that it attempted to take the
point of view of "the people," it was not popular in the sense of having a
mass audience. Although the policy of low-budget independent production seemed sound, nothing could guarantee the film's being *shown* in a
market dominated by North American conglomerates. If the masses were

Grande Otelo in *Macunaíma* (1969)

often on the screen, they were rarely in the audience. The filmmakers linked to Cinema Novo, consequently, began to see the making of popular films as, in Gustavo Dahl's words, "the essential condition for political action in cinema."[10] In cinema as in revolution, they decided, everything is a question of power, and for a cinema existing within a system to which it does not adhere, power means broad public acceptance and financial success.

In their efforts to reach the public, Cinema Novo adopted a two-pronged strategy. First, with producer Luiz Carlos Barreto, they founded a distribution cooperative: Difilm. Second, they began making films with more popular appeal. Leon Hirszman's *Garota de Ipanema* ("The Girl from Ipanema," 1967), the first Cinema Novo feature in color and the first to attempt the new strategy, explored the myth of the sun-bronzed "girl from Ipanema" in order to demystify that very myth. Joaquim Pedro de Andrade's *Macunaíma* (1969), however, was the first Cinema Novo film to be truly popular in both cultural and box-office terms, offering a dialectical demonstration of how to reach the public without compromising a left political vision of Brazilian society.

Macunaíma is generally classified as part of the third phase of Cinema Novo, the so-called "cannibal-tropicalist" phase.[11] Tropicalism in the cinema begins around the time of the 1968 *coup*-within-the-*coup* and the promulgation of the Fifth Institutional Act (initiating an extremely repressive period of military rule) and extends roughly to the end of 1971. Because of rigorous censorship, the films of this period tended to work by political indirection, often adopting allegorical forms, as in Andrade's *Macunaíma*, Rocha's *Antônio das Mortes* (1968), dos Santo's *Azyllo Muito Louco* ("The Alienist," 1969), Guerra's *Os Deuses e os Mortos* ("The Gods and the Dead," 1970), Diegues's *Os Herdeiros* ("The Heirs," 1969), dos Santos's *Como Era Gostoso Meu Francês* ("How Tasty Was My Little Frenchman," 1970), and Jabor's *Pindorama* (1971). An artistic response to political repression, Tropicalism, at least in the cinema, developed a coded language of revolt. *The Alienist*, for example, made subversive use of a literary classic. Based on *The Psychiatrist* by Machado de Assis, it tells the story of a mad psychiatrist-priest who constantly changes his standards for placing people in the local madhouse, a story with obvious implications for military-ruled Brazil. *How Tasty Was My Little Frenchman*, a kind of anthropological fiction, suggested that the Indians (i.e., Brazil) should metaphorically cannibalize their foreign enemies, appropriating their force without being dominated by them. At the same time it criticized the government's genocidal policies toward the Indian as analogous to seventeenth-century massacres.

Tropicalism, a movement that touched music and theater as well as the cinema, emphasized the grotesque, bad taste, *kitsch*, and gaudy colors. It

Carlos Diegues's *The Heirs* (1969)

played aggressively with certain myths, especially the notion of Brazil as a tropical paradise characterized by colorful exuberance and tutti-frutti hats à la Carmen Miranda. The movement was not without its ambiguities. Roberto Schwarz, a Brazilian intellectual then living in Paris, interpreted the movement in an article published in *Les Temps Modernes*, "Remarques sur la Culture et la Politique au Brésil, 1964-1969." Tropicalism, he suggests, emerges from the tension between the superficial "modernization" of the Brazilian economy and its archaic, colonized, and imperialized core. While the Brazilian economy, after 1964, was becoming integrated into the world capitalist economy, the petite bourgeoisie was returning to antiquated values and old resentments. "The basic procedure of such a movement consists in submitting the anachronisms (at first glance grotesque, in reality inevitable) to the white light of the ultra-modern, presenting the result as an allegory of Brazil."[12]

Concurrent with the third phase of Cinema Novo, there emerged a radically different tendency—*Udigrudi*, the Brazilian pronunciation of "Underground." As Cinema Novo decided to reach out for a popular audience, the Underground opted to slap that audience in the face. As Cinema Novo moved toward technical polish and production values, the Novo Cinema Novo, as it also came to be called, demanded a radicalization of the esthetics of hunger, rejecting the dominant codes of well-made cinema in favor of a "dirty screen" and "garbage" esthetics. The Underground proclaimed its own isolation in the names they gave their movement: marginal cinema, subterranean cinema. Although they were intentionally marginal, identifying socially downward with rebellious lumpen characters, they were also *marginalized*, harassed by the censors and boycotted by exhibitors. The movement nurtured a love-hate rela-

Júlio Bressane's *Killed the Family and Went to the Movies* (1970)

39

tionship with Cinema Novo, at times paying homage to its early purity, while lambasting what it saw as its subsequent populist co-optation. In *The Red Light Bandit*, Rogério Sganzerla symbolically puts to flame the St. George triptych from *Antônio das Mortes*, while he spoofs the multi-layered soundtrack of *Land in Anguish*. Some of the important names and titles in this diverse and prolific movement are: Rogério Sganzerla (*O Bandido Da Luz Vermelha*; "The Red Light Bandit," 1968); Júlio Bressane (*Matou a Família e ao Cinema*; "Killed the Family and Went to the Movies," 1970); João Trevisan (*Orgia ou o Homen Que Deu Cria*; "Orgy, or the Man Who Gave Birth," 1970); Andrea Tonacci (*Bangue Bangue*; "Bang Bang," 1971); André Luiz de Oliveira (*Meteorango Kid: O Herói Intergaláctico*; "Meteorango Kid: Intergalactic Hero," 1969); José Mojica Marins (*À Meia-Noite Encarnarei No Teu Cadáver*; "At Midnight I Will Incarnate Your Corpse," 1967); Ozualdo Candeias (*A Margem*; The Margin," 1967); Neville Duarte d'Almeida (*Jardim de Guerra*; "War Garden," 1970); and Luiz Rosemberg Filho (*America do Sexo*; "America of Sex," 1970). (See Robert Stam's article on avant-garde cinema in this volume.)

Toward the end of what we have called the Tropicalist phase, Cinema Novo entered into a politically engendered crisis of creativity that reached its nadir in 1971-1972. As censorship and repression worsened Glauber Rocha, Rui Guerra, and Carlos Diegues left Brazil for Europe. As funding became more problematic, several directors undertook co-productions with other countries or completely financed their projects abroad. Joaquim Pedro de Andrade's *Os Inconfidentes* ("The Conspirators," 1972) was produced by and for Italian television. Nelson Pereira dos Santos's *Quem é Beta?* ("Who Is Beta?" 1973) was a co-production with France. Gustavo Dahl's *Uirá, um Indio a Procura de Deus* ("Uirá, an Indian in Search of God," 1973), was a co-production with Italian television.

Around this time, a flood of vapid erotic comedies—*pornochanchadas*—rushed into the vacuum left by political censorship and departing filmmakers. Taken together, these films offer a cinematic portrait of the sexual alienation of the Brazilian petite-bourgeoisie; they exalt the good bourgeois life of fast cars, wild parties, and luxurious surroundings, while offering the male voyeur titillating shots of breasts and buttocks. Their titles give some indication of their vulgarity: *Um Soutien Para Papai* ("A Bra for Daddy"), *Essas Mulheres Lindas, Nuas e Maravilhosas* ("Those Beautiful, Naked, Marvelous Women"), *Mais ou Menos Virgem* ("More or Less Virgin"), *As Secretárias . . . Que Fazem de Tudo* ("Secretaries . . . Who Do Everything"), and *A Virgem e o Machão* ("The Virgin and the Macho"). Sexist and reactionary, these films are also anti-erotic and moralistic. Rather than deliver on the erotic promise implicit in their titles, they offer instead frequent nudity and perpetual *coitus interruptus*. The military regime, phenomenally alert to violations of "morality" in the films of the more politicized directors, has hypocritically tolerated, indeed encouraged, these productions.

Jean-Pierre Léaud and Nara Leão in *The Heirs* (1969)

Brazilian Cinema: Up to the Present

Brazilian cinema not only survived the crisis of 1971-1972 but also went on to thrive and prosper; its "recovery" is explicable by a series of convergent factors. First of all, important political changes occurred after 1972, changes that weakened the military government but strengthened the cinema. The ferocious repression of the crisis period, applied "democratically" to workers, peasants, and intellectuals, boomeranged by alienating the Brazilian people and isolating the regime. More important, the predatory economic model imposed by the junta was proving bankrupt and unworkable, enriching foreign companies and their local allies, but impoverishing the Brazilian masses by runaway inflation (80% at a conservative estimate in 1980) and a 50 billion dollar foreign debt. The "economic miracle" of 1967-1973—in fact a brutal transference of wealth from the bottom to the top—was challenged by popular opposition and undermined by the sudden quadrupling of oil prices. While the government offered promises of liberalization and "responsible democracy," recent years have been marked by the victory of the opposition party (MDB: Brazilian Democratic Movement) in the 1974 elections, by mounting pressure against censorship, by working-class militancy and strikes, and a general call for constitutional government, amnesty for political

Arnaldo Jabor's *Tudo Bem* (1978)

prisoners and exiles, and for "democracy without adjectives."

Since 1972, all of the Cinema Novo directors have returned to Brazil. Glauber Rocha returned in 1976 and quickly assumed the role of ideological gadfly to both left and right. His short film *Di*, about the Brazilian painter Di Cavalcânti, was made in Brazil in 1977 and won a documentary prize at the Cannes Film Festival. Rocha has completed his *Idade da Terra* ("Age of the Earth") in cinemascope, direct sound, featuring prestigious actors in the roles of Christ, the Pope, and diverse allegorical personages. Meanwhile, Nelson Pereira dos Santos (*O Amuleto de Ogum* ["The Amulet of Ogum"], 1974); *Tenda dos Milagres* ["Tent of Miracles"], 1977); Carlos Diegues (*Joana Francesa*, 1974; *Xica da Silva*, 1976; *Chuvas de Verão* ["Summer Rains"], 1978; *Bye Bye Brasil*, 1980), Arnaldo Jabor (*Toda Nudez Será Castigada* ["All Nudity Shall Be Punished"], 1973; *O Casamento* ["The Wedding"], 1975; *Tudo Bem* ["Everything's Fine"], 1978), Leon Hirszman (*São Bernardo*, 1973), Joaquim Pedro de Andrade (*Guerra Conjugal* ["Conjugal Warfare"], 1975; *Vereda Tropical* ["Tropical Path,"], , 1978), Paulo César Saraceni (*Anchieta, José do Brasil*, 1978), Walter Lima Jr. (*A Lira do Delírio* ["Delirious Lyre"], 1978), and Rui Guerra (*A Queda* ["The Fall"], 1977), have all been active. The Cinema Novo directors, it should be added, also trained new directors. Many young assistant directors, photographers, and editors of Cinema Novo films made their own first films in the early or mid-seventies, notably Eduardo Escorel (*Lição de Amor* ["Lesson of Love"], 1975), Carlos Alberto Prates Correia (*Perdida* ["Woman Astray"], 1976), Luis Fernando Goulart (*Marília e Marina*, 1976), and Bruno Barreto, whose *Dona Flor e Seus Dois Maridos* ("Dona Flor and Her Two Husbands," 1976) has made significant inroads in the American market.

The seventies have also been marked by the emergence of a significant number of women and black directors. Among the films by women are Maria do Rosário's *Marcados para Viver* ("Branded for Life," 1976), shown in the New York Women's Film Festival; Tânia Quaresma's *Nordeste: Cordel, Repente, Canção* ("The Music and People of the Northeast," 1975); and Teresa Trautman's *Os Homens Que Eu Tive* ("The Men in My Life," 1974), a sexually subversive film banned, until recently, in Brazil. Meanwhile, Ana Carolina Teixeira Soares, after making eleven documentaries largely on political subjects, made her first fiction film in 1977—the witty, surreal, incendiary *Mar de Rosas* ("Sea of Roses"). Although blacks have been featured prominently as actors, it is only now that there are black directors. Antônio Pitanga, actor in many Cinema Novo films (*Barravento, The Big City, Joana Francesa*) directed *Na Boca do Mundo* ("In the World's Mouth," 1977) and Waldyr Onofre, another actor, directed *As Aventuras Amorosas de um Padeiro* ("The Amorous Adventures of a Baker," 1975).

With current production at roughly one hundred feature films per year, Brazilian cinema has achieved industrial quantity and quality without, paradoxically, having ever become an industry. The most important single factor in this evolution of Brazilian cinema today is the role of the state film enterprise—Embrafilme—in production and distribution. Founded in the late sixties to replace the National Cinema Institute (INC), Embrafilme began playing a decisive role in 1974 when President Geisel named filmmaker Roberto Farias as director. Prior to that time,

Anecy Rocha in *A Lira do Delírio* (1978)

Embrafilme had been little more than a minor bureaucratic agency that redistributed funds (from taxes levied on theater tickets) to film producers. Farias, the chosen candidate of the Cinema Novo directors, gave the entity new strength by implanting a program of co-productions with independent producers. He also developed the largest distributor in Latin America, headed by Cinema Novo veteran Gustavo Dahl. Many of the most important films now being made in Brazil are at least partially financed by the organization, and some, like Guerra's *A Queda* ("The Fall," 1977), are distributed, although not produced, by Embrafilme.

Embrafilme's involvement in distribution goes back historically to the decision of independent producers in the 1960s to struggle collectively against the multinational film corporations. Despite some successes, they soon realized the limits of their own power vis-à-vis wealthy, highly-organized foreign concerns. The solution, they discovered, was, first, to combine the know-how of such producers with the economic power of the state, and, second, to press for legislation reserving a portion of the market for Brazilian films. As of today, all movie theaters in Brazil must show national films at least 133 days per year. Legislation—fought bitterly by foreign concerns (especially by Jack Valenti with the Motion Pictures Export Association)—also requires the screening of one Brazilian short along with each foreign feature, an essential measure since short films serve as a training ground for new directors and technicians. Still, much remains to be done. Luis Carlos Barreto, for example, calls for new theaters in the poorer urban areas, and for cinemobiles (à la Cuba) for the rural poor who have not yet seen *any* cinema.

Although most Brazilian filmmakers acknowledge the need for a state role in film production and distribution, satisfaction with the current

Sonia Braga in *Lady on the Bus* (1978)

structure is neither universal nor complete. Joaquim Pedro de Andrade, while basically supporting Embrafilme, calls for a democratization giving filmmakers themselves a stronger role in decision making. He and some 40 other directors have founded an exhibition cooperative as an alternative for independent filmmakers. Meanwhile, filmmakers from São Paulo (Francisco Ramalho Jr., João Batista de Andrade) complain of favoritism toward Rio de Janeiro. Underground filmmakers, for their part, object that Embrafilme promotes commercial superproductions while it neglects low-budget and avant-garde films.

Some critics pose more radical objections. Rui Guerra, who recently accepted an invitation by the government of Mozambique to participate in the formation of the National Cinema Institute, and who is therefore familiar with socialist alternatives, makes the obvious point that in a capitalist society one cannot expect a state organ to promote anti-capitalist films. Yet Guerra's own *The Fall*, which is highly critical of Brazilian capitalism, is being distributed by Embrafilme. But it is filmmaker-critic Paulo Chaves Fernandes who makes the most radical critique of all. The dominant tendency in Brazilian cinema, he argues, with all its talk of "national objectives," rigorously avoids talking about social contradictions:

> This cinema, protecting itself with certain nebulous concepts and redeeming promises such as "national interests," "Brazilian culture," and "conquest of the market," accepts the corporativist game and patriotically pursues the triumphalism of "national-popular art," digestive, cheerful, and above all profitable. History repeats itself with its customary irony: populism returns, this time through the very "radicals" who contested it so vigorously in the sixties.[13]

While the danger to which Chaves points—that of a vacuous bourgeois nationalism—is very real, it is equally true that many Brazilian films *do* talk about social contradiction. In *Tudo Bem* and *The Fall* social contradiction occupies center stage, while in *Tent of Miracles* social contradiction is evoked *through* cultural struggle. As for the charge of "populism," Carlos Diegues argues that Embrafilme is a victory, not a retreat, for the anti-populist radicals of the sixties. Cinema Novo, he claims, had always called for an entity like Embrafilme. While opposed to the present *government*, Diegues sees a state contribution to national cinema as a popular right—like the nationalization of resources—to be seized. In any case, many filmmakers argue that without Embrafilme foreign films would immediately reoccupy Brazilian screens and that would be a tragedy for filmmakers of *all* tendencies.

What has been gained and what lost since Cinema Novo? First, to speak of the indisputable victories, Brazilian cinema has won its own public; it now speaks directly to the Brazilian people rather than to a national and international elite. Second, it has achieved unprecedented levels of technical excellence. Third, it has gained a pluralistic diversity of style and genre, broad enough to include avant-garde experimentation (Sganzerla's *O Abismo* ["The Abyss"]), political documentary (Lauro Escorel's *Os Libertários* ["The Libertarians"]), militant film (João Batista de Andrade's *A Greve* ["The Strike"]), anthropological fiction (Gustavo Dahl's *Uirá*), historical reconstruction (Geraldo Sarno's *Delmiro Gouveia*), surreal fantasy (Ana Carolina's *Sea of Roses*), carnivalesque celebration (*Xica da Silva*), intimist dramas (*Marília And Marina*), science fiction (José de Anchieta's *Parada 88*), and critical realism (*São Bernardo*).

Films like *Macunaíma* disinhibited Brazilian cinema and thus brought it closer to the Brazilian people. Brazilians, after all, share a lively sense of humor and repartee, combined with an historically exacerbated alertness to the absurd, traits one rarely senses in first and second phase Cinema Novo films. The right, which monopolizes so much according to Carlos Diegues, need have no monopoly on humor or joy. Arnaldo Jabor recalls the days when Brazilian directors were harassed by what he calls "the culturalist superego":

> There was a strong culturalist pressure on Brazilian cinema. Everytime a filmmaker was going to place the camera, the filmmaker would muse: Straub would put it here, Godard would put it there, Losey would have a travelling shot, Jancso would have a ten-minute travelling shot, Welles would take a wide-angle lens and put it on the floor . . . in short, there was a certain hesitation at the level of cinematic language. . . .[14]

Uirá, um Índio a Procura de Deus (1974)

Jofre Soares in *Conjugal Warfare* (1975)

Jabor sees Brazilian cinema as liberating itself from this "castrating figure called fictive mise-en-scène" and from the fantasy of gaining entry to a cinematic pantheon which begins with Eisenstein and extends to Godard and Straub. Brazilian cinema is finding its own political and stylistic voice.

The successes of Brazilian cinema have not been without their ambiguities. At times the "esthetic of hunger" seems to have degenerated into an esthetic of gluttony, with high-budget features and well-told tales that have won their market, but to no purpose.[15] A crucial debate now taking place in Brazil centers on the nature of the *popular*. Brazilian cinema is now popular in the sense of drawing a large public. The debate focuses on whether the current films are truly "popular" or merely "populist" and "popularesque." The idea of popular cinema, quite widespread in the early sixties, was resuscitated in 1974 by Nelson Pereira dos Santos's "Manifesto for a Popular Cinema," written to accompany the release of his *Amuleto de Ogum*. In general terms, this manifesto advocates the affirmation and defense of Brazilian popular culture through cinema, popular culture being defined here as the spontaneous cultural expression of the people, i.e., of the vast marginalized majority of the Brazilian population. According to dos Santos, it is important to celebrate this culture since "it is different from other superficial, elitist cultural forms that follow antiquated, colonized models." Defending popular cultural expression, filmmakers also defend popular political ideas. Dos Santos

Saraceni's *Anchieta, José do Brasil* (1978)

took religion as a starting point since it provided him with a "global vision and a way of thinking in relation to all of Brazilian society." Rather than impose elitest preconceptions on popular culture, dos Santos seeks to adopt the perspective of the people. Unlike earlier Cinema Novo positions, this view comes close to suggesting that the popular vision is always right, a position echoed by Pedro Archanjo, the protagonist of dos

Santos's *Tent of Miracles*, when he tells the ponderous Marxist professor that "love for the people" is more important than political "dogma."

Dos Santos's position is a salutary provocation for those left intellectuals who speak of "the people" and of "popular culture" in the abstract, yet who in the concrete frown on virtually everything "the people" do and believe. On the other hand, the unproblematic celebration of popular culture is charged with ambiguities, the same ambiguities that characterize carnival in Brazil. If it is true, as Mikhail Bakhtin suggests, that carnival represents the utopia of the common people in which official ruling-class hierarchies are overturned and people gain brief entry into the sphere of utopian freedom, it is also true that carnival—like football, samba, religion, and the cinema—can function as an escape valve, a means of masking oppression and making it bearable.[16]

To Glauber Rocha's famous phrase, *uma idéia na cabeça e uma câmera na mão* (an idea in your head and a camera in hand), Nelson Pereira dos Santos has added *e o povo na frente* (and the people in front). Rui Guerra has further amended the phrase: "the people in front, certainly, but *não em festa*" (not only in their festivities). For Guerra, a popular cinema must not only deal with popular themes, but must create a political relationship with the people; it must reach the potentially revolutionary classes: the urban proletariat and the rural masses. Brazilian cinema has never been "popular" in these terms, since the exhibition circuits have historically served the middle class. Given the capitalist structures of production, distribution, and exhibition in Brazil today, a popular cinema in the sense advocated by Guerra and others remains a utopian idea unless accompanied by a popular transformation of

Geraldo Sarno's *Coronel Delmiro Gouveia* (1978)

society, a truly radical change in its political and economic structure. Given the impossibility of making truly popular films within the present system, Guerra sees many current films as trying to reconcile the contradictions inherent in such a project and falling into a populist trap by showing the people in festive moments rather than in their daily work and struggle. *Candomblé* and other religious forms, for Guerra, are alienated cultural expressions, and their unqualified celebration represents an abdication of the intellectual's role in cultural and political life.

Brazilian cinema has much to offer. At its best it points the way to the dialectical transcendence of a number of false dichotomies. A radical avant-garde cinema that few see versus a commercially degraded popular cinema? Films like *Macunaíma* and *The Fall* are, in different ways, avant-garde *and* popular. Self-referential distanciation versus emotional participation? Many Brazilian films — *Land in Anguish, The Gods and the Dead* — are rigorously Brechtian *and* intensely participatory. Serious didactic films versus frivolous entertainment? *Macunaíma* and *Tudo Bem* are politically radical *and* extremely funny. It is this synthesis of energy and consciousness, emotion and dialectics, humor and political purpose, perhaps, which is most impressive in Brazilian cinema.

Notes

1. Paulo Emílio Salles Gomes, "Cinema: Trajetória no Subdesenvolvimento," *Argumento* 1 (Rio de Janeiro: Paz e Terra, October 1973): 58.
2. See Vicente de Paula Araújo, *A Bela Época do Cinema Brasileiro* (São Paulo: Editora Perspectiva, 1976).
3. Georges Sadoul, *Dictionnaire des Cinéastes* (Paris: Seuil, 1965), p. 158.
4. Rogério Sganzerla, "Ganga Bruta," *O Estado de São Paulo (Suplemento Literário)* (6 February 1965).
5. Carlos Roberto de Sousa, *Jornal do Brasil* (14 May 1977).
6. Ibid. Humberto Mauro went on to a prolific career, making hundreds of documentaries for the National Institute of Educational Cinema and directing scores of feature films up through *O Canto da Saudade* ("Song of Nostalgia," 1952). He also collaborated on Nelson Pereira dos Santos's *Como Era Gostoso O Meu Francês* ("How Tasty Was My Little Frenchman," 1972) and Paulo César Saraceni's *Anchieta, José Do Brasil* (1978).
7. Carlos Roberto de Sousa, "A Fascinante Aventura do Cinema Brasileiro," *O Estado de São Paulo* (25 October 1975).
8. For a discussion of this period see Maria Victória de Mesquita Benevides, *O Governo Kubitschek: Desenvolvimento Econômico e Estabilidade Política* (Rio de Janeiro: Editora Paz e Terra, 1976).
9. From the Difilm Distribution notes to *O Bravo Guerreiro*.
10. Gustavo Dahl, et al., "Situation et Perspective du Cinéma d'Amerique Latine," *Positif* 139 (June 1972):2.
11. The cannibalist metaphor goes back to the Brazilian modernist movement of the twenties. "Only cannibalism unites us," proclaimed modernist poet-novelist-dramatist-critic Oswald de Andrade, "Tupi or not Tupi — that is the question." Through the metaphor of cannibalism, Brazilian artists thumbed their nose at their own "palefaces" and at over-cultivated Europe, while heeding surrealism's call for "savagery" in art.
12. Roberto Schwarz, "Remarques sur la Culture et la Politique au Brésil: 1964–1969," *Les Temps Modernes* 288 (1970): 52.
13. Paulo Chaves Fernandes, "Cinema Novo: Força Total para Embrafilme, Ordem e Progresso," *Beijo* 1 (January 1978): 12.
14. From an unpublished interview with Arnaldo Jabor.
15. It would be quite possible in this connection to trace the significance of hunger in the diverse

phases of Cinema Novo. Quite literal in first phase films like *Barren Lives* and *The Guns*, it becomes semi-metaphorical in second-phase films like *Land in Anguish* and *Hunger for Love*, grotesquely allegorical in such tropicalist films as *Macunaíma* and *Brasil Ano 2000* ("Brazil Year 2000), finally giving way to the lavish banquets and feasts of *Xica da Silva* and *Tent of Miracles*.

16. See Mikhail Bakhtin, *Rabelais and His World*, trans. Helene Iswolsky (Cambridge, Mass.: M.I.T. Press, 1968).

Part II
The Theory of Brazilian Cinema: The Filmmakers Speak

Introduction

Brazilian Cinema, and especially Cinema Novo, shares with Soviet film of the twenties, Italian Neo-Realism, and the French *nouvelle vague* a penchant for theorizing its own cinematic practice. These three film movements represent more than a mere parallel, of course; they constitute concrete historical influences as evidenced in frequent allusions by the Brazilian directors to Eisenstein and Vertov, Rossellini and Zavattini, Truffaut and Godard. The unusually close link between theory and practice in Brazil derives as well from a number of other convergent factors: the generally abstract and theoretical bent of intellectuals in Latin coun-

Joaquim Pedro de Andrade

tries; the fact that many of the filmmakers, as with the *nouvelle vague*, began as film critics; and finally, the specific pressures of the Brazilian situation that made filmmakers feel "responsible" for their country's cinematic development and that led them to theoretically justify their own production. As a result, each Cinema Novo film became more than an isolated artistic event; each became an experiment within a broader field. Of each film it was asked: How does this film alter the field? Are its strategies cinematically advanced and politically progressive? Can its strategies be generalized?

Brazilian filmmakers tend to politicize their discussion of film to a degree that might surprise many non-Brazilians. Critic-historian Paulo Emílio Salles Gomes was among the first to see that the struggle for film production in Brazil was inseparable from a general political struggle. In two seminal articles published in 1961—"The Owner of the Market" and "A Colonial Situation"—he analyzed the social, economic, political, and psychological barriers that had prevented the flourishing of a truly national cinema. In all of these areas, he found the cruel marks of neo-colonial dependency. Throughout the sixties, this fundamental insight was deepened. Brazilian left intellectuals generally, and filmmakers particularly, began to see themselves as part of the emerging Third World. They became conscious of both the structural oppression and the revolutionary potential of Brazil and other Third World countries. Events such as the Cuban Revolution in 1959, Algerian independence in 1962, and the struggle of the Vietnamese led Brazilian filmmakers to identify with a "tricontinental" revolution.

Unlike Brazil, the history of American cinema has played itself out against a backdrop of relative political stability. While Americans have known over 200 years of constitutional government, Brazilians have been subjected to swift changes in political climate and economic fortune, changes that have inevitably left conspicuous traces in the films themselves. What is generally true of film—the impossibility of separating filmic text from social context—is perhaps more obviously true in the case of Brazilian cinema. Military rule, for example, has often brutally affected filmmaking in Brazil. Cultural organizations like the Popular Center of Culture have been closed; some filmmakers have been arrested; others have gone into temporary exile. Censorship has physically mutilated certain film texts and prevented others from being disseminated. Self-censorship, meanwhile, has harmed Brazilian cinema in less visible but equally destructive ways. As a result Brazilian filmmakers have never enjoyed the luxury of regarding themselves as "apolitical."

The documents included in this part of the book are intended to give some sense of the filmmakers' own vision of Brazilian cinema, of how film practice in Brazil has been thought and theorized by those who have participated in it. The documents range from theoretical articles about culture and politics (Estevam), to general articles about Cinema Novo by the directors themselves, to manifestoes, both individual (Rocha) and collective (*Luz e Ação*). Taken together, these texts give a notion of the voice of the filmmakers and the theories that animated them. At the same time, they provide a kind of capsule documentary history of Brazilian cinema over the last two decades.

While responding to precise events and issues, these documents also develop an ongoing problematic, a set of interrelated questions asked repeatedly and answered diversely. Some of these questions are:

1) How could cinema best express what the filmmakers were fond of calling "Brazilian reality?" What areas of Brazilian experience had been neglected or distorted in cinema? How could cinema show Brazil its true face?

2) How were films to be produced and financed? What strategies were most appropriate to Brazil's situation as a neo-colonized country? What was the role of the independent producer? What was the role of the state? Was the state the disinterested protector of national cinema vis-à-vis powerful foreign interests, or was it indirectly allied with them and with conservative social classes in Brazil?

3) How could Brazilian cinema conquer its domestic market from Hollywood's domination? What distribution strategies would be most effective?

4) What cinematic language was most appropriate for Brazilian cinema? Should it imitate the Hollywood continuity and production values to which the public was accustomed? Or should it make a radical break with Hollywood esthetics in favor of "an esthetic of hunger?" Should Brazilian cinema, as Glauber Rocha put it metaphorically, sell Coca-Cola or coconut milk? Or should it sell coconut milk in Coca-Cola bottles? To what extent should cinema incorporate popular cultural forms like those of the *samba, candomblé,* or *cordel* literature? To what extent should the films be anti-illusionistic, anti-narrative, anti-spectacular, avant-garde?

5) What was the relation between the filmmakers (largely middle-class intellectuals) and the "people" whom they purported to represent? Should they be a cultural vanguard speaking for the people by proxy? Should they merely be the mouthpieces of popular culture, or the unrelenting critics of its alienations?

1
"For a Popular Revolutionary Art"

Introduction

One of the first Cinema Novo films, *Cinco Vezes Favela* (1961), was produced by the Popular Center of Culture of the National Students' Union. Subsidized by the Ministry of Education and Culture prior to 1964, the PCC attempted to establish a cultural and political link with the Brazilian masses by putting on plays in factories and working-class neighborhoods, producing films and records, and by participating in literacy programs. Many of the original members of Cinema Novo, including those who directed the five episodes of *Cinco Vezes Favela*, were active in the PCC.

Carlos Estevam's "For a Popular Revolutionary Art," while not dealing specifically with cinema, outlines the political and cultural positions of the Popular Center of Culture. Written in mid-1962 by its executive-director, the article reflects the political ambiance in which Cinema Novo arose. Politically radical, Estevam's theory is marked by the combination of a sometimes mechanistic Marxism with a populist brand of voluntarism. He proposes a "popular revolutionary art" while at the same time disdaining the cultural production of the people as "coarse," "clumsy," "backward," and devoid of artistic quality. Truly popular art, according to this theory, is that made by middle-class students and intellectuals who have taken it upon themselves to lead the people to revolution. This elitist conception of social transformation, reflected, perhaps, in *Cinco Vezes Favela*, was quickly attacked by Cinema Novo as paternalistic. Glauber

Tânia Quaresma's *Music and People of the Northeast* (1975)

Rocha and Carlos Diegues maintained an often virulent polemic with Estevam in the pages of various student publications. In the cinematic arena, the PCC advocated collective discussion of film projects, a position Glauber Rocha rejected as "collective censorship." The Popular Center of Culture, together with the National Students' Union, was banned by the military regime after it took power in 1964.

"For a Popular Revolutionary Art"

CARLOS ESTEVAM

The positions of the Popular Center of Culture on the fundamental questions of popular art and art in general do not derive exclusively from reflection about esthetic problems. We, the artists and intellectuals of the Popular Center of Culture have arrived at our esthetic conceptions starting from other areas of reality. We think and act as we do because we feel that art and other higher manifestations of culture cannot be understood as an incommunicable island independent of the material processes that structure social existence. Nor do we believe that artists, simply because they are artists, deserve to live in a universe apart, free from ties to the community and to the contradictions, struggles, and victories of our national history. Before becoming artists, they are human beings among other human beings, participating in common limitations and ideals, responsibilities and efforts, defeats and victories. No one asks artists if they prefer to live in or outside of society. They are asked, rather, how they will orient their life and production within the society to which they inevitably belong. To ignore this question or deny its validity does not resolve it or eliminate it from the set of speculations at the origin of all authentic artistic activity. Artists who do not take conscious social positions evade this duty only in an indirect and illusory manner since in their work, in their productive activity, they define themselves as members of the social body. What is not declared explicitly by the alienated artist is asserted implicitly in alienated work. Willingly or not, knowingly or not, artists always find themselves confronted with a radical option: either to act decidedly and consciously, interfering in the shape and destiny of the social process, or be transformed into the passive and amorphous material on which this process supports itself in order to advance; either declare themselves subjects, active centers of deliberation and action, or be objects, dead elements that suffer without knowing, decide without choosing, and are determined without determining. . . .

What conception of form and content orients the artistic production of the PCC? Here it is necessary to differentiate the art of the people from popular art and both of these from the art practiced by the PCC, which we call *popular revolutionary art*. The three kinds of art have in common the fact that their public does not consist of the cultural minorities, but beyond this similarity they maintain marked differences.

The "art of the people" is predominantly a product of economically backward communities, flourishing primarily in rural or urban contexts that have not yet reached the life styles that accompany industrialization. In it the artist is indistinguishable from the mass of consumers. Artists and public live integrated in the same anonymity, and the level of artistic elaboration is so primary that the act of creation does not go beyond the simple ordering of the most patent data of a backward popular consciousness. "Popular art," on the other hand, is distinguished from the art of the people not only by its public, made up of the population of the developed urban centers, but also due to the division of labor that makes the masses the non-productive receiver of works created by a professionalized group of specialists. The artists thus constitute a social stratum different from their public, reduced to a mere consumer of goods whose elaboration and divulgation escape its control. The art of the people and popular art, when considered from a culturally rigorous point of view, scarcely deserve to be called art and from the point of view of the PCC, are neither truly "popular," nor "of the people."

In reality, the art of the people is devoid of artistic quality and cultural pretensions, rarely going beyond a coarse and clumsy attempt to express trivia filtered through a dull sensibility. Naive and backward, it has no real function other than satisfying a need for diversion or ornamentation. Popular art, meanwhile, albeit more refined and more technically elaborated, does not qualify as a legitimate artistic experience since its purpose is merely to offer the public entertainment, an inconsequential occupation for leisure time; it never proposes for its public the project of confronting the fundamental problems of existence. Resulting from the general democratization of contemporary society, popular art consists of the mass production of conventional works whose supreme objective is to distract rather than inform, to entertain and dazzle rather than awaken its public for reflection and self-awareness. Popular art does not attempt to substantially transform its public; it is as if the goal of this art were to maintain the people in a state of immobilization. In its multiple manifestations an escapist attitude is always visible which pretends to resolve the world's conflicts by pretending that they do not exist. . . .

The artists and intellectuals of the PCC have chosen another road, that of *popular revolutionary art*. For us everything begins with the people, and we understand that artists can bring the essence of people to life only when they confront the naked fact of ruling-class domination and the consequent powerlessness of the people themselves, reduced to a mass controlled by others and for the benefit of others. Art that does not start from this awareness is neither revolutionary nor popular, because to revolutionize society is to pass power to the people. Radical as it is, our revolutionary art strives to be popular by identifying with the fundamental aspirations of the people, by uniting itself to the collective strength that intends to carry out the project of the people, which can only be to cease to be "the people" as it is presented in class society, i.e., people who do not direct the society of which they form a part. If the fact of the people's powerlessness is glaringly obvious, it is equally obvious that in this historical stage the people can free themselves only through destructive actions that abolish their own enslavement. In revolutionary action, the people negate their negation, restore to themselves their own possession and become the subjects of their own drama. This movement generates all of the raw material necessary for popular revolutionary art, since the content of this art can only be the rich process by which the people frees itself and forges its collective destiny.

That is why we affirm, in this country and in this time, that *outside of political art there is no popular art*. If the people represent a universal fact, they can only be presented as the people, and therefore as universal, in works that analyze human questions in the light of a political perspective. Simply expressing actions and situations of an apolitical type does not show the people as the protagonist of its own drama and promoter of its own destiny. If politics is not our source of inspiration, if politics does not form the substance of the situations of conflict that we formalize, then our works will no longer speak directly and in revolutionary terms to the people as such, to the people as a collective entity that needs to escape as a whole from its circle of misery and that finds in organized and unified political action the only path of redemption. There cannot be two distinct programs, one for taking power, another for making popular art; the two must be linked.

For this reason we repudiate the romantic conception held by many Brazilian artists who dedicate themselves with simple abnegation to bringing the people closer to art and for whom popular art is merely the formalization of the spontaneous manifestations of the people. For such groups the people are like a bird or a flower, an esthetic object whose potential for beauty, primitive strength, and Biblical virtue has not yet been duly explored by erudite art; we, in contrast, see the people above all in their heroic quality as future combatants in the army of national popular liberation. Since in moments of struggle we do not behave as artists but as active members of the popular forces, we can evaluate the importance of cultural weapons in the victories and defeats of the people and the value of ideas when they penetrate the consciousness of the masses and are transformed into power. That is why we affirm the necessity of concentrating our art on the situation of the Brazilian people in terms of a double challenge: understanding the world in which they live — the objective being of the nation in its structures, its movements, its tendencies and potentialities — and arming them with the will, the values, the revolutionary feelings, and all of the subjective elements that will help them overcome the present situation of material oppression. Rather than isolate people in their individuality, lost forever in the intricate wanderings of introspection, our art should bring to the people the human significance of petroleum and steel, of political parties and class associations, of rates of production and financial mechanisms. For our art the burning of tons of coffee is more urgent than the petty passions of a betrayed husband or the alienated despair of those who see in existence a motive for failure and impotence. For the people, however, it is not sufficient that their knowledge of the world toward which they will direct their transforming action be rich and diverse: our art needs to offer them the motives that forge and impel revolutionary action. It needs to reformulate and endow with a new anthropological meaning the notions of merit and demerit, heroism and villainy, virtue and vice, self-awareness and alienation. When the people ask of our art: "Who are we?" we should respond first with their objective position in society, with their role in the causal connections between phenomena, with the challenge posed by the material articulations to which their being is subordinated in its essential belonging to the world; and secondly, we should respond with the attitudes, predispositions, beliefs, and hopes that will make possible their liberation.

Through investigation and analysis of the objective world, our art can transform consciousness and make the public aware of a radical new possibility: the concrete comprehension of the process through which the external world is de-alienated and the apparent naturalness of things is dissolved and transmuted. With our art we can communicate to the people, in a thousand ways, the idea that the forces that crush them merely appear to be objective, but they possess nothing of a blind and invincible fatality since they are, in truth, products of human labor. Popular revolutionary art finds in this its principal axis: the transmission of the concept of the inversion of praxis, the concept of the dialectical movement according to which the people appear as the true authors of the historical conditions of their existence. The world, the antithetical term to humanity, is turned upside down and its true nature is discovered as dialectical moment, as human deed rather than absolute fact; and human independence is revealed in the final analysis as the people's dependence on itself. No art can propose a higher goal than to align itself with the forces that favor the passage from the realm of necessity to the realm of freedom.

2
"Cinema Novo"

Introduction

The polemic between the Cinema Novo filmmakers and the Popular Center of Culture reached a peak in 1962-1963 through disagreements over the question of the *auteur*. While the Popular Center of Culture favored collective discussion of film projects, Cinema Novo opted for a more personal, albeit no less political, form of expression. As Glauber Rocha was to explain, "if commercial cinema is the tradition, then *auteur* cinema is revolution. The politics of a modern *auteur* are revolutionary politics" (*Revisão Crítica do Cinema Brasileiro*). Because of its political commitment, Cinema Novo's use of the *politique des auteurs* differs radically from that espoused by the *Cahiers du Cinéma* critics in the late fifties.

Carlos Diegues's "Cinema Novo," published originally in *Movimento 2* (May, 1962), the journal of the National Students' Union, is one of the first formulations of the basic project of Cinema Novo. The article reflects the youthful enthusiasm of the movement while showing awareness of the long history of Brazilian cinema and the difficulty of trying to reach a market controlled by foreign interests. Diegues also indirectly expresses the movement's adoption of the *politique des auteurs* and the influence of Italian Neo-Realism when he observes that the Cinema Novo filmmakers, in their individual and personal investigations, have taken their cameras and "gone out into the streets" to film the marginalized majority of the Brazilian people in the ambience in which they live.

"Cinema Novo"

CARLOS DIEGUES

Cinema Novo has no birthdate. It has no historic manifesto and no week of commemoration. It was created by no one in particular and is not the brainchild of any group. It has no official theoreticians, no popes or idols, no masters or guiding lights. Cinema Novo is not *novo* merely because of the youth of its practitioners. Nor does *novo*, in this context, suggest novelty or modishness. Cinema Novo is only part of a larger process transforming Brazilian society and reaching, at long last, the cinema.

In the beginning there were Humberto Mauro, Mário Peixoto, Adhemar Gonzaga, and other pioneers of our cinema. Despite obstacles, they left a body of work. Humberto Mauro, for example, remains an important model for anyone making films in Brazil. Then came the *chanchadas*, mid-year comedies or carnivalesque celebrations. A specifically Brazilian genre, it offered some valid alternatives, but, at the same time, was defiled by bad taste and by the most sordid commercialism, representing finally, a form of cultural prostitution. Then Vera Cruz was founded, a bizarre structureless monster, without roots in our culture, nourishing itself on the dream of a European cinema in an illiterate and impoverished Brazil. Its failure was both financial and cultural. In its wake, the *chanchada* once again dominated Brazilian production, with "serious" cinema—sometimes cerebral and often ridiculously pretentious—running a very distant second.

At the same time foreign producers, distributors, and the exhibitors allied to them (and who were at times the same people) continued to dominate the market. Co-productions, invented as a kind of salvation for Brazilian cinema, resulted only in an absurd cost increase for *all* cinematic production in Brazil. There were also experiments with protectionist laws, and the state timidly turned its attention to the small, independent producer.

The independent producer arrived just in time. He became angry, stuck out his chest, closed his eyes, opened his hands, and threw his scanty resources into the cinematic adventure. He discovered miraculous ways of creating adequate technical conditions, begged for raw film stock, contracted capable people (discovering that Brazil was very well supplied in terms of excellent and inexpensive talent), outwitted the distribution mafia, exhibited his films, and made just enough money to be able to make more films. Gradually, the independent producer began not only to share his experience with others, but also to incorporate, with the same drive and audacity, the ideas of others. Soon, independent producers took on considerable importance.

Low-budget productions, while lowering the technical level of films, nevertheless offered the conditions—in conjunction with a policy of freedom of creation, invention, and treatment—for the emergence of Cinema Novo.

Brazil and its people became the central preoccupation of the new group of Brazilian filmmakers. They avoided both the touristic and picturesque attitudes that characterized co-productions and the cultural alienation inherent in an enterprise like Vera Cruz. Their goal was to study in depth the social relations of each city and region as a way of critically exposing, as if in miniature, the socio-cultural structure of the country as a whole. To take the people as theme, to give human form to fundamental conflicts, to make the people the center and master of the cinematic instrument. A critic from São Paulo, taking this option to its logical conclusion, exploded: "We don't want to make films. We want to hear the voice of Man." And the human voice will have to be heard in the northeast, in the southern latifundia, in Rio's *favelas*, in São Paulo's factories, and on the beaches of the fishermen of Bahia, indeed in all that is authentic and experiential.

Cinema Novo is a committed cinema, a critical cinema, even when, because of the youth and inexperience of its members, this commitment and this critical attitude become somewhat naive and lacking in analytical focus. But even this naiveté is valid, for Cinema Novo is, above all, freedom.

Freedom of invention, freedom of expression. Because Cinema Novo is not a school, it has no established style. On the contrary, a unanimous style makes a movement retrograde, bourgeois, frivolous, manifested merely, or at least most intensely, in the formal, artisan aspect of its expression. In Cinema Novo, expressive forms are necessarily personal and original without formal dogmas, because form is merely one of the terms of a totality of simultaneous instruments directed toward the communication of a truth.

Without wasting time on the relative merits of close versus long shots, without worrying about whether the specifically filmic resides in the camera or in editing, without slothful theorizing, but rather technically rationalizing the practical questions of cinema, Brazilian filmmakers (principally in Rio, Bahia, and São Paulo) have taken their cameras and gone out into the streets, the country, and the beaches in search of the Brazilian people, the peasant, the worker, the fisherman, the slum dweller. Many have already presented the results of their work, but the great majority will release their first films this year.

1962 will doubtless be a key year for national cinema, the year of Cinema Novo. In Bahia, *A Grande Feira* ("The Big Market"), by Roberto Pires, has already been released. The same director is now preparing *Tocaia no Asfalto* ("Asphalt Ambush"). Glauber Rocha is ready to exhibit *Barravento* and is preparing a film about peasants in the state of Rio along with Paulo César Saraceni. Rex Schindler, producing these Bahian films, will probably soon direct a script of his own. Nelson Pereira dos Santos is preparing *Barren Lives* in the northeast. In Rio, Guerra's *Os Cafajestes* has already reached the theaters. *Assalto ao Trem Pagador* ("Assault on the Pay Train"), by Roberto Farias, and *Cinco Vezes Favela*, by five young directors (Joaquim Pedro de Andrade, Marcos Farias, Miguel Borges, Carlos Diegues, and Leon Hirszman) are being readied for distribution. In São Paulo Roberto Santos is finishing his adaptation of Guimarães Rosa's *Matraga*. And there are many other projects either in preparation or in production. Cinema Novo is also defending itself with short films, a recent phenomenon in Brazilian cinema that contributes, for its part, to the training of filmmakers: Linduarte Noronha, Orlando Senna, Glauber Rocha, Paulo César Saraceni, Rex Schindler, Mário Carneiro, Joaquim Pedro de Andrade, Sérgio Ricardo, Paulo Huchmacher, Marcos Farias, David Neves, Affonso Henriques, and many others. Unfortunately, these shorts will probably not have commercial distribution.

Thus Cinema Novo is being created with spirit and invention and without official policies, cliques, or snobbery. Turned toward Brazil and its people, Cinema Novo is ready to take the streetcar of national cinema that has been off track for too many years.

3
"An Esthetic of Hunger"

Introduction

"An Esthetic of Hunger" was first presented in Genoa, Italy, in January, 1965, as part of a retrospective survey of Latin American cinema. It was published in *Revista Civilização Brasileira* in July, 1965, and was subsequently translated into French and published in *Positif* as "L'esthétique de la violence." Although written during the second phase of Cinema Novo, Glauber Rocha's manifesto sheds light on the first phase as well. In the notes to the Portuguese version, Rocha sums up the films of the first phase: "From *Aruanda* to *Barren Lives*, Cinema Novo has narrated, described, poeticized, discussed, analyzed, and stimulated the themes of hunger: characters eating dirt and roots, characters stealing to eat, characters killing to eat, characters fleeing to eat." Rocha contrasts Cinema Novo and its "gallery of starving people" with what he calls "digestive" cinema: "films about rich people with pretty houses riding in luxurious automobiles; cheerful, fast-paced, empty films with purely industrial objectives." In tones that recall Frantz Fanon's *The Wretched of the Earth*, Rocha denounces Brazil's neo-colonial oppression, calling on Brazilians to take both their political and cinematic destiny in their own hands. Like Fanon, Rocha sees violence as the authentic cultural expression of a hungry people. Rejecting the condescending praise of European critics who are merely "nostalgic for primitivism," Rocha proudly asserts the international stature and importance of the Cinema Novo movement. But the truly seminal contribution of this essay was to call for a style appropriate to the real Brazil, to articulate a social thematic together with a production strategy into a truly revolutionary esthetic.

"An Esthetic of Hunger"

GLAUBER ROCHA

Dispensing with the informative introduction so characteristic of discussions about Latin America, I prefer to examine the relationship between our culture and "civilized" culture in broader terms than those of the European observer. Thus, while Latin America laments its general misery, the foreign onlooker cultivates the taste of that misery, not as a tragic *symptom*, but merely as an esthetic object within his field of interest. The Latin American neither communicates his real misery to the "civilized" European, nor does the European truly comprehend the misery of the Latin American.

This is the fundamental situation of the arts in Brazil today: many distortions, especially the formal exoticism that vulgarizes social problems, have provoked a series of misunderstandings that involve not only art but also politics. For the European observer the process of artistic creation in the underdeveloped world is of interest only insofar as it satisfies a nostalgia for primitivism. This primitivism is generally presented as a hybrid form, disguised under the belated heritage of the "civilized world," a heritage poorly understood since it is imposed by colonial conditioning. Latin America remains, undeniably, a colony, and what distinguishes yesterday's colonialism from today's colonialism is merely the more polished form of the colonizer and the more subtle forms of those who are preparing future domination. The international problem of Latin America is still a case of merely exchanging colonizers. Our possible liberation will probably come, therefore, in the form of a new dependency.

Os Inconfidentes (1971)

69

This economic and political conditioning has led us to philosophical weakness and impotence that engenders sterility when conscious and hysteria when unconscious. It is for this reason that the hunger of Latin America is not simply an alarming symptom: it is the essence of our society. There resides the tragic originality of Cinema Novo in relation to world cinema. Our originality is our hunger and our greatest misery is that this hunger is felt but not intellectually understood.

We understand the hunger that the European and the majority of Brazilians have not understood. For the European it is a strange tropical surrealism. For the Brazilian it is a national shame. He does not eat, but he is ashamed to say so; and yet, he does not know where this hunger comes from. We know — since we made these sad, ugly films, these screaming, desperate films where reason does not always prevail — that this hunger will not be cured by moderate governmental reforms and that the cloak of technicolor cannot hide, but only aggravates, its tumors. Therefore, only a culture of hunger, weakening its own structures, can surpass itself qualitatively; the most noble cultural manifestation of hunger is violence.

Cinema Novo shows that the normal behavior of the starving is violence; and the violence of the starving is not primitive. Is Fabiano [in *Barren Lives*] primitive? Is Antão [in *Ganga Zumba*] primitive? Is Corisco [in *Black God, White Devil*] primitive? Is the woman in *Porto das Caixas* primitive?

From Cinema Novo it should be learned that an esthetic of violence, before being primitive, is revolutionary. It is the initial moment when the colonizer becomes aware of the colonized. Only when confronted with violence does the colonizer understand, through horror, the strength of the culture he exploits. As long as they do not take up arms, the colonized remain slaves; a first policeman had to die for the French to become aware of the Algerians.

From a moral position this violence is not filled with hatred just as it is not linked to the old colonizing humanism. The love that this violence encompasses is as brutal as the violence itself because it is not a love of complacency or contemplation but rather of action and transformation.

The time has long passed since Cinema Novo had to justify its existence. Cinema Novo is an ongoing process of exploration that is making our thinking clearer, freeing us from the debilitating delirium of hunger. Cinema Novo cannot develop effectively while it remains marginal to the economic and cultural process of the Latin American continent. Cinema Novo is a phenomenon of new peoples everywhere and not a privilege of Brazil. Wherever one finds filmmakers prepared to film the truth and oppose the hypocrisy and repression of intellectual censorship there is the living spirit of Cinema Novo; wherever filmmakers, of whatever age or background, place their cameras and their profession in the service of the great causes of our time there is the spirit of Cinema Novo. This is the definition of the movement and through this definition Cinema Novo sets itself apart from the commercial industry because the commitment of Industrial Cinema is to untruth and exploitation. The economic and industrial integration of Cinema Novo depends on the freedom of Latin America. Cinema Novo devotes itself entirely to this freedom, in its own name, and in the name of all its participants, from the most ignorant to the most talented, from the weakest to the strongest. It is this ethical question that will be reflected in our work, in the way we film a person or a house, in the details that we choose, in the moral that we choose to teach. Cinema Novo is not one film but an evolving complex of films that will ultimately make the public aware of its own misery.

New York, Milan, Rio de Janeiro

January, 1965

Translated by Randal Johnson and Burnes Hollyman

4
"Criticism and Self-Criticism"

Introduction

During the second phase of Cinema Novo the question of the political efficacy of cinema became much more crucial and immediate. As part of a general re-evaluation of left politics in light of the events of 1964, Cinema Novo, which had previously attempted to put the urban and rural proletariat on the screen, now turned inward toward self-analysis and self-criticism.

In "Criticism and Self-Criticism," an interview-discussion that took place shortly after the release of his *The Priest and the Girl* (1966), Joaquim Pedro de Andrade examines with Alex Viany the accomplishments and failures of Cinema Novo. The starting point of the discussion excerpted here is the question of the political effectiveness of the adoption of the *politique des auteurs*. There can be no tranquil consciences in the current conjuncture, Andrade suggests; simply declaring a politically progressive position is not sufficient. In order to be politically effective films must communicate with the potentially revolutionary classes. Cinema Novo has its public, composed mainly of university students and intellectuals, but has alienated the traditional public of Brazilian cinema. Cinema Novo in this regard is not unlike the Brazilian Modernist Movement of the twenties, which called in theory for a democratization of art but in practice remained an elitist form of expression. Joaquim Pedro de Andrade suggests that Cinema Novo should re-examine the Modernist Movement in light of the current situation in order to break through the homogeneous artist/spectator relationship that had characterized the early years of Cinema Novo.

This article is the first of those presented here to mention military rule in Brazil. The filmmaker painfully acknowledges that if Cinema Novo were to become an effective revolutionary instrument it would be very quickly repressed.

"Criticism and Self-Criticism"

JOAQUIM PEDRO DE ANDRADE AND ALEX VIANY

Viany: . . . is it true that the so-called auteur theory could lead to alienation? It is said that the filmmaker, in search of this auteurism, of this personal affirmation, could be fleeing from true popular art.

Andrade: Politics, within the process of the material and cultural development of Brazil, has assumed more direct, explicit importance. None of us ever stops being a political being, perhaps even primarily a political being. Politics is for us one of the principal materials of speculation, revealing all of the problems of behavior that we debate on the immediate and mediate levels. In political terms, and with reference to Cinema Novo, none of us can have a clear conscience. Merely taking a position, merely defining oneself politically, resolves nothing. It is not enough for a filmmaker to verbally assume a progressive position. If he is truly honest about his position, he must attempt to be politically effective, that is, he must make his film an effective political and social instrument. This has simply not happened. For a film to be a truly political instrument, it must first communicate with its public. If cinema is to be revolutionary, it must reach the potentially revolutionary classes.

Alienation is always a factor in the process of the composition of the film. This problem is manifest in the film's exhibition. We see it clearly in the box-office failures of some films, and even better in the distribution of profits, when films made from a supposedly revolutionary position fail precisely in the theaters located in areas inhabited by the potentially revolutionary classes. Political efficacy is obviously not being achieved. No one's conscience can remain tranquil simply for having verbalized a socially progressive position: often such a position is clear only to those who know the filmmaker. If he assumes this position and is involved in transforming the current situation, he has to reflect on these problems, attempting to make his instrument effective. This has never been, in fact, an object of serious thought and discussion resulting in practical solutions. Now that Cinema Novo has gone beyond the phase of first films and is entering the phase of second and third films, with new filmmakers appearing all the time, some directors have arrived at this point with positive results. Having made their first films they now begin to see the

73

problem with greater clarity and try to resolve it in a truly effective way. Leon Hirszman, for example, is going to make *Garota de Ipanema*, in which he uses a popular stereotype to establish contact with the masses, while at the same time he demystifies that very stereotype. Leon is thus formulating the problem in practical terms.

This change in relation to the Brazilian public and, by extension, to Brazilian reality, arises from the problems connected with auteurism. Auteurs assume total responsibility for their work. All of us here in Brazil — authors of films, books, plays — continually receive information from the cultural vanguard throughout the world. We are obviously affected by this information. There is always a degree of interpenetration and communication between the intelligentsia of more developed and less developed countries. This phenomenon is a perennial one. The modernists of 1922, for example, attempted to deal with this problem by rejecting all imported values and techniques not relevant to our reality in favor of authentically Brazilian processes that would be, in principle, communicative and unalienating. The works produced by this movement, according to this rationale, should have had a greater degree of communication than they in fact had. Despite the good intentions of their program, the movement's complex intellectual processes and intellectual pretension made such communication impossible. We would do well to re-examine the movement of 1922 in terms of the present situation.

Once the filmmaker is absolutely convinced that the most pressing task is political and social action, the only option is to act in consequence, searching honestly and immediately for communication with the potentially progressive classes in order to transmit useful messages. Not all of Cinema Novo has assumed this position. We must respond on the basis of all the knowledge and information available to us; we cannot, for moral reasons, push such values out of our field of cogitation or practical action. For me, the most progressive position is one of complete honesty. If, at a given moment, we hide something because it is not tactically convenient, then that action, extended to its logical conclusion, becomes criminal. The most legitimate progress comes through a dialectical process, through discussion, through the conflict of values, through individual and collective investigation of ideas. The fear of heresy is negative, cowardly, and retrograde. The creation of a body of doctrines that gradually assume the aspect of dogma is anachronistic.

Viany: Anything that leads to stagnation is undialectical by definition. You referred very opportunely to the movement of 1922. Truly, that movement tried to find Brazilian esthetic solutions to better reach the people. The Week of Modern Art undoubtedly made a real effort to find a Brazilian language for Brazilian art, which should have aided this art in reaching more of our people. Although that did not happen the movement of 1922 had enormous importance. It fulfilled its role, influencing where it could among the educated classes, which began to use their investigations and teachings. In a country like Brazil, where illiteracy is widespread and where those that reach the university level constitute a privileged minority, it is in fact very difficult to achieve the transmission of ideas, particularly new and revoultionary ideas. . . .

There is no doubt that Cinema Novo alienated the first audience that Brazilian cinema had conquered, that is, the popular audience of the *chanchada*. This audience simply does not see Cinema Novo films. When it sees them it neither accepts nor understands them. Cinema Novo conquered a whole, vast, new sector of more intellectualized spectators, principally young people and students. Unfortunately, it was unable to combine the two audiences. I sometimes doubt that it intended — despite certain declarations, some sincere and others demogogical — to reach large sectors of the public. As Nelson Pereira dos Santos has observed, one of the first goals of Cinema Novo was to dignify the filmmaking profession in Brazil, to give cinema a dimension, until then denied it, of a legitimate cultural manifestation. The professional and cultural valorization of cinema was achieved. Brazilian cinema had an international impact but the problem of a Brazilian audience for that cinema remains unresolved. Intentionally or not the question was put aside temporarily. But in any case certain postions have been conquered. . . .

Andrade: In our films, the propositions, positions, and ideas are extremely varied, at times even contradictory or at least multiple. Above all they are increasingly free and unmasked. There exists a total freedom of expression. Our films are rich in contradictions; even the most traditional, conventional, negative, out-moded, and reactionary ideas can be found in them. All of these elements are transparent in Cinema Novo films. That is why they provoke such strange discussions, attacked by critics of the right and left and serving as material for a very broad debate. At first glance this would seem to indicate some internal incoherence within the Cinema Novo movement. But in reality I think it indicates a greater coherence: a more legitimate, truthful, and direct correspondence between the filmmaker — with his perplexities, doubts, and certainties — and the world in which he lives. Finally, it would be useful to relate our conversation to the current moment in Brazil. At first glance this type of discussion may seem alienating, even Byzantine, when the immediate reality is so brutal. The situation in fact does not permit us to put these speculations into practice. If a program of revolutionary action — through films, theater, or even books — were successful, truly reaching the masses, that program would be repressed immediately. Even without such a program repression exists. We are thus faced with a tactical problem: given the present situation how do we re-elaborate these questions?

5
"The Tricontinental Filmmaker: That Is Called the Dawn"

Introduction

Published in *Cahiers du Cinéma* in November, 1967, this text represents a further step in the radicalization of Cinema Novo. The twin references in its title, to Che Guevara's "tricontinental" revolution and to Luis Buñuel's *Cela s'appelle l'aurore*, reflect the double thrust, at once political and cinematic, of the manifesto. Che Guevara coined the term "tricontinental" in the late fifties to refer to the three continents — Asia, Africa, and Latin America — that had suffered colonization and that were now ripe, in his view, for revolution. Rocha's rhetorical violence responds to an increasingly repressive political climate within Brazil. He speaks metaphorically of "guerrilla" cinema at a time when Brazilian leftists, reacting to the closing of the political system, began to promote guerrilla actions in the cities and countryside of Brazil. Apart from its political interest, however, the essay also illuminates Rocha's own progression as a filmmaker. It renders explicit what was implicit in his stylistic evolution from *Barravento*, to *Black God, White Devil*, and *Land in Anguish*: a search for an avant-garde, self-reflexive esthetic that would fuse the didacticism of a Brecht or a Godard with the magic and violent anger of the Third World. Rocha simultaneously rejects both socialist realism and empty formalism as models for the tricontinental filmmaker: formal research without political thrust is impotent, while political messages wrapped in bourgeois forms communicate only alienation.

Júlio Bressane's *Agonia* (1973)

"The Tricontinental Filmmaker:
That Is Called the Dawn"

GLAUBER ROCHA

For the Third World filmmaker, commitment begins with the first light, because the camera opens on to the Third World, an occupied land. Choices must be made, in the street, in the desert, in the forest, or in the city, and even when the material might be neutral the montage transforms it into discourse. A discourse that can be imprecise, diffuse, barbarous, irrational, but one in which even refusals are significant.

These films from Asia, Africa, and Latin America are films of discomfort. The discomfort begins with the basic material: inferior cameras and laboratories, and therefore crude images and muffled dialogue, unwanted noise on the soundtrack, editing accidents, and unclear credits and titles. And on the screen a desperate body writhes, advances jerkily only to hunch over in the rain, its blood confounded.

The tools belong to Hollywood as arms belong to the Pentagon. No filmmaker is completely free. Even when not the prisoner of censorship or financial commitments he remains a prisoner until he discovers within himself the tricontinental man. Only this idea liberates him, for within it the perspective of individual failure ceases to be important. Che Guevara said: "our sacrifice is conscious; it is the necessary price of freedom."

All other discourse is beautiful but innocuous; rational but fatigued; reflexive but impotent; "cinematic" but useless. Lyricism is born with words gliding in the air; but it is immediately structured into passive form in a sterile conspiracy. . . .

There is a great deal to do today. A national cinema that concentrates on didactic films makes a contribution: the de-intoxication from socialist realism.

> Simplifying the terms of these polemics, which involved some artists and functionaries, some defended a kind of socialist realism, while others (mostly artists) defended an art which would not renounce all the conquests of the avant-garde. The rejection of the first tendency was made clear in Che Guevara's essay, "Man and Socialism in Cuba," which condemned socialist realism without finding a completely satisfying alternative: for him, it had to be transcended. But to go further, one must begin from somewhere, and the avant-garde seems to be the best point of departure. (Jesus Diaz, "Partisans," no. 137)

Other Latin American countries, meanwhile, can only use their cameras to make official newsreels showing generals and their medals.

Tupi, Cangaço, Bossa

I. Brazil speaks Portuguese. In order to understand the phenomenon called Cinema Novo it is important to know that the Portuguese are less fanatical and more cynical than the Spanish: we have a heritage that is not as nationalistic as the Spanish. Brazilian filmmakers have lost their "awe" for cinema. They have laid their often awkward hands on cameras without asking anyone's permission. Although intellectuals used to say, to the point of convincing critics and intimidating filmmakers, that "Portuguese is an anti-cinematic language," Cinema Novo decided to take the daily speech and music of Brazil as its material. Peopled by long-winded, chattering, energetic, sterile, and hysterical individuals, Brazil is the only Latin American country that never had a bloody revolution like Mexico, or the baroque fascism of Argentina, nor a real political revolution like Cuba, or guerrillas like those found in Bolivia, Colombia, or Venezuela. So as sad compensation Brazil has a cinema that turned out sixty films this year (1967) and will double that figure next year. More than a hundred young filmmakers have presented films in 8mm and 16mm at the last two amateur film festivals in Brazil, and the public, disappointed by the last soccer match, discusses each film with passion. In Rio, São Paulo, Bahia, and other cities, there are art cinemas, cinematheques, as well as 400 different film clubs. From Rio to São Paulo, Godard is as popular as De Gaulle. Cinematic madness abounds in the land.

II. Tupi is the name of an Indian nation in Brazil. Its characteristics: intelligence and artistic incompetence. Cangaço is a mystic, anarchist guerrilla: the word cangaço describes violent disorder. Bossa is a dance: it is also the art of feinting toward the right while attacking from the left, coming together in a dance with rhythm and eroticism. This tradition, whose values are questioned in the films of Cinema Novo, make up the tragic caricature of a melodramatic civilization. For Brazil has no historic density: there have been only a few military coups and counter-coups carried out in the name of imperialist interests and the national bourgeoisie. The populist left always ends up by signing a pact with the repentent right, advancing once more on the path towards "redemocratization." It is noteworthy that the political avant-garde of Latin America is always led by intellectuals and that poems frequently precede gunshots. Popular opera, music, and revolution all go hand in hand; that is our Iberic heritage. Today, in the Brazil of unforeseen reconciliations, the urban left is known as the "Festive Left." There one discusses Marx to the sound of the samba. But that doesn't stop students from descending into the streets to join violent demonstrations where professors are arrested, universities are closed, and intellectuals write protest manifestos.

III. Cinema Novo represents thirty percent of all cinematic production in Brazil. The collective nature of the movement allows for control over publicity, distribution, and criticism. Confronted with a relatively uncultivated (or at least, less literate) audience, a Tricontinental cinema has to overcome immense obstacles to create a means of meaningful communication in popular language and stimulating revolutionary feelings. A Cinema Novo film is polemical before, during, and after it is projected. A Cinema Novo film inevitably shocks the paradise of inertia of its public. Thus, *Vidas Secas* gives information concerning the peasants; *The Guns* goes beyond *Vidas Secas* to become an anti-militarist film. *Black God, White Devil* raises the protest of *The Guns* to a frenzied, fanatical level that is repeated in *O Desafio*. *Ganga Zumba* deals with blacks, *Os Cafajestes* is the urban version of *Vidas Secas*. From *Plantation Boy* to *Land in Anguish*, or from *Land in Anguish* to *The Brave Warrior*, Cinema Novo seems to lose its central thrust through the difficult exercise of individual expression; it could be said that still, taken as a whole, Cinema Novo forms a concerto that, as a kind of permanent, ongoing polemic, constitutes a political action.

Cinema

I. The past and present cinematic technique of the developed world interests me to the extent that I can use it the way the American cinema was used by certain European filmmakers. Certain cinematic techniques have transcended both individual auteurs and the films in which they operate to form a sort of vocabulary of cinema: if I film a *cangaceiro* in the *sertão*, it belongs to a montage tradition that is linked to the western, more than to individual auteurs like Ford or Hawks. On the other hand, imitation need not be perceived as a passive act, a need to take refuge in the established language of the form, in an attempt to "save" a film. In an interview Truffaut said: "All of the films that imitate Godard are unbearable because they lack the essential. They imitate his casualness, but they forget his despair. They imitate his wordplay but not his cruelty." Most films made today by young filmmakers suffer from *mal de Godard*. But it is only by encounters with reality and by the exercise of one's profession that one can go beyond imitation. Brazilian films like *The Deceased, Vidas Secas*, and *The Guns* show how the colonized film-maker can use technique to express himself. The problem is different for Americans or Europeans, but even films from socialist countries are anything but revolutionary. The attitude of most filmmakers degenerates into a kind of calligraphic cinema that betrays a contemplative or demagogic spirit. And the short films that are shown at international film festivals all seem to have been made in the same mold, manufactured (innocently?) on the editing table and distributed in projection booths, part of a cinematic production line.

II. Cinema is an international discourse and national situations do not justify, at any level, denial of expression. In the case of Tricontinental cinema, esthetics have more to do with ideology than with technique, and the technical myths of the zoom, of direct cinema, of the hand-held camera and of the uses of color are nothing more than tools for expression. The operative word is *ideology*, and it knows no geographical boundaries. When I speak of Tricontinental cinema and include Godard in this grouping, it is because his work opens a guerrilla-like operation in the cinema; he attacks suddenly and unexpectedly, with pitiless films. His cinema becomes political because it proposes a strategy, a valuable set of tactics, usable in any part of the world. I insist on a "guerrilla cinema" as the only form of combat: the cinema one improvises outside the conventional production structure against formal conventions imposed on the general public and on the elite.

III. In the case of *Barravento, Black God, White Devil*, and *Land in Anguish*, I think that I have taken the first steps toward this guerrilla cinema. I see in these films the disasters of a violent transition. But it is through this rupture that I have come to see the possibilities for Tricontinental cinema. The goal of epic-didactic cinema cannot replace the epic-didactic mise-en-scène of a true revolutionary like Che Guevara, it can only fuse itself with it. If Buñuel's films displace the conventions of the continental cinema, the Tricontinental cinema must infiltrate the conventional cinema and blow it up. At the moment when Che Guevara's death becomes legend, poetry becomes praxis.

Translated by Burnes Hollyman and Robert Stam

6
"Cannibalism and Self-Cannibalism"

Introduction

Joaquim Pedro de Andrade's *Macunaíma* (1969), based on the novel of the same name by Mário de Andrade (1928), is generally considered to be the high point of the Tropicalist movement in Brazilian cinema. While

How Tasty Was My Little Frenchman (1971)

certainly a response to the political contradictions of post-1964 Brazil, Tropicalism also resurrects Oswald de Andrade's *Movimento Antropófago* (Cannibalist Movement) of the modernist period (1922-1930) in terms of the social and political realities of the late sixties.

The Cannibalist Movement of the twenties advocated the creation of a genuine national culture through the consumption and critical re-elaboration of both national and foreign influences. Imported cultural influences were to be devoured, digested, and reworked in terms of local conditions. Oswald de Andrade's anthropophagous program was influenced by Levy-Bruhl's concept of the primitive mind as being at a pre-logical stage as well as by Keyserling's idea that the true barbarian is not the "primitive," but rather the "civilized" alienated by technology. The Cannibalist program expresses a utopian desire for a return to a mythical matriarchal Golden Age when tribes, rather than enslaving their enemies, ate them. Oswald de Andrade's cannibal is not the Romantic ideal of the noble savage, but corresponds rather to Montaigne's cannibal who devours his enemies as an act of supreme vengeance.

Joaquim Pedro de Andrade's *Macunaíma*, released less than a year after the promulgation of the extremely repressive Fifth Institutional Act, is an ideological radicalization of Mário de Andrade's original text and perhaps the most successful re-evaluation and re-elaboration of the Brazilian Modernist Movement. Its coded language of revolt represents an extremely aggressive attack on the continued exploitation of Brazil by the international capitalist system. The following text, written as an introduction to the film for the 1969 Venice Film Festival, forms part of the English version of the film.

"Cannibalism and Self-Cannibalism"

JOAQUIM PEDRO DE ANDRADE

Cannibalism is an exemplary mode of consumerism adopted by underdeveloped peoples. In particular, the Brazilian Indians, immediately after having been "discovered" by the first colonizers, had the rare opportunity of selecting their Portuguese-supplied Bishop, Dom Pedro Fernandes Sardinha, whom they devoured in a memorable meal.

It is not by accident that the revolutionary artists of the twenties — the Modernists — dated their Cannibal Manifesto "the year the Bishop Sardinha was swallowed." Today we can clearly note that nothing has changed. The traditionally dominant, conservative social classes continue their control of the power structure — and we rediscover cannibalism.

Every consumer is reducible, in the last analysis, to cannibalism. The present work relationships, as well as the relationships between people—social, political, and economic—are still basically cannibalistic. Those who can, "eat" others through their consumption of products, or even more directly in sexual relationships. Cannibalism has merely institutionalized itself, cleverly disguised itself. The new heroes, still looking for a collective consciousness, try to devour those who devour us. But still weak, they are themselves transformed into products by the media and consumed.

The Left, while being devoured by the Right, tries to discipline and purify itself by eating itself—a practice that is simply the cannibalism of the weak. The church celebrates communion by eating Christ. Victims and executioners are one and the same; devouring themselves. Everything, whether it be in the heart or in the jaw, is food to be consumed. Meanwhile, voraciously, nations devour their people.

Macunaíma is the story of a Brazilian devoured by Brazil.

7

"Everybody's Woman"

Introduction

The late sixties were marked by a burgeoning Underground film movement. One of the key figures in this movement was Rogério Sganzerla, author of one of its seminal films: *Bandido da Luz Vermelha* ("Red Light Bandit," 1968). In an act of cultural cannibalism, Sganzerla's films, and generally those of the Underground movement, devour international cinema in order to appropriate its force and then re-elaborate it in an irreverent camp style. The films become parodic, making fun of the most cherished fetishes of Brazilian official culture. The Underground directors even made fun of Cinema Novo, which they regarded as too academic, well-behaved, and serious. In contrast, the Underground developed techniques of aggression, fragmentation, and provocation. The following text, written in 1969 as a kind of preface to Sganzerla's film *A Mulher de Todos* ("Everybody's Woman"), gives some idea of the polemical tone and satirical spirit of the movement.

"Everybody's Woman"

ROGERIO SGANZERLA

Fortunately or unfortunately, *A Mulher de Todos* is more intelligent than the critics, a sin not easily forgiven. Nevertheless, nothing is easier than making films more intelligent than their critics.

I understand perfectly that the critics do not understand. No one is obliged to agree with me. It is all part of a game: I proclaim the obvious but few people realize it. The fault is neither mine nor that of our pious South American critics, but simply of the culturalist prejudices that the new decade will destroy. Until then, stupidity comes cheap.

My next little films will be exactly like *A Mulher de Todos*, neither better nor worse, designed for the internal consumption of underdevelopment. From now on, I intend to plagiarize every last frame of my own work, because what interests me now is not *pastiche* but rather *auto-pastiche*. I am still the world's biggest fan of Radio Nacional and Mayrink Veiga.* I will never deliver clear ideas, eloquent speeches, or classically beautiful images when confronted with garbage—I will only reveal, through free sound and funereal rhythm, our own condition as ill-behaved colonized people. Within the garbage can, one must be radical. Whence my love for Brazilian cinema as it is, poorly made, pretentious, and without redeeming esthetic illusions. Crushed and exploited, the colonized can only *invent* their own suffocation; the cry of protest emerges from the abortive *mise-en-scène*. No one can think purely and esthetically on an empty stomach.

I continue to make an underdeveloped cinema, both by condition and vocation, a barbarous indigenous cinema, anticulturalist, striving for that toward which the Brazilian people have been aspiring since the days of the *chanchada*—to make Brazilian cinema the worst in the world. Ah, how marvelous and reasonable it would be!

It all forms part of an ignoble game: Brazilian critics repudiate everything marginal (Júlio Bressané, Neville d'Almeida, a film like Fernando Campos's *Voyage to the End of the World*) in order to promote the official manifestations of Cinema Novo and hillbilly expressionism, and principally that old school which seeks to falsify our reality by mediocre academicism and astronomical budgets.

After all, my films are above all obvious self-criticisms that intellectuals could never understand. My films *are* their defects. My films are exactly that which their production could not achieve and that I could never film because, as everyone knows, Brazilian cinema is the greatest precisely because it is impossible.

*A major Brazilian radio network.

8
"From the Drought to the Palm Trees"

Introduction

First published in *Positif* in March, 1970, "From the Drought to the Palm Trees" represents a report to Europeans on the state of Brazilian cinema. The title, in Rocha's typically allusive way, evokes the passage from Cinema Novo's first phase, with its esthetic of hunger and thematic of drought, to its third phase: the lush exuberance of Tropicalism. It recalls, at the same time, the apocalyptic symbolism of both *Black God, White Devil* and *Antônio das Mortes*: "The sertão will become sea, and the sea sertão." Symbolically, the current drought of political repression will give way to an oasis of freedom. Rocha catalogs the seemingly insuperable political and economic obstacles that confront filmmakers in Brazil, even as he glories in their successes despite the obstacles. In the elliptically allegorical language that was to become increasingly characteristic of his writing he proudly rejects paternalistic "advice" from would-be European mentors. He defends Cinema Novo in its Tropicalist incarnation when some critics and filmmakers were beginning to argue that the term "Cinema Novo" had become obsolescent. At the time of this article, Cinema Novo was under attack from both left and right while being challenged by a burgeoning Underground movement. The article displays an essentially ambivalent attitude toward the Underground movement. On the one hand, Rocha salutes the arrival of "young Brazilian filmmakers" such as Bressane, Sganzerla, Tonacci. On the other, he chides them for their naiveté in wanting a completely anti-industrial cinema. And he asks that they be mindful of their cinematic forebearers: ". . . they are filmmakers because Cinema Novo opened the way for them."

"From the Drought to the Palm Trees"

GLAUBER ROCHA

HEADLINE:
Cinema Novo in 1970 is not dead.
The situation in Brazil is painful. Making films there is an economic risk. The market is dominated by the Americans and the Europeans. Making Cinema Novo films is also a political risk, because for the right Cinema Novo represents subversion, while for the left it constitutes a useless distraction. The National Institute of Cinema dislikes Cinema Novo. Most Brazilian intellectuals (and the bourgeoisie) are enraged; they think "we must get rid of these upstarts who want to make films in a country that does not even have stars like Gary Cooper."
But Cinema Novo is still alive.
Luis Carlos Barreto has a realistic vision. "Our distribution house is like a political party with its organization, its discipline, and its freedom of creation." And in Europe our friends ask: "If you have no money, no official protection, no freedom, how in the world can you still make films?"
ECONOMY
We are the peasants of cinema. Before, in 1962, we planted on dry ground; we put our fears aside to accomplish our task. In 1969 we have *Macunaíma, Brazil Year 2000, The Heirs, Memories of Helen, The Alienist, Antonio das Mortes.* After the drought and before the palm trees we were involved in resistance: *The Challenge, The Big City, Plantation Boy, The Priest and the Girl, The Deceased, Public Opinion, Matraga, Land in Anguish, The Brave Warrior.*
And others came as well: Bressane, Gomes Leite, Neville d'Almeida, Fontoura, Escorel, Calmon, Farias, Sganzerla, Bernardes, Tonacci, Sarno, Moniz, Santeiro, Gil Soares, Capovilla, André Luiz.
1960: It is impossible for us to make films.
1968: Nelson Pereira dos Santos begins Cinema Novo all over again with *Fome de Amor.*
1969: More than thirty new filmmakers and seventy films.
Perhaps the cinema is no longer important. But the existence of Cinema Novo constitutes proof of our country's cultural power.
In Brazil people are full of doubts. So I ask them: "How is it possible to organize production without money or protection, and with censorship and imperialist domination? How? With class consciousness. Cinematic peasants have to organize in order to work the earth and sell their products on the market. But people prefer imported canned food; no one has the courage to say that coconut milk is *better* than Coca-Cola. The in-

tellectuals (the technicians) give their advice: "You should sell coconut milk, but in Coca-Cola bottles." At least we have constructed our own concession within the film marketplace: Difilm. . . . Our goal: to overthrow American, European, and Brazilian consumer cinema and replace it with a dialectical cinema. We are underdeveloped. We do not love either this absolute hunger or the chronic illness that we all carry since birth.

The phrase "political cinema" comes cheap. We Brazilian filmmakers are too busy dying and producing to waste our time participating in the grand demogogic international celebration.

All we want is the international market.

Our public is the victim of international cinema.

Our bourgeoisie has been colonized by Neo-Realism and the nouvelle vague. This colonization threatens to continue even after the revolution. Fox, Paramount, and Metro are our enemies. But Eisenstein, Rossellini, and Godard are also our enemies. They crush us. Our only friends are the critics in Brazil and elsewhere, who have done important work for, or rather with, us.

DIARY

In Venice Carlos Diegues said that we were already too old to be young filmmakers. Rui Guerra added that we should put an end to Cinema Novo, but that nevertheless we had to go back to Brazil to film. I wonder if we should put an end to Cinema Novo in its Tropicalist incarnation. Let's wait for the fire next time. Fire must devour Cinema Novo as Iara devours Macunaíma. But before being devoured, Cinema Novo must devour the Brazilian market, itself devoured by imperialist cinema. It should also devour the stupid snobbery of our intellectuals, devoured by "culture." Cinema Novo should provoke fiery indigestion, be devoured by its own fire, and be reborn from its own ashes. . . .

NEWSREELS

A few young Brazilian filmmakers want to do away with Cinema Novo because it has no esthetic-political program. But in fact it is exactly the films, including the films of these new filmmakers, that constitute the program of Cinema Novo. The program: conquer the market and maintain economic independence in order to sustain freedom of production. It is useless to denounce the system if one has no means to sabotage the system. We can no longer make a moralistic critique of the system; we have to transform it, knowing full well that one does not shoot a film as one writes verses. Even when cinema is anti-industrial it remains an industry.

SITUATION

There are centers of production in Rio, São Paulo, Bahia, Paraíba, Pernambuco, Brasília, Paraná, Rio Grande do Sul, and Minas Gerais. New centers are emerging from the Amazon to the Pampas. More than 300 films in 16 millimeters and in super-8 were presented at the Festival of Amateur Cinema sponsored by the *Jornal do Brasil*. Thomas Farkas directs a team that is in the process of making 100 16 millimeter documentaries, with direct sound and in color. At the School of Communications of the University of São Paulo, Roberto Santos and Rudá de Andrade make films with students. A number of writers and painters are changing their profession and beginning to make films.

MANIFESTO

Cinema Novo is starting to take on the look of Brazilian cinema itself. That is why I insist: even if we find that the expression "Cinema Novo" is obsolete we cannot do away with a spirit that is greater than our will. But the young should know that they cannot be irresponsible about the present and the future because today's anarchy can be tomorrow's slavery. Before long imperialism will start to exploit new raw materials. If Brazilian cinema now has palm trees of Tropicalism, the peasants who have lived through the drought have to be on guard so that Brazilian cinema doesn't become underdeveloped.

The only way of fighting is to produce: the filmmaker who doesn't see this reality is either blind or idiotic. Filmmakers of the Third World have to organize national film production and expel imperialist cinema from the national market.

If each Third World country sustains production with its own national market, then revolutionary cinema is possible.

The Third World filmmaker shouldn't be afraid of being "primitive." The true naiveté consists in imitating the culture of domination or in chauvinism. The filmmaker must be dialectical and cannibalistic.

The people colonized by the commercial-popular esthetics of Hollywood, the populist-demogogic esthetics of Moscow, and the bourgeois-artistic esthetics of Europe, must see, hear, and comprehend a new, popular, revolutionary esthetic. This is the only justification for the Third World cinema. We must create this new esthetic.

The seizure of political power by the colonized is fundamental. But the seizure of power is not enough.

The creation of a popular revolutionary esthetic is the most revolutionary task at hand because all political powers are afraid of a dialectical criticism. Exceptions?

The popular revolutionary esthetic remains a Utopia.

Tropicalist cinema is the virgin coast of that Utopia.

The Tricontinental filmmaker should burn the theories that the neocolonialist left tries to impose on us.

Third World filmmakers are tortured by the police. They can be shot.

A true international relationship should be founded upon these principles: no more paternalism, no more sentimental solidarity, no more humiliation, no more gratuitous aggression, and above all, no advice!

Images don't need translation and leftist words cannot save rightist images.

Translated by Robert Stam and Burnes Hollyman

9
"The *Luz e Ação* Manifesto"

Introduction

"The *Luz e Ação* Manifesto," published in July, 1973, is the joint work of a number of Cinema Novo directors: Carlos Diegues, Glauber Rocha, Joaquim Pedro de Andrade, Leon Hirszman, Miguel Faria, Nelson Pereira dos Santos, and Walter Lima Jr. The title—"Light and Action"—evokes both the processes of cinematic production and, metaphorically, the light of theory and the action of praxis. The manifesto denounces governmental repression and cinematic mediocrity; more importantly, it points up the link between the two phenomena. Without mentioning them by name, it scores the commercialism of *pornochanchadas* (cheap erotic comedies) as politically and esthetically retrograde. The success of films like *Macunaíma* and *How Tasty Was My Little Frenchman* showed that the public was ready for artistically valid and politically progressive films. It should be remembered that the state cultural apparatus at this time was promoting patriotic films based on literary classics and historical events. In 1972, the Ministry of Education and Culture proposed an annual prize for films adapted from literary works by "dead authors." This necrophilic preference for the defunct carried with it certain practical and ideological consequences, for it implicitly favored the production of innocuous costume dramas set in a safely distant past. Some directors outwitted the cooptive intentions of this policy: Andrade's *Os Inconfidentes* ("The Conspirators," 1972) gave a decidedly non-official reading of a famous historical incident (an abortive revolution in the eighteenth century) and Leon Hirszman's *São Bernardo* (1973) took a literary classic, already highly politicized, and made it relevant to Brazil of the seventies. "The *Luz e Ação* Manifesto" in some ways marked a turning point in

Xica da Silva (1976)

Brazilian cinema. To a situation of general malaise, it opposed a collective "Basta!" and proposed a new departure.

"The *Luz e Ação* Manifesto"

LUZ E AÇÃO

Since 1968/69, our films have been victims of the cultural exorcism that has swept the country. New tendencies and emergent standards — official or not — have stifled us, but at the same time have permitted us time for reflection. And we have been silent.

The silence has animated old rancors and has permitted the "vengeance" that has lasted now for four years. In the cultural desert in which Brazil has been transformed, solitary megalomaniac *cangaceiros* ride the beast of their neuroses, firing wildly at whatever shows signs of life.

We've had enough.

We are no longer willing to peacefully coexist with the slothful silence and suspect aggression that have conspired against our films. We are no longer willing to tolerate the mental leukemia that is threatening Brazilian culture.

Mental leukemia: white corpuscles have swallowed red corpuscles, blood no longer warms the body. Leukemic intelligence is manifested through complacency, laziness, and mechanical imitation.

We reject the bureaucratic cinema of statistics and pseudo-industrial myths. Films like *Macunaíma* and *How Tasty Was My Little Frenchman* have broken box-office records. Nothing can justify low-level commercialism.

We reject "the public at any price" blackmail. It has led Brazilian cinema to the most abhorrent deformations: easy laughs at the expense of the weak, racism, sexuality as merchandise, scorn for artistic expression as a scientific and poetic form of knowledge. And we affirm this rejection with the authority of those who have worked consistently and constantly toward a dialectical relationship between spectacle and spectator.

Our most recent films show our desire for a vast and just redistribution of the cultural wealth of the nation. We are opposed to its concentration in the hands of asceptic experimentalism, the self-serving vanguard, and socialite clowns.

For us cinema only has meaning as a permanent invention, on all levels of creation—the search for new modes of production, new thematic areas, new techniques, and linguistic experimentation.

Permanent invention is what distinguishes a good film from a bad one. The pleasure of form, the great utopias, the "sentiment of the world," are rights and duties of the artist. Because one thing, as Drummond says, is always two: the thing itself and its image.

In the name of this permanent invention our cinema formulated the most radical theses to emerge from Brazilian culture during the sixties. A general political and ethical position produced an original and revolutionary esthetic that gained international prestige and influenced modern cinema.

We want to generate new ideas for new situations, and thus keep Brazilian cinema from transforming itself into the newest "old" industry, or the youngest decadent culture, in the world.

We refuse to justify silence or impotence with hypocrisy. Progressively expanding these limits through the exercise of freedom, we will further deepen our work, making it rain in the desert.

As Brazilians, this is our fundamental situation: if we do not put Brazil in our films, they will have failed.

We therefore convoke the cultural producers of the country, particularly those of cinema, to an open dialogue. We repeat: we want to generate new ideas for new situations. This is not a group manifesto, but a collective text of provocation, intended to ignite debate.

Brazilian culture should not have to choose between complaints and conformism, cynicism, and vulgarity. The *new* is beyond these alternatives.

10

"Toward a Common Market of Portuguese- and Spanish-Speaking Countries"

Introduction

Throughout its history Brazilian cinema has had to confront the domination of its internal film market by foreign concerns. As a result, it has often called on the state for support and protection. Legislation guaranteeing a portion of the internal market for Brazilian films was first passed under the government of Getúlio Vargas in the mid-thirties and since that time many laws have been implemented regulating the market and the film industry. Such legislation has given Brazilian cinema the needed impetus to develop despite its unfavorable position in its own market.

By the mid-seventies Brazilian cinema, led by a strengthened state film enterprise (Embrafilme) under the direction of filmmaker Roberto Farias, was not only in a position to compete on more favorable terms with foreign cinema, but was also able to reach limited foreign markets, especially in Latin America and Africa. In an attempt to further decolonize the Brazilian film market and to exhibit its films abroad, Embrafilme promoted in 1977 an international Congress on the Commercialization of Films in Portuguese and Spanish. Brazil proposed the creation of a Common Market among Portuguese- and Spanish-speaking countries, suggesting that each country open, by legislation, twenty percent of its film market to other Common Market countries. The implementation of such a proposal would help break the stranglehold of American cinema on most of the local markets and guarantee each country a broader market for the development of a national film industry. "Toward a Common Market of Portuguese- and Spanish-Speaking Countries" is Roberto Farias's closing address at the 1977 conference.

"Toward a Common Market of Portuguese- and Spanish-Speaking Countries

ROBERTO FARIAS

The implementation of a "new world order," proclaimed by the United Nations in 1974, will inevitably have to be based on studies that UNESCO has been making in the thirty years since its founding about inequalities between developed and underdeveloped countries.

These inequalities, more than evident in social and economic sectors, are just as evident when analyzed from a cultural perspective. One cannot remain indifferent to the abysmal disequilibrium between the production and consumption of information in the world. Because information — as Makaminan Makagiasar, sub-director general of Cultural Affairs and Communications of UNESCO warns — "constitutes today not only a technological power but also a political one, both on the national and international levels."

Cinema is an important part of the communications complex by which information is transmitted. An image is information, and information is culture. Subject to a unidirectional flow of information through all media — the press, radio, television, books, cinema — developing countries are condemned to the annulment of their most precious national values and to the consequent decharacterization of their own cultures.

By proposing the creation of a Cinematographic Common Market of Portuguese- and Spanish-speaking countries, I have adhered, *ipsis literis*, to the recommendation of UNESCO that groupings of countries be formed in the cultural defense of their heritage "to promote the free circulation of ideas through words and images."

The Nineteenth General Conference of UNESCO, held in Nairobi in 1976, denounced the role of information as a new form of domination in which poor countries become increasingly alienated by new information agencies, films, and the profuse television programming exported by rich countries. We thus consume — as Nidha Najar, a communications technician from Tunisia, observes — information that tends to maintain the inhabitants of developing countries in a state of alienation, while wealthy countries live in dangerous ignorance of these peoples, with reckless faith in the industrial, technological, and cultural superiority of their civilization.

Cultural products originating in wealthy countries are fashioned to the tastes of the public of the producing market, that is, the public of the country of origin. They are almost always entertainment products imposed, through their low price, on poor countries. For example: a film for television whose cost, in the wealthy country, may vary from $500,000 to $1,000,000 can be sold to an underdeveloped country for as low as $500.

Normally, wealthy countries hold and disseminate, deliberately or not, a distorted image of the reality of poor countries. This image is commercialized and maintained through films and television programs, contributing to the transformation of the cultural vision that poor countries have of themselves.

From the perspective of the dominant market, the Mexican is generally lazy and drunk at the door of a tavern, protecting himself from the sun with his prodigious *sombrero*; the Brazilian, in striped shirt and tambourine in hand, is always twisting and turning in a samba school and — even worse — also in a *sombrero*.

—Why don't you make another *Black Orpheus* in Brazil?

This question is often asked of Brazilian directors and producers abroad. For many foreigners, Brazil represents nothing more than the Amazon, coffee, samba, and soccer. *Black Orpheus* happens to be a French film.

The controllers of information look for only what is exotic and picturesque in underdeveloped countries. In a country like Brazil they expect us to make films only about wild animals and *macumba*. They import, for the enjoyment of their public, the image they have created of us, while at the same time they impose their own reality on us.

These considerations lead me to propose the creation of the Common Market. Brazilians want to be known as they are, which might even include the exotic and the picturesque. But we also want to know our Latin American, Africa, and Portuguese brothers and sisters just as they are.

Our proposal offers poorer countries, including those that have not yet fully developed their cinema, access to an enormous market that will place them on the same level in the Common Market block as the more advanced countries.

The Brazilian proposal is neither neo-colonialist nor paternalistic. It is founded rather on respect for regional cultures and on the policy advocated by the Organization of American States of non-intervention and self-determination for the peoples of the world.

Cultural and economic policies cannot be independent of each other. Cultural cooperation leads to economic liberation and, therefore, to political emancipation. I am convinced that our possibilities in this undertaking are great. Brazil does not speak alone, because opposition on the part of receiving countries to the unidirectional flow of information from transmitting countries is world-wide.

The Nineteenth UNESCO Conference emphasized the need for rich and poor countries to strengthen their sense of international responsibility through a system of equitable communication.

We have begun by proposing the Cinematographic Common Market because we are convinced that it will work. Providing an opportunity to all countries, it will neutralize the influence of a one-way flow of information. It will lead to political emancipation and to an awareness of the freedom that each people must have to express itself.

The cultural identification between Portuguese- and Spanish-speaking countries is the greatest trump card we possess in this campaign. The Bantu dialect, for example, spoken by significant numbers of African slaves, helps maintain a bridge of reciprocal interest between Angola and Brazil. Remains of Inca culture or of the Aztec empire form part of the contemporary civilization of the Spanish colonizer while each region retains its cultural particularities. The Luso-Brazilian community is very close to the Latin American community.

In our inaugural speech we proposed to open twenty percent of the Brazilian film market to Angola, Argentina, Colombia, Spain, Mexico, Paraguay, Peru, Portugal, Uruguay, and Venezuela.

The response to our proposal has exceeded all expectations, partially due to the good fortune of having as counterparts figures who not only have the highest personal and professional qualifications in the cinematic media but also represent the highest levels of their respective governments.

Although we were very close, we hardly saw one another; although we were allies in the same cause, we did not know it. Without any pretension of rewriting history, we have recognized that our roots are much deeper than we had thought.

The First Congress on the Commercialization of Films in Spanish and Portuguese has permitted member countries to meet, debate, and propose solutions to problems that are common to us all. From this arises the need for interchange, for the unity of developing cinemas against cultural and commercial domination by multinational corporations. The original document of this Congress underlines an important political lesson: no people should underestimate its own potential.

We can no longer permit the absurd practice of block-booking, that is, the system by which the exhibitor, in order to profit from the astronomic box-office success of a *King Kong*, must passively accept dozens of low-quality films.

Other mature cinemas, paradoxically—such as the French and Italian—lacking the distribution network of a traditionally dominant cinema, can only enter Brazil at a fixed price. This system results in an absurd situation: films that are underpromoted and bought for approximately $1,000 often generate an income of $1,000,000 in Brazil alone.

The Brazilian formula for reoccupying our own market does not exlude the future possibility of the entrance into the Cinematographic Common Market of countries like France and Italy, with whom we share our Latin roots. In that case a market of 1,250,000 spectators per year would expand to more than 2,000,000.

Currently, due to laws of compulsory exhibition, Brazilian cinema occupies thirty percent of the internal market opposed to seventy percent occupied by foreign cinemas, above all American. With the gradual implementation of the Common Market among Portuguese- and Spanish-speaking countries, twenty percent of the market would be reserved for the cinemas of the community, with the exception of the importing country, so that competition would be equalized: fifty percent for strong foreign cinemas and fifty percent for national cinema and those of the Common Market.

The spirit of free enterprise will be preserved even in the reserved minimum of twenty percent, to be disputed in open competition by the members of the block.

We must immediately open a part of the foreseen quota in our market to member countries since at least two of them have already signed bilateral accords with us.

The Common Market will provide an alternative to unidirectional information. It will decentralize production. We will no longer be passive consumers, tacitly complicit with the distortion of our own image.

In the execution of such an ambitious project, we will have to create mechanisms of distribution—such as the formation of an enterprise, probably of mixed economy—with which the countries of the community will associate themselves. Representatives should also meet annually in one of our countries to examine the comportment of the Common Market in relation to its members. I am certain that after agreements on film exhibition, we will eventually deal with television, the single most powerful vehicle of communication, which constitutes one of the major preoccupations of the "receiving" countries faced with a deluge of canned programs filled with violence and eroticism.

11
"Popular Cinema and the State: Two Views"

Introduction

The two interviews excerpted here, originally published in 1977 in the film journal *Cine-Olho*, reflect the growing debate among Brazilian filmmakers concerning the role of the state in the national film industry. A major question in this debate revolves around the possible political cooptation of the original Cinema Novo group due to their collaboration with Embrafilme. Carlos Diegues's latest films have been co-produced by the state enterprise, and Rui Guerra's *The Fall* is distributed by Embrafilme.

Comparing the present situation with the early days of Cinema Novo, both Diegues and Guerra partially blame the movement's initial failure to develop a truly popular cinema on the youth of the directors, then in their 20s. Diegues lauds the stylistic pluralism of Cinema Novo. Embrafilme, for him, represents a victory in Cinema Novo's struggle against the multinational film corporations, and has democratized Brazilian cinema by giving it access to a broader public.

For Guerra, on the other hand, popular cinema involves much more than box-office statistics. A truly popular cinema must reach the potentially revolutionary classes with a viable political program, something that Brazilian cinema has never done due to the existing structures of distribution and exhibition. Such a cinema can only go hand in hand with a general social transformation. As a state enterprise, Embrafilme merely reflects the contradictions of the Brazilian political and economic system. It is utopian, Guerra suggests, to expect Embrafilme to support film pro-

Os Inconfidentes (1971)

jects that threaten dominant interests. He also discusses the problems of self-censorship and economic censorship in the current conjuncture.

"A Democratic Cinema"

CARLOS DIEGUES

Q: How do you see the participation of the Cinema Novo group in the current phase of Brazilian cinema, a phase in which a state enterprise, Embrafilme, co-produces and distributes its films?

Diegues: Let's answer this question in parts. First of all, what is Cinema Novo? Cinema Novo began as a group of persons of the same generation who created a certain kind of cinema in Brazil. With Cinema Novo, it must be remembered, personal friendship is fundamental. We have known each other since childhood. But what united this group? First of all, the decision to make Brazilian films in Brazil, films with a critical vision, understanding Brazilian reality not only in its apparent social form, but also in its spiritual and cultural forms.

Another fundamental characteristic of Brazilian cinema and of Cinema Novo was that this cultural action would be made through films that were individual and personal expressions. Thus, despite the programmatic unity of making Brazilian films in Brazil with a critical perspective, there were in each film and in each auteur well-defined and very clear personal positions, styles, tendencies, and forms. This movement evolved as each auteur followed a personal road. Some even followed several different roads. One of the fundamental qualities of Cinema Novo was this pluralism, this capacity to be one thing and a number of things at the same time. The development of the auteurs of Cinema Novo coincided with the evolution of Brazilian cinema and of Brazil. Today one can only talk about Cinema Novo in nostalgic or figurative terms, because Cinema Novo as a group no longer exists, above all because it has been diluted into Brazilian cinema. When I made my first film in 1963, the production of that year had been twelve films. It was seventy films in 1975. So what do ten or twelve filmmakers, the Cinema Novo group, represent within this production? They are diluted within Brazilian cinema, which is itself not a unified whole. It is a mistake to talk about a single economic project of Embrafilme. The great quality of Embrafilme is the pluralism that ranges from Rui Guerra's *The Fall* to an expensive, glamorous film like *Dona Flor and Her Two Husbands*. It ranges from *Vida e Morte Severina* to *Ajuricaba*, a fantasy about Indians, a cinematic poem by Oswaldo Caldeira. The range of Embrafilme is vast, which I regard as positive. A state enterprise cannot determine the cinematic project without exerting censorship.

The Cinema Novo group is not identified with Embrafilme. Supporting Embrafilme does not exclude recognizing its weaknesses. It's like Petrobrás;* one may be opposed to a specific policy, but one does not oppose Petrobrás. Petrobrás is a necessity, regardless of the government in power. The country needs such an enterprise. It may be poorly administered or perhaps commit absurd errors. I defend Embrafilme as fundamental at this moment in the economy and development of Brazilian cinema. It is the only enterprise with sufficient economic and political power to confront the devastating voracity of the multinational corporations in Brazil. This does not mean that Embrafilme is without flaws. It lacks a program for short films. It should enter exhibition. One must criticize the weaknesses of Embrafilme. I am not definitively committed to everything Embrafilme does, but I staunchly defend its existence, since it is in reality a project of Cinema Novo.

Embrafilme did not come from heaven, it is not an offer or a present from the state or the government to Brazilian filmmakers. Embrafilme is the result of the struggle of Brazilian filmmakers since Alberto Cavalcânti and Getúlio Vargas talked for the first time in 1954 about such an enterprise. Cinema Novo inherited his idea, struggled, and finally realized it. The government did not give it to us. And we must distinguish here between the government and the state. As citizen-filmmakers, we have the right to use the state as one uses commuter trains or the Bank of Brazil. But this right does not imply a commitment to a specific government.

Q: When you spoke of Cinema Novo, you spoke of a critical perspective. Do you think that Embrafilme, as a state enterprise, is diluting this critical perspective?

*Brazilian State Petroleum Industry.

Diegues: No, I do not. Cinema Novo has always proposed a popular cinema. The popular cinema was not achieved for several reasons, including the immaturity of the directors. Every director had difficulties with expression. I made my first film when I was twenty-two; Glauber Rocha at twenty-three. But don't reject the importance of the films of Cinema Novo. I am not ashamed of the films I made. I think that the changes in the films correspond to a more democratic conception of cinema. Just as there is no democracy without the people, there can be no democratic cinema without a public. And we have always thought and struggled for the ideal of a democratic cinema.

"Popular Cinema and the State"

RUI GUERRA

Q: The question of a popular cinema has been discussed since the days of Cinema Novo. How do you conceive of popular cinema within the current conjuncture?

Guerra: There is a great deal of confusion about popular cinema. Many people see popular cinema merely as one that reaches a large public. But on a deeper level, we must examine popular cinema in terms of the type of public that sees the films and the function of cinema vis-à-vis that public. I don't consider a film popular merely because it is seen by many people unless it creates a political relationship with them. A popular cinema must reach the most oppressed segments of the population — the low-income sectors, the proletariat, the rural masses — and must be inserted in a political project for the transformation of society. In this sense Brazilian cinema has never been a truly popular cinema because it has never had the opportunity to become one. The system of distribution prevents films from reaching the popular classes. When films manage to penetrate these sectors they generally have a purely capitalist, commercial purpose rather than a political project for transformation. Thus, there has never been a popular cinema in Brazil. Cinema Novo was said to be elitist, but its elitism was never really tested. It was rarely seen outside of middle and upper-middle class areas. . . .

Cinema Novo attempted in its first phase to be popular solely on an ideological level, and continues to do so today. But at that time there was good faith, a true desire to be popular both thematically and in terms of cinematic language. The critical demystifications proposed then were more acute and consequential. Today the "popular" is being used merely as an alibi for better marketing. The concern is more with the potential return on capital investments than with the political transformation of society. . . .

It is very difficult to make a popular cinema in Brazil when the structures of financing, distribution, and exhibition exist within a truly violent capitalist context. Popular cinema is a contradiction in which filmmakers walk a tightrope between the will to make a certain kind of cinema and the ability to concretize this will in practice. But I think that the idea of an effective popular cinema in Brazil is utopian without a real social transformation or at least some liberalization.

Q: How do you see the problem of self-censorship?

Guerra: It's not exactly a question of self-censorship. *A posteriori* censorship, even though it is reflected in and influences the whole process of production, is not as violent as economic censorship. Official, political censorship forms only a small part of a whole process of restriction within the broader context of an economic project that makes a certain kind of cinema viable. A certain economic control, exercized by distributors, producers, and exhibitors, constitutes a repressive scheme within the overall colonial situation of Brazilian cinema. The financing of certain kinds of films is impossible, even without censorship, because the structures that would give access to popular sectors do not exist. So one cannot develop political projects, but merely commercial ones. This context does not allow a truly critical cinema, for even if its films got by the censors, they would not be viable as commercial products. Official censorship is less harmful than the extremely violent economic censorship that results from a structure completely dominated by the foreign film, by large distributors, by exhibition networks, all of which is reflected on the level of production.

Q: Does Embrafilme exert economic censorship?

Guerra: No, but Embrafilme reflects the political and economic system. We cannot expect — once again it would be utopian — a state organ to act against the ruling classes and the official government line. A popular cinema would go against the interests of the current government, because today every economic program is directed toward increasing the wealth of the few and maintaining great social inequities, and it is hard to imagine that Embrafilme would oppose such a program. It tries at best to be liberal within this context. . . .

The filmmaker trying to make a popular cinema has to adapt to this situation, an impossible, almost mythical task! That would be like living in a popular democracy and making films defending capitalism. Here it is almost the same thing. Our cinema is supported by a vehicle for capitalism, a state enterprise. The contradiction is obvious. Imagine going to Cuba and defending capitalism with the help of ICAIC! But that is precisely the situation of the Brazilian filmmaker who has no other source of capital and who tries to justify certain films, allegorical, elitist, and almost masturbatory in their form of expression, in an attempt to reconcile this contradiction.

Q: You spoke of the difficulties of creating a popular cinema when confronted with an adverse political and economic conjuncture. How would you pose this problem in terms of the earlier period of Cinema Novo?

Guerra: Cinema Novo had very little time to develop. We began making our first films in 1962, and in 1964 there was the *coup d'état*. So we had only two years. From 1964 to 1968 there was a limited political and economic space for a certain kind of production, but it became increasingly difficult to make films. In truth the birth, apogee, and decline of Cinema Novo came in a very short period of time. Furthermore, the economic conditions that permitted the financing of Cinema Novo ceased to exist after 1964.

There was never, in fact, much economic and political space for Cinema Novo. We were all making films for the first time, experimenting with forms of language but limited by a lack of knowledge of ourselves and of our cinematic instrument. This resulted in a number of personal exorcisms, a need to experiment with language. The process of depuration within this experimentation initially rendered the films less clear. One can hardly use Cinema Novo as a concrete point of reference because it was itself very divided. With all these contradictions and the 1964 coup, Cinema Novo simply had no time. When it began to reach its apogee, it was already in a descending curve due to existing political conditions.

Today it is much easier to make films because of Embrafilme's line of credit but contradictions of a political order also limit the possibility of making certain films. At the same time, these contradictions are not so acute that they completely exclude projects turned toward a political vision antagonistic to the official line. One can test some things, but not really make a film with a truly popular program. This is visible in the films now being made; most of them are populist films because of their attempt at compromise. They are not popular films, but rather films that use the people instead of defending them. They show the festivities, the dances, the people seen from an entirely paternalistic viewpoint — and what is populism if not political paternalism? It is within this scheme that we manage to make films, but it is also difficult to create political links with the people because it is almost impossible to take the project to its logical conclusion.

12
"Embrafilme: Present Problems and Future Possibilities"

Introduction

Shortly after becoming director of Embrafilme, Roberto Farias named filmmaker Gustavo Dahl (*The Brave Warrior, Uirá*) to head its distribution agency. Temporarily abandoning his filmmaking career, Dahl, who is Argentine by birth, quickly transformed Embrafilme into the largest film distributor in Latin America, responsible for more than 200 films. By 1978, however, disagreements arose between the two men about the role of the distributor, and Farias asked for Dahl's resignation late in the year. In this interview, published in the newsweekly *Veja* on 13 December 1978, Gustavo Dahl discusses some of the reasons for his impending resignation and his vision of the future role of Embrafilme in distribution. He feels that Embrafilme must strengthen its role in distribution in order to counter the tremendous power of the multinational distributors in the internal Brazilian market. He speaks as well about the implication of Cinema Novo's collaboration (and his own) with the government of President Ernesto Geisel (a topic also dealt with by Carlos Diegues and Rui Guerra in the previous document in this volume). In March, 1979, Geisel was succeeded by General João Batista de Figueiredo and Farias by career diplomat Celso Amorim. Finally, Dahl speaks of the legacy of Cinema Novo and the "cultural dictatorship" that it maintains even today in Brazilian cinema.

"Embrafilme: Present Problems and Future Possibilities"

GUSTAVO DAHL

Veja: Why did you submit your resignation to Embrafilme?

Dahl: I had the feeling that my work had finished. When I entered Embrafilme, four years ago, the distributor was merely one department of the sector of operations; today it is itself a superintendency with 150 employees, 10 branches, and a budget of over $5,000,000 per year. At this point a reformulation and a deep discussion about the problem of distribution is necessary. Roberto Farias and I disagree about distribution. I think that the distributor cannot remain dependent on an endowment or on the whims of a bureaucrat. He sees the project of distribution with undefined growth as dangerous, running the risk of being concentrated in the hands of a single group. For this reason he proposes the reactivation of private distributors. I disagree. I think that the answer to a market structured by large theater chains is precisely a strong distribution organ that can offer a sizeable volume of programming — or else we will be swallowed by the large monopolies. This divergence of opinion, by the way, is not only with Roberto, but also with a number of other leaders of Brazilian cinema.

Veja: Who are these leaders and what kind of criticisms have they made of your position?

Dahl: It is difficult to establish who they are because there is no face-to-face discussion; positions are known more on the basis of "so-and-so said. . . ." But one of the criticisms that the distributor frequently receives is that it favors exclusively big films like *Dama do Lotação* and *Tudo Bem*. But it is utopian to believe that if we spend a million *cruzeiros* on the publicity of all films each of them will behave in the same manner on the market. We, the distributor, must establish the margin of risk that each film can handle.

Veja: What has been the price of the filmmaker's alliance with the state?

Dahl: During the Geisel period, there was a political pact between cinema and the government that implied the existence of a certain unity to be maintained at all cost. I believe that this formula had a very strong social result, permitting a new flourishing of Brazilian cinema. This unity, however, had its price: the total neutralization of debate. But such neutralization is increasingly linked to the past. Now the whole country is debating its future. Brazilian cinema meanwhile, is still grasping at a ragged unity, as if it were the price of its material existence and as if the political pact had not been exhausted.

Veja: What do you expect from the next government?

Dahl: A permanent dialogue with the cinematographic class, the maintenance of a policy aimed at the occupation of the internal market, action in the area of exhibition, attempting, at the very least, to double the market, the utilization of electronic means of communication for the diffusion of our cinematic culture, the penetration of the Brazilian film in Latin America, Africa, and also in the American market. And above all: that the funds given cinema be compatible with the service it performs for the nation.

Veja: The political pact you refer to has been considered by many to be a cooptation. . . .

Dahl: When the money for films came from the National Bank of Minas Gerais no one talked about cooptation. Nevertheless, we could say that filmmakers were just as coopted then as now. In truth, there is a profound ignorance about the process of film production, principally in an emergent country. Films have to be made either with foreign capital or with the money of the state. Here in Brazil there is no such thing as a professional producer. The problem of capital for cinema did not begin with the current boom. Personally, I think that the return to bourgeois democracy, in which films are made with funds raised in banks and co-signed by millionaire friends, is a frightening perspective. Equally frightening is the hypothesis of a cinema totally controlled by the state, as in socialist countries.

Veja: What was, in reality, the collaboration of Geisel's government with cinema?

Dahl: The investment of Geisel's government in cinema was a task of cultural restoration. No easy adherence was being bought. The people's memory is very short. In the last moments of the Goulart period, a whole phase of literary films was being conceived: *Matraga, Plantation Boy, The Priest and the Girl*. The cinematic project of the government was that of valorizing the director, rather than production as such. What pushed Brazilian cinema in the direction of big films was the situation of the market. Few moments in the history of cinematic production have had the freedom to produce as did Brazilian cinema during the Geisel government.

Veja: Can you give an example of this freedom?

Dahl: Glauber Rocha dragged the script of *A Idade da Terra* around for five years. He proposed it in Los Angeles, Paris, Rome, Mexico, and Venezuela. Only in Brazil did he find the possibility of making it. The greatest freedom that we had was that of exercizing language, of using the vehicle. There is nothing more corrupt, more damaging to a cineaste, than not making films. That is true censorship: censorship at the source. This type of barrier—silence—was overcome during the Geisel government.

Veja: But what about censorship?

Dahl: It is impressive that there was much more freedom to make than to judge. We have had cultural production, but not much discussion. The responsibility is not of censorship, but of the intellectuals.

Veja: Why then did today's cinematic production cease being critical as in the days of Cinema Novo?

Dahl: The term "critical" always has a negative meaning. What was incredible about Cinema Novo was its desire to build the country through cinema. But building a country through cinema does not eliminate its hunger, but merely gives it an identity. That is what was missing. People need to feel free and responsible for the social group in which they live, which is what happens in any Indian village. What bothers me deeply, today, is this opposition between individual and collective destiny, this lack of coincidence between them.

Veja: Why has this desire to build the country been lost?

Dahl: This desire was also capricious: believing that the film was a magic wand that, thrown on the screen, would change people's minds. This loss is a worldwide phenomenon. Pasolini said that the sixties was a decade of destruction and that the seventies would be one of restoration. I think that we have also lost contact with world cinema.

Veja: But isn't censorship to blame in this case?

Dahl: No! Police censorship plays its part, but the laws of the cinematic market play an equal part. Today, in Brazil, two thirds of the market is dominated exclusively by American cinema. This is not a problem of police censorship, but of economic realities. The fact that it has become uneconomical to import a film by Godard is a censorship just as violent as the cuts made in Bertolucci's *1900*.

Veja: In relation to the pact with the military government, some filmmakers have been accused of collaborating with the dictatorship.

Dahl: It is necessary to say once and for all that you cannot have a country like Brazil, with 120,000,000 inhabitants and 4,000 kilometers of coastline in the South Atlantic, without the political presence of the military. Through the professional activities of the Army, the military is linked to a project for the nation. For some, this project is seen as fascist. Others, including myself, see it as a road to independence, autonomy, and liberation. There is no great cinema without a national project, and vice-versa. In this sense, Brazilian cinema is something that goes beyond governments and regimes.

Veja: It is said that, with the pretext of defending nationalism, filmmakers have adhered to the dictatorship.

Dahl: I did not collaborate with the Geisel government unconsciously. I believe that the end of torture, the liberalization of the press, and the resignation of General Sylvio Frota have generated profound modifications that the country has not yet understood. Nothing has been sold or exchanged. A job was merely done. I don't like the dictatorship, but neither do I like the bourgeois democracy that kills millions of Brazilians with a smile. One should not confuse democracy with freedom for the national bourgeoisie to continue living off the public coffers while defending free enterprise. The same bourgeoisie that today longs for a socialist party is the same one that, several years ago, was marching with God for liberty.*

*A reference to the extreme right-wing Tradition, Family, and Fatherland organization that was active in Brazil in the 1960s and early 1970s.

Veja: How do you see the kind of cinema being made today in Brazil?
Dahl: There are only two types of cinema: industrial and experimental. They sometimes mix. *Tudo Bem* is an example of a film conceived as experimental, but that came to life within the parameters of industrial cinema. In Brazil we have not yet had our *La Dolce Vita* or *Lola Montes*; great films of spectacle that also exploded cinematic language. Today there are no movements in Brazil. There is no group of directors working in a common direction with an affinity of themes, language, cinematic vision. Brazilian cinema has not yet been able to digest its last movement. It still lives under the cultural dictatorship of Cinema Novo. After fifteen years, the most enthusiastically awaited films are those of the Cinema Novo directors.

13
"Jack Valenti's Brazilian Agenda"

Introduction

Brazilian director Arnaldo Jabor began as a theater critic and playwright before becoming involved with Cinema Novo. His films include *Opinião Pública* ("Public Opinion," 1967), *Pindorama* (1971), *Toda Nudez Será Castigada* ("All Nudity Will Be Punished," 1973), *O Casamento* ("The Marriage," 1975), and most recently, *Tudo Bem* ("All's Well," 1978). Jack Valenti is the president of the Motion Pictures Association of America. His 1977 visit to Brazil "happened" to coincide with the impending adoption of a number of legal measures designed to protect Brazilian cinema against foreign domination. Wielding sticks (reportedly threats of a blockade by American distributors) and carrots (offers to exert pressures on the U.S. Congress to avoid the passage of commercial laws prejudicial to Brazil), Valenti tried to overturn the measures. Like the British colonialists of the nineteenth century, he argued "free trade," which in the Third World is a code word for "exploitation" and "domination." Valenti had reason to worry, of course, since Brazilian films like *Xica da Silva* and *Lúcio Flávio* were outgrossing Hollywood blockbusters like *Jaws* and *The Exorcist*. The Brazilian public for Brazilian films, in fact, went from 30,000,000 in 1974 to 52,000,000 in 1976. Jabor's poem constitutes a veritable Third World "Essay in Film Criticism." With satiric tones that recall both the Vertov manifestoes and the Beat poets, he excoriates the political, economic, and esthetic influence of Hollywood films in Brazil.

Aleluia Gretchen (1976)

"Jack Valenti's Brazilian Agenda"

ARNALDO JABOR

At exactly six in the afternoon
as the American dream closes its lilac eyes
and the great American night begins,

a golden cloud of danger hangs over the horizon of Sunset
    Boulevard
and the smooth rumbling of forty thousand neutron bombs
rocks the children of Los Angeles like a gentle earthquake,
today,
now that the "American dream" is cause for irony at
Fifth Avenue cocktail parties
and guilt is visible in elegant New York restaurants
though no one flings their slim and very bloody Marys in despair
and though the crimes of imperialism are tolerated as an evil
necessary for the good life,
at exactly this moment
Jack Valenti,
with Republican grin, star-spangled tie,
diamond smile and the pale/solid semblance of the perfect executive
hints of Dick Tracy, George Wallace, Westmoreland, Liberace,
Billy Graham, and so many other robots of infinite guffaw,
at exactly this moment,
with his solid portfolio of indestructible designs
and the audacity that our Foreign Debt has lately given
international executives,
Jack Valenti will descend from his astral airplane
into the land of promised and overdue payments.

In the Brasília morning Mr. Valenti will grant interviews
and cameras will explode
and behind a ritual cordiality
dragging on for 400 years and not to be transgressed
a thousand faces will dance in the daily press
white teeth, shaking hands, poisoned cologne[1]
will intoxicate our cabinet heads
and Broadway lights will blind our technocrats
and then,
under Valenti's non-Brazilian shoes
the red carpets of hospitality
will roll
and no one will see the cinematic crimes in the air
nor the remains of our poor dead minds,
no one will see the wounds
since there will be no corpse
no coroner to discover the bruises in our soul
purple wounds, pink wounds, rainbow wounds
stardust in our eyes, the tattooed people we have become
of Hollywood's thousand and one adventures
invisible victims of a thousand dazzling fairy wounds
Eastmancolor burns
seven-colored napalm
kodak-yellow of our hunger.
Everything hidden behind the colonial *frisson* of our Ministers of
    State ah . . . how well I know that colonial *frisson* . . .

the pride of touching an illustrious *bwana*
habitué and creator of *lobbies*
and they will say, between the swimming pools and frozen daquiris
"Let me be like you, *boss, cowboy*, big shot, *silver dollar, big
     daddy*."
In a few hours,
Valenti will take from his portfolio of indestructible designs
the most sacred values of the imperial Occident:
logic, symmetry, continuity,
beginning, middle, end,
the *happy end*, the "individual," and
the sinister American vision of goodness.
We will attempt to flee, but from the portfolio of indestructible
     designs
will grow the King Kong of our Unconscious
and he will grow
with each fluttering of fingers
with each click of the opening valise
he will grow
the *papier-mâché* monster of our colonized Desire,
genie of the lamp with Roman warrior's legs,
De Mille's Moses, the Red Sea on his heels,
tablets of the Law in hand, Statue of Liberty face,
luminous thighs of Marilyn Monroe, *kitsch frisson* of our
     cinephiles,
Las Vegas' lips,
Las Vegas' luminous eyes and
luminous vagina
phallus blinking in incandescent neon
mouth of infinite kisses
and the mad floating dream of Manhattan.

And like some poisonous milk from the great breast of California
our TV antennas will drink for year on end
the colored milk of the most infernal lie yet invented
and they will come
with celluloid teeth
with Raquel Welch breasts
with Carrie eyes spreading death in the theaters
they will come
to Jack Valenti's bloody cocktail party
with somnambulant extras
but they will not bring Busby Berkeley's birds of paradise
nor the wings of Fred Astaire,
nor the sweet soar of Gene Kelly,
they will come to the funeral of our culture
with the heavy lead of Tom's machine guns
and Jerry's slender dagger
and the great white shark with Jean Harlow's silks bleeding be-
     tween its teeth

and their robot filmmakers will come:
Coppola, Bogdanovich, Spielberg, de Palma,
limping along sordid with crutches stolen
from the masters Ford, Hawks, Hitchcock, and Vidor
while Nicholas Ray falls drunk in a Toulon alley
and Orson Welles does whiskey commercials in Amsterdam,
they will come to sell their freshest fish,
at the end of the American dream
the last reel of the American dream
on the last dirty shore of the last dirty wave of the dregs of New
    York
they will come with the patches of their mended myths
the shabby mannequins, sewn by hand, fallen eyes, cloth feet,
ragged silks of phoney dolls, auctions of studio scrap;
they will come
to produce here
to bleed our sky, salt, south
just as Carlo Ponti came, expulsed from Italy
husband of the Roman she-wolf of the seven pendant breasts
who came to freeze her daiquiris with ice cubes
from the multinational's *frozen funds.*
They will come
for the ball of the fiscal island of our nationality
and they will explode their Titanics in millionaires'
    swimming pools
and Linda Blair will turn her head to the four winds
and all of them will come,
white with plaster make-up
plastic, smiling
phosphorescent overcoats
selling the last vestiges of an ancient hope
with Las Vegas balanced on their head like a Carmen
    Miranda turban,
but they will not bring Carmen Miranda, fallen dead in a
    Paramount gutter
nor Judy Garland, suffocated by executives
injections in her red lips
nor Marilyn floating in the blue-poisoned pool of her last screen
    test
nor will they bring James Dean's demolished car
nor the scenes cut from Stroheim's "Greed"
nor the mutilated photograms of "1900"
nor Buster Keaton's corpse
nor anything else.
Here comes the last bionic generation
Jack
bionic
kodak heart
napalm brilliantine
Lyndon Johnson's transplanted kidney
Nixon's claws;

and when the orchestra of *"cubancheros brasileños"*
picks up its maracas to play "That's Entertainment"
all the social columns will dance
skeletons with roses between the vertebrae
covers of Vogue
advertising models spewing marshmallows
monumental hairdos of dandruff shampoo
they will dance the broken waltz with congressmen from
   Piauí[2]
while outside
a crane floating in Catete's skies[3]
sends to the North 40 million dollars
of tickets sold
under the eyes of passers-by who understand nothing.

Rio de Janeiro
11 October 1977

Translators' Notes

1. An untranslatable pun. "Cologne" in Portuguese, *água de colônia*, translates literally as "water from the colony."
2. Piauí is a poor state in northeastern Brazil.
3. Catete is the section of Rio de Janeiro that housed, until the construction of Brasília, the Presidential Palace. Jabor probably chose this word due to its connotations of power as well as the fact that it is an indigenous term, thus creating an image of the destruction of national culture.

Part III
Cinema Novo and Beyond: The Films

Introduction

The real history of Brazilian cinema does not consist of the declared intentions of filmmakers but rather of the filmic texts themselves. The following essays examine some of the landmark films of the last two decades. Our selection has been motivated by diverse criteria. First of all, the films covered in this section are currently in distribution in Europe and the United States or are likely to be in the near future. Many have developed a certain reputation, and some, like *Macunaíma* and *Antônio das Mortes*, have a veritable cult following. The selection is also structured chronologically with the films summing up the major historical periods of Brazilian cinema since the beginning of Cinema Novo. *Vidas Secas*, *Os Fuzis*, and *Deus e o Diabo na Terra do Sol* brilliantly exemplify the first "hungry" phase of Cinema Novo; *Land in Anguish* and *Fome de Amor* illustrate the self-referentiality and introspection of the second phase; *Antônio das Mortes*, *Macunaíma*, and *How Tasty Was My Little Frenchman* display the colorful exuberance of Tropicalism; and *São Bernardo*, *Lição de Amor*, *Xica da Silva*, and *Tent of Miracles* demonstrate some of the strategies adopted in recent years. The interest in these films goes beyond the merely historical. Some are adaptations of major Brazilian literary classics like *Vida Secas* and *Macunaíma*. Others, like *Land in Anguish*, inflected the very course of the esthetic and narrative development of Brazilian cinema.

In these essays we have sought a degree of methodological rigor. Each tries to deal with a filmic text in the richness and complexity of its signification. The essays focus not only on the textual (i.e., the specifically cinematic operations of the text), but also on what Julia Kristeva, borrowing from Mikhail Bakhtin, calls the "intertextual," i.e., the film's insertion into the broad historical weave of discourse, the way they respond to other texts, filmic and non-filmic. Some of the films highlight their

117

own intertextuality, through specific references to the international cinematic tradition: *Land in Anguish* alludes to *Potemkin*, *Macunaíma* to *Footlight Parade*. At the same time they draw on other arts and media: opera in *Land in Anguish*, cordel literature in *Antônio das Mortes*, musique concrète in *Fome de Amor*, television in *Tent of Miracles*. The approach is at the same time contextual. The analyses place the films within a broad cultural and political conjuncture. Finally, many of the essays examine the relationships between the spectator and the text. What reactions do the texts encourage or preclude? Do they favor distanced rationality or emotional identification, passive consumerism or active collaboration?

These texts are methodologically diverse. The analysis of *Vidas Secas*, besides concentrating on the transposition of literary into cinematic codes, also examines the relation between subject (drought, poverty) and treatment, for the achievement of that film was precisely to match a thematic to an esthetic appropriate not only to its specific subject but also to Third World film in general. Roberto Schwarz's essay on *The Guns* delineates the subtle play of identification and distance between the filmic text and its middle-class spectator. Using categories drawn from such thinkers as Hegel, Althusser, Sartre, Fanon, especially the mirror image of master and slave from Hegel's *Phenomenology of Mind*, he explores the complexity of our own reactions to Guerra's aggressive text, revealing at the same time its deeper structural logic. Ismail Xavier's article on *Black God, White Devil* offers a rigorous account of the textual operations of that film, focusing less on the diegesis than on the mediations through which it is constructed. The essay on *Land in Anguish* places that film within a broad discussion of politics and esthetics, showing its insertion as well in a wide cultural field that includes literature, opera, samba, architecture, and other films. Elizabeth Merena and João Luiz Vieira examine *Fome de Amor* both within the personal trajectory of its director and in relation to the mainstream movement of Brazilian cinema. Partially filmed in the United States, *Fome de Amor* translates a moment of political repression and emotional disintegration by means of aggressive dissociative techniques. The essay on *Macunaíma* studies the essential codes — specifically cinematic, artistic, cultural — operative in its textual system and delineates the subtext of cannibalistic imagery that structures this singularly dense and subtle film. Terry Carlson details the weave of the cultural tapestry that is *Antônio das Mortes* and examines the "structures of alienation" in that film. Cannibalism, subtext in *Macunaíma*, becomes text itself in *How Tasty Was My Little Frenchman*. Richard Peña explores the film as an ironic fable in which cannibalism becomes a metaphor for diverse forms of cultural assimilation in a colonial and a neo-colonial context. The analysis of *São Bernardo* focuses on the film's esthetic strategies and on its thematic of social reification. The study of *Lesson of Love*, a film seen by many critics as somehow "un-Brazilian," demonstrates the way in which its director deliberately "decinematizes" a highly cinematic novel. The essay on *Xica da Silva* applies Mikhail Bakhtin's category of the Carnivalesque to an exuberant and controversial film of the mid-seventies. Marsha Kinder's article on *Tent of Miracles* accounts for the multi-dimensional appeal of the film. The essay on Rui Guerra's *The Fall*, finally, explores a thematic — working-class and sexual politics — and its formal articulation via highly innovative anti-illusionistic strategies.

14
"The Cinema of Hunger: Nelson Pereira dos Santos's *Vidas Secas*"

ROBERT STAM AND RANDAL JOHNSON

Even before Glauber Rocha coined the expression "an esthetic of hunger," Nelson Pereira dos Santos embodied that esthetic in *Vidas Secas* (1963). With its soberly critical realism, its sterling austerity, and its implicit optimism, it represents first phase Cinema Novo at its best. Rarely has a subject—in this case hunger, drought, and the exploitation of a peasant family—been so finely rendered by a style. Rarely have a thematic and an esthetic been quite so fully adequate to one another.

In some crucial respects Graciliano Ramos's novel on which the film is based elicits comparison with John Steinbeck's *The Grapes of Wrath*. Published only a year apart (*Vidas Secas* in 1938; *The Grapes of Wrath* in 1939), both are established literary classics in their respective countries, and both form part of what may broadly be called the naturalist tradition. They treat, furthermore, an identical subject: drought and migration. The droughts of the dustbowl drive the Joads from Oklahoma to California, just as the droughts of the Brazilian northeast drive Fabiano and his family to the cities of the south. In both works the trajectory of a single family comes to encapsulate the destiny of thousands of oppressed people. In one case the oppressors are real-estate companies and agro-businessmen; in the other, landowners and their accomplices.

There are, on a purely sociological level, contrasts as well as similarities between the two novels. The Okies of *The Grapes of Wrath*, while an oppressed minority within the United States, enjoy relative affluence. The Joads have a broken-down truck and some basic necessities; Fabiano and family have only their blistered feet and a single trunk for their possessions. The Okies may be only barely literate, but they are presented as loquacious home-spun philosophers, forever discoursing on the oversoul and the survival powers of the people. The peasants of *Vidas Secas*, meanwhile, are not only illiterate, but they also have a tenuous grasp even on spoken language, communicating only in gestures, grunts, and monosyllables. The Okies, consequently, are better equipped to combat their oppression. Fabiano has only confused resentments and an inarticulate impulse to revolt; Tom Joad is equipped with literacy and a degree of class consciousness.

The distance that separates John Ford's 1940 adaptation of Steinbeck's novel from Nelson Pereira dos Santos's adaptation of *Vidas Secas* is the distance that separates Southern California from the *sertão* and Hollywood studio production in the forties from Third World filmmaking in the sixties. With *Vidas Secas*, as for many other works from the first phase of Cinema Novo, the word "hunger" characterizes not only the film's subject and its esthetic, but also its production methods. Too often we as First World spectators tend to transfer conventional expectations

Maria Ribeiro as Vitória in *Vidas Secas* (1963)

based on the output of wealthy and sophisticated film industries to works from countries that lack the means to produce such films. The total production cost of *Vidas Secas*, for example, was $25,000, compared to thirty times that figure for *The Grapes of Wrath*. The film rights to the Steinbeck novel alone cost three times the total cost of *Vidas Secas*. And these differences in production inevitably inflect both the ideology and the esthetics of the films. *Vidas Secas* could afford no highly paid star for its central role, and thus poverty loses some of the glamor associated with a Henry Fonda.

If there was any production model for Nelson Pereira dos Santos it was not the Hollywood system that produced *The Grapes of Wrath*, but rather Italian Neo-Realism, one of the most important film movements to have emerged in the years separating the two films. Nelson Pereira dos Santos sums up the influence of Neo-realism as follows:

> The influence of neo-realism was not that of a school or ideology, but rather as a production system. Neo-realism taught us, in sum, that it was possible to make films in the streets; that we did not need studios; that we could film using average people rather than known actors; that the technique could be imperfect, as long as the film was truly linked to its national culture and expressed that culture.[1]

Vidas Secas, then, has certain affinities with Neo-Realism, affinities that extend even to a thematic level. Like many Neo-Realist films, *Vidas Secas* makes the story of a few ordinary individuals the springboard for a discussion of a larger social problem. Just as the lone bicycle thief of *Ladri di Bicicletta* "speaks for" the armies of the unemployed in post-war Italy, so the single peasant family of *Vidas Secas* sums up the lives of the millions of northeasterners who migrate to the cities of the south. The film's final title—"and the *sertão* would continue to send to the city strong people like Fabiano, Vitória, and the two boys"—merely renders explicit the film's basic procedure of socially generalizing its meanings.

A comparison of *Vidas Secas* and its novelistic source is also instructive. The novel consists of 129 pages (in Portuguese) segmented into 13 chapters.[2] The film consists of 652 discrete shots articulated into 69 sequences for a duration of 120 minutes.[3] The novel was originally published as a series of fairly autonomous short pieces whose unity derived from a common milieu and the continuity of the characters. The film manipulates this basic material into a coherent, rather more linear narrative. For example, it groups some chapters that are separate in the novel. The events of chapter three ("Jail") and chapter eight ("Feast Day"), both set in town, are joined. A flashback in chapter ten ("Accounts"), where Fabiano remembers previous difficulties with the town's tax collector, has been placed before the other events set in town. Although both works develop a city-country opposition, in the film the town assumes a more threatening visage than in the novel. Fabiano goes to town twice. The first time he is cheated by the landowner and bullied

Vidas Secas (1963)

by the tax collector and a soldier. The second time, on Feast Day, he is pressured into joining a card game and subsequently arrested and beaten by the soldier. Fabiano, a ranch hand, simply does not know how to survive in town. The film offers Fabiano an option not available in the novel. The young *jagunço*, who soothes Fabiano's wounds in jail and later offers him his horse, invites Fabiano to join his band. A shot of Fabiano holding a rifle intimates the possibility of armed struggle, however remote, an option Fabiano rejects in order to remain with his family.

The film also modifies the novel by historically dating the action — 1940 at the beginning of the film, 1942 at the end — whereas the novel left the date unspecified. The date corresponds roughly to the time of the publication of the novel, but its meaning goes beyond that elementary fact. The historical specificity constitutes a kind of ironic provocation on Nelson Pereira dos Santos's part. Superficially he has set the film in a safely distant past. We know from interviews, however, that he intended the film to be an intervention within the contemporary political conjuncture, in this case as part of the debate then raging in Brazil concerning agrarian reform. The precise dating of the film suggests, with a subtlety quite typical of its director, that a situation denounced by Graciliano Ramos decades earlier continued to exist. Peasants like Fabiano continue to be oppressed by landowners and are still being forced to migrate from the northeast. It is precisely the lack of change in the intervening years that constitutes the scandal.

Nelson Pereira dos Santos also joined entirely new episodes to the material of the novel. One documentary-like segment alternates shots of Fabiano in jail with shots of the villagers celebrating the *bumba-meu-boi* ceremony in front of the mayor and the landowner. In this traditional folkdance pageant, the people symbolically divide an ox and offer it to the local dignitaries. The *bumba-meu-boi* can be seen in this context as the ceremonial representation, the *mise-en-scène* of a situation of oppression, for they offer what is in some sense the product of their labor to the oppressors. Popular culture, the director seems to be saying, is politically ambiguous. On the one hand, it offers a counter pole to elite culture, represented in the film by the classical violin lessons for the landowner's daughter. On the other hand, it can alienate the people by simply representing, rather than challenging, their own oppression.

One area in which the film is imaginatively "faithful" to the novel concerns point of view. The Ramos novel is written from what might be called a subjectivized third-person point of view. It uses an indirect free style, i.e., a mode of discourse that begins in the third person ("he thought") and then quietly modulates into a more or less direct, but still third person, presentation of a character's thoughts and feelings. The discourse of *Vidas Secas*, like that of Flaubert's *Madame Bovary*, is highly subjectivized in that most of the verbal material is articulated via the point of view of characters. Five chapters are named for the personage whose vision colors their presentation; four others are dominated by Fabiano. At the same time, within particular chapters, a kind of subsystem organizes point of view that passes down a hierarchy of power from Fabiano to Vitória to the two boys and, at times, to the dog Baleia.

The novel *Vidas Secas* is characterized by an intense imaginative empathy whereby the author projects himself into the minds and bodies of characters very different from himself. Graciliano Ramos displays the kind of empathetic power that allowed Keats to imaginatively transform himself into a "sparrow pecking around in the gravel." He brings us into the very physical being of his peasant subjects. In a tour de force, Ramos even psychologizes the dog Baleia, going so far as to give him visions of a canine afterlife. At some points, obviously, he does not strictly limit himself to the consciousness of his characters, but rather includes and transcends them. He makes allusions, for example, which would undoubtedly have been beyond the ken of his characters (e.g., Fabiano's comparison of himself to a "wandering Jew") or he details their confusion (Fabiano's semi-comic attempt to compose an appropriate lie for Vitória concerning his loss of money in a card game) while making it clear that he as author does not share his confusion.

In the film interior monologue in the indirect free style disappears in favor of direct dialogue. Fabiano's internal wrestle with language itself, for example, is dropped; we are given only the fact of his inarticulateness. Fabiano and Vitória's lack of verbal communication is related through a "conversation" as they sit by the fire and listen to the rain outside while both of them talk simultaneously without hearing each other. But Nelson Pereira dos Santos does retain what one might call the democratic distribution of subjectivity. Fabiano, Vitória, the two boys, and the dog are all subjectivized by the film. This subjectivization operates by playing on diverse cinematic registers. Classically, and most obviously, the film exploits point of view shots that alternate the person seeing with what the person presumably sees. Such shots are associated with each of the four human protagonists and with the dog. One sequence alternates shots of Baleia looking and panting with shots of cavies scurrying through the brush. The film also subjectivizes by camera movement; hand-held travelling shots evoke the experience of traversing the *sertão*; a vertiginous camera movement suggests the younger boy's dizziness and fall. Other procedures involve exposure (an overexposed shot of the sun blinds and dizzies the character and the spectator); focus (Baleia's vision goes out of focus as Fabiano stalks him, as if the dog were bewildered by his master's behavior); and camera angle (as the boy inclines his head to look at the house, the camera inclines as well). It is also noteworthy that the camera films the dog and the children at their level, without patronizing them, as it were, by high angles.

Like *The Grapes of Wrath*, *Vidas Secas* elaborates the analogy, characteristic of naturalist fiction and rooted in nineteenth-century biologism and social Darwinism, between human beings and animals. The twist in *Vidas Secas* is that it is not in the descriptive passages that the novelist brings up the metaphor; rather, he has the characters themselves make the comparison, conversely reinforced by the author's "humanization" of animals. While Fabiano and Vitória constantly complain that they are forced to live like animals, the dog Baleia is given almost human qualities and is totally integrated into the family. The human characters are very much aware of their inability to communicate through language, but when Vitória kills the parrot to eat, she justifies her action by saying that it was worth nothing, "it didn't even talk." A leather bed takes on overweening importance for Vitória because it represents the ideal of ceasing to live like animals. While animals hide in the forest and sleep on the ground, "real people" sleep in beds. Thus Graciliano Ramos avoids the reductionism that characterizes many naturalist novels, in which characters become the mere playthings of biological and economic forces, the objects of a grim determinism. In Ramos it is social structures that "animalize" people, while the characters consciously resist their own animalization.

Apart from being a highly intelligent reading of a classic novel *Vidas Secas* also makes a specifically cinematic contribution. Graciliano Ramos's style, a style ideally suited to the rendering of physical sensation and concrete experience, is transmuted into film. Luis Carlos Barreto's cinematography is dry and harsh like the *sertão*. Indeed, he has been credited with "inventing" a kind of light apppropriate to Brazilian cinema. The film's soundtrack, meanwhile, is ingenious, providing, as Noel Burch points out in *The Theory of Film Practice*, an instance of the "structural use of sound." The non-diegetic sounds of the creaking wheels of an ox cart accompanying the film's credits are subsequently "diegetized" as we see an ox cart simultaneously with the sound. At another point, the sound forms part of an aural pun as the creaking of the cart modulates in-

Atila Iorio as Fabiano in *Vidas Secas* (1963)

to the (diegetic) sound of a scraping violin. Through the course of the film the sound of the ox cart becomes a kind of auditory synecdoche that encapsulates the northeast, both by its denotation (the ox cart evoking the technical backwardness of the region) and by its connotation, the very unpleasantness of the sound constituting a certain structure of aggression. Simultaneously the wheel of the ox cart operates metaphorically, recalling in its circularity the cyclical droughts and never-ending misery of the region.

The opening shot of *Vidas Secas* intimates aggressiveness toward the spectator. A static camera records the slow progress of four human figures and a dog across an inhospitable landscape. Their slow approximation suggests the cultural distance between the peasant characters and the middle-class urban spectators who constitute the audience. At the same time, the quite unconventional prolongation of the shot in time (four minutes) serves as a warning to the spectator not to expect the fast pacing and density of incident that characterizes most fiction films. The spectator's experience, in short, will be as dry as that of the protagonists. The relative fidelity to the tempo and duration of peasant life forms part of the film's meaning.

Third World peasants form the majority of the world's population, yet they are drastically underrepresented in the cinema. When they are represented they are frequently sentimentalized and pastoralized according to the bourgeois ideology of the western film industry. It is to Nelson Pereira dos Santos's credit that he avoided the pitfalls common to many treatments of similar subjects. Rather than sensationalize his subject by concentrating on pathetic incidents and dramatic confrontations, he portrays, generally, only the most quotidian of events. His characters, rather than being rude transcendental poets, strumming guitars at streamside and mouthing the rustic wisdom of the simple folk, are moving in their very inarticulateness, in their unequal struggle with language. Rather than make them the exemplary victims of a quasi-metaphysical injustice or the patient sufferers of human cruelty, his characters are simply oppressed by a social situation; they are neither more nor less noble than other people. Rather than relieving the austerity of the images with a lush musical score, his soundtrack offers only occasional diegetic music (the violin lessons for the landowner's daughter, the music of the *bumba-meu-boi* ceremony), along with extremely harsh sounds (the squawking of a parrot, the grating creak of the ox cart); there is no non-diegetic musical score at all. Too often such scores serve to render poverty palatable as the spectators lose themselves in the music and forget the provocative rawness of the facts depicted. Rather than emphasize picturesqueness, having the scenery compensate for the aridity of the subject, Nelson Pereira dos Santos presents images as harsh and inhospitable as the landscape; the spectator lives there only at the price of a certain discomfort. The relentlessly blinding light of Luis Carlos Barreto's camera leaves the spectator, like the protagonists, without respite. *Vidas Secas* elicits no pastoral nostalgia for a simpler time and place—an attitude frequently projected by city dwellers onto rural people—and entertains no mystical attitude toward "the land." The spectator hungry for conventional sensations, in sum, goes away unfulfilled, but the spectator hungry to learn goes away well nourished.

Notes

1. Quoted in "*O Cinema Novo no Jogo da Verdade,*" *Manchete* 20 (November 1965): 120.
2. Graciliano Ramos, *Vidas Secas* (1938; São Paulo: Editora Martins, 1972). Translated into English by Ralph Edward Dimmick (Austin: University of Texas Press, 1973).
3. Information from "Roteiro de Vidas Secas" elaborated by students at the University of Brasília. Published by the Escola de Comuniçãoes e Artes, University of São Paulo, 1970.

15
"Cinema and *The Guns*"

ROBERTO SCHWARZ

Just as the cinema can take us to the savannah to see lions it can also take us to the northeast to see drought victims. In both cases, proximity is a product, a technical construction. The film industry, with the world and its image at hand, can bring the savannah and the drought to our neighborhood screens. Since it guarantees a real distance, however, the constructed proximity is proof of its power: it offers intimacy without risks; I see the lion, but it does not see me. The lion may seem close and convincing, but still more impressive is the miraculous technical power of our civilization. The real situation, however, is not one of confrontation between man and beast. The spectator is a protected member of industrial civilization and the lion, composed of light, was in the eye of the camera. It could just as well have been in the sight of a rifle. With films about wild animals our privileged situation becomes clear. Without it, we would not stay in the theater. Through this prism, however obvious, there emerges a true notion of our power; the fate of animals becomes our responsibility. In other cases, however, the evidence is less clear.

Proximity mystifies, establishing a psychological continuum where there is no real continuum: the suffering and thirst of the northeastern peasant, seen in close-up and from a privileged angle, become ours as well. But human sympathy impedes our comprehension because it cancels out the political nature of the problem. Through identification the true relationship is obscured, the nexus between the northeast and the chair in which I am sitting disappears. Provoked by the image, I feel

Nelson Xavier as Mário in *The Guns* (1963)

thirst, I hate injustice, but I do not really feel responsible. I witness suffering, but I am not guilty. I do not leave the theater as the beneficiary, which I am, of a constellation of forces and exploitative undertaking. Even important films with serious intentions, such as *Black God, White Devil* and *Vidas Secas* fail at this point, leaving a feeling of malaise. Esthetically and politically compassion is an anachronistic response. Cameras, laboratories, and financing do not commiserate, they transform.

Rui Guerra's masterpiece, *The Guns*, does not try to *comprehend* misery. On the contrary he films as if it were an aberration, and this distance deprives it of its emotional impact. At first glance, it is as if two incompatible films were alternating: a documentary of drought and poverty and a fiction film. The difference is clear. Following the sacred ox with its devout followers, the speech of the blind man and the mystic chants, the entrance of the soldiers, motorized and talkative, comes as a rupture in style. The documentary sequences reveal the misery of the local population. In the fiction sequences the work is done by actors; these characters are from a world not of hunger, but of rifles and trucks. In the facial mobility of the actors, who are not starving, one encounters desire, fear, boredom, individual will, and a freedom inexistent in the opaque faces of the drought victims. When the focus passes from one sphere to the other the very reach of the image is altered: expressive faces are followed by those that express nothing; the brutish peasants are to be looked at, but plot, psychology, and humanity can be read only on the mobile faces of the soldiers. Some faces are there to be looked at, others are to be understood. This rupture and the theme of the film converge. The actors are to the non-actors as the city dwellers with their technical civilization are to the evacuees, as possibility is to pre-determined misery, as plot is to inertia. The visual effectiveness of *The Guns* derives from this codification.

The eye of the cinema is cold, a technical operation. It produces a sort of ethnocentricity of reason, in the face of which, as with contact with modern technology, that which is different cannot be tolerated. The violent effectiveness of capitalist colonization, in which reason and superiority are combined, is transformed into an esthetic model: it permeates our sensibilities, which become equally implacable. "Everything that is fixed and callous is dissolved, but the retinue of traditions and archaic conceptions . . . profanes that which is sacred, and men are forced, finally, to see with sober eyes their positions and relationships."*

From the beginning of *The Guns* misery and technological civilization confront each other. The former is slow, excessive, an aggregate of defenseless people, discredited through the spiritual and real mobility—the trucks—of the latter. Although the misery seems pervasive and strong, its causes do not matter; it is one side of a relationship, carrying a negative sign. By showing it frontally and from the outside, the film refuses to see more than anachronism and inadequacy. This distance is the opposite of philanthropy: short of transformation there is no possible humanity; or, from the perspective of plot, short of transformation there is no difference that matters. The mass of miserable evacuees ferments but does not explode. What the camera shows in the abstruse faces, or better said, what makes them abstruse, is the absence of explosion, the action that has not been taken. There is therefore no plot, but merely the weight of their presence, remotely threatening. The political structure has been translated into an artistic structure.

The soldiers, in contrast, look as if they could do anything. In the city they are ordinary men of a lower class. In the small town, however, uniformed and godless, they saunter through the streets as if they were gods—the men that came by jeep from the outside. They talk about women, laugh, and do not depend on a sacred ox; it suffices that they are a new element. In long sequences their haughtiness recovers, for us, the privilege of being *modern*; to be from the city is to be admirable. The same holds for the warehouse owner and the truckdriver. Their actions matter; they are on the level of history, whose local levers—the warehouse, rifles, transportation—they control. Even their unfulfilled intentions are important: their ambivalence concerning their own role, for example, suggests that the final outcome of the conflict might have been very different. In other words, where there is transformation of individual destinies, everything matters: there is plot. A space of freedom has been

* Source of quote not specified by author.

opened, we feel at home. The nature of the image has been transformed. Psychology colors every face, evoking a sense of justice and injustice, individual and understandable destinies. The soldiers are like us. Moreover, they are our emissaries at the locale, and, whether we like it or not, their practice carries out our implicit politics. It is with them that we identify, much more than with the suffering and superstitious drought victims.

From a narrative perspective the solution is perfect; it precludes emotional reactions and favors responsible reflection. Concentrating on the soldiers, called from the city to defend a food warehouse, the plot forces antipathetic identification and self-awareness: we feel compassion for the drought victims, but identification with the police. The displacement of the dramatic center from the victims to authority renders the film's material more intelligible and better articulated. For the peasants the world is a homogeneous and diffuse calamity in which the sun, the boss, politics, and Satan have equal roles. The soldiers, meanwhile, participate in a precise but transformable situation. The distance between the drought victims and private property is guaranteed by the guns, which, however, could cross over to the other side. The image, as Brecht would have it, is of a changeable world: rather than stress the moral injustice, the film focuses on its concrete mechanism and human guarantors. Our feelings go far beyond mere sympathy. While we identify, we also despise; so that compassion comes only through the destruction of our emissaries and, by extension, of the existing order of things.

The soldiers strut arrogantly through the small town, but from the perspective of the city from which they come they are quite modest. They are simultaneously the guardians of private property and mere salaried workers. Soldiers by circumstance, they might have been involved in other forms of work; the truckdriver too had been a soldier. They give orders, but they themselves must obey. Seen from below they represent authority, but from above they are "the people." This system of contradictions forms the boundaries of the plot. The logic of this conflict appears for the first time in what is perhaps the most powerful scene in the film: a soldier, in front of his companions, explains to the townsmen the functioning and efficiency of a rifle. The reach of the shot is X; it will penetrate so many meters of pine, so many sacks of sand, six human bodies. The information is intended to threaten. By naming each part, he wants to stupefy. The technical vocabulary, impersonal and precise by nature, is passionately enjoyed as a sign of personal and even racial superiority: we are of another species, a species it is wise to obey. Contrary to its supposed vocation of universality, knowledge merely exploits and consolidates difference. The contradictions of this situation, a microcosm of imperialism, involve bad faith. Insisting on technical language, inaccessible to the townsmen, the soldier provokes the animosity of his companions. The specialized vocabulary, mystifying for some, is commonplace for others; to successfully exalt himself the soldier requires the complicity of his companions, who in turn need his humiliation to regain their

The Guns (1963)

freedom. His insistence becomes ridiculous and soon traps him: the ignorance of others no longer proves his own superiority, but he must insist
and trample the townsmen even more, in order to retain, through their
common condition as oppressors, the fugitive solidarity of his irritated
companions.

The soldiers see in each other the mechanisms of the oppression of
which they are agents. Because they are not merely soldiers, their complicity, necessary to the superior race, has limits; and because they are
soldiers they do not reach a radical unmasking. Their position vacillates,
as a result, between haughtiness and vileness. They confront two permanent dangers: the arbitrary destruction of the drought victims and their
own violent disintegration. Later conflicts repeat this pattern: the murder
of the villager, the fight between the soldiers, and the love scene, close to
rape in its brutality.

This series of events culminates in the violent persecution and death of
the truckdriver. The food is to be transported out of the city, far from the
drought victims, who look on impassively. The soldiers stand guard, ter-
rified by the masses of starving people, but also exasperated by their
passivity. The truckdriver, an ex-soldier who himself is hungry, does what
the soldiers could have done as he tries to stop the transport of the food.
Hunted by the whole detachment he is finally caught and riddled with
bullets. The frenetic excess of shots, as well as the sinister joy of the chase,
makes the exorcism clear: in the ex-soldier the soldiers kill their own
freedom, their anxiety about passing to the other side.

Refracted in the group of soldiers the real problem, that of private property, ultimately reduces to a psychological conflict. The collision of consciences, with its own movement, is outlined and incited gradually until

the final gun battle. A partial dialectic erupts, one that is merely moral, based on fear, shame, and fury, restricted to the soldiers, even though caused by the presence of the drought victims. It is therefore an *innocuous dialectic*, bloody as the struggle may be, since it does not involve the starving masses that should be its true subject. It is as if, in view of the central conflict, the dramatic development were off center.[1] The climax does not really resolve the conflicts of the film; even though the gun battle represents the culmination of one conflict, it does not govern the sequence of episodes, which always alternates and separates the world of the plot and the world of inertia. At first glance this decentered construction is a defect: of what value is the crisis if it is a dislocated and distorted version of the primary antagonism? If the crisis is moral and the antagonism political, of what use is their approximation? It serves, in *The Guns*, to mark the discontinuity between the two worlds. It serves as a critique of moralism since it accentuates both moral responsibility and its insufficiency. The important link, in this case, is in the very absence of a direct link.

Even in the final scenes, which parallel the soldiers and the drought victims, the hiatus between the two is carefully preserved. The slaying of the sacred ox does not result from the death of the truckdriver. It is an echo, a degraded response. The persecution and the gun battle, although they may have a political substratum, do not transmit awareness or organization to the drought victims; but they do transmit excitement and movement, a vague impatience. The bearded prophet threatens his sacred ox: "If it does not rain soon, you will no longer be sacred, you will no longer be an ox." A continuous act, the edible holiness, which had been preserved, is transformed, as Joyce would say, into Christeak. The victims, inert up to this point, in this final moment are like piranhas. The group of peasants is explosive, and the moral position of the soldiers is untenable. The moral crisis, however, does not feed the hungry, nor can it be resolved by what they have done. The relationship between the two forms of violence is not one of continuity or proportion, but neither is it of indifference; it is aleatory and highly flammable. In the fictional sequences, which represent our world, we witness oppression and its moral cost; the close-up is of bad faith. In the sequences about misery we witness the conflagration and its affinity with lucidity. The close-up is obscure, and if it weren't it would be frightening. In the supposed *defect* of this construction, whose elements do not mix, is fixed a historical fatality: our western civilization foresees with fear the horror of itself and the eventual access of the plundered to justice.

Note

1. My argument and vocabulary are taken from a study by Althusser, "Notes sur un Theatre Matérialiste," in which he describes and discusses a structure of this type, "assymetrical and decentered." Cf. *Esprit*, December 1962.

16
"*Black God, White Devil*: The Representation of History"

ISMAIL XAVIER

Accusations of "formalism" are often addressed to films in which the work of narration, rather than being effaced, is made present and visible. Such films foreground their own narrative operations; the discursive operations of the text come to the surface and, as a result, the usual immersion in a fictive universe is rendered difficult or impossible. While conventional films allow the spectator to witness the unfolding of an imaginary world that gradually takes on the density of the "real," *Black God, White Devil* offers no such satisfaction. An adequate analysis of the film, therefore, must go beyond the represented fiction (the diegesis) if it is to account for the wealth of significations. The film cannot be reduced to the subjective whims of an auteur, nor to simplistic labels such as the "baroque," presumably expressing some hypothetical Brazilian "essence." This reading focuses, therefore, on the complex play of relations between the fictional world posited by the film and the work of narration that constitutes that world. The film's densely metaphorical style virtually pleads for allegorical interpretation even while its internal organization frustrates and defies the interpreter searching for a unifying "key" or implicit "vision of the world." And this resistance to intepretation is by no means incidental; it structures the film and constitutes its meaning.

The "fable" of *Black God, White Devil* is organized around a peasant couple, Manuel and Rosa. The film speaks of their social condition, their

Othon Bastos as Corisco in *Black God, White Devil* (1964)

hopes and representations, and their links to two forms of contestation: messianic cults and what Hobsbawm calls "social banditry" (*cangaço*). We can identify, and the narrator clearly distinguishes, three stages in their evolution. In the first stage, the cowherd Manuel lives with his wife Rosa and his mother on a backwoods plantation. He takes care of the local landowner's cattle in exchange for a small portion of the herd. Rosa, meanwhile, cultivates the crops necessary to their survival. The first "break" in this stage occurs when Manuel, cheated out of his due allotment of cattle, kills the landowner (Colonel Morais) whose henchmen pursue him and murder his mother. Hounded by the powerful and seeing his mother's death as a sign from heaven, Manuel joins the followers of Sebastião, the miracle-working saint (*beato*), the black God. In the second stage Manuel, ignoring Rosa's objections, places his destiny in Sebastião's hands. To prove his devotion, he performs the necessary purification rites. Sebastião's cult, meanwhile, begins to preoccupy both the local landowners and the Catholic Church. Together, they call on Antônio das Mortes — "killer of *cangaceiros*" — to repress the movement. The break in this stage occurs when Antônio das Mortes agrees to exterminate the *beatos*. At the same moment that Antônio massacres the beatos, Rosa slays Sebastião, ending his domination of Manuel. In the final stage, blind singer Julião leads Manuel and Rosa, the lone survivors of the massacre, to Corisco, survivor of another massacre, that of the *cangaceiro* Lampião and his band. Manuel transfers his faith to Corisco, whom he sees as another divine emissary. He and Corisco discuss the role of violence in the struggle to master destiny. A poetic "challenge" (*desafio*) revolves around the relative grandeur of Sebastião versus Lampião, an argument that comes to absorb all the protagonists: Manuel, Rosa, Corisco, and Dadá, his mate. The final break occurs when Antônio das Mortes fulfills his promised mission of eliminating Corisco. With both the black God (Sebastião) and the white Devil (Corisco) slain, the *sertão* opens up to the headlong flight of Manuel and Rosa.

The three phases outlined here do not occupy equal intervals in the temporal development of the narrative. The first is relatively short, suggesting a kind of prologue. Already in this phase, however, the film develops its central procedure: the synthetic representation of social existence. This procedure distinguishes *Black God, White Devil* from films like *Vidas Secas* whose scenic conventions derive from the Neo-Realist tradition. The "prologue" of *Black God, White Devil* already "condenses" ordinary activities and situations, making them emblematic of a mode of existence. This process occurs, for example, in the scenes beginning with Manuel's return to his farm when he tries to communicate the shock caused by his first encounter with Sebastião and that ends with his traversal of the small-town corral to meet Colonel Morais. At the same time, this scene, by its precise way of preparing the spectator to grasp the dramatic significance of the dialogue with Colonel Morais, fully demonstrates a style of narration announced in the prologue and reasserted throughout the film.

The film's credits — superimposed over shots of the arid *sertão* — announce the narrative style. The crescendo of Villa-Lobos's "Song of the *Sertão*" coincides with images (two close shots of the decomposing skull of an ox) emblematic of the drought afflicting the region. Contrasting in scale with the preceding long shots, these images are still reverberating in our mind when we first see Manuel. These brief shots, then, concentrate a dramatic charge of information concerning the drought and the precarious conditions of *sertão* life. The drama erupts, and dissolves, rapidly. The synthetic style and the information-laden shock-image condensing a broad range of significations already anticipate the film's constant modulation of contrasts and energetic leaps.

This modulation becomes clearer in the sequence of dialogue with Colonel Morais. Rather than evoke tension through a conventional play of shot-reaction shot, Rocha exploits composition within the frame and the slow movement of the actors. The tension is primarily created by the dilatation of the scene over time, especially in the long hiatus preceding the conflict's resolution. Manuel's violence responds to the colonel's violence; it discharges the accumulated tension, finding resonance in the montage as long takes give way to a rapid succession of short duration jump-cut shots. The narration "short-hands" the struggle between Manuel and the colonel, the chase by a cavalcade of *jagunços*, and the exchange of gunshots leading to the death of Manuel's mother. At the same time, coincident with this discontinuous visual montage, silence gives way to a saturated soundtrack that superimposes the sounds generated by the action with the music of Villa-Lobos. This aural saturation is proleptically "triggered" by the stomping hooves of the cavalcade, heard even before the colonel's death. This rush of sounds and events then give way to the prolonged shot in which Manuel, after closing the eyes of his murdered mother, slowly rises while looking back at the house. Complete silence, broken only by the singer's hushed lament, translates the pensive immobility of the character. Within this sequence, then, dilated time, relative immobility, and silence "frame" a more contracted time of multiple actions and crucial decisions in a contrastive scheme typical of the entire film. Rosa's mounting exasperation with Manuel's idolization of Sebastião, for example, transforms itself into a scream that "cues" Antônio's exuberant entrance into the film.

The sequence in which Manuel performs penance by carrying a boulder up an interminable slope brings dilation to the exasperation point. At the altar, Sebastião quietly tells Manuel to bring his wife and child to the sacrifice. The film opposes the interior of the chapel, space of ceremonial silence and equilibrium, to the exterior, space of hysteria and agitation, evoked by the permanently gyrating hand-held camera and the strident cries, amplified by the blowing wind, of the *beatos*, in the same dialectic of rarefaction-excess that commands the narrative as a whole. In the chapel, the ritual evolves in a silence marked by fixed glances and stylized gestures. The itinerary of the camera's glance, meanwhile, gradually transforms the central instrument of the rite (the dagger) into the center of the gravity of the composition. The hieratic disposition is broken only with Rosa's slaying of Sebastião and the fall of icons and candles from the altar, the clatter of which "signals" the eruption of gunfire and cries originating from the scene of the massacre. Extremely brief shots render the agitation and fall of the devout under the relentless fire of an Antônio das Mortes multiplied in a montage effect that recalls Eisenstein's *October* and even "quotes" images from the Odessa steppes sequence of *Potemkin*. The massacre completed, the film reverts to slow camera movements over the victims, as shots of a pensive Antônio install a new phase of reflection.

This dialectic of scarcity and saturation marks the temporality of *Black God, White Devil* as a whole. On a semantic level, this narrative organization might be seen as metaphorizing the psychology of the characters, here taken as typical representatives of the peasant class. The exasperating passivity, the verbal awkwardness, the atmosphere of hesitant rumination, alternating with sudden explosions of violence, characteristic of peasant life, thus find resonances within the narrative style. This metaphor could be extended to the environmental conditions of the *sertão* with its rude challenges to human survival, where drought alternates with deluge. More important than these plausible homologies between character and milieu, however, is the conception of temporality, historical in one of its dimensions, inherent in this modulation. The narrative, in its very texture, molds time so as to privilege disequilibrium and transformation. What seems immobility is in fact accumulation of energy, moments of apparent stasis that mask and express hidden forces. The slow passages are not neutral moments of pure extension; they engender the strong moments and the qualitative leaps. The internal movement of the narrative, in its swift changes and irreverent lack of measure, asserts the discontinuous but necessary presence of human and social transformation.

Functionally, this modulation opens "breaches" for the diverse interventions of the narrative voices, creating space for explicit commentary on the imaginary world represented in the film, and making possible the autonomous development of sound and image tracks. What guides the movement of the images, apart from the unifying "stage" of Monte Santo, is the contrasting articulation of Sebastião's messianic discourse versus Rosa's disbelief. We accompany the play of questions and answers on the soundtrack; it matters little that a sentence spoken during one scene is completed in a different scene. The same criteria operate in the *cangaceiro* episodes. The film emphasizes the rhetorical elaboration of Corisco's argument; the changes of tonality are always subordinated to the discourse rather than to the action.

Black God, White Devil is dotted with ritual stagings of its own central ideological debate. The succession of phases weaves an overall movement of reflexion, and everything in the film—the *mise-en-scène*, the montage, the singer-narrator, the dialogue, the discursive use of image and sound—foregrounds this movement. Although the film speaks of historical struggles, it never reproduces those events through naturalistic spectacle. The film is not preoccupied with the reconstitution of appearances, or with showing events as they actually transpired. Unlike spectacular, expensive, dominant cinema, it does not seek "legitimacy" in the illusory transfer of the "real" life of another epoch to the imaginary universe of the screen. In its refusal of the dominant industrial esthetic, *Black God, White Devil* affirms the basic principles of "the esthetic of hunger." The film attunes its style to its own conditions of production and thus marks its esthetic and ideological oppositon to the colonizing discourse of the film industry. Its very texture expresses the underdevelopment that conditions the film, transforming its own technical precariousness into a source of signification. And within this multiple operation, it adds a crucial element: it uses as the mediating figure of the discourse, the central narrative instance of the film, a poet from the oral tradition, a personage belonging to the same universe that constitutes the film's object of reflection.

This mediation, if not the only source of the film's cavalier attitude toward historical data, at least partially explains the fact that the film speaks of Corisco, Lampião, Antônio Conselheiro, and Padre Cícero without seeking any rigorous fidelity to the official history of dates and documents. The "figural" method of the film transforms history into a referential matrix covered with layers of imaginary constructions. The mediation operates as a kind of permeable membrane that allows passage only to selected fragments and transfigured characters. This precipitate of the popular imagination takes the form of exemplary tales whose purpose is not fidelity to fact but rather the transmission of a moral. The historical process is represented as a parable that retains only what the narrator sees as essential, in a style reminiscent, in its criteria of selection and its narrative poetics, of *cordel* literature. In the film, this tradition is embodied by the singer-narrator, although it would be simplistic to see the narration as merely the expression of his values. Popular poetry is but one of the multiple mediations that inform *Black God, White Devil*, for the film exploits all the parameters of the medium. The material of its representation (industrialized sound and image) is not homogenous to the material of oral literature and its conditions of production are not those of the *cordel* tradition. To state the obvious, *Black God, White Devil* is a film, with all that this fact implies. The mediation of *cordel* literature, resulting from an impulse of identification with popular art, interacts with the other processes involved in the film's construction, and this interaction generates the displacements that render the discourse ambiguous. The story of Manuel and Rosa "transfigures" the accumulated experiences of the peasant community. These experiences, schematized and encapsulated within an individual linear trajectory, are mediated by a narrative instance that constantly shifts its position. In this sense, the film constitutes a decentered and problematic reflection on history itself, in which the memory of peasant revolts is both revealed and questioned from diverse points of view.

The singer's narration, the work of the camera, and the musical commentaries of *Black God, White Devil* are not always in accord. In the sequence of Manuel's first encounter with Sebastião, for example, the image of the sky coincides with the singer's first chord on the guitar. While the camera pans vertically to frame Sebastião, the singer begins his song. He presents the characters and anticipates the special character of the encounter. The initial camera movement seems to define a unity of perspectives: sound and image define the saint as blessed by God. As Manuel approaches on horseback, however, the voice of the singer is stilled and the visual composition interprets the encounter in a way that anticipates the subsequent unmasking of Sebastião. Manuel excitedly circles Sebastião and his followers, staring at the saint. The play of shot/counter shot, however, underlines Sebastião's indifference to Manuel. The subjective camera shows that the saint does not look at Manuel, who becomes present to him only when Manuel places himself directly before the saint's impassive eyes. This treatment helps characterize Manuel by discrediting in advance his account of the incident in the following scene. At the same time, the image does not support the singer's description of Sebastião ("goodness in his eyes, Jesus Christ in his heart"). There is a total divorce between the actor and the camera, and the distance that characterizes the play of glances only becomes more pronounced as the film progresses. In these encounters, Sebastião remains an enigma as the camera identifies more and more with the perspective of Rosa, the focus of skepticism. Sebastião, for his part, stimulates this skepticism by his vain air of aristocratic indifference and by a certain sadistic touch in his ministering of the ceremonies. His behavior culminates in an inglorious, almost cowardly, death, the ordinary humanness of which contrasts with his former haughtiness and definitely unmasks him in our eyes. Only minutes before Rosa's attack, after all, had not this same man resolutely murdered a child?

This process of demystification, however, hardly exhausts the film's account of the social phenomenon of messianism. Manuel's "surrender" to Sebastião is constructed so as to celebrate a religious force capable of uniting the peasant masses. The camera anticipates Manuel and Rosa climbing the mountain up to Sebastião's domain, thus providing a rare moment of apotheosis. Processions of banners and symbols outlined against the sky and agitated by the wind find an echo in the symphonic music of Villa-Lobos. The solemn grandiosity of the scene comes, interestingly, not from the cordel-singer's voice but rather from the music of a non-regional "universal" composer. Even here, however, the figure of Sebastião is treated with great subtlety, since the camera emphasizes the pomp and circumstance surrounding him, ignoring his "good eyes" in order to emphasize the collective force of religious ecstacy. The following sequence points up the hysterically repressive side of this same religion by showing ritual humiliations and flagellations. The violent confrontation between the beatos and the larger society is rendered in a kind of strident shorthand, and the critique of messianism implicit in this passage is subsequently confirmed by the extended sequences on Monte Santo, locus of retreat and contemplative longing. Metaphorically exploring the topography of the mountain, the narration crystalizes the idea of proximity to heaven and imminent ascension, of retreat to a kind of antechamber to Paradise (the island that constitutes Sebastião's fundamental promise). In this privileged space, detached from the earth and its sordid involvements, the possibility of direct intervention in the world

Geraldo del Rey as Manuel in *Black God, White Devil* (1964)

ceases to be a goal. Messianic rebellion takes the peasants out of the process of production and distances them from the official church. It frees
them from the domination of landlord and boss, but in their place proposes only the passivity of prayer and the initiatory rituals that will define
them as elect in the moment of cataclysm.

After the massacre, Manuel continues to be faithful to Sebastião. The
saint's demystification takes place within the work of narration, without
the knowledge of the characters. With the appearance of Corisco,
however, the *mise-en-scène* changes significantly. An element from
within the diegesis now becomes the focus of critical reflection. As master
of ceremonies, Corisco's reflection is directly addressed both to us as spectators and to Manuel within the fiction. From this point on, the extended
passages of rarefied action involve the characters' discussion of their own
experience, a discussion in which Corisco collaborates. A new kind of
dialogue appears with the insertion of the singer himself, or of his double,
within the scene. At the same time, image and sound, by repeating similar
elements within apparently opposite conditions, suggest that Sebastião
and Corisco are merely two sides of the same metaphysic; in the symmetry
of their inversions lies a deeper unity.

The same voice (Othon Bastos) delivers the words of both Sebastião
and Corisco. And the same Villa-Lobos music consecrates Sebastião's
triumph on Monte Santo and Manuel's initiation—by castrating the
fazendeiro—into *cangaço* violence. The same metaphor marks the
horizon of their practice: "The *sertão* will become sea, and the sea
sertão." Both speak in the name of Good and Evil. The unity that
underlies their contradictions is expressed in symmetrical presentations;
Corisco too is announced as a kind of advent ("as fate would have it") in

versification similar to that of the beginning of the film.

At the same time, there are significant inversions; the vertical pan from sky to earth associated with Sebastião becomes a creeping horizontal pan over the *sertão* with Corisco. This inversion opposes Corisco's rootedness in the "lower" world of "that devil Lampião" to the "elevated" world of the saint. The *beatos'* straight-lined progression toward Monte Santo, furthermore, is replaced by the back and forth movements of Corisco's violent rituals. In long shot, he promises vengeance, as his circular movements underline the clearly limited space of his action on the close-cropped *sertão*. The perspectival view of his stage, staked out by his immobile henchmen, project on his figure the shadow of a closing and an absence of horizons that will only be reaffirmed and rendered explicit as the film progresses.

In its theatricality, the *cangaceiro* phase of the film takes on the tone of a ritual of the living dead, of survivors without hope or prospect. While Manuel lives the experience as an optimistic present, Corisco stages the events in a very different spirit, as the accomplice of the very forces that condemn him. More than once it is he who defines this condition of living death. In the metaphor of the two heads (one killing, the other thinking) he sees himself as a repetition of Virgulino, as the vestige of an historically condemned practice that he carries to its foredoomed conclusion. Corisco himself represents the limitations of social banditry on his backlands stage. His most daring strokes seem like ritual expositions of a doctrinaire solution, without practical consequence but relived symbolically as a hymn of praise to violence as a form of justice. This violence involves no program beyond "turning things upside down," and its loyalties and vengeance are based only on circumstance and personal connection. They become legitimate only when enlisted in the service of "Good" and "Evil." Corisco sees himself as the agent of Good and the figure of the just avenger (he is Saint Jorge, the people's saint, versus the dragon of wealth) and as the agent of Evil in the figure of the condemned man, who, when confronted with the greater indignity of death by starvation, chooses violence. He takes on his destructive task in the name of justice, knowing that it involves, by the ironic economics of destiny, his own condemnation. His discourse is caught in self-defeating circularity; it creates a short circuit of means and ends, an alternation of revolt and accommodation with the enemy. The exuberant rhetoric with which Corisco demystifies Sebastião (Manuel's myth) implies the demystification of Virgulino (his own myth).

In its simultaneous praise and demystification of both Sebastião and Corisco, the narration discredits messianism and *cangaço* as practices likely to generate a more just human order. The underside of the metaphysic of Good and Evil is exposed in the equivocal expression of its rebellion. The film clearly favors the willed defeat and exemplary revolt of the White Devil to the radical alienation of the Black God, whence the similarity between Corisco's discourse and that of Antônio das Mortes, figure of infallible efficacity. Like Corisco, Antônio defends his own violence as a kind of euthanasia—the people must not die of hunger. He defines himself, furthermore, as the condemned agent of destiny within the same logic of "kill and be killed" proposed by Corisco. But while Corisco exposes his contradictions in a frenetic back-and-forth movement, Antônio is enigmatic and laconic, mysterious in his physical presence and contradictory in his words. His hesitation in accepting the task proposed by the priest and the colonel implies that he understands the conversation on some other level ("it is dangerous to meddle with the things of God"). When he accepts with the words "Sebastião is finished," his tone of voice, suggesting both power and resignation, impresses solemnity on the moment. And in the conversation with blind Julião he posits once and for all the larger meaning of his acts, a meaning that his conscience intuits but that he never really explains.

Our task now is to reflect on this "larger order" affirmed by the symbolic recapitulation of the peasant revolts and their religious ideology, along with its narrative elaboration. By foreseeing the outcome of the encounter between Manuel and Sebastião, the singer suggests the idea of Destiny. The *beato* enters Manuel's life without Manuel having done anything to provoke the encounter. At the same time, Manuel's revolt is perfectly explicable in more earthly terms—the material conditions of his life, the social relations of his work, his visionary tendencies, Rosa's despair. To explain Manuel's violence, one need only assume a minimal notion of right and wrong and an elementary aspiration to justice. Angered by an obvious fraud and frustrated in a very precise hope (the possession of land), Manuel fails to understand the structural nature of his oppression, and therefore invokes metaphysical entities to explain his adversity and justify his revolt. Sebastião's presence in this moment of revolt encourages Manuel to adopt the saint's interpretive system. Manuel attributes the tragedy to a divine plan that requires his devotion to the saint, an option that placates his guilty conscience and protects him from police pursuit.

The singer's authority remains ambiguous, not only because he says nothing about the destiny supposedly manifest in these events, but also because image and sound reveal situations that hardly require supernatural stratagems to explain them. The providential presence of Sebastião remains the focus of this ambiguity; he offers Manuel, at precisely the right moment, the option for which his consciousness is prepared. It is the narrator, admittedly, who brings Sebastião to Manuel, but Manuel must also play his part for destiny to be fulfilled. It this coincidence, this complexity, which triggers movement and concretizes the first moment of rupture in the film.

In the second major rupture, the intervention of Antônio, also a stranger to the devout world of Monte Santo, coincides with Rosa's act of violence. Her act too is explicable in terms of her own situation. She does not kill the saint to serve some transcendent design, but rather in her own name. Antônio's intervention, already ambiguous in itself, becomes doubly ambiguous by this precise coincidence with Rosa's violence. In the two moments of rupture, external forces and human actions converge to create a turnabout that projects the characters into a new phase of life. Transformation arises from this correspondence, which marks a double determination: the narrative creates a situation in which the characters, unconscious of the stratagems mounted against them, and moved by both personal and extra-personal motives, act at the right time, participating actively in a process controlled by these same stratagems. Everything moves toward a goal that remains unthinkable for Manuel and Rosa but that is palpably clear to the spectator.

In reality, events do not evolve according to Manuel's expectations. The narration works, in fact, to discredit his interpretation, suggesting instead the existence of a pre-ordained end. After the Monte Santo massacre, the projection of the singer (blind Julião) into the fiction, visibly conducting Manuel and Rosa, makes palpable the presence of the agents of the grand plan behind the whole arrangement. In his first dialogue with Julião at the crossroads, Antônio explains that he allowed Manuel and Rosa to survive so they could "tell their story." He thus reinforces the notion that he collaborates with the larger order that controls individual destinies. He makes the protagonists the spokesmen of his own legend, bastions of the oral tradition that organizes the film. He hints, then, at the very level at which the narration is engendered, for it is in the nature of the narratives to organize themselves within a certain teleology. *Black God, White Devil* "confesses" this condition and comments on it, even as it fulfills it.

The *cangaceiro* phase inaugurates a new system. Corisco arrives via the voice of the singer, and the couple comes to Corisco via blind Julião. Manuel, after the encounter, has his reasons for carrying out the predetermined; he joins the *cangaço* in order to avenge Sebastião. Prepared for violence, he sets out on a new trajectory of equivocations, in which his actions follow one design (that of a dimly glimpsed teleology) while his consciousness imagines another (based on the very metaphysic being discredited). Without knowing it, Manuel completes a circle; he descends from his messianic flight only to return to the down to earth practicality of Rosa. At this point, however, a subtle dislocation distances Manuel and Rosa from the central events of the fable. Although they remain present to the end of the film, their survival is determined by Antônio ("I didn't kill once, and I won't kill again"). In the final sequence, the most relevant fact within the larger order is the duel between Corisco and Antônio; the song makes no reference to Manuel and Rosa. For the couple, survival marks a new opening and the reassertion of immediate natural bonds. Their conscious future consists in liberation from both Sebastião and Corisco in favor of the life-oriented immediacy of Rosa.

If Manuel initially shows capacity for revolt, the Manuel of the end shows only minimal initiative. Corisco gains strength, paradoxically only in so far as he participates in the ritual representation of his own inevitable defeat. Antônio das Mortes, despite his infallibility, relinquishes all personal ambition, seeing himself as merely the doomed agent of a predestined scheme. None of the characters in the film consciously make their own history and the film advances no project for taking control of destiny. The narration moves in the opposite direction, from initial ambiguity toward explicit definition of a teleology. Initially, this teleology is merely suggested by the singer and by the *mise-en-scène*, while the characters retain some initiative. With the dialogue between blind Julião and Antônio, however, this teleological scheme, implicit in Corisco's style of representation, becomes explicit. Antônio, by his infallible action, consummates the scheme; his revelatory word evokes the final term of the overall movement: "the great war, without the blindness of God and the Devil." His own behavior, furthermore, favors this progression from implicit to explicit teleology. His slaying of the *beatos* is explicable, on one level, by his earthly code of money, but his enigmatic attitude hints at more transcendent considerations. His duel with Corisco is not commercially motivated — killing *cangaceiros* is simply his destiny. The film refers only to his commitment to the future whose teleology leads to a great war whose preparation is the only motive proposed for Antônio's action. The overall development of the film, and Antônio's specific course, suggests that progress is not determined by human beings. In this sense, the film moves toward a determinism whose focus is outside of the characters whose consciousness is completely alienated, at worst, and capable, at best, only of vague intuitions of a more comprehensive order. And it is precisely Antônio who most clearly professes this radical agnosticism.

There are, then, two major criss-crossing movements in the film: the questioning of a dualistic metaphysic in the name of the liberation of human beings as the subjects of history is superimposed on the gradual affirmation of a "larger order" that commands human destiny. This coexistence does not develop along parallel paths, but rather through a fundamental interdependence: the very person who furthers liberation and humanistic values is also the fated agent of a dim larger order. Antônio, incarnating this short circuit of alienation-lucidity, constitutes the nucleus of both movements, in which History advances along the correct path thanks to ambiguous and equivocal figures. Antônio's repressive violence is not an unfortunate incident but a basic necessity, not a *despite* but a *through* by which History-Destiny weaves itself. Messianism and *cangaço* are moments through which human consciousness moves toward lucid acknowledgment of human beings themselves as the source, the means, and the end of transforming praxis. This ascension to consciousness does not take place, however, within the perspective of the protagonists. There is a hiatus between their experience and the final term, the revoluntionary *telos* around which the narrative organizes its lesson. Manuel need not complete this trajectory because he does not liberate himself alone; he is not the center of his own trajectory. The horizon of History is not delineated by Manuel or even by Rosa; the "larger order" requires that the certainty of the end be affirmed through incompletion.

The dominant voice in the fable of *Black God, White Devil* is that of the narrator. He composes the story as a propedeutic recapitulation of a historical process (peasant revolts) that the narrator understands as propedeutic, as incorporating the movement toward the "great war," an essential subterranean movement that the recapitulation, by its symbols, tries to make clear and palpable. This "making palpable" is realized by the transfiguration of the Marxist idea of "historical necessity" into the idea of "Destiny" — a version of "necessity" familiar to popular oral traditions and to *cordel* literature. The carrying out of the revolutionary telos is a certainty, but its mechanisms remain ambiguous. The crucial point is that, under the form of Destiny, the film paradoxically affirms the apparently opposite principle of human self-determination.

This paradox is clearly inscribed in the final sequence. Antônio arrives at the duel, observing Corisco without being seen. He easily aims his rifle, but before shooting, he hesitates. It is only with the beginning of the singer's ballad that Antônio resumes his arbitrarily frozen gesture. His raising of the rifle is synchronized with the words "surrender, Corisco!" in the song. From this point on, the montage schematizes the diegetic action in such a way as to make it illustrative — by its rhythm and tonality, and by its chivalric style — of the song. *Cordel* literature dominates the representation. The singer draws the moral of his own story: "this world is ill-divided — it belongs to Man, and not to God or the Devil." He affirms a conception of change that places history in the hands of human beings themselves, thus confirming Antônio's allusions to the "Great War" and completing the demystification of the metaphysical based on both Black God and White Devil. The hope of transformation, or rather its certainty, is reasserted by the refrain: "the *sertão* will become sea, and the sea *sertão*." Manuel and Rosa's headlong *corrida* toward the sea — the first straight-lined vector within a trajectory marked by a constant circling of glances, movements, and even thoughts — reinforces the projection toward a dimly glimpsed future. The narrative discourse, however, does not end with their *corrida*. It offers one last reversal by celebrating revolutionary certainty in such a way as to challenge the secular humanism implicit in the singer's final words. By an imagistic leap, the narration visually realizes the metaphor of transformation used by both Sebastião and Corisco: the surf invades the screen; the *sertão* becomes the sea. The ritual sounds and voices of the Villa-Lobos music elaborates the transformation. The waves break again and again, connoting omnipresence, domination. The image strengthens and renders actual the telos that guides the entire film, lending to Manuel's *corrida* on the level of immediate appearance nothing more than a blind flight across the *sertão* — a note of hope.

The discontinuity between this narrative leap and Manuel's trajectory situates the certainty of transformation on the level of the Universal ("Man") and reaffirms the hiatus between his lived experience and his meaning as a figure within the frame of the stratagems of destiny. His trajectory constitutes an oblique, transfigured representation of the certain-

Lídio Silva as Sebastião in *Black God, White Devil* (1964)

ty, just as Antônio's "repression," finally, both liberates and represents this same certainty. Everything in *Black God, White Devil* denies the possibility of thinking in terms of lost trails, irrecoverable detours, or insurmountable gaps. The redemptive power of its teleology is radical. The story evolves as the fulfillment of Destiny, at the same time that it grants humanity the condition of subject. Everything in the story only reaffirms this problematic condition, as it is expressed in the contradictory movement of the film.

The winds of History are ubiquitous. Its modulations are palpable in moments of violence, and there is no doubt about its final direction. But who or what impels it? *Black God, White Devil* gives no univocal response to this question, and it would be obtuse to require one, for what is fundamental in the film is the very heterogeneity of its representations. The interaction of voices renders ambiguous the principle of its revolutionary lesson, thus creating an unresolved tension, deriving from the criss-crossing movements in which "Man" and "Destiny" struggle for primacy. There is no definitive answer concerning the knowledge that sustains this certainty because the mediations in the film mark the debate with different systems of interpretation of the human experience within history.

Crystallizing an esthetic and ideological project that affirms popular forms of representation (as a focus of cultural resistance, and a *logos* where national identity is engendered) and striving for social transformation, on the basis of a dialectical vision of history, the film neither idealizes nor downgrades popular culture. Rather than dismiss popular forms in the name of ideological correctness, Rocha uses them even as he questions the traditional character of their representation. Cinema Novo confronted this task—of reelaborating popular traditions as the spring-board for a transformation-oriented critique of social reality—in diverse ways. *Black God, White Devil* is a key film because it incorporates within its very structure the contradictions of this project. It avoids any romantic endorsement of the "popular" as the source of all wisdom, even as it discredits the enthnocentric reductionism that sees in popular culture nothing more than meaningless superstition and backward irrationality, superceded by bourgeois progress and rationalism. Adopting the didactic formula, *Black God, White Devil* decenters the focus of its lesson and, contrary to the "edifying" and dogmatic discourse of the "models for action" school, challenges us with an aggressive fistful of interrogations. Rather than offer, in a single diapason, an insipidly schematic lesson about class struggle, it encourages reflection on the peasantry and its forms of consciousness, and more important, on the very movement of History itself.

17
"Land in Anguish"

ROBERT STAM

Terra em Transe ("Land in Anguish," 1967) is a watershed film within the history of Brazilian cinema. It brings to its paroxysm the anguished self-scrutiny of second-phase Cinema Novo and opens the way both for the aboveground "official" Tropicalism of *Macunaíma* and the subterranean Tropicalism of "Udigrudi." An explosive study of art and politics in the Third World, it is also Glauber Rocha's most personal and brilliant contribution to political cinema. The film is especially germane to any discussion of a revolutionary esthetics in the cinema, for it points the way to a possible political cinema that avoids the twin dead ends of a condescending populism on the one hand and an aridly theoretical reflexivity on the other. Populism (*Burn!, Z, State of Siege*) wraps a radical message in Hollywood packaging in an attempt to be "accessible," while reflexive cinema à la Straub makes us aware of the medium by self-consciously investigating its own processes. Rocha's film is reflexive—a veritable essay on the intersection of art and politics—but it is neither bloodless nor dispassionate. While allowing for the role of emotions in political life, it never falls into the trap of merely personal outburst. Although saturated with anger, eloquence, personal and collective hysteria, it is in no sense a manipulative film, for it investigates rather than exploits its emotions.

The events of *Terra em Transe* take place in the imaginary state of Eldorado. Felipe Vieira, governor of the province of Alecrim, refuses to resist a coup led by the rightist Porfirio Diaz.[1] After an angry discussion

Land in Anguish (1967)

with Viera, the protagonist-narrator Paulo Martins, accompanied by Viera's secretary Sara, flees the governor's palace and is mortally wounded by the police. As his life ebbs away, he recalls the events that led to this personal and political defeat. Four years earlier he had been the poet-protégé of Diaz, before leaving him in order to explore a more political kind of poetry. He goes to Alecrim to work with the communist militant Sara in the gubernatorial campaign of Vieira, a liberal populist politician. They win, but the governor-elect, because of his ties to absentee landlords, violates his campaign promises and unleashes his police against the peasants. Disillusioned, Paulo throws himself into a life of orgies and existential nausea.

Later, when Sara asks him to make a televised report in order to destroy Diaz, now allied with Explint (read imperialism), Paulo accepts out of love for Sara and makes a film, *Biography of an Adventurer*, recounting Diaz's successive political betrayals. Denounced as a traitor by Diaz, Paulo joins Vieira's presidential bandwagon. In an atmosphere of popular celebration marred by repressive violence, the people dance the samba and contribute to the gathering momentum of Vieira's populist campaign. The right, fearful of electoral defeat, begins to prepare its *putsch*. Brought back to the starting point of the film, we see Paulo offer Vieira a gun, which Vieira refuses. Cross-cutting alternates Paulo's final dying moments with the coronation of Diaz and a long last shot shows a silhouetted Paulo with uplifted rifle.

Organized around Paulo's memories as he lies dying, the narrative of *Terra em Transe* consists of the lucid recital of a life dominated by political illusions and thus conforms to what has been called the "Quixotic formula of systematic disenchantment." As if to highlight this structure of enchantment-disenchantment, Paulo speaks in both the prologue and epilogue of the impossibility of his naive and impotent political faith. The first object of his faith is Porfirio Diaz, whose very name has divine resonances, whom Paulo calls the "god of his youth." The second object of his faith is his "leader," the populist demogogue Vieira. The word "leader," in fact, reverberates ironically throughout the film, culminating in Paulo's explosion of disgust against Vieira when he fails to resist the coup: "You see, Sara? . . . Our leader! . . . Our great leader!" What is new in Rocha's elaboration of the Cervantic formula is the precise political meaning he gives to it. Paulo comes to be disaffected from all the bourgeois political leaders, whether rightists like Diaz or liberals like Vieira. In his disappointment, he is doubled by people like the journalist Alvaro and by communist militants like Alto and Sara. Paulo shares his disenchantment with the people, who "can believe in no leader." (Like the peasant leader Felicio, Paulo goes from faith in Vieira's promises to disillusionment and death.)

Land in Anguish as a whole elaborates what might be called the theme of "the apparent difference." Vieira and Diaz appear to occupy opposite ends of the political spectrum, but the parallel montage of their electoral campaigns, superficially contrasting them, on a deeper level ironically equates them. The "nationalist" press magnate Fuentes thinks himself different from Diaz; historical forces make their roles converge. Paulo fondly thinks that he is not an oppressor; but on occasion he acts as Vieira's policeman. Sara and the militants seem farther to the left, but their actions only reinforce Vieira, and ultimately, Diaz. Linked by their common ties to the bourgeoisie, all these political figures, with the exception of Diaz, nurse the illusion of their own purity. The film's doubling procedures, however, constantly expose their subterranean affinities with their supposed enemies.

At times the struggle beteen Paulo and Diaz seem less ideological than psychological, a case of the artist wrestling with his alter ego. Paulo nurses a kind of oedipal hatred toward Diaz, his political and spiritual father. The oedipal note is sounded in the final ironic words of the *Biography of an Adventurer*—"Here is the father of our country." A bizarre, almost sexual bond links Paulo and Diaz. At one point, Paulo imagines himself fighting with Diaz and abandoning him, while Diaz cries hysterically, in the accents of desperate and unrequited love: "You left me alone, alone!" The film's editing reinforces the parallels between Paulo and Diaz ("Diaz, dying like me . . . ."). At another point, the off-screen voice of Paulo is superimposed on the image of Diaz, whose lips are moving, as if Paulo were somehow speaking *through* Diaz. This identification of Paulo with Diaz has a social as well as a psychological dimension. Diaz personifies the imperial origins of Brazil. He carries the cross of the Portuguese navigators and the black flag of the Inquisition. Here, the film suggests, is the historical source of the bourgeois class in Brazil.

These are the "rotten roots" to which Paulo refers. Paulo tries to disown these roots by crying: "He is not in my blood!" He imagines himself killing Diaz, but in so doing he is not so much eliminating an individual as liquidating his own personal and historical past. For socially speaking, he is what Alvaro calls him, "a dirty copy of Diaz."

The central dialectic of *Terra em Transe* involves art on the one hand, and social reality on the other. The dialectic is summed up in the poem that comments on Paulo's death:

> He failed to sign the noble pact
> between the pure soul and the bloody cosmos,
> a gladiator defunct but still intact—
> so much violence, yet so much tenderness.

> —Mário Faustino
> *Epitaph of a Poet*

The bloody cosmos and the pure soul, violence and tenderness, politics and poetry—these are the poles around which *Terra em Transe* revolves. The film shows the degradation of the ideal in the real world, where "purity rots in tropical gardens." Romanticism, the film suggests, is out of place in a world where the political earth is in convulsion. Poets like Paulo, who cultivate the private sensibility in the world of the *putsch*, do not survive in places like Eldorado. In *Terra em Transe*, social violence is constantly intruding on private tenderness, just as the soundtrack superimposes the crackling fire of machine guns on the tender harmonies of the Brazilian composer Villa-Lobos.

To the intellectual hunger for the ideal of romanticism, *Terra em Transe* opposes the real physical hunger of the Brazilian masses. When Paulo, quoting Chateaubriand, speaks of his "hunger for the absolute," Sara brings him back to earth by asserting simply: "Hunger." While Paulo bemoans "the misery of our souls," Sara is more preoccupied with *social* misery. Rocha's art refuses to obscure the fact of hunger. It develops what his most important declaration of artistic principles calls "an esthetic of hunger." His films treat hunger as subject and as pervasive metaphor; they are hungry in their urgency as well as in their enforced technological poverty.

Paulo represents the poet abroad in the world of class struggle and coups d'etat. His habitual mode of speech, simultaneously frenetic and solemn, is poetic.[2] The lava of his words repeatedly erupts into apostrophe, incantation, curses. His poetry, ubiquitous in *Terra em Transe*, punctuates, interrupts, and counterpoints the action. Most often, however, it expresses his inner voice, rather like the soliloquies in *Hamlet*. Paulo recurrently appears in closeup with voice off, in a technique reminiscent of the Orson Welles adaptations of Shakespearean tragedies. Paulo, furthermore, shares significant traits with Hamlet—an overheated imagination, a perverse virtuosity of language, a rigorous skepticism coexisting with exasperated idealism, and the view of himself as the legitimate heir of power. Like Hamlet, he is the more or less lucid critic of an ambient corruption in which he himself participates. His almost obsessive references to death, to worms, to a people whose sadness has rotted its blood, reinforce the atmosphere of suffocating malaise. *Terra em Transe* is Shakespearean in its intense interplay of the personal and the political, in its frequent ruptures of tone, with lyric calm preceding explosions of violence, and in the complex interaction of love scenes and political scenes, whereby the two come to color and "contaminate" each other.

Apart from putting poetry to diverse rhetorical uses, *Terra em Transe* also pinpoints the diverse political uses to which poetry can be put. While working as Diaz's protege, Paulo timidly expresses a desire to speak of politics in a new kind of poetry. Diaz condescendingly suggests that everyone feels radical in their youth. Paulo subsequently offers his services to the apparently more receptive Vieira. The country needs poets, Vieira remarks, like those romantics whose voices stirred the crowds. He applauds Sara's recitation of a poem ("The street belongs to the people, as the sky belongs to the condor") by Castro Alves, a Brazilian romantic poet who fought for the abolitionist cause. The poem highlights the historical ambiguity of Romanticism; the same movement that produced the self-indulgent narcissism of Lamartine also engendered the socially conscious poetry of Percy Bysshe Shelley and Castro Alves. Vieira's allusion to "those romantics" evokes a moment in Brazilian history when political and artistic movements acted in symbiosis. The subsequent events of the film, however, show the precise political limits within which poetry, and art generally, operate. It becomes obvious that Vieira prefers his political poets to be safely buried in the past. When Paulo tries to dissuade Vieira from using the police against the peasants, a voice-over sings the Castro Alves poem. The street may belong to the people in the world of poetry, the film suggests, but in fact it belongs to their oppressors.

Terra em Transe criticizes the naive notion that art in itself can create a revolution. Paulo Martins loses his initial faith in political poetry, concluding that "words are useless." Sara, who generally represents the best face of orthodox communism, tells Paulo that poetry and politics are too much for one man. Literal-minded critics, taking Sara's judgment as the film's final verdict on the question of art and politics, fail to appreciate the dialectical relation between poetry and politics in the film. They also miss the obvious irony, since the film itself not only "includes" poetry but also proceeds poetically, constituting the cinematographic equivalent of poetry.

Cinema has accustomed us to filmmakers who include in their films surrogates for themselves (for example, the magic lanternist in Bergman's *The Magician*) or analogues for their art. In the references to poetry in *Terra em Transe*, one must read as well art in general, and cinema in particular. Paulo's talk of new poetic forms in which to speak of politics

Paulo Autran as Porfirio Diaz in *Land in Anguish* (1967)

inevitably calls up Rocha the filmmaker, creating new forms of political cinema. Who would know better than he that established power prefers servile pens — and cameras — to aggressive and radical ones? Both his enthusiasm for poetry and his reservations about its social efficacy apply as well to cinema. One moment in the film effectively equates the two. In a shot whose backlighting and rectangular composition recall Godard, we see Paulo aim his camera out of his apartment window and take a photograph, while his off-screen voice comments: "I, for example, devote myself to the vain exercise of poetry."

Paulo, we must remember, is a journalist and filmmaker as well as a poet. He makes *Biography of an Adventurer* in order to destroy his fallen idol Diaz, who is shown laughing while the off-screen commentary tells of the successive betrayals behind his rise to pre-eminence. In one sense, *Biography of an Adventurer* is a kind of microtale that resumes and recapitulates the film as a whole, for the film-within-the-film, like *Terra em Transe*, recounts Diaz's rise to political power. On a deeper level, however, *Biography of an Adventurer* tells a story that resembles that of another "adventurer" — Paulo himself in *Terra em Transe*.

Important differences, however, prevent the film-within-the-film from being a mere replica in miniature of the film as a whole. The "Biography" is a piece of militant journalism sponsored by one political force in order to destroy another political force. It is the kind of film that politically committed filmmakers often make or are encouraged to make — clear, factual, militant, and immediately "useful." The dialectical juxtaposition of two kinds of political film brings out the strengths and weaknesses inherent in each. The "Biography" is direct, "effective," but also unsubtle, manipulative, and slick. *Terra em Transe* as a whole is complex, all nuance and subtle contradiction, but at the same time dif-

154

ficult of access, full of subjectivity, somewhat confusing. Thus the film-within-the-film critiques the totality of the film, and the film as a whole points up the limitations of the film-within-the-film.

Terra em Transe shares a number of features with *Citizen Kane* — its flashback structure, its journalistic subject, its verbal and visual exuberance, and its baroque density. The "Biography," for its part, is modelled on the "March of Time" newsreel in Welles's film. Like the newsreel, it exposes the duplicity and treachery of people in power. Diaz represents an underdeveloped, third-world Hearst; both are wealthy, arrogant, and demagogic. In both films, the metallic staccato voice of a news-reporter hammers home points with heavy-handed irony. Both of the films-within-the-film, furthermore, are situated in a precise political context. In *Citizen Kane*, the masters of a new kind of journalism finance a film in order to "bury" the older journalism of the Kane-Hearst empire. Paulo makes his film to politically bury Diaz. *Terra em Transe* sensitizes us to the social context of filmmaking. Films do not emerge full-blown from the heads of their creators; Paulo makes his because certain political enemies of Diaz pay for him to make it. Paulo, having offered his humble pen first to Diaz and then to Vieira, now offers his humble camera to those who would destroy Diaz. If Paulo's poetry was already conditioned by political ends, his film — since cinema by its very nature is immersed in socio-economic process — is even more profoundly affected by political and material interests. The film exposes the illusion of the self-determining artist who thinks he's using the apparatus that is in fact using him.

Both films are treated reflexively. The newsreel in *Citizen Kane* is shown as part of a discussion among the participating journalists. We are shown a projection room and the projectionist who adjusts his equipment. The journalists discuss possible changes in the film. We are made aware that film is artifice, a collective creation, the end product of innumerable esthetic and political decisions. The "Biography" highlights the artifice of film in a different way. As an off-screen voice delineates his perfidies, Diaz laughs as if he were conscious of the soundtrack but unmoved. The footage has obviously been manipulated, for Diaz performs in a film whose political ends he could not conceivably have approved. The technique illustrates Godard's notion that the distinction between documentary and fiction film is an arbitray one; all films are fiction films, for they are all fabrications.

This reflexivity sheds light on a puzzling fact about *Terra em Transe* — our lack of identification with its central hero. As narrator and protagonist, Paulo is the only personage granted subjectivity. His sensibility colors all the events of the film. His lyric poems — and lyric poetry is the privileged mode of personal feeling — punctuate the action. Voice-over monologues combined with close shots, surely the cinematographic equivalent of the lyric mode, recur throughout the film, Paulo would seem to incarnate the conventional cinematic hero. Young, handsome, dynamic, sensitive, articulate, and sexually attractive, he offers an ideal

155

José Lewgoy (left) as Vieira and Mário Lago in *Land in Anguish* (1967)

object for identification. Yet the identification never takes place. We neither identify with his life nor weep over his death.

Terra em Transe is linked to one of the least realistic of artistic genres: opera. Rocha has often expressed fondness for the "cinema-opera" of Welles and Eisenstein. Opera itself, especially Verdi and his Brazilian counterpart Carlos Gomes, pervades the soundtrack. Paulo's death, co-extensive with the film, recalls the protracted agonies of opera, where people die eloquently, interminably, and in full voice. As if to call attention to the operatic reference, the wounded Paulo twice declaims: "Eu preciso cantar (I must sing)!" Paulo does not try to escape or locate a doctor, and Sara does not bind his wounds; such basely material preoccupations have no place in cinema-opera. The exalted stylized speech of the film also recalls opera. Although some of the dialogue is naturalistically rendered, the world of the film remains one where people find it natural to address one another in poetry.

In his famous essay on the significance of a revitalized opera for the creation of epic theater, Brecht speaks of his desire to make opera contemporary and democratic. He claims that opera, while procuring a certain realism, annihilates it by having everyone sing. If we apply the terms of his comparison of epic and dramatic theater, we find that *Terra em Transe* invariably falls into the epic category. Rather than incarnate a process, it tells its story with narrative distance. Rather than involve the spectator, it transforms him/her into a critical observor of the contradictions of character. We are in a sense Paulo; yet at the same time we see him critically, much as we see a figure like Mother Courage, simultaneously from within and without. Paulo, like Mother Courage, ultimately learns very little from the disasters that befall him, but we as an audience can learn much by observing him. He is, as Walter Benjamin said of Galy Gay, the protagonist of Brecht's *A Man's a Man*, "an empty stage on which the contradictions of our society are acted out."

The mechanisms that subvert our identification with Paulo are extremely complex. Paulo is less a rounded character than a political figure, the point of convergence of various political and cultural forces. Our interest in him, consequently, is always subordinated to our interest in the political realities in which he is enmeshed. The title reads *Terra em Transe*, not *Paulo em Transe*. The film aborts our natural tendency to idealize Paulo, for he is always seen critically, and first of all by himself. At one point he denounces his own bourgeois class as weak and decadent. He derides himself as "a romantic," and other characters echo his auto-critique. The communist militants berate his political irresponsibility, while Sara always brings him back to concrete social reality. To his temptation for facile heroism, she responds: "We don't need heroes." When he laments having sacrificed his profoundest ambitions, she reminds him what real sacrifice means—thankless political work, childlessness, imprisonment, and torture. The film also insists on the scorn that Paulo displays toward the very people he wants to liberate. While clinging to a romantic notion of "the people," he shows only contempt for them in his everyday life. It is as if Rocha has anticipated within the film itself, all possible criticisms of his protagonist. His refusal of heroes reflects both his analysis of the Brazilian political situation as well as his programmatic opposition to Hollywood conventions of character.

This critical undercutting of Paulo's status as hero does not, however, fully explain our failure to identify with him. The failure derives rather from the basic esthetic strategy of the film—its refusal of the techniques of dramatic realism. *Terra em Transe* underlines its anti-realistic intentions by the ultimate implausability—the posthumous narrator. Everything conspires, furthermore, to diminish any feeling of suspense. The film is framed by a prologue and epilogue, both of which treat the coup d'etat, Paulo's flight and his subsequent death. We know from the outset both the how and why of Paulo's death. Rocha is less interested in the outcome of the conflict than in its "anatomy." He has called *Terra em Transe* an "anti-dramatic film, which destroys itself by a *montage à répétitions*." The narrative is constantly derailed, deconstructed, re-elaborated. The incidents of the film are exploded, analyzed into a play of political forces.

The world of *Terra em Transe* is one of spatio-temporal discontinuity. There are no establishing shots to situate us. We are further disoriented by dizzying camera movements and an unorthodox variety of camera angles. Even in sequences characterized by spatial homogeneity, there is discontinuity in the cinematographic treatment of the unified space. We are given fragments that defy organization into a narrative whole. In the various orgy and cabaret sequences, for example, it is impossible to divine any pre-existing fiction which has been treated elliptically. We ourselves have to create the spatiality and the temporality of the scene.

Terra em Transe proliferates in jump cuts and violations of orthodox "continuity." Two different shots, for example, show Sara entering the same door twice in a row in what the film itself designates as a temporally impossible repetition. Violence, above all, is consistently de-realized by the editing. Guns are omnipresent but they are never coordinated with their sounds. A policeman on a motorcycle presumably shoots Paulo, but we see no wound. Violence is treated in a fragmented and anti-realistic way, in keeping with Rocha's expressed desire to reflect on violence rather than make a spectacle of it.

An autonomous, discontinuous soundtrack further undermines realism, creating contradictions, for example, between visual and aural "scale." We see Fuentes in long shot but hear his voice in aural close-up. We see pistols and hear machine guns. We see Alto fire a machine gun, but we hear nothing; yet the people quiet down, as if *they* had heard it. Then Rocha suspends the soundtrack to an unnaturally total silence.

The same autonomy that characterizes the soundtrack also marks the camera movements. The camera does not generally accompany the action, rather, it performs its own autonomous ballet of stylized, geometricized, and choreographed movements, creating a tension between the mobility of the personages and that of the camera. The work of the camera is extremely "visible" and the visibility is designated as such by the inclusion in certain shots of the equipment involved in making a film. At one point, for example, we see a cameraman filming exactly the shot — of the murdered man of the people — that we have just seen in the film.

Terra em Transe refuses transparence and illusionism in yet another sense, by always making us aware of the rhetorical and stylistic mediation of the story. The film exhibits a conflict of cinematographic styles, so that

Jardel Filho as Paulo Martins in *Land in Anguish* (1967)

the meaning partially emerges from the creative tension between diverse methods of filmic writing. Alongside the Wellesian influence, two other specifically cinematographic styles can be discerned. One is the style of direct cinema, obvious in the hand-held camera, in the frequent use of direct sound, and in the preference for ambient light. The technique, when this style predominates, seems to operate by chance; people block the camera's access to key personnages, as if the camera were capturing spontaneous moments of everyday life. Coexisting with this direct style is the style of Eisensteinian montage, which reconstructs the action as a function of the director's political intentions. The Eisensteinian style is visible in the jump cuts and deliberate mismatches between shots, in the use of socially emblematic personages (Felicio *the* peasant, Geronimo *the* union official, Vieira *the* populist), in the graphic stylization, and in the use of non-synchronous sound.

Glauber Rocha does not merely cite the cinematic tradition; he uses it and transforms it. One moment, for example, recalls the sequence from *Potemkin* when the goateed Doctor Smirnov, responding to complaints by the sailors, uses his glasses as a kind of magnifying glass to examine maggot-covered meat, which he pronounces "perfectly healthy and ready to be eaten." Rocha has his senator, after lavishing grandiloquent praise on Eldorado's perfect society, use his glasses in an identical fashion to examine the corpse of the murdered man of the people. The analogy is clear—in both cases the corrupt representatives of established power deny the most glaring evidence of social ills. The senator's empty and swollen phrases mask sordid political realities. He too pronounces a visibly sick society, a maggot-ridden corpse, "perfectly healthy."

Just as Eisenstein drew on the popular theater of his day—his "montage of attractions" originally referred to the "attractions" in a circus; tightrope, lion tamer, clown—so Rocha turns to account various popular traditions and "lower" forms. Vieira's electoral campaign is treated as an ambulatory circus, aptly metaphorizing the bread and circuses of populist politics. Thus Rocha exploits the theatricality inherent in certain privileged moments of Brazilian collective life—circuses, carnival, samba schools, political rallies, processions.

Terra em Transe operates a double demystification—one political, the other esthetic. It deconstructs two styles of representation. Populism, after all, constitutes a style of political representation. In its Latin American version, certain progressive and nationalist elements of the bourgeoisie enlist the support of the people in order to advance their own interests. *Terra em Transe* performs the *mise-en-scène* of the contradictions of populism. The character Vieira represents a composite political figure, combining the traits of a number of Brazilian populist leaders. His speech of resignation echoes Vargas's famous suicide letter denouncing international conspiracies against him. Indeed, his trajectory toward the left recalls the extraordinary historical transformation of Vargas from head of the oligarchy to national leader of the workers. Like João Goulart, Vieira is a gaucho and is deposed by a right-wing coup. His description of himself as self-made politician recalls Jânio Quadros, while other traces recall both Miguel Arraes and Leonel Brizola. His manners, meanwhile—smiles, embraces, unaffected manner and dress—reflect a generalized Brazilian political style, marked by populism, calculated to create the illusion of egalitarian contact between the elites and the people.

The film exposes the fatal compromises Vieira makes as well as his failure of nerve in moments of conflict with the extreme right. The sequence of confrontation between the peasants and Vieira's police, in this sense, is emblematic. It unmasks the contradiction between the electoral promises of populism and its real commitments. To Paulo's question—"I wondered how the governor-elect would respond to the promises of the candidate"—the sequence gives an unequivocal answer: the governor-elect responds with guns and billy clubs. Populism sets a trap for the people. It offers the illusion of participation. It incites the people to speak, but represses them when their voices of protest become too strident. It invites the people into the palace, but murders them if they become too militant. In the populist zigzag betwen democracy and authoritarianism, paternalistic encouragement often precedes brutal repression.

On another level, *Terra em Transe* rejects an esthetic style of representation might also be labelled "populist." The populist esthetic is paternalistic. It claims that art should speak to the people in simple and transparent language, at the risk of not "communicating." It practices the sugar-coated pill theory of art. It is sweet in order to be useful. To get its message across, it gives the public its habitual dose of cinematic gratifications—an intrigue, a love story, spectacle. It treats the public as slightly retarded, in need of a simplistic and prettifying art, just as Vieira speaks demagogically of justice and the power of the people, while doing nothing to advance the political maturation of the people. With populist cinema, as with populist politics, the people lose their collective identity as a class, and become an amorphous mass of submissive individuals. Populism treats the people as mere extras; it wants its spectators to be passive.

Just as important as this work of demystification is the fact that *Terra em Transe* renders the "feel" of political experience. The film recognizes the importance of human feelings in politics—the euphoric camaraderie of a political campaign, the resentments that arise when fragile alliances disintegrate, the provisional relative moralities of political combat, with its betrayals and problematic commitments. *Terra em Transe* communicates the anguished excitement of political action in a brutally repressive Latin-American context. The film conveys an atmosphere of menace and the pervasive odor of imminent death.

Terra em Transe portrays what Rocha has called the "tragic carnival" of Brazilian politics. The carnival ambiance is omnipresent in *Terra em Transe*. Fuentes, in carnival costume, declaiming to his fellow orgiasts, declares the state of permanent happiness in Eldorado. While the people, again in costume, dance the samba, the senator declares that neither hunger nor illiteracy exist in Eldorado's best of all possible worlds. "*Transe*," in Portuguese, simultaneously connotes frenetic movement, personal delirium and collective hysteria. It evokes as well the trance of African religious cults, like the music of *candomblé* which opens and closes the film. At the same time, the apparent movement of carnival (and of populist politics) is shown as alienated and factitious, a dead-end frenzy. The word *transe* itself conveys this paradoxical simultaneity of stasis and movement. The carnival is seen through disabused eyes, and the hysteria is ultimately mastered by the distancing technique. The film alternates distanced analysis with psychic explosions. Like Paulo, the spectator goes in and out of the *transe*.

Terra em Transe is a provocative, aggressive, intentionally difficult film, an advanced lesson in reading political and cinematographic significations. It consistently violates our expectations, it withholds spectacle when the story demands it, and denies romance where plot conventions would require it. Even its orgies are anti-erotic. Where we expect sharp political definition, the film gives us poetic, imagistic freedom. It creates a world of systematic contradiction, between and within the personages, between sound and image, between cinematographic styles. Brutal ruptures in editing keep the spectator off balance, incapable of identifying in the conventional way. For Glauber Rocha to have proceeded in any other way would have radically compromised his message through the very artistic codes by which it had been mediated. *Terra em Transe* is a piece of revolutionary pedagogy. Its methodology and vision are dialectical; it offers no correct line or pat answers. The solution lies in the spectator becoming conscious, and acting on that consciousness.

Notes

1. A word on the prototypes for the political figures in *Terra em Transe*. Porfirio Diaz, named after the Mexican dictator, embodies the Latin American version of Iberic despotism, while his political career parallels that of the Brazilian politician Carlos Lacorda, evolving from youthful leftism to an almost religious anti-communism. Viera combines the traits of a number of Brazilian populist leaders. Sara and her militant friends represent the communist party, whose policy it then was (and still is) to support populist politicians like Vieira, seeing itself as a kind of midwife for a bourgeois revolution which would logically precede an authentic proletarian one. Explint (Company of International Exploitation) obviously represents foreign (mainly North American) economic forces, and especially multinational corporations, which were involved in the coup against João Goulart.

2. A word on the English subtitles for *Terra em Transe*. The English titles for *Terra em Transe* are incompetent at best and disastrous at worst. When Paulo speaks in poetry for example, the titles not only do not translate his words into poetry—that is admittedly difficult—but they do not communicate the fact that he is speaking in poetry, with the result that the spectator takes what is in fact heightened, lyrical speech for an inept attempt at naturalistic dialogue. At other times, the text is distorted or simply impoverished. "I abandon myself to the vain exercise of poetry" becomes "I, for example, write poetry."

18

"Hunger for Love"

ELIZABETH MERENA AND JOÃO LUIZ VIEIRA

Hunger for Love is a unique film in Brazilian cinema and in the career of Nelson Pereira dos Santos, whose name is generally linked to more conventional films such as *Vidas Secas* (1963) and *Tent of Miracles* (1977). *Hunger for Love* was made in an atmosphere of extreme political repression and increased governmental censorship. It can be understood as a partial reflection of the despair that had engulfed Brazil in 1968. More specifically, the film exposes the anguished impotence of the Brazilian intellectual in a muted political allegory. For Dos Santos this meant a changed filmic strategy: a pre-coup cinematic language could not express the conflicts of the post-coup situation. Whereas *Vidas Secas* had used a precise objective style, *Hunger for Love* employs a radically different approach. The complexity of the film derives from its anti-illusionistic narrative structure. Instead of the neo-realist continuity of *Vidas Secas*, *Hunger for Love* proposes discontinuity. In its puzzling way of organizing images and in the often autonomous soundtrack we sense a disruptive avant-garde impulse.

We come to know the film's main characters through their very confused, cynical relationships that move from complicity to aggression and even violence. The film harshly criticizes their dissipation and exposes their alienation. In the character of Alfredo (Paulo Pôrto), we can read a pointed reference to the current position of Brazil's intellectuals: isolated, exiled, politically defeated. He who had once known how to struggle is now mute, blind, and deaf. Alfredo's wife, Ula (Leila Diniz) explains that he was the victim of an assassination attempt. He now spends his days playing chess, silently contemplating strategies in diverse languages chosen for the opposing sides: Russian, Chinese, Spanish. One day, it is hoped Alfredo will again be able to speak, but Ula is doubtful.

She married Alfredo four years before. Since the film was released in 1968 one infers that he had been politically active around 1964 — the year of the military coup — and that he had been involved with the left. This association is reinforced by subsequent references to his scientific (botanical) career, all evoking the idea of revolution: "By the age of thirty he had published five books about a small plant that grows in the northeast . . . . His thesis was a true revolution [here Ula pauses and then adds] . . . in botanics. That's why we travelled so much. We've even passed through Viet Nam. . . "

Ula seems unaware that their travels had any purpose other than scientific. She married Alfredo "for love"; the viewer eventually realizes she is totally ignorant of her husband's political associations. Later, she even writes the Brazilian government for information concerning him.

His retreat to the island, after the attack, has made Ula bitter. She prefers to indulge her desire for amusement. She confronts each day, tests each new situation, and arrives at the same conclusion; since life on the island is meaningless she will cater to her whims. If Alfredo attempts to interfere or communicate, he shall be silenced with a slap. Negation of their past and obliteration of their future is Ula's self-determined remedy to the problems that surround her.

A somewhat similar outlook comes to be shared by Felipe (Arduino Colasanti), a young Brazilian painter (and friend of Ula and Alfredo's)

Irene Stefânia as Mariana in *Hunger for Love* (1968)

who has recently returned to the island from New York. While working in the United States his hope had been to develop an expressive and personal artistic style, but he encountered only frustration. Foreign influences and styles only promoted confusion rather than serving as inspiration. What Felipe did gain, however, was money—in the form of a cultivated young woman named Mariana (Irene Stefânia) who pays, among other things, for their return trip to Brazil.

Mariana and Felipe's relationship is complex. The opening flashback, set in Central Park, establishes the two as a couple, but as the film progresses this unity is dissolved. Each memory sequence provides further insight into the gap between the two. Triggered by events on the island, these flashbacks subtly clarify to what extent Mariana and Felipe's contrasting frames of reference stem from their different socio-economic backgrounds. Even the first love-making scene set in Brazil epitomizes their basic differences. The film intercuts shots of Felipe's misty island with shots of Mariana's recently arrived piano. The piano suggests a different cultural and intellectual habitat, another "island." The visual interplay between the island and the piano mimic the alternating English and Portuguese words spoken by Mariana and Felipe as they make love: "Come. . . . Came. . . . Alone. . . . Together." The fragmentation of the scene evokes the distance between them.

Mariana belongs to the landed aristocracy; Felipe made his living by serving this class. When they first meet, he is a waiter and she is the customer to whom he must cater. A flashback sequence set in the Museum of Modern Art in New York points up basic differences. The image track is spatially and temporally dislocated: scenes from the sleek and contemporary sculpture garden of the museum are intercut with those of an abandoned monastery in Brazil. The unkept gardens and graffiti-laden corridors of the latter (representing Felipe) subtly undermine the propriety of Mariana's adopted New York culture garden. At another point the voluptuousness of a female sculpture at MOMA is juxtaposed with three naturalistic, extremely thin Brazilian icons.

Hunger for Love's narrative is elaborated through point-of-view shots, effective flashbacks and projected imaginary shots. Most of the point-of-view shots are associated with Mariana, leading us to identify with this character. It is through her that we find out Alfredo's identity: Ula and Felipe already know. They offer Mariana different accounts of him, leading her to create an image that is transmitted to the spectator. Ula's interpretation seems naive; she doesn't remember where she has traveled with Alfredo, nor the name of the plant that caused a revolution in botanics. Felipe's account of Alfredo apparently comes from direct and recent contact. Back in Brazil, he tells Mariana that he had been working for Alfredo in the United States. His version reveals admiration and respect: "When the day of the explosion comes, no matter where, we will be with him." "At the same place; in the same hour." Mariana portrays Alfredo as the ideal revolutionary.

Alfredo's point of view is non-existent. What better metaphor for the state of the revolution than this lack of expression? He has been forced into silence, the silence of the left in times of political repression. The director therefore limits himself to exploring the point of view of Mariana and her class. He presents the contradictions of a class that begins to acquire political consciousness abroad, but that retains (rather like the frustrated protagonistist of Bertolucci's *Before the Revolution*) a strong bourgeois heritage. With the left temporarily silenced and the hopeless sons and daughters of the bourgeoisie inhabiting a dead-end island the film is one of the most powerfully pessimistic cinematic statements concerning Brazil of 1968.

Mariana is often seen reading political literature. She ponderously formulates her ideas of revolution. As her consciousness is "raised" however, she loses contact with Felipe and Ula. Political musings become her being; instinctively she is drawn to Alfredo. His mystique, his past efforts, affect her almost spiritually.

The alliance between Mariana and Alfredo is evoked through complex cinematic and narrative means. Having rejected an offer from Ula and Felipe to visit the city, Mariana remains alone. The solitary musical note that consistently punctuates events concerning her throughout the film is re-introduced on the soundtrack. It is the same note that was heard when Mariana first met Alfredo but it now seems to penetrate and draw her toward him. She hesitates, as if interpreting this signal, and then starts up the path leading to his "botanical" retreat. The music foreshadows their bond; it represents their cryptic pattern of intellectual interaction. Subsequently they make love. The over-exposure of the shot however, suggests two things: Mariana has become both "illuminated" and blinded. Her idealism has weakened her grasp on reality. Felipe and Ula, annoyed with vacuous political philosophizing, have united against Mariana and Alfredo. Mariana, confused and anxious, senses their hostility and wants to leave. Despite her withdrawl from Ula and Felipe, their unspoken aggressivity pressures her subconsciously, to the point that she imagines them taking direct action against her. The viewer becomes witness to her nightmares.

The most bitter statements in the film are made during an after-dinner debauch. Costumes are brought from the cellar, drinks are consumed and the party acquires a morbidly carnivalesque spirit that allows latent hostilities to rise to the surface. Alfredo is the last to receive a costume. Ula chooses the outfit for him; it brutally mocks his political stance: he is made to look like Ché Guevara. "The Santa Claus of Latin America," she cruelly declares.

Felipe is furious; he angrily attacks Ula. For him it is too painful to see the man he respects so highly treated in such a way. He circles Alfredo and shouts: "He can be anything we invent now. . . . Don't you see? What *was* he? A priest? A revolutionary? A professor? A man? He could be anything, because now he is nothing. *Nothing*." Felipe has clearly

165

Hunger for Love (1968)

become disillusioned. Alfredo no longer provides him with political inspiration. The truths revealed in this carnivalesque setting also affect
Mariana. She drunkenly claims to have "crucified Marxism-Leninism in
her head." She seems to understand, at least temporarily, that her
knowledge of revolution is merely theoretical, not practical.

The morning after this all-night masquerade shows Mariana far from
the island on which Felipe, Ula, and the guests are sleeping. As the final
zoom pulls away, we see that she leads Alfredo around their "own" island.
Derisive laughter from the just-awakened group of derelict carnival-
makers fades out as we hear Mariana's voice over. ". . . The duty of all
revolutionaries is to make revolution." In conjunction with these words
the soundtrack, for the first time, offers folkloric Brazilian music. The
implication clearly concerns future hope for a unified nation.

Hunger for Love, while sometimes highly praised, has also been
criticized as imprecise, confusing, and esoteric. In *Hunger for Love* solutions are not easy to find, but one must ask: Is *Hunger for Love* difficult
or are the *questions posed* difficult?

One pivotal sequence provides us with a better understanding of
Mariana's failures as a "potential" revolutionary and once again places
the spectator within her point of view. This complex sequence merits
detailed description. Mariana walks on the beach reading Mao while her
subjective voice-over occupies the soundtrack. Felipe is preparing their
boat for a short trip and invites her to come with him. When she refuses,
he forces her into the boat. In the next shot Mariana imagines that Felipe
is attempting to kill her. Then a shot of Mariana sitting in the restaurant
at MOMA is interjected, providing the spectator with a possible clue for

166

understanding the entire sequence as a recreation of her decision to return to Brazil. The following shot, a pan over the Brazilian islands; coincides with Mariana's voice on the soundtrack: "I want to go back to my island, to my people; exploited, drained . . . corpses dismembered by hunger . . . that's it . . . I see children drowned in their own excrement . . . I must renew my will of vengeance . . . ." The pan ends with Felipe and Mariana looking at the islands. He asks her: "Was the trip worth it?" She doesn't answer, and on the soundtrack one now hears the continuation of her earlier voice-over concerning Mao. Felipe walks toward the ocean and Mariana, deep in thought, desperately asks: "The people . . . . Where are the people?" The next shot brings the answer: The people, depicted in her mind as poor children, are too far away. All she can do is wave awkwardly at them.

The director's sympathetic yet critical treatment of Mariana recalls Godard's stance toward Veronique (Anne Wiazemsky) in *La Chinoise* (1967). The spatio-temporal discontinuities of the New York/Brazil sequences are reminiscent of Resnais, and a Felliniesque decadence surrounds the masquerade party on the island. The film's complex editing style articulates the fragmented narrative and accounts for the feeling of disorientation provoked by the film. As in many of Resnais's films such fragmentation has an affective quality. In the spatio-temporal discontinuity between the sequences depicting Brazil and New York, it is usually Mariana's point of view that is suddenly projected on the screen. At times disruptive sequences are linked to dialogue. Elsewhere editing is based on a principle of thematic associations. A sequence of three consecutive shots, for example, reveal the significance that Mariana has for Felipe;

The party sequence in *Hunger for Love* (1968)

i.e., that she is rich and can thus support him. Although spatially and temporally discontinuous, the sequence possesses continuity of action — Mariana signing checks. The first shot shows her at a counter in a New York bank; in the next she continues signing, but in Brazil, on Felipe's chest. Money and Mariana's financial power form the thematic link. At other times voice-overs provide continuous development while the image is fragmented.

The visual style of *Hunger for Love* is designed to look random, technically "imperfect," almost careless. The photography is often grainy and over-exposed. A hand-held camera is often used. This procedure reflected an emerging tendency in Brazilian cinema, which purposefully turned its back on the "respectable" cinema of strict literary adaptation, elaborate sets, and production values. *Hunger for Love* finds, in its "garbage esthetic," a new way of portraying Brazil. Rather than identifying with the art of the developed world it expresses the poverty and sorrow that remain hidden behind polished surfaces.

As a corollary to this anti-illusionistic style, self-referential devices call attention to its director, and to one of his future projects. Felipe mentions to Mariana that a friend of his is planning to shoot a film about the Tupinambas Indians later in the film. This is an obvious reference to dos Santos's *How Tasty Was My Little Frenchman* (1971), which was shot in the same area as *Hunger for Love*, and also employs Arduino Colasanti (Felipe) in its major role. Dos Santos also briefly appears in *Hunger for Love*.

Hunger for Love opened new political and esthetic paths for Brazilian cinema. The film criticizes and exposes the "progressive" bourgeoisie. But, time has passed and the political context has changed. Brazilian cinema now chooses to travel less dangerous roads.

19
"Antônio das Mortes"

TERENCE CARLSON

Populist art tries to justify its primitivism with "good conscience." The populist artist always claims: "I'm not an intellectual . . . I'm with the people. . . . My art is good because it communicates, etc. . . ." But what does it communicate? In general it communicates the people's own alienation. . . . Truly modern art which is ethically and esthetically revolutionary must be opposed, in its language, to the dominant language. . . . The only solution is to revolt, through the pure aggressivity of . . . art, against all the moral and esthetic hypocrisies which lead to alienation.[1]

—Glauber Rocha, 1968

Glauber Rocha's *Antônio das Mortes* exemplifies the aesthetic and political goals of Cinema Novo, as well as the established traditions of Brazilian Modernist art. The film, set in Brazil's northeast, addresses the realities of its people. It is very specifically Brazilian in its mythic and folkloric background, in its codes, in its music, poetry and dance, as well as in its political thrust. To apply North American or European values to the film in an attempt to give it some kind of political universality or cross-cultural applicability is to misread the film and to deprive oneself of an enormous share of its richness.

To combat the alienation of "populist" art (that which only serves to reinforce the alienation of the people), Rocha creates his own cinema of alienation. By using emblematic characters whose actions are stylized and

Othon Bastos as the Professor and Maurício do Valle as Antônio in *Antônio das Mortes* (1968)

theatrical, along with Brechtian techniques of distanciation, he insists on our awareness of the *form* of his art. A close analysis of Rocha's characterizations in *Antônio das Mortes*, followed by an examination of specific cinematic techniques, will illustrate both the aesthetic and political aspects of Rocha's work, as well as the Modernist spirit through which his creativity operates. The real triumph of *Antônio das Mortes* is realized in the ways by which Rocha amalgamates myth, mysticism, and reality into a filmic whole that is both epic and lyrical.

Each character in *Antônio das Mortes* represents a synthesis of actual or fictional people, ideas, movements, or mythical/mystical elements. Characterization is very complex, and no attempt should be made to interpret the film as allegory based on one-to-one relationships. As René Gardies points out:

> Rocha's heroes take shape in a world which eliminates their existence as individuals. They retain only what reveals the real nature of society, those subterranean and open antagonisms which constitute the social fabric and ensure its organic evolution.[2]

Thomas Kavanaugh claims that the vision of *Antônio das Mortes* is based on the integration of apparent opposites, " . . . a confluence of contrasts: Indian and colonial, black and white, Christian and pagan, industrial and agricultural, intellectual and mystical."[3] But Rocha goes even further and delves deeply into Brazilian history and legend for the composites of his characters. "Palmares" (a black revolt) and Canudos (a mystic/peasant' revolt) are two of the greatest uprisings in Brazilian

170

history. It is entirely possible that these revolts are part of the background of *Antônio das Mortes*. Canudos was a religious colony established by Antônio Conselheiro, a mystic who led one of Brazil's religious millennial movements. The story is the subject of Euclides da Cunha's *Rebellion in the Backlands* (Os Sertões). Canudos is described as:

> . . . a stereotype of the dubious form of social organization that prevailed among the earliest barbarian tribes. The simple sertanejo, upon setting foot in the place, became another thing, a stern and fearless fanatic. He absorbed the collective psychosis and even ended by adopting the name . . . *jagunço*. [4]

The idea of a "collective psychosis" seems to be at work in Rocha's film — not only the representatives of the *cangaceiro/jagunço*, but also with the *beatos* who faithfully follow in the footsteps of the Santa. Rocha also feels that at least part of the strength of the masses in Brazil lies in mysticism, in "an emotional, Dionysiac behavior" that he sees rising from a mixture of Catholicism and African religions.[5] Thus, there is a very high level of integration in *Antônio das Mortes* — one that includes folklore, literature, revolution and social history.

The following briefly describes the characters of *Antônio das Mortes* and their interrelationships:

Antônio	A *jagunço*, or hired killer, employed by the colonel to protect his property and kill the *cangaceiros*, bandits who threaten the rich. Antônio is a wanderer of the *sertão*, a solitary figure, a romantic hero, who bridges the gap between oppressor and oppressed. In the course of the film he is converted from a *jagunço* to a *cangaceiro*.
Horácio	(The Latifundista) The blind (physically and metaphorically) landowner who stubbornly resists agrarian reform, denounces the peasants, and believes that his injustices are compensated by occasional charitable acts.
Coirana	A *cangaceiro*, or wandering gunman, who dies at the hands of Antônio. A hero of the oppressed, Coirana represents *all cangaceiros* and especially Lampião. Coirana speaks mostly in verse.
The Santa	(Saint) Representing Brazilian messianism, the Santa leads the *beatos* (her

	followers) in their uprising and influences Antônio. The Santa seems to embody a religious solution to the social and economic problems of Brazil. She speaks in oracles and metaphors and wears the white dress of purity.
Antão	This figure, who accompanies the Santa, represents black revolt in Brazil as he undergoes a transformation from passive *beato* to active warrior. He is associated with African religions.
The Teacher	Like Antão, this character is converted from passive escapism (alcoholism, intellectual malaise) to active and violent participation.
Laura	A Bahian prostitute who has become Horácio's mistress.
Mattos	A modern-day Horácio, Mattos is the politician-oppressor of the poor. He wants to industrialize the *sertão* and bring in foreign investments.
Mata Vaca	A ruthless *jagunço*.

If there is a single concept that gives unity to these diverse and somewhat unintegrated characters, it is death or murder as an instrument for resolving conflicts. Death involves every character in *Antônio das Mortes* — from the murdering *jagunços* of Mata Vaca's band to the Teacher whose potential for violence is more internal, intellectual. Rocha presents a dialectic of violence. As the *beatos* are massacred, so are Mata Vaca and his *jagunços*. Coirana's death is followed by that of Mattos and finally, Horácio, the last of the old dragons. From all of this bloodshed emerges the new conflict: Antônio versus the enormous foreign corporate dragons (represented by modern trucks on a highway).

The motif of Saint George and the dragon is encountered on the first, most evident mythic surface of *Antônio das Mortes*. At various points in the film, Antônio, Coirana, Antão, and even arguably the Teacher, all take on the heroic proportions of the Saint George role. The film is enclosed by a triptych of Saint George and the dragon in the opening credits and the three-part rapid montage shots of Antão spearing Horácio at the end of the film. The triptych anticipates Rocha's use of threes in *Antônio das Mortes*, as well as his stylization. In addition to the three Saint George figures, three religious figures, and three millennial movements represented by the Santa, there are also the three men slain by Antônio — Lampião, Coirana, and Mata Vaca. Again, the Santa, Antão, and Coirana are the three immediate representatives of political struggle.

The ambiguity of many characterizations in *Antônio das Mortes* results from the many elements Rocha integrates in these figures. Gardies points out that Antônio plays a pivotal role in that he shifts from serving as an "instrument of power" (as a *jagunco*) to fulfilling the role of "revolutionary" (as a *cangaceiro*).[6] Similarly, the black warrior Antão plays a very passive, inactive role until he mounts a horse and rides off to slay Horácio. As a variation of Saint George, the black man dressed in red is an amalgam of Oxosse, the African god of the hunt, and Ogum, a god of war in the rites of *macumba*. We learn, however, from the film's dialogue that Rocha also associates Coirana with Ogum — hence, a racial integration within the fighting revolutionary figure.

Antão shares a religious role with the Santa, who represents three millennial movements in Brazilian history (Sebastianism, the campaign of Antônio Conselheiro, and the period of Padre Cícero). Antão and the Santa together present a blend of African ritual and Catholic ceremony. Their stylized movements and gestures are derived from hieratic codes of the carnival. The priest, a third religious figure in the film, is an exaggerated version of the ineffectualness of Antão and the Santa. Rocha acknowledges the importance of the existence of religion in Brazilian culture and society, but at the same time is critical of it. Antão may succeed in killing Horácio (*after* Mata Vaca and his band are killed by Antônio and the Teacher), but in the film's final sequence, as the priest leads away the horse bearing Antão and the Santa, Rocha suggests that their direction (or future effectiveness) is highly questionable.

Kavanaugh calls Antônio a "living suicide" because by killing Coirana, he kills a part of himself — the *cangaceiro* he could have been in the past had his political conversion occurred sooner. On another level we may view Antônio's murder of the *jagunço* Mata Vaca as revenge for the murders of Lampião and Coirana — murders that Antônio *himself* committed. This again is the "suicide" of a former identity; however, it is a positive, progressive act.

The idea of the "living suicide" in *Antônio das Mortes* recalls the themes of cannibalism and self-destruction in Brazilian literature. As Macunaíma is "consumed by Brazil" at the end of the novel and film, so Antônio commits destructive and suicidal acts as a representative of social/political struggle. And Antônio is probably destined for death at the hands of yet another Mata Vaca, or perhaps the new industrial dragon represented by Shell Oil, and will himself finally be "consumed by Brazil." The Santa does prophetically announce (three times), "The endless war will begin," and Antônio has been condemned "to walk the burning paths of the earth forever." Clearly Antônio is an anachronism in Rocha's scheme, and the Santa talks to him as if he were responsible for the deaths of all *cangaceiros* of the past and for many deaths to come.

Rocha's integration of diverse social and political elements in his characterizations in *Antônio das Mortes* is at times so complex that spectators not well informed in Brazilian cultural and political affairs will find them indecipherable. For instance, when Coirana is mortally wounded by

Antônio das Mortes (1968)

Antônio, it is the unlikely threesome of the Teacher, Laura, and Mattos who gently convey the body of the bleeding *cangaceiro* into a house. At this point in the film the Teacher is a drunkard whose cynicism has stifled his political consciousness; Laura is a Bahian prostitute-turned-mistress of Horácio; Mattos is the ultimate opportunist and heir apparent to Colonel Horácio's social position. Their benevolent behavior toward Coirana is incomprehensible, but Rocha undoubtedly includes in these composite characters elements of the social origins from which they rose before they betrayed those origins. At least they are not yet blind like Horácio.

In a similarly enigmatic sequence the Teacher viciously beats Antão for no apparent reason. Prior to the sequence Antão talks of leaving Brazil and returning to the shores of Africa. The Teacher, newly inspired by Antônio's conversion and now armed with Coirana's gun, has taken it upon himself to provoke the passive Oxosse/Ogum figure to action.

Rocha's characterizations in *Antônio das Mortes* are an integral part of his cinema of "alienation." The development of plot is minimized by the radical transformations and unanticipated actions of characters like Antônio, Antão, and the Teacher. The spectator's conventional expectations are dashed when the *beatos* are murdered and all seems hopeless. However, through Rocha's dialectic of violence, the deaths of the *beatos*, followed by the deaths of Mattos, Horácio, and Mata Vaca's cutthroats, take on a new context and sense of purpose as Antônio moves on to face the larger industrial dragons of the highway. Suddenly the social/political struggle is seen as something that goes beyond the village of Milagres, the *sertão*, and landowner-peasant disputes to that which is a greater menace to Brazil. Rocha refuses merely to reiterate the age-old agrarian injustices ("the people's own alienation") and instead redefines the direction of political struggle.

The very first shot (opening credits) of *Antônio das Mortes* is significant in terms of Rocha's cinematic experimentation in the film. In a static shot of the wide-open *sertão*, a *jagunço* (Antônio) is seen firing a gun toward a point (we assume toward a person) off screen. The opening is a direct quotation from Rocha's *Black God, White Devil*. There initially is a sense of involvement with the *jagunço*'s activity, but the spectator is deprived of half of the scene — in spite of the great space (deep and lateral) within the shot. As a wounded man stumbles within the frame of the shot to die a most stylized death, we realize that what we have before us is something not necessarily *real*, but something vast and grand and even operatic.

Aside from the use of highly emblematic characters, cinematic articulation in *Antônio das Mortes* should be noted in Rocha's camera movement and editing. To a certain extent the two are interrelated. Rocha's camera movement is best defined as a kind of "searching." Highly self-conscious editing creates a conflict between the spectator's sense of "participation" and the distancing effects of abrupt cuts and spatial ellipses. Rocha makes very limited use of montage in *Antônio das Mortes*, and only occasionally does he employ any conventional editing. Instead he uses long takes, slow pans, and long travelling shots. The idea of a "searching camera" is partially suggested by the duration of shots, because Rocha seems to be seeking answers — solutions to the mystery of the *sertão* and its complex mixture of races, cultures, religions, and myths; reasons for political inactivity during a time of struggle against oppression. The baroque, carnival-like sequence in which Antônio and Coirana fight with swords is particularly long, and is a good example of what is accomplished by Rocha's searching camera. The *beatos*, led by the Santa, Coirana, and Antão, sing and dance in random movements. The camera follows these movements in similarly irregular patterns. The lengthy shots are punctuated by sounds and bright splashes of color and abrupt, intrusive movements. The long take serves to provide cohesiveness — to make a whole, a kind of poem, of the mixture of images.

Closely related to Rocha's use of a searching camera technique is the sense of exaggerated space in *Antônio das Mortes*. Long travelling shots in particular (but also static long shots) take in enormous amounts of space. The vastness of the *sertão* is suggested, of course, but there is also a surreal quality given to actions that are carried out in larger-than-normal cinematic space. The sequence in which Laura and the Teacher embrace passionately over the body of Laura's castrated, dead lover (Mattos) is an interesting variation of Rocha's use of space. Mattos's body has been dragged into a barren area of the *sertão* — into a large, arid, lifeless space. The camera follows the frantic movements of the priest as he tries to put a stop to this most bizarre behavior (and to warn the Teacher that Mata Vaca is about to slaughter the *beatos*). The camera shoots within very tight space (close-ups and medium close-ups of Laura and the Teacher) through most of this sequence, yet the spectator is still aware of the *large* space (primarily the effect of a wide-angle lens) within which this activity is occurring. Again this is a deliberate misrepresentation of space, but in this case the exaggeration is accomplished essentially through distortion.

Basically, Rocha distances his spectators with techniques that emphasize the medium through which he is working. He uses off-screen space; he pointedly interrupts the flow of sound and movements with silence and stasis. Rocha uses direct sound for greater authenticity, but this also serves to make us more aware of the distancing effects created by lapses of sound. Action in certain scenes is so very stylized that all sense of realism is suspended. Rocha juxtaposes medium shots and close-ups with long and extreme long shots of the same subject (e.g., the Santa sitting near a lone gnarled tree in large open space). He also juxtaposes sequences that are radically different in tone and visual content (the city parade and the carnival-like procession in Milagres—an interesting comparison between the passivity of the parade's spectators and that of the *beatos*).

Rocha uses techniques of distanciation to increase our awareness of the searching camera. If it is true that Rocha encourages an awareness of the searching camera (that which *involves* us), then participation and distanciation are inextricably related and, in fact, occur simultaneously. The procession sequence is again the best example, but discussion of it needs further elaboration. As the camera weaves among the dancing and singing *beatos*, we are involved. We, with Rocha's camera, seek some explanation for this unusual gathering of festive yet somber *beatos* who are led to town by a saint, an African war god, and a *cangaceiro*. In the midst of the frenetic activity (moving camera/movement within the frame/loud music), Rocha cuts to a static, iconographic shot of Coirana. The shot of the *cangaceiro* in the midst of all the confusion underlines Coirana's real isolation and the futility of his mission. At another point the Santa steps forward with her dagger to prevent Antônio from striking another blow at Coirana. The action is so highly symbolic that it, too, serves to distance. The alienating techniques within the sequence have an impact that prevents any sense of total involvement and instead enhances an awareness of a limited participatory role. By using distancing techniques Rocha is addressing us, his spectators, but he only calls attention to the fact that we are viewing a film and makes us cognizant of our "role" in the narrative.

One further example may clarify the idea of simultaneous participation/distanciation in *Antônio das Mortes*. In the film's climactic sequence, Antônio and the Teacher do battle with Mata Vaca and his band of *jagunços*. Rocha parodies the American western shootout. Rocha dashes any sense of involvement as the scene becomes ridiculous. Antônio and the Teacher take on super-heroic dimensions, and twenty or thirty dead *jagunços* lie at their feet in a matter of moments. Similarly, when Antão (as a Saint George figure) rides up on a white horse to slay the dragon Horácio, Rocha is playing with another typical Hollywood motif that draws heavily on audience emotions (the villain meets his doom at

Antônio das Mortes (1968)

the hands of the hero). Again, this action is so highly emblematic that it calls attention to itself as stylization at the same time that it thrills us.

Antônio das Mortes unquestionably reflects the spirit of Modernist art in Brazil, as well as the more contemporary goals of Cinema Novo. Esthetically the film is Rocha's political/revolutionary statement on the potentially volatile link between hunger and violence in Brazil. This link is realized in Rocha's dialectic of violence — a tool that challenges conventional cinematic articulation at the same time that it defines new aesthetic and political directions.

Notes

1. Glauber Rocha, "Cinema Novo: The Adventure of Creation." A paper presented at Pesaro in 1968.
2. René Gardies, "Structural Analysis of a Textual System: Presentation of a Method," *Screen* 15 (1974):13.
3. Thomas M. Kavanaugh, "Imperialism and the Revolutionary Cinema: Glauber Rocha's *Antônio das Mortes*," *Journal of Modern Literature* 3 (April 1973):212.
4. Euclides da Cunha, *Rebellion in the Backlands*, trans. Samuel Putnam (Chicago: University of Chicago Press, 1944), p. 148.
5. James Roy MacBean, "*Vent d'est*; or Godard and Rocha at the Crossroads," *Sight and Sound* 40 (Summer 1971):150.
6. Gardies, p. 14.

20
"Cinema Novo and Cannibalism: *Macunaíma*"

O presente vem de mansinho/de repente dá um pulo/cartaz de cinema com fita americana

— Carlos Drummond de Andrade (1925)

Joaquim Pedro de Andrade's third feature-length film, *Macunaíma* (1969), released in the United States with the inane title "Jungle Freaks," is the culmination of the first three phases of Cinema Novo and the pacesetter for subsequent developments of Brazilian cinema. Adapted from Mário de Andrade's modernist novel of the same name (1928), *Macunaíma* is perhaps the first Cinema Novo film to be formally innovative, politically radical, *and* immensely popular with the Brazilian masses.

In a 1966 interview, Joaquim Pedro de Andrade suggested that the Cinema Novo filmmakers would do well to reexamine the Brazilian Modernist Movement of the twenties in terms of the socio-political situation of the country in the late sixties.[1] Such a revaluation burst on the Brazilian cultural scene in 1967-68 with the Tropicalist movement in theater, popular music, and cinema. Cinema Novo is, in fact, deeply rooted in the problematic faced by literary Modernism, which had attempted to democratize Brazilian art through a stance of cultural nationalism, rejecting a critical imitation of European models in favor of an interest in popular forms of expression and the culture of native Brazilian peoples. Many Modernist poets incorporated the rhythms of indigenous languages into their work, and their *Revista de Antropofagia* ("Cannibalist Review," 1929) frequently included articles on folklore, native languages, and culture. Perhaps more than any other Modernist, Mário de Andrade (1893-1945) undertook extensive research into music, dance, folk festivities, and rituals as well as popular and indigenous myths and legends. *Macunaíma*, widely considered his masterpiece, is the aesthetic apex of Mário de Andrade's attempts at fusing popular sources and erudite literary forms.

Mário de Andrade classifies his *Macunaíma*, written in one week in 1926, revised in 1927, and published in 1928, as a rhapsody (in the musical sense), i.e., a free fantasy "of an epic, heroic or national character."[2] In this work, the author orchestrates popular and folkloric motifs, creating what Florestan Fernandes calls a compendium of Brazilian folklore.[3] *Macunaíma* combines popular expressions, proverbs, elements of popular literature, and folklore with indigenous legends collected by German ethnologist Theodor Koch-Grünberg in the headwaters of the Orinoco in Northern Brazil and Southern Venezuela between 1911 and 1913.[4] Through the combination of such heterogeneous elements, the novel attempts to create a synthesis of Brazil. The author negates the limitations of provincial regionalism by including, in his many enumerations, elements from all regions of the country (e.g., fish from the north and the south in the same body of water), by dissolving spatial limitations, placing Macunaíma, in his various journeys, in one part of the country at one moment and in another in the next, by suspending temporal limitations, allowing his hero to roam through Brazil's history, and by combining, in the *macumba* episode, elements of Afro-Brazilian religious cult ceremonies from several parts of the country.[5]

The novel's Macunaíma is a composite of several heroes found in Koch-Grünberg's legends: Kone'wó, a courageous and astute hero; Kalawunseg, a liar; and Makunaíma, the tribal hero.[6] Makunaíma's contradictory and ambivalent nature is contained within his very name, composed of the root "maku," meaning "bad" or "evil" and the suffix "-ima," meaning "great" or "large." When translating the Bible for indigenous proselytization, English missionaries translated "God" as "Makunaíma."[7] Makunaíma, as a hero, is both good and evil, courageous and cowardly, capable and inept. Mário de Andrade maintained these same characteristics in his composition of the novel, subtitled "the hero without a character." Linked to the folk tradition, *Macunaíma*, in its jocose examination of the Brazilian psyche, fuses symbols, satire, and free fantasy and melds the real and the fantastic into a unified fictional universe.

The film maintains the basic narrative structure of the novel, which has been so thoroughly analyzed by Haroldo de Campos in his *Morfologia do Macunaíma*.[8] Born full grown in the jungle, Macunaíma and his

Macunaíma (1969)

brothers, Jiguê and Maanape, leave for São Paulo after the death of their mother. In the city Macunaíma encounters Ci, an urban guerrilla who likes to "play around" with him. After living joyously with her a short time, and after she gives birth to a black "baby," Ci explodes with her home-made bomb. The *muiraquitã*, Ci's good-luck talisman, explodes with her. Macunaíma mourns heroically and one day discovers that the stone has been recovered by Venceslau Pietro Pietra. After several unsuccessful attempts, Macunaíma finally defeats the villain and recovers the *muiraquitã*. He returns to his homeland carrying the trappings of modern civilization. Due to his laziness and unwillingness to search for food, he is abandoned by his brothers. Finally, he is devoured by the Uiara in the river near his home. The narrative core of both works reduces, in accordance with the structuralist terminology of Vladimir Propp, to three basic functions: 1) the villainy (the "theft" of the talisman), 2) the struggle with the villain (Macunaíma versus Venceslau Pietro Pietra), 3) the liquidation of the misfortune caused by the villainy (Macunaíma recovers the talisman). The filmmaker, however, introduces significant differences on other levels of the film's discourse, including that of the characterization of the story's *dramatis personae*. The adaptation is not merely an attempt at expressing the ideas of 1928 work in a different medium. Rather, it is a critical reinterpretation and an ideological radicalization of Mário de Andrade's rhapsody cast in terms of the social, economic, and political realities of the late sixties.

Mário de Andrade's "hero without a character," like his model in Koch-Grünberg's legends, is a great transformer. He turns himself into a handsome white prince, into an ant, and, at the end of the narrative, into the constellation Ursa Major. He frequently transforms his brother Jiguê into the "telephone machine," either to call a local cabaret to order "lobster and French women" or to curse the villain, Venceslau Pietro Pietra. He transforms an Englishman into the "London Bank machine" and, before returning to his homeland, he transforms the city of São Paulo into a giant, stone sloth. He dies several times and is revived through the use of magical agents.

Joaquim Pedro de Andrade eliminated all magical transformations except two: Macunaíma becomes a handsome white prince and later turns white permanently. In neither case, however, is Macunaíma himself the agent of transformation. In the first case, Sofará (Jiguê's first "companion") gives him a magical cigarette that causes his transformation into a prince. In the second, a fountain magically appears that turns him white. The only other "magical" episodes maintained in the film are the "Currupira" episode and the scene in which Macunaíma uses *macumba* to give Venceslau a beating. In neither of these episodes, however, do magical powers emanate from Macunaíma, who is thus demystified as a hero. He has no more powers than any ordinary man. He survives largely due to his own wits. At no time does Macunaíma, in the film, use magical agents of any kind in his face-to-face struggles with the villain. Furthermore, while in the novel the hero is characterized ambivalently with both positive and negative traits, in the film he is characterized only negatively. The director himself has observed that his Macunaíma is "a hero without purpose and without destiny."[9]

Ci, the "Mother of the Forest" of the book, has become Ci, urban guerrilla, in the film. Joaquim Pedro de Andrade's transformation of Ci into an urban guerrilla is linked directly to the historical events of the period in which he made the film, when urban guerrilla warfare was one result of the closing of the political system by the military in 1964. Macunaíma, after meeting and "conquering" Ci, becomes an object of desire for the dominating subject Ci, unlike the book, where he becomes the "Emperor of the Virgin Forest." His role vis-à-vis Ci is represented visually: the design on the robe he wears in her house is that of the male genital organs. Macunaíma also prostitutes himself sexually for money. The film-maker thus inverts values typical of Brazilian society and unmasks the myth of male dominance.

The villain, Venceslau Pietro Pietra, is much the same in the film and the novel. While the novel stresses the fact that he is the cannibalistic giant Piaimã (once again a composite figure from indigenous legends and the imagination of the novelist), in the film he is introduced as a giant of industry and commerce and as a champion of free enterprise. He is a wealthy industrialist, but one in dependent relationship to the United States. As he shows reporters around his factory, he tells them that "all of these machines are new—second-hand American."

Other magical, fantastic, animated creatures inhabiting the world of Mário de Andrade's narrative have been transformed by the filmmaker into the outcasts of Brazilian society. The director's basic strategy in the adaptation is thus the simplification and condensation of the book's narrative and the concretization of its magical and fantastic elements. The film enters a critical dialogue with the novel, rendering explicit that which is implicit in the original and radicalizing many latent political aspects of the novel. Through this strategy Joaquim Pedro makes the film relate more directly to modern Brazilian social, political, and economic reality. In this sense, the film represents a step toward realism vis-à-vis the novel.

The textual system of a film is an integration of both cinematic and extra-cinematic codes, a productive practice. The codes of a text intermingle and interplay creating a multiplicity of meanings articulated across many different codes. The textual system of *Macunaíma* is one of the inversion, if not subversion, of established hierarchies, social mores, and, perhaps more importantly, spectator expectations. With its complex cultural coding, it is a radically subversive text. The space of *Macunaíma* is one of incongruity, discontinuity, and *non sequitur*. Macunaíma is born full grown, son of an old woman (played by a man). The family is racially mixed: one of his brothers (Jiguê) is black, the other (Maanape) white. While members of an apparently primitive Indian tribe, Macunaíma's mother uses an umbrella to protect herself from being urinated on by her son, who sleeps in the hammock above her. Sofará, Jiguê's girlfriend, wears a white sack dress with an Alliance for Progress emblem on it. Temporal discontinuity is achieved precisely through the use of such disparate elements. In the initial sequences Macunaíma wears a sixteenth-century European dress shirt, Jiguê an African robe and headdress, Maanape a worn and torn priest's frock. The implication is that the clothes' previous owners have been eaten by the family. The film is replete with cannibals: an ogre (the Currupira) who cuts off a piece of his leg for Macunaíma to eat, an Italo-Brazilian industrialist (Venceslau Pietro Pietra) who tries to persuade Macunaíma to join (literally) their banquet meal, the villain's wife who refers to the hero as a "duck" she has captured and begins preparing him in a large pot before he manages to escape, and the Uiara, an incarnation of a Brazilian folk legend, a "mermaid" who finally devours Macunaíma at the end of the film. There are bums who speak Latin, geese that defecate silver, trees with many different kinds of fruit on the same branches, orgies, political speeches, street battles with the police, transvestites, black magic, and a generous dosage of bad taste (kitsch).

The image track of *Macunaíma* consists of 65 segments or sequences, each accounting for a specific episode of the plot. These sequences, in turn, are divided into 283 separate shots, not counting the black screen that both precedes and follows the image track *per se*. The number of shots is surprisingly low considering the rapid pace of much of the film.

Nelson Pereira dos Santos's *Vidas Secas*, a much slower, more deliberate film, consists of 652 shots. Macunaíma, as the hero, is present in every segment except two. The montage is rather traditional, and there is a general preoccupation with smooth transitions between shots and sequences. An omniscient narrator introduces the film, comments on the action, reveals and explains elements not clear in the image track alone, and functions as a transitional device between shots and sequences. The narrator intervenes thirty-three times in the film. At times his remarks are redundant in terms of the image seen; other times he comments ironically on the action of the film or presents a false reality that the visual image undercuts. The novel *Macunaíma* also uses an omniscient narrator.

Macunaíma's basic focus is apparent in its very first moments, i.e., during the titles and credits. The credits are set on a green and yellow background, obviously representing a jungle area (the Amazon). Green and yellow are Brazil's official colors and are the colors of the country's flag. The music accompanying the credits and background is a patriotic march by nationalist composer Heitor Villa-Lobos that seeks through its lyrics to glorify the heroes of Brazil. Before the initial shot of the image track, therefore, its basic theme is articulated across three distinct codes: a chromatic code (green and yellow with all their connotations of nationalism), a musical code (the patriotic march), and a linguistic code (the march's lyrics). The film thus links immediately with the epic tradition, or, more precisely, with the comic-epic tradition, as it proposes to deal with the problem of Brazil and the Brazilian hero.

If, in the novel, Macunaíma is characterized in folktale fashion by rapid growth, in the film he is born full grown. The film adapts the deformed, comic, fatherless birth of the novel with an additional grotesque charge. Macunaíma is born head first when he falls out from under his mother's dress and is, in a sense, born of the earth (i.e., he is firmly planted on the ground when he is born, his color is that of the earth). His mother is old and masculine (played by actor Paulo José, who later plays white Macunaíma). The ambivalent characterization of the mother (old age giving birth) is typical of a carnivalesque attitude toward the world, an attitude that, according to Mikhail Bakhtin, maintains a grotesque image of the body:

> The grotesque image reflects a phenomenon in transformation, an as yet unfinished metamorphosis, of death and birth, growth and becoming. The relation to time is one determining trait of the grotesque image. The other indispensable trait is ambivalence. For in this image we find both poles of transformation, the old and the new, the dying and the procreating, the beginning and the end of the metamorphosis.[10]

The carnivalesque is profoundly subversive of the official, dominant ideology, since it abolishes hierarchies, levels social classes, and creates an alternative, second life, free from the rules and restrictions of official cultural life. Macunaíma's humorous and grotesque birth thus serves to subvert the ideology suggested by the theme song and background colors of the credits. The film is dealing with a Brazilian hero, but not the kind envisioned by the dominant ideology. The use of actor Grande Otelo, who, together with Oscarito, epitomizes the *chanchada* in Brazilian cinema, as Macunaíma-child creates an immediate empathy among the spectators for the character, an identification important for the potential success of the film as a political statement. (Cultural code: reference to Brazilian cinema: *chanchada*.)

Macunaíma passes more than six years without speaking, and his entertainment during his childhood is decapitating ants. While the narrator informs that Macunaíma likes to behead ants, the hero appears sucking on a pacifier and eating dirt, a common, disease-causing occurrence among children in Brazil's impoverished interior (an element absent from the novel). The scene is repeated after Macunaíma returns to his homeland in a kind of mirror image. The film thus develops on two levels: a superficial, humorous, irreverent level and a serious, profound, referential level, referring to the reality of modern, underdeveloped Brazil. The referential force of the image thus undercuts the superficial, humorous image received by the spectator.

If Mário de Andrade's rhapsody satirizes foreign influence and cultural dependence, Joaquim Pedro de Andrade denounces cultural and economic imperialism. Much of the director's critique of imperialism, capitalism, and modern Brazilian society is transmitted through a subcode or sub-text of cannibalistic imagery. Cannibalism pervades both works, but gains importance in the film as the guiding force behind its message. It is synonymous, in the film, with exploitation, especially the exploitation of underdeveloped Brazil by the international capitalist system.

Macunaíma (1969)

184

In a text written as a presentation of the film for the 1969 Venice Film Festival and later included as a preface to the version of the film distributed in the United States, Joaquim Pedro observes:

> Every consumer is reducible, in the last analysis, to cannibalism. The present work relationships, as well as the relationships between people — social, political and economic — are still basically cannibalistic. Those who can, "eat" others through their consumption of products, or even more directly in sexual relationships.[11]

Throughout the film an erotic code interweaves with the film's political code, almost always within a broader context of the director's concept of cannibalism.

Early in the film, for example, Macunaíma and Sofará go into the woods to set a trap for a tapir. After setting the trap, Sofará takes a magical cigarette out of her crotch (erotic code) and gives it to Macunaíma. When he takes a puff, he immediately becomes a handsome white prince. Sofará and Macunaíma then run deeper into the woods for a sexual romp to the sound, on the musical soundtrack, of an old carnival march entitled "Peri e Ceci." Peri and Ceci are characters in José de Alencar's famous Romantic novel, O Guarani. Peri is the noble savage with whom the young European (or Europeanized) girl, Ceci, falls in love. An opposition thus develops, on the level of a musical/linguistic code, between the native Peri (Macunaíma) and the foreign Ceci (Sofará).

Macunaíma's transformation into a prince, however, is only superficial. His clothes are made of gaudily colored crepe paper, and he soon reverts to the black "baby" who amuses himself by sucking on a pacifier and eating dirt. He is no more than a paper prince.[12] The filmmaker's characterization of Macunaíma-prince is thus different from Mário de Andrade's Macunaíma, who, through his own powers of transformation, becomes a "fiery prince."

The trap that Macunaíma and Sofará set is successful, and we soon see Jiguê dividing the cooked animal among the members of the family while the hero boasts of his exploits. All that Macunaíma receives of the tapir he trapped are the intestines. Most critics have overlooked one detail in these two episodes: Sofará is wearing a sack dress with an Alliance for Progress emblem on it. On a deeper level, then, it is the foreign Alliance for Progress (North American imperialism) that gives Macunaíma (Brazil) an appearance of development (the so-called "economic miracle"), but when the goods are divided, all Macunaíma receives is tripe. Just as Sofará/Ceci wants to consume Macunaíma/Peri sexually, American capitalism attempts to consume Brazil economically. The political allegory is clear, albeit superficially outlined here.

Cannibalist imagery continues after a devastating flood that leaves Macunaíma's family hungry. The hero has hidden some food, but refuses to share it with his brothers. His mother, therefore, abandons him with the admonition: "You stay alone here and don't grow any more, stupid!"

Shortly thereafter, Macunaíma runs upon the Currupira who, from the narrative point of view, serves as a hostile donor who tries to trick the hero in order to eat him. In Brazilian folk legends, whence Mário de Andrade borrowed the episode, the Currupira is a god who protects the forests.[13] Although essentially a visualization of the corresponding episode in the novel, the Currupira sequence is much more aggressive and violent in the film due to the act of cannibalism shown when the ogre cuts off a piece of his leg for Macunaíma to eat. The Currupira then shows Macunaíma the wrong way home, and a chase begins. As the hero runs from the Currupira, the ogre yells to the flesh from his leg, now inside Macunaíma's stomach. The meat answers, indicating the hero's route to the ogre. Finally, Macunaíma realizes what is happening and vomits the meat into a mud puddle on the ground in front of the Cotia's house (the Cotia is a benevolent donor who shows the hero the way home).

The last shot of the sequence shows the puddle, with the meat still trying to respond to the Currupira's calls, but in reality only gurgling in the muddy water. The puddle, as filmed, forms, together with the film's frame, the design of the Brazilian flag: a rectangle enclosing a diamond shape, within which is a globe with stars on it. The frame represents the flag as a whole, the puddle is diamond shaped, and the meat, gurgling and making concentric circles, is the flag's globe. The connotations and implications are multiple. The image is at once a comment on the state of Brazilian politics under the military regime and a cannibalistic image, as Brazil (here, the earth and the flag) devours part of the Currupira. In this sense the image echoes earlier scenes in which Macunaíma had attempted to "consume" Sofará under water while the family bathed together in the river and foreshadows the consumption (again in the water) of Venceslau Pietro Pietra later in the film. The muddy flag also foreshadows the final shot of the film in which Macunaíma dies while his green jacket spreads over the water like a flag.

Macunaíma soon finds his way back home. He tells his mother: "Mother, I dreamed I lost a tooth." She responds: "A relative will die." In literal respect for the proverb (something akin to "step on a crack, break your mother's back"), she immediately drops dead in a shot reminiscent of the famous insert in Truffaut's *Shoot the Piano Player* in which the gangster's mother drops dead. While the family mourns their mother's death, the narrator explains that "Macunaíma mourned heroically," but the image undercuts the seriousness of his words: Macunaíma is standing in the door of their dwelling rubbing Iriqui's (Jiguê's new "companion") derrière.

After their mother's death, Macunaíma and his brothers depart for the city. They soon come upon a magical fountain that turns the hero white. The transformation is ironically accompanied by an old, romantic song entitled "Sob uma cascata" ("By a Waterfall"), the Brazilian version of a song used by Lloyd Bacon in his *Footlight Parade* (1933), a film featuring musical numbers directed by Busby Berkeley (cultural code: reference to

American cinema, *chanchada*, cultural imperialism). On arriving in the city, where Iriqui becomes a prostitute, Macunaíma faces another problem: he is unable to distinguish men from machines. After much contemplation, he determines in typical carnivalesque fashion that the men are machines and that the machines are men, a wry comment on the alienation of modern man in technological society.

Macunaíma soon encounters Ci as she does battle with the police. After witnessing her victory, discarding severed arms in the struggle, Macunaíma pursues her into a parking garage and "seduces" her (with the help of Jiguê, who hits her over the head with a large rock). She wakes up, finds herself irresistibly attracted to the hero, and takes him home with her. Like many other elements in the film, the episodes involving Ci represent an inversion of established values and social hierarchies of patriarchal Brazilian society. While Macunaíma is interested in Ci sexually, Ci in reality dominates and determines their relationship. In their initial struggle, Ci soundly defeats Macunaíma. Later, Macunaíma, not Ci, prostitutes himself for money. Six months after their first encounter Ci gives birth to a black baby (once again played by Grande Otelo, thus repeating the initial situation of the film), but it is Macunaíma who must rest. Macunaíma's role as a sexual object is reinforced by the clothes he wears while in Ci's house (a purple robe with male genital organs designed on it) and by the fact that his part of the house, the bedroom, is painted in pink and other tones of red. Ci's part of the house is green, yellow, and blue (Brazil's colors). While Ci goes out to fight the forces of repression, Macunaíma, the anti-hero, stays home resting. But Ci herself, a subject in relation to the object Macunaíma, also becomes an object—an object for mass consumption, a pop song, a poster on the wall. She later literally self-destructs, blowing up with her own bomb, thus participating in what Joaquim Pedro de Andrade refers to as the "self-cannibalism" of the left.

Before her death, Ci had promised to leave Macunaíma a precious stone, the *muiraquitã*, as an inheritance. The talisman is lost with the explosion of Ci's bomb. After her death, Macunaíma learns that the stone has been found by an Italo-Brazilian industrialist, Venceslau Pietro Pietra. Frustrated in his initial attempts at recovering the talisman, Macunaíma tries a new tactic: he goes, in drag, to Venceslau's house, pretending to be a "recently divorced" French woman who collects rare stones. In this episode the characters are stylized, exaggerated, caricatured, as each one plays out his role: Macunaíma as the seductive, alluring French woman; Venceslau as the seducing, worldly, wealthy industrialist (decadent bourgeoisie). Venceslau is patently absurd in his purple smoking jacket over green boxer shorts and garters. As Macunaíma enters, the episode is choreographed to the sounds of an Argentine tango. Through vain promises, Venceslau convinces Macunaíma to take off his/her clothes while they watch a pornographic movie, "based precisely on the book you are reading," Venceslau explains, "a free adaptation," an obvious reference to the film we ourselves are watching, a free adaptation of Mário de Andrade's rhapsody. After

Macunaíma has taken off all his clothes and hands Venceslau the oranges he had been using as breasts, he runs, nude, out of the room to Venceslau's entreaties. The villain, it seems, has no specific sexual preference. The entire episode is a tour de force of carnivalesque inversion and ambivalence.

The final battle between Macunaíma and the giant takes place only after several other misadventures: Macunaíma uses *macumba* to give Venceslau a beating; he is captured and almost eaten by Venceslau's wife, Ceiuci; he gives a patriotic speech on the "plagues of Brazil" in a public plaza; he chases a *cotia* through the stock market; he attempts to get a scholarship to pursue the giant, who is in Europe convalescing from the beating; he is tricked by a bum into smashing his testicles ("sic transit," remarks the bum); he is tricked into buying a goose that "defecates money"; he sees a juvenile delinquent rob a shoe-shine boy, asks what happens, then robs the rest of the money; he seduces Jiguê's third "companion," Suzi; and he takes a walk in the local leper colony. Finally, invited by the giant to participate in a *feijoada* (Brazil's national dish) to commemorate his younger daughter's marriage, Macunaíma returns to the villain's mansion for the final confrontation. The *feijoada*, in a large pool, is a cannibalistic one in which the traditional sausages, dried beef and pork ends have been replaced by human bodies, intestines, and appendages, a far cry from the pools used for geometric synchronized swimming in Bacon's *Footlight Parade*. After much peril, Macunaíma finally defeats Venceslau, who falls into the pool of *feijoada*. Before he goes under, however, he yells: "It needs salt!" Macunaíma's victory is complete.

But what is Macunaíma's victory? Looking at the action of the film to this point, one might be tempted to see the struggle between Macunaíma and Venceslau Pietro Pietra as a rather bizarre allegory of class struggle with the industrial bourgeoisie defeated by the disinherited masses. Such an interpretation, however, is soon undercut. Macunaíma, his brothers and Princesa (Macunaíma's new companion) leave the city with a wagon filled with electrical appliances: fans, televisions, stereos, blenders, electric guitars. His dress gives him away. He is wearing a green and yellow (symbolic of Brazil) buckskin cowboy suit and hat (North American cultural imperialism). Taking back to the jungle with him products of multinational corporations (e.g., a Philco television set) and dressed as he is, Macunaíma has been totally co-opted by North American cultural dominance. He has assimilated the values of urban, bourgeois, capitalist society. In the jungle, all of his electrical appliances will be totally useless to him.

Upon arriving at his birthplace, Macunaíma refuses to help the others find food, preferring instead to sleep, and is soon abandoned. The hero cannot understand the silence, and one day a talking parrot appears to keep him company. And soon, Macunaíma awakes "with a new feeling in his muscles" and goes to the river to take a swim. There he encounters the cannibalistic Uiara in the form of a beautiful, nude woman. He jumps in the river after her, and the last shot shows his green jacket afloat with blood gushing up from under it, as Villa-Lobos's patriotic march once again begins to play. In the novel, Macunaíma, mutilated by piranhas, tires of living on earth and is transformed magically into Ursa Major.

The final shot of the film is of Macunaíma's death. His coat, olive green, floats on the water, slowly spreading out as if it were a flag, while blood surrounds it. The shot echoes all of the earlier scenes of cannibalism, including Venceslau Pietro Pietra's death in the *feijoada*. The patriotic march in the background continues through the final credits, set, once again, on a green and yellow background, until the screen becomes black. Accompanied by the music the black screen continues for several seconds before the film finally ends. Blackness and death thus surround the film (it may be remembered that before the first shot *per se* of the image track the screen is black). In this sense, the film's message is a very pessimistic one.

Throughout the film Macunaíma undergoes a process of demystification. His generally anarchistic attitude must certainly offend the dominant ideology, but at the same time he is not the kind of hero envisioned by those who oppose the dominant ideology. Through his own laziness and egoism, Macunaíma largely defeats himself. He becomes, in fact, his own antagonist. He is a failed hero. The director has frequently observed that *Macunaíma* is a film about a Brazilian devoured by Brazil, but since Macunaíma so frequently represents Brazil itself, one can say that the underlying theme is that of "self-cannibalism": Brazil devours its citizens through poverty and underdevelopment, its citizens devour Brazil, and Brazil, consequently, devours itself. In this sense the film radicalizes ideological positions latent in the novel, just as Cinema Novo radicalizes

The cannibalistic *feijoada* in *Macunaíma* (1969)

and takes to their ultimate conclusions many issues first raised by the modernist movement.

Notes

1. Joaquim Pedro de Andrade, "Crítica e auto-crítica: O Padre e a Moça," *Revista Civilização Brasileira* 1, no. 7 (May 1966), pp. 251-65. See "Criticism and Self-Criticism" in this volume.
2. *Harvard Dictionary of Music*, 2d rev. ed. (Cambridge: The Belknap Press of Harvard University, 1969), p. 728.
3. Florestan Fernandes, "Mário de Andrade e o Folklore Brasileiro," *Revista do Arquivo Municipal* 12, vol. 106 (São Paulo: 1946): 135-58.
4. Theodor Koch-Grünberg, *Vom Roroima zum Orinoco: Ergebnesse einer Reise in Nord Brasilien und Venezuela in den Jahren 1911-1913*, vol. II: Mythen und Legendun den Talipang und Arekuna Indianes (Stuttgart: Verlag Ströcker and Schröder, 1924).
5. Mário de Andrade, "Anotações Para o Prefácio," in Telê Porto Ancona Lopez, *Macunaíma: A Margem e o Texto* (São Paulo: Editora de Humanismo, Ciencia e Technologia/Secretaria de Cultura, Esportes e Turismo, 1974), p. 94.
6. Lopez, *A Margem e o Texto*, p. 3.
7. Theodor Koch-Grünberg, "Mitos e Lendas dos Indios Taulipang e Arekuná," trans. Henrique Roenick, *Revista do Museu Paulista* 7 (1953): 21.
8. Haroldo de Campos, *Morfologia do Macunaíma* (São Paulo: Perspectiva, 1973).
9. Quoted in "La cara fea," *Análisis* (Buenos Aires, 28 July 1970): 428.
10. Mikhail Bakhtin, *Rabelais and His World*, trans. Helene Iswolsky (Cambridge: M.I.T. Press, 1968), p. 24.
11. Joaquim Pedro de Andrade, "Sobre Macunaíma: Antropofagía y Autofagía," *Hablemos de Cine* (Lima) 49 (September/October 1969): 10.
12. Heloísa Buarque de Hollanda, "Heróis de Nossa Gente" (M.A. Thesis, Universidade Federal do Rio de Janeiro, 1974), p. 120.
13. M. Cavalcánti Proença, *Roteiro de Macunaíma* (Rio de Janeiro: Civilização Brasileira, 1969), p. 319.

21
"How Tasty Was My Little Frenchman"

RICHARD PEÑA

How Tasty Was My Little Frenchman concerns the exploits of a French-man, in the service of the French Huguenots (then settling the area around what is today Rio de Janeiro), who is captured by a tribe of Tupinamba and sentenced to death. Tribal custom allows such a prisoner to live as a member of the tribe prior to his execution. The French-man is given a wife, and he soon takes part in tribal work, wars, and even religious ceremonies. After a brief attempt at escape he is finally killed and cannibalized by his former hosts. The original source for the film was the diary of a German adventurer named Hans Staden, who, while in the service of the Dutch colonizers of Brazil was similarly captured by some tribesmen, but escaped to tell the tale. Much of the early literature of Latin America exists in the form of diaries and letters concerning contact with the native American peoples. The idea of the author or narrator as captive, as opposed to a conqueror as in Bernal Diaz's *The Conquest of New Spain*, lends a peculiar power to writing like that of Staden's which later writers of fiction would use as a standard narrative device. In this sense the narrative of *How Tasty Was My Little Frenchman* harks back to a sub-genre of adventure or travel literature called the "captive witness." The captive witness differs from other witnesses to alien cultures in that he is to die at a prescribed time, and therefore his captors offer him in-sight into their culture, confident that he will carry such secrets only to

191

How Tasty Was My Little Frenchman (1971)

the grave. There is no need to act or dissemble before him; thus, the account offered by the captive witness is unsullied by alien defensiveness. Melville's *Typee* also falls into this sub-genre and, in recent years, both science fiction and detective literature have appropriated the device.

The film begins with a declaration: "Latest news from Terra Firme." This statement falls outside of the body of the letter that follows, and thus forms part of the screenplay written by the director, who here begins to establish one of the film's major themes: the possible implications of this story about the colonial past for the Brazil of today (Terra Firme was one of the colonial names of Brazil). The film is announced as the "latest news," suggesting that in a way we must see it as a statement about the present. This motif of "presentness" or actuality is especially reemphasized throughout by the exceptional camera work of Dib Lutfi. The long, uninterrupted hand-held shots, quick zooms, and use of natural light are clearly reminiscent of the techniques of cinema verité. The film's approach to the Frenchman owes much to the branch of cinema verité called the "portrait film," such as D.A. Pennebaker's *Don't Look Back* and Ed Pincus-David Neuman's *Portrait of a McCarthy Supporter*. The portrait film gives a view or a description of a certain character or type of character, so that we can "know" and hopefully understand them. Directors like Pennebaker or Pincus and Neuman totally avoid the interview: the characters are never allowed to verbally present themselves to us. Rather we are forced to come to our own conclusions about the subjects of the portrait on the basis of our view of their actions in the world. Often these actions seem contradictory, making it difficult to assess our feelings about the characters without considering the pattern and larger implications of their actions, and finally the sources of our own feelings. This approach might well have been a model for the relationship its director hoped to create between his projected audience and the Frenchman.

Following this statement comes a voice-over reading of a letter from Villegaignon, leader of the French Protestant settlers of Guanabara Bay, to John Calvin. Immediately, the contradictions between the verbal descriptions of "Terra Firme," and the images on the screen become apparent. Instead of a man being drowned after an attempted escape from justice, we see that man being murdered, or at least being subjected to a murder attempt. The official version of the conquest and colonization of Brazil—official in the sense that documents like the Villegaignon letter do indeed form the colonial historical record—is certainly not what we are being shown. Immediately thereafter we are given the film's first intertitle. The intertitles consist of quoted extracts from the colonial legacy of documents, letters, and diaries used as ironic, "historical" counterpoints to the events depicted. Often, the action of the film makes us look at, or interpret, these quotations in a new light.

The first intertitle describes the structure of alliances in force at the time of the story, as set down in the official record: French and Tupinamba versus Portuguese and Tupiniquim. The story of the Frenchman exposes the basic falseness of these alliances: in his shifting relations to these groups, and in his acceptance and rejection by them, the film actually implies that the primary conflict was always Europeans versus Americans, despite appearances or alliances. The final intertitle in which we are told of the slaughter of the Tupiniquim by their allies the Portuguese, gruesomely validates this theory with the only historical quotation used in the film that needs little further interpretation.

In the documents and "official histories" of the colonial past, the focus is always clearly on the acts and deeds of the white, European colonizers, presumed to be the ancestors of present-day Brazil. It is this easy assumption that the film wishes to challenge. In the first shot after the intertitle, we see the Frenchman coming up out of the water and on to land, dragging with him the heavy ball and chain that was meant to drown him. It is significant that the camera's—and thus our—point of view for this scene is from *on land*, from behind bushes, at a low height. When he is discovered by the Tupiniquim and Portuguese a few shots later, they will have been observing him from a similar vantage point. Yet while this point of view does link our initial view of the Frenchman with that of the land dwellers, the native Americans or Brazilians, the film avoids any sort of facile presentation of the "Indian's point of view" on colonization or on the narrative action, as we might find, say, in a film merely "sympathetic" to native American rights. The narrative of the film concentrates on the figure of the Frenchman in a way that is at once allied to the point of view of the tribespeople and also separate from them: the camera at several points declares its independence from the point of view of any character. The camera's attention to the Frenchman is not justified by, for example, the interest of the tribespeople in him; on the contrary, they seem remarkably disinterested and accepting. The concentration is in a sense *our* interest in the Frenchman: our interest in determining who he is, or what he is, and what our relationship to him might be. Most of the audience for this film, in Brazil, would be white-skinned descendents of Europeans who, due to their emotional and intellectual formation, would "naturally" tend to identify with the Frenchman. Just as Rocha's *Land in Anguish* might be said to be obsessed with the figure of Paulo Martins, and yet is distanced and critical of him, so too *How Tasty Was My Little Frenchman* attempts to be critical of the facile, ethno-centric response to the figure of the Frenchman as the "hero" of the film. On the contrary, as the title, *How Tasty Was My Little Frenchman*, it attempts to include us in his destruction. The links between the present-day Brazilians and the cannibalistic tribespeople can be seen as one of the influences of the Tropicalist Movement in the film.

The attempt to define the Frenchman occurs throughout the film. Soon after he is captured by the Tupiniquim and the Portuguese, his captors are attacked and overcome by some Tupinamba warriors, who are the Frenchman's supposed allies. The fury and the chaos of the attack is beautifully conveyed by the frantic camera work, consisting of short, jabbing camera movements and quick zooms, with a playing-in-reverse sound track. In order to determine whether the Frenchman is actually French or Portuguese, the Tupinamba submit him to a kind of language test while the captured Portuguese recite different steps in a recipe (a joke in Brazil, where the Portuguese have a reputation for gluttony). The Frenchman recites, in French, a brief passage that translates as "The savages walk totally naked, and we walk unrecognized." The ambiguity of this sentence points to some of the difficulty in assessing the Frenchman: the need to get beyond mere surface appearances. The "savages" walk about naked and are thus easy to recognize, as savages, in their nudity; the French, however, who presumably walk about fully clothed, are unrecognized as "savages." The squabble between the two Tupinamba warriors for the Frenchman, a fight that seems in many ways comical, anticipates the more tragic fight between the Frenchman and the old trader later in the film, a fight in which the Frenchman's "savagery" is clearly shown. Finally, the inability of Cunhambebe, the chief, or any of the other warriors to tell that the Frenchman is indeed French and therefore an ally further points to the stronger dichotomy of European versus Brazilian that exists as opposed to the system of alliances mentioned in the first intertitle.

The first scenes of the Frenchman's life as a Tupinamba captive tend to stress his separation and distance from them. He is blond, bearded, and at least partially clothed and soon after his capture he is given over to the women. When he thinks that the women are trying to remove his beard, he loudly objects, as if trying to cling to his "Europeanness." In these first scenes he is always pictured as being separate from his captors, off in his own space in the frame or forcibly "tied" to them by ropes.

How Tasty Was My Little Frenchman (1971)

His relation to the Tupinamba soon changes, however. The primary cause for this is the arrival of the old French trader who, ironically, is introduced by another historical intertitle that speaks of the love that the native American people have for these "good and virtuous people, who have so many wonderful things." Immediately, the economic basis of this relationship is implied, a subject that the subsequent scene will explore. The physical differences between the old trader and the Tupinamba exaggerate those of the Frenchman; it places the Frenchman in a position, figuratively speaking, somewhere between the European and the Americans.

In this scene we are first introduced to the structure of colonial trading: the exchange of a few relatively worthless manufactured items, such as mirrors, combs, and jewelry for large quantities of brazilwood, pepper, and other primary materials that were extremely valuable on the European market. Beyond the mirrors and other goods, however, is the promise of gunpowder, the desire for which will grow into a sort of dependence as tensions between the native American tribes — in this case the Tupiniqim and the Tupinamba — were exacerbated by the Europeans. This creation of a dependence economy, a dependence based upon a kind of technological superiority of the Europeans, would give the Europeans an upper hand in any commercial dealings with the tribespeople.

The old trader's flat refusal to acknowledge the Frenchman as one of his countrymen—"Go ahead and eat him"—is symbolic of the Frenchman's separation from Europe and the colonial metropolis. He is, in a sense, rejected by the Europeans as one of *them*, he is permitted, though, to assume a "special role" in the new land, a role within the economy whereby he will be a sort of "private entrepreneur" with special and separate ties to the colonial metropolis, and a promise that someday he will be "reaccepted" by that metropolis. The Frenchman, physically and economically, is thus cast into a state of abeyance, somewhere between being a real American and a European. Significantly, it is the old trader, a European, who explains to the Frenchman the terms of his captivity in America.

The next scene, after the old trader's departure and an intertitle stating the importance of brazilwood in the early colonial trading economy, shows the Frenchman at work in the jungle with Sebiopepe, the woman who has been designated by the tribe as his wife. It is the first time that we see the Frenchman in any kind of relation to the Tupinamba other than that of captive. The two seem to work together comfortably but separately. As the two stop their work to take a swim, in one of the film's curiously erotic scenes, the romantic atmosphere is temporarily interrupted by the Frenchman's discovery of the gold piece in Sebiopepe's navel. He approaches her with an interest not seen up until then and he discovers that there is more where that came from. Nelson immediately cuts to a shot of the two sleeping together: their marriage, in effect, consummated, as the Frenchman sees that their knowledge of the presence of more gold will be his way of getting the upper hand with the old trader. He has discovered a way of using the tribespeople against the European. When Sebiopepe asks him to get up and go with her to look for more wood, he refuses, preferring to stay at home today—"chez moi," as French creeps back into his dialogue. This signifies his affirmation of his own Europeanness, as he now imagines himself to be, with the gold, on equal footing with the old trader, instead of someone to whom terms can be dictated, as they are to the Tubinamba.

The narrative use of the chance discovery of hidden wealth seen in this passage is part of a theme that runs throughout the film. Brazilwood, pepper, and gold all seem to be found simply "in the wild" in this new land and ripe for the taking, unnoticed by that land's inhabitants until their value is announced to them by outsiders. The chief can hardly believe that the old trader has travelled many miles "just to get wood"; similarly, Sebiopepe openly discusses with the Frenchman how she came upon the gold piece, and even shows him where she got it. The idea of hidden wealth that almost seems to spring out of the ground is related to the development of Brazil's own economic history, which has been based upon a series of "chance discoveries" of brazilwood, gold, diamonds, rubber, and other materials, which all led to regular boom-and-bust cycles of economic development too well known throughout the Third World. The manipulation of this discovered wealth, though, is totally in the hands of the outsiders, the Europeans, who give a value to the wood, pepper, and gold, create a need, and thus a value, for the gunpowder.

As the Frenchman attempts to embark upon a new relation with the old trader, he too attempts to imagine for himself a new relation with the Tupinamba. This new relation is revealed immediately after he refuses to go to work with Sebiopepe. He asks her to tell him the story of Mair, the great Caraiba, the "great ancestor." As she begins her recounting of this tribal myth, Nelson cuts to a shot of Sebiopepe behind the gauzy material of the hammock, as if, with the start of the tale, she had entered a kind of "dream world." In view of this, the cut immediately after this shot is a bit startling, because instead of any kind of visual "continuation" of the dreamy quality of the preceding shot, the image we see of Sebiopepe and the Frenchman by a pool of water has the same cinematographic quality as the rest of the film: the same bright natural lighting. The myth of Mair will not be acted out in a mythical time and place, but in the world of the film, the Brazil of 1568.

Sebiopepe's voice-over narration—the second such narration in the film—recounts in Tupi a Promethean myth of the Tupinamba "ancestor," Mair, the great Caraiba, who elevated the tribe from an animal-like existence to a more human-like one. In her telling of the tale Mair teaches the Tupinamba how to build fire and how to move out of the caves within which they were hiding. While she is speaking we see, for the first time, the Frenchman with his head shaved in the manner of the Tupinambas, beardless, and naked. He only seems to stand out in his whiteness. Suddenly, the Frenchman's voice, speaking in French, takes over the narration. He details how the god built a new kind of house, better than the other ones, and how he taught the Tupinamba to organize their villages. All the time that we hear these further deeds of the god, we see the Frenchman himself acting out this part, performing all the works ascribed to the god Mair in the myth. Sebiopepe, then, resumes the narration, again speaking in Tupi, and completes the tale: the Tupinamba revolt against the god, and forsake his works. As she speaks we see the works that had appeared in the Frenchman's portion of the narration being destroyed; they burn his house, and treat him as they would any other prisoner, making him run through fire. We then see and hear Cunhambebe vowing that the Tupinamba will never forget who their enemies are. Sebiopepe then speaks of the killing of the god and its consequences: meanwhile, we see the Frenchman swimming and diving in a pool, in a shot that recalls the earlier pool scene between Sebiopepe and the Frenchman, at a time when he had been more fixed within his old role as captive.

In this sequence, Nelson again makes further usage of the European accounts of the conquest and colonization of America. One of the most common legends concerning the initial contacts between Europeans and Americans is that the Europeans were worshipped by the native Americans, as they were believed to be gods whose return had long been prophesied. One of the principal features by which the god might be recognized would be his whiteness. The Frenchman, as he tells his version of the myth of Mair (in French), imagines himself as a kind of god in relation to his captors, bringing to them the blessings of his civilization. In the Tupinamba version of this myth, spoken by Sebiopepe, the European vision of themselves as gods is rejected, as the works of the Frenchman/God are rejected, and the Tupinamba are reminded by their chief never to forget their enemies. They have not been fooled, and in their rejection of him and his works they affirm something about themselves and their civilization: their self-sufficiency and integrity. Sebiopepe's conclusion of the myth, in which thunder and lightning issue forth from the head of the god after he is slain, is a sort of grim prophecy of the eventual destruction of the Tupinamba by the European cannons and musket fire.

The attempt at being a god having failed, the Frenchman next attempts to achieve some kind of full acceptance by the tribe, albeit in some special capacity, as he holds the secret of how to make the captured cannons fire. It is to this attempt at assimilation that the last half of the film is devoted. We see the Frenchman take an enthusiastic part in the tracking down and killing of some Portuguese: one of the most remarkable moments in the film occurs when the Portuguese turns to face the white-skinned "savage," now fully recognizable, complete with bow and arrow, yelling at him to halt in French. Later in the film, he will take part in tribal religious ceremonies, join the tribe in its attack on the Tupiniqim, and even rehearse his own execution with Sebiopepe. The old trader, during his second visit, mocks the Frenchman in reference to his appearance by asking him if he would like some beads.

The second scene with the old trader deserves special attention for its expansion of some of the themes mentioned earlier. The Frenchman attempts to assume a position whereby he deals in primary materials (gold) to the old trader, and in manufactured commodities (gunpowder) to the Tupinamba, becoming a kind of economic middleman. The defilement of the grave, with a skull and some pieces of gold framing the bottom edge of the screen, makes the act of extracting the "hidden wealth" a kind of unholy plunder. The fight between the two men is ludicrous, as has been mentioned, yet takes on a rather tragic tone as the old trader has his skull split open by a shovel. The killing serves several functions: it helps to further destroy any sympathy we might feel for the Frenchman, it further separates the Frenchman from the Europeans (the old trader being his second European victim), and finally, it eliminates the older kind of "foreign agent" — the European who looks like a European, who deals in manufactured commodities — and replaces him with a new kind of agent, curiously still a foreigner, yet one who looks, at least on the surface, like an American or Brazilian. The struggle between these different types of agents is in many ways a battle between father and son, as the latter type was certainly spawned and rejected by the former. Curiously, Nelson Pereira dos Santos cast in these two roles an actual father and son (Manfredo and Arduino Colasanti).

The next scene is in many ways the most problematic in the film. After extracting the gold and jewelry from the grave, and burying the old trader, the Frenchman starts to paddle his canoe towards the European ship. Sebiopepe calls to him from shore, and after a series of eye-line matches, he decides to paddle towards shore. He tries to bring Sebiopepe alone with him, but she struggles out of his grasp. By the time she seemingly agrees to go with him, the boat has sailed out of reach. While there are several possible interpretations of his decision, his paddling back to shore when he had a clear opportunity to escape suggests that he no longer can escape. He has lost his Europeanness and cannot, finally, go home again. His sense of being suspended between cultures gives the second part of the film a pervasive air of melancholy. There is a boredom or sadness in his speech; the only time that he breaks into a smile during this part of the film is during the rehearsal of his execution with Sebiopepe as if he were fascinated and delighted at the prospect of his own demise. In one of the final shots of the rehearsal scene, the film cuts to an extremely large close-up of the Frenchman's face — an unusual shot within the context of this film — smeared with a reddish dye so that, for the first time, his skin color approaches that of the Tupinamba. Ironically, his assimilation into the tribe occurs on the eve of his own destruction. There really is no "middle ground." Assimilation of a European into the Tupinamba means, essentially, the destruction of the European.

It is in this light that we must see the film's final act of cannibalism as a gesture of defiance, a special kind of revolt. It represents the ultimate kind of assimilation: one that in the process of assimilation definitively transforms that which is being assimilated. The Frenchman does, finally, become part of the tribe, but in such a way that we no longer perceive him as a Frenchman. Significantly, Cunhambebe accuses the Frenchman's "people" of having cannibalized Tupinamba.

The final shot of Sebiopepe, the zoom in to her face while she is eating the Frenchman, bears this out: she eats him emotionlessly. Despite her warm relationship with him she recognizes that he is an enemy who must be destroyed. Destroyed, however, in such a way that he is not simply gotten rid of but rather incorporated into the tribal body.

22
"*São Bernardo*: Property and the Personality"

ROBERT STAM AND RANDAL JOHNSON

Property renders its owner enormously stout, endlessly avaricious, pseudo-creative, and intensely selfish.

— E. M. Forster

Property is theft.

— Proudhon

Leon Hirszman's *São Bernardo* can best be understood within the complex relationship between Cinema Novo and the Brazilian artistic movement called Modernism (1922–1945). Cinema Novo is an heir of Modernism and parallels it in many ways. Both movements reacted against the dominant codes in their respective areas of signification: Modernism against the calcified discourse of a Parnassianism that mirrored the archaic class structure of Brazilian society; Cinema Novo against the *chanchada* and the academic "serious" films of Vera Cruz. In contrast to the colonized, inconsequential vision of their antecedent movements, both Modernism and Cinema Novo struggled to decolonize Brazilian culture through a posture of critical nationalism. But the initial impulse of Cinema Novo is linked not so much to the initial phase of Modernism

(1922-1930) as it is to the second phase (1930-1945) with its critical consciousness of Brazilian social and political life. The literature of this period was dominated by socially committed novels in the critical realist mode. Significantly, one of the most important Cinema Novo films was drawn from this tradition: Nelson Pereira dos Santos's *Vidas Secas*, based on Graciliano Ramos's 1938 novel of the same name.

While Modernism evolved from irrationality (in opposition to the rationality of Parnassian poetry) to rationality (the novelistic "Neo-Realism" of the thirties), Cinema Novo moved in the opposite direction. Due partially to circumstances beyond the filmmaker's control, the initial commitment to realism gave way to the allegorical, even hermetic stance of films like *Pindorama* and *Os Deuses e os Mortos*. In the late sixties, these metaphorical, "Tropicalist" films served a double function: decolonizing cinematic language by liberating Latin America's "magical" Unconscious, and providing an outlet for the frustrations caused by a closed political system. In the midst of this metaphorical outpouring under harsh military rule, *São Bernardo* stands out as anomaly for its return to a critical realism in some ways reminiscent of early Cinema Novo.

São Bernardo maintains continuity with the movement's original project not only by drawing, like *Vidas Secas*, on one of the most socially conscious novelists of the thirties, but also by its narrative and esthetic posture. Based on Graciliano Ramos's 1934 novel, the film was made in 1971/1972, but released only in 1973. It was held up by the censors for seven months, a delay that speeded the bankruptcy of its production company. In their negotiations with the censors, the filmmakers argued that the film was a scrupulously faithful rendition of a literary classic and a fitting tribute to Graciliano Ramos on the eightieth anniversary of his birth. They added, with Brechtian cunning, that the novel had been *required* reading for college entrance examinations the year before.

Both novel and film open with an economic metaphor. In the novel, protagonist-narrator Paulo Honório proposes to write a novel based on the division of labor. The local priest is to handle the moral aspects and the Latin quotations, while other acquaintances are to be responsible for punctuation, orthography, typesetting, and literary composition. Paulo Honório himself will provide the outline, the knowledge of agriculture and livestock, the financial backing, and the name on the cover. The film *São Bernardo*, meanwhile, opens with the image of a Brazilian Cruzeiro bill, thus keynoting the central theme of both works: the reification of human beings in a society where the accumulation of property and capital diminishes the possibilities for human dignity, where human warmth and contact are "drowned" in what Marx called the "icy waters of selfish calculation."

São Bernardo recounts the transformation of Paulo Honório (Othon Bastos) from the illegitimate son of a poor peasant into a powerful plantation owner. Both novel and film are narrated by Paulo himself in flashbacks during a period of introspection and psychic disintegration.

Othon Bastos as Paulo Honório in *São Bernardo* (1972)

Paulo rises from abject poverty to become the master of a plantation, São Bernardo, where he had formerly been brutalized as a hired hand. His methods of self-advancement range from ruthless bargaining and petty cheating to bribery and even murder. The process of construction of São Bernardo simultaneously causes his destruction as a human being, and this tension between construction and destruction permeates the entire film. Filtered through Paulo's point of view and mediated by his memory, the narration is his attempt to reconstruct his life, to find some kind of retrospective human meaning in his past actions. He is, however, caught in a dilemma, for even as he tries to construct a new persona based on self-understanding, he simultaneously destroys his essential being as a man of property.[1]

After he successfully acquires and develops São Bernardo, Paulo resolves to marry, not out of love but out of abstract economic necessity: he needs an heir for his property. Without loving any particular woman, without being provoked, as he puts it, by "any passing skirt," he settles on a schoolteacher, Madalena (Isabel Ribeiro) because he is impressed with her frugality, common sense, and "refinement."

Accustomed to dominating people through force and money, Paulo cannot understand Madalena, nor can he comprehend the embryonic feelings of tenderness she arouses in him. Although his intentions in marrying are abstract, Madalena is not an abstraction but a complex person who refuses to be just another of Paulo's possessions. Intelligent and intellectually curious, she reads voraciously and learns by conversing with all those who pass through São Bernardo. Her humanizing instincts clash with Paulo's quantification of others.[2] Preoccupied with justice, she rebukes Paulo's cruel treatment of his hired hands.

Paulo, who learned to read and write in jail, cannot understand Madalena's language. He mentally transforms her innocent conversation with his associates into cause for jealousy, precisely the emotion that combines a distorted kind of love with an exacerbated notion of property. He tyrannizes her with his obsession and shoots into the night at imagined rivals. His jealousy, interestingly, confounds itself with his paranoid fear of communism for it is her political discussions with his assistant Padilha that trigger his rage. Madalena ends up a virtual prisoner in her own home, and finally opts for a suicide that amounts to an act of resistance, a radical refusal of oppression.

Women, for Paulo, are "strange animals. . . difficult to dominate." Although he presumably feels some sort of inarticulate affection for Madalena — fissures of sensitivity in his hardened human shell — Paulo sees love as irrational and suspectly unamenable to his quantifying vision of the world. His incipient tenderness distorts itself into pathological jealousy, finally rendering him deaf and blind to the world around him. When Madalena criticizes him for beating the hired hand Marciano, Paulo can only interpret her concern for his worker as proof of an affair. After all, he himself has slept with Marciano's wife. Paulo's *idée fixe* finally oppresses even him, a fact evoked brilliantly by the image of an insomniac Paulo mounting guard against his chimerical enemies.

But Paulo is not alone in objectifying Madalena. Even before he meets her his male acquaintances talk about her legs and speculate about her age as if she were a radio being bargained over in a flea market. The men in São Bernardo cannot speak of women without mercantile language creeping into the discourse. Madalena is "worth a lot" "a beautiful acquisition," "a marvelous ornament." Marriage is a "good deal," and when Madalena initially rebuffs Paulo's marriage proposal by insisting that they wait a year, he protests that business deals, after a year, cease to be valid. Everything in Paulo's life is subject to the profit-and-loss logic of the ledger book. For him, to be is to possess. Money and power pervert all of the relationships into which he enters. Friends, neighbors, lovers, sons, become nothing more than raw material for exploitation. Paulo sees Padilha, the commercially inept heir of São Bernardo, as someone to be tricked out of his property, "a rat to be trapped." He sees Mendonça, his farmer-neighbor, as a rival to be done away with. He regards his workers as congenitally worthless "animals" and his son as a mere posthumous receptacle for his wealth.

The central conflict of the film, however, is that of Paulo with himself. Although he is in some ways a brutal, prototypical capitalist, he is never painted as a villain. His moral bankruptcy is quite unconscious. He simply carries certain dominant values to their logical conclusion. His commentaries betray his values in moments of inadvertent self-revelation: "I

Isabel Ribeiro as Madalena in *São Bernardo* (1972)

could never make sense out of the idea of good and evil, because sometimes my bad acts brought me profits and sometimes my good acts brought me losses." He can accuse Madalena without irony of being a "materialist," because of her interest in socialism. In fact, he is the materialist, in the conventional sense of the word, who superficially admits the existence of a God, who will reward those who are ill paid on earth (and thus relieve Paulo of the responsibility), and the Devil, who will punish those who rob him.

While admittedly an extreme example of alienation, Paulo is also a typical case, a schematic exaggeration of deeper social tendencies, a heightened instance in which the fundamental logic is laid bare. He becomes, as Walter Benjamin said of Brecht's personages, "a stage on which the contradictions of the age are played out." Oppressed as a child, Paulo comes to hate those who oppressed him, even while he adores and covets all they revere: property and political power. He hates the people who oppressed him but respects the system that allowed them to oppress. Rather than destroy the system, he seeks merely to occupy what he sees as a more advantageous position within it. But through his success he self-destructs as a human being. His final self-criticism only heightens his alienation.

São Bernardo is a profoundly dialectical film. The dialectic operates on many levels. First, the film, like the novel, creates a dialectical tension between Paulo's history and his confession. The film alternates sequences that show Paulo contemplating his own ruin with sequences that narrate his version of the events leading up to his ruin. All of his actions are relativized by the fact that we know the final outcome of his frenetic pursuit of property. His progress is exposed as a long march toward solitude and emotional desolation. He is paradoxically impoverished by his wealth, just as he is unmanned by his machismo. His greed is insatiable by definition. *São Bernardo* captures the treadmill quality, the frustration inherent in material "success." But Paulo's success leaves him utterly alone, a small-scale Kane in a third-world Xanadu. The film's final images, contrasting Paulo reflecting *alone* while his workers toil and sing *together*, imagistically underline his solitude.

The film develops a creative tension between sympathetic intimacy with Paulo and critical distance from him. The whole story is told from his point of view; virtually everything in the film is filtered through his consciousness; the facts are told as remembered by him; he in fact constructs the narration. When he tells us that he could not hear what Madalena and Padilha were saying, we as spectators do not hear it either. The film literalizes the idea that jealousy prevents Paulo from "hearing" Madalena; we see her speaking in close-up but do not hear her. Similarly, we hear Paulo's son crying but never see him, presumably illustrating the extent of Paulo's dehumanization since he does not even "see" his own child. Despite this systematic adherence to Paulo's point of view, however, we never really identify with him. We are constantly and subtly made to be critical of him. The close shots of his face do not subjectivize Paulo or make us identify with him, as they conventionally might. They confront us rather with the evidence of his anxiety. The film thus develops a confrontation between Paulo and the spectator, who is forced to reflect on how he or she might be like or unlike Paulo.

Much of *São Bernardo* consists of long, beautifully handled one-shot sequences, a technique appropriate to the meaning of the film. The generally static camera and the primacy of the one-shot sequence translates the immobility of the protagonist and leaves space for spectatorial reflection, at the same time that it creates a specifically cinematic equivalent to the spare, elliptical style of the novel. Often the shots continue after the "action" has stopped. When Paulo fires on his imaginary rivals, for example, the camera remains fixed on him and Madalena in bed. The film continues where most films would have stopped because the action has been completed. But in *São Bernardo*, reflection is as essential as the action.

The distancing dialectic of *São Bernardo* is cinematically realized in a number of ways. The cinematography alternates between abstraction (frontal angles, geometrically composed shots, fields ploughed in abstract patterns) and sensuality (lush colors, delicate backlighting, close attention to the textures of faces), thus creating a dialectic of sentiment and reason. Image also plays against sound. When the soundtrack is inactive, the camera begins to move or the editing becomes more rapid. When the image is static, the soundtrack becomes animated. The sound and words of one sequence often reverberate ironically backwards over the material of the preceding sequence. The sequence in which Paulo, pacing up and down in front of a church altar, contemplates marriage, is immediately followed by a sequence that opens with Padilha's words, "it's theft, that's what it is," and even though his words have a different context, we retrospectively apply them to the institution of marriage itself.

The cinematography of *São Bernardo* is never merely decorative. The exquisite long shots of the plantation, while beautiful, also inform us about the state of the crops, the progression of borders, the improvements in the property. Similarly, the music, consisting of Caetano Veloso's stylization of the work songs and vibrato style of the region in which the film is set, functions as a structuring device, an aid to reflection, rather than a merely agreeable "support" to the image.

São Bernardo (1972)

While *São Bernardo* on one level makes a universal statement about the relations between property and personality, on another it makes a very specific statement about Brazil. The property São Bernardo is a microcosm of Brazil, and although the story is set in the late twenties, its social and economic structures resemble those of Brazil in the early seventies. Hirszman himself has suggested, "Graciliano Ramos's novel is so rich that it surpasses its temporal limitations and reaches through to our days in its unveiling of the process of a man who gears himself toward capitalistic consolidation." Paulo reflects upon his own actions, and thus assumes a position of antithesis through which "the audience itself becomes aware of the general and social process, by force of which the character cannot become aware of himself and therefore lives his tragedy. This is a situation that could happen either in 1927 or in 1977."[3] Paulo, not unlike Brazil's military rulers at the time the film was made, comes to power through force and intimidation, bribery and murder. He practices arbitrary rule ("I don't have to explain anything to anybody!") and censorship (he rifles through Madalena's books and papers). Hysterically anti-communist and physically violent, he forms a kind of grotesque double of the military regime in Brazil. Furthermore, *São Bernardo* was made at a time when there was much talk in the international press of the Brazilian "economic miracle." The film exposes the miracle for what it was: a cruel deception. Paulo rises economically by a kind of miracle, but the miracle benefits only himself, just as the Brazilian economic miracle enriched an elite few at the expense of the oppressed majority. If *São Bernardo* is, as Leon Hirszman claims, a "concrete analysis of a concrete situation," the terms of its analysis can be extended from a plantation in the twenties to present day Brazil as a whole.

Finally, *São Bernardo* represents more than a simple return to the critical realism of early Cinema Novo. The self-reflexivity of its novelistic source, the distancing strategies of the film itself, and its microcosmic critique of contemporary Brazil make it politically and esthetically more advanced than the earlier films.

São Bernardo anatomizes the effects of acquisitiveness on the human personality, as well as the psychic violence and physical destruction that follow from the values by which its protagonist lives. It examines the social defects of what Hirszman calls "a kind of living fossil, an agent of the pre-history in which we are all living." *São Bernardo*, as a probing analysis of social alienation in which every image and sound is thought dialectically, without becoming either inaccessible or propagandistic, is a model political film.

Notes

1. See Antônio Cândido, *Ficção e Confissão* (Rio de Janeiro: José Olympio, 1956), pp. 25-37.
2. Luiz Costa Lima, "A Reificação de Paulo Honório," in *Por Que Literatura* (Petropolis: Vozes, 1966), pp. 51-72.
3. Quotation by Hirszman taken from MOMA notes, *Cineprobe*, 5 June 1978.

23
"Lesson of Love"

RANDAL JOHNSON

In 1962, during the ferment of the first years of Cinema Novo, the Swedish documentarist Arne Sucksdorf gave a six-month course on film-making in Rio de Janeiro's Museum of Modern Art. Among those who studied with Sucksdorf was Eduardo Escorel, whose first feature film, *Lição de Amor* ("Lesson of Love," 1975), was among the most highly praised films released in Brazil in 1976. Between 1962 and 1975 Escorel made several short films and established himself as the foremost editor in Brazilian cinema, working with many of the original participants of the Cinema Novo movement. Among the many films that he has edited are Glauber Rocha's *Land in Anguish* (1967) and *Antônio das Mortes* (1968), Carlos Diegues's *The Heirs* (1969) and *Joana Francesa* (1974), and Joaquim Pedro de Andrade's *Macunaíma* and *Os Inconfidentes* (1971).

Lição de Amor is based on the novel *Amar, Verbo Intransitivo* (written in 1924; published in 1927; translated into English as *Fraulein*), by Mário de Andrade, author of *Macunaíma* (1928). Set in São Paulo of the twenties, the film deals ostensibly with the sexual initiation of a sixteen-year-old boy by a German governess who has been hired by the boy's father, a wealthy landowner and incipient industrialist. In reality, it is a beautifully subtle analysis of the defense mechanisms of the bourgeoisie and of the reality that underlies the appearances of certain forms of bourgeois behavior. The director himself observes that "in the final analysis, it is a film about a repressive form of behavior, about a certain way of exercising repression."[1] It is a deliberately limited proposal, undertaking a low-

208

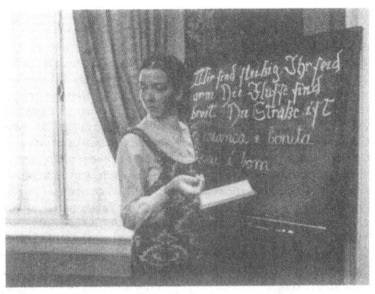

Lilian Lemmertz as Elza in *Lesson of Love* (1975)

key analysis of the most basic political unit, the family.

The novel on which it is based is anything but low-key. Midway in Mário de Andrade's text, there is a scene in which the adolescent Carlos, after much painful and awkward hesitation, finally embraces and kisses Elza, the German governess hired by Carlos's father to sexually initiate the boy. Carlos thinks to himself: "I wonder what those kisses in the movies taste like?" In the next paragraph, the constantly intervening narrator refers to the encounter between Elza and Carlos as a "filmic moment." These two successive references to cinema reveal at least two things: Mário de Andrade's own conception of his work as a cinematographic novel, and the self-reflexivity that characterizes the novel from beginning to end.

Amar, Verbo Intransitivo, characterized by its author as an idyll, is cinematographic primarily due to the segmentation of the narration in "sequences," without an apparent concern for continuity or smooth transitions between them. Such narrative fragmentation characterizes the novel's overall organization as well as its internal structuring of the flow of images. The novel consists of seventy-two rapidly changing scenes ranging from one line to some thirteen pages in length, as if each one were a filmic sequence. Many of the sequences themselves are partially composed of rapid successions of disparate and often unexpected images, as if each image were but one shot in a larger sequence.

In reality, *Amar, Verbo Intransitivo* is cinematographic more through the author's desire for it to be so than because of any profound, inherent affinity with cinema itself. We cannot in truth say that the fragmentation of a novel into episodes or scenes is a technique that began only with the advent of cinema. The principal link between this novel and film are Mário de Andrade's continued references to cinema. As one of the leading figures in the Brazilian Modernist Movement, Mário was concerned that his art be in tune with the modern world, and by the time he wrote the novel in 1924, cinema was well on its way to establishing itself as one of the major art forms of the twentieth century. Many participants in the Modernist Movement reflected an interest in cinema. Both Guilherme de Almeida and Menotti del Picchia later became film critics for São Paulo newspapers, and Menotti even made several films. In *Amar, Verbo Intransitivo*, Mário de Andrade reveals an awareness of the tremendous psychological and social influences exerted by cinema when, toward the end of the story, the narrator suggests that Carlos recovered quickly from the blow of losing Elza through the helpful influence of Tom Mix!

The novel's self-reflexivity reveals the influence of Machado de Assis, especially the Machado of *Memórias Póstumas de Brás Cubas* ("Epitaph of a Small Winner"). Among the many metalinguistic techniques used by Mário de Andrade are the detailed commentaries concerning the process of the narrative's construction, the constant analysis of the narrator's own attitude toward the language used, the all-too-frequent narrator interventions to comment on the action, to converse with and allude to the fictitious public posited as creative readers, and to defend the narrative solutions employed in the work, and, finally, the long expository digressions that explain psychological motivations and reactions not obvious in the narrative itself.

The so-called cinematographic aspects, the self-reflexivity, the apparently free and fragmented narrative structure, the novel's false ending, and the changing narrative perspective, characterized especially by the use of a free indirect discourse that approaches stream-of-consciousness techniques, are all elements that the Modernists of the twenties considered to be the great novelties of modern literature. They represent attempts to break away from the realist, linear structures of the nineteenth-century novel and may indeed be called typically Modernist solutions to the problems of narrativity.

Rather than try to maintain these Modernist solutions in his adaptation of the novel, however, Eduardo Escorel did just the opposite. He, in a sense, "de-cinematized" the novel, creating an historical link not with the self-reflexivity of *Memórias Póstumas de Brás Cubas*, but rather with the elegant sophistication of Machado de Assis's masterpiece, *Dom Casmurro*. Rather than use an intervening narrator and a free narrative structure, Escorel opted for a classical, linear narrative that turns attention away from the process of artistic construction and toward the interrelationships that develop between members of a family enclosed within a limited space. He eliminated all of those elements that in the twenties were considered to be the great "novelties" of cinema and Modernist literature. His rationale for doing so is very simply that fifty years of cinema have led to the exhaustion of such techniques. In Escorel's words, "the challenge that is before those who make films today is one of rediscovering cinema through a return to certain things that are already stratified, a classical narrative, and through this narrative set out toward a new discovery. The avant-garde solutions of the twenties seem to have arrived at a limit beyond which one cannot go without paying the price of destroying cinema."[2] The director is quick to add that he already has such avant-garde experience in the editing of Glauber Rocha's *Severed Heads* and *The Lion Has Seven Heads*, both of which were made during Rocha's self-exile from Brazil. The result of Escorel's strategy is an elegant film that is rich in ambiguity and is infinitely more subtle and low-key than the novel on which it is based. One São Paulo critic has referred to the film as a "de-complicated" Mário de Andrade.

In a pre-credit sequence, landowner-industrialist Sousa Costa (Rogério Froes) finalizes his deal with Elza (Lilian Lemmertz), assuring her that his wife, Dona Laura (Irene Ravache), knows of his intentions (she does not). Elza will ostensibly serve as governess, teaching piano and giving German lessons to Carlos (Marcos Taquechel) and his two younger sisters. In reality, her function is to give Carlos a "lesson of love" in the safe and apparently favorable atmosphere of their bourgeois home. Sousa Costa wants to protect his son from the outside world, which he sees as dangerous, uncontrollable, and above all threatening to the privileged, yet isolated, world he has created for his family. He himself is well aware of the "dangers" of the outside world, for his nocturnal forays reveal his own hypocrisy and double standard. As one Brazilian critic puts it, Sousa Costa creates the conditions for a "camouflaged process of consented

Lesson of Love (1975)

decadence" within the walls of his own home.[3]

Elza goes about her task with extreme dignity, momentarily interrupted only when Dona Laura begins to suspect her real intentions, and the governess learns that Sousa Costa had not informed his wife of her function. Dona Laura, normally silent and stoic, is, along with Carlos and Elza, a victim of the repression of patriarchal society. After Sousa Costa assuages his wife's fears by exaggerating the possible dangers of letting nature take its own course, Elza is allowed to finish her assignment. One night, while Carlos is in Elza's bedroom, Sousa Costa feigns discovery of this "outrage" and sends the governess away as planned. Carlos will soon recover from the loss, but Elza, who inevitably mixes her emotions with her professional role, is the real loser. Her lesson of "pure, sincere love, the intelligent union of two people based on mutual understanding" clashes with the repressive pedagogical process forced on Carlos by his father. For Sousa Costa, with his mercantilist perspective, Elza is no more than another commodity, a hired prostitute, and his family is something to be controlled and dominated at all costs. Elza's conception of her role thus clashes as well with Sousa Costa's view of her, and she cannot help but believe, at least to an extent, that he may be right. Her apparently noble goals are debased by the paid relationship itself.

The filmmaker thus retains what might be called the backbone of the novel's narrative. The entire story, with two brief exceptions, takes place within the walls of the Sousa Costa home. Escorel thus creates a closed universe that permits a more abstract analysis than would a more "faithful" adaptation of the novel. In *Amar, Verbo Intransitivo*, Mário de Andrade satirized the bourgeoisie of his own time. His satire was to be much more aggressive and grotesque in *Macunaíma*, which was filmed by Joaquim Pedro de Andrade in 1969. *Lição de Amor* is not so much a satire of São Paulo's bourgeoisie of the twenties—especially since such a satire would mean little to today's film audience—as it is a subtle analysis, on the family level, of the bourgeoisie as an historically dominant class, an analysis rare in Brazilian cinema, where the bourgeoisie is commonly dealt with only in its superficial aspects. By focusing attention on the "outsider" Elza, on the relationships between family members and on breaks in the idyllic harmony of the family's universe, the director is able to see through the surface appearances of bourgeois behavior to the motivating reality underlying it. To this end, the director also eliminated many of Mário de Andrade's long expositions dealing with the two faces of the German race and the differences between Europeans and Brazilians, although such an element is suggested in Elza's constant dissatisfaction as she tries to earn enough money to return to Germany. In other instances, Escorel found specifically cinematic equivalents for aspects of the novel he considered relevant to modern Brazilian audiences. He thus transmits through the suggestion of facial expression, gestures, scenography (by Anísio Medeiros), and spatial relationships what Mário de Andrade transmitted through his expository digressions.

Lição de Amor is a very well balanced, almost symmetrical film. It begins with Elza's arrival at the Sousa Costa home and ends with her departure. The first and last shots of the image track per se (post-credits) show Elza in her taxi with the Sousa Costa home in the background. The film is thus circular in terms of its overall composition. The center of the story, Carlos's sexual initiation, is not shown in the film, which is thus constructed around an absent narrative core. Such a tactic is justifiable initially since the scene is not described in Mário de Andrade's original version either. The narrator intervenes at that point and tells the reader about the relationship between Elza and the Japanese servant, Tanaka. In the film, the director cuts at that moment to the foot of Carlos's parents' bed. The idea of not showing Carlos's sexual initiation is not, however, merely an attempt to be faithful to the novel. Referring to this aspect of the film, Escorel explains that within the context of much current Brazilian film production, where this type of theme is dealt with in an extremely degrading and disrespectful manner (and he refers specifically to the erotic comedies that make up much of Brazilian cinema today), the idea of constructing the film around something that is not shown was both a narrative challenge and a way of thwarting the spectator's voyeurism.[4] When the film cuts to the foot of Carlos's parents' bed, the audience still believes that it will see what happens between Elza and Carlos. The camera then pans to show Sousa Costa and his wife, Dona Laura, thus directing attention away from Carlos's sexual initiation, which is not really the most important aspect of the film, and toward his parents and the role they are playing in the narrative situation. The structuring absence of the story's core serves as a starting point from which many elements explicit in the novel are suggested discreetly in the film.

The narrative is constructed around its absent center through scenes that are repeated in almost mirror fashion, modifying their original intent with each repetition. Carlos's sexual initiation is enclosed by two shots of him in the shower. The first time he is bathing after having masturbated; the second time after having his first sexual relation with Elza. The first bath is thus a guilty one; the second, innocent or joyous. The film's development is accompanied by the progressive competence of the performance of Mozart's "Turkish March," which Elza is teaching one of Carlos's sisters to play. Near the beginning of the film it is poorly played. Later it is played more satisfactorily, and toward the end of the film it is well played. The final version of the march coincides with a shot of the family posed formally for a photograph. At this moment, the film reaches a point of stability: the march is well played, Elza has completed her mission, and the family is united and posed formally. This stability occurs immediately prior to the final rupture in which Sousa Costa pretends to discover his son's relationship with Elza and sends her away.

Throughout the film there is a disjunction between surface appearance and underlying reality. Nothing is quite what it seems. Carlos, for example, appears to be an innocent adolescent discovering the pleasure of his sexuality for the first time. In reality, he has already been sexually initiated — by a prostitute in São Paulo's red-light district. Elza seems to be a cold professional, interested only in her payment, but she cannot help getting at least somewhat emotionally involved with Carlos. Carlos's sisters, for their part, seem to be blissfully ignorant of Elza's true function, but shots of broken dolls and of one of them tearing a butterfly apart reveal their own bitterness and frustration. The parents recognize Carlos's physical needs, but are incapable of seeing that their daughter might have similar needs. But Sousa Costa, not Carlos or Elza, is the key figure in the film. He provokes, motivates, and, to a certain extent, guides the narrative's action. On the surface it seems that he is a very modern and understanding father, offering his son sexual initiation in a favorable and safe environment. In reality, he is exerting an extremely castrating authority over his son in order to protect the private world that he has created within the walls of his house and, by extension, to protect the continuation of his economic interests. His family relationships are based on the oppression and hypocrisy that derive from his mercantilist mentality. The disjunction between appearance and reality, as well as the ultimate fragmentary nature of Sousa Costa's bourgeois world, is represented visually through a number of shots in which doorways or other physical objects split the screen, each side presenting one facet of the situation, and by repeated shots of staircases that serve as metaphors of isolation and fragmentation.

Like many of Machado de Assis's works, *Lição de Amor* has been accused by its critics of not being Brazilian. One American critic has gone so far as to say that the film might as well take place on the North Pole

Lesson of Love (1975)

since it is so divorced from Brazilian reality. The film's central narrative situation, however, is firmly rooted in Brazilian culture, going as far back as the colonial period when masters slept with their slave women and continuing to the present when modern-day masters frequently take sexual advantage of their maids. The film has also been criticized in Brazil precisely because it is well made, sure of itself, balanced, and patient. Such criticism reflects, according to Escorel, a "conception that the Brazilian film must not only show misery but must also be miserable. It must be poorly made, poorly photographed, out of focus. It was often said that 'the film is so well made that it doesn't seem Brazilian.' So, if it's well made and doesn't seem Brazilian, then it's poorly made. A strange equation."[5] The scenography of *Lição de Amor*, designed by Anísio Medeiros, is one of the most exquisite historical re-creations in the history of Brazilian cinema. With music by Francis Hime, the film's discretion, subtlety, and restraint represent a high point in recent cinematic production in that country. Eduardo Escorel provides not only a "lesson of love," but also a lesson of cinema for Brazilian audiences.

Notes

1. From an unpublished interview with Eduardo Escorel, recorded in New York in October, 1977.
2. Ibid.
3. Orlando L. Fassoni, *Folha de São Paulo*, reprinted in "Dossiê Crítico: *Lição de Amor*," *Filme Cultura* 29 (May 1978): 96.
4. Unpublished interview with Eduardo Escorel.
5. Ibid.

24
"Carnivalesque Celebration in *Xica da Silva*"

RANDAL JOHNSON

Cinema is not the reproduction of reality. It implies the creation of a parallel, alternative and verisimilar universe. This verisimilitude nourishes itself more on the spirit and ideology of the spectators than on their daily experience.

—Carlos Diegues

Carlos Diegues refers to his sixth feature film, *Xica da Silva* (1976), as a "multi-colored glass butterfly resting on the solemn wall of a colonial church."[1] The image is appropriate, for the film is a dynamic, colorful, noisy, playful celebration of a little-known historical figure made in a political context that perhaps gives less cause for joy and commemoration. It is an ode to the creative spontaneity of the Brazilian people, a spirit that, the director suggests, transcends any specific political situation. It reflects a renewed optimism and faith in the vitality of the Brazilian people in the process of liberation. The film's popular reception in Brazilian was enormous. It was seen by over 8,000,000 spectators in its first two and a half months of exhibition. It was equally well received by popular critics. The film is not, however, without its detractors, who base their critique on political problems they see as inherent to the film. Such diverse reactions derive, ultimately, from the ambivalence of the film's very conception: a comedy about slavery, a defense of the irrational set in a political context, a historical reconstruction in which fantasy and myth are more important than historical accuracy.

Xica da Silva is a fictional re-creation of events that occurred in the state of Minas Gerais in eighteenth-century colonial Brazil. Like Diegues's first feature, *Ganga Zumba* (1963), it deals with slavery and the possibility of freedom. In the second half of the eighteenth century, the Portuguese crown inaugurated a system of contracts for the extraction of diamonds and other precious stones from the rich mineral areas of Brazil's interior. Such contracts guaranteed a monopoly for a Portuguese capitalist of the King's choosing. The most famous of the successive holders of contracts for diamond extraction was João Fernandes de Oliveira, who first obtained his contract in 1739. João Fernandes implanted modern, efficient (if corrupt) systems of extraction, discovered rich new beds of precious stones, and accumulated a wealth approaching that of the Crown itself. His wealth and power were soon seen as threatening to the Crown, and he was forced to return to Lisbon in 1773. While in Brazil, João Fernandes took as his lover the slave woman Francisca (Xica) da Silva, freed her, and made her into one of the most powerful people in the state of Minas Gerais. For several years, until João Fernandes's downfall, Xica da Silva literally dominated the politics, economics, and fashion of the region. Her rise to power and frequent extravagant and vindictive behavior—in retaliation for humiliations suffered while a slave—scandalized the bourgeoisie of the diamond-mining region as well as the Portuguese court. Very little is known about Xica da Silva since after her fall the people of Diamantina (then Arraial de Tijuco) undertook a virtual exorcism, burning most documents concerning her. The myths surrounding Xica and her love of freedom are the bases of Carlos Diegues's film. If *Ganga Zumba* was a story of the love of freedom, *Xica da Silva*, observes Diegues, is about the possibility of freedom through love.

The film's first sequence develops the political space through which the story's major contradictions are worked out. In a rather bucolic scene shot in soft focus, João Fernandes (played superbly by Walmor Chagas), travelling to Tijuco to assume his position as contractor, stops along the road and plays flute with a couple of itinerate musicians. The European music is strangely out of place in the rugged interior of Brazil, and a major opposition develops: the incongruous refinement and "solemnity"[2] of European culture contrasted with the "primitive," yet authentic, vitality of Brazilian things. The musicians comment upon the economic and political situation of the region until they realize with whom they are speaking. One of them then looks directly at the camera and says, excusing himself: "Artists shouldn't be involved in politics, isn't that right?" Such a statement is certainly reflective of the dominant ideology's posi-

Zezé Motta as Xica da Silva

tion, here in the figure of João Fernandes, but is certainly not reflective of Carlos Diegues's viewpoint. The director himself suggests that *Xica da Silva* is perhaps even more political than some of his earlier films (e.g., *Ganga Zumba*) since it is a reflection on the nature of power and how one enters the different arenas of power. The film is political, albeit not in the traditional sense of political cinema. A rigid political analysis fails to account for the film's originality and vitality. In it the existing political, economic, and moral hierarchies are upended in ribald fashion by the exuberant and quick-witted Xica. The film's politics are of festive, carnivalesque commemoration.

During medieval folk festivals and carnivals, from which the carnivalesque derives, existing social hierarchies were abolished, there was no distance between actors and spectators; participants led, so to speak, a second life, free from the rules and restrictions of official cultural life (i.e., the restrictions imposed by the dominant ideology). According to Russian scholar Mikhail Bakhtin, the people achieved a temporary liberation from the established order through the suspension of hierachical rank. The carnival spirit "offers the chance to have a new outlook on the world, to realize the relative nature of all that exists, and to enter a completely new order of things."[3] In the carnivalesque, a material bodily principle, especially of the body's "lower stratum" (including eating, drinking, copulation, defecation, and other bodily functions) prevails as a positive force. Folk laughter, another important element in the carnivalesque, represents universalism (communication between all people without regard to social rank), freedom, and the people's unofficial truth (as opposed to the "official" truth of the socially dominant classes). Such laughter "presents an element of victory not only over supernatural awe, over the sacred, over death; it also means the defeat of power, of earthly kings, of the earthly upper classes, of all that oppresses and restricts."[4] In Diegues's film, Xica da Silva participates in a profoundly carnivalesque attitude toward the world.

Xica (Zezé Motta), a slave belonging to Arraial de Tijuco's master sergeant, appears before João Fernandes's arrival in the town. She is first seen sitting on the ground of the courtyard of her master's house and is soon interrupted by the sergeant's son, José, who later runs off to Vila Rica, the capital of the region, to join a rebellion against colonial rule. The rebellion, which is not seen but merely mentioned in the film, is an obvious reference to the "Inconfidência," an unsuccessful revolt that took place in the eighteenth century. José, like his father, takes sexual advantage of Xica, who is portrayed as having certain unrevealed sexual abilities that make her unique in the region. Her rise to power is based precisely on her sexual prowess. While such a characterization may be sexist in the light of modern feminist ideology, it is also typical of the carnivalesque, since copulation is a major element of the material bodily principle.

The film deals with Xica's rise to power, her vindictiveness and extravagance while in power, and her subsequent fall from power. She is an object of the desire of the most important men in the village, including the intendent (the holder of civilian power) and, finally, the contractor himself. She first attracts João Fernandes's attention, which leads to his purchase of her from the master sergeant, through the premeditated exposure of her body as the contractor is meeting with the intendent and the master sergeant. Soon after buying Xica, João Fernandes's other slaves comment wryly that he has become her sexual slave. Social hierarchies are thus comically overturned through Xica's frontal, festive attack on the ruling classes' solemnity. Diegues's apparent rationale in this characterization of Xica is that as a slave she has no possessions except her own body, and throughout most of the film she exercises control over it. Thus, in addition to being an object of the desire of the most powerful men in the village, she is also an acting subject in relationship to them. There are many indications that she, not her partners, controls and determines the sexual relationships she maintains. Even though she has no economic, military, or political power, she exercises the power of Eros, erotic power.

As Xica ascends, rumors abound of her strange behavior, both in the mining district and in Lisbon. While she pretends to enjoy herself on her private sailing ship (built by João Fernandes after she complained of having never seen the sea; the ship can only be used by blacks—no whites allowed except as musicians and servants—another social inversion), we learn that José, who had earlier left for Vila Rica, has been accused of subversion against the colonial regime and is now hiding in a local monastery for black monks. We also learn that a dam built by João Fernandes to aid in the extraction of diamonds has burst and killed many workers. The contractor had been warned of such a danger earlier but obviously preferred profit to safety and failed to heed the warnings. The intendent's wife—a pale, whiny, petty woman—begins to conspire against Xica out of jealousy and overt racism.

Shortly thereafter, a pompous revenue agent—with the equally pompous name of José Luis de Menezes Abrantes Castelo Branco de Noronha, the count of Valadares—arrives from Lisbon to inspect João Fernandes's management of the diamond extraction business and to investigate reports of Xica's behavior. He and Xica have an immediate, mutual dislike and distrust of each other. He makes racist jokes about her color saying that things should be cleared up (in Portuguese, the word for "clear," *claro*, also means "light colored"). Xica reacts in high carnivalesque fashion by wearing white-face makeup to dinner and suggesting that the count not eat the chicken with "brown sauce." The count, dressed in European finery and an absurd white wig, is totally out of place in tropical Brazil and constantly refers to the primitive and strange customs he witnesses. Yet as has been the case throughout Brazilian history, those who hold the most power over the local population have the least in common with that population.

Realizing the danger the count represents to João Fernandes, Xica tries to enlist the bandit Teodoro in an effort to organize an army to protect the contractor. Rather than convincing him (through her sexual "favors") to organize an army, she instead unknowingly leads the count's militia to Teodoro's hiding place. Teodoro is captured and tortured. When João Fernandes tries to stop the torture, the count tells him that "you have to decide once and for all which side you're on." He decides to remain loyal to the colonial regime. Xica's venture into the traditional political realm thus ends in failure and, ultimately, in her fall.

Xica makes one last attempt to convince the count to go back to Lisbon and leave the situation as it is: she prepares an exotic African banquet ("More picturesque-ness," responds the count) and performs a sensual dance to seduce him. The seduction succeeds, but the scheme fails, and the next morning the count publicly reads the decree that João Fernandes has been recalled to Lisbon. It is at this point that the true limits of Xica's erotic power are revealed. After João Fernandes rides off, the townspeople turn on her, and some of the boys begin to stone her.

She does, however, have one last chance. She flees the town and goes to the monastery where the rebel José has been hiding. She feels that her life is over and that she is nobody once again. José tries to convince her that she herself is life and that they together will show "that this country is not made up only of weaklings. We're going to get out of this together and piss on the king and his followers." Xica then begins to feel dizzy (a common occurrence when she becomes sexually excited) and chases José up the stairs of the monastery to make love with him. The film ends with a replay of shots of Xica going happily to the church carrying in her hand the papers granting her freedom. She thus reverts to her previous car-

Xica da Silva (1976)

nivalesque attitude toward the world.

The importance of Xica's trajectory from slave, to powerful free woman, to social outcast rests on the contrast that she represents to the rigidity of the representations of the ruling class. She disrupts their corrupt political machinations and their social rituals. She parodies and ridicules their staid yet hypocritical behavior. She creates an alternative "second life" for those who are repressed by the ruling classes. She enters the "official" strata of power only to subvert it through what Bakhtin might call her "gay relativity." She ridicules the hypocrisy of the church and even suggests that it be painted black. She takes public and hilarious revenge of those who had earlier humiliated her.

Many critics failed to recognize the profoundly liberating character of Xica's carnivalization of social relationships. Some claim that the film deals in cultural and racial stereotypes: the black woman with some sort of unspecified, yet extraordinary, sexual capabilities, the slave who aspires to whiteness, imitating the values of the oppressor, the woman who reacts emotionally to people and events, the oppressed who, on becoming free, becomes an oppressor. Xica da Silva is described as a "sexual opportunist," and the film is criticized for not developing fully another ostensibly viable alternative for oppressed slaves in colonial Brazil: the *quilombo*, or communities of escaped slaves, the most famous of which was the Republic of Palmares, dealt with by the director in *Ganga Zumba*. Such an alternative is suggested in the figure of Teodoro, but in reality he is never described as an escaped slave. He is portrayed throughout as a freeman who is successful in competing with João Fernandes, albeit illegally, in the extraction of diamonds. Finally, Diegues is accused of not being historically accurate, a strange accusation considering the dearth of historical material concerning his subject.[5]

While these criticisms may be valid from a rigorous political perspective, it cannot be truthfully said that Xica is portrayed only in a negative fashion. Although she does briefly become a petty, vindictive tyrant who functions emotionally, she is also a dynamic, creative, personable, and quick-witted woman who exudes tremendous vitality and energy. In this sense she is a very positive figure, even though the path she chooses for her own liberation is fraught with contradiction. By following her trajectory throughout the film, Diegues attempts to demystify her chosen path. The people will not achieve liberation by depending on the ruling classes, but rather must depend primarily on themselves.

Brazilian anthropologist Roberto da Matta suggests that relationships of power must be seen in relative terms.[6] The ruling classes attempt to find ways to control the masses and yet have them content enough to avoid revolts. There are several levels of power evident in the film: military power (the sergeant), civilian power (the intendent), spiritual power (the priest) and economic power (João Fernandes and, later, the count). Matta points out that it is exactly when the holder of economic power is asserting himself that Xica da Silva enters into action to change her situation in life. Through the premeditated exposure of her body (disrupting an "official" discussion among the holders of power), Xica manages to align herself with the most powerful man in the village, most powerful since he is closest to the seat of power, the Portuguese court. She is a slave who is aware of the value of her body, the only thing she possesses. Matta also points out that it is precisely João Fernandes who feels most strongly the contradiction between individual rights and authoritarianism since it is he who must reconcile his personal enrichment with that of the crown. In his freedom of economic movement, in opposition to the desires of the crown, João Fernandes creates a link with the bandit Teodoro. The conflict comes to a peak when he has to decide whether or not to link with Teodoro in the formation of an army to fight the count. He of course rejects such a possibility.

Xica herself does not enter the spheres of power through political knowledge and action, as does the rebel José, but rather through the use of her body. If José has an intellectual, political knowledge of Brazil, Xica has a *practice* of Brazil. Matta suggests that she is a repressed individual in political terms, but at the same time is remarkably free in terms of her own carnivalesque sensuality and sexuality. He observes that Xica has "the power, in short of giving pleasure, joy and strength" to those with whom she relates [*sic*]. That is her most powerful weapon. The politically powerful men she deals with exercise the power of the strong; Xica the power of the weak. Her power is carnivalesque since it results in the leveling of social forces and hierarchies. By herself, however, she is unable to consolidate such an inversion and make it lasting. That is where José comes in. The link between José and Xica is meant to show that Xica's "magic vitality" alone is not enough; such vitality must be linked to the

Marcus Vinicius (Teodoro) and Zezé Motta in *Xica da Silva* (1976)

politics of revolution, which revolts not against people, as does Xica, but against the oppressive and mystifying institutions of colonial rule. It is Xica who shows us the road to *practice*, it is she who is victorious in the end as José himself expresses in carnivalesque terms ("piss on the king") a future program of action.

Although the portrayal of Xica as a sexual creature does have racist overtones, there is also, to Diegues's credit, a critique of racism throughout. Racism pervades the power structure pictured in the film, especially the church and the representatives of the Portuguese Crown. The intendent's wife is perhaps the most petty incarnation of racism in the film. Lily white, she feels threatened by Xica's vitality and ascent. Although many critics have been troubled by Diegues' comic treatment of slavery, the careful observer will notice that as João Fernandes rides into town he passes a slave in chains. When he rides out, the slave is still chained in the same position. *That* is the reality of slavery in Brazil. Xica's link with the ruling classes has changed nothing. *One* slave (Xica herself) has been liberated. The film's ending, though offering no concrete solutions, opens to the possibility of other forms of social and political transformation.

The film often evokes political struggle through cultural differentiation. The director develops this struggle through an opposition between the stodginess of alien European culture (i.e., "official" culture) and the vitality of Brazilian popular culture (the people's "unofficial" truth). Through the valorization of dance, music, and cuisine, the film inverts the existing social and economic hierarchies. Banquet images are typical of the carnivalesque, and in the tropical banquet that she offers the count, Xica ridicules his greed and hypocrisy. As Xica ascends, she becomes increasingly alienated from her own culture, even to the point of ordering other slaves to desist with the "noise" of their highly rhythmic, percussion-based music. Only after her fall from the "graces" of official culture is she restored to the fulness of her previous self. The situation is once again inverted, and Xica can begin a life anew with José.

Perhaps the most important and salutary aspect of *Xica da Silva* is the debate that it has helped spark concerning the nature and role of the "popular" in Brazilian cinema. Not only has the responsibility of filmmakers vis-à-vis popular culture come into question, but also the role of film criticism has been fiercely debated. Diegues is opposed to what he calls "ideological patrols," i.e., certain sectors of left criticism which reject any manifestation of artistic expression that does not follow narrow, orthodox ideological prescriptions. Diegues feels that Brazilian cinema will only be a strong cinema when filmmakers of all tendencies have the freedom to explore and develop myriad themes in a multiplicity of styles. In this sense, *Xica da Silva*, with it carnivalistic celebration of a heretofore little-known historical figure, is indeed a landmark film for Brazilian cinema.

Notes

1. "Nota Introdutória," in João Felício dos Santos, *Xica da Silva* (Rio de Janeiro: Civilização Brasileira, 1976): xv.
2. The idea of Xica's disruption of official solemnity is developed by Brazilian critic José Carlos Avellar in "Uma Grande Festa," *Filme Cultura* 29 (May 1978): 89-92.
3. Mikhail Bakhtin, *Rabelais and His World*, trans. Helene Iswolsky (Cambridge: M.I.T. Press, 1968), p. 34.
4. Ibid., 92.
5. All of these critiques are from a series of articles published in *Opinião*, 15 October 1976.
6. Matta's article, "A Hierarquia do Poder dos Fracos," is in *Opinião* 15 October 1976.

25

"*Tent of Miracles*"

MARSHA KINDER

Nelson Pereira dos Santos's *Tent of Miracles* (1977) is one of a rare breed — a brilliant political film that succeeds in raising the consciousness of its audience and yet is thoroughly enjoyable to watch. Its appeal is multi-dimentional — it confronts us directly with *ideology*, moves us with its narrative through a wide range of emotions, amuses us with satire, both blatant and subtle, dazzles us with visuals, stirs us with sambas, baffles us with magic, catches us in stereotyped responses, and demystifies the Brazilian social structure. The film develops a consciousness that is painfully aware of the pervasive injustice, corruption, and hype and yet, instead of righteously denouncing all characters who are in any way tainted with these vices or cynically rejecting all values and efforts because they are limited, it powerfully affirms human life and perceptively evaluates various positive steps that can be taken to build a better world. Its comprehensive social analysis is combined with a comic tolerance and penetrating humanism that are reminiscent of Renoir.

Although *Tent of Miracles* is primarily focused on racial issues (most particularly, the struggle to retain Brazil's African heritage), it masterfully blends them with sexual politics on at least three levels. The film explicitly identifies sex as an ideological weapon — for the primary position of its hero Pedro Archanjo is that racial crossbreeding is the best way to solve Brazil's political problems. Narratively, visually, and musically, it celebrates sexual vitality as a major national resource, particularly as it is embodied in Archanjo, who couples with women of all colors, and Ana

Tent of Miracles (1977)

Mercedes, a fiery mulatta who is called the best living example of Ar chanjo's theory. More implicitly, the film explores sexual stereotypes, frequently making visual contrasts between males and females in the same situation and narratively linking the dynamics of sexism and racism. At every level of style and content, the film reaffirms crossbreeding — in its characterizations, its mixture of conventions and tones, its highly varied music that ranges from African drums and hot sambas to ponderous operatic arias, and its openness to every combination — of ideology and instinct, logic and magic, materialism and music, dogma and dance.

Although the story adapts a novel by Jorge Amado, the structure of the film is reminiscent of *Citizen Kane*. The first scene with Archanjo, set in the forties, shows us how he dies. The rest of the film tries to explain who he was, incorporating multiple contradictory perspectives. The search is led by a man working for a newspaper, who eventually makes a movie about "the great man." At the end we are left with the sense that the full truth about him lies far beyond the consciousness of both his friends and his biographers. In adapting it to his Brazilian subject Nelson Pereira dos Santos politicizes his structure. Unlike Welles's hero Kane/Hearst, Pedro Archanjo is not great, powerful, or infamous in a conventional sense. Rather, he is an obscure sociologist-philosopher without degrees — a skinny, plain featured, toffee-colored mulatto who does not look like a hero. The problem in *Tent of Miracles* is how to make this man, who is an anti-hero by conventional standards because he is poor, black, unknown, unambitious, and ordinary looking, into a popular hero of a commercial film that can be successfully sold and distributed within a capitalist society. His true extraordinary qualities—intelligence, originality, courage, openness, flexibility—unfortunately won't help much. This marketing miracle is accomplished through a frame story, in which poet Fausto Pena makes a film about Archanjo. This frame is not just another fashionable example of self-reflexiveness, but is used very cleverly to raise the political consciousness of the filmmakers and their audience.

The stories of Archanjo the scientist and Pena the artist make the same political point because they grow out of the same society that is dominated by the same forces. Brazilians are ashamed of their culture and want to pretend they are white. Thus, the intellectual elite never heard of Archanjo until he is mentioned in an interview by a white Nobel Prize winner named Dr. Livingstone—an American anthropologist from Columbia University, whose handsome appearance (a masculine pipe jutting out of a well-trimmed blond beard and a muscular build in well-fitted tweeds) immediately qualifies him as a scientist/hero. Although this blue-eyed devil speaks with a comic nasal inflection that establishes him as a fool, he nevertheless utters the truth—viz., that Archanjo is an important philosopher, that it's absurd that Brazilians have never heard of him, that Ana Mercedes is living proof that he was right. Despite the fact that his anthropological training has theoretically enabled him to avoid ethnocentrism, he behaves more like his missionary namesake. Livingstone turns out to be a hateful gringo who callously exploits the Brazilians he supposedly admires, turning Ana Mercedes into his whore and Pena, her fiancé, into his flunky research assistant, the same subservient role that Archanjo was forced to play at the University. Because appearances may or may not be deceiving (the magnetic beauty of Ana Mercedes is authentic while Dr. Livingstone's is all "frosting," yet the unheroic ordinariness of Pena and Archanjo is misleading in both cases) and because of the contradictory nature of what we are told (that Ana Mercedes is a whore, a glittering idiot, and the best example of cross-breeding; that Pena is a celebrated poet, a cowardly cuckold, and a reactionary fool who prostitutes his talent; that Livingstone is a Nobel Prize winner and stupid gringo; that Archanjo is the greatest scientist in the world and a powerful magician/priest, an irresponsible gambler and a glamorous black stud), we are forced to take a critical attitude toward everything we see and hear and to actively evaluate these characters for ourselves.

The first question raised by the film is: who is the Hero or what is the central focus? The images behind the opening titles introduce the key polarities that lie in the film's historical background; we see a progression of still photographs of Brazilian ancestors contrasting European masters and African slaves, men and women, black and white and color. Then we are exposed to the material reality of the film medium—a ribbon of celluloid moving through an editing machine. Finally, we meet our first candidate for protagonist; Fausto Pena sits at the editing table, clearly in control while watching footage of his film on Archanjo with his assistant named Dada, who functions like an audience. Deep in the background we glimpse Ana Mercedes, who can be seen either as a muse or distraction, but in either case, like most women in conventional movies, she seems to be playing a subordinate role. Dada explicitly tells us that Pena could pass more readily for a hero than his subject Archanjo. But both agree that the one who really looks the part is Dr. Livingstone, who stars in the first footage we see from the inner film. The scene is a press conference where the American first informs both the Brazilians and us in the audience that Pedro Archanjo is the authentic hero both for the society and for the film. At the press conference, Pena and Ana Mercedes are part of the audience. When Ana Mercedes immediately rushes forward to Livingstone like a groupie, another woman calls her a whore and Pena retreats in shame. On one level, of course, the charge is just. Ana Mercedes trades her body for an exclusive interview with the scientist, but it turns out he is more interested in photographing her like a rare species of animal and she is the one with the stronger sexual desire. Pena perceives what is happening but lets the gringo sleep with his fiancée in exchange for a job. While at first he might appear to be acting as a pimp, from another perspective it is actually Ana Mercedes who is pimping for Pena, whose writing talents are being bought. The film forces us to see the complicity of all its characters while still recognizing their values: the gringo speaks the truth and supports Archanjo's political ideas; Ana Mercedes is more sexually liberated and honest than the men around her; Pena grows as an artist in the process of making his film.

All of these characters are measured against Archanjo, who emerges as the Super Protean hero capable of many transformations — philosopher, priest, scientist, magician, drunkard, stud, gambler, godfather, journalist, brawler, anthropologist. He is the rebellious *Archangel* who succeeds in fighting fascist tyranny at all levels of society — from the university faculty to Hitler's Third Reich. He celebrates crossbreeding because it produces strong individuals who can "master despair and misery by being creative in daily life." Extraordinary creatures like Archanjo, who can absorb and in some sense transcend ideology and still remain open to other individuals and cultures. In contrast to the courageous Marxist professor who defends our hero at the Academy, Archanjo has lost his faith but not his spirit for he insists on loving the people instead of dogma. Within him he carries the sound of the drums just as the Marxist carries his books. Hence, Archanjo can function as a priest without being restricted by religious doctrines; he has a sincere passion for the ceremonies and rituals, which he uses in his political struggles. Just as he is both black and white, Archanjo is capable of holding two contradictory theories at the same time; he tries to retain the tribal practices and spiritual power of his African heritage and to unify them with Western rationalism and science. He warns his Marxist friend that his rigid materialism might transform him into a policeman or fascist. Although the Marxist retains his radical ideas and humanistic instincts, he begins to lose his courage when his social position rises and he has more to risk. But as Pena emphasizes, since Archanjo's identity is never fixed in any one social role or persona,

Juarez Paraiso (Pedro Arcanjo) and Janete Ribeiro in *Tent of Miracles* (1977)

he remains true to his ideas and courageously stands up at the key moments of crisis throughout his life. Although *Tent of Miracles* succeeds in selling Archanjo as a mythic hero, the film simultaneously demystifies the process of myth-building by showing its corruption. We can all readily scoff at the commercial for a male deodorant called "Fresh Black," the essay contest for first graders telling why Archanjo is a great man, a shopping center that uses his name, and a centennial celebration that tries to transform him into another profitable Jesus. The exploitative nature of Pena's film is more ambiguous. Although he gets the idea while doing a commercial newspaper story, gathers the research while working for Livingstone, and distorts or omits some of the facts in order to please the distributors, his film nevertheless grows increasingly responsible as Pena becomes more involved with Archanjo. He starts out selling the date of Pedro's birth to the promoters and ends up insuring that the myth retains the most important truths. Archanjo, Pena and dos Santos are no purists, and neither are we viewers — that's the whole point. The film celebrates crossbreeding and mixed forms as the best solution to racism, democracy, and filmmaking.

This process is dramatized in the scene where Pena and his film crew tape a brainstorming session on Archanjo, in which they try to reconcile the conflicting aspects of his character and behavior. In trying to explain the hero, each character reveals a great deal about him or herself and their own conception of freedom. This scene encourages us in the audience to do the same and yet forces us to be conscious of our own limitations in the process. As his name suggests, Fausto Pena is the masochistic scholar who is willing to sell his soul and sacrifice his woman in order to gain greater knowledge and power. In this scene, he is most concerned with gathering as much data as possible from the others to enrich his own vision of Archanjo. When one young crew member, who is proud of his radicalism, has great difficulty understanding how Archanjo could have had an affair with a Scandinavian woman, Ana Mercedes insists it was a question of lust without reference to color. Although we might suspect her of projecting her own ideas of sexual freedom onto the hero, we realize that many members of the audience would condemn her sexuality simply because she is a woman. Like Archanjo, Ana Mercedes enjoys lovers of all races and classses; convincingly played by Sonia Dias, who looks like a young Lena Horne, she possesses an extraordinary range of sexuality that is expressed in the way she moves, especially at the candomblé where she is highly responsive to the magical forces of the samba. Pena promises Ana Mercedes that she can play all of Archanjo's women — the magical Rosa de Oxalá, whom Ana Mercedes suspects was Pedro's great love; Dorothea, the young mother of Tadeu, who inherits his father's intelligence and turns out to be the right-hand man of the mayor of Rio; and even the blond-braided "white beetle" named Kirsi, whose son Pedro hopes will grow up to be the King of Scandinavia. While Pena uses this promise as a bribe for sexual favors, it still reaffirms what the gringo Livingstone could perceive — that Ana Mercedes possesses the same kind of protean, transformational power as Archanjo. While her use of it is restricted primarily to sexuality, she nevertheless has a positive receptivity that, as Wilhelm Reich suggested, is almost instinctive in women but that can offer a valuable political lesson to men — a lesson that was strongly urged by Pedro Archanjo and that is demonstrated in the brainstorming session. When the discussion is interrupted by the mother of one of the crew members, we at first expect that she will make a fool of herself because she looks like a conventional upper-middle-class housewife. But, when she delivers a stirring speech about Archanjo, reminding us that he was always poor and socially oppressed, we are forced to confront our own prejudices against her based solely on her sex and her class.

In *Tent of Miracles*, the audience repeatedly encounters female characters, whose appearance and social personae make us assume that they are objects of satire and ridicule, but whose basic instincts turn out to be more progressive than those of the men around them in the same class or condition. In the scene where the police chief is on his death bed, the white doctors dressed in black stand on one side of the bed reciting their useless medical jargon while the black maids in white express their grief in chants and prayers to Oxalá; the female members of the dying man's family cross class and racial lines to join the women in their outcries of pain. This pattern is developed more fully with the countess of Brusca and Mrs. Edelweiss.

The countess first appears as a grotesque caricature of a frivolous Francophile. As we hear mocking bird calls, we see a painted, befeathered middle-aged woman flirting with our hero and asking to be taken to a macumba. When she actually attends one (to celebrate Tadeu's graduation from engineering school), instead of doing a samba, she performs a ludicrous cancan. Yet, this eccentric Brazilian aristocrat, who turns out to be the cousin of Archanjo's chief academic enemy Nilo Argolo, strongly supports Pedro's arguments for crossbreeding by exposing the African roots of her own family and class. When Pedro's son Tadeu marries Lou Gomes, the daughter of one of the best so-called "white" families, the countess holds the reception in her home; like a Matisse painting, the decor presents a riotous clash of conflicting patterns and textures, combining artifacts from all over the world. It provides exactly the right setting for this interracial coupling.

We first see Mrs. Edelweiss, an attractive bourgeois intellectual, at Livingstone's press conference, where she is enchanted with the hero like the rest of the audience. The commercial promoters of the Archanjo centennial select her as president of their committee, undoubtedly seeing her as an appealing and easily manipulated figurehead. Delighted with her new job, she earnestly proposes a Seminar on Brazilian Racial Democracy as the main event of the celebration; clearly she is a naive liberal who is taken in by their hype. Up to this point, she seems to be an object of satire (who cannot be taken seriously). When she comes to the office of the promoters to discuss her plans, they also refuse to take her seriously; they treat her, not as a human being or as a professor (which we only *now* learn that she is), but as a woman. Putting on their jackets and their false

Tent of Miracles (1977)

231

smiles, they graciously kiss her hand, shower her with compliments, and flirtatiously sidle up beside her, before giving her the bad news—that her seminar must be cancelled. Then we cut to a close-up of her face, which suddenly drops the simpering smile of her social persona and reveals her sincere disappointment. Her consciousness continues to be raised in a later scene where she learns of their plans for exploiting Archanjo and demands explanations; realizing that all their answers are bullshit, she drops her polite mask and bluntly tells them, "Fuck you!" At this moment we see a quick montage of three female images— a close-up of Edelweiss's angry face, a glamorous poster of a sex symbol like Ursula Andress posed seductively with a deadly weapon, and the cute little first grader reciting her winning essay on Archanjo. The humanity of Edelweiss has been revealed despite the social stereotypes that would make us dismiss her as a sex object or child. The film ends with Edelweiss at the celebration for our hero, frowning at the distortions and the hype but applauding his authentic contributions to Brazilian Racial Democracy. She emerges as the model for the bourgeois members of the audience, whose political consciousness is to be raised and whose authentic feelings and humanity are to be liberated from restrictive social personae.

Nelson Pereira dos Santos's visual and audio choices are very effective in developing his political theme and reinforcing Archanjo's ideas.

For example when Pedro's son Tadeu asks Captain Gomes for the hand of his daughter Lou, the two men stand on opposite sides of a window, through which they see the serene pastel landscape and hear the sound of the waves. At the same time, we hear operatic singing, used periodically through the film to deflate the "white" Brazilian's sense of racial purity, precisely the force that keeps the young lovers apart.

Later, when Captain Gomes informs his wife of Tadeu's outrageous proposal, the aristocrats symmetrically stand facing the young black man on opposite sides of an open doorway, through which we see a cross on a religious altar, which sanctifies their rejection. Beside each parent is a formal portrait—the captain stands in front of a gentleman, his wife in front of a lady—as if these still works of art provide the models for their behavior. Meanwhile, the opera continues on the sound track, as if setting the tone for the captain's impassioned dismissal of Tadeu.

This scene also echoes visual choices in earlier sequences. For example, in a café the screen is neatly bisected by a wall, separating Pena on the left, with pictures representing his Christian heritage hanging on the wall behind him, and Ana Mercedes seated on the right in front of pictures of her black ancestors. This use of still photographs ultimately goes back to the images behind the titles at the opening of the film, which clearly established the historical roots of the drama. They also provide visual irony for the final sequence at the centennial celebration, where we see Archanjo immortalized in one of these formal portraits that clothes him in respectable academic robes, strips him of his vitality and uniqueness, and transforms him into a conventional "national hero." This frozen image contrasts sharply with Pena's picture of Pedro Archanjo, which is moving is both senses of the term. As if to insure that Archanjo lives on as the spirit of Bahia, behind the titles at the end of the film we see the vital moving images of a Bahian Independence Day celebration — the rich mixture of races, sexes, classes, colors, and styles that gives modern Brazil its creative energy.

26
"Formal Innovation and Radical Critique in *The Fall*"

ROBERT STAM

Rui Guerra and Nelson Xavier's *The Fall* (1978) combines political consciousness with highly experimental technique. A sequel to Guerra's *The Rifles* (1964), the film traces the subsequent careers of three characters from the earlier film—Pedro, José, and Mário, the soldiers sent to "protect" rich landowners' food stores from possible seizure by hungry peasants. One soldier, Pedro (Paulo Cesar Pereio), has remained with the army, because, as he says, "nowadays a man without a uniform is worth nothing." The other two—José (Hugo Carvana) and Mário (Nelson Xavier)—have become hardhat construction workers building the Rio de Janeiro subway system. José falls to his death—whence the title—and his tragedy sets in motion the pivotal events of the film. Mário tries to obtain justice for José's widow Lindalva (Maria Silva), but management refuses to grant her fair compensation or even acknowledge its own culpability in José's death. Mário's stuggle precipitates a domestic crisis with his wife Laura (Isabel Ribeiro), whose father, Salatiel (Lima Duarte) is a foreman on the same construction site. Although Salatiel, as a worker, understands Mário's point of view, he also values his own career. He connives with the bosses in getting the company off the hook, a service for which he is duly rewarded in promotions and raises. The film's climax is neither simplistically upbeat nor needlessly gloomy; rather, it is realistically hopeful about the possibilities of love and solidarity.

Hugo Carvana as José in *A Queda* (1978)

This synopsis gives no inkling, however, of the highly original way the story is constructed, or better, of the five *different ways* in which it is constructed. First, the story is told through a pre-credit prologue, a kind of metaphorical Eisensteinian prelude, which presents four kinds of images: a building implodes and collapses; famished people pick through garbage for scraps of food; oxen are put to death in a slaughterhouse, while the managers drink the blood of the slaughtered in an official ceremony. Planted as seeds in the spectator's minds, the meaning of these images comes to fruition only as the story unfolds. The images suggest that the society portrayed in the film is imploding from its own contradictions; that the workers who constructed the building, and who will build the subway for which it presumably makes way, are the principal victims of this implosion (as the Brazilian working-class has, in fact, been the principal victim of the contradictions generated by Brazilian society); that some people, even more destitute than the workers, survive on scraps thrown out by the well fed; and that the mechanisms of this society, as in the society characterized by an identical metaphor in Eisenstein's *Strike*, resemble those of a slaughterhouse, in which the workers are the slaughtered and the owners symbolically drink their blood. The slaughter of the oxen also constitutes an intertextual reference to *The Rifles*. That film ended with the slaying of the sacred ox by the peasants. *The Fall* begins with the mechanized, industrialized slaying of the same animal.

The story is told, secondly, by a startlingly novel procedure—the "quotation" of entire sequences from *The Rifles*.[1] The device, paradoxically, both strengthens and subverts realism. The quoted passages reinforce realism by implying that the characters in *The Fall* somehow preex-

235

isted the film we are seeing. Since they have a filmically available past, their lives are given a kind of fourth dimension—a temporal and experiential density. At the same time, the quoted sequences undercut illusionism by denaturalizing the filmic medium: the vivid color of *The Fall* sets off the pale black and white footage of *The Rifles*; and the deliberate pacing (appropriate to the northeast) of the earlier film contrasts strikingly with the quick nervous "urban" rhythms of the latter film. The quoted footage constitutes a personal, historical, and cinematic flashback, triggering multiple reflections in the mind of the spectator. First, the soldiers, manipulated oppressors in the service of the oligarchy in *The Rifles*, have joined the ranks of the oppressed in *The Fall*; secondly, the earlier film—and in this it is typical of first phase Cinema Novo—is set in the northeast, while the contemporary story takes place in the urban industrialized south; and thirdly, the army, in which the soldiers play a subordinate role in *The Rifles*, has taken control of the Brazil of *The Fall*. It is suggested that cinematic history and "real" history have been running along on their parallel tracks during the fourteen intervening years.

The third narrative strategy in *The Fall* involves the utilization of *La Jetée*-like still photographs for the sequences in which management discusses its response to the crisis provoked by José's death. Thus the film depsychologizes the capitalist managers; it concentrates on their social function rather than explore the nuances of their private sensibilities. The film abstracts and depersonalizes them, not because Guerra-Xavier regard them as less than human, but because it is not with management that their interest or solidarity lies. They abstract management for social-historical reasons, much as Goya depersonalizes Napoleonic soldiers in his paintings, or as Eisenstein depersonalizes the tsarist forces of repression in *Potemkin*. The workers, meanwhile, are shown *in movement* for *they* are the dynamic class, the catalyst for movement and progressive change. The film also aurally contrasts workers and owners; the owners' voices are post-synched in a kind of echo-chamber effect, suggesting a protected, "studio" existence, while those of the workers must compete with well-nigh intolerable ambient noise.

The fourth and principal way the story is told is in color, with direct sound, in the manner of *cinéma vérité*. *The Fall* was filmed in sixteen millimeter—in line with Guerra's theory that light, portable equipment facilitates, indeed virtually obliges, a closer, more epidermic contact with real social situations—and subsequently blown up to thirty-five millimeter. The production was low cost, independent, cooperative, and rapid (the film was shot in twenty-two days). The film is not a "well-made film" with "high production values." It does not have a bourgeois appearance, that well-upholstered look that in itself often cradles illusions while it softens and cushions radical messages. *The Fall* shares with *cinéma vérité* its frequently hand-held camera, its long takes and one-shot sequences, and its reliance on ambient light (with no attempt to light even nighttime sequences artificially). Next to this staged *cinéma vérité*, there exists, finally, a fifth style, that of authentic *cinéma vérité*: direct-to-camera interviews with actual workers. The *cinéma vérité* style is saved from the naive mushiness of *cinéma vérité* ideology, however, by the rigorously dialectical structure of the film as a whole and by the formal contextualization and relativization of the *vérité* style.

Guerra, who has always been fond of pyrotechnically complex camera movements, literally places the camera at the side of the workers; it follows them through the mud of the construction site, it squeezes with them through the narrow corridor that circles the workplace, and it ducks with them from low-hanging beams. When José plummets to his death, the camera becomes anxious and restless with the workers; it suffers anthropomorphically, as if it were risking a good deal simply by putting itself in contact with life as lived by a substantial portion of humanity.

If Brazilian cinema has often neglected the working class, *The Fall* compensates that lack with a fiery political vengeance. The film paints a brutal and unsentimental picture of the lives of workers in Brazil—it catalogues, and more important, analyzes, the hidden and not so hidden injuries of class. Thrown into an equipment-strewn mudhole, clinging precariously to shaky scaffolding, subject to intolerable noise, without access to law or power, the Brazilian worker—embodied by Mário—is daily environed with misery. Mário's trajectory is presented as typical; his migration from the drought-ridden northeast to the industrialized south encapsulates the lives of millions of Brazilians, and specifically, the lives of the northeasterners who form the majority among construction workers in Rio and São Paulo.

Mário plays a bitter game of class struggle, and although neither he nor his class really win, he does at least learn in preparation for future com-

A Queda (1978)

bat. Initially, he naively trusts bourgeois legality. His co-worker has died, he reasons, and the law assures his widow the right of compensation. But the construction firm cares little for such legalisms. What for the worker is a question of life and death is for management an exercise in adroit public relations. Involved in a competition for another contract, and therefore under pressure to finish the work rapidly, their overriding goal is to avoid scandal and maximize profits. The film suggests that the powerful have economic and political control, and the powerless are confronted with a choice — to sell themselves, to keep silent, to speak up and lose their jobs, or — and this alternative is only *implied* in the film — to organize as a class.

Mário's muddy work site becomes a microcosm for Brazil as a whole, a springboard for a comprehensive and radical critique of capitalism in its fascistic sub-equatorial variant. What was loftily metaphorized as the Brazilian economic "miracle," the film suggests, was in fact a disaster, a fall — the fall of a free press and human rights, and the fall in living standards for the working class. The film demystifies the Brazilian model for development. The carrot-and-stick capitalism that typifies Mário's workplace, pervasive in all capitalist societies, takes especially grotesque and predatory forms in the Third World. For those not sufficiently motivated by its carrots — bonuses, bribes, consumer products — the system reserves its sticks — dismissal, brutality, imprisonment, death.

Rui Guerra has always excelled in exposing the mechanisms of power as they operate in everyday life, especially during moments of crisis. What most impresses in *The Fall* is not its anger but its subtlety. No manicheanism pits haloed workers against diabolic bosses. Rather, the film highlights the contradictions that riddle *all* our lives, including those that rend the working class itself. Rather than choose a facile enemy — for example, the *foreign* capitalist — *The Fall* concentrates on Brazilian capitalism and *its* contradictions. The film reveals an intricate hierarchy of corruption, with a large gray area between worker and boss. The system tries to grind out opportunistic workers as efficiently as it grinds out products, and here Salatiel, the foreman, serves as a kind of negative exemplar. Having grown up a rural worker, he is astonished by the easy success that comes with betraying his class and collaborating with the bosses. He urges the same path on Mário, telling him to "think modern," (i.e., to forget about antiquated notions like friendship and loyalty to one's co-workers) and thus reap the rewards of complicity and acquiescence. Thus are friendship and solidarity drowned in the icy waters of selfish calculation. Salatiel inhabits that gray zone, the social no-person's-land, where labor and management appear to blur together, a zone of ambiguous loyalties where people of working-class origin become bourgeois in aspiration. People like Salatiel would like to cross a magical class line beyond which they will enjoy affluence and respect. But while Salatiel wins an apartment, a car, and some consumer goodies, he remains a tool in the hands of the real owners. He will never really cross that magical line, and he will never be free of a nagging feeling of class betrayal.

The contradictions of the work place inevitably spill over into the domestic life of Salatiel, Mário, and Laura (Salatiel's daughter and Mário's wife). Laura, played with wrenching power by Isabel Ribeiro, suffers the domestic fall out of Mário's oppression as a worker. At one point, Mário virtually rapes his own wife, and the rape is followed not by the sexist cliché of coy reluctance giving way to ecstatic abandon, but rather by visible bitterness on her part. At the same time, Mário is never characterized as a purely oppressive "heavy" in their relationship. Although Laura chafes under male-imposed strictures, and although she resents certain of Mário's actions, one senses a complex experiential bond, a desperate tenderness and anguished communication, between them.

The most powerful sequence in the film involves Mário, Laura, Salatiel, and sexual politics. The three of them, and their families, are celebrating Mário and Laura's acquisition of a new apartment, indirectly made possible by Salatiel's collaborationism. In response to Mário's questions, Salatiel whispers vague reassurances about how the apartment was obtained. Laura, overhearing snatches of the conversation, tries to find out more and Salatiel cuts her off. Laura insists angrily on her right to know about where *their* house came from, and to know about anything that might affect her and her husband. After trying to silence her with paternalistic kisses, her father-foreman scolds her for not respecting her husband's authority and for not emulating the submissive example of her own saintly mother, who never meddled in affairs beyond her ken. He plants a kiss on the saintly mother, who turns away with irritation and embarassment. Mário, meanwhile, paces around the apartment, transparently ill at ease. Laura then explodes with articulate rage, her voice crackling with emotion. Enraged to be treated like a retarded child, with no right to know about the inner workings of issues that touch her

Nelson Xavier as Mário and Isabel Ribeiro as Laura in *A Queda* (1978)

239

most closely, she articulates a woman's anger with rare power, even as the film, through her, highlights the political and sexual contradictions of everyday life.

This sequence, perhaps better than any other, exemplifies the synthesis of political consciousness and emotional force in *The Fall*. Guerra-Xavier somehow fuse the visceral affectivity of a Cassavetes with the political cunning of a Brecht. The camera pursues the improvising actors, its gaze guided only by the tension in their voices. The acting performances have the gut-level immediacy one associates with films like *Faces* or *A Woman under the Influence*, yet the political understanding of the emotions is immeasurably deeper. Isabel Ribeiro's performance turns into an outcry against patriarchal oppression, against her father's infantilization of her and against her husband's complicitous silence in the face of this infantilization. Yet the sequence fits into the overall logic of the film, which is a cry — but a well-reasoned cry — against all kinds of oppression — sexual, political, and economic.

The Fall as a whole, like the cited sequence, combines the emotional urgency of deeply felt improvisational acting — obvious in the lack of a preestablished text, in the indecision of some of the gestures — with a cogent and well thought out overall structure. What saves the film from being merely phenomenological and descriptive is its ways of socially *generalizing* its meanings. At one point, Mário, reflecting on José's death, tells Laura that "this is no way for a person to die." His remark is followed by a montage of shots of consumer stores and television images. The reality of his life contrasts starkly with the promises of consumerist bliss proffered by the media. José's death, the montage suggests, is a consequence of the choices inherent in the Brazilian economic model. A TV station logo forms the map of Brazil, and we hear the government slogan: "We are constructing Brazil." In fact, the film suggests, it is José, Mário, and Laura who are constructing Brazil, and it is the system that tries to destroy them.

Brazilian cinema at its best has been a cinema of demystification. It has demystified class society by laying bare the internal structure of its social relations. At the same time, it has demystified the cinema itself by means of anti-illusionist strategies that lay bare the process of construction of the text itself. By combining a thematic of construction with an esthetic of *de*construction, *A Queda* constitutes a remarkable prolongation of this tradition.

Note

1. The technique of self-quotation has been used in poetry, for example by T.S. Eliot in *The Waste Land*, and the technique of *retour des personnages* has been employed in the novel, notably by Balzac. Although Godard "quotes" his earlier work (for example, *Tout Va Bien* cites dialogue from *Le Mépris*), he does not use quoted footage to function both as subjective and historical flashback (showing the same actors at the earlier stage playing the same characters), as well as a clearly marked authorial intrusion.

Land in Anguish (1967)

the Villa-Lobos music with its European-Brazilian tensions additionally suggests the dilemma of a man torn between elitist and popular politics.

There are a good many percussion effects throughout the film, used particularly to suggest the suppressed violence of an oppressed people about to break forth: an ominous piece for drums, cymbals, and piano dominates the scene where Felicio confronts Vieira over the land question; a hollow-sounding gong pounds relentlessly throughout the scene where the widow and friends of Felicio, ranged about his dead body, proclaim Vieira as responsible; and loud cymbals and a fast drum rhythm are heard through Paulo's vision of Felicio's supporters blaming first himself and then Vieira.

A film denouncing populism and advocating armed revolution could hardly embody its critique within a populist film style. Above all, Rocha sought to avoid a film where

> . . . everything was worked out to minimize any conflict for the spectator . . . grind everything down to its basic ingredients, blend in the ideology and give the whole thing to the public pre-digested.[5]

The music plays its part in the "impurely aggressive"[6] style of the film. Rocha avoids musical bridges forming smooth transitions from one scene to another, and favors sudden jolts of sound. For example, the music of the scene where Paulo hurls Felicio to the ground is quite arbitrarily cut mid-phrase with the change to Paulo's apartment, while the silence of the latter scene is suddenly rent by a howl of anger and mourning with a sudden cut to the scene of the peasants around Felicio's body. Similarly a drum roll or a cymbal stroke will emphasize a cut. Within scenes, too, music abruptly stops or starts as in Vieira's popular meeting, or percussion effects arbitrarily punctuate the action as in the scene on the roof-terrace of Fuentes's television building.

Antônio das Mortes (1969), Rocha's next film, transplants the most significant character from *Black God, White Devil*, which immediately preceded *Land in Anguish*, and thus the two invite consideration together.

Black God, White Devil is Rocha's most powerful film primarily because of its simple, balanced structure. This structure is determined basically by its music, in particular a ballad song recounting the fortunes of the sertão dwellers, Manuel and Rosa. Composed by Sérgio Ricardo in the style of popular *cordel* literature, the ballad functions like a Greek chorus, foretelling and commenting upon the action contained in the images, and in addition, acts as a Brechtian distanciation device. The characters here are more fully developed psychologically than those of the later *Antônio das Mortes*, but they are nonetheless basically emblematic; they resume the history of an oppressed people seeking deliverance, appealing now to *beato*, now to bandit. Rocha's view here is that such deliverance lies not in religious ecstasy nor in disorganized violence, but in a conscious decision for action and struggle. This is the function of the *jagunço*, Antônio das Mortes, in the film: killer of both *beatos* and *cangaceiro*, he provides Manuel with freedom and the opportunity to make such a decision.

This representative function in the characters is suggested by the ballad commentary. Blindness is the traditional state of the visionary seer, and the tale of the blind ballad singer, Julio, here gives a timeless, epic quality to the story. The two encounters—with Sebastião and Corisco—are introduced by almost identical lyrics, suggesting that both offer similarly ineffective forms of revolt: "Then one day for good or evil, the saintly Sebastião, the devilish Corisco, entered their lives." Just as Sebastião embodies the tradition of Sebastianism and religious mystics such as Conselheiro and Padre Cicero who offered hope to the oppressed poor, so Corisco incorporates all *cangaceiros*. Specifically, Corisco sees himself as the descendant and avenger of Lampião, a quiet portion of the ballad suggesting Corisco's meditation on the latter's death: "Lampião died in the middle of the night/Maria Bonita at break of day." Furthermore, Corisco's fight is linked with that of St. George with the dragon, another part of the ballad speaking of him as "Corisco of St. George."

The ballad, in fact, functions in many ways within its use as an overall structuring device. It can provide a change of tone: the plaintive tune and sparse guitar accompaniment as the singer tells of Manuel and Rosa in the sertão "working the land with their hands" changes later to a brisk section as Sebastião is described, suggesting new hope; later there is another change to a dirge as Manuel closes the eyes of his mother who is killed in the struggle with Morais's men. It can take the place of dialogue:

in the final, wordless duel between Corisco and Antônio, the balladist sings, "Surrender, Corisco!/No I won't surrender! I'm not a bird to live in a prison." It can direct the camera movement as in the introduction of Corisco: as the balladist sings, "the devilish Corisco entered their lives," the camera pans right to frame Corisco as if the words had directed its attention. Finally, it can suggest the significance of the whole, most obviously, of course, towards the end of the film as the singer concludes,

> So I've told my story
> Made of truth and imagination,
> And I hope you've all drawn your lesson from it,
> That a world so badly divided
> Is headed the wrong way
> And that the earth is man's
> And not God's or the devil's.

Complementing the ballad song and the solo voice and guitar of Sérgio Ricardo are the orchestral and choral pieces of Villa-Lobos. Here, Rocha uses the *Bachianas Brasileiras*, Numbers 2, 4, and 5—pieces that have their root in the sertanejo region—as well as the *Magníficat Alleluia* for chorus and orchestra. These are employed not merely as accompaniment but also to comment upon image and action. For example, the opening music, the *"canção do sertão"* (the "aria" movement from *Bachianas Brasileiras No. 2*) establishes underneath the credits the setting of the tale before the film proper starts and the ballad begins, "Manuel and Rosa lived in the sertão." The dramatic opening of this *canção* later erupts in a burst of sound as the sertanejo's name is changed by Corisco to Satanás. The "dansa" movement from the same piece provides a sardonic comment on the fight to the death between Manuel and Morais, while at the same time its conflicting rhythms are appropriate to those of the struggle. And as Antônio tells the blind singer that the death of Corisco, like that of Sebastião, is necessary because soon there will come a great war "without the superstition of god or devil," the *"canção do sertanejo"* (the "prelude" of the *Bachianas No. 2*) marks his journey towards Corisco: it is this abandonment of god and devil in order to fight one's own war that must be the real sertão dweller's "song" and which Antônio's action will make Manuel see.

Antônio is introduced by means of the "dansa" from the *Bachianas No. 4*. A quick montage of shots of a cloaked and hatted figure firing a gun establishes the idea of *"jagunço"* while the gay music makes its ironic comment (the piece's subtitle is "Mindinho" or "little"), the gun shots falling on its strong beats. The ballad song then takes over to explain that it is "Antônio das Mortes, killer of *cangaceiros*." Another section of this fourth *Bachianas*, the "aria," is used as Rosa follows Manuel climbing the Monte Santo to Sebastião. The scene gains in significance if we are aware that this *Bachianas* is based on a famous song from Paraiba, "Oh sister, let me go . . . Oh sister, I'm leaving alone/Oh sister let me go to the sertão of Pianco."

The most famous of the *Bachianas* is the fifth, a song of the freedom of love, its lyrics and theme connected with the sertão. The serenely beautiful opening movement where the soprano voice soars above the pizzicato cellos in a wordless cantilena is used as Corisco holds his wife in a long, final embrace before they face Antônio. It is one of the film's few tender moments.

Villa-Lobos's *Magnificat Alleluia* provides a number of occasions for ironic image/sound counterpoint, usually in relation to the messianic cult of Sebastião. The painfully slow pan up the path to the Monte Santo and the initial statement of the loud hymn of praise on the sound track is both the subjective, awe-stricken viewpoint of the followers of the cult and also the filmmaker's comment on their mistaken zeal. The piece occurs again triumphantly at the end of the film over shots of the sea and of Manuel running alone. Music and seascape recall Sebastião's promise to make a sea of the sertão; yet the image of the free-running Manuel shows that it is only the man freed from god and devil who will do this and who is worthy of an "alleluia." God and devil are furthermore equated by means of the *Magnificat Alleluia*: it bursts forth suddenly as Manuel castrates a man at Corisco's bidding. We recall the initial association of the music with Sebastião, the man who bid Manuel kill his son as a similar test of loyalty. Finally, this same castration scene contains the most sardonic use of music in the film. Corisco disrupts a wedding feast, rapes the bride, and forces Manuel to geld the groom. This gruesome interaction of the four is accompanied by a Villa-Lobos quartet, the allegro non troppo movement from the No. 11.

Antônio das Mortes (1969)

Antônio das Mortes employs music in a similar way to *Black God, White Devil* but with one important exception: an overarching structure such as the blind singer's ballad is missing. It is in any case a very different film, reflecting five years of tightening military control. Now *beato*, *cangaceiro*, and *jagunço* are all seen as possible revolutionary forces together with priest, intellectual, and people.

The most poignant moment of the film is a song. A long close-up dwells on the magnificently intense face of the wounded Coirana as he sings a ballad recounting his life: journeying south in a pau-de-arara in the hope of making money; working as a slave in the Mato Grosso; encountering the religious mystic settlement at Joazeiro; and retreating finally to the sertão. Coirana, as revealed in his story, is not only the spiritual descendant of Corisco, as he mentions in the last line, but a summation of the history of the oppressed *nordeste*. The *beatos'* lament upon Coirana, "Ogum is dead," reinforces this. Ogum is the *candomblé* equivalent of St. George, the warrior saint with which Coirana, like Corisco, links himself in the fight with Antônio, the dragon of evil. Toward its end, Coirana's ballad changes its point of view. The first-person narrator changes to a third person who speaks of meeting Coirana and giving him his name. At this change, the camera viewpoint also changes from the close shot of Coirana to a long shot of him dying on the rock while beside him, black Antão continues the song. The voice, however, does not change nor does the guitar accompaniment give way to the log drum Antão is playing. In the same way as he takes over Coirana's song, Antão also takes over his role as St. George, killing the real dragon of evil, Horácio, with lance and white charger like the saint of the triptych under the opening credits.

Coirana's song exemplifies the major functions of music in *Antônio das Mortes*—to suggest, as in the earlier film, the emblematic nature of the characters, and to structure scene or sequence and comment upon it.

The approach can be seen again in a scene between Laura and Matos. The two sing Pixinguinha's *Carinhoso* whose saccharine melody and debased, romantic lyrics epitomize bourgeois escapist entertainment. And indeed, Laura, significantly a prostitute from Bahia and clad throughout in diaphanous lilac, represents the middle class, allying itself now with the landed class (Horácio), now with the civil and political power (Matos) as seems expedient, and ready to brutally stab one or the other. The title ("full of tenderness") and the references in the lyrics to "kindness" and "sincerity" also provide an ironic commentary on the action as Matos loads Laura with a succession of pieces of jewelry. The music dictates the structure of the scene and provides its "dialogue," a parody perhaps of Démy and Legrand.

Church and intellectual and their potential contributory role in armed revolution are also embodied in the characters of the film. The teacher, for example, progresses from a fog of drunkenness and hilarity to a state where he sees clearly, the latter portrayed with simple directness as the teacher opens his eyes wide and looks straight at the camera. Songs chart the course of this development. In the scene where he indulges in a political discussion with Matos over a game of billiards, he sings a song-samba. The contrast between the melancholy words ("How I've wept, how my soul has been tormented") and the gay rhythm suggests the teacher's inner conflict, the turmoil that lies beneath the mocking banter and raised glass. Rocha regards the samba as "violent and anarchistic"[7] and presumably intended its use here to suggest where the teacher's eventual allegiance will lie. Toward the end of the film when Antônio halts the teacher's flight and brings him back to commitment, a bright pop tune erupts upon the sound track. Its jaunty rhythm and the fatuous moral tone of its lyrics ("Get up, shake off the dust, start climbing up the path . . . a strong man doesn't stay down") are deliberately at odds with the painful progress of the two up the hill.

The non-realistic, emblematic nature of the characters of the film as a whole leads Callenbach[8] to interpret Antônio as representing the army, causing a series of miscalculations both in his own conclusions and later those of Hans Proppe and Susan Tarr.[9] The character is emblematic but quite simply of the tradition of *jagunços*, hired killers with a conscience who, like Antônio, changed sides according to where right seemed to reside. The conjunction of image and reprise of the relevant part of Sérgio Ricardo's ballad makes this clear. As the song describes the killer of *cangaceiros* who "prays in ten churches but has no patron saint," the camera pans across the dusty land in a wide sweep in extreme long shot. Certainly Antônio is there in the shot, but he is a tiny figure almost invisible in the vast landscape.

The *cordel* or ballad poem that Ricardo's song imitates is a typical musical form of the northeast heard from itinerant singers who do not hesitate to unite traditional and contemporary elements. They are often available in printed pamphlet form, illustrated by woodcuts. It is a cordel on one of the most popular subjects, the *cangaceiro* Lampião, which Rocha uses to provide a structure for the last sequences of the film.

From the moment that Antônio places Coirana's body in an upright, cruciform position in the tree, the Lampião *cordel* dominates the sound track, telling of the revolution he caused in hell, burning Satan's empire and setting free the oppressed. It binds together the scenes of those who take over the cause of the oppressed from Coirana and liberate the people from their own Satanic oppressor, Horácio.

During the first part of the cordel relating how Lampião argued with the gatekeeper, threatening to wreck the place if refused entry, the teacher commits himself to Coirana's cause, solemnly taking both gun and sword from the body spread-eagled on the tree trunk. The ballad is silent for the most solemn, ritualistic moment as all those who will resurrect the armed struggle assemble: the priest goes to minister to Coirana in the background while in the middle ground, Antônio, Santa, and Antão stand in a ceremonial line as Santa slowly hands rifle and hat to Antônio who walks away to join the priest.

As the *cordel* resumes, there is a long shot of Mata Vaca's men carrying Horácio in a litter, a nice visual summation of the extent to which the

Antônio das Mortes (1968)

power of the landowning class rests upon armed banditry. The shot is an extraordinarily lengthy one, continuing long after its point has registered and seems designed to allow us to savor the words of the *cordel* and their relation to the image: Satan, the singer tells, upset that Lampião's reputation as a hardworking thief will bring down the value of his property, gives orders to "get the black folks together" to resist his entry.

Another silence takes place for the confrontation between Mata Vaca's men and the combined forces of Antônio and priest, but as Antônio challenges Mata Vaca to single-handed combat, another cordel strikes up, relating the story of the battle between the two. The words, telling of events in the past have a distancing effect upon these images of the present before us. The Lampião ballad, however, cuts off the other, before being submerged in an avalanche of gun fire as the duel gives way to a Peckinpah-style gun battle in which Mata Vaca's men are slaughtered.

As Antão completes the process by killing Horácio, the cordel continues once more, detailing Lampião's destruction of hell. The singer describes the latter in terms of a vast capitalist enterprise with stores, time clock, book of rules, and a depressed work force. In the images, the priest ritually leads the horse carrying Antão and Santa around Antônio. Image and *cordel* are united by the recollection that Coirana, whose heirs are Antônio and Antão, regarded himself as the spiritual heir of Lampião. The final images however are Antônio's alone, and the jaunty Lampião *cordel* gives way to the sadder *cordel* of the man with no patron saint.

In a way similar to the use of the Lampião *cordel*, a variety of choral songs with drum accompaniment link the scenes of the *beatos* dancing and surrounding their spiritual leaders. As a result, these are highly stylized scenes, their action choreographed, their dialogue poetic. The songs themselves, combining Christian and African elements in typical macumba fashion, express the people's faith in those who are fighting their cause.

The third scene of the film introduces the *beatos* dancing around Coirana, their colorful costumes, in tropicalist splendor, interspersed with studded leather *cangaceiro* hats. The songs, accompanied by a frenzied drum rhythm, gives way to a batucada, a piece for a variety of percussion instruments—here drums, makeshift cymbals, gongs, and bells—as Santa encircles Coirana in a ritualistic movement, followed by silence for Coirana's pronouncements in verse.

The second *beatos* scene (interrupted by the billiard games scene) shows the dancers retreated to a rocky hillside gradually revealed by a lengthy zoom out. Their song honoring St. Cosme and St. Damian and asking "What has happened to Jau and Orixá?" (two Macumba saints) gives way this time to a hummed chorus as Coirana, as he has sworn, pronounces it is time to descend upon the town. He is opposed by Antão, as yet innocent of his future active role, and at this point advocating passivity in a manner recalling a slave of the Brazilian Empire.

For the scene in the square when the beatos have descended from the rock, the Cosme and Damian song activates the dance, the words suggesting that a period of renewal is about to come: "Cosme gives the medicine, Damian is the healer, Cosme claps his hands, Damian beats the drum." The song is cut arbitrarily for the desafio: as Antônio and Coirana face each other, the alternate lines of their challenge are spoken in rhymed verse. There is another sudden cut, and the *beatos'* song begins as the two face each other within the length of Antônio's pink scarf, its ends held between the teeth of each. As the *beatos* sing "Oxossi is king," associating Coirana, the anticipated victor, with the macumba god of the hunt, the clangs of the choreographed sword fight fall on the strong beat of the song until the final frenzied thrusts and wounding of Coirana. The song continues relentlessly as Laura, priest, and professor go to Coirana's aid and the three carry him up the Alvorada Bar, while Horácio makes a conciliatory gesture of a food handout from the store.

Very different from the macumba songs is the Marlos Nobre music that links the scene comprising the second climax of the film—the scene over Matos's body, the slaughter of the *beatos*, and the carrying of Coirana's body to the sertão by Antônio. Scored for small ensemble including piano, contralto and soprano voices used as instruments, and electronic tape, the music has a bizarre nightmarish quality vaguely reminiscent of Schoenberg's *Pierrot Lunaire*. It begins as the teacher drags Matos's body out to open ground followed by Laura, her lilac dress blotched with red patches of blood, and carrying a bouquet of bright red and yellow paper flowers. The priest attempts to recall the teacher with the news that Horácio has ordered the death of the *beatos*, but he remains, fascinated by Laura as she embraces the dead Matos, finally rolling upon the body with her in a desperate embrace. It is a scene reflecting the tropicalist movement in its deliberate "bad taste"—the bizarre excesses of the action, the garish mixture of colors, and the cacophony of the music. The music continues during the two inserts of Mata Vaca's men rejoicing as they prepare to slaughter the *beatos* seen on the hill behind them. It provides a weird counterpoint to the beatos' songs and the cheers of the killers. The vocal parts of the music dominate the last shots of the sequence: the slaughter of the *beatos*, Antônio embracing Coirana's body that he has carried to the sertão, and Mata Vaca laughing at Santa and Antão, the sole survivors, standing amid the strewn corpses of the beatos. During this last shot, the singers perform great vocal leaps like shrieks of lamentation, the contralto intoning the first words to be used in the music, "Have pity on those who have invaded our land." The sequence ends with Mata Vaca backing away in awe of Santa's intense gaze.

Throughout these four films, Rocha has shown a consistent attitude toward the function of music in film. While he does not despise the use of music as accompaniment, he requires it to perform other tasks as well—to structure, comment on, and extend the meaning of image, scene, and even whole film; and to expand the reference of the film's protagonists beyond individual psychological studies to emblematic resumes of Brazil's history.

Notes

1. Interview with Glauber Rocha in *Image et Son*, no. 236, February 1970.
2. John Willet, ed., *Brecht on Theatre* (New York: Hill and Wang, 1964), p. 203.
3. Interview with Glauber Rocha in *Les Lettres Françaises*, 25 October 1967.
4. *Grove's Dictionary of Music and Musicians*, vol. 3, p. 707.
5. Glauber Rocha, "Cinema Novo: The Adventure of Creation," a paper given at Pesaro, 1968.
6. Ibid.
7. *Image et Son*, no. 236, February 1970.
8. Ernest Callenbach, "Comparative Anatomy of Folk-Myth Films: *Robin Hood* and *Antônio das Mortes*" in *Film Quarterly*, Winter 1969/70.
9. Hans Proppe and Susan Tarr, "Cinema Novo: Pitfalls of Cultural Nationalism" in *Jump Cut*, no. 10/11.

32
"On the Margins: Brazilian Avant-Garde Cinema"

Introduction

Like the United States, Brazil displays a vital avant-garde cultural tradition. Throughout the history of Brazilian film, more specifically, many directors have searched for alternatives to the dominant esthetics and the dominant mode of production. In the late sixties, an Underground Movement, influenced by international avant-garde currents but also characteristically, even defiantly, Brazilian, emerged in full force. The following essay traces the historical antecedents of the current movement, sketches its present-day outlines, and examines some of its most notable films.

"On the Margins: Brazilian Avant-Garde Cinema" *

ROBERT STAM

Recent avant-garde cinema in Brazil has been diversely labelled. Sometimes called "Udigrudi," in a parodically Brazilian corruption of

*I would like to express my appreciation to Ismail Xavier for our long discussions concerning Brazilian avant-garde films. I am especially indebted to him in my discussion of *Bandido da Luz Vermelha*, *O Anjo Nasceu*, and *Rei do Baralho*.

English "underground," its practitioners and critics also refer to it as "Marginal Cinema," "Subterranean Cinema," and "Garbage Cinema." This most recent flowering of the avant-garde, which first emerged in the late sixties and that continues to the present day, actually extends a long and combative tradition within Brazilian cinema. Already in the twenties, the heyday of literary modernism, there were occasional avant-garde films. European city-symphony films like Walter Ruttmann's *Berlin, die Symphonie einer Grossstadt* (1927) and Alberto Cavalcânti's *Rien que les Heures* (1926) inspired a number of Brazilian imitations. Humberto Mauro made a short symphony film about his native city of Catagüases, and Adalberto Kemeny and Rodolfo Lustig made *São Paulo: Sinfonia de uma Metrópole* ("São Paulo: Symphony of a Metropolis," 1929). The latter film is a cinematic poem-tribute to what the Paramount press releases call the "thundering rhythms of progress" of the "brain-city of Brazil." The press releases, like the film itself, employ the language of heroic urbanism: "iron and steel jutting defiantly against the sky . . . all the feverish activity of São Paulo unfolding before our astonished eyes." Fourteen months in production, *São Paulo: Symphony of a Metropolis* animates a collage of material ordered chronologically (beginning at dawn and proceeding to dusk) and thematically (vehicles, men in uniform). In the film's final segment a shot transparently modelled on Millet's *The Angelus* shows a man in silhouette contemplating the city from a distance. An intertitle reads: "The Angelus, and Man Contemplating his Superb Work." The following shot—of an Angelus bell in a church tower overlooking São Paulo—literalizes what had been implicit. In the following shot, animated airplanes fly over a modernist cityscape drawn in the expressionist style of Fritz Lang's *Metropolis*. An intertitle speaks of the Brazil of the future, followed by a shot of an hourglass, which dissolves to a spinning globe, dissolving, in turn, to the globe inscribed on the Brazilian flag, on which is written the meliorist national device (equally reflective of the film's structuring ideology): "Order and Progress."

Mário Peixoto's *Limite* ("Limit," 1930), is a landmark film within the history of the Brazilian avant-garde. Although seen by very few people in Brazil because Peixoto withdrew it from circulation, *Limite* soon acquired the status of myth as *the* early Brazilian experimental film. Only nineteen when he made the film, Peixoto became conversant with the European avant-garde during his diverse trips to England and France. The film explores a situation—three strangers lost at sea in a small boat—and three separate but inter-related narrations. The opening image, held for over a minute, of a woman in handcuffs announces the unifying theme of bonds, imprisonment, limits. The film then successively recounts, in an oblique and fragmented manner, the stories of the three castaways and their diverse entrapments. A light-haired woman, who, we learn later, has escaped from prison with the complicity of a guard, flees, only to find herself trapped in another situation of oppression—work as a seamstress. Successive shots of her work instruments—spools, buttons,

Taciana Rei in Mário Peixoto's *Limite* (1930)

scissors, measuring tape — all bathed in a kind of dusty light, evoke the tedium of her job. If the images recall Vertov's *Man with a Movie Camera*, the political attitude emphatically does not. Then the second dark-haired woman tells her story. After the prolonged walk through a fishing village, she returns home, where her depressed-looking husband awaits her at the top of the stairs. Later, a clip from Charlie Chaplin's *The Adventurer*, watched by a montage of laughing mouths, recapitulates in microcosm the structuring idea of the film. The clip shows Charlie tunneling out of prison to discover that he is at the feet of a guard: he excapes one set of limits only to encounter others. Then the man tells his story. A hand-held camera follows his promenade with a woman whose face we never see. He accompanies the woman home, then walks to a cemetery where a man (Mário Peixoto) tells him that the woman has leprosy. Gnarled trees and shots in negative evoke the narrator's inner torment, and frenzied pans express his dizziness. A storm arises, and the man commits suicide. Appropriate to a film in which work, love, and marriage have been revealed to be diverse forms of imprisonment, *Limite* ends with the same shot that opened the film — a woman in handcuffs.

Thematically, *Limite* seems designed to illustrate P. Adams Sitney's contention that the avant-garde finds its spiritual origins in nineteenth-century Romanticism, although the Romanticism here is more of the Francophonic variety then influential in Brazil. The anguished meditation on memory and loss, and the heavy atmosphere of emotional crisis, recall Lamartine, while the sea and landscapes recall Victor Hugo. At the same time, the film is imbued with a metaphysical *soif de l'absolu* worthy of Chateaubriand; the human imagination seems to butt against its epistemological and ontological limitations. The use of "sympathetic weather" as climatic analogue to mental states, finally, invokes a characteristic romantic strategy.

Sergei Eisentein, who saw *Limite* in London in 1932, called it "an extremely beautiful film which one should submit oneself to right from the very first moments, as to the agonizing chords of a synthetic and pure language of cinema."[1] On a specifically cinematic level, *Limite*, while clearly not an experimental breakthrough film like *Man with a Movie Camera*, is fairly audacious. Imagistically, the film tends toward abstraction, often recontexting objects through excentric framing and disorientingly outsized close-ups. The plastic beauty and a senuous tactile quality of the images contrast strikingly with the structural pessimism of the film. Shots of fishing nets anticipate, by their graphic composition, certain shots in *Que Viva Mexico*. Peixoto and his cameraman Edgar Brasil seem especially sensitive to the play of light rippling over watery surface, glinting off scissors or "glowing" within a glass of beer. The occasionally frenzied camera movement and swish pans recall Kirsanoff's *Menilmontant*, which Peixoto presumably saw while living in Paris. The editing places identical shots in diverse syntagmatic contexts, structurally varying their meaning. Visual analogies link train wheels and sewing machines, telegraph wires and trees, a fish and a boat's prow. And the climactic, tour-de-force storm sequence consists of roughly seven shots of crashing surf and eddying swirls of water, edited into a frenzy so as to suggest a tempest on the high seas.

There is little evidence of an avant-garde in Brazil during the thirties and forties. Brazilian-born Alberto Cavalcânti was called to Brazil in 1950 to head the Vera Cruz production company, but the Cavalcânti invited to Brazil was not the director of the French avant-garde period (*Rien que les Heures*) but rather that of the post-war English period (*Nicholas Nickleby* and *They Made Me a Fugitive*). In Brazil, Cavalcânti and Vera Cruz made precisely the kind of film that would subsequently be denounced both by Cinema Novo and by Underground Cinema. Vera Cruz offered a "classy" cinema with high production values, completely ignoring the economic realities of Brazil, while both Cinema Novo and the Underground favored an esthetic that would dialectically transform a negative condition — underdevelopment — into a positive source of signification, by integrating into their very language the difficulty of making films in Brazil.

The Cinema Novo movement that emerged in the early sixties attempted to fuse political and esthetic avant-gardism. Like the Soviet filmmakers of the twenties, Cinema Novo sought to simultaneously decolonize cinematic language and liberate its people from oppressive political and economic structures. Just as Vertov lamented the penetration of Hollywood films in the Soviet Union, "impressing the magnanimous figure of the American millionaire upon the stern hearts of the Russian proletariat," so Cinema Novo formulated its opposition not only to the ideology and esthetics of Hollywood, but also to its distribution chains. At the same time, Cinema Novo challenged Brazilian commercial cinema; rather than exploit the tropical conviviality of *chanchada* or the imitative glossiness of Vera Cruz, its directors searched out the squalid corners of Brazilian life. Although partially inspired by the auteurist production strategies of the *nouvelle vague*, Cinema Novo was politically and esthetically far more radical than the French movement. Politically, it was Fanonian, eager to give voice to the wretched of the earth. Esthetically, it strove for a definitive break with Hollywood models, invoking instead the precedents of Eisenstein, Vertov, and Brecht. The most advanced practitioners of what Glauber Rocha called "an esthetic of hunger" rejected the suave continuities and rapid tempo of culinary cinema in favor of self-reflective technique and harshly aggressive images and sounds.

The opening shot of Nelson Pereira dos Santos's *Vidas Secas* may be taken as emblematic of this avant-garde impulse even within the more traditional "Neo-Realist" Cinema Novo films. In a shot reminiscent of the final segment of *Zorns Lemma*, a static camera records, for a duration of four minutes, a peasant family's slow traversal of a barren landscape, as the wheels of a non-diegetic oxcart scrape and grind on the soundtrack. Other films of this period reverse the procedure of *Vidas Secas*. Rather than combine a static camera with movement in the shot, they weave pyrotechnically complex camera movements around a relatively static object. In *Os Cafajestes* ("The Hustlers," 1962) Rui Guerra winds spiralling car-borne travelling shots around Norma Benguel's nude body for nearly ten minutes. And in *Deus e o Diabo na Terra do Sol* ("Black God, White Devil," 1964), Rocha combines choreographed movement within the shot with an autonomous camera ballet, all orchestrated to the music of Villa-Lobos's *Bachianas Brasileiras*.

Underground Cinema burst noisily on the scene during the latter part of the second phase (1964–1968) of Cinema Novo, in an atmosphere of worsening political repression combined, paradoxically enough, with radical experimentation in the arts. In 1967, José Celso Martinez Correia staged his brilliant theatrical version of *O Rei da Vela* ("The King of the Candle"), based on a thirties play by modernist poet-playwright Oswald de Andrade. The preface-manifesto to the play called for a theater of "cruel and total provocation" whose political efficacy was to be measured not by the norms of sociology but by the "level of aggressivity." A calculated attack on São Paulo's "stupid and provincial bourgeoisie," the manifesto defended deliberate bad taste as the ideal expression of "Brazilian surrealism."

O Rei da Vela was dedicated to Glauber Rocha, and the high point of the Underground movement coincides with the general cultural movement called Tropicalism, the movement in which both *Terra em Transe* and *Rei da Vela* play a key role. The Tropicalists drew partial inspiration from the anarchic Bohemian avant-garde of the twenties, and particularly from the experimental attitudes and social irreverence of Oswald de Andrade. It especially appreciated his notion of "anthropophagy" as metaphorically applied to cultural products. For Modernists like Oswald,

How Tasty Was My Little Frenchman (1971)

cannibalism was an authentic native tradition as well as a key metaphor in their own struggle for artistic independence, a way of thumbing their noses both at their own "palefaces" and at colonizing over-cultivated Europe, while heeding surrealism's call for "la sauvagerie" in art. "Only cannibalism unites us," Oswald de Andrade proclaimed and, paraphrasing one of the most illustrious of the palefaces, "Tupi or not Tupi, that is the question." The Cinema Novo directors revived the cannibalist metaphor in works like *Macunaíma* and *How Tasty Was My Little Frenchman*. But while their approach to cannibalism was discreetly distanced — *Macunaíma* was based on an acknowleged literary classic and *How Tasty Was My Little Frenchman* was set in the sixteenth century — the Underground directors were less circumspect, more angry, more audacious.

The Underground Movement, in this sense, constitutes both a rejection and a radicalization of Cinema Novo. For the Underground, Cinema Novo had become *embourgeoisé*, respectable, paternalistic, overly cautious both in its thematics and in its cinematic language. Just as Cinema Novo decided to reach out for a popular audience, the Underground opted to slap that audience in its face. "If the reader-spectator doesn't agree with what we are saying and doing," said filmmaker-critic Luiz Rosemberg Filho, "we recommend a strong dose of Tatu insecticide." And if the public did not appreciate "the most interesting films on this planet," Julio Bressane shouted, "too bad for you, squares!" The Underground was no less aggressive toward the Cinema Novo filmmakers, and their hostility was often reciprocated. Neville

Duarte d'Almeida blamed Cinema Novo and its "bourgeois intellectualism" for bringing Brazilian Cinema to "its humiliating, subservient, and culturally underdeveloped condition of subproduct of the Hollywood-Cinecitta-Rive Gauche circus."

As Cinema Novo moved toward relatively high-budget films characterized by technical polish and "production values," the Novo Cinema Novo (the New New Cinema) as it came to be called, demanded a radicalization of the "esthetic of hunger." Cinema Novo, they taunted, had become Cinema Novo Rico (nouveau riche cinéma). As Cinema Novo moved increasingly into color, "covering" its apparent retreat to a more commercial esthetic by the "alibi" of Tropicalism and its camp emphasis on gaudy colors, the Underground remained faithful to black and white. The Underground turned out inexpensive films in remarkably swift succession, rejecting a well-made cinema in favor of a "dirty screen" and "garbage esthetics." A garbage style, they argued, was the style most appropriate to a Third World country picking through the leavings of an international system dominated by First World monopoly capitalism. The films, consequently, bore the marks of economic oppression, inscribing into the films themselves — by inaudible grating sound and grainy images — the very precariousness of their own production.

The first indisputably Underground film, both in its production methods and in its thematic, was Ozualdo Candeias's prophetically titled *A Margem* ("In the Margin," 1967). The film has to do with "margins" in all the diverse overtones of that word. It is set, first of all, along the margins of São Paulo's irredeemably polluted Tietê river (surely the least noble estuary to water a major metropolis) where diverse "marginals" improvise their daily survival by begging, prostitution, and junk collecting. Along the river a highway, known in Portuguese as "the Marginal," also generates its marginal life. *A Margem* tells two surreally poignant love stories. The first involves a black prostitute and a bourgeois *déclassé*. Disappointed in her hopes, the prostitute unceasingly perambulates the riverside *favela* in her immaculate wedding dress, as a kind of tropical Miss Havisham. The second love story involves a blonde woman and a divinely touched madman who haunts the garbage dumps. Although the madman visually recalls the retarded children of Buñuel's *Las Hurdes*, he gradually assumes heroic, Chaplinesque dignity.

A Margem unpretentiously communicates a feeling of rare poetry and subdued audacity. Its subtle modulation of fantasy and realism recalls the Vigo of *L'Atalante* and there is even a fairly surreal wedding procession reminiscent of that film, set, like *A Margem*, on a riverbank. The film literalizes the metaphor of a "garbage esthetic," eliciting flowers from evil and stealing beauty from squalor. Candeias's subtle sense of lighting turns the miasmal exhalations of the Tietê into ethereal mists, and his gift for composition transforms riverside pipes, bridges, hulks of ships, and skeletal buildings into wonderfully abstract compositions.

With Candeias one is often on the brink of the conventional, yet at the same time oddly distanced from it. What might have been a banal shot of birds taking flight, conventional sign for "freedom," shifts its meaning because the birds are vultures and their flight ascends from a garbage dump. The film is replete with what at first seem to be conventional subjective shots, except that the shots are eccentric in their angulation and often only retroactively defined as subjective. Candeias seems particularly intrigued by the space that separates human faces from the recording lens; time and time again, hands extend themselves into the camera's field of vision in a gesture of communication that aptly metaphorizes the basic impulse animating the film itself.

A Margem treats its lumpen characters with great warmth and respect. The image of a slum dweller patiently extracting lice from her mate's hair is treated with immense tenderness, as an act of love equal to any other. *A Margem* suggests, to paraphrase a revolutionary slogan from May 1968, that "nous sommes tous des marginaux." The film denounces as a cruel mystification the notion that marginals are somehow "outside" society. In fact, they are its product and its distorting mirror image, the repressed other that reflects the truth about the larger social body. At the same time, the film hints at an analogy to cinema itself. There is no single valid cinema, in relation to which all other cinemas are to be belittled as marginal and inferior. For Candeias, all cinemas are created equal as all human beings are created equal. It is this quiet but radical egalitarianism that gives force to Candeias's work and makes him, in some ways, the conscience and founder of Underground Cinema.

Working in the low-life district of São Paulo called Boca do Lixo (Mouth of Garbage or "Garbage Zone" whence one of the other labels for Underground Cinema—Mouth of Garbage Cinema), Candeias initiated a number of filmmakers into a method of filmmaking whereby virtually the only expenses were the film itself, the laboratory work, and the camera. By 1971, the movement could claim a significant number of filmmakers and at least thirty feature films, including Rogério Sganzerla, *Bandido da Luz Vermelha* ("The Red Light Bandit," 1968); Ozualdo Candeias, *A Margem*, 1967; *Meu Nome é Tonho* ("My Name is Tonho," 1969); Júlio Bressane, *Matou a Família e Foi ao Cinema* ("Killed the Family and Went to the Movies," 1970); João Trevisan, *Orgia: Ou o Homem Que Deu Cria* ("Orgy: Or the Man who Gave Birth," 1970); Andrea Tonacci, *Blá-Blá-Blá*, 1968; *Bangue-Bangue* ("Bang-Bang," 1971); André Luiz Oliveira, *Meteorango Kid: O Herói Intergaláctica* ("Meteorango Kid: Intergalactic Hero," 1969); Neville Duarte d'Almeida, *Jardim de Guerra* ("War Garden," 1970); and Luiz Rosemberg Filho, *América do Sexo* ("America of Sex," 1970).

While they were in some respects intentionally marginal, the Underground directors were also marginalized, harassed by censors, and boycotted by exhibitors. They had difficulty getting their films screened not only because a censorious government banned some films (Neville Duart d'Almeida's *Jardim de Guerra*), or demanded unacceptable cuts in others (João Trevisan's *Orgia: Ou o Homem Que Deu Cria*), but also

Luiz Rosemberg Filho's *Crônica de um Industrial* (1978)

because exhibition was monopolized either by Cinema Novo or by government-encouraged soft-core porn films (*pornochanchadas*). When their films were seen, therefore, it tended to be in special showings, in cine-clubs, or at the diverse cinematheques.

While one hesitates to make facile generalizations about such a diverse movement, one can discern tendencies. The Underground films are generally violent, irreverent, iconoclastic; their very titles explode with polemical violence. In the hour of maximum repression, they strive to keep the spirit of anarchic revolt alive. Many films make reference to the climate of repression and torture then reigning in Brazil. *Matou a Família* includes an apparently gratitous torture sequence, while in *Jardim de Guerra* a marginal is pitilessly tortured by a right-wing organization, to the sound of Gounod's "Ave Maria." In these films, desperate lumpen anti-heroes embark on a mad search for personal and collective liberation, and sex and drugs become metaphors for freedom. At the same time, the films seem pessimistic about possibilities for real change, leading some critics to condemn the Underground as "suicide-cinema." In these films, an ineluctable hemorrhage seems to extend the protracted agony of Paulo Martins in *Land in Anguish*. Images of impotence and self-aggression proliferate. In Neville Duarte d'Almeida's *Piranhas do Asfalto* ("Asphalt Piranhas") a character castrates himself. The protagonist of *Bandido da Luz Vermelha* ("Red Light Bandit") dies electrocuted, and the two women of *Matou a Família e Foi ao Cinema* ("Killed the Family and Went to the Movies") kill each other joyfully as part of a homoerotic suicide pact.

The Underground is stylistically pluralist, but here again certain characteristic strategies appear. Conventional linear narrative tends to be subverted, but in diverse, often contradictory ways. Andrea Tonacci's *Blá-Blá-Blá* has virtually no "action" whatsoever; the film simply juxtaposes three discourses (three kinds of bla-bla-bla): that of a caricatural populist politician, that of a politicized worker, and that of an idealistic petite bourgeoise. The same director's *Bangue-Bangue* musically replays, with variations, two central actions: a quarrel between a taxi driver and his passenger, and the discussion of a couple in a bar. In other films, however, such as *Bandido da Luz Vermelha*, conventional narrative is subverted by a hyperbolic, parodic density of narrative incident. Editing styles in Underground films, similarly, tend to be anti-academic, but in different directions, ranging from the long static one-shot sequences of a Júlio Bressane to the deliriously rapid editing and frenzied movement of a Rogério Sganzerla. Many of the films use found footage; *Bandido da Luz Vermelha* cities American B-films and *Blá-Blá-Blá* uses newsreel footage of demonstrations in Paris and Peking. Others constitute generic parodies or conflations. *Bangue-Bangue* and *Meu Nome é Tonho* parody westerns. Ozualdo Candeias defines his *A Herança* ("The Inheritance") meanwhile as "a western based on *Hamlet* in which dialogue is replaced by the sounds of birds and animals."

Many Underground films take Cinema itself as theme. In João Trevisan's *Orgia: ou o Homem que Deu Cria* ("Orgy: Or the Man who Gave Birth," 1970) a gallery of figures, collectively representing Brazilian cinema in its diverse genres and incarnations, make a picaresque voyage through Brazil in an attempt to rediscover the country. In this very carnivalesque film (surely worth of a Bakhtinian analysis), a transvestite imitates Carmen Miranda, a *cangaceiro* gives birth, a film-critic (Jean-Claude Bernardet) sits naked on a pile of books, and cannibalistic Indians devour children. In other films, the self-referential theme is announced in the title. Andrea Tonacci's *Bangue-Bangue* translates as "Bang-Bang" or "Western," and Jairo Ferreiro defines his *O Vampiro da Cinemateca* ("The Vampire of the Cinematheque") as a "science-fiction film concerning experimental cinema."

Rather than attempt an exhaustive account of the subsequent evolution of a movement embracing more than a score of directors, it seems more useful, at this point, to examine a chronological sequence (1968–1974) of representative features, highlighting three of their defining characteristics: their intertextual relation to other films, their character as metacinema, and their aggressive stance toward the spectator. Rogério Sganzerla's *Bandido da Luz Vermelha* ("Red Light Bandit," 1968) is an ideal starting point, for it is a seminal Underground film and one which typifies certain of the movement's strategies. Only twenty-three when he made *Bandido*, Sganzerla came to filmmaking as a critic from a prestigious São Paulo newspaper, and his films are obviously the product of a critic and a cinephile. He calls *Bandido* a "western about the Third World." Its characters are, once again, marginals: thieves, drug addicts, smugglers, prostitutes, and artists. The film's protagonist is Jorge, an urban hustler of dubious origins who joins the underworld of Boca do Lixo and who attacks the wealthy in the sanctity of their homes. He gains his sobriquet in virtue of his novel approach to theft: he invariably carries a red lantern and has long parleys with his victims. A thief and a killer who enjoys his work, he is as unsentimental as a film noir psychopath. Despite a general dragnet by the police, he circulates freely, supremely bored by the ineptitude of the police. The sensationalist press amplifies his exploits, calling him the Zorro of the Poor. He spends his stolen money on extravagant clothes, excursions to the beach, and long evenings with prostitutes in tasteless cabarets. He frequents cinemas full of furtively trysting homosexuals (cf. *Masculin, Féminin*) where he looks at the screen through binoculars. The police finally catch up with Jorge, but not before he does himself in. When his persecutor, Inspector Cabeção, finds his corpse, the inspector accidentally electrocutes himself by the very apparatus that he had rigged up for Jorge.

Such a plot summary, however, makes *Bandido* seem more linear and of a piece than it in fact is. The film exploits a common Underground strategy: generic conflation. Sganzerla calls the *Bandido* a "film-summa: a western, a musical documentary, detective story, comedy, *chanchada* and science fiction." He wanted to meld "the sincerity of documentary (Rossellini), the violence of the gangster film (Fuller), the anarchic rhythm of comedy (Sennett, Keaton), the brutal narrative simplification of the western (Hawks) and the love of long shots and open spaces

(Mann)." This improbable collage of incompatible genres makes the film inevitably anti-illusionistic, turning it into a compilation of pastiches, a kind of cinematic writing in quotation marks. In his list of models for the film, Sganzerla neglects a crucial one — Jean-Luc Godard. In some ways, *Bandido* is Sganzerla's *À Bout de Souffle*. Like that film, *Bandido* renders homage to the B-film. Its principal actor (Paulo Villaça) physically resembles Belmondo and shares with him his flip style, a Humphrey Bogart at two removes. The film's wildly tilted angles recall certain shots in *Bande à Part*; the slapstick violence evokes *Weekend*, and Jorge's mode of self-annihilation is modeled on *Pierrot le Fou*. The overloaded, hyperactive soundtrack, meanwhile, recalls *1 plus 1*. Like Godard, Sganzerla emphasizes written language in the form of headlines, news tickertapes, and shaving cream graffiti. At one point, Jorge writes "Merci" on the back of one of his victims; a sardonic subtitle obligingly translates the word into Portuguese. Again like Godard, Sganzerla makes personal appearances in his film, once as a spectator in a movie theater, and once in the form of a childhood portrait. All these self-referential devices — the virtuoso display of homages, the omnipresent film posters, the cinematic citations — recall Godard.

Bandido's soundtrack is densely overlaid with intertextual references, a veritable anthology of Hollywood programmatic music, classical sym-

Rogerio Sganzerla's *Red Light Bandit* (1968)

phonic pieces, and Brazilian and American camp materials. Often three or four pieces of music play simultaneously. Beethoven's Fifth is fused with the Brazilian folksong *Asa Branca* in a provocative leveling of "high" and "low" art. But the film's most important innovation has to do with its off-screen narration. The narrators of *Bandido* have the affected metallic delivery of radio announcers. At times, the voices recall the aggrandizing tones of movie previews; amplified by an echo-chamber, the narrators declaim the hero's prowess, so that the film becomes a self-mocking advertisement for itself. At times the narration anticipates events; often it seems to lose itself entirely. The different narrators cut each other off progressively, and lapse into a verbal perplexity that is the sign of the film itself.

The narration of *Bandido* is decentered; it lacks a diegetic core. The off-screen narration is out of synch with what is happening on the screen, and the diverse narrations, with their multiple focuses, contradict one another. Within this heterogenous collage of discourses, the character becomes nothing more than a palimpsest of quotations. At one point, a subtitle intervenes: "my last bomb." It is characteristic of the film's discourse that we have no idea whether the "my" refers to the protagonist or the director.

Underground Cinema often displays an Oedipal hostility to its cinematic parent, Cinema Novo, a hostility clearly marked in the title of Bressane's *Killed the Family and Went to the Movies*. *Bandido* too stands in parodic relation—parody being that mode which reconciles affectionate emulation and mordant critique—to Cinema Novo. The director pointedly sets fire, at one point, to the famous Saint George triptych that opens *Antônio das Mortes*. At another point, the narrator mentions a girl who liked to go to proms and talk about Cinema Novo. The film's initial images and sounds demonstrate this tendency to simultaneously cite and criticize Cinema Novo. It shows black slum children dancing around garbage dump fires on the outskirts of São Paulo. On the soundtrack, Sganzerla quotes the powerful *candomblé* music from Glauber Rocha's *Land in Anguish*. This audio-visual montage constitutes both a tribute and a critique. The apocalyptic energy suggests Rocha at his best, but at the same time, Sganzerla seems to be saying that these images, and not the stylized allegorical images of Rocha's films, tell the truth about underclass life in Brazil.

While prolonging certain preoccupations of Cinema Novo, *Bandido* criticizes its characteristic modes of expression. The flip humor of the film indirectly critiques the humorless didacticism of some of Cinema Novo, while the brilliantly reckless camera work and unorthodox editing mock what Sganzerla sees as Cinema Novo's "academicism." *Bandido* is full of socially motivated black humor and satiric touches. A brilliantly drawn populist politician in the film proclaims his platform: giving Chiclets to the poor and constructing homes for unwed fathers. The narration tells of two slum dwellers trying to steal the other's wallet, only to discover that neither even *has* a wallet. As a bourgeois woman is being robbed by the Red Light Bandit, she protests meaninglessly that she will not "talk to strangers." In all this one detects a kind of pop attitude, a refusal of Cinema Novo's high art seriousness.

Bandido develops, and modifies, one of the primary narrative and esthetic procedures of Cinema Novo — the erudite elaboration of the materials of Brazilian popular culture. But whereas the popular culture that interested Cinema Novo was largely rural and literary, the Underground is more interested in urban popular culture and especially in the mass-media. (Cinema Novo, it should be added, is largely Rio de Janeiro based, while the Underground is centered in São Paulo.) *Bandido* draws on the degraded material of the Third World mass-media, both in its local forms (the sensationalist press, the radio) and in its imported forms (American B-films and TV shows). The subproducts of an imperialized mass culture, the film suggests, now form part of popular culture in Brazil and these subproducts are more real to most Brazilians than the blind singers and folk dancers that peopled many Cinema Novo films.

André Luiz Oliveira's *Meteorango Kid: O Herói Intergaláctico* ("Meteorango Kid: Intergalactic Hero," 1969) was directly inspired, according to its director, by *Bandido da Luz Vermelha*. Like the Sganzerla film, it weaves cinematic *clins d'oeil* and pop references into a fragmented and discontinuous audio-visual tapestry. The film's loose narrative structure revolves around a day in the life of a revolted teenager from Bahia named Lula, including both the outer world of his actions (smoking dope, discussing politics, visiting a film producer, celebrating his birthday), and the inner world of his subjectivity. Like some of the protagonists of the English New Wave — Morgan, Billy Liar — Lula nurtures all sorts of vindictive and self-aggrandizing fantasies from the movies and the mass-media. The opening images show him, made up to look like the pictorial Jesus and haloed by backlighting, being crucified on a palm tree. Lula embroiders his daily routines with daydreams, successively imagining himself as Tarzan, Batman, and other figments of the imagination of the cultural industry.

Meteorango Kid is what Brazilians call a "filme de curtição," a film to groove on. It is a sensual hymn, or better, a cine-samba, to the counter-culture. Dedicated, symptomatically, to the filmmaker's own hair, its tone recalls that of Dylan in "Mr. Jones"; the spectator, especially the square spectator, suspects that something is happening, but is unsure as to precisely what it is. The film orchestrates an orgy of Brazilian and Anglo-American pop references: Caetano Veloso, Gilberto Gil, the Beatles, Jimi Hendrix, and Frank Zappa, seated magisterially on his countercultural toilet. The hero is "intergalactic" not only in the sense that he fantasizes himself as a science-fiction hero but also because his imagination is deeply involved with international cinematic and pop music "stars." The film itself speaks a kind of mass-media Esperanto — the

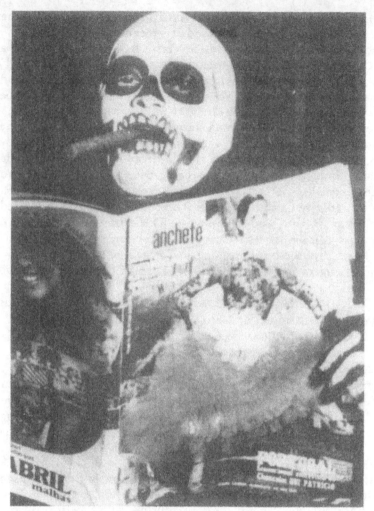

A$$untina das Amérikas (1977)

cultural language that simultaneously channelled and co-opted the socially aggressive impulses of late sixties youth. It was in this period, it should be noted, that the mass-media "invaded" cities like Bahia, until then on the periphery of Brazilian capitalist development, thus leading to a situation of enforced cosmopolitanism and to the heightened awareness of international pop culture. That the film merely registers this situation without really analyzing it is attributable, perhaps, to the director's youth (twenty-three) or to a conscious option for the sensuous and playful as opposed to the politically didactic.

The oeuvre of Júlio Bressane, one of the most prolific and brilliant of the Brazilian Underground filmmakers, constitutes a protracted exercise in metacinema. The very title of his *Matou a Família e Foi ao Cinema* ("Killed the Family and Went to the Movies," 1970) evokes the preoccupations and tone of many of his films: the Oedipal violence of "killed the family," the self-referentiality of "went to the cinema," and the scandalous parataxis of the copulative that promiscuously equates the stuff of antique tragedy (patricide and matricide) with the witless search for entertainment. The provocative amorality of the title announces a film in which stomach-turning brutality is registered with icy indifference. The murders promised by the title are delivered, with virtually no additional spectatorial preparation, during the first five minutes. The film elicits, and then dissipates, its enigmas, in what amounts to a kind of perverse hermeneutics; it refuses to slowly and coyly remove the garments of the plot in the conventional narrative striptease.

Having "killed the family," Bressane's nameless protagonist "goes to the movies." He sees, more precisely, a film called "Perdidas de Amor" ("Lost Women of Love"). At this point, the film becomes a Chinese box of representations within representations, for the film never clearly opens or closes the quotation marks around the film-within-the-film. It is never clear which film we are seeing: *Matou a Família* or *Perdidas de Amor*. At one point one of the women characters, presumably from "Perdidas de Amor," speaks of seeing a film consisting of "crimes in dirty places without any connection," a description that applies equally well to *Matou a Família* itself. Thus a play of doublings and mirror images is set up, an infinite regress of representations in which the spectator loses his/her bearings and is forced to reflect on the factitious status of filmic representation itself.

Matou a Família — by its "faulty" technique, its gratuitous dialogue, its disjunctive soundtrack, its caricatural acting — "exiles" its own spectators. It lays end to end autonomous sequences with only minimal connection, some characterized by horrendous violence and others by vacuous banality. We as spectators feel equally exiled in both instances, for the film provides no dramatic or characterological center, no perspective from which to judge the banality or the horror. This decentering occurs, for example, when Bressane superimposes Carmen Miranda's effervescent version of "What a great country for partying" on images of unredeemed squalor. It occurs, again, in the film's final sequence, where the two women, tenderly, playfully, lingeringly, murder each other, to the sound of a Brazilian pop singer endlessly entoning the same hackneyed phrase, while the camera maintains its aggressively laconic attitude.

Bressane's *O Anjo Nasceu* ("The Angel Is Born"), released the same year as *Matou a Família*, develops certain variations on these structural aggressions. If *Matou a Família* is perverse in its hermeneutics, *O Anjo Nasceu* is perverse in its syntax. The film maintains the facade of a linear tale: two bandits — one black and one white — steal and murder. The perversity consists in the film's ellipses. First of all, it often inverts the conventional process by eliding not the superfluous but rather that which the conventional spectator would regard as most essential. The white bandit, at one point, is obviously wounded, but the film never explains how he received his wound. Secondly, *O Anjo Nasceu* refuses the conventional narrative legerdemain that suggests that the events of the film form part of a temporal continuum extending beyond the film itself, with an implied "off-screen" anteriority (a setting, a situation) and futurity (the projected conjugal bliss of classical happy endings). The opening shots of a slum, for example, seem to promise the kind of sociological definition one might expect from a conventional realistic film, and more precisely, from a Neo-Realist or early Cinema Novo film. Instead, the film abruptly changes setting and the slum is forgotten. The initial shot is retroactively exposed as a pseudo-establishing shot, a sociological red herring. The film refuses to imply some social or psychological substratum on which the film rests.

By its refusal to make any comment on its marginal characters, *O Anjo Nasceu* grants them a kind of understated solidarity. The two criminals might be seen, in this sense, as recalling the radical criminality evoked by the figure and the work of Saint Jean Genet, comedian and martyr. Their crime simply exists, without forethought, without program, without redemption. Its tranquil self-confidence becomes clear in the sequence where they break into the house they plan to use as a hideout. They enter the house in the most natural way, without surreptitiousness, exploring it with unaffected curiosity, as if there were never any question that it belonged to them as much as to its "owners." At another point, the two bandits watch the televised transmission of the first astronauts landing on the moon. Richard Nixon, the earthly representative of official power, occupying a small rectangle to the left of the screen, congratulates the astronauts with perfunctory clichés about peace and progress. The black bandit comments: "They're really out of it. Why do they go to the moon, when I've already been there for a long time?" As Brazilian critic Fernando Mesquita suggests, the bandits, in their lunar solitude, represent the hidden face of the official earth. The film implicitly identifies with this hidden face; the film itself represents a cool and tranquil kind of criminality, an audio-visual assault and battery. Like the crimes depicted, it simply exists in all of its provocative gratuitousness, a nihilistic gesture directed against the hypocritical discourse of power.

The film's final shot typifies its refusal of all teleology and redemption. A static shot, held for eight minutes, shows a deserted highway stretching toward the horizon. On the soundtrack: a Brazilian folksong with no clear relation either to the image or to the "story" of the bandits. Virtually nothing occurs within the image, except that at one point the camera zooms in, abruptly and uselessly, as if in an attempt to take the vanishing point by surprise. The zoom, a conventional signifier of a movement of attention, here signifies nothing. Unlike the forty-five-minute zoom of Michael Snow's *Wavelength*, which at least culminates in a visual pun referring back to the film's title, the zoom in *O Anjo Nasceu* has no

Paulo Cesar Pereio in *Bangue-Bangue* (1971)

diegetic or structural justification whatsoever. It is simply there. One need only think of the countless "meaningful" highway endings of films—from Chaplin's final iris-ins to Paulo's upraised rifle in Rocha's *Land in Anguish*—to realize how radical *O Anjo Nasceu* is in its resolutely proffered negations.

Andrea Tonacci's *Bangue-Bangue* (1971) is perhaps even more audacious in its metacinematic subversions. The title refers, in Portuguese, to any violent film and especially to westerns, but its author defines the film as a "Maoist detective comedy." Like many of Bressane's films, *Bangue-Bangue* constantly promises a story that never arrives, which is perpetually derailed and interrupted. The film consists of fifteen segments, many of them composed of one-shot sequences, and involves five characters: a central figure, who frequently dons a monkey mask, chased by three gangsters and a magician who makes the characters appear and disappear by stop photography, as the auditory logo of Twentieth Century-Fox plays on the soundtrack. One of the gangsters is blind; he shoots around him indiscriminately, providing the film with the titular bang-bangs and establishing a robust atmosphere of incompetent marksmanship. The chase structure of the film is mere pretext, a tenuous thread on which to hang images and sounds. This tenuousness becomes obvious when, fairly late in the film, one of the gangsters (a transvestite) begins to offer what seems a distorted synopsis of the film: "Once upon a time there were three bad bandits. They say that one was the mother, but no one knows for sure." Suddenly, the plot is abruptly cut short by a cream pie, coming from behind the camera, thrown in the face of the storyteller, in a gesture that aptly expresses the filmmaker's scorn toward conventional plot.

Bangue-Bangue, according to its director, is partially inspired by Umberto Eco's *Oeuvre Ouverte*. The film constitutes a structured play of changes on given situations and images, variations on the theme of virtually nothing. Three sequences especially recapitulate, in a kind of *mise-en-abîme*, the film's structural logic. In one, an extended one-shot sequence, the central character argues with a taxi driver about the best route to a given destination, as a camera placed behind both characters records the taxi's confused itinerary through the streets of Belo Horizonte. The sequence, which recurs in a slightly different form later in the film, implicitly compares the film experience itself to a taxi ride, with its driver-director and its passenger-spectator, in which both the destination and the route are not simply given but must be argued over. The question is process, not product, passage, not destination. Another sequence proposes a different analogy for the film experience. A man and a woman initiate, five times in succession, the same conversation, concluding that the word "Hi" should be substituted for expressions like "How are you" and "Good morning." The sequence implicitly compares the film experience to discourse, to conversation. It consists, more accurately, of metadiscourse, discourse on discourse, just as the film is metacinema. The point of the discourse, furthermore — the desirability of using as few words as possible — is contradicted by the articulation of the discourse, which is wordy and redundant. What matters, the sequence seems to be saying, is not the message but the articulation, or better, the inseparable connection between the two, a point that is illustrated when the same conversation is played once with harsh ambient noise and then again with harp music, to completely different effect.

The third "microcosmic" sequence is a five-minute "chase" in which the camera pursues a jeep over a Monument Valley-like landscape. The accompanying music represents a kind of pop version of Ravel's *Bolero* in the sense that it maintains a threshold of slowly accelerating excitement that never reaches a climax. Like the film as a whole, the sequence mocks the spectator who demands explanations (the long ride is never "justified" narratively) and who insists on some sort of narrative orgasm, rather than this frustrating plateau of artificially prolonged tumescence, an orgasm that the film, in its perpetual coitus interruptus, rigorously denies.

In a number of sequences of *Bangue-Bangue* the principal character dons a monkey mask and looks at himself in the mirror. The spectator is confronted with an ignoble double, a grotesque repository for a spectatorial identification, in an image whose Lacanian implications might well be explored. At the same time, we occasionally see the camera reflected in the mirror or in the eyes of the ape man. When we do not literally see the camera or, as at one point, the entire filmmaking crew, we see the shadow of the camera. *Bangue-Bangue*, from its title to its final image of the soundstrip passing through a movieola, simply never lets us forget that we are spectators at a film.

Júlio Bressane's *Rei do Baralho* ("King of the Cards," 1973), like

Bangue-Bangue, might be said to consist of scraps from the junk heap of cinematic history. What Tonacci does with the gangster film, Bressane does with the *chanchada* (the frivolous Brazilian genre in which Carmen Miranda made her debut). *Rei do Baralho* is a metachanchada, a parody of a parody in the sense that *chanchada* already tended to parody, at times unconsciously, American musical comedies. *Rei do Baralho* was filmed in studios specifically associated with the *chanchada* tradition — the Cinédia studios in Jacarepaguá — and exploits that studio's decor. The film provides a collage of stereotype scenes, each associated with a specific set: a ship, a casino, a cabaret. The decors are minimal and impoverished, in the style of *chanchada*, and one shot reveals the totality of the space, revealing it as forming the self-chosen parameters of much of the film's fiction. The "plot" centers on a discreet romance between Grande Otelo (the black actor best known in the United States for his role in *Macunaíma*) and a blonde Jayne Mansfield look-alike. The film weaves between them a ludic-erotic play of promises, delays, detours, and interdictions, a kind of *Last Year in Jacarepaguá*. The title and its card reference already announces the film's aleatory serial organization, in which specific shots, gestures, scraps of dialogue, situations, become cards to be shuffled at the filmmaker's will. Despite its numerous frustrations for the spectator, *Rei do Baralho* does offer one conventional satisfaction. In the final shot, the two principals, who up to this point have barely touched, exchange a prolonged, and very Hollywoodean, kiss. Bressane has shuffled his cards in such a way as to deal out at least this one final, if ironic, *frisson*.

Artur Omar's *Triste Trópico* (1974) might best be defined as a metacinematic anthropological documentary. Its title, transparently inspired by Lévi-Strauss's ethnographic memoir about Brazil, triggers an evocative chain of cultural associations. While Lévi-Strauss went from Europe to Brazil only to discover, in a sense, the ethnocentric prejudices of Europe, the human subject of *Triste Trópico* goes to Europe — and here his trajectory parallels that of innumerable Brazilian artists and intellectuals — only to discover Brazil. Thus the film inserts itself within the extended discussion of Brazil's problematic cultural relationship to Europe — its colonizing mother — a discussion undergoing frequent metamorphoses and changes of etiquette: "Nationalism," "Modernism," "Tropicalism." *Triste Trópico* is not a Tropicalist film, however; it is rather a distanced reflection on the whole notion of the "tropics" as Europe's other, as something exotic.

Triste Trópico disorients by constantly altering its relation to the spectator. The opening shots — traffic in São Paulo, old photographs — and their musical accompaniment, make us expect a fairly innocuous documentary. An off-screen narrator, with the confident tone and stilted language to which documentaries have accustomed us, tells us that the film concerns a certain Arthur Alvaro de Noronha, known as Dr. Arthur, who returned from studies in Paris to practice medicine in Brazil.

Artur Omar's *Triste Trópico* (1974)

Footage, presumably dating from the period of Dr. Arthur's life, shows a man with his family; we infer that the man in the image is Dr. Arthur. In Paris, we are told, the doctor became friendly with André Breton, Paul Eluard, and Max Ernst, our first clue that a truly surreal biography awaits us. As the film continues, two things happen. First, the narration becomes progressively more improbable and hallucinatory. The doctor becomes involved with Indians, compiles an almanac of herbal panaceas, becomes an indigenous Messiah, and finally degenerates into sodomy (an exclamatory intertitle underlines the horror) and cannibalism. The narrated descent into a Brazilian Heart of Darkness coincides with our own descent into a tangled jungle of cinematic confusion. Secondly, the images progressively detach themselves from the narration, becoming less and less illustrative and more and more chaotic and apocalyptic. We begin to suspect that we have been the dupes of an immense joke, as if Borges had slyly rewritten Conrad and that the illustrious Dr. Arthur is merely the figment of the imagination of the director, whose name, we should remember, is also Arthur.

The central procedure of *Triste Trópico* is to superimpose an impeccably linear (albeit absurd) narration on extremely discontinuous sonorous and imagistic materials. While the narration is coherent within the limits of its implausibility, all the other tracks of the film—image, music, noise, titles—form a kind of serial chaos, an organized delirium. The image track consists of the most heterogenous materials: amateur movies from the twenties, contemporary footage from Europe, shots of Rio's carnival, staged scenes, archival material, clips from other films, engravings, book covers, and almanac illustrations. The music constitutes a chaotic anthology of Brazilian, American, Argentinian, and Cuban music, inserted briefly and discontinuously as if someone were rapidly switching the radio dial. Within this audio-visual bricolage we encounter certain Lévi-Straussian binary oppositions; some specifically cinematic (black-white versus color; two-dimensional versus three-dimensional; old footage versus new; static versus moving) and some broadly cultural: coast and interior ("raw" Brazil and "cooked" Europe; classical Apollonian order and Dionysian Carnivalesque frenzy; *la pensée sauvage* and *la pensée civilisée*).

Triste Trópico is a Brazilian *Witchcraft through the Ages*, and the primary object of its attack is the witchcraft of cinema itself. The film constantly surprises us in our naive belief that seeing is believing, that what we hear is what we see, and that what we see is what we hear. The narration's constant attempt to validate itself with dates, statistics, citations, and archival footage is a joke on the suspect authenticating procedures of cinema itself and on our own implicit faith that narrators will not abuse our credulity. The good Doctor Arthur Omar does not offer us a magic potion. He does not celebrate witchcraft; rather, he exposes the craft behind its rituals. Rather than have us become magicians, he would have us all become our own anthropologists.

The most recent productions of the Brazilian avant-garde, in sum, define themselves by a series of refusals — of linear narrative, of closure, of technical "competence," of conventional continuity. Their relation to the spectator is one of aggression, creating what Ismail Xavier has called a "festival of discomfort." Rather than entertain, they create a salutary disease.

33
"Seeing, Hearing, Filming: Notes on the Brazilian Documentary"

Introduction

Cinema Novo was deeply concerned with presenting a realistic visage of Brazilian society, so it is not surprising that the movement arose largely within a documentary mode of production. Linduarte Noronha's *Aruanda* (1960) provided the young filmmakers with an early model, and many of the initial Cinema Novo films were themselves documentaries. Even after establishing the fiction-feature as the dominant mode, Cinema Novo filmmakers continued producing documentaries, including the seminal *Maioria Absoluta* ("Absolute Majority," 1964), by Leon Hirszman; *Integração Racial* ("Racial Integration," 1964), by Paulo César Saraceni; *O Povo do Velho Pedro* ("The People of Old Pedro," 1964), by Sérgio Muniz; *Em Busca de Ouro* ("In Search of Gold," 1965), and *O Circo* ("The Circus," 1965), by Arnaldo Jabor. In 1964 Thomas Farkas produced four films that later combined in the feature-length *Brasil Verdade* ("Brazil Truth"): *Viramundo*, by Geraldo Sarno, *Nossa Escola de Samba* ("Our Samba School"), by Manuel Giménez, *Subterrâneos do Futebol* ("The Subterranean World of Soccer"), by Maurício Capovilla, and *Memória do Cangaço* ("Memories of the Cangaço"), by Paulo Gil Soares. Around the same time, Joaquim Pedro de Andrade made Brazil's first attempt at direct cinema in *Garrincha Alegria do Povo* ("Garrincha, Joy of the People," 1963). Later, between

1969 and 1971, Thomas Farkas produced a series of twenty-two short documentaries by Paulo Gil Soares, Eduardo Escorel, Sérgio Muniz, and Geraldo Sarno, in an effort to cinematically "map" the northeast.

Despite such continuous production, the documentary has existed precariously without a substantial market to guarantee a return on investments. It has thus remained a largely artisan form of cinematic practice. In 1973, the documentary was included in protectionist legislation reserving a portion of the market for national films, a measure that stimulated them and provided them a limited amount of stability. The documentary continues to be one of the most dynamic and politically progressive modes of production in Brazilian cinema.

In this article, José Carlos Avellar, film critic of the *Jornal do Brasil*, traces changes in the documentary over the last twenty years, focusing particularly on the evolution of the camera's attitude toward the profilmic reality in a constantly shifting political context.

"Seeing, Hearing, Filming: Notes on the Brazilian Documentary"

JOSÉ CARLOS AVELLAR

In *Viramundo* (Geraldo Sarno, 1964), the camera goes to the São Paulo train station to record the arrival of a train carrying northeastern migrants. These migrants had abandoned the countryside for the uncertain promise of employment in the big city—in civil construction, metal industries, or in some more marginal activity such as collecting paper, glass, or scrap iron—that would guarantee them enough income to support their generally numerous families. Initially, the camera is static. It sees the migrants leaving the station, leaning against the wall, with a somewhat startled expression when faced with the policemen who check their suitcases or bundles of clothing. The camera then begins to move slowly. It passes over the faces, examines the baggage check, closes in, and, finally, begins to talk with the people. It asks about life in the northeast, about work in the countryside, about their reasons for fleeing to the city, about the hope they brought along with their tattered baggage. From that point on, *Viramundo* is organized like a dialogue.

There are direct conversations in which the interviewer and the interviewee are together in the image and in which the spectator hears the interviewer's questions. There are also indirect conversations in which only the person interviewed appears as well as those resulting from the montage of two or three separate interviews, so that what one person says is complemented by others, as if in a natural conversation.

What orients these two kinds of conversation is the camera's concern

Segunda-Feira (1975)

with not acting merely as a machine for seeing and hearing, but rather with reacting as a person: participating in the conversation, cutting a sentence in the middle if the emotional reaction to what is said so requires, and placing one statement beside another in order to complement or contradict it, just as one might do in conversation.

After documenting the arrival of the train and identifying the passengers as they begin their search for work and housing, *Viramundo* advances like a dialogue unsatisfied with the immediate information. It also attempts to investigate the mechanisms created more or less spontaneously by the city to receive, temporarily absorb, and then expel this mass of unskilled workers who are accustomed only to a hoe in a field. The conversation ranges from the arriving migrants to the industrial owners, to centers of social assistance and charity, to forms of religion, to northeasterners who have adapted and found stable employment, to those who move from job to job without learning a skill, and finally to those who, expelled by the lack of opportunities, return to the station to take a train back to the dry northeast.

In *São Caetano, Imigração Italiana* ("São Caetano, Italian Immigration"), made by Tânia Avieto ten years later, the camera goes to the gate of a metal industry to record the workers leaving the factory, some sons and daughters of Italian immigrants, and others who came from the northeast and managed to learn a profession. Initially the camera is static, but here it remains immobile throughout, focusing on the gate with a telephoto lens from across the street. The workers, out of focus in the background, approach, pass through the gate, and disappear from the frame. Sometimes they pass through the image without noticing the camera on the other side of the street. At times they slow their pace, surprised at the camera's presence.

The shot is at times crowded, and other times empty. The workers leave the factory in silence, in groups, talking, or walk toward a doorman or some other person beyond the frame. The surprised look of some of them toward the camera is at times especially evident, often provoking a comment or a smile, but none of this interferes with the camera's comportment. It remains still and watches. The shot remains on the screen a little more than three minutes, a time that seems much longer due to the camera's immobility, its apparent indifference toward what it sees, and due to the sound accompanying the image: we do not hear the worker's voices or any ambient noise; no footsteps, no factory whistles, not even the sound of the buses and cars that, from time to time, cut across the image. We hear only a smooth and slow piano piece.

The shot begins and ends at a given moment. Workers leaving the factory is no more than a slice of reality, almost a cinematic in-joke, or perhaps an attitude vis-à-vis the real. Midway in the shot, relatively hidden by other workers, a man passes through the gate wearing a shirt strangely painted with the design of an eye surrounded by the phrase "don't look at me like that." He crosses the frame like the other workers and is not isolated by the camera. The spectator probably does not see what is written on the shirt when viewing the film for the first time. But the film sees itself, manages to read itself, without being aware of the commentary that reality itself is making about the camera's comportment. It continues to look in the same manner, distant, from the other side of the street, without interfering, just as one might look without seeing, perhaps because the senses are all attuned to the music, the smooth and slow piano piece.

The comparison of these two attitudes vis-à-vis similar themes clearly exemplifies what has happened in the Brazilian documentary film over the last few years. The camera, we might say, has taken a step backwards, planted itself in a firm, almost defensive position in order to observe reality, to see without interfering in the object being seen, in sharp contrast to what was attempted in the sixties. Initially an attempt to pronounce, to act, to participate in the situation being filmed, the documentary assumed an apparently more simple position of revealing the fragment of reality before the camera, as if the object being filmed could explain itself and the spectator could visually grasp all of its meanings.

What one perceives with the simple examination of the camera's attitude toward the workers of *Viramundo* and *São Caetano, Imigração Italiana* becomes even more evident if we compare the use of music in the two films. While the second film attempts to achieve a sound that weds harmoniously with the image and does not clash with the contemplative attitude it proposes, the first film uses a contrastive sound. The music enters with evident sonority at the beginning, the end, and in the middle of the narrative to separate two blocks of interviews. This sung poetry, written especially for the film, functions as a text for the analysis of the situation, for despite its being written in the third person (as if it were another migrant being interviewed), it provides a general vision of the problem of northeastern migration to São Paulo, presenting a global understanding that transcends many of the partial depositions. The music acts, qualifies, completes, dialogues, and interferes in the spoken texts.

The music of *São Caetano, Imigração Italiana*, on the other hand, remains in the background as an accompaniment so the spectator can *see*. Cinema seems to be revealing something hidden or prohibited, as if, in this long period of rigid censorship, seeing — seeing anything, opening one's eyes — were a subversive act. After all, if the immediate divulgation of events and the simple relating of everyday facts had been prohibited, then reality itself must possess something that endangers the survival of the dictatorship. Cinema thus went out to see this "revolutionary" reality. It went to see without asking anything beyond that, without asking about possible points of view for registering this or that fragment of reality, without asking if the relationship between the camera and the people or objects filmed was the most effective possible. Faced with pressures of all kinds, there was no time for questions. The important thing was to see, to assume this subversive and threatening attitude.

According to Jom Azulay, his documentary *Os Doces Bárbaros* ("The Sweet Barbarians," about a musical tour interrupted by the arrest of one of the singers — Gilberto Gil) is a film that made itself. "It seemed that everything was already made, leaving us only the honorable and humble task of collecting the events as they were happening. I did not choose any of the scenes of the film; they just happened, and we took care so that, as one of the film's editors would say, the bubble would not burst."

In this attitude the director intends that which many documentaries made in the seventies also intended: to use the camera as if it were an absolutely objective instrument, capable of transmitting directly, without interference, an event that the spectator cannot see in person. The filmmaker does not interfere so as to not burst the bubble; his personality is manifested only through the choice of the subject to be filmed. Starting from this point, he glues his eyes to the lens, his ears to the microphone, and attempts to behave like a machine. The framing, the duration of the shot, the position of the microphone, the recorded sound, and the noises that may or may not interfere, in short, all the formal characteristics of the film, are determined by the events themselves. At first glance an impersonal, formalist attitude that from time to time reappears in the history of cinema or photography, becoming especially strong when people first sang their fascination for mechanized rather than artisan production, for the representational fidelity to the external aspects of the material world permitted by the machine, by photography, by the lens, by the mechanical eye.

But in reality this stance represents a personal attitude, a taking of a position against censorship and against everything that is symbolized by the allegorical language installed by the regime: the smooth movements

Os Doces Bárbaros (1976)

of a zoom, the low-contrast light of the sunset, the calm voice and didactic text of the so-called "subjects of educational interest," pieces of
governmental propaganda that are obligatorily screened before newsreels
and exhibited with regularity on all television channels. Seeing directly,
without imposing an artistic treatment on the object being seen, was
often the most immediate, the purest, and the most subversive response.

In the mid-seventies, when the expulsion of the northeastern labor
force from São Paulo became more violent, and the jobless and homeless
immigrants were randomly installing themselves beneath the city's
modern viaducts, João Batista de Andrade made *Migrantes* (1973), a five-
minute black-and-white documentary using direct sound and hand-held
camera. The film consists merely of an interview that does not exceed the

333

direct knowledge of any São Paulo resident. It interviews a woman and her children waiting for their husband/father who had gone out looking for work. It also interviews two or three curious residents, attracted, perhaps, by the camera. The questions are simple: the migrants are asked where they are from and why they are there. The passers-by are asked what should be done with the migrants. Nevertheless, this simple situation, when compared with the colorful and slick governmental films, provokes a sharp contrast. It alters the visual sensibility of the spectators, teaches them to see many details of Brazilian daily life that, although they desperately call attention to themselves in the street, continue to be unseen, hidden by the shadow of the great governmental works — viaducts, stadiums, highways, and bridges.

On presenting the documentary *Acidente de Trabalho* ("Work Accident," 1977), made in collaboration with the Metalworkers' Union of São Bernardo, its director Renato Tapajós defines the question very well:

> It does no good to elaborate an extremely brilliant, new cinematic language if that language has no resonance in the public to which the film is directed. The language we are searching for starts from the daily life of the worker — the work accident, unfortunately, is part of this life — in order to create in the worker audience a certain sense of "strangeness." This public identifies with this daily life, but suddenly begins to see it with other eyes. In an exhibition of the film, a worker told me that he thought it was excellent that we showed a foot pressing the pedal of a machine. It is something he does every day, but he can never stop and look at his own foot pressing the pedal.

In this period, the person filmed, the spectator and the filmmaker all seem to participate in a common sensation: that cinema surrounds what it registers with a kind of magic. On the screen things are seen differently; vision explicates, reality is amplified. Things that in daily life go unnoticed (because the system, or censorship, has invented a number of devices to make people myopic) can then be seen directly and in detail, since one does not perceive the presence of an intermediary, but merely the existence of a mechanical eye (and ear) that sees (and hears) better because it is objective. The language remains as invisible as the language of the traditional fiction film. By trying to eliminate every possible formal manipulation of the objective world, films end up reflecting a most evident and intentional subjectivity.

Much of the most significant Brazilian cinematic production is situated exactly in his imprecise border between documentary and fiction. The Brazilian cinema made since the early sixties has a certain documentary tone, in the sense that the artist searches for the bases of a form of expression in direct contact with the social and political context. The artist does not become an artist through academic training; cinema is not learned from the study of classical models, but rather from an immediate response to the surrounding reality. All production — fiction or documentary — is concerned with taking an esthetic model from reality itself and with mapping the country.

It is difficult, for example, to separate the documentary from the fictive in Orlando Senna's *Diamante Bruto* ("Uncut Diamond," 1977). We are apparently faced with fiction (a situation determined by the camera) filmed as if it were a documentary (by a camera that lets itself be led by improvised actions and the elements of the real world that condition the improvisation). Half of the film is taken from the novel *Bugrinha*, by Afrânio Peixoto: a television star returns to his home town and re-encounters his childhood girlfriend, the poor daughter of diamond prospectors. The other half is documentary, inspired by the presence of a famous television actor in a prospecting region.

It is even more difficult to separate the documentary from the fictive in another film co-directed by Orlando Senna, Jorge Bodansky, and Wolf Gauer, *Iracema*, 1975, that takes place in the Amazon region and concerns a truck driver who cuts through the Trans-Amazonic highway transporting cattle and wood. Here, there is not even an identifiable story, but rather merely isolated events revolving around the prostitution of minors along the road and the deforestation of the Amazon region for the construction of the trucks' refueling stations.

In these two films a professional actor mixes with non-actors who live their daily life or personages they know not through the study of methods of interpretation but rather through direct contact with real people. The professional actors play their own roles as strangers in the community: a television actor, a truck driver who came from the south to make money on the road. People of the region play their own roles: the daughter of a prospector, in love with the great television actor; the orphan girl who sees roadside prostitution as her only option. The mode of these "natural" actors transmits the sensation of something really lived, since the gestures are not studied, the dialogues are not precise and correctly spoken, and the movement within the form is not conventional. The personages make, so to speak, the wrong gestures and speak with the wrong words, as anyone would in natural conversation.

Such gestures thus yield new information for the professional actors, who elaborate them into strongly significant gestures; they take their mode of representation from reality. But, from the point of view of documentary, what interests us is the montage solution adopted in these films. Since the actors (or better, the non-actors) fail to express themselves with the precision common to professional actors, the montage (or the tone of the photograph, or the framing) should have, as in the documentary, an interpretive function.

In a certain moment of *O Xente, Pois Não* ("Why, of Course!"), a documentary by Joaquim Assis about an agriculture cooperative in the northeast, a small pond covered with minuscule green leaves covers the screen. A woman approaches and clears away the leaves to get water. After she walks away the camera remains focused on the water and

Iracema (1975)

registers, in a close shot, the movement of the leaves, which regroup until once again covering the open space with green, like a grassy lawn or a piece of land covered with vegetation. Accompanying this slow reassemblage of green leaves is a text with a single meaning composed of a series of individual depositions about the birth of the idea of cooperative work:

The drought united our hearts here. While we were isolated, life was different. We avoided each other. A time of crisis made us understand each other's value. In our land, here, whoever sees someone suffering and doesn't help is not a human being. A person who has something helps those who have nothing. One person knows one idea and the others know different ones. We are learning that everyone has a world in his own head. In his head he brings me a world. In my head I give a world to you. Every day in this life changes us. I am 54 years old and in these 54 years I have lived more than 54 lifetimes.

In the image are real things, green leaves floating on a body of water filmed without ornamentation. On the soundtrack there are real things as well, diverse depositions, people speaking in a more or less poetic mode about the formation of an agricultural community. The association of image and sound, produces a representation that goes beyond the limits of immediate knowledge of things seen and heard. The green specks that unite cease being leaves in the water and become symbolic of the formation of an agricultural community.

In *Viva Cariri* ("Long Live Cariri," 1970), by Geraldo Sarno, a documentary about the attempt to industrialize the *sertão* of Cariri, around Joazeiro, the city founded by Padre Cícero, a rancher (*fazendeiro*) pulls out a revolver and shoots three times in the air, a signal for his employees to gather in front of the porch to be filmed. The conversation before the shots (a pleasant talk about the size of the *fazenda* and the number of employees) is not heard. Another soundtrack, superimposed over the first, offers a different deposition about this same rancher, protesting with irritation against the conditions of life on the *fazenda*. We hear the sound of an image that does not appear on the screen. The shots thus appear as a reaction to the protests. When the *fazendeiro* takes his revolver from the holster, the irritated voice ends, and we hear the amplified sound of the shots in the foreground.

In another shot of *Viva Cariri* a thin man with a tired expression continuously beats a wooden mortar in an imprecise and darkened room. The camera enters the room and approaches the man's face. In yet another shot, near the end of the film, an old woman sitting on the ground eats manioc flour, taking it from the gourd with the tips of her fingers and throwing it slowly and precisely into her mouth, while she looks fixedly toward the camera.

We have here three rather expressive examples — regardless of their meaning at the moment of filming and despite the objectivity of the camera — that can only be apprehened within the dramatic structure that organizes the images. What is important is not only to make the spectator see the filmed situations as if he had been there, in place of the camera, as if he himself were a camera, but to make the spectator feel these images exactly as they were felt by the person behind the camera.

The important thing is to create (starting with the visual impressions registered by the camera) a dramatic structure leading the spectator to an effective understanding (and not to a merely visual recognition) of the filmed reality. In this sense the man who beats the mortar in the dark room is, at the same time, that which can be recognized visually — a thin, sick, hungry worker like so many others from the northeast — and also what he signifies in context, in the midst of other elements of the Cariri Valley: a representation of the mechanisms of the society in which he lives, which beats repeatedly, always with the same dry and muffled sound.

Suddenly all of the real characteristics of the image are overtaken by a sensation that surpasses the real. We see beyond the objectivity of the camera. We see only the repeated movement of his beating. Two distinct depositions, edited one over the other in a single image of a rancher who shoots in the air, results in a more faithful picture of reality than the direct registering, because it concentrates two distinct attitudes in one shot. The image of the old woman who throws bits of manioc flour in her mouth, an isolated unexplained shot, is more than a simple picture of one of so many elderly women who can be found on a street corner of any village in the *sertão*. She is the representation of the only gesture possible for poor people: the small movement with the hand to throw in the mouth portions of food picked up with the fingertips.

A mixture of these two impulses — seeing without questioning camera placement and ordering the filmed material as something to be manipulated for the construction of a cinematic narrative — is found in the films of Wladimir Carvalho, who perhaps best represents Brazilian documentary cinema in the last few years.

He produces his own films, with extremely simple technical resources

Raoni (1978)

and means, which circulate almost exclusively in film clubs and the cinematheques of Rio and São Paulo. Behind an appearance of extreme naturalism, he covers his documentation with a narration unconcerned with direct information (*A Bolandeira*, a short film about sugar mills, and *O País de São Saruê* ["The Country of Saint Saurê"], a feature-length film about the Peixe River Valley in Paraíba, have verse narrations).

In *O País de São Saruê*, the camera is often static, and what it films is equally still: the face of an old man, a religious print hanging on a wall, a dry landscape, and branches without leaves. But on the screen everything moves, because the amplified grain of the image breaks it into thousands of agitated points on a screen.

In *A Bolandeira*, the image remains focused throughout on the gears of the sugar mill, on the cane syrup dumped in wood boxes, on the smoke from the oven, and on the burning wood. The accompanying text, meanwhile, refers to the system of labor, the hard work of the employees, and the regalia of the mill owners. What the spectator sees, then, is no longer a static landscape, but rather an internally disintegrating reality, agitated but not really moving, like something compressed and ready to explode. The gear mechanism that squeezes the cane and transforms it into dry bagasse imagistically represents the labor system supporting the sugar plantations and mills.

Despite the lack of an organized system of production and exhibition, Brazilian filmmakers have been turning out documentaries of this type for the last twenty years. Such questions as composition of the shot are determined by technical possibilities or concrete conditions at the moment of filming. The filmmaker's proposed dramatic structure (i.e. the interpretation of the reality to be filmed) does not totally command the work of filming, either because the structure only becomes clear during the filming itself, or because it is solidified later, i.e. in the process of editing. But once the work of documentation is completed, and the footage is ready, it is all manipulated like a fragment of a possible film. And what determines this manipulation is not a concern with obeying all the rules of correct cinematic composition. The concern is not merely formal; it consists, rather, in the human impulse to go beyond the limits of the camera's merely objective vision.

34
"When Women Film"

Introduction

Feminist film critics have only recently alerted us to the strong current (often subterranean) of women filmmakers in world cinema such as Jeanne Roques (Musidora), Alice Guy Blaché, and Lois Weber. This article offers a contribution to this ongoing research project by focusing on women filmmakers in Brazil. Elice Munerato and Maria Helena Darcy de Oliveira, as part of a project ("Matinée Muses") financed by the Carlos Chagas Foundation, in cooperation with the Ford Foundation, were able to study most of the feature fiction films — at least those of which copies exist — made by women in Brazil. They reveal, first of all, that the tradition goes at least as far back as the twenties. As for the current boom in films by Brazilian women, the authors come to a surprising conclusion — that the recent films too often inherit, although in a subtly disguised manner, some venerable stereotypes.

"When Women Film"

ELICE MUNERATO AND MARIA HELENA DARCY DE OLIVEIRA

The history of Brazilian women's participation in the cinema is no exception to the rule: they have often performed in *front* of the camera, but they have but rarely worked *behind* it. The first film directed by a woman in Brazil was, most probably, *O Mistério do Dominó Negro* ("The Mystery of the Black Domino," 1930), by Cléo de Verberena, an actress who reportedly sold her own jewelry and property in order to finance her only film. (The means of financing was not as unusual as one might think, since most of the pioneer Brazilian filmmakers financed their films in similar ways.) It is quite possible, however, that there was a good deal of filmmaking by women during the early period (i.e., from the beginnings through 1940) that was simply never registered as such. Since most of the first productions of Brazilian cinema were precariously financed domestic undertakings, in which the husband was director, the wife and children actors, and a friend was cameraman, it is reasonable to assume that women often took on important functions in the production process. The actress Georgina Marchiani claimed to have filmed a number of sequences of *O Guarani*, made in São Paulo in 1916, since there was no regular cameraperson on the crew. Almery Steves and Rilda Fernandes, meanwhile, were associates of Aurora films, principal producers of what came to be called "the Recife cycle" (1925-1931).

The public came to love Carmen Santos in the twenties, largely through the film magazine *Cinearte*, since the three films in which she worked as an actress had never been screened publicly (*Urutau*, 1919; *A Carne*, 1924; and *Mademoiselle Cinema*, 1925). The producer of the first film disappeared with the negative, and the remaining two films are supposed to have been destroyed by fire. Another version of the incident, however, suggests that Antonio Seabra, with whom Carmen Santos lived and later married, and who financed the productions in which she participated, prohibited the film's exhibition for fear of "complications." *A Carne* ("Flesh"), based on the novel of the same name by Júlio Ribeiro, was considered rather risqué for its time, and *Mademoiselle Cinema* is supposed to have provoked difficulties with the police.

Carmen Santos, a film enthusiast, partially financed Humberto Mauro's *Sangue Mineiro* ("Minas Blood," 1928), a film in which she also worked as an actress, in order to assure its completion. In the same year she acted in and produced Mauro's never-to-be completed *Lábios sem Beijos* ("Lips without Kisses"). In 1930 she starred in *Limite*, Mário Peixoto's seldom seen but often praised avant-garde film. It was perhaps the very obstacles that Carmen Santos encountered during her career as an actress that led her to establish her own production company — Brasil Vita Filme — in 1932, with comfortable studios installed in Rio de Janeiro. In this period, Carmen Santos was responsible for the production of some of Humberto Mauro's most significant films, notably *Cidade Mulher* ("Woman City," 1934), *Favela de Meus Amores* ("Favela of My Loves," 1934), and *Argila* ("Clay," 1940). She also produced Otávio Mendes's *Onde a Terra Acaba* ("Land's End," 1932) and Luís de Barros's *Inocência* ("Innocence," 1949) and *O Rei do Samba* ("King of the Samba," 1952).

Carmen Santos directed only one film: *Inconfidência Mineira*

Carmen Santos

("Rebellion in Minas") in 1948. The film's production, according to some scholars, lasted from seven to ten years. Apart from producing and directing the film, Carmen Santos was also scriptwriter and actress. The film was a modest success, but unfortunately only a few fragments have survived. More a film enthusiast than a businesswoman, Carmen Santos left a will, before her death in 1952, stipulating that her studios never be destroyed.

In the early period of Brazilian cinema, women were primarily actresses, although they presumably also participated in such matters as art direction, decor, costume, makeup, in short, in tasks that merely extended what were regarded as the perennial obligations of women and that were therefore acceptable for a woman at the turn of the century. The lack of documentation for this kind of participation can be explained either by a certain scorn for such "minor" technical responsibilities or by the fact that it was not considered proper for women's names to appear in the credits, since cinema, like the theater before it, was still regarded as a *métier* incompatible with a decent reputation. It is only in 1941 that Gita de Barros is credited as the scriptwriter of the films by her husband Luis de Barros, with whom she had been working since 1914.

It as also in the forties that Gilda de Abreu, a key figure in the history of Brazilian cinema, came into prominence. With her husband, Vicente Celestino, she had her own production company that staged light operas in Rio theaters. Together they became known as a kind of Brazilian Jeanette MacDonald-Nelson Eddy duo. An extremely dynamic and productive woman, she not only performed as a singer and actress in radio, theater, and cinema (for example, in *Bonequinha de Seda* ["Little Silk Doll"] in 1936), she also wrote and adapted novels, plays, and musical numbers. Her first film as director, *O Ébrio* ("The Drunkard") in 1947, adapted a successful play by her husband, based on one of his musical compositions. The film was a huge box-office success. Five hundred copies of the film were made, it was shown throughout Brazil, and even today remains a popular success. Subsequently, Gilda de Abreu scripted *Pinguinho de Gente* ("Tiny Tot," 1949), which she directed in the following year, but without the same popular response. In 1951, she founded her own company, Pro-Arte, in order to make *Coração Materno* ("The Maternal Heart").

By her own account, Gilda de Abreu found filmmaking in the forties extremely difficult. The technicians were reluctant to take orders from a woman and doubted her ability to direct. On the set of *O Ébrio*, consequently, she wore slacks, in order to make herself the visible equal of men. Even after the immense success of her first film, she had difficulties with the filmmaking crew. It was only when she herself produced *Coração Materno* that the situation became more manageable. Her achievement was enormous, since besides directing, she also contributed as an actress. She subsequently abandoned filmmaking because, as she put it, the "romantic era of cinema had come to an end." In 1955, however, she did accept the task of scriptwriting *Chico Viola Não Morreu* ("Chico Viola Didn't Die"), and in 1973 she became involved once again, adopting one of her own plays, *Mestiça*, for the woman director Lenita Perroy. Shortly before her death in June 1979 (at the age of seventy-four), Gilda de Abreu was still writing novels and dreaming of finding a producer to finance a film biography of the Brazilian turn-of-the-century composer Carlos Gomes.

Between 1940 and 1960, one encounters an increasing number of women working as "script-girls" (obviously one of the few positions traditionally "monopolized" by women), as choreographers (also not surpris-

Gilda de Abreu as actress in her own *Coração Materno* (1951)

ing, since the role of *bailarina* was always seen as "typically feminine"), as editors, and production assistants. Only rarely, however, does one encounter women directors. It is in this phase that Brazilian cinema goes beyond the familial mode of production and begins to be produced by ambitious studios—Atlântida, Vera Cruz—with large crews, and whose principal products were, respectively, *chanchada* and melodrama. These products were often made with a decidedly Italian accent, a fact attributable to the massive importation, in the fifties, of Italian directors and technicians. Among them were two women, Carla Civelli, director of *É um Caso de Polícia* ("A Case for the Police," 1959), and Maria Basaglia, director of *Macumba na Alta* ("Macumba in High Society," 1958) and *O Pão que o Diabo Amassou* ("The Devil's Bread," 1958).

The decade of the sixties represents something of an anomaly. For good or for ill, women in the preceding decades had managed to direct one or more films. In the sixties, however, we find only one feature-length fiction film directed by a woman: *As Testemunhas Não Condenam* ("The Witnesses Do Not Condemn") by Zélia Costa. The contribution of women to the cinema in the sixties was more noticeable in the increased number of women involved in editing, production, assistant camerawork, and music, not to mention, of course, the ever-present "script-girls" and makeup people.

The women who became directors in the seventies generally gained their apprenticeship through short films and documentaries (Tereza Trautman, Ana Carolina), or as actresses (Vanja Orico, Rosângela Maldonado). The number of feature films directed by women increased dramatically in this decade. Some of the directors and their films include: Vanja Orico's *O Segredo da Rosa* ("Rosa's Secret," 1974); Lenita Perroy's *Mestiça* (1971) and *A Noiva da Noite* ("Bride of the Night," 1974); Rosa Lacreta's *Encarnação* ("Incarnation," 1974); Vera de Figueiredo's *Feminino Plural* and *Samba da Criação do Mundo* ("Samba of the Creation of the World," 1979); Maria do Rosário's *Marcados para Viver* ("Branded for Life," 1976); Luna Alkalay's *Cristais de Sangue* ("Crystals of Blood," 1975); Ana Carolina's *Mar de Rosas* ("Sea of Roses," 1977); and Rosângela Maldonado's *A Mulher que Põe a Pomba no Ar* ("The Woman Who Lets the Bird Take Flight," 1978).

According to our research, throughout the history of Brazilian cinema, there are only twenty feature fiction films known to be directed by women. We analyzed the sixteen films of which copies still exist. In nine out of the sixteen films, the plot centers on amorous relations in which the women characters form part of triangles. Such is the case in *O Ébrio, Pinguinho de Gente, Coração Materno, Macumba na Alta, Mestiça, Os Homens que Eu Tive* (1973), *Marcados para Viver, Mar de Rosas,* and *A Mulher que Põe a Pomba no Ar*. Although the films also show women involved in stable relationships apart from any amorous triangle, these relationships are peripheral to the plot; they do not form the point of departure for the action of the films.

In the films whose stories are not centered on amorous relations (*O Pão que o Diabo Amassou, É um Caso de Polícia, O Segredo da Rosa, Encarnação, Cristais de Sangue, Feminino Plural* [1977], *Samba da Criação do Mundo*) such questions as marital status, evolving relationships with lovers, romance and so forth, are irrelevant to the development of the plot. The presence of partners serves only to characterize the protagonists without limiting or expanding their field of action. In any case, fifty-five of the seventy women characters in the films being analyzed exist largely, as fictional figures and as human beings, in explicit or implicit relation to men. Among the fifteen exceptions to this rule, five of the characters are children and adolescents.

Most of the women characters are between twenty and thirty years of age. They invariably obey current fashion trends, and their physical attributes respect to the letter conventional ideals of beauty. Since socially speaking only their bodies are emphasized, it becomes essential that they be young and beautiful.

In these films women who are older or "ugly" are given secondary and often caricatural roles. Two of them (in *Pinguinho de Gente*) are shown as uninvolved in any relationship, thus swelling the list of exceptions along with children and adolescents. There is a notable transgression of this rule in the film, entitled, significantly, *Feminino Plural* ("Feminine Plural"). Since the feminine is precisely one of the major preoccupations of the film, the only older woman in the film sees in the wrinkles of her face not a depressing sign of degeneration but rather something positive, the mark of her struggles during a long life.

The women who form part of triangles, in the majority of the films analyzed, do so, in large part, for the love of a man; the norm is for women to be dependent (existentially, socially, diegetically) on their male counterparts (husbands, lovers, parents). And to mark this feminine competition there are punishments for the "losers." For women, that is to say, even love does not justify competitive behavior. The punishments vary from vertiginous falls on the social ladder (Marieta and Lola in *O Ébrio*) or, to what the films see as more serious, condemnation to celibacy and solitude (Ruth in *Coração Materno* and Matilde in *Pinguinho de Gente*). The opposite never occurs; no man suffers additional punishment for having lost in amorous dispute. And it is the punishment of "evil actions" committed by women that regulates and "normalizes" the happiness of the couples.

The destruction of triangles and the sanctioning of the couple is the rule in all the films. Although each decade has its specificity, the rule spreads across the history of Brazilian cinema. In the films of Gilda de Abreu, the triangle has to be undone in order for the misunderstandings to be cleared up. Beginning in the fifties, with *Macumba na Alta*, the structure becomes much looser. Triangles are no longer the only alternative for the characters. Instead, the films offer intermediate situations leading to recomposition and the formation of new couples. In the seventies, with the exception of *Mestiça*, set in nineteenth-century Brazil, and *A Mulher que Põe a Pomba no Ar*, which treats the question of marital infidelity, the triangles are experienced by the characters as something positive. In *Os Homens que Eu Tive*, and *Marcados para Viver*, we encounter the simultaneous coexistence of various triangles. The triangle does not have to disappear to make way for the happiness of the couple. The third member of the triangle is often displaced, allowing the couple to exist, but there are no supplementary punishments, nor is the displaced member condemned to solitude as punishment.

The emotional universe of most of the characters under discussion is limited to home and family, since the woman is conventionally expected to assure the proper functioning of the domestic machinery (the tradi-

346

Maria do Rosario's *Marcados para Viver* **(1976)**

tional "feminine" duties), and also to realize her "supreme vocation" of bearing children. With offspring, supposedly the most sublime moment of their lives, their work proliferates. Preparing meals, watching over the children and their education, taking care of the home and its inhabitants — all these tasks are somehow not considered to constitute productive labor. They are seen, rather, as "natural" activities, for which the only recompense needed is the security offered by the home and the supposed personal satisfaction that comes with the status of wife and mother. What would be truly "natural" of course would be to rationally collectivize domestic work or at least divide it equally among the partners. In fact, however, this whole problematic is never touched upon because in these films, as in Brazilian middle-class life generally, these tasks are performed by domestics.

Curiously, traditional mothers are rare in these films, and the few who do exist have but a superficial relationship with their children. Nor do we see wives doing housework. The absence of these elements might be seen as a refusal, perhaps unconscious, of the narrow world to which women have been confined. Or it could be explained by something rather more trivial, i.e., by the simple transcription to the screen of a social fact, that as Brazilians rose on the social ladder they often came to enjoy the privilege of having maids and servants.

However fundamental, these domestic tasks are rarely given due attention in these films. Occasionally there appears an exception to prove the rule, and in this case there are interesting distinctions to be noted according to sex. When performed by men (servants, butlers) they are white, and fairly refined. Conversely, the women who perform domestic work tend to be black or mulatta, are often fairly elderly, and almost invariably semiliterate.

In sum, the traditional feminine world is seen in a singular manner, in the sense that the wives are not primarily concerned with domestic affairs nor with the education of their children. On the other hand, these women do not seek any autonomous space outside of the domestic sphere. Apart from the maids, only eleven women characters are shown as involved in any kind of work. Only seven are attributed a specific profession — past, present, or future — but these professions are not represented on the screen. It goes without saying that these women are generally involved with the "nurturing" service professions: a nurse, a seamstress, a manager of a small hotel, a manager of a grocery store, a television publicity woman, a madame, a fair saleswoman, a secretary, a film editor, two prostitutes, a street vendor, a love counselor, a smuggler, and a psychiatrist.

Given the fact that most characters work only in order to survive (e.g., maids), once the woman ascends socially, generally through marriage, she ceases to work. It is curious, furthermore, that love often serves, in the films of the forties and fifties, to reconcile class differences. Thus, poor but pretty girls marry rich men (Marieta in *O Ébrio*, Maria Lúcia in *Pinguinho de Gente*, Lena in *Macumba na Alta*), while only the poor orphan Carlos, in *Coração Materno*, is able to conquer the aristocratic heart of Violeta while another Carlos, the rising popular singer in *Macumba na Alta*, seduces the psychiatrist Irene who leaves her profession in order to become her husband's impresario and take care of *his* career.

In the seventies, we encounter this situation only in *Mestiça*, where the principal character, a slave, marries her overseer, the son of wealthy landowners. It is worth nothing that Mestiça is the only feminine character who has to bring to her marriage any dowry other than her own beauty. As her nickname indicates, she is in fact a "mestiça" and therefore has to become rich thanks to an inheritance (to which she had the right as an illegitimate daughter) in order to marry the young man. Races are reconciled, then, across class lines.

Doing nothing either at home or outside of it, the women characters devote their energies to defending and maintaining their emotional bonds to the principal stars in their amorous galaxy — men. It is hardly surprising, therefore, that they cease to work upon marrying, and return to work only when they separate or lose their husbands. The implicit assumption: work, which offers dignity to men, offers no special gratification to women.

Beginning in the late sixties, with increased education for women and the consequent broadening of professional opportunities, women began to struggle with men over their share of the labor market. Even in the films produced after the sixties however, one rarely encounters women

Ana Carolina's *Mar de Rosas* (1978)

who work by personal choice, and only one (Vitória in *Feminino Plural*) who goes to the university. The universe of the emotions, once again, predominates in the representation of women characters.

One new feature in the films of the seventies is an unprecedented solidarity among women. In *Marcados para Viver*, we find the only case of homosexual love between women — the prostitute Rosa and the street vendor Jojo. Until this time, women in Brazilian films had been isolated creatures with only the most tenuous of links to their sisters; on the contrary, even those who claim to be friends often end by committing acts of disloyalty, since their friendships are often based on some kind of selfish interest (Violeta and Ruth, in *Coração Materno*, Maria Lúcia and Matilde in *Pinguinho de Gente*).

In the seventies, women come, for the first time, to the foreground. This change, however, brings little change from the films of previous decades, in the sense that the axis around which everything else revolves continues to be affective relations. The evolution of the women characters is limited to the level of non-traditional behavior. The innovation is restricted to the proposal of new models of amorous relationships, while work life continues to be as circumstantial and superfluous (except in the case of lumpen characters — in *O Segredo da Rosa* and *Marcados para Viver*) as in the films of the forties and the fifties. This unconventional behavior, in any case, eventually comes to be co-opted by the reigning morality. Rosa in *Marcados para Viver* and Felicity in *Mar de Rosas* are punished by death, while Piti in *Os Homens que Eu Tive* opts for maternity with a man whose relation to her reproduces the classic dichotomy of wife and lover.

349

Many of the pertinent questions concerning the relations of the sexes in contemporary society, questions raised by the diverse feminist movements beginning in the sixties, remain untouched by the most recent productions of Brazilian cinema. Admittedly, as two women filmmakers told us in an interview, it is difficult to bring these issues — issues of which these filmmakers themselves are highly aware — to the screen, partially because of a lack of cinematic models. In 1979, we might add, women involved in film production as directors, actresses, technicians, and so forth, joined together in an association whose purpose is to discuss the specific relation between the profession of filmmaking and their condition as women. This association, one hopes, is the embryonic form of a collective of women filmmakers, which will work toward a participatory cinema that transmits a more realistic and contemporary image of women, in the context of an egalitarian and non-sexist future.

Note

1. Maria Basaglia is mentioned in Sharon Smith's *Women Who Make Movies* as the director of *Sua Altezza Ha Detto No* (1954) and *Sangue di Zingara* (1956), both produced in Italy.

35
"Hollywood Looks at Brazil: From Carmen Miranda to *Moonraker*"

Introduction

Many filmgoers have an implicit faith that the cinematic portrait of foreign countries corresponds, on some level, to the truth. The image of Brazil, for many non-Brazilians, is a bewildering potpourri of piranha-infested waters, samba and romance, carnival and coffee, *Black Orpheus* and Carmen Miranda. Brazilian critic Sérgio Augusto is widely conversant with both American and Brazilian cinema and is therefore ideally placed to discuss the image of his country in Hollywood films. In this article, he wittily traces the evolution of Southern California's portrayal of the largest of the South American "neighbors." He catalogues some of the more striking ethnographic, linguistic and even topographical blunders to be encountered in these films and, more importantly, disengages the condescending attitude behind them.

"Hollywood Looks at Brazil: From Carmen Miranda to *Moonraker*"

SÉRGIO AUGUSTO

"You have beautiful horses, darling."

Thus spoke Lana Turner to her beloved Ricardo Montalban almost three decades ago, and in Portuguese, thanks to tongue-twisting lessons from a bewildered teacher hired for the occasion. Down in Rio with her wealthy American beau (John Lund), she had fallen irrevocably in love with the city. Love at first breath, one might add, for her first reaction upon arriving in Brazil was to suggest that the romantic atmosphere of Copacabana beach be bottled for export, presumably as a sure-fire aphrodisiac. But while hyping Rio's glowing beauty and the excellence of its studs, not to mention their thoroughbred horses' beauty, Mervyn LeRoy's *Latin Lovers* (1953) turned out to be — due to the inanities of the plot, LeRoy's frequently abulic *mise-en-scène*, and a fistful of ethnographic and topographic blunders — just one more insult to the sensitivities of the Brazilian audience.

Latin Lovers includes a tango along with the customary pseudo-samba, or rather, a Hollywood rhumba, entitled "A Little More of Your Amor," crooned by Carlos Ramírez, the only masculine counterpart to Carmen Miranda ever to come out of Colombia. Some members of the cast, furthermore, continually refer to Montalban's farm as an "hacienda," which actually does mean "farm," but in Spanish. Perhaps a guilty Joe Pasternak wanted to placate Argentinian-born Fernando Lamas after having replaced him as Lana Turner's *carioca* sweetheart just a week before shooting began, following a gleefully publicized brawl involving the two restless stars during a party at Marion Davies's.

But let us leave aside gossip mongering and ethnic nitpicking in order to focus on MGM's topographical blunders. Such slips are commonplace in maudlin tearjerkers like *Latin Lovers*, most notably in a scene in which Lana Turner must have kindled the envy of more mortal tourists by managing to glimpse both Sugar Loaf and Corcovado from the single window of a hotel located *behind* these two scenic attractions. American cinematic pragmatism, once again, has come to the aid of nature.

Latin Lovers is, admittedly, sheer schlock even by camp standards, but it would be criminal not to mention the film's sole fillip to the moral regeneration of its genre. Even though the Andrews Sisters, only five years before in Norman Z. McLeod's *The Road to Rio*, had said it was completely superfluous, Lana Turner did, at least, try to "know the language," thus anticipating Audrey Hepburn, alias Holly Golightly, in *Breakfast at Tiffany's*.[1] And the language, "hacienda" notwithstanding, was not Spanish, just as the capital of Brazil was no longer Buenos Aires, as many Americans had long believed, although not exclusively through

Carmen Miranda

the fault of Hollywood. Since 1933, when Fred Astaire, Ginger Rogers, and Dolores Del Rio (no relation) had flown down to Rio, Hollywood knew—and therefore Americans must have known—that Brazil was not part of Argentina.

The confusion partially derives, presumably, from the fact that Spanish is spoken in all of the countries of Latin America with the exception of Brazil. In the decades prior to the First World War, furthermore, the United States limited its geo-political obsessions to the Caribbean, since it was the English who pulled the strings from the "Rum and Coca-Cola line" downward. Between 1914 and 1929, when United States investments in Latin America rose from seventeen percent to forty percent of the total, due to Great Britain's inability to maintain its edge in the loan and bond markets, there occurred a general shift toward increased investment in South America. Argentina received the highest percentage, going from three percent in 1913 to eleven percent in the late twenties, while Brazil's part in the total rose from four percent to nine percent. For a long time Argentina enjoyed first place. To the point that Carmen Miranda made her debut in American cinema performing in a Buenos Aires nightclub, in *Down Argentine Way* (1940). More envious and Jacobin Brazilians might respond that, after all, the most respectable films using a Banana Republic as backdrop—*Notorious* (1946)—was filmed in Rio, although by a second unit and therefore without the physical presence of Alfred Hitchcock, Cary Grant, Ingrid Bergman, etc.[2] Their Argentinian counterparts might remind them, of course, that in the same year, Gilda put the blame on Mame not in Rio but in Buenos Aires, and that just a few months before Cary Grant began to enlist Ingrid Bergman as a counterspy against Nazi uranium smuggler Claude Rains, Dick Powell had already gone to Argentina to track down the wartime murderer of his wife, in Edward Dmytryk's *Cornered*.

Rio triumphed over Buenos Aires in the long run, however, especially as the paradise of Yankee imperialism. Charlie Chan came in 1941, followed by Orson Welles in 1942. Tarzan put in an appearance in 1965; Brenda Starr made a stopover on her way to the Amazon in 1973; and, more recently, James Bond (*Moonraker*) almost got himself killed on the Sugar Loaf cable car. Blondie, we might add, passed close by in 1941, and Charlie's Angels never reached the port of Rio only because the "singles" cruiser on which they had embarked a year before was hijacked en route by a band of gangsters. At this rate, Brazilians will soon be hearing shouts on the beaches of Ipanema: "Look! Up in the sky! Is it a piranha? Is it Pelé? No, it's Superman!"

The magic spell of Rio, they say, is everywhere. "At night, when the sun goes down . . . when the sky pales and the pale light fades, and the thick-clustering tropical stars come out, and are met below by the semi-circle of warm yellow sparks . . . you will find yourself holding on to the picture almost fiercely with your eyes, for fear that they shall ever lose it." So goes Cole Porter's account of his impressions of Rio, when he passed through with his buoyant *coterie* aboard the Franconia Cruise over four decades ago, and in homage to its splendor composed the delightful *It's De-Lovely*.[3]

There is something about Brazil that fascinates heels on the run. At the end of *Ocean's Eleven* Frank Sinatra suggests to Angie Dickinson that they escape to Brazil after their Las Vegas caper is over. In *The Steel Trap*, a fairly entertaining yarn directed by Andrew L. Stone in 1952, Joseph Cotten steals a small fortune from his bank with the *idée fixe* of fleeing with his wife to Brazil, the only friendly country without a criminal extradition agreement with the United States. But Rio primarily fascinates itinerant Romeos and Juliets. Could it be that Rio offers a special brand of moonlight? Apparently, for Jane Powell and Ann Sothern evoke it in Robert Z. Leonard's *Nancy Goes to Rio* (1950) in their duet *Magic Is in the Moonlight*, during a break in their interminable dispute over Barry Sullivan's heart.

Robert Leonard's *Nancy Goes to Rio* (1950)

Thus Rio was mystified as the ideal site of enraptured romance, repeating what had already been done (and is still being done) with Paris, Rome, Venice, Hong Kong, and even Marrakesh: sentimental Shangrilas all, where, to continue quoting Cole Porter, one can hear mother nature murmuring low: "Let Yourself Go." That is exactly what Alice Faye tried to do—with *two* Don Ameches—in Irving Cummings's *That Night in Rio* (1941), paving the way for Jane Powell, Ann Sothern, and later, Jill St. John and Carol Lynley (in Henry Levin's *Holiday for Lovers*, 1959), and finally Marisa Berenson, Margaux Hemingway, and Karen Black in Anthony Dawson's *Greed* (1978). Each of these films contributed, in its way, to consolidating the blatantly insulting, if not racist, vision that the cultural colonizers of California always had of their colonized subjects south of the border. A vision that, given the heights from which Latin America was contemplated, could only be blurred, without depth, one-dimensional. Whence the spreading "haciendas" on the outskirts of Rio and the orgy of tangos, rhumbas, congas, mambos, and cha-cha-chas, dressed up in phony Brazilian rhythms in soundtracks smelling more of *chili con carne* than *feijoada*.

Things did not, curiously enough, improve with time. In the latest version of *The Champ*, Jon Voigt dreams of becoming rich and flying to Brazil to dance the cha-cha-cha. In the first version of *My Sister Eileen* by Alexander Hall in 1942, Rosalind Russell and Janet Blair's nutty basement in Greenwich Village is invaded by a horde of frisky young officers, who force them to dance a frenetic conga. Nothing surprising, since the officers were part of a war-bound South American flotilla, where they spoke Spanish among themselves. In the generally literal remake directed by Richard Quine in 1955, however, the officers who invade the apartment of Betty Garrett and Janet Leigh are members of the Brazilian navy, for motives as obscure as the origins of the conga that they have the audacity to present as a typical product of the land that gave birth, just a few years later, to Bossa Nova, the Latin sound to end all Latin sounds.[4] As far as music is concerned, it strikes me as unfair to place the entire blame on Carmen Miranda and the bastardized samba that she served up, not without a certain voluptuous pleasure, for the international palate, as the condition *sine qua non* for her own success in the American market as the epitome of *latinidad*. It is important to remember, that before her, Vincent Youmans, Edward Eliseu, and Gus Kahn had invented "the Carioca," a new, supposedly Brazilian dance, a kind of slow-tempoed *maxixe* that elicited only bemused smiles on the faces of Rio spectators when Thornton Freeland's *Flying Down to Rio* was released in the city in whose honor it was conceived.[5] The cariocas subsequently endured, with equal nonchalance, the stowaway carnival musician played by Bob Hope, alias Hot Lips Barton, in *The Road to Rio*. All of which hardly justifies Italian director Anthony Dawson (alias Antonio Margueriti) for infesting the placid bay of Angra dos Reis—the beach where Rio's *haute bourgeoisie* relishes its summers and weekends—with piranha fish. Providentially, the bionic Lee Majors discovers in time a means of distracting the insatiably voracious fish, by offering them a succulent diet of raw beef.[6]

It all began, apparently, with that viscerally commercial production *Flying Down to Rio*. The man who proposed the project to RKO boss Merian C. Cooper (better known as the creator of *King Kong*) was producer Lou Brock. He knew that Cooper could not resist a project whose principal ingredients coincided with Cooper's chief delights: aviation and South America. Cooper was elated to learn that the film would end with an extravagant aerial ballet over Rio (partly dubbed by Malibu beach), conceived by Busby Berkeley disciple Don Gould, and with pin-up girls fastened to the wings of the clipper that Sirorsky had recently designed for Pan American Airlines. Cooper happened to be a member of the board of directors of Pan Am, a company that in 1933 was beginning to expand its routes to the coastal capitals of the south of the continent. Rio

Cary Grant and Ingrid Bergman at Rio's Jockey Club in *Notorious* **(1946)**

was the number one attraction in the area, and, as the ads boasted: "the lovely ladies catch your eyes/by the light of a million stars in evening sky." Very tempting indeed.

But there is more. At one point in the film we see Dolores Del Rio and the American aviator Gene Raymond sending wires to Rio, courtesy of RCA Communications. RKO at that time was affiliated with RCA; together they owned Radio City Music Hall, where *Flying Down to Rio* was the special attraction of Christmas in 1933. Americans appreciated this joyful mystification, and some undoubtedly believed that Mexican actress Dolores Del Rio, alias Belinha de Rezende, was every bit as Brazilian as her fiancé Raul Roulien,[7] who gives her up to Gene Raymond with the same elegance with which Georges Guétary would lose Leslie Caron to Gene Kelly in *An American in Paris*, eighteen years later. The disillusioned Roulien parachutes from a seaplane and lands, very coincidentally, on the patio of the Copacabana Palace where Fred Astaire and Ginger Rogers, mere supporting actors in their first effort together, are dancing and who finally earn the right to the final and prophetic fade-out of the film.

More coincidences: 1933 was a key year in the long history of the cultural and economic invasion of Latin America by the United States. It was in this year that Franklin D. Roosevelt was inaugurated as president and established the basic tenets of the Good Neighbor Policy. At last the time had come to win the hearts and minds of Latin America. In fact,

357

very little effort was required, since Latin American hearts and minds were already the captive audience of the "entertainment" manufactured and exported by the big brother to the north, not without provoking the revulsion of certain nationalistic intellectuals, one of whom went so far as to call Americans "civilized barbarians" and "Genghis Khan with a telegraph." The historian Alonso Aguilar is certainly right in arguing that the Good Neighbor Policy involved, by its very nature, serious contradictions. "While, on the one hand, it showed respect, previously nonexistent, for the Latin American nations" — he wrote — "on the other hand, it manifested itself as an effort to further subordinate them to United States economic needs. Even Roosevelt himself believed in 1940 in the advantage of increasing investments in Latin America 'in order to develop sources of raw materials needed in the United States.' "[8]

In 1935 Nelson Rockefeller made his first trip to Latin America, in order to visit a museum of modern art in Venezuela. He was already regarded as an expert on the region, due to his service as head of the foreign department of the Chase Manhattan Bank and to his well-known familiarity with the health activities of the Rockefeller Foundation in Latin American countries. With the emergence of Hitler and the capitulation of France in 1940, Roosevelt decided to run for a third term and became wholly absorbed by foreign affairs. Brazil was living, at the time, under the dictatorship of Getulio Vargas, visibly enthusiastic about the Nazi-Fascist regimes of Europe. In order to dissuade him from continuing to buy arms from the Germans, Washington went so far as to promise Vargas's war minister free cases of whiskey and cartons of Lucky Strikes. To convince Vargas to break with the Axis and join the war as an ally, Roosevelt invited him to visit the United States, where, according to Assistant Secretary of State Sumner Welles, he would be received as no head of state had ever been received before. Vargas politely refused, preferring to hold his trump card for a more propitious occasion. When Brazil finally broke with the Axis, Vargas had already been assured American financing of a gigantic steel plant.

Before that, on 16 August 1940, the coordinator of Inter-American Affairs was established by executive order of the Council of National Defense. Headed by Nelson Rockefeller, the CIAA (an indubitably ominous acronym) was primarily concerned with commercial and financial problems in the Latin American countries. But with the creation of the Board of Economic Warfare, the CIAA was free to devote full attention to cultural matters. The CIAA was clearly a war information agency.[9] Its motion pictures division, created in October of the same year and operating under the aegis of Rockefeller's close friend John Hart Whitney, set up a string of committees in Hollywood to help the film industry people develop a "better understanding" of Latin America, in order to prevent "irritating things from cropping up in films about South American countries and customs." Strangely enough, some of those irritating films, made with Rockefeller's encouragement, had been booed or laughed off the screen all over Latin America for their spurious absurdity. In his monograph on Orson Welles, Charles Higham suggests that Rockefeller was forced to give Darryl Zanuck $40,000 of CIAA money to reshoot portions of *Down Argentine Way* offensive to Argentinians. Even some of Walt Disney's projects had to be supervised. No risks could be taken now that Latin America had become the only strong foreign market left after the closure of Europe.[10]

By the time Disney visited Brazil with his staff to gather background material for a series of Good Neighbor[11] cartoons — among them *Saludos Amigos!* (1941) and *The Three Caballeros* (1944) featuring the naughty "Brazilian" parrot Zé Carioca — Carmen Miranda had already been launched with enormous élan among the biggest and most powerful of hemispheric "Neighbors," first on Broadway, then in Hollywood, where she was to appear in fourteen comedies, some intermittently pleasant like Walter Lang's *Weekend in Havana* (1941), some tropically surrealist like Busby Berkeley's *The Gang's All Here*, and only two (*That Night in Rio*, and *Nancy Goes to Rio*) set in Brazil. Even today, Carmen Miranda remains the focus of heated polemics. Many Brazilians stigmatize her as the passive instrument of North American cultural imperialism, while others regard her as a kind of force of nature, somehow beyond good and evil. Beginning in the sixties, she became the object of an international cult, when a fraternity of nostalgic camp-oriented cinephiles, almost invariably gay, rediscovered her films.

Disney's *The Three Caballeros* (1944)

Carmen Miranda constituted a most remarkable caricature of women. Behind the peerless vulgarity of her costumes and ornaments — tutti-frutti hats and necklaces, frilly sleeves, and multi-colored skirts — lurked the incubus of a transvestite. Epitomizing the energy of the early forties perhaps better than any other star, she had at least been raised in Brazil after leaving Portugal as a child, unlike innumerable gringos transformed by Hollywood into apocryphal Brazilians, including, we might add, people like the Mexican singer Tito Guizar in S. Sylvan Simon's *The Thrill of Brazil*, produced two years after his equally dispensable appearance in Joseph Santley's *Brazil* in 1944.

Before Disney even began packing for his trip, Rockefeller had decided that Orson Welles would serve as cultural ambassador to Latin America, with the special mission of cleaning up after the CIAA — and thus was born the ill-fated Pan-Americanist documentary *It's All True*. Rockefeller thought that the film should begin with a long description of Rio's carnival. In order to film it, Welles arrived in Brazil on 13 February 1942. He stayed for five months, travelling up and down the country, and not always with luck in his favor. While a second-unit crew was filming the recreation of an adventurous 1650-mile voyage undertaken by four fisherman (*jangadeiros*) from the Brazilian northeast to the port of Rio de Janeiro, on the high seas and without a compass, the leader of the group fell off their frail tree truck raft (*jangada*) and disappeared under the waves. Welles was unfairly blamed for the tragedy and the film never recovered from the shock. *It's All True* was never finished and most of the footage was dumped into the Pacific by Paramount film librarian Hazel Marshall. Around 30,000 feet of excerpts survived, however, enough to convince Charles Higham, who had the good fortune to see the material on a movieola, that *It's All True* was "the cinematic equivalent of the treasure of King Solomon's mines or the lost city of the Incas."

The moral of the story: even with the best of intentions Hollywood had trouble treating Brazil the way it deserved to be treated.

Notes

1. In the film, Audrey Hepburn falls in love with a Brazilian coffee millionaire, played by Spanish ham José Luiz Villalonga. The Portuguese lessons are given via phonograph records in which the accent is indisputably that of Continental Portuguese.

2. Hitchcock, with his diabolical creativity, shows in *Notorious* (above all a model of scenario construction) how to make a city come alive on the screen, even when it consists only of a series of back projections. James Agee was perhaps the first to notice this Hitchcockian talent, when he noted that Hitchcock "has a strong sense of the importance of the real place and the real atmosphere; the shots of Rio de Janeiro are excellent and one late-afternoon love scene is remarkable in its special emotion and the grandeur of excitement it gets away with and in communicating the exact place, weather and time of the day." (*The Nation*, 17 August 1946.) It is a pity that Charles Higham and Joel Greenberg did not read Agee before reducing *Notorious* to a "story of spies in Buenos Aires" in their generally more accurate, *Hollywood in the Forties* (South Brunswick and New York: A. S. Barnes, 1968), p. 44.

3. See Brendan Gill, *Cole* (New York: Holt, Rinehart and Winston, 1971), p. 133.

4. Bossa Nova constitutes a kind of feedback samba, unquestionably influenced by jazz, an influence that partially explains the facility and rapidity with which it was absorbed abroad, and especially in the U.S.

5. The Rio-born *maxixe*, generally considered "the Brazilian tango," was introduced in the U.S. by Vernon Castle in 1941. According to Arlene Croce, "the maxixe never caught on, but strangely enough the carioca did. People paid to have it taught to them in dance schools." *The Fred Astaire and Ginger Rogers Book* (New York: Outerbridge and Lazard, Inc., 1972), p. 27.

6. Regarded by many as the most dangerous fish in the world, piranhas are found only in South America, and especially in the Amazon region, where they proliferate in the tepid waters of its rivers. Although carnivorous, they never attacked the creature from the Black Lagoon, a monster as unbelievable and seductive as the notion that there exist lagoons along the Amazon. During the same era that *The Creature from the Black Lagoon*'s pathetic gillman was caged by Richard Carlson's crew while hankering for Julia Adams, forty-square miles (*sic*) of vengeful and symbolism-laden ants invaded the splendid tropical plantation of Charlton Heston in another corner of the Amazon depths in Byron Haskin's *The Naked Jungle*. Two years later another creature turned up there: *Curuçu, Beast of the Amazon*, a Curt Siodmak delirium that has yet to find its cult audience. The flora and the fauna of the Amazon have perhaps even more right to protest the predatory actions of the American cinema than the cariocas. On two different occasions, John Farrow disturbed the tranquility of the region by dumping a half-dozen neurotic plane-crash survivors, first in 1939 (*Five Came Back*) then in 1956 (*Back from Eternity*) thus giving birth to a sinister genre whose most recent manifestations were Harvey Hart and Thomas Carr's *Sullivan's Empire* and Joseph Leytes's *Valley of Mystery*, both filmed in 1967. In the late fifties, Siodmak's fertile imagination spawned a devilish matriarchal tribe in the same region (*Love Slaves of the Amazon*, 1957) presumably not very far from the place where Mel Ferrer's naive pretentiousness transformed his muse Audrey Hepburn into an anthropomorphic parody of Bambi, in *Green Mansions* (1959). Henry Fonda's safari up the Amazon in the opening scenes of Preston Sturges's *The Lady Eve* (1941) was, if memory serves, quite benign.

7. *Flying Down to Rio* was the tenth out of fifteen films in which the authentically Carioca Raul Roulien participated as an actor in Hollywood, where he arrived in 1931, with a letter of introduction, an audition — filmed in the Cinedia studios in Brazil — and a lot of nerve. Before him, many Brazilians had gone to Hollywood — Syn Conde, Arquimedes de Lalor, Olimpio Guilherme, and the beautiful brunette Lia Torá. The latter two were the winners of an international contest promoted by Fox in 1927. Together, they performed in Wallace MacDonald's *The Low Necker* (1927), Alfred E. Green's *Making the Grade* (1928), and participated as masters of ceremony in the Brazilian version of John Murray Anderson's *King of Jazz* (1930). Although she had appeared with distinction in more than a half-dozen films, Lia Torá's rise to stardom was interrrupted by the advent of sourd. Olimpio Guilherme's career was equally infelicitous. He left only one film, albeit a rather respectable one: *Hunger*, a raw depiction of 1929 Hollywood, filmed by himself with a kind of candid camera, which a number of American film historians regard as a little-known precursor of the realist documentaries of the thirties and of Italian Neo-Realism in the forties.

8. Alonso Aguilar, *Pan-Americanism from Monroe to the Present* (New York: Monthly Review Press, 1968), p. 70.

9. See Richard Dyer McCann, *The People's Films* (New York, 1973), p. 148.

10. *The Films of Orson Welles* (Berkeley: University of California Press, 1970), p. 85.

11. In 1941, Ray McCarey's *Cadet Girl*, a musical vehicle for blonde Carole Landis, included a song by Ralph Rainger and Leo Robin whose title, "She's a Good Neighbor," would be echoed the following year by another song, composed by Roger Edens, entitled simply "Good Neighbor" and included in the score of Norman McLeod's *Panama Hattie*. In David Butler's *Thank Your Lucky Stars*, released in 1943, Dennis Morgan and Alexis Smith sang "Good Night, Good Neighbor" with lyrics by Frank Loesser.

36
"The Rise and Fall of Brazilian Cinema, 1960–1990"

RANDAL JOHNSON

It was easy to chase the public away from the cinema; it's difficult to bring it back.

— Júlio Bressane

Either we internationalize Brazilian cinema or they will internationalize us.

— Murilo Salles

Brazilian cinema is dead.

— Arnaldo Jabor

From almost its very beginnings the Brazilian film industry has suffered a chronic lack of continuity, causing it to develop erratically, either in isolated and short-lived cycles far from the country's major metropolitan centers (e.g., the efforts, in the 1920s, of Humberto Mauro in Cataguases, Gentil Ruiz in Recife, or Eduardo Abelim in Porto Alegre), or in unsuccessful attempts at industrialization based on a studio model (Cinédia in the 1930s, Atlântida in the early 1940s, Vera Cruz in the late 1940s). This lack of continuity is also evident in the careers of many Brazilian filmmakers, some of whom have appeared with great promise only to make subsequent films with tremendous difficulty, if at all. The example of Lima Barreto, whose *O Cangaceiro* (1953) was a double prize-winner in Cannes, is a case in point.[1]

Recognizing the historical lack of continuity in Brazilian cinema and the inadequacy of a Hollywood-style studio model in a country with such a small domestic market, the internationally acclaimed Cinema Novo sought, starting in the early 1960s, to develop new modes of cinematic production, opting for an auteur cinema based on an independent and inexpensive mode of production using, initially, small crews, location shooting, and nonprofessional actors. Cinema Novo represented not only a new start for Brazilian cinema but also a new definition of the social role of the cinema, no longer conceived as a mere form of entertainment but rather as a mode of artistic and cultural intervention in the country's sociohistorical conjuncture. As such, it became an important site of resistance against the military regime imposed on the country in 1964. In the 1970s, Cinema Novo's alliance with the state through Embrafilme created a situation in which it seemed that Brazilian cinema would finally manage to solidify itself as an industry with the real potential for self-sufficiency.[2]

Yet in the mid-1990s, some thirty years after Cinema Novo first appeared on the scene with its harsh portrayals of Brazilian reality and twenty-one years after the founding of Embrafilme, the national film industry faces the most severe crisis of its history. Brazilian film production is now at its lowest level since the early 1940s, with no more than a dozen feature-length films under way.[3] Even worse, between 1981 and 1988 hardcore pornography accounted for an average of almost 68 percent of total production (see table 1). In 1988 twenty of the thirty top-drawing Brazilian films were pornographic (table 2).[4]

Table 1
Brazilian Film Production, 1978–1988

Year	Total	Pornographic	Embrafilme	Others	% Porn
1978	100	15	13	72	15
1979	93	7	16	70	8
1980	103	32	18	53	31
1981	80	63	16	1	79
1982	85	59	22	4	69
1983	84	62	18	4	74
1984	90	64	22	4	71
1985	87	59	NA	NA	68
1986	112	69	NA	NA	62
1987	82	43	NA	NA	52
1988	90	68	NA	NA	76

Source: Embrafilme, *Jornal da tela,* Edição especial: "Proposta para uma política nacional do cinema" (March 1986): 3; and Concine, *Relatório de atividades,* Segundo Semestre 1988 (1989): 219–23.

Table 2
Top-Drawing Brazilian Films, 1988

Title	Spectators
1. Os Heróis Trapalhões	3,080,000
2. Os Fantasmas Trapalhões	2,689,380
3. Super Xuxa contra o Baixo Astral	1,627,667
4. O Casamento dos Trapalhões	1,351,038
5. Banana Split	716,530
6. A Menina do Lado	490,271
7. Feliz Ano Velho	468,021
8. Luzia Homem	345,876
9. Os Trapalhões no Auto da Compadecida	233,930
10. As Aventuras de Sérgio Malandro	222,936
11. A Dama do Cine Shangai	195,861
12. Eles Comem Crú	177,298
13. Dedé Mamata	162,387
14. Coisas Eróticas	162,387
15. O Delicioso Sabor do Sexo	157,345
16. Senta no Meu que Eu Entro no Teu	147,291
17. No Calor do Buraco	142,810
18. Eternamente Pagu	141,253
19. Gemidos e Sussurros	137,627
20. Aluga-se Moças	115,824

Note: Some films were originally released prior to 1988. In these cases, figures do not represent total number of spectators.
Source: Concine. *Relatório de atividades,* Segundo Semestre 1988 (1989): 12.

In terms of the size of the market, the number of theaters in the country dropped from 3,276 in 1975 to less than 1,100 in 1988. Attendance figures for Brazilian films dropped from 1978's high of 60 million to less than 24 million in 1988. During the same period, the total number of spectators in the Brazilian market for both foreign and national films dropped from around 211.5 million to 108.5 million (table 3). Attendance figures for 1984 represent only 43 percent of the 1978 figure (Concine, 13).

Brazilian cinema is in many ways back to square one, a retrogression echoed — but not caused — by Fernando Collor de Mello's 1990 extinction of Embrafilme, Concine (the Conselho Nacional do Cinema), and the Fundação Brasileira de Cinema in one of his initial acts as Brazil's first democratically elected president since 1960. Given the increasing depth of the crisis that has faced Brazilian cinema over the past decade, Collor's action was more symbolic than real in its effects, since Embrafilme had long since ceased to be an effective agency of film industry development and, as filmmaker Eduardo Escorel has put it, its invest-

Table 3
Film Spectators in Brazil, 1974–1988

Year	Brazilian Films	%	Foreign Films	%	Total
1974	30,665,000	16	170,625,000	84	201,290,000
1975	48,859,000	18	226,521,000	82	275,380,000
1976	52,046,000	21	198,484,000	79	250,530,000
1977	50,937,000	25	157,398,000	75	208,335,000
1978	61,854,000	30	149,802,000	70	211,656,000
1979	55,836,000	29	136,072,000	71	191,908,000
1980	50,689,000	31	114,085,000	69	164,774,000
1981	45,911,000	33	92,981,000	67	138,892,000
1982	44,965,000	36	82,948,000	64	127,913,000
1983	33,774,000	32	72,762,000	68	106,536,000
1984	30,638,000	34	59,301,000	66	89,939,000
1985	21,928,000	24	69,372,000	76	91,300,000
1986	29,337,000	23	98,266,000	77	127,603,000
1987	25,123,713	21	91,806,019	79	116,929,732
1988	23,987,515	23	84,580,576	77	108,568,091

Source: Concine, *Relatório de Atividades,* Segundo Semestre 1988 (1989): 12.

ments in the industry had largely ceased to be recognized as socially legitimate. One might say that yet another cycle has come to an end.

Over the past few years, numerous commentators, including many film industry professionals, have attempted to analyze the crisis and to offer potential solutions. Most point out quite correctly that in immediate terms the current crisis of Brazilian cinema reflects the larger crisis of the national economy in a period when the so-called economic "miracle" of the 1967–1973 period, characterized by high growth rates and relatively low inflation, was replaced by an economic nightmare with a $100 billion foreign debt and near hyperinflation. The economic crisis forced the government to impose severe restrictions on imports, making film production costs rise dramatically and accentuating what is often called the "dollarization" of the film production process. Film production costs increased rapidly at a time when the market was shrinking, thus accelerating the process of decline, and ticket prices, which have long been controlled by the government, have not kept pace with inflation, further reducing the industry's income. The constant and massive presence of foreign — largely North American — films in the domestic market has only served to exacerbate the situation.

Many additional reasons exist for the decline of the Brazilian film industry since the early 1980s. High inflation rates have made filmgoing a luxury for much of the Brazilian population. Television, which has been so successful during this same period (due in part to considerable infrastructural public-sector investments in the telecommunications industry), has provided Brazilians with inexpensive yet generally high-quality entertainment in the comfort of their homes. At the same time, unlike the United States and Western Europe, television has not provided the national film industry with a significant additional source of income since historically there has been little integration between the two media. By and large, the Brazilian television industry either produces its own programming — there have been few coproductions with the film industry — or broadcasts imported programming. It has rarely provided space for independent production, including that of the national cinema. In 1984, of 1,967 feature-length films shown on Brazilian television stations, only eighty-two were Brazilian.[5]

But the crisis goes beyond mere economic considerations. Many commentators have pointed to the relationship between cinema and the state as a major contributing factor, focusing primarily on the corporativist and paternalistic nature of that relationship as it developed over the last twenty-five years. Along these lines I have argued elsewhere (*The Film Industry in Brazil*) that the crisis represents the bankruptcy of the state-supported model of film production that led Brazilian cinema, in the mid-1970s, to truly remarkable levels of success, a model that did not derive from a far-sighted vision of the future of Brazilian cinema and was authoritarian in many of its particulars, especially in relation to the exhibition sector. Although the policy contributed to the viability of many important film projects, including most of the Brazilian films distributed in the United States in recent years, it ultimately failed to reconcile the state's cultural and industrial responsibilities vis-à-vis the cinema and contributed to the meteoric fall of the Brazilian film industry during the last several years.

In this essay I will attempt to put the crisis in perspective, discussing in some detail a number of its fundamental causes. My focus will be on the shift in state policy toward the cinema in the early 1970s within the context of other cultural initiatives of the regime of Gen. Ernesto Geisel and, in a broader sense, the political conjuncture that contributed to the shift. I will argue that the policy failed primarily because of its clientelistic nature, which led it to respond to the demands of clients who occupied dominant positions in the cinematic field rather than attend to the real needs of the industry and provide infrastructural support which could have strengthened the industry as a whole. In addition, without placing blame or denigrating the multiple accomplishments of the Cinema Novo movement, I will suggest that the roots of this orientation are to be found in Cinema Novo's (and, by extension, Brazilian cinema's) insistence on an auteur model of cinematic practice and on the anti-industrialism of the movement's earliest phase, both of which contributed to a marked increase in hostility between the production and exhibition sectors.

The story of the rise and fall of Brazilian cinema is thus one filled with paradoxes, not the least of which is the alliance between a radical and highly creative film movement and the authoritarian state. Equally paradoxical is the fact that government support of the industry would come into being only during a period of military rule opposed by most sectors of the industry and that it has waned following the reinstitution of a more democratic system of government. Furthermore, the state model of support for the film industry ultimately had a result that was precisely the opposite of its original intentions.

Although the state claimed that its goal was to make the cinema more competitive in its own market, the screen quota and the various forms of financial assistance it provided in fact suspended the rules of the marketplace for national films, which ceased to compete against foreign films in the domestic market and began to compete against each other in the reserve market. Embrafilme became the major source of production financing, creating a situation of dependence between the state and "independent" filmmakers, and it itself became a marketplace where filmmakers competed against each other for the right to make films, thus exacerbating tensions within the industry and creating a situation in which the play of influences was often more important than the talent of the filmmaker or producer.[6] It is equally paradoxical that one of the few solutions to the crisis now appears to be association with foreign companies or with national exhibition groups, both of which have long been considered "enemies" of Brazilian cinema.

Cinema and the State in Brazil: A Historical Overview

To put the discussion in context, a brief overview of the historical development of state policy toward the film industry is in order. State intervention in the film industry dates from the early 1930s, when Getúlio Vargas implemented the first of what would turn out to be a long series of protectionist measures, most in the form of a screen quota for national films, designed to give the industry a modicum of stability for future development in a market long dominated by foreign cinemas.[7] Since the 1930s, and especially after 1964, the state role evolved from that of regulator of market forces to active agent and productive force in the industry, especially through its various programs of film production financing (low-interest loans, advances on distribution, and coproduction with private companies).

The state began its direct financial support of the film industry in 1966 with the creation of the Instituto Nacional do Cinema (INC). The institute, created by an executive decree of the Castello Branco regime, was the result of a long struggle by most sectors of the film industry (*The Film Industry in Brazil*, 107–12). It administered three major programs of support: first, a subsidy program providing all national films exhibited with additional income based on box-office receipts; second, a program of additional cash awards for "quality" films, selected by a jury of critics and film industry professionals; and third, a film-financing program in which the institute administered coproductions between foreign distributors and local producers using funds withheld from the distributor's income tax.[8] Although the first two were ultimately inadequate in terms of the amount of additional income offered, these programs were available for all interested filmmakers and thus tended to support the production sector as a whole.

The coproduction program ended in 1969 with the creation of Embrafilme, which was originally intended to promote the distribution of Brazilian films in foreign markets, and the funds withheld from the distributor's income tax became a major source of the agency's budget. As early as 1970 Embrafilme began granting producers low-interest loans for film production financing, and between 1970 and 1979, when the loan program was phased out, Embrafilme partially financed over 25 percent of total national production in this manner. Carlos Diegues's *Bye Bye Brasil* (1980) was the last film financed under this program.

As initially formulated, decisions to grant production financing were ostensibly made on purely technical grounds, taking into consideration the size of the company, its production history, the number of awards it had won in national and international festivals, and its experience. Such a policy may seem reasonable for most economic sectors or most industries, but the film industry is different in that its product transmits cultural, social, and ideological values, and such "neutrality" was seen as unacceptable by many segments of Brazilian society. The influential *O Estado de São Paulo,* for example, editorialized on 28 January 1972 that Embrafilme should *not* be a merely technical agency but rather should finance only films of high quality which contribute to the "moral foundations" of Brazilian society. Since a more neutral policy designed to foster Brazilian cinema as a whole led to the production of films deemed undesirable by many social sectors, including the military — and here I refer to the rash of *pornochanchadas* (erotic comedies) that began to appear in the early 1970s, many partially financed by the state — a reformulation of Embrafilme's production policy became inevitable.

The Reorientation of State Cinematic Policy

In 1975, during the Geisel regime, Embrafilme was reorganized and at that time absorbed the executive functions of the now-defunct INC. The Conselho Nacional do Cinema (Concine) was created the following year to assume INC's legislative role.[9] In 1973 Embrafilme had created its own nationwide distributor, long a goal of Brazilian producers, and in 1974 it initiated a program of coproduction financing that gradually replaced the loan program. As initially formulated, the enterprise participated in selected film projects with up to 30 percent of total production costs and received in return a 30 percent share of profits. With an advance on distribution of another 30 percent, the state could cover up to 60 percent of a film's production costs. In the late 1970s, Embrafilme began providing up to 100 percent of a film's financing in some cases.[10]

Several factors explain the shift in state policy toward the film industry. I have already mentioned the fact that the state cinematic apparatus had come under severe criticism from diverse sectors of civil society and the state because of its financing of films of questionable quality. From a different angle, Renato Ortiz sees increased state investments in culture (including the cinema) during the 1973–1975 period as one result of the economic optimism produced by the "miracle" of 1967–1973 as reflected in the Second National Development Plan (1974). Previous governments had focused primarily on economic aspects of development, although they had given lip service to the need for the "humanization of development" or for "psychosocial development" to accompany economic development. The Geisel regime, according to this analysis, attempted to put such ideas into action and thus gave more attention to the area of culture (Ortiz, p. 82).

Although there is no doubt some truth in Ortiz's interpretation, other factors are clearly of equal or greater importance. The years between 1969 and 1975 were the most repressive of military rule. Sparked by an impasse in its constitutional relationship with Brazil's Congress, on 13 December 1968 the Costa e Silva regime decreed the Fifth Institutional Act (AI-5), which "granted the president authority to recess legislative bodies, to intervene in the states without limit, to cancel elective mandates and suspend constitutional guarantees . . . [including] the right of habeas corpus" (Schneider, p. 274). The AI-5 led to the imposition of the harshest censorship yet known in Brazil and forced a number of political leaders, intellectuals, and artists, including some filmmakers, into exile. The appearance of armed movements in opposition to the regime led, in turn, to the institutionalization of torture and a national campaign by the military against "subversion."

This period of repression and censorship exacerbated the military's crisis of legitimacy, especially in relation to the intellectual-cultural field, and the increased activity in the cultural arena can be interpreted as one response to this crisis. In August 1973, General Médici's Minister of Education and Culture, Jarbas Passarinho, initiated a Program of Cultural Action which, according to Sérgio Miceli, was designed to provide financial (and political) credit to some areas of cultural production that had previously been ignored by the government and which constituted an official attempt to improve relations with artistic and intellectual circles (p. 56). Film producer Luiz Carlos Barreto, who was closely associated with Cinema Novo from the beginning, has explained that the reformulation of Embrafilme's program of production financing in the early 1970s grew out of conversations he and other film industry professionals, especially those associated with the Cinema Novo group, had during this period with Jarbas Passarinho (*Jornal da Tela*, March 1990, p. 14).[11]

The state's attention to culture intensified under the Geisel regime with the creation of Funarte (Fundação Nacional de Arte), the revitalization of the Serviço Nacional de Teatro (SNT), the reorganization of Embrafilme, the creation of Concine, and the publication of the document "Política nacional de cultura," which formalized the regime's cultural policy (Ministério de Educação e Cultura, MEC).[12] The cultural offensive in the mid-1970s focused primarily on those areas — the plastic arts, music, theater, and the cinema — with a reduced market potential and a more personalized or even artisan mode of production (Miceli, p. 64).

Geisel's Minister of Education and Culture, Ney Braga, managed to recruit cultural administrators who were either identified with the left of the cultural field or who had the confidence of the left (Roberto Farias and Gustavo Dahl in Embrafilme, Orlando Miranda in the SNT, Manuel Diegues Jr. — filmmaker Carlos Diegues's father — in the Departamento de Assuntos Culturais, which functioned as an umbrella agency within MEC with responsibility for overseeing all of the government's cultural activities). The optimism that reigned in the cultural field at this time, despite the repression, was due in part to the feeling among different cultural sectors that they not only had the support of the government but that they were finally able to influence the shape of state policy toward their respective areas:

> CARLOS DIEGUES (1975): "The current government has shown, in contrast to all other post-Vargas administrations, that it has a program for a cinematic infrastructure, and this is fundamental. I believe in Embrafilme's mission and in the aims of its current leadership, although I know that there are still many things to improve or create." ("As Esperanças")

> NELSON PEREIRA DOS SANTOS (1977): "All artists, not only in cinema but in theater and popular music also, who are considered to be of the left . . . were obligated to be more flexible, and we participated with independent producers on a common program and were able to place Roberto Farias, himself a filmmaker, as president of Embrafilme. Therefore, in reality, cinema today is a 'front populaire'. . . . We do not participate in the decision making, but we have a great influence in the composition of forces within Embrafilme." (Johnson, "Toward a Popular Cinema," p. 228)

Miceli correctly points out that the success of this cultural offensive would have been impossible without a strong Minister of Education and Culture with legitimacy in both the military government and the cultural field. A retired army general, Ney Braga consolidated his political career through successive electoral victories in the state of Paraná (mayor of Curitiba, 1954; federal deputy, 1958; state governor, 1960) and service in nonmilitary positions of the post-1964 period (he was Minister of Agriculture under Castello Branco). In Paraná his political legacy included many important cultural initiatives, including the Fundação Educacional do Paraná, the Teatro Guaíra, and the Companhia Oficial de Teatro.

In addition, he was the central figure in what was then considered to be one of the strong civilian political "clans" in the country, which included such government officials as Karlos Rischbieter (president of the Banco do Brasil), Reinhold Stephanes (director of the Brazilian social security system), and Maurício Schulmann (director of the Banco Nacional de Habitação), among others. Together, Braga's group was said to control almost half the national budget. The group also counted on the support of then secretary of Planning, João Paulo dos Reis Velloso, who was seminal in obtaining increased funding for Embrafilme (Miceli, pp. 64–66).[13] This strong government support contributed significantly to the remarkable success of the Brazilian film industry in the late 1970s. Unfortunately, neither the support nor the success lasted.

The coproduction program described above marked a fundamental redirection in state policy toward the industry, much in line with what producers had proposed to Jarbas Passarinho in 1972. With this program, the granting of production financing became much more selective. When the state decides to coproduce a limited number of films, it must inevitably decide *which* Brazilian cinema it will support. This causes the state, on the one hand, to enter into competition with nonfavored sectors of the industry and, on the other, to become a site of contention for competing groups. The reorientation of the state's financial assistance to the industry exacerbated conflicting positions among filmmakers (Ramos, chap. 4).

Two conflicts are particularly relevant to the present discussion: cultural versus commercial views of the state role, and "independent" versus concentrationist views of the proper industrial model the state should support. On the cultural side were filmmakers who felt that the state should support films based on their cultural importance, with no regard to commercial potential. In Brazilian film circles, this kind of film is known as a *miúra*. At the extreme of this position were documentarists such as Sílvio Tendler (*Os Anos JK,* "The JK Years," 1980; *Jango,* 1982) and some state bureaucrats who wanted Embrafilme limited to the production of cultural and educational films, much like the Instituto Nacional do Cinema Educativo, which was created by Getúlio Vargas in 1937 and later absorbed into INC. On the other side of this conflict were filmmakers and producers who thought that commercial potential should be the only thing that concerned the state enterprise in its attempts to support the industry's development. Pedro Rovai, known as a producer and director of *pornochanchadas,* argued that Embrafilme should finance production companies, much as the state

371

does in other economic sectors, and not individual film projects. He saw the cultural-commercial division as a false dichotomy and believed, quite correctly, that once a film is projected on screen it transmits cultural values (Bernardet, *Cinema Brasileiro,* p. 57).

The idea that only commercial potential should be considered derives from the notion, oft-repeated by exhibitors, that the public is the final judge of the value of cultural production. Such a notion does not consider historical distortions in the transmission and reception of cultural goods in a dependent, peripheral context. When film production began in Brazil on a fairly large scale after the turn of the century, the formal uses to which the highly technical cinematic apparatus could be put had already been largely determined. The early domination of the Brazilian market by foreign film industries fostered in the audience certain expectations concerning a film's quality as the foreign film became the standard against which all films would be judged. Although Brazilian films were relatively successful in the domestic market in the first decade of the century, they were by and large unable to attain the production values of foreign films and thus came to be seen by the Brazilian public as of poor quality and unworthy of support. The massive presence of foreign — largely American — films in the Brazilian market has tended to reinforce audience bias in their favor. This creates, for the Brazilian filmmaker, the dilemma of whether to imitate foreign films or attempt to create new modes of cinematic discourse based on what he or she perceives to be "national" values. The cultural-commercial dichotomy is one expression of this complex and perhaps unresolvable dilemma.[14]

Acutely aware of this dilemma, some directors (such filmmakers as Joaquim Pedro de Andrade, Nelson Pereira dos Santos, Carlos Diegues, Arnaldo Jabor, Leon Hirszman, Geraldo Sarno, Tizuka Yamasaki, and Hector Babenco, among others) attempted with varying degrees of success to combine the cultural and the commercial, making films that spoke to the Brazilian people in culturally relevant terms and were also successful at the box office. Embrafilme attempted to please both camps. It set up programs for the production of cultural films and documentaries and financed beginning directors and others such as Glauber Rocha and Júlio Bressane, whose films have limited commercial appeal.

The "independent"-concentrationist split grows out of the cultural-commercial dichotomy. "Independent" filmmakers have no firm commercial structure and few sources of production financing other than the state, and yet they have contributed decisively to the critical success of Brazilian cinema over the last twenty years.[15] Their production companies often consist of little more than a small office, a desk, and a telephone. They normally do not own complete filmmaking equipment, yet they constitute the vast majority of Brazilian cinematic activity.[16] Although they are not opposed to making successful films, they see commercial success as secondary to cultural or social relevance. By financing individual films rather than production companies, Embra-filme tended to support these "independent" filmmakers, reinforcing an atomized model of production rather than turning, as did Mexico, to a production model based on large studios.

In the 1970s the concentrationist group (and I use the term "group" very loosely) gained considerable strength and power within Embra-filme. The group is composed of medium-sized production companies which have complete or almost complete filmmaking facilities and fairly large and permanent staffs. Unlike the "independents," they normally produce several films a year (sometimes directed by "independents"), often in partnership with private investors, both national and foreign. They called on Embrafilme to adopt a more entrepreneurial attitude leading to increased capital accumulation in the industry. As a means to that end, they favored the concentration of Embrafilme's resources in a few films with strong commercial potential. Some of them wanted Embrafilme, or at least its profitable sectors, to be sold to private con-cerns.[17]

The existence of such tensions, when set against the traditionally clientelistic nature of the Brazilian state, of which the agency was part, resulted in a general lack of direction in Embrafilme's policy. Since the state's precise role in relation to the film industry was never truly defined, Embrafilme tried to be too many things to too many people, often under the forms of political pressure inherent in a clientelistic framework, the result being that it did few things as well as it might have been able to do under different circumstances and with different operating principles. Embrafilme made viable many important film projects and contributed decisively to Brazilian cinema's becoming, for a brief period, the premier cinema in Latin America, but its policies obviously did not lead to the consolidation of Brazilian cinema as a self-sustaining industry.[18]

Among the perhaps unintended effects of state policy toward the film industry were the bureaucratization of cinematic practice and a dramatic increase in production costs. The former, which led, in objec-tive terms, to Brazilian cinema being an officially sanctioned cinema (i.e., sanctioned by the state), is evident in the number of certificates a film needed to be recognized as a film, to benefit from cinematic legisla-tion, and to legally enter the exhibition circuit. According to the legisla-tion compiled by Alcino Teixeira de Mello, among such certificates have been a Censorship Certificate, a Certificate for Compulsory Exhi-bition, a Certificate of Origin, a Certificate of Brazilian Production, a Certificate-Guide for the obligatory "contribution" for film industry development, and a Certificate of Registration. In other words, a film does not exist as such in Brazil until legally recognized by the state bureaucracy.

On at least one occasion this process became a *de facto* form of censorship. In 1975 Jorge Bodansky and Orlando Senna codirected *Iracema*. The film was shot in 16mm using a type of stock that Brazilian laboratories were apparently ill-equipped to develop. Consequently, the film was developed in West Germany, where the film had been picked up for distribution on German television. Since it was not developed in Brazil, the film did not technically conform to the legal definition of a "Brazilian film" and was therefore denied the necessary Certificate of Brazilian Production, without which it could not be exhibited in the country. *Iracema* thus entered a sort of catch-22 situation; it could not be exhibited as a Brazilian film and enjoy the rights thereof (e.g., participation in the reserve market under the protectionist compulsory exhibition statutes), nor could it be submitted as a foreign film, since it was obviously Brazilian. The bureaucratic interdiction lasted until 1980 when it was finally released by Embrafilme as a Brazilian film. It also won top honors in that year's Embrafilme-sponsored Brasília Film Festival. Although bureaucrats argued that the film's interdiction was a technical legal matter, there is no doubt that its controversial nature had something to do with its problems with the state.

Another effect of the shift in policy toward the financing of selected film projects was, it is often said, to "socialize losses and privatize profits" (Schild). Since the state assumed the lion's share of the financial risk involved in film production, many directors and producers tended to be less concerned with keeping costs down and, at least to some extent, with public acceptance of their films. This problem was compounded by the political favoritism or clientelism that came to characterize the selection process. Many critics and filmmakers have commented on the situation:

SÉRGIO AUGUSTO: "The worst thing was the damage caused by the corporative and cartorial policy [Embrafilme] fostered. Access to whatever funds were available for production was only easy — and at times too easy — for those who had political contacts or who screamed the loudest. Talent for making good or successful films became a secondary factor in Embrafilme's entrance exams."

HERMANO PENNA: "Embrafilme has a paternalistic relationship [with the industry], with the total collusion of cinematographic professionals, because their relationship to the agency is not clear, partly because a film industry has never really been established in Brazil. It's a two-way street: the agency paternalizes, but filmmakers also have a tendency to expect it." (*Jornal da Tela,* March 1990, p. 13)

JÚLIO BRESSANE: "Embrafilme preserved and exacerbated all the defects of state enterprises: nepotism, malversation, overcharging, in sum, all the characteristics of an organized gang, and it thus chased the public away from the cinema and destroyed the market." (*Jornal da Tela,* March 1990, p. 14)

LUIZ PAULINO DOS SANTOS: "Another thing that is terrible in Embrafilme, besides the fact that one administration simply reverses the policies of the previous one, is the lack of criteria in the choice of productions, which are always selected in the most subjective way possible by special interest groups." (*Jornal da Tela*, March 1990, p. 15)

EDUARDO ESCOREL: [Even after its 1987 reorganization] "the paternalistic nature of state support continued, through subsidized investments with no hope for return given the conditions of the market. Embrafilme's public image ended in tatters after being bombarded for years by accusations of favoritism and having even the legality of its operations questioned. Even so, filmmakers refused to admit that the agency had a fatal illness. Tested chameleons, directors and producers tried to go about business as usual as if nothing had happened. Despite their chronic dissatisfaction, they preferred to maintain their relationship of dependency with the state instead of admitting that Embrafilme . . . had ceased to serve the true interests of Brazilian cinema. Struggling to reach an illusory life raft — the signing of a contract with Embrafilme — they continued to participate in the farce: while they cursed Embrafilme in public, in private they fought tooth and nail for their slice of its meager resources. On the one hand the agency approved projects with no apparent criteria; on the other filmmakers pressured to sign contracts they could not fulfill." ("Cinema e Estado")[19]

Embrafilme's coproduction program undeniably improved the technical quality of Brazilian cinema — virtually all the Brazilian films exhibited in the United States during the last decade were produced under such programs — but by doing so it allowed production costs to be inflated to levels far above the market potential for return in the domestic market. According to Concine's own calculation, at an average cost of $500,000 a film would need to be seen by 1,800,000 paying spectators to break even. In 1988 only two films, both by the Trapalhões comedy team, reached that level, although a third, *Super Xuxa contra o Baixo Astral* ("Super Xuxa Against the Bad Vibes"), came close (table 2; Concine, 130–31). While the process of rapidly increasing production costs was taking place, Embrafilme/Concine did little to improve and strengthen the industry's infrastructure. Its focus, at least in terms of financial support for the industry, was almost exclusively on production and on its own distribution sector.

By the mid-1980s it was increasingly apparent that the existing mode of state-supported cinematic production was obsolete and transformation of the relationship between cinema and the state was necessary. The urgency of the restructuring became clear — and Embrafilme once again the object of severe public criticism and debate — when the *Folha de São Paulo* published, in early 1986, a series of articles on the enterprise's management.[20] In an editorial titled "Cine catástrofe" (20 March 1986), the newspaper referred to Embrafilme's activities as a "moral, economic, and artistic disaster." Many film industry professionals recognized the need for a reevaluation of the relationship between cinema and the state. Cinema Novo veteran Carlos Diegues (*Bye Bye Brasil*), for example, referred to the enterprise as a "cultural Medicaid system that treats cancer with Band-Aids," and Embrafilme director Carlos Augusto Calil (1985–1987) asserted that the state could no longer attempt to substitute for private enterprise and that the existing model was simply no longer viable.[21]

Although minor changes in policy had occurred throughout the late 1970s and early 1980s, the next major attempt at transformation took place during the Sarney administration, with Celso Furtado as Minister of Culture. Sarney restructured Embrafilme, separating its cultural and commercial activities, by creating a mixed-ownership enterprise (Embrafilme — Distribuidora de Filmes S.A.) housing all the firm's commercial activities and transferring its other sectors into a foundation (Fundação Brasileira de Cinema). In the past, some 15 percent of Embrafilme's capital has been designated for nonprofit cultural activities, creating what many feel to be a financial burden on an enterprise designed to engage in entrepreneurial activities in support of the national industry *qua* industry. Even under this new structure, Embrafilme's fundamental orientation — the support of individual film projects rather than the industry as a whole — remained unchanged, and the general situation of the Brazilian film industry continued to deteriorate.[22]

The Exhibitor as Enemy

One of the major reasons for the crisis, and one that has yet to receive the serious public discussion it deserves, is the tension, if not outright antagonism, between the state-supported production sector and the exhibition sector. This antagonism goes back to the very beginnings of Brazilian cinema. In the early 1900s producers and exhibitors were normally one and the same. The development of independent distributors drove a wedge between producers and exhibitors, and the exhibition sector began to function almost exclusively for the benefit of foreign cinemas. In the 1930s exhibition groups fought legislation initiating a timid screen quota for Brazilian short films, just as they have fought every attempt to expand the quota until today, arguing free trade and open markets in opposition to state intervention and manipulation of the rules of the marketplace.

Without a screen quota and other protectionist measures, Brazilian cinema would very likely have existed only on the most crass commercial basis. At the same time, state policy toward the film industry clearly contributed to a loss of profits for exhibitors and was at least partially responsible for the decline of the exhibition sector, which has been pernicious for the Brazilian film industry as a whole.

The relationship between the state and the exhibition sector deteriorated steadily over the last two decades and especially since the reorientation of state policy toward the industry described above. In 1974 *O Estado de São Paulo* ran an article with the headline "The Great Duel of National Cinema," referring to the duel between exhibitors and state-supported producers as analogous to a Western movie, with the producer as hero, the exhibitor as villain, and the state as sheriff. The "duel" would by 1980 become a "war," fought largely in the courts, as exhibition groups, sometimes in conjunction with distributors, continually filed suit and frequently obtained at least temporary injunctions against various aspects of state policy, especially the compulsory exhibition law (screen quota). In its report for the second half of 1988, Concine lists suits filed by thirty-two exhibition companies (not counting multiple colitigants) representing over 10 percent of the total number of theaters in Brazil (Concine, 314–17).

The "war" between exhibitors and producers was fought not only in the courts but also in the theaters. Jorge Schnitman suggests that "historically, whenever exhibitors were forced to exhibit a large number of national films, they attempted to produce their own" (p. 67, n. 1). As early as 1971, exhibition groups began joining together to form production companies with the expressed intention of making films to meet the requirements of the compulsory exhibition law. The result was the rash of poor-quality *pornochanchadas* that began to flood the reserve market in 1972–73, leaving even less room for more culturally serious films. In the 1980s such production would become even more noxious as the soft-core *pornochanchada* was replaced by hard-core pornography. Table 1 not only indicates the astonishingly high percentage of pornographic films after 1980 but also the nonexistence of independent sources of film production financing as well as the almost total dependence of the production sector on either exhibitors (i.e., pornography) or the state.

Rather than go into more detail or discuss the merits of exhibitors' arguments, it is important to summarize legislation regarding the exhibition sector to attain an at least partial understanding of its situation. Brazilian cinematic legislation stipulates that exhibitors must show national films at least 140 days per year, regardless of the number of Brazilian films produced in a given year or the quality of those films. Although exhibitors negotiate with distributors of foreign films, they are obligated to pay a minimum of 50 percent of net income for Brazilian films, and they must make payment within fifteen days of exhibition. They must show a national short subject as part of each program of foreign films, purchase standardized tickets and box-office income recording sheets from Embrafilme at inflated prices, and keep Brazilian films in exhibition as long as the average of total spectators for two weeks or more equals 60 percent of the previous year's weekly average.

In return, exhibitors have received virtually nothing from the state except the disdain which has long characterized producers' attitudes toward the sector. Although it was among Embrafilme's attributes to attend to the needs of the sector, it refused to divert funds from production and did not even provide subsidies or low-interest loans to help them renovate their equipment and theaters. The result of the authoritarian imposition of these unwelcome measures has been a decline in income and a deteriorating sector, which has led to the closing of many theaters, especially in the interior of the country, and to the current crisis of Brazilian cinema. The proof of the failure of state policy toward the exhibition sector — and toward Brazilian cinema as a whole — is the dramatic decline in the number of theaters in operation in the country, now slightly over one thousand for a country of 140 million. Today the only films that can cover costs in such a small market are children's films using popular television stars as actors (Xuxa, Sérgio Malandro, the Trapalhões).

Cinema Novo, Exhibitors, and the Public

If the politically radical Cinema Novo movement was able to reach at least a tacit understanding with certain segments of the military regime regarding film production financing and the creation of a nationwide distributor within the framework offered by Embrafilme, why, then, was it unable to effect a rapprochement with the exhibition sector on mutually beneficial grounds? It would be simplistic to lay blame exclusively on the relationship between exhibitors and foreign film distributors, although there can be no doubt that that relationship has been a major contributing factor. For a full understanding, one must also go back to the origins of Cinema Novo, especially its attitude toward modes of cinematic practice and toward traditional film industry structures, and to the internal dynamics of the movement as it evolved in the 1960s.

An integral part of Cinema Novo's conception of social action through the cinema was a new attitude toward the development of the national film industry, based on a rejection of the studio model, which had failed so dismally with Vera Cruz, and an insistence on the importance of an auteur model. In his seminal 1963 book *Revisão Crítica do Cinema Brasileiro*, Glauber Rocha aligns himself and the movement with the French Nouvelle Vague and its struggle to free itself from the rigidity of industrial cinema and its norms, while at the same time politicizing the Nouvelle Vague's concept of auteur. The auteur, according to Rocha, revolts against the mercantilist mentality of industrial cinema, which puts profitability and easy communication above art. Rocha proposed an opposition between "commercial cinema," equated with illusionistic technique and untruth, and "auteur cinema," characterized by freedom of expression and a dedication to truth.

Cinema Novo thus rejected the studio system, a model borrowed from the "metropolis," as being dedicated by definition to the falsification of reality. Because of an extreme scarcity of finance capital for film production, Cinema Novo could not hope to equal the technical level of most foreign films. So rather than imitate dominant cinema, which would make their work merely symptomatic of underdevelopment, they chose to resist by turning, in Ismail Xavier's words, "scarcity into a signifier" (p. 18). The critical realism of films marked by the "aesthetic of hunger" served an important tactical and political function by expressing the radical "otherness" of Brazilian cinema in relation to world cinema. In short, as part of their project for "decolonizing" Brazilian cinema and attempting to create a critical consciousness in the Brazilian people in opposition to the alienated consciousness supposedly fostered by Hollywood, Cinema Novo adopted a new attitude toward the industrial development of Brazilian cinema and a new attitude toward film aesthetics, privileging ideas over technical perfection, politics over commercial potential.

Despite the movement's real contributions along these lines, a paradox also appears in its strategies. Although it opposed traditional modes of cinematic production and the aesthetic forms accompanying them, its participants made no real attempt to create alternative or parallel exhibition circuits. Rather, they released their films in established commercial circuits which had been developed primarily for the exhibition of foreign films. The Brazilian public, long conditioned by Hollywood's products, was generally unreceptive to the films of Cinema Novo, which became in many ways a group of films made by and for an intellectual elite and not for broad sectors of the Brazilian people or even of the filmgoing public.

Filmmaker Gustavo Dahl discussed the relationship between Cinema Novo, the public, and exhibitors in two 1966 articles, "Cinema Novo e Estruturas Econômicas Tradicionais" and "Cinema Novo e seu Público." In the first, Dahl argues that the Cinema Novo's initial success among intellectual elites allowed its participants to glimpse "the possibility of *making the old structures of Brazilian cinema collapse* through a strategy of internal prestige and commercial success abroad. . . . [It] was a question of destroying the artistic and cultural vices of [Brazilian] cinema from the inside out" (p. 197; emphasis added). Using the prestige gained in international film festivals, the movement's participants began making their first features with money from private patrons or borrowed from banker José Luís de Magalhães Lins's Banco de Minas Gerais. But "since the new filmmakers found themselves unconnected to the traditional structures of the Brazilian market — '*et pour cause*' — nothing could prevent the repetition of the errors of São Paulo's attempt at studio-based industrialization: the production of films that had no guarantee of exhibition" (ibid.). In other words, Cinema Novo hoped to destroy traditional cinematic structures but paradoxically found itself at an impasse because of the lack of alternative or parallel structures of distribution.

Cinema Novo participants had naively overestimated their ability to penetrate foreign markets beyond the festival circuit and, given their frequently nonexistent capital base, directors and producers came to depend on distributors and even exhibitors for postproduction financing. Dahl explains that "the exhibitor took advantage of this situation by diminishing the producer's percentage, releasing the film without publicity and using the film only to fulfill his compulsory exhibition quota. The cultural prestige and artistic success obtained by the films were insufficient to overcome either the pressure of the exhibitors or the traditional estrangement between the public and the *serious* Brazilian film" (pp. 197–98).[23] In other words, the ultimate cost of Cinema Novo's new attitude toward modes of cinematic production, film industry development, and film aesthetics was its inability to penetrate the existing film market, where, at least implicitly (and objectively), *less serious* Brazilian films did find success. Dahl's initial and most explicit explanation for this inability addresses what he calls the "greatest problem" of the national cinema: "the struggle of Brazilian exhibitors and foreign distributors against Brazilian producers and distributors" (p. 200).

The problem with this argument is that it fails to link the exhibitors' resistance — they frequently argued that Cinema Novo films were too intellectual and hermetic for success in the marketplace — to the widely recognized fact that the public by and large did not accept the movement's films. If the public refused to see the films, the exhibitors argued, why should they be forced to exhibit them? The problem of public acceptance would perhaps be of less significance if the movement had created stable parallel circuits for the exhibition of its films, but it did not, choosing, rather, to attempt to penetrate traditional circuits where deeply rooted economic interests and cultural habits fostered traditional forms of cinema *qua* entertainment, precisely the type of cinema that Cinema Novo, at least initially, virulently opposed.

In "Cinema Novo e seu Público," Dahl acknowledges that the movement's films did not reach their intended public (which he does not define but which apparently includes the filmgoing public as a whole) and asks whether that public would accept their films even if they saw them. The public Cinema Novo did manage to reach — estimated at around 50,000 people in Rio de Janerio — was composed largely of students, liberal professionals, intellectuals, artists, film enthusiasts, and even "some sectors of the bourgeoisie." But, Dahl suggests, "even this public is not satisfied with the films produced by Cinema Novo. Although it follows the movement with interest, it has one criticism: it does not make films that please the public!" This supportive yet restricted public recognized Cinema Novo as an important cultural movement, but it regretted its hermeticism and its "divorce from the masses." Thus the major question facing the movement: "how to resolve the contradiction between a socially and aesthetically responsible cinema and its acceptance by the public" (p. 194).

Dahl does not have an answer to this question. Rather, he shifts to the level of idealistic explanations ("film is an art. . . . No one asks [composer Pierre] Boulez how many records he has sold") by comparing Cinema Novo filmmakers (Rocha, Saraceni, Guerra, and Andrade, in this case) to Antonioni, Godard, and Resnais, whose films are frequently unsuccessful at the box office but who, unlike the Brazilians, are able to salvage the situation through international sales or, in the case of Godard, low budgets. Dahl thus displaces the argument from the concrete question of Cinema Novo's relationship with the public to the importance of linguistic experimentation in modern auteur cinema, using Godard as the paradigmatic example (p. 195). Implicit in his formulation is a charismatic, Romantic vision of the artist and an essentialist view of the film as an *objet d'art*.[24] The importance of Cinema Novo, he suggests, consists in "its ambition to be part of a worldwide search for a new cinema" (p. 198).

The basic problem remains unresolved. Cinema Novo, in its initial phase, was not accepted by the Brazilian people, and the movement did not seriously address "the fundamental question of the films' lack of communication with the public and its repercussions on the levels of language and ideology" (p. 199). Who was to blame? Not the filmmakers; certainly exhibitors and foreign film distributors, and perhaps even the public. After all, in "Cinema Novo e Estruturas Econômicas Tradicionais," Dahl had written that "the Brazilian public had followed the changes in taste of the worldwide public in its unbridled search for sex and violence, found in the plays of Nelson Rodrigues and *cangaceiro* adventures" (p. 198).[25]

In "Cinema Novo e seu Público" he continues the argument, recognizing the disjunction between the movement's political intentions and its objective inefficacy: "At first, the illusion was held that it would be sufficient to place the people in front of the films, as if before a mirror, for them to become aware of their alienation. Experience demonstrated exactly the opposite: the more they recognized themselves in their negative aspects, the more they protested. *It's dangerous to affirm that the public is not always right*" (emphasis added). Some films of the movement's second phase — *Menino de Engenho* ("Plantation Boy," 1966), *São Paulo S.A.* (1965), *Matraga* (1966), and *A Grande Cidade* ("The Big City," 1966) — had more success, partially because they "overcame the exasperating slowness considered one of the characteristics of Brazilian cinema," but at the cost of a "dilution of ideological substance." Others, such as *O Padre e a Moça* ("The Priest and the Girl," 1965), *A Falecida* ("The Deceased Woman," 1965), and *O Desafio* ("The Challenge," 1966), with their "intransigent fidelity to the conceptions of an auteur cinema, their stylistic rigor, and their conspicuous personality . . .

381

disconcerted the public" (p. 200). The people, Dahl continues, "do not want to be made aware of their unhappiness and inferiority in relation to other nations. It is necessary . . . to reveal both their weaknesses and their strengths in order to prevent them from falling into either depression or euphoria. We must learn to entertain them with their problems, which is not easy, and make them believe that one day they will find a solution, which is even more difficult" (p. 202).

One can clearly see in Dahl's statement of the problem the paternalistic didacticism of early Cinema Novo based, ultimately, on a Romantic vision of the artist (the auteur) as possessing a superior form of social and cultural knowledge as well as a self-attributed mission for making the people aware of their alienation and their supposed inferiority to other peoples as a means of helping them overcome their weaknesses and use their strengths to find solutions to their problems. If the people did not accept Cinema Novo's message, the difficulty must surely rest with them — or with the "colonial situation" which inculcated certain cinematic preferences — and not with the message itself or its aesthetic packaging.

In "A Crise do Cinema Brasileiro e o Plano Collor," critic Jean-Claude Bernardet discusses the insistence on an auteur mode of cinematic practice as a significant contributing factor to the crisis. Bernardet argues quite correctly that this insistence, combined with the inability or unwillingness to develop more stable modes of cinematic production — what he calls a "cinema de produtor" or a "producer's cinema" — led the independent cinema of the early 1960s to gradually become an "auteur-cinema-dependent-on-the-state." As Bernardet writes, "The model of auteur cinema comes from the days of silent film and reached its apogee with Cinema Novo and Marginal Cinema and its dependence on the state, which was consolidated in the 1970s. This does not mean that beautiful films do not occasionally appear, but rather that the model does not offer a structural solution, that is, a form of production that attracts a public and is able to recuperate its means of production." In other words, the insufficiencies of the auteur model itself were a factor in the failure to develop a self-sustaining film industry with a strong financial basis through the support of the Brazilian public.[26]

Cinema Novo was left with two options: play by the exhibitor's rules and make popular films (in box-office terms) or change the public's viewing habits and preferences. Given the difficulty if not impossibility of the second (Dahl suggested, in "Cinema Novo e seu Público," that such a change could occur only as a consequence of deep social transformations when the people would be "freed of the oppression of misery"), many of the movement's participants recognized that the production of more popular films became imperative if Cinema Novo was to continue to exist. To this end, it took a number of steps. First, producers and directors formed a distribution cooperative as a strategy for placing their films more easily in the market. Second, they began to make films they hoped would have a more popular appeal, turning more systematically toward literary classics and admitting comedy as an acceptable mode of discourse (early Cinema Novo, one might recall, was almost totally humorless).[27] In addition, they appealed to the state to guarantee, indeed *impose*, what the films themselves were unable to obtain: access to the market and a return on investments. One result of this appeal was the creation, within INC, of subsidy and coproduction programs, another the increased screen quota for foreign films — but also the increased hostility between, and polarization of, producers and exhibitors.

The exhibitor was irreversibly cast in the role of villain with whom no dialogue was possible. In the I Congresso da Indústria Cinematográfica (First Film Industry Congress, 1972), the exhibitors' syndicate presented a twenty-one-point proposal concerning the problems faced by the sector and focusing on financial assistance, standardized tickets and income reporting devices, and the compulsory exhibition law. Although many of the proposals were reasonable — such as a modification of the compulsory exhibition law so that no theater would be obligated to show a national film that had already been exhibited at another theater within a one kilometer radius — none was accepted.[28] It was as if the exhibitors had no legitimate concerns to be addressed in a serious manner.

The future of Brazilian cinema is currently up in the air. Virtually all the ideological alibis used in its defense over the last thirty years have crumbled along with the decimation of the domestic film market, the collapse of the production sector, and the at least temporary elimination of state support. The only solution to the current crisis — if there is one — may well be association with those long held to be the enemies of Brazilian cinema: foreign producers and exhibitors. More importantly, however, if it is to survive the current crisis and remain a significant form of cultural expression, Brazilian cinema must reexamine and redefine its relationship to the public and the state as well as its own position in the broader field of social relations.

Notes

1. After *O Cangaceiro* Barreto was able to make only one other feature, *A Primeira Missa* ("The First Mass," 1961). Even award-winning Cinema Novo directors have been less than prolific, due primarily to structural and conjunctural problems. Joaquim Pedro de Andrade (*Macunaíma*, 1969) made only six features, including one documentary, between 1960 and his death in 1988, and Leon Hirszman (1938–1988) only four.

2. The evolution of Cinema Novo's relationship to the state is outlined in Randal Johnson, *The Film Industry in Brazil*, esp. chaps. 4–6. The unprecedented level of stability and prosperity attained during this period is evident in the following statistics: between 1974 and 1978 the total number of spectators for Brazilian films doubled from 30 million to over 60 million, and total income increased by 288 percent, from $13 million in 1974 to over $38 million in 1978. Brazilian cinema's share of its own market increased from around 15 percent in 1974 to over 30 percent in 1978. From "Lei Básica do Cinema Brasileiro," *Filme cultura* 33 (May 1979): 114–16.

3. Given the complexity of the film production process, it is virtually impossible to know precisely how many films are currently under way. The figure given derives from conversations I had with a

number of filmmakers in Rio de Janeiro and São Paulo in July 1990. Most of the films now in production are being financed by European television industries or by the municipal government of São Paulo.

4. The "twenty out of thirty" statistic actually sheds a favorable light on the real proportion. Of the top-grossing one hundred Brazilian films of 1988, only around twenty were *not* pornographic. Of the fifty top-grossing foreign films during the same period, none were pornographic. See Concine, *Relatório de Atividades*, pp. 76–77, 91.

5. The situation has improved slightly since 1984, especially as other networks have begun to mount more serious challenges to the Globo network's virtual monopoly, but not enough to significantly change the situation.

6. Journalist-critic Sérgio Augusto sarcastically refers to those filmmakers who were able to obtain financing primarily through political contacts rather than talent and who depended almost entirely on the state for their sustenance as "Embrafilme's orphans."

7. The evolution of the screen quota was: *1932:* one short for each program of foreign films; *1939:* one feature per year; *1946:* three features per year; *1951:* one feature for every eight foreign films; *1959:* 42 days per year (i.e., that Brazilian films must be shown); *1963:* 56 days per year; *1969:* 63 days per year (provisional); *1970:* 77 days per year (provisional); *1970:* 112 days per year (not implemented); *1970:* 98 days per year (not implemented); *1971:* 84 days per year; *1975:* 112 days per year; *1978:* 133 days per year; *1980:* 140 days per year (Johnson, *The Film Industry in Brazil*, p. 185).

8. Among films financed under the coproduction program were Joaquim Pedro de Andrade's *Macunaíma* (1969), Carlos Diegues's *Os Herdeiros* ("The Heirs," 1968), and Nelson Pereira dos Santos's *Como Era Gostoso o meu Francês* ("How Tasty Was My Little Frenchman," 1971). For a complete listing, see Johnson, *The Film Industry in Brazil*, pp. 202–204.

9. The texts of the decree laws that founded and subsequently reorganized Embrafilme and founded Concine are in Mello, *Legislação* 1:11–29, 53–58.

10. Examples of such films are Glauber Rocha's *A idade da terra* ("The Age of the Earth," 1980) and Leon Hirszman's *Eles Não Usam Black Tie* ("They Don't Wear Black Tie," 1981).

11. Barreto and other producers formulated and presented to Passarinho a five-point program proposing, among other things, the restructuring of Embrafilme (Johnson, *The Film Industry in Brazil*, p. 150).

12. According to the "Política Nacional de Cultura," the Brazilian government's cultural policy is founded on a number of basic principles that reflect the historical, social, and spiritual values of the Brazilian people. The document says explicitly that the state role includes support of spontaneous cultural production and in no way implies that the state has the right to direct such production or to impede in any way freedom of cultural or artistic creation. The state's responsibility, in other words, is ostensibly to support and stimulate cultural production, not control it. The document is infused with a nationalist sentiment that is broad enough to include virtually all Brazilian cultural production. It formulates a desire to construct a harmonious "national identity" on a symbolic level based on respect for regional and cultural diversity and the preservation of the nation's cultural and historical patrimony.

13. Velloso, who was an avid film fan and a friend of Cinema Novo veteran Nelson Pereira dos Santos, has explained the Geisel regime's support of the film industry in the following terms: "Our objective was not to make an experimental, formally sophisticated and hermetic type of cinema. Not that that was excluded, but it wasn't our primary objective. We had to make a kind of cinema that really reached the people, a culturally dignified cinema. . . . From the beginning there was an understanding that the government would not culturally restrain anyone. The filmmaker would have artistic freedom to make his film, but at the same time I warned them that although political cinema is certainly legitimate, they should not make a doctrinaire, propagandistic cinema" (quoted in Tendler, "Cinema e Estado," 164).

14. See Johnson, *The Film Industry in Brazil*, pp. 19–23, 33–34.

15. The term "independent filmmaker" came into being with the Cinema Novo movement to distinguish between its mode of production and traditional modes of production based on a studio model. With the increasing dependence of such filmmakers on the state, the term has lost its original meaning and is in contradiction with their objective position in the cinematic field. Thus the quotation marks.

16. In an extensive interview granted after the release of his internationally acclaimed *Pixote* (1980), director Hector Babenco described his production company in the following manner: "My office is shameful. I have a typewriter I'm still making payments on and two telephone lines. . . . I don't have anything, not even a lease . . . 'HB Filmes'! In fact, it's just me, an office and a secretary. When I'm sick, HB is sick; when I'm broke, HB is broke." In Naves et al., "Hector Babenco," *Cinema*, no. 5 (Fundação Cinemateca Brasileira, Spring 1980): 15. An abbreviated English translation of this interview can be found in *Studies in Latin American Popular Culture* 7 (1988): 241–54.

17. See, for example, comments by Luiz Carlos Barreto in *O Estado de São Paulo*, 12 September 1984.

18. Between 1974 and 1985 Embrafilme coproduced 194 feature films. For a complete listing, see Johnson, *The Film Industry in Brazil*, Appendix E, pp. 213–20.

19. An important distinction is in order. Since Embrafilme's central offices were located in Rio de Janeiro, the agency was much more susceptible to pressure from Rio-based filmmakers than from those living in other parts of Brazil. São Paulo directors tended to use collective approaches to Embrafilme, devising more equitable forms of competition for funds within film industry organizations. Ozualdo Candeias describes their strategies in the following terms: "We in São Paulo never approach Embrafilme directly and say 'look, I have a film project for you to see.' We are united in an organization [the Associação Paulista de Cinema or APACI], and it is not our habit to act individually in relation to Embrafilme, perhaps partially because its relationship with São Paulo filmmakers has never been very good" (*Jornal da Tela*, March 1990, p. 16). In the same issue, see additional comments by São Paulo filmmakers João Batista de Andrade and Sérgio Toledo.

20. See also, in the *Folha:* "L. C. Barreto Diz que É Credor da Embrafilme," 17 March 1986; Renata Rangel, "Co-produção Aumenta Déficit da Embrafilme," 18 March 1986; "Nova Declaração de Massaini," 18 March 1986; "Cineastas Pediram o Fim da correção," 19 March 1986; Carlos Diegues, "De Quem É Mesmo o Dinheiro da Embra," 20 March 1986; "Calil Investe no Cultural e Comercial," 21 March 1986; Sérgio Santeiro, "O Modelo Cinematográfico Opressor," 21 March 1986; "Furtado Quer Mudar Embrafilme," 22 March 1986; "Embrafilme Responde à Reportagem da *Folha*," 23 March 1986; Luiz Gonzaga Assis de Luca, "Embrafilme, o Consumidor É Quem Paga," 23 March 1986; "Decreto de Sarney Determina o que É o Filme Brasileiro," 25 March 1986; Sérgio Toledo and Roberto Gervitz, "Embrafilme É um Antídoto," 30 March 1986.

21. Diegues's remark came in an interview to the *Jornal do Brasil*, 23 February 1985, and Calil's in an interview to that same paper on 23 March 1986.

22. In fact, the Fundação Brasileira de Cinema was never funded, and during its brief existence its budget came from Embrafilme.

23. Glauber Rocha describes this situation in some detail in *Revisão Crítica do Cinema Brasileiro*, esp. pp. 140–41. Rocha's own solution to the problem of market access involves two steps: first, a reserve market of 51 percent for national films, and second, increased censorship under the aegis of the Ministry of Education and Culture. A censorship commission, made up of "intellectuals, critics, professors, and men with a proven capacity for the cultural understanding of the cinema" rather than "ignorant police officials and puritan women," would screen both imported films and national films on the basis of "quality." His formulation constitutes an appeal for authoritarian solutions to the industry's problems (or at least for the problems of the "independent" directors and producers with whom Rocha was associated).

24. In an earlier article, "Algo de Novo entre Nós" (1961), Dahl wrote that "before being an industry, the cinema is an art," and "Art derives from the artist, the artist is the man [sic] who exists in freedom. The cinema, which is of man and Man [sic], is free, free above all from the economic pressure that industrial organization brings with it." The individual expression of an artist or auteur thus has priority over all other considerations.

25. It is perhaps ironic that one of the films Dahl mentions as being intransigently faithful to the original conceptions of Cinema Novo and the tenets of auteur cinema — and a box-office failure — is Leon Hirszman's *A Falecida* (1965), based on a play by Nelson Rodrigues. The first film by a Cinema Novo director drawn from Rodrigues was Nelson Pereira dos Santos's moderately successful *Boca de Ouro* ("Gold Mouth," 1962). In the 1970s and 1980s films based on Rodrigues would constitute a rich vein (culturally and economically) in Brazilian cinema, with such works as Arnaldo Jabor's *Toda Nudez Será Castigada* ("All Nudity Will Be Punished,"1973) and *O Casamento* ("The Wedding," 1975), Neville d'Almeida's *Dama do Lotação* ("Lady on the Bus," [1978] and *Os sete gatinhos* ("The Seven Little Kittens," 1980), Braz Chediak's *Bonitinha mas Ordinária* ("Cute but Vulgar," 1981), and Bruno Barreto's *O Beijo no Asfalto* ("Kiss on the Asphalt," 1981), among others.

26. A São Paulo critic once suggested to me that Brazilian cinema suffers from a "Godard syndrome" in that filmmakers tend to be more interested in aesthetic experimentation and, consequently, in being recognized as a "new Godard," than in making films that might please a broad public. Although one should be careful not to make excessively broad generalizations (there are *many* cases where this does not apply), the critic is certainly correct in some instances.

27. Toward the end of the 1960s the situation was in fact beginning to change, with Andrade's *Macunaíma* being the paradigmatic case of a film that was both politically radical and successful at the box office. In Nelson Pereira dos Santos's words, "The big turnaround came with *Macunaíma*, [which constituted] a rupture with didactic cinema, an anthropological openness and the end of the limiting stances of pre-conceived intellectual schemes" (Bojunga).

28. For a more detailed description of the exhibitors' proposals, see Johnson, *The Film Industry in Brazil*, pp. 147–50.

Works Cited

Augusto, Sérgio. "Governo Estuda Incentivos para Filmes Brasileiros." *Folha de São Paulo*, 5 July 1990.

Bernardet, Jean-Claude. *Cinema brasileiro: Propostas para uma História*. Rio de Janeiro: Paz e Terra, 1979.

――――. "A Crise do Cinema Brasileiro e o Plano Collor." *Folha de São Paulo* (Letras F3), 23 June 1990.

Bojunga, Cláudio. "Nelson: Do Beco, da Boca, do Humor entre Dentes, do Corpo Fechado." *Jornal da tarde*, 31 October 1974.

Concine, *Relatório de Atividades*. Segundo Semestre 1988 (1989).

Dahl, Gustavo. "Algo de Novo entre Nós." *O Estado de São Paulo* (Suplemento Literário), 7 October 1961.

――――. "Cinema Novo e Estruturas Econômicas Tradicionais." *Revista Civilização Brasileira* 1, nos. 5–6 (March 1966): 193–204.

――――. "Cinema Novo e seu Público." *Revista Civilização Brasileira* nos. 11–12 (December 1966–March 1967): 192–202.

Diegues, Carlos. "As Esperanças do Cinema Brasileiro." *Opinião* 26 (December 1975): 21.

Escorel, Eduardo. "Cinema e Estado." *Jornal do Brasil*, 10 April 1990, Caderno 1, p. 11.

Folha de São Paulo. "Cine Catástrofe." 20 March 1986.

Johnson, Randal. *The Film Industry in Brazil: Culture and the State*. Pittsburgh: University of Pittsburgh Press, 1987.

――――. "Toward a Popular Cinema: An Interview with Nelson Pereira dos Santos." *Studies in Latin American Popular Culture* 1 (1982): 225–36.

Jornal da Tela (Embrafilme). Edição especial ("Proposta para uma Política Nacional do Cinema"), March 1986.

Jornal da Tela (Embrafilme). Edição Documento ("Embrafilme 20 Anos"), March 1990.

"Lei Básica do Cinema Brasileiro." *Filme Cultura* 33 (May 1979): 114–16.

Mello, Alcino Teixeira de. *Legislação do Cinema Brasileiro*. 2 vols. Rio de Janeiro: Embrafilme, 1978.

Miceli, Sérgio. "O Processo de 'Construção Institucional' na Área Cultural Federal (anos 70)." In Miceli, ed., *Estado e cultura no Brasil*. São Paulo: Difel, 1984.

Ministério de Educação e Cultura. "Política Nacional de Cultura." Brasília: MEC, 1976.

Naves, Sylvia Bahiense et. al. "Hector Babenco." *Cinema* (Fundação Cinemateca Brasileira), no. 5 (Spring 1980): 9–22. (An abbreviated version, " 'Beauty Must Be Convulsive': An Interview with Hector Babenco," trans. Randal Johnson, appears in *Studies in Latin American Popular Culture* 7 [1988]: 241–54.)

Ortiz, Renato. *Cultura brasileira e Identidade Nacional*. São Paulo: Brasiliense, 1985.

Pereira, Luiz Carlos Bresser. "Cultura e Estado." *Folha de São Paulo*, 13 May 1990.

Ramos, José Mário Ortiz. *Cinema, Estado, e Lutas Culturais*. Rio de Janeiro: Paz e Terra, 1983.

Rocha, Glauber. *Revisão Crítica do Cinema Brasileiro*. Rio de Janeiro: Civilização Brasileira, 1963.

Schild, Susana. "Embrafilme, um Modelo Falido." *Jornal do Brasil*, 23 March 1986.

Schneider, Ronald M. *The Political System in Brazil: The Emergence of a 'Modernizing' Authoritarian Regime, 1964–1970*. New York: Columbia University Press, 1971.

Schnitman, Jorge. *Film Industries in Latin America: Dependency and Development*. Norwood, N.J.: Ablex, 1984.

Tendler, Sílvio. "Cinema e Estado: Em Defesa do Miúra." M.A. thesis, Pontifícia Universidade Católica, Rio de Janeiro, 1982.

Xavier, Ismail. "Allegories of Underdevelopment: From the 'Aesthetics of Hunger' to the 'Aesthetics of Garbage'." Ph.D. diss., New York University, 1982.

Part V

The Shape of Brazilian Cinema in the Postmodern Age

ROBERT STAM, JOÃO LUIZ VIEIRA, AND ISMAIL XAVIER

The first two editions of *Brazilian Cinema* (Associated University Press, 1982; University of Texas Press, 1988) pursued their subject up through the late 1970s. This Columbia reprint therefore calls for up-dating to cover Brazilian cinema productions through the 1980s and mid-1990s.[1] The first and most obvious point to make about this recent period is that the optimism expressed in the 1982 edition concerning the future of Brazilian cinema was to some degree unwarranted. The original manuscript was finalized (in 1980) at a high point for Brazilian cinema: 100 features were produced in 1978 and 103 in 1980. Just a few years before, Bruno Barreto's *Dona Flor and Her Two Husbands* (1976) had been seen by ten million people in Brazil, outdone in that same year only by the record-setting *Jaws*. With the support of Embrafilme, founded in 1969 as a distributor but empowered to fi-nance film production in 1973, Brazilian cinema had become commer-cially viable, partially thanks to an unsigned pact between left-leaning cultural nationalists and a conservative and authoritarian state.

In 1994 the situation is very different and in some ways more bleak. In March 1990, then President Collor abolished Embrafilme as part of a "scorched earth" policy toward any cultural production not regulated by "the market." The telegenic man that George Bush dubbed "Indiana Collor" also abolished Concine (the legal agency regulating film activi-ties) and suspended the "Sarney Law" (the tax benefit accorded those investing in cultural projects). The consequences of this cultural "Thatcherization" were devastating. Gone were the legal quotas pro-tecting Brazilian film, along with the inspection and reappropriation of box-office receipts and the obligation to make distribution prints of foreign films in Brazilian labs.

But Collor was not the sole cause of the crisis. Economic changes — galloping inflation, increases in production costs, the "dollarization" of filmmaking, the power of Hollywood distribution and pro-Hollywood exhibitors, the shrinking of the internal market, the impoverishment of the lower-middle-class audience, the closing of many movie theaters, the growing popularity of television and of home video — also played a role. The hostility of elite journalists, meanwhile, and the failure of Brazilian filmmakers to find the secret of popular communication, further exacerbated the crisis. As a result of all these factors, Brazilian film production has declined precipitously — down to thirteen features in 1990 and only three in 1993, with a resurgence, as we shall see, in 1994/1995. Brazil is not going through this crisis alone, of course; similar crises also afflict Great Britain, Italy, Germany, and most film-producing countries in the world. Few national cinemas, the United States and India being the exceptions, are completely autonomous, and most survive partially thanks to major state support. In Europe, perhaps only France retains a strong commercial cinema based primarily on its own internal market — whence its nationalist hostility to the cultural "globalization" implied by the GATT accords. (At the end of this essay we will explore some of the Brazilian responses to the crisis and the glimmerings of hope presently on the horizon.)

A second point to make about the recent period is that it is now impossible to analyze the cinema separate from television and other audiovisual media. While Brazilian film production has become more precarious, Brazilian television has largely escaped the negative effects of the crisis. By 1962, the same year that Cinema Novo was garnering its first international prizes, videotape was already rationalizing TV production in Brazil. Also in 1962, the Congress passed Law 4117, the "Brazilian Telecommunications Code," endorsing the idea of national security and development through television. The hope was to link all of Brazil through reliable telephones, telex, and televisual systems, accompanied by the provision of the technological infrastructure required for national networks. In 1965 the government created Embratel (Brazilian Enterprise for Telecommunications) to carry out this task, and in 1967 it created the Ministry of Communications as the bureaucratic agency providing financial and logistical support for the project. Brazilian television was then linked to Intelstat satellites, thus achieving its dream of addressing all Brazilians at the same time. The ideology of "national security" prodded the regime into modernizing communications for purposes of "national integration." In the era of the "economic miracle," furthermore, TV, unlike the cinema, directly served the national economy by absorbing consumers into a world-market economy. As a result, Brazilian television flourished, becoming a virtual paradigm of commercial success in a dependent Third World context — Brazil's TV Globo is now the fourth largest private network in the world in audience and resources — while Brazilian cinema suffered the triple whammy of runaway inflation, urban crisis, and governmental neglect. And as the coup de grace, Brazilian television, unlike many of its European counterparts, has virtually boycotted national films. (In 1986, for example, out of 2,170 films screened on Rio's six television channels, only 35 were Brazilian.)[2]

All these factors generated an immense gap between the two media;

while TV was consolidated as a mass vehicle in the 1960s, cinema reached quasi-industrial status only in the 1970s, a temporal retard whose consequences still linger. While Brazilian cinema has achieved only a modest portion of the internal market — going from a high point of 36 percent in 1982 to less than 10 percent in 1994 — Brazilian television dominates the domestic market with huge *telenovela* hits such as *Escrava Isaura, Roque Santeiro, Vale Tudo, Pantanal,* and *Maria Moura* (many seen by a daily audience of over 70 million people). In the 1971–1983 period, the percentage of foreign TV programming actually declined from 60 percent to 30 percent (and during prime time to only 23 percent), a proportion placing Brazil on a par with or above such European countries as France, Italy, and the United Kingdom.[3] While Brazilian cinema existed under the fragile protection of the underfunded Ministry of Education and Culture, Brazilian television was linked to the powerful Ministry of Communications. And while Brazilian films are screened sporadically in international film festivals and only exceptionally distributed abroad, Brazilian TV programs are systematically exported to Latin America, Portugal, Italy, France, Poland, and even China.[4] Television has thus become the most significant shaper of the image of Brazilian national identity, both internally and externally.

The long-term implications of these processes could hardly be clear to the young filmmakers of the 1960s. Their auteurist project with its artisanal utopia of "a camera in hand and an idea in the head" merely postponed, as it were, a deeper reflexion on the role of cinema within a broader "culture industry." Indeed, early Cinema Novo formulations largely avoided the question of the evolving nature and role of the mass media in Brazil. How was one to develop a national cinema while rejecting the market and consumerism? How was Glauber Rocha's Brechtian-style attack on "digestive cinema" and his denunciation of the "public-at-any-price" mentality to be reconciled with the desire to reach the popular audience? How could an anti-industrial and even avant-garde cinema meet the challenges thrown up by mass-mediated culture and the consciousness industry?

The struggle against authoritarian militarism after 1964, meanwhile, in some ways distracted attention from deep structural changes in the Brazilian cultural economy, masking the fact that the military regime did in some ways constitute a modernizing force, even if a perverse one, which consolidated capitalism, energized the media, and facilitated the circulation of "cultural goods." It was the precise terms of this modernization that led to colossal national debt and a high misery index in terms of illiteracy, malnutrition, criminality, and infant mortality. At the same time, leftist intellectuals continued to see even a right-wing state as a means for confronting foreign domination, whence their support for Embrafilme. The period of military rule was ironically marked by a dramatic expansion in cultural production — books, journals, TV programs, films — as part of a general industrialization of culture. But Cinema Novo theorizations symptomatically favored Frantz Fanon, with his notions of liberatory violence and national fulfillment, and Antônio Gramsci, with his ideal of the "organic intellectual," over those schools and theorists that focused on the culture industry. Only in the late 1960s, when it became obvious that the audiovisual economy was revolving around television, did such issues come to the foreground, and by then the theme of debate was not the promise and potentialities of the cinema but rather its crisis. The consolidation of the hegemony of the cultural industry, in this period, was accompanied by a few compensatory mechanisms (for example, the state financing of historical epics and prestigious literary adaptations) favoring the media marginalized by that hegemony. But in general, the cinema, forced to suffer passively the whims and vicissitudes of official cultural policy, saw itself outperformed by other cultural sectors (such as television and popular music) whose internal dynamics were more attuned to transnational capitalist currents. Indeed, the segregation between TV and cinema in Brazil has cost the latter dearly, and the current consensus (at least among film professionals) is that the two media must cross-fertilize and collaborate both artistically and economically (as is already the case in much of Europe and elsewhere) if Brazilian cinema is to survive.

The challenge confronting Brazilian filmmakers must be seen in the light of the socioeconomic transformations triggered by what might be called "conservative modernization," a model that promotes industrial expansion built on repressed wages, the proletarianization of the middle class, and a general shift toward "postindustrial" jobs in administration, communications, and services. It would therefore be inaccurate to see the current crisis as the simple product of "twenty years of dictatorship." Brazilian cinema has always survived within a situation of scarcity, dependency, undercapitalization, and inadequate technical infrastructure. The crisis engendered by economic neocolonialism and by Hollywood's stranglehold on the market preceded the dictatorship — indeed, it was precisely that crisis which prodded Cinema Novo's search for alternative methods of production. What the post-1964 period did bring was the additional "nuisance" of political censorship as the most visible aspect of repression, along with raids on cineclubs, the interruption of "leftist" film production, the banning or delayed exhibition of films, and the forced or voluntary exile of numerous filmmakers. The illusion was to imagine that the mere removal of the dictatorship would bring with it a radical change in the development model, one that would quickly "correct" the perverse consequences of the earlier process.

The negative effects of the conjunction of economic crisis and political censorship on the cinema were not "automatic," moreover, any more than the positive effects of the redemocratization known as "abertura" (opening) were automatic. (Unlike the situation in Argentina, the end of dictatorship in Brazil did not bring with it a sudden cinematic resurgence.) In Brazil, some of the liveliest moments of creativity and debate coincided, paradoxically, with the periods of the most intense repression. The cultural hegemony of the left, in terms of publication, filmmaking, and cultural production generally, was ironically stronger during the dictatorship than it was later with redemocratization. The brutally repressive 1969–1974 period produced more provocative films than the subsequent period of liberalization. While the earlier, more repressive period offered the tropicalist subversion of *Macunaíma* (1969), the ironic cannibalism of *Como Era Gostoso Meu Francês* ("How Tasty Was My Little Frenchman," 1971), the distanced (Brechtian) analysis of *São Bernardo* (1973), and the formal subversion of *Triste Trópico* (1974), the *abertura* period generally featured more conventional works, such as the relatively "safe" literary adaptations of major Brazilian writers such as Jorge Amado and Nelson Rodrigues.

The third point to make about Brazilian production since the late 1970s — and this will be our emphasis here — is its remarkable diversity. While it was relatively easy to posit a unifying thread to account for early Cinema Novo (the call for national liberation in general and for cinematic decolonization in particular), the sequel offers no such clarity. Brazilian cinema has become much more dispersed and eclectic. Even if one sets aside the "hillbilly" films of Amâcio Mazzaropi (thirty-two films before his death in 1981) and the popular children's films by the comedy team "Os Trapalhões" (roughly, the "Four Morons," with thirty-six features between 1965 and 1990), and the soft- and hard-core porn films, one is confronted with a wide spectrum of productions. These range from ongoing work by veteran Cinema Novo directors (especially Nelson Pereira dos Santos, Arnaldo Jabor, Carlos Diegues, and Rui Guerra), and by the "sons and daughters" of Cinema Novo (Tizuka Yamasaki, Ana Carolina, Carlos Alberto Prates Correia, Jorge Bodansky, Lauro Escorel, Eduardo Escorel, Bruno and Fábio Barreto), to that of the Underground (Júlio Bressane, Rogério Sganzerla, Andrea Tonacci, Luiz Rosemberg Filho), and the new wave of young filmmakers from São Paulo (Chico Botelho, Djalma Limongi, Ícaro Martins, José Antônio Garcia, Sérgio Toledo, Wilson Barros, Sérgio Bianchi, Carlos Reichenbach, Guilherme de Almeida Prado), not to mention the work by makers of short fiction films, militant documentaries, and art videos. Rather than a unifying thread, we can now establish little more than a common substratum of concern, a broad problematic of interrelated questions. Our goal in this final section will not be to cover the entire spectrum, but rather to point to salient trends, while lingering on some films of special interest.

The Question of the National

In a landmark 1986 essay, Fredric Jameson argued that all Third World texts are "necessarily allegorical," in that "even those texts in-

393

vested with an apparently private or libidinal dynamic . . . necessarily project a political dimension in the form of national allegory; the story of the private individual destiny is always an allegory of the embattled situation of the public third-world culture and society." [5] Brazilian intellectuals, for their part, had been working with something like the concept of national allegory at least since the debates revolving around "tropicalism" in the late 1960s, and arguably even since the debates concerning the national character conducted by "modernismo" in the 1920s. [6] Without endorsing Jameson's somewhat hasty totalization of all Third World texts as "necessarily" allegorical — it would be problematic to posit any single artistic strategy as uniquely appropriate to the cultural productions of an entity as heterogeneous as the "Third World" — and without denying the analytical relevance of allegory for all national cinemas (including First World cinemas), one can argue that Brazilian films, even the most frivolous, have often had an allegorical dimension, with allegory here conceived in a broad sense as any kind of oblique or synecdochic utterance soliciting hermeneutic completion or deciphering. The 1950s *chanchadas*, in this perspective, can be seen as parodying successful Hollywood films of the period in order to allegorize both the "inferiority" of Brazilian cinema vis-à-vis the dominant model and the impulse to transcend the conditions imposed by economic dependency. The films of first-phase Cinema Novo, similarly, constitute "allegories of underdevelopment," where history is shown as the unfolding of a progressive teleological design and where an "aesthetic of hunger" turns scarcity itself into a signifier. The avant-garde films of the late 1960s and early 1970s (for example, Rogério Sganzerla's *Bandido da Luz Vermelha* — "The Red Light Bandit," 1968), meanwhile, become allegorical in another, more modernist sense, as "fragmentary discourses" expressing a "crisis in representation," where the very notion of historical and cinematic teleology becomes suspect. [7] The early 1960s metaphor of hunger, evoking the victim finding self-redemption through Fanonian violence, gives way to the late 1960s metaphor of an "aesthetic of garbage" as being appropriate to a Third World country picking through the detritus of an international system dominated by First World monopoly capitalism. The diverse strategies we will encounter over the last two decades of Brazilian cinema — metacinema, carnivalization, "*abertura* naturalism," and national allegory — can be seen as responses to a new historical juncture where there is little place for the messianic optimism of early Cinema Novo or even for the aggressive nihilism of "Marginal Cinema."

Because of Brazil's neocolonized Third World status, its intellectuals — and the Brazilian filmmakers discussed here largely see themselves, and are seen as, intellectuals — have necessarily been concerned with the ramifications of nationalism. Of course all films, as the products of national industries, as produced in national languages and recycling national intertexts, are on one level national. But if First World filmmakers have enjoyed the luxury of appearing to be "above" petty nationalist concerns, it is because they can take for granted the projection of a national power which facilitates the making and the dissemination of their films. In Brazil, in contrast, national power does not provide a quiet substratum of confidence; rather, a sense of national powerlessness generates a Sisyphysian struggle to conquer an elusive "authenticity" to be constructed anew with every generation. The cultural and ideological environment in which Brazilian filmmakers operate forces them to juggle diverse concerns — the desire for personal expression, a preoccupation with certain themes, an engagement with film language, an attitude toward the spectator — while never losing sight of the question of the "national." Brazilian filmmakers, even those who affect disinterest in the issue, remain haunted by the specter of cultural colonialism, of being too imitative, too servile toward the dominant model. (That this specter came to haunt virtually all Brazilian filmmakers constituted a victory for Cinema Novo since, during the first four or five decades of Brazilian cinema, copying the foreign model implied no shame.) Given the foreign domination of the market, and given the immense obstacles to making films, the cinema, for better or worse, has been habitually evaluated in terms of its service to "development" and "national liberation." The filmmakers express their creative personalities, but they also see themselves as part of a larger collective project: the consolidation of a national cinema.

The concept of the national, however, is hardly unproblematic. Quite apart from the historical ambiguities of nationalism — the slippage between its original meaning as racial group and its later meaning as politically organized entity, the oscillation between its progressive and regressive poles — there are also cultural and intellectual ambiguities at work. The early discussions of nationalism took it as axiomatic that the issue was simply one of expelling the foreign to recover the national, as if the nation were a kind of "heart of the artichoke," to be found by peeling away the outer leaves, or as if, to change the metaphor, the nation were the ideal sculpted form lurking within the unworked stone. Roberto Schwarz calls this view the "national by subtraction," i.e., the idea that the simple elimination of foreign influences will automatically allow the national culture to emerge in its native glory.[8] The project of eliminating the foreign and recuperating the national was shared, incidentally, by both left and right, except that each gave the words *national* and *foreign* a distinct political inflection. For right-wing "national-security" ideologists, it was an "alien" Marxism that had to be excised for the nation to regain its integrity, while for the left it was imperialism and the multinational corporations.

While the deficiencies of the right-wing analysis are perhaps obvious, the ambiguities of the left's position deserve exploring. First, the topos of a unitary nation elides the realities of class, camouflaging the possible contradictions between different sectors of Brazilian society and distracting attention from the internal mechanisms of Brazilian capitalism. Second, the exaltation of "the national" per se fails to provide criteria for distinguishing exactly what is worth retaining in the national tradition. A blind nationalism that exalts patriarchal social institutions simply because they are "ours" (as in the case of the Jorge Amado character who claimed to feel Brazilian only during carnival and when he was beating his wife) can hardly be seen as progressive. Third, even apart from the question of class, there are many "Brazils" — urban and rural, male and female, indigenous, African, European and Asian immigrant. The view of the nation as a unitary subject muffles the "polyphony" of social and ethnic voices characteristic of a heteroglot culture. In Brazil the "real" country evoked by the word *povo* ("people") is understood to be the dark-skinned nation of the poor, the precariously literate and the ethnically stigmatized, in sum, the victims of diverse forms of exclusion. Fourth, the precise nature of the national "essence " to be recuperated is extremely elusive and chimerical. Some nationalist purists locate this essence in the past (e.g., prior to North American, or British, or Portuguese influence) or in the rural interior of the country, or in a prior stage of development (the preindustrial), or in a non-European ethnicity (the indigenous substratum, Afro-Brazil). But in the case of Brazil, even the most prized national symbols come with the mark of the foreign. Palm trees came from India, soccer came from England, and the samba traces it roots to Africa. The Brazilian nation must therefore be envisioned as an "imagined community," to borrow Benedict Anderson's phrase, just as many of the traditions valorized by Brazilian nationalism must be seen as what Hobsbawm calls "invented traditions."[9] Any definition of Brazilian nationality, then, must be anti-originary (seeing the nation as narrated, constructed, diacritically forged within difference), must take class into account, must allow for racial, gender, and sexual difference, and must be dynamic, seeing "the nation" as an evolving, imaginary, deferred construct rather than as an originary essence.

The Penchant for Reflexivity

Symptomatic of its allegorical-modernist tendencies, Brazilian cinema since the late 1970s shows a clear penchant for metacinema and reflexivity. We use these terms here in their broadest possible sense, to refer to films that foreground the filmmaker, or the film's intertext, or its textual procedures, or its reception, or its production.[10] Taking themes from the cinematic universe, these films generate an iconography marked by the presence of projectors, cameras, movie posters, and theaters, combined with constant recourse to narrative formulae self-consciously drawn from the cinematic archive. One finds reflexivity, to take just a few examples, in *Fulaninha* ("What's Her Name," 1986), David Neves's film about a filmmaker in love; in *Sonho Sem Fim* ("Dream

Without End," 1986), Lauro Escorel's film about Brazilian film pioneer Eduardo Abelim; in *Brás Cubas* (1985), Júlio Bressane's reflexive adaptation of a Machado de Assis novel; in the self-flaunting MGM-style artifice of Rui Guerra's *Malandro* (1986); in the cinematic obsessions and stagy films-within-the-film of Hector Babenco's *Kiss of the Spider Woman* (1985); in the metalinguistic exercises of popular composer Caetano Veloso's *Cinema Falado* ("Talking Cinema," 1986); in the mixed documentary-fiction modes and filmmaker-within-the-film of Tizuka Yamasaki's *Patriamada* (1985); in the metavoyeuristic focus of Guilherme de Almeida Prado's *Dama do Cine-Shanghai* ("Lady of Cine-Shanghai," 1987) and *As Taras de Todos Nós* ("Everybody's Vice," 1987); in the anagrammatic title of Reichenbach's *Filme Demência* (1986); in Carlos Diegues's *Dias Melhores Virão* ("Better Days Will Come," 1988), a film about (and released on) television; and in the reflexion on documentary processes in Eduardo Coutinho's *Cabra Marcado para Morrer* ("Twenty Years After," 1984).

It is as if the filmmaker, conscious of working with issues having a long history of formulation in a body of filmic and extrafilmic texts, becomes necessarily reflexive, dialoguing with the received body of belief and methodology, directly or indirectly discussing the cinema within the films. Each film becomes a methodological sample of a possible approach, at once "about" a subject and "about" itself. Here Brazilian cinema is in step, of course, with international cinema, with its ever-increasing tendency to reflexivity, whether modernist (early

Cláudia Ohana in *Malandro* (1986)

Godard), Brechtian (late Godard) or postmodernist (Atom Egoyan). But there are also national and continental specificities at work, rooted in the special status of the Latin American artist-intellectual and in the marginal and syncretic nature of the Latin American cultural experience. First, the Latin American artist-intellectual is virtually obliged to commit what Michel Foucault calls the "indignity" of speaking for others. Given the power of the state apparatus and the relative weakness of civil society, the intellectual becomes a mediator between what Carlos Fuentes calls the "power elite" and the "critical elite." Artists-intellectuals thus come to speak "in lieu of" repressed institutions and groups. Second, the Latin American artist-intellectual is almost necessarily multicultural, at once inside and outside, defined as at the margins yet thoroughly penetrated by the center. As the product of cultural and ethnic *mestizaje*, Brazil, especially, forms a veritable palimpsest of diasporas — blacks kidnapped from Africa, indigenous peoples made alien in their own land, immigrants from Europe, Asia, and the Middle East — whence the appropriateness of the title of Tizuka Yamasaki's first film, *Gaijin* (Japanese for "stranger"), in stressing the primordial foreignness of all Brazilians. As an (at least) tricultural people, Brazilians tend to be language- and culture-conscious, inhabiting a peculiar realm of irony where words and images can seldom be taken at face value.

Whatever the root cause of the phenomenon, metacinema has been ubiquitous in recent Brazilian cinema. But even here we find a remarkable plurality. Among the most commercially oriented films, for example, metacinema takes the form of parodies of Hollywood films or American television programs. These parodies, as was argued earlier in this volume, tend to take as their parodic object Hollywood high-tech spectacles rather than equally popular but less spectacular films such as *Love Story* or *Kramer versus Kramer;* they parody, in other words, precisely those films whose production values Brazilian filmmakers find most difficult to emulate. Many of the most successful high-tech Hollywood films of the past two decades have attracted the parodic interest of Brazilian cineastes: *Bacalhau* ("Codfish," 1976) parodies *Jaws; A Banana Mecânica* ("The Mechanical Banana," 1973) parodies *A Clockwork Orange; O Jeca Contra o Capeta* ("The Bumpkin Against the Devil," 1976) parodies *The Exorcist* and so forth. These films can properly be termed allegorical, as we have seen, in that they explicitly thematize the relatively weak position of Brazilian cinema vis-à-vis Hollywood, either by directing laughter against dominant cinema in a kind of aesthetic exorcism or a part of a ritual of self-degradation.[11]

In the 1980s a number of independent films demonstrate the creative power of intertextual parody for generating fiction through metafiction. Ivan Cardoso's *O Segredo da Múmia* ("The Secret of the Mummy," 1982), for example, throws together prototypical characters from diverse films within cognate genres as an economical means of recycling generic materials. Here the intertextual references — to the *chanchada,* to *Red Light Bandit,* to the B-film, Andy Warhol, and Mel Brooks (especially *Young Frankenstein*), to Val Lewton and Boris Karloff — serve not as mere homage but rather as structural armature for an attack on Hollywood illusionism. The collage appropriates not only the residue of genre films but also the leftovers of other films, reportedly picked up from editing-room trash cans in what amounts to a literalization of the "garbage can" aesthetic. This spliced assemblage of heteroclite materials, which includes clips from Atlântida newsreels, shots of lightning and thunderstorms, segments of B-films, emphasizes the artificiality of the process of narrative construction. The assemblage calls attention to the surprisingly wide range of archival material available in Brazil, and thus demonstrates the infinity of ways such material can be artistically recuperated. The images include the landing of an old airplane from the now extinct Brazilian Royal Airlines, and the election of Marta Rocha as Miss Brazil in 1954 (with an homage by modernist poet Manuel Bandeira) — cherished images, in other words, for the Brazilian popular unconscious. The minimalist approach of the film is also exhibited in the deployment of stills and postcards. The title "Cairo 1954" appears over a postcard image, while a clichéd piece of "exotic" orchestral music evokes an orientalized Egypt. The flagrant intention is to deploy such hackneyed strategies as part of a parodic defamiliarization that "lays bare the device."

The same method of ironic hybridization operates in Júlio Bressane's *Tabu* ("Taboo," 1982), a film that continues the project begun in *Rei do Baralho,* to wit, the "transvaluation" of the codes of the *chanchada.* Bressane posits a hypothetical meeting or "threshold encounter" (Bakhtin) between popular 1920s composer Lamartine Babo and the modernist poet Oswald de Andrade (played by Colé, the *chanchada* veteran familiar from *Carnaval Atlântida*). Babo here invokes the spirit of popular culture and carnival (a point underlined by casting popular singer-composer Caetano Veloso as Babo), while Andrade embodies the avant-garde theorization and elaboration of popular culture. This suggestive structural mechanism enables a retrospective rapprochement between the popular carnival music of Rio and the erudite literary vanguardism of São Paulo. At the same time, the film elegiacally celebrates the Rio of the 1930s as a tropical paradise by associating it with interpolated footage from Murnau's *Tabu* (1931). One remarkable audiovisual montage superimposes a carnival song about the daily chores of fishermen, delivered by *chanchada* star Emilinha Borba, on Murnau's images of Tahitian dancers. By spreading the spirit of carnival to the South Pacific in a kind of joyful heterotopian contamination, Bressane demonstrates the inexhaustible suggestiveness of a tradition rooted in anthropophagic modernism and its latter-day incarnation, Tropicalism.

We find still another kind of metacinema in Rogério Sganzerla's documentary-fiction feature *Nem Tudo É Verdade* ("It's Not All True," 1985), a film that works through Sganzerla's obsession with Orson

Welles Reconsidered in *Nem Tudo É Verdade* **(1985)**

Welles and specifically with the never-completed *It's All True,* which Welles began filming during Rio's 1942 Carnival, the lost footage of which was rediscovered in a Paramount warehouse in the mid-1980s.[12] *It's Not All True* recreates Welles's Brazilian experience through a sound-image collage, combining documentary-style material (footage from *It's All True,* footage of Welles in Rio, citations of *Citizen Kane* and *The Lady from Shanghai,* newspaper accounts, period photos, interviews with participants in the film) with staged reconstructions in which Brazilian avant-garde musician Arrigo Barnabé (who physically resembles the young Welles) plays Welles himself in his encounters with Brazilian celebrities and studio executives. Sganzerla portrays Welles as the rebellious victim of the Hollywood studio system, the press, and North American and Brazilian politicians. Welles's utopian dream of real industrial and artistic collaboration between North and South America, Sganzerla suggests, violently challenged the neocolonial assumptions of the time and was therefore cut short.[13]

São Paulo Metacinema

Metacinema is also a constant in the world of São Paulo filmmaker Carlos Reichenbach, author, since 1968, of eleven features and a number of short films. "I make films about cinema," Reichenbach claims, "but which don't speak of cinema."[14] In Europe, Reichenbach is well known as the "tropical Fassbinder," but only a few of his films, notably *Liliane M* (1975) and *Anjos do Arrabalde* (1987), have been screened in the United States. Because of the foregrounding of eroticism in his work, Reichenbach has often been mistakenly considered a porn director, but the real goal of his "intellectual pornography" is the critique and transvaluation of porn. Reichenbach forms part of a generation of filmmakers who began their careers with producers in São Paulo's "Boca de Lixo"("mouth of garbage") district, a group less inspired by neorealism than by American B-films and the Japanese films of Oshima and Imamura screened in the Japanese neighborhood of São Paulo. Reichenbach's first feature, *Corrida em Busca de Amor* ("Race for Love," 1971) is a raucous parody of American beach-party movies which melds cinematic in-jokes with the anarchistic socialism of Proudhon and Bakunin. Within Reichenbach's metapornography, eroticism is always distanced and voyeurism always short-circuited. In his episode for the film *Audácia*, for example, Reichenbach has a lovemaking couple repeatedly interrupt the "action" to discourse on the role of sexuality in the cinema. The Borgesian *Ilha dos Prazeres Proibidos* ("Island of Forbidden Pleasure," 1979), meanwhile, presents its diegesis as a narrative emerging from an erotic novel read by one of the characters. A character named Luc Moullet confesses to having murdered Lemmy Caution in Godard's *Alphaville* (1965). The love scenes, in this meta*pornochanchada*, are invariably more comic than titillating, as when we are shown sunburned tourists pawing each other at a beach picnic while lipsynching Nelson Eddy's "Indian Love Call." [15] In 1975 Reichenbach directed *Liliane M — Relatório Confidencial* ("Lilian M, Confidential Report"), under the self-confessed influence of the Jean-Luc Godard of *Vivre sa Vie* and the Samuel Fuller (affectionately known as "Samuca" in São Paulo) of *The Naked Kiss* (1964). The narrative develops via flashback confessions, recorded by an always visible Nagra tape recorder and an invisible camera whose function it is to erase the differences between the narration and the facts narrated. The film tells the story of a woman from the country who arrives in São Paulo full of ambitious dreams but who winds up as an object in the hands, in socially descending order, of an Italian businessman, a German industrialist and his salesman son, a government bureaucrat, and an auto mechanic. Nostalgic for rural life, she ultimately has little choice but to continue as a high-class urban prostitute. This apparently linear story is told, however, in multiple and seemingly contradictory styles. While the female protagonist is treated in a realist style reminiscent of early Cinema Novo, the other characters are treated in a stylized and quasi-caricatural manner. The mix of naturalism and stylization fractures the diegetic world, disturbing the conventions of sociological realism and unsettling the spectator looking for easy answers.

Reichenbach made *O Império do Desejo* ("The Realm of Desire," 1980) in less than a month on the São Paulo coast, using only twenty-three cans of negative film stock. Its title a clear reference to Oshima's *In the Realm of the Senses* (1976), the film critiques the *pornochanchada* from within the genre itself. Produced by Antônio Polo Galante, the Roger

Corman of the Boca de Lixo (the red-light district of São Paulo), its fast pacing evokes the freely associative spirit of the *chanchada* by promoting an anarchic mélange of cheap melodrama, horror, and gangster thriller, all incongruously infused with poetic flights and political ruminations. The diegetic pretext for this subversion of the canonical *pornochanchada* is apparently quite simple. A young hippie couple hitchhiking to the coast is picked up by a wealthy widow, who invites them to stay at her beach house. Upon arriving, the hippies learn that peasant squatters are about to be expelled by the police with the help of the widow's lawyer. Nearby there lives a visionary prophet and murderer who constantly quotes Maoist philosophy and finally sets fire to his own house. After the widow is killed by her lawyer and the young couple has left, the peasants return to occupy the house.

Here again Reichenbach juxtaposes naturalized and stylized elements within the same scene. The insider trio of main characters within the house behaves according to the conventional standards of mimetic representation, but the "outsiders" wreak havoc with such codes. The lawyer, for example, sports 1930s-style clothing and hyperbolically theatrical makeup. The prophet sets fire to his cabin to the words of a poem by a Portuguese Jesuit, while simultaneously devouring a Chinese woman in an anthropophagic banquet. The effect is one of blatant *ostrenanie* (estrangement), of playful incongruity, mingling references to the high art of Ingmar Bergman and the low culture of the *pornochanchada*. The most aggressive gesture, however, is directed at the narrative convention that makes voyeurism central to the *pornochanchada*'s decoupage. Playing on the titillating coitus interruptus structure typical of the genre, Reichenbach subverts the usual identification with the male hero by making the male the sexual object. At one point, an "outside" woman, depicted in long shot and from a frontal angle, corners the protagonist in the house. She orders him to kiss her while she looks at the camera and addresses supposedly erotic commentary to the audience. He complies with her requests, but the woman's returned gaze, and the stylization of the gestures and language, undercut conventional identification.

Reichenbach's work corrects a perennial problem in Brazilian film — the cinematic neglect of one of the world's largest and most cosmopolitan metropolises — São Paulo. *Anjos do Arrabalde* ("Suburban Angels," 1987), Reichenbach's drama about three schoolteachers and a manicurist takes a step toward social realism in its portrayal of the São Paulo of the working-class poor. Dalia (Betty Faria) is a closeted lesbian; Rosa (Clarisse Abujanra) is the mistress of a married man, the school supervisor; while Carno (Irene Stefânia) is oppressed by an authoritarian husband who does not want her to work. The "suburb" of the title is a recently incorporated neighborhood where middle-class teachers can barely conceal their elitist superiority to their "country" charges from the Northeast and the interior of São Paulo. The film references not only the work of Paulista director Luis Sérgio Person (the school central

São Paulo as backdrop in *Anjos do Arrabalde* (1987)

to the narrative is named after him) but also the work and methods of Shohei Imamura, with its quasi-anthropological revelations of life on the outskirts of Tokyo. (The debt is acknowledged by the inclusion of posters from *Eijanaika* and *Vengeance Is Mine*.)

Two São Paulo metafictions by other directors deal with the role of sound in the cinema. Walter Rogério's *Voz do Brasil* ("Voice of Brazil," 1981) — the title refers to a widely detested official radio program — foregrounds the difficulties of a young filmmaker waiting for Embrafilme to finance his script. This drama is intercut with a series of episodes having no intrinsic link to the story except that they have to do with the world of São Paulo filmmaking. One sequence shows an American TV series being dubbed in Brazilian Portuguese in a sound studio. As the film loop of an action-packed scene passes on the screen, the dubbing technicians do their work and exchange trivialities. We are struck by the disjunction between the glamorous American stars on the screen and the ordinary Brazilians lending their voices. The provocation of the film, then, is to reveal the hidden face of the normally offscreen dubbers, rendering visible the effaced labor of a particular cinematic process while revealing the technical supports of cultural neocolonialism. The "voice," to go back to the title, is that of Brazil, but the images and the mentality and corporate structure behind them are not.

Ícaro Martins and José Antônio Garcia's *Estrela Nua* ("Nude Star," 1985), meanwhile, parlays the issue of postsynchronization into a complex tale of exchanged identities. When the well-known actress Angela

403

dies without having dubbed her last film, the television dubber Glória is called to lend her voice to the image of the original actress. She delights the filmmakers by enacting the role as if truly possessed by the deceased actress's spirit, until they realize that the possession has become quite literal and destructive, as Glória's life slowly comes to coincide with that of Angela, leading ultimately to her death. *Estrela Nua* proliferates in modish self-referential devices in the postmodernist mode of proxy sensibility, but what is finally most interesting is the film's way of linking the technical question of postsynchronization to larger psychic questions of human identity, transference, and possession.

The Rediscovery of the *Chanchada*

A number of late 1970s and 1980s films renew contact with the *chanchada*, now seen as the highest symbol of successful communication with the Brazilian public, fount of a cinema at once nationalist, pragmatic, and popular. This process of revalorization began with Tropicalism's aggressive leveling, in the late 1960s, of high (erudite) and low (mass) culture. As expressed in music, theater, and film, Tropicalism provocatively mingled the folkloric and the industrial, the native and the foreign; its favored technique was the collage of disparate discourses, the result of a "cannibalistic" ingestion of the most heterogeneous cultural stimuli. The latter-day filmic incorporation of the *chanchada*, as seen earlier, dates from Sganzerla's *Red Light Bandit* (1968) and Joaquim Pedro de Andrade's *Macunaíma* (1969). The socially conscious recycling of *chanchada* actors (Grande Otelo, Zezé Macedo), music, and strategies enabled *Macunaíma*, especially, to realize a goal long inaccessible to Cinema Novo directors — the reconciliation of political and aesthetic avant-gardism with popular and box-office appeal.

In the field of criticism and film history, meanwhile, film historian Paulo Emílio Salles Gomes furthered the revalorization of the *chanchada* in his essay "Cinema: A Trajectory Within Underdevelopment," by arguing that the *chanchadas* were not only of vital importance for having retained the loyalty of the Brazilian audience but also that all Brazilian films, even the most imitative, remained authentically Brazilian, thanks to the Brazilian "creative incapacity for copying."[16] Once dead, the *chanchada* becomes history and therefore available for nostalgic or critical reelaboration, a legitimate urban tradition to be incorporated much as rural folklore was incorporated by Cinema Novo in an earlier period. Within the filmic revitalization of the *chanchada*, we find a wide diversity of trends. At times the *chanchada* is taken up in a romantic vein, as in Carlos Diegues's *Quando o Carnaval Chegar* ("When Carnival Comes," 1972), and at times in a conceptual-reflexive vein, as in Bressane's stylistic exercises, and at still other times in a comic-parodic-erotic vein, as with Ivan Cardoso's *Segredo da Múmia* ("Secret of the Mummy," 1982) or *As Sete Vampiras* ("The Seven Vampires," 1986). Cardoso favors a genre he himself dubs "Terrir" — a play on "terror" and "rir" (laugh) which builds on cinematic codes already internalized by the spectator, specifically those of the classical horror film. With Cardoso we have a parody of parody, since the *chanchada* was already parodic. In a Brazilianized synthesis of Roger Corman and Mel Brooks, Ivan Cardoso gives new life to generic clichés, vampirizing, as it were, preexisting films and genres, absorbing and transforming the "blood" of other texts. [17]

By appropriating an existing discourse but introducing into it an orientation oblique or even diametrically opposed to that of the original, parody is well-suited to the needs of oppositional culture, precisely because it deploys the force of the dominant discourse against itself. Joaquim Pedro de Andrade's *Vereda Tropical* ("Tropical Paths," 1980) provides a striking example of this strategy. It was made at the height of the popularity of the *pornochanchada*, when films with titles like *A Bra for Daddy*, *The Secretaries Who Do . . . Everything!* and *The Virgin and the Macho* were proliferating in the movie theaters. The military regime, phenomenally alert to violations of "morality" and "decency" in the more politicized films, hypocritically tolerated and even encouraged the *pornochanchadas*. In Andrade's meta*pornochanchada*, the object of desire takes the form of a watermelon — the protagonist literally loves them. *Tropical Paths* demystifies the *pornochanchada* by assigning to the watermelon the function usually accorded the woman in such films. The protagonist seduces the watermelon as if it were a frightened virgin, deflowers it ritualistically, and subjects it to sadomasochistic perversities. A series of shots even achieves what has remained inaccessible to more conventional nonvegetative pornography — shots from inside the pink wetness of the watermelon itself. Thus the film deconstructs the *pornochanchada*'s Pyrrhic victories over visual taboos. The fantastic voyage into the heart of the watermelon is in every sense a hollow victory, revealing little more than the hidden totalitarianism of masculinist pleasure.

Tropical Paths also switches the terms of secondary identification of the *pornochanchada*. The woman character, usually cast as the coy sex object, is here the spectator's delegate who asks the protagonist precisely those questions we would have liked to ask. Nor does she ever undress. The watermelon-loving protagonist, meanwhile, is scarcely an ideal figure for male projection. While *pornochanchada* protagonists were generally playboys driving the latest sports cars and living in luxurious apartments, the protagonist of *Tropical Paths* is physically unattractive and professionally incompetent. Hardly the macho sexual athlete of the *pornochanchada*, he suffers from premature ejaculation even with his watermelons. In sum, *Tropical Paths* answers the male voyeur's implicit request for a female sex object by offering an ironically reified, vegetative exemplar of pure alterity. (The Brazilian military government, sensing the insult to machismo in a film completely devoid of nudity and heterosexual or homosexual lovemaking, banned the film, while tolerating the much more explicit *pornochanchadas* that *Tropical Paths* so acerbically mocked.)

The Emblem of Carnival

The symbolic energies of carnival and parody animate countless Brazilian films in the period of our discussion. But this "recarnivalization" takes variegated form. At times the revolution itself is regarded as a kind of carnival, as with Zé Celso's Living-Theatre-like approach to an absurdist Brazilian theatrical classic, Oswald de Andrade's *Rei da Vela* ("King of the Candle," written in 1933, staged by Zé Celso in 1967 and filmed in 1985), where the revolution becomes a fete or collective communion. More often, however, the filmmakers are less concerned with militancy. They abandon the old puritanical-leftist equation of party-carnival with alienation and escapism, as, for example, in *Cinco Vezes Favela* ("Five Times Favela," 1962), where the popular classes were exhorted to abandon the samba in favor of union activism. Instead, the directors revalorize carnival as an emblem of national identity, a culturally rooted master-trope, the crystallization of a richly syncretic culture that still has a place for an orgiastic ritual at once sacred and profane. Carnival, in these films, is not simply metaphoric. Carnival, specifically in the form of Rio's "samba schools," are a quite literal presence in Walter Lima, Jr.'s *Lira do Delírio* ("Delirious Lyre," 1978), Vera Figueredo's *Samba da Criação do Mundo* ("Samba of the Creation of the World," 1979), Glauber Rocha's *Idade da Terra* ("Age of the Earth," 1980), and Paulo César Saraceni's *Natal da Portela* (1987). In other cases, carnival forms part of the wider circulation of popular and erudite culture. The stories of Diegues's *Xica da Silva* (1976) and Walter Lima, Jr's *Chico Rei* (1982), for example, were first presented as samba-school pageants for Rio's carnival. Indeed, Diegues has said that he conceived both *Xica da Silva* and *Quilombo* (1984) as "samba enredos" (theme sambas), i.e., as analogous in their procedures to the collection of songs, dances, costumes, and lyrics that form part of the popular narrative form called the samba-school pageant. Fernando Cony Campos's *Ladrões de Cinema* ("Cinema Thieves," 1977) foregrounds this analogy by having his *favelado* protagonists steal filmmaking equipment from American tourists visiting Rio for carnival. The *favelados* conceive the film they plan to make with the stolen equipment — about an abortive eighteenth-century revolt against Portuguese colonialism — as a kind of samba-school narration.

At times carnival comes to form part of a larger recuperation of popular culture, a constellation of values that includes sensuality, *malandragem* (quick-witted hustling), popular religious practice, and even soccer. Early Cinema Novo films such as *Subterrâneos do Futebol* ("Subterranean Soccer," 1962) and *Garrincha, Alegria do Povo* ("Garrincha, Joy of the People," 1963) tended to denounce soccer as a modern form of "bread and circuses" exploited by the ruling class to divert and demobilize the people. *Garrincha, Alegria do Povo,* for example, pointedly placed the World Cup loss of 1950 *after* the 1962 victory in order to emphasize the ephemeral and ultimately futile nature of sports triumphs. Djalma Batista's *Asa Branca, Um Sonho Brasileiro* ("White Wing, a Brazilian Dream," 1981), in contrast, sees soccer as positive energy invested in a creative dream. The film reveals the limitations of the dream and the human price paid by the soccer-player protagonist, but it also pays uninhibited homage to the festive poetry of athletic contest. Other films emphasize the famous Brazilian *jeitinho* (streetsmart transcendence or clever way out of apparently intractable problems) associated with the fast-thinking *malandro* (urban hustler). We find the *malandro* figure in the films of actor-turned-director Hugo Carvana, notably in his *Vai Trabalhar, Vagabundo* ("Go to Work, You Bum," 1973) and *Se Segura Malandro* ("Cool It, Hustler," 1978), as well as in Rui Guerra's musical comedy entitled *Malandro* (1986), a film adaptation of Chico Buarque's play *Ópera do Malandro,* itself based on John Gay's *The Beggar's Opera* and Bertolt Brecht's *Threepenny Opera.*[18]

All these reapproximations with popular culture reflect a renewed identification, on the filmmaker's part, with the more perennial features of Brazilian cultural life, a compromise formation that allows for a discussion of the function of the intellectual-filmmaker *and* the possibility of assimilation to the people's worldview. At its best, this strategy leads to a popular-yet-pedagogic cinema that combines social critique with carnival-style joy. At times, it turns into the affirmation of putative Brazilian character traits and the Brazilian national style. Real conflicts are played down in favor of the celebration of the "cordiality" of the fun-loving Brazilian. At its worst, an apolitical version of Bakhtin's subversive carnival celebrates the Brazilian capacity for political conciliation, mocked by Glauber Rocha as the historical tendency for the now-repentant right to hold hands again with the now well-behaved left, while "tudo acaba em samba" (everything ends in the samba).

Two young directors, Ana Carolina and Carlos Alberto Prates Correia, emphasize humor and transgression — a quasi-carnivalization — without ever reducing their films to calculated market-driven products. Their work reconciles commercial viability, guaranteed by sensuality, humor, and technical competence, with risk-taking and invention. Ana Carolina's first feature *Mar de Rosas* ("Sea of Roses," 1977) anatomizes a grotesque family, consisting of squabbling parents and an anarchoterrorist daughter with whom the film clearly sympathizes, set in an atmosphere of surreal banality à la Ionesco. It is as if, as Paulo Perdigão put it, "Jules Feiffer's black humor and Samuel Beckett's dramaturgical

Ana Carolina

absurdity were made to rendezvous on the Via Dutra [the highway that links Rio with São Paulo]."[19] Her second feature, *Das Tripas Coração* (idiomatically, something like "Bending Over Backwards," 1980), analyzes a girls' school as a site of hypocrisy and sexual repression. The entire film extends into one hundred minutes of film time a government inspector's dream just before he signs the order to close the school. Finally, *Sonho de Valsa* ("Waltz Dream," 1987) plays with the religious prohibitions and sexual transgressions generated by a Catholic girlhood.

The work of Carlos Alberto Prates Correia similarly reconciles the drive for auteurist expression with the constraints of the market. Born in the state of Minas Gerais, land of (now exhausted) mineral wealth and the brilliant prose-poetry of Guimarães Rosa, Prates Correia's films translate the peculiar beauty and somewhat archaic social life of the region. *Perdida* ("Lost Woman," 1975) traces the trajectory of a country girl who leaves rural Minas to become a maid and prostitute in the city, registered in a style that fuses the understated frontality of Godard with the laconic flipness of the Brazilian Underground. The title of *Cabaret Mineiro* ("Cabaret in Minas," 1980), taken from a poem by Carlos Drummond de Andrade, emphasizes the regional aspect of the film, set in the area of the old railroad lines, a reminder of the glory days of the region. Around a tale of an elegant adventurer's love for a red-haired beauty, Prates Correia spins a tale of rural fantasy and eroticism. The cineaste acts as a kind of voyeur-stager of an audiovisual mosaic made up of sultry insinuations and languorous afternoons. In *Noites de Sertão* ("Sertão Nights," 1984) — we are symptomatically far from the oppressed northeastern sertão of *Vidas Secas* and *Black God, White Devil* — he explores the Minas plantation universe and its figura-

Carlos Alberto Prates Correia's *Perdida* **(1975)**

tions of desire, foregrounding the conflict between patriarchal order and anarchic sexuality, in a filmic "translation" of the spirit of Guimarães Rosa. (Correia's most recent film is called *Minas Texas* [1986], in homage both to Wim Wenders' *Paris, Texas* (1984) and to his own native region.)

The Voice-of-the-Other Documentary

Some of the most experimental work within Brazilian cinema has been done within the documentary. Glauber Rocha's seminal film *Di*

(1977), a documentary homage to the Brazilian painter Di Cavalcânti, had already reflexively mocked the conventional "art documentaries" favored by Brazil's cultural bureaucrats, while Artur Omar's *Triste Trópico* (1974), as seen earlier, had pioneered the "fictive documentary," anticipating Woody Allen's *Zelig* by more than a decade. In some documentaries, reflexivity becomes a kind of *political* obligation. Whereas 1960s documentarists discoursed confidently about otherized victims (worker, Indian, black) from a presumed superior position, 1970s documentarists began to doubt their own right and even capacity to speak "for" the other. The "documentary" films of Arthur Omar, in this sense, interrogate the very possibility of the cinema's relaying without distortion a cultural experience alien to the filmmaker. The title of his *Congo* (1972) seems to promise a conventional treatment of a typical documentary subject of the period — folklore, and specifically the Afro-Brazilian dance called "congo" or "congada" — yet the film itself offers no image referring to the film's ostensible theme. The film's real subject, then, is the impossibility, for the white urban intellectual filmmaker, to truly apprehend that which is rural, black, and of the people. Omar returns to this theme in his video *A Coroação de uma Rainha* ("The Coronation of a Queen," 1993), where he films a Congo ceremony in an industrial neighborhood of Belo Horizonte, emphasizing the contrast between the daily life of a lower-class Afro-Brazilian woman and her regal enthronement within the privileged space of the sacred. Impoverished circumstances provide the social frame for ecstatic beauty. Other filmmakers, disenchanted with all condescending sociologistic approaches to "the people," strive for a more dialogical and reciprocal relationship between observer and observed. Thus filmmaker Andrea Tonacci, in his work for television, simultaneously registers the encounter of urban white Brazilians with freshly contacted indigenous groups and reflects on the recording of that encounter.

Sérgio Bianchi's documentary *Mato Eles?* ("Should I Kill Them?" 1983) takes a more ironic approach. The film's subject — the desperate situation of the last surviving remnant of certain indigenous groups in Brazil — does not at first glance seem amenable to parodic treatment. Yet the film completely deconstructs the conventional approach (in Brazil and elsewhere) to this kind of topic. Instead of the customary realist depiction of the local habitat, interspersed with talking heads and disembodied voice-over expressing the enlightened consciousness of non-Indian filmmakers, Bianchi satirically undermines not only the official discourse concerning the Indian but also the traditional *bonne conscience* of the "denunciation documentary." Indeed, the film constitutes a relentless assault on the assumptions and sensibility of the middle-class spectator accustomed to documentaries that flatter his/her narcissistic sense of humanist compassion.

Mato Eles? is structured around a series of apparently whimsical multiple-choice quizzes addressed to the spectator. The Brechtianism of these quizzes, in their implicit call for spectatorial collaboration and the "rendering of a verdict," is tinged here with bitter irony, for both question and answer tend toward the mutually contradictory and the absurd. One question reads: "Very few Indians remain from the once numerous Xeta tribe. What happened to the others? Choose one of the following: (1) They all intermarried with the white population and are now living in the cities; (2) They all died due to infectious diseases and litigation concerning land rights; (3) They are all on vacation in Europe; (4) The Xeta Indians never existed. This documentary is false; (5) All the above are correct." Another quiz poses three unpalatable alternatives: "The extermination of the Indians should be (a) immediate; (b) slow; (c) gradual." The questions and answers leave no comfortable space for the "progressive" spectator; rather, they confront the audience with the reality of extermination, in a manner that initially provokes laughter but subsequently elicits reflection and self-doubt.

Mato Eles? also deconstructs the official "Indianist" discourse predominant in Brazil since the time of the nineteenth-century Romantics, for whom the Indian was the idealized symbol of national difference. But the descendants of the "bravos guerreiros" (heroic fighters) celebrated in countless songs, poems, and novels, *Mato Eles?* suggests, are now shackled by a dreary cycle of disease and powerlessness. Bianchi mocks the heroicizing vision of the Indian by announcing a film-within-the-film, an Indianist epic entitled, in transparent homage to James Fenimore Cooper, "The Last of the Xetas." The lush strains of *O Guarani*, from the equally Indianist opera by Brazilian composer Carlos Gomes, further swells our expectations for an epic spectacle. Instead, Bianchi shows us the sole surviving, literally "last" member of the tribe, presented in a series of photographs strongly reminiscent of police mug shots. The "brave warrior" of romanticism has become the despised object of the official discourse of police photos coldly registering the reality of genocide.

Nor does Bianchi exempt himself from criticism. At one point, a venerable Guarani Indian surprises the filmmaker by asking exactly how much money he will make on the film. This inconvenient question, which normally would have found its way into the editing-room trash can, segues to an authorial voice-over in which Bianchi speculates about other avenues for financially exploiting the Indian — anthropological scholarships, photograph albums, arts and crafts shops, showing films in Europe. Thus the "Voice-of-God" offscreen narration is used, against the grain of conventional practice, to mock the filmmaker himself. The condescending voice of monologic Truth here deconstructs itself, thus closing the film's circle of multiple ironies directed at the power structure, at the filmmaker, and at the canonized formulae of the liberal documentary.

The convergence of a more commercially oriented cinema with the moment of political liberalization (*"abertura"*) led in the 1980s to what might be called "*abertura* naturalism," in films that focused not only on sex and violence but also on the repressed political experience of the two decades of dictatorship. The first tendency led to a proliferation of "explicit sex" films — hardcore exploitation films that made the *pornochanchadas* look positively sentimental and authentically Brazilian in comparison — as well as to the intimist existential-artsy films of Walter Hugo Khoury (e.g., *O Prisoneiro do Sexo* ["Prisoner of Sex," 1983], where neurotic males exorcize their erotic obsessions) and to the jet-set eroticism of Neville d'Almeida's *Rio Babilônia* (1984), where the Rio elite and international stars shuttle in sports cars from orgy to orgy, all staged in palatially modernist houses invariably offering dazzling scenic views of Rio de Janeiro. The second tendency, focusing on the remembered experience of dictatorship, meanwhile, led to a new genre: detective thrillers focalizing themes related to political repression. Whereas the Cinema Novo–derived films of the 1970s dealt with repression and physical violence through allegory, as in Nelson Pereira dos Santos's *Um. Azyllo Muito Louco* ("The Alienist," 1970), or through poeticized grotesquerie, as in Antônio Fontoura's *Rainha Diaba* ("Devil Queen," 1974), or through the detached observation typical of the Foucauldian "institutional case study" approach of Eduardo Escorel's *Ato de Violência* ("Act of Violence," 1980), the new films were frankly entertainment-oriented, favoring action-filled plots accompanied by a modicum of "redeeming social value." Hector Babenco's *Lúcio Flávio: O Passageiro da Agonia* ("Lúcio Flávio: Passenger of Agony," 1977) constitutes a particularly effective example of the genre. Babenco risked offending the junta's censors by focusing on a controversial case involving police complicity with Rio's notorious "death squads." The film's rhetoric, meanwhile, systematically opposes the "truth" of cinema to the "lies" of the print and electronic media. Naturalism becomes part of a seductive strategy associating cinematic spectacle with authenticity and even audacity in presenting the raw data of everyday life.

Babenco's *Pixote* (1980), in this same vein, forms part of an international genre — the street urchin film — that includes not only De Sica's *Shoeshine* (1946) but also Buñuel's *Los Olvidados* (1951) and Mira Nair's *Salaam Bombay* (1988). *Pixote* shares with the Buñuel film its topic (delinquent children), its source (sociological documentation), its setting (the Third World metropolis), its style (documentary-inflected), its casting strategies (a mix of professional and nonprofessional performers), its focalization (the children themselves), and even its episodic structure. The film follows some Brazilian slum kids, synecdochic samples of that country's three million homeless children, from police round-up to reform school to a life-endangering "freedom" on the streets. After a didactic prologue by the director himself, the film zooms in to isolate a few typical figures: the ringleader "queen" Lilica; the grass-loving Fumaça ("Smoke"); the sensitive, searching Dito; and Pixote himself, the smallest and most vulnerable of the group. Pixote combines pubescent energy with precocious street smarts, and behind his hauntingly feral face one glimpses what might have been, under less Darwinian circumstances, a normal child. That both the young actor Fernando Ramos da Silva, who plays Pixote, and his brother were themselves both subsequently killed by the police in dubious circumstances sadly attests to the film's veracity. Indeed, the film was prescient in anticipating a situation in which over one thousand children would be slain every year between 1989 and 1991, usually by police (on or off duty) or by death squads.[20]

The first half of *Pixote* is set in a microcosmic detention center, a ritualized universe of authoritarian power trips and sordid sexual humiliations. Babenco exposes an array of abuses: gang rapes by the inmates themselves, and exploitation and even murder by the authorities, "covered" by glib lies to investigating agencies. The film vividly illustrates the perennial metaphor of prison as a "school for crime." Armed with wooden guns, the children play-act bank holdups, and rehearse techniques of torture learned from the authorities, who are in some ways presented as the real criminals. Apart from exposing the Dickensian oppression of the reform school, the film uncovers the human suffering masked by bland abstractions like "abandoned minors" and "juvenile delinquency."

Prison as school for crime: *Pixote* **(1980)**

413

When Pixote and his friends escape, the film metamorphoses generically from social pamphlet into a picaresque tale of tragicomic misadventures. "Freedom," the boys discover, bears an uncanny resemblance to their previous confinement. The escapees form a makeshift family surviving through petty assaults and drug deals. (As in *Los Olvidados*, we find a poignant adolescent yearning for the lost mother: Marta in the Buñuel film, Sueli in *Pixote*.) Having little in common beyond their own marginalization, the group is perpetually threatened by internal and external pressures. The children forge a precarious solidarity, seizing fleeting moments of tenderness in the face of insurmountable odds. Pixote is finally stripped of his companions, left as the last survivor of a diminished tribe. At the same time, he undergoes a process of desensitization, showing little emotion not only at the deaths of "their" prostitute Sueli's despised johns, but even at the accidental slaughter of his friend Dito. That the film renders this melancholy slide into degradation believable is one of its achievements. Babenco treats his adolescent protagonist without moralism. Neither monster nor victim, he is an urban survivor, denied the luxury of conventional morality.

Pixote tends to indict specific institutions as ghettoized scenes of local abuse rather than designate the social system that makes such abuses virtually inevitable. The film's deployment of point of view is also somewhat problematic. Our identification with the children — guaranteed through narrative focus, point-of-view shots, empathetic music — is usually so total that we lose all critical distance. The characters that middle-class spectators would normally identify with — the doctors, the teachers, the social workers — are all one-dimensional figures unworthy of sympathy, while the victims of Pixote and company are noxious tourists or low-life types, equally unworthy objects of identification. Thus the film lets the middle-class spectator (who in real life might be either the oppressor or the victim of the Pixotes of the world) off the hook. The film skirts the question of the spectator's location within this story. We sympathize with the children and are viscerally affected by their story, but we are given little sense of our relation to what we see or what might be done about it. The emotional impact leaves little analytical residue in its wake.

Despite the lack of a global analysis, *Pixote* is startlingly effective in purely aesthetic and cinematic terms. Babenco's funky Third World expressionism turns the film into a montage of repulsions, a series of horrific images: Pixote forced to drink spittle out of a cup; prepubic adolescents witnessing a gang rape; Sueli's aborted fetus speared by a knitting needle and dumped in a bathroom wastebasket. At the same time, Babenco snatches beauty from squalor. Smoking dope and sniffing glue inspire kaleidoscopic visions of paperweight saints, intimations of an ephemeral transcendence. Babenco is fond of quoting André Breton's aphorism, "Beauty will be convulsive or it will not be," and *Pixote* does achieve a kind of wrenching beauty which artfully juxtaposes apparent opposites. The sordid milieu becomes the backdrop for

Longing for the mother: *Pixote*

epiphanies of tenderness in the form of sexual connections made across lines of age, race, and class. At times, the erotic merges with the lethal. "See if this makes you come," taunt the kids as they poke a revolver in the face of a prostitute's john. Although lacking in political analysis, *Pixote* does expose the abuses of governmental correctional institutions and achieves, at its best, a convulsive beauty reminiscent of Buñuel.[21]

Within this same naturalistic vein, we also find less agile films where the social analysis is severely compromised by the felt need for traditional formulae: classical dramatic structure, Manichean hero-villain schemas, the imperative for constant "action." Such is the case of Oswaldo Caldeira's *0 Bom Burguês* ("The Good Bourgeois," 1983), based on the story of a wealthy businessman who gave financial and logistical support to the leftist guerrillas sought by the junta, as well as of the controversial *Para Frente Brasil* ("Forward Brazil," 1983) by veteran filmmaker Roberto Farias. Although the Farias film provoked the wrath of the junta (and even triggered the fall of the then head of Embrafilme) by dramatizing the military apparatus of repression and torture, in fact the film is politically ambiguous in seeming to contrast local "rogue" sadists with a benign and concerned federal government. A more successful instance of this tendency, Murilo Salles's *Nunca Fomos Tão Felizes* ("We Have Never Been So Happy," 1984), tells the story of a clandestine leftist militant forced to hide his own activities even from his own bewildered son. Here the interest is displaced from the political

415

drama per se to the psychological investigation of the son's isolation and his truncated relationship to a father he cannot understand, as well as to the implied complementary dilemma of a father eager to love his son but prevented by political circumstance from fully doing so. Jorge Durán's *A Cor do Seu Destino* ("The Color of Your Destiny," 1986), finally, also politicizes the father-son relationship in its evocation of the lives of a Chilean family exiled in Brazil and torn between affection for their new homeland and anguished nostalgia for a Chile brutalized by the Pinochet dictatorship. In a suggestive matching between technique and theme, the film has the artist-son superimpose spray-painted images of Chile on the TV screen in Brazil, thus rendering visually the superimposed subjectivities of the exile experience. The generational tension between the old leftist father and the relatively apolitical son — pinpointed by Oedipal echoes from *Hamlet* — finally gives way to the politicization of the son, who penetrates the Chilean Embassy in Rio in order to douse a portrait of Pinochet with symbolic blood-red paint.

The Emergence of the Worker

While the Cinema Novo of the 1960s, despite its revolutionary concerns, had largely ignored the working class,[22] certain late 1970s films register the impact of workers' struggles, partly as a result of the immense coming-to-consciousness and political mobilization of the workers in São Paulo, culminating in the strikes that paralyzed the city in 1978. This theme too is expressed in a variety of styles and formats. João Batista de Andrade's *O Homem que Virou Suco* ("The Man Who Turned into Juice," 1980), first-prize winner at the Moscow Film Festival, for example, develops a popular narrative tone, mingling humor with pathos in its story about a worker who also writes *folhetos* (handout fiction). Thus the film treats, on another register, the theme often elaborated in the work of Nelson Pereira dos Santos — the distance between the cultural producer (a projection of the filmmaker himself) and his public.

A film that articulates these themes — strikes, work conditions, political tensions, assassinations — and that received distribution in the United States, is Leon Hirszman's *Eles Não Usam Black Tie* ("They Don't Wear Black Tie," 1981). The film updates the 1950s play of the same title by Gianfrancesco Guarnieri, a play that both marked and fostered the emergence of a politicized theater in the mid-1950s. Hirszman filters the play through an aesthetic reminiscent both of Italian neorealism and of early Cinema Novo. Retroactively compensating for Cinema Novo's slighting of the working class — Cinema Novo always seemed to prefer those both lower (the *favelados*) and higher (the elite) on the social ladder — the film offers an impressive gallery of proletarian

Mother and son in *They Don't Wear Black Tie* **(1981)**

characters, ranging from the old leftist Otávio (played by Guarnieri himself) and his wife Romana (Fernanda Montenegro), through the impatient radical Sartini (Francisco Milani) to the courageous black unionist Bráulio (Milton Gonçalves) to the wavering but never completely despicable son Tião (Carlos Alberto Ricelli), his resourceful and courageous wife Maria (Bete Mendes), along with the predictable assortment of scabs and informers.

Black Tie mingles a family story, which contrasts the militant father's lucidity with the son's confused opportunism, and the story of a strike. In political terms, the film supports, in the end, a cautious nonadventurist militancy, a disciplined struggle for small local victories while condemning the "irrational excesses" of the radicals. Subtextually, the veteran militant filmmaker "corrects" the lost generation of the dictatorship, and in this sense distorts history. For in fact the São Paulo strikes were the product of a new generation typified by Luis Inácio da Silva ("Lula") and his Workers' Party, rather than of the traditional left. Indeed, the character Bráulio, who is killed by a police agent and whose death is commemorated by a massive funeral procession at the end of the film, is modeled on Santos Dias, a militant within the Workers' Party. But the realism of *Black Tie* ultimately consists less in strictly accurate historical depiction (if such were possible) than in the social dynamic of the characters. Hirszman presents the working class not as an idealized monolith but rather as a complex totality subject to external repression and rent by internal conflicts along gender and ideological lines. His vision is neither prettifying nor denigrating; instead, it communicates a feeling of knowledgeable intimacy with workingclass life.

Hirszman's films have always been remarkable, within Cinema Novo, for their solidarity with women characters and their sensitivity to women's issues. *Black Tie* features a number of strong and dynamic women characters. The mother, Romana, practices the creativity of everyday life; she mediates between father and son, cares for family and friends, and confronts the police to get Otávio out of jail. Maria, meanwhile, is very much strengthened in comparison with the Maria of the play. Reflecting the evolution of attitudes since the 1950s, the film promotes her professionally (from domestic seamstress to factory worker) and shows her as having the courage to demonstrate in the streets and the pride to choose working-class principles over the facile attractions of conventional marriage.

What saves *Black Tie* from being mere agitprop or political melo-drama is its lack of Manichaeism. Rather than pit an idealized Labor against a villainized Capital, Hirszman focuses on the tensions and conflicts within the working class. Although the logic of the narrative clearly favors the moderate leftists, the film also treats political adver-saries with a certain generosity. All the major characters have their reasons, even when their actions merit censure. Otávio, who more than anyone else embodies the history of principled popular struggle, has his reasons for throwing Tião out of his home, since "this is not the home of a strike-breaker." But Tião has his reasons as well for pursuing personal and family advancement rather than participate in risky oppo-sitional politics. Although politically mistaken, his choice is humanly comprehensible. As a practiced expert in survival, Romana is also right to repeat her litany of proverbs and admonitions about "staying out of trouble." Maria's rejection of Tião, meanwhile, has as much to do with his domineering machismo as with his political incorrectness. The characters all have hesitations; they are not mere projections of the filmmaker, although one might fault the film's tendency to attribute political insight to older men such as Otávio and Bráulio while denying it to younger men like Tião and Sartini. Here one suspects a nostalgi-cally patriarchal undercurrent in a clearly left-hearted film.

Black Tie excoriates police violence, a subject that would have been taboo only a few years before. The film also suggests that a dispropor-tionate share of the victims of this violence are black. We are shown a world in which the working class is not racist but the police are: "Get the black guy," the informer tells the policeman just before the latter kills Bráulio. The murder is shown as both political and racial. Here too *Black Tie* breaks new ground. Black characters in earlier Cinema Novo tended to be anarchist free spirits like Firmino in *Barravento* or Calunga in *A Grande Cidade* ("The Big City," 1966), but Hirszman presents Bráulio, who was not featured in the original play, as a coura-geous leader and martyr.

As a veteran theater director, Hirszman was always known for his work with actors — one need only think of Othon Bastos's Paulo or Isabel Ribeiro's Madalena in *São Bernardo* — and this film is no excep-tion. The excellent ensemble acting melds brilliant individual perfor-mances into a powerful whole. Guarnieri, who at twenty-four played

Milton Gonçalves as Bráulio in *They Don't Wear Black Tie*

the role of the son in the original production, here plays the role of the father, in a manner that seems to incorporate the political maturation of a fictive character. Fernanda Montenegro is self-effacingly charismatic; she makes solidarity palpable. Unlike many of the more allegorical and distanced of the Brazilian films, *Black Tie* captures Brazilian affectivity in a naturalist style. Although hardly innovative in aesthetic terms, the film is moving and efficacious. Within the democratic realism of this epic of everyday life, Hirszman has managed to fuse political consciousness and popular emotion, marshaling the force of feeling in the service of enlightenment.[23]

The Latter-Day Allegories of Cinema Novo

Cinema Novo has been relentlessly allegorical since its first films in the early 1960s in the sense that it has always favored the filmic treatment of microcosmic situations which evoke Brazil as a whole, developing a fragmentary discourse to insinuate coded political messages. We have seen allegory in the millenary Marxism of Rocha's *Deus e o Diabo na Terra do Sol* ("Black God, White Devil," 1964), in the synthetic political figures (the populist, the fascist, the leftist intellectual) of *Terra em Transe* ("Land in Anguish," 1967), as well as in the "cannibalist" fables of *Macunaíma* and *How Tasty Was My Little Frenchman.* This alle-

419

gorical tendency became exacerbated during the period of extreme political repression in the early 1970s. Joaquim Pedro de Andrade, in *Os Inconfidentes* ("The Conspirators," 1972), for example, allegorized the defeat of the left in contemporary Brazil by displacing current issues onto the events of another century, specifically the abortive eighteenth-century revolt against Portuguese colonialism led by Tiradentes.

Any number of 1970s and 1980s films by Cinema Novo veterans offer a globalizing vision of society as expressed in ironic allegories of underdevelopment and modernization. Both Guerra and Xavier's *A Queda* ("The Fall," 1977) and Jabor's *Tudo Bem* ("Everything's Fine," 1977), for example, elaborate the metaphor of "construction" to make a general statement about Brazilian modernization. *The Fall*'s story about hard-hat construction workers building Rio's subway system, as seen earlier, is made to resonate more generally about the overall movement of Brazilian society in the era of consumerist models, national integration via satellite transmission, huge foreign debt, and the restructuring of urban space wrought by advanced capitalist development. More recently, Wladimir Carvalho's exposé documentary *Conterrâneos Velhos de Guerra* ("Old Compatriots Tired of War," 1992) archaeologically unearths a vast array of archival material to disinter the scandals buried beneath the construction of Brasília by (largely Northeastern) construction workers. The construction metaphor also underlies the allegorical *Tudo Bem,* in which a bourgeois couple invites construction workers to remodel their Copacabana apartment. As the construction workers and maids take over the apartment (the "shanties," in Glauber Rocha's felicitous phrase, "invade the Master's House"), the apartment becomes a symbolic microcosm, the site of interaction of opposing class discourses and interests.

Carlos Diegues's *Bye Bye Brasil* (1980), for its part, weaves a picaresque allegory in which the "Caravana Rolidei" — a motley troupe of ambulatory artists — wanders around Brazil to witness, not without melancholy, the advance of modernization. Here the social contradictions compressed into a single apartment in *Tudo Bem* are anamorphically splayed out over the wide screen of Brazil, moving from the arid Northeast (Piranhas, Maceió), through the Amazon forest (Altamira, the Transamazonian Highway) to the Central Plateau (Brasília, Rondônia). En route, the troupe confronts internal obstacles (amorous complications) and external ones, most notably the television that leads the troupe's audience to passively consume the insipid fare of Rio and São Paulo TV stations. National television flattens regional diversity and renders obsolescent the troupe's old-fashioned entertainment. Alongside its self-flauntingly theatrical core fiction, *Bye Bye Brasil* presents a kind of seismological documentary that registers the aftershocks of the "multinationalization" of the Brazilian subcontinent. The exploitation inherent in the Brazilian model of development takes especially predatory form in the interior. The Amazon region, the government's trump card ("After all, there's always the Amazon") is being transformed into a vast bordello administered by a legion of hustlers and entrepreneurs. The transformation of the "Rolidei" truck into an ambulatory neon-lit whorehouse in this sense metaphorizes a much broader process. American millionaires such as Daniel Ludwig try to extract profits from cheap Brazilian labor through "floating factories" shipped from Japan. The futurist city of Brasília, designed by the Communist Oscar Niemeyer during the developmentist euphoria of the 1950s, is now ringed by the minislums into which two of the characters are graciously ushered by a social welfare assistant. The interior, the site of perennial hope, has merely telescoped and amplified Brazil's historical contradictions.

The key to *Bye Bye Brasil* lies in its title. The film bids farewell to what it sees as outmoded visions of Brazil — not only to rightist dreams of capitalist development but also to leftist dreams of popular resistance. The film's Indians, for example, do not play the symbolic role conventionally assigned them in Brazilian art and in the Brazilian collective unconscious. They are not heroic representatives of quintessential Brazilianness, as they were for the Romantics, nor are they symbols of anticolonial resistance cannibalizing Europeans in allegorical meals. *Bye Bye Brasil* breaks with this metaphorical discourse by showing Indians in the process of physical extermination and cultural annihilation. The Cruari Indians in the film, last remnants of a once proud tribe, now are thoroughly impacted by modernity, as encapsulated in the image of the chief's mother with her ears glued to a transistor radio. Neither mythical heroes nor stereotypical victims, the Indians are presented simply as members of the urban poor, trying to survive with dignity.

Bye Bye Brasil provides visual confirmation of the Americanization pointed out in the lyrics of the title song: pinball machines in the jungle, Indian chiefs sporting designer jeans, backlands bands that

José Wilker in *Bye Bye Brasil* (1980)

421

sound like the Bee Gees. One sequence especially lampoons this kind of cultural colonialism. Lord Cigano anoints his audience with a bogus snowstorm (actually shredded coconut) to the accompaniment of Bing Crosby's "White Christmas," thereby realizing the "dream of all Brazilians" — to have snow like the "civilized countries." At the same time, the film highlights a process of reciprocal cultural anthropophagy which is not without its positive side-effects. Even the name of the traveling caravan — "Caravana Rolidei" — a phonetic transcription of the Brazilian pronunciation of "holiday" — illustrates the Brazilian "creative incapacity for copying." The loudspeaker of the refurbished caravan plays Frank Sinatra's version of a Brazilian song ("Aquarela do Brasil"), rendered in the style of American swing, much as Bossa Nova musicians melded the sounds of cool jazz with those of samba. The Americanization of Brazilian music, that is to say, goes hand in hand with the Brazilianization of American music, detectable in artists as diverse as Aretha Franklin, Paul Simon, Stevie Wonder, David Byrne, Pat Metheny, Michael Franks, and Al Jarreau. The problem, for Diegues, is not the intermingling of different cultural traditions but rather the exploitative terms under which these exchanges too often take place.[24]

The same observation about unequal exchange applies to the other media treated in the film. One sequence has a provincial mayor place a TV set on a kind of altar in a public square, to be worshipped as a fetish of modernity. Television, the image suggests (in an analysis reminiscent of Frankfurt School depictions of the narcoleptic audience) has inherited the ideological role of religion as mass opiate. Northeasterners watch "Dancin' Days" (the original title, again, was also in English), a Rio de Janeiro–based soap opera set among the disco crowd. The program encodes a double form of cultural colonialism: that of Brazil by the United States — since one of the show's functions is to disseminate American "top forty" hits — and that of the poorer Brazilian North by the more developed South. But the film is not monolithic in its critique of television. First of all, the film uses TV soap opera stars (most notably José Wilker and Betty Faria) to make contact with the TV audience. And although TV fosters cultural homogenization, it also brings the events of the world into the lives of rural people.

Bye Bye Brasil also speaks of the cinema itself. The crisis situation of the ambulatory troupe evokes that of cinema, also challenged by the ubiquitous fishbones (antennas) of TV. Lord Cigano functions as a fictive surrogate for the cineaste. He represents a latter-day incarnation of a typical Cinema Novo character, the mediator, the *magister ludi* (e.g., Firmino in *Barravento*) at once inside and outside the fiction. His self-description as a magician capable of realizing the dreams of all Brazilians echoes Diegues's own view of himself as the interpreter of the "utopias of the people." The film's central concerns (What is the current state of Brazil? What is popular culture? What is cultural colonialism? What is the relation between artist and public?) are largely inherited from earlier stages of Cinema Novo, but Diegues clearly rejects the "aesthetic of hunger" in favor of relatively high production values. Beginning with its pop-pastel credits, *Bye Bye Brasil* is lush, colorful, sensuous, and its soundtrack is elaborate and polished. A film about poor people, for Diegues, need not look poor. And unlike earlier Cinema Novo films, *Bye Bye Brasil* offers no omniscient political analysis, no models to be followed. Instead, it displays a Renoir-like tenderness for all its characters, without completely forgetting the social contradictions in which they are enmeshed. [25]

The metaphor of civil construction, familiar from *Tudo Bem* and *The Fall*, reappears in Glauber Rocha's *Idade da Terra* (1980), but this time in the biblical image of the people exploited by Pharaohs in the edification of tombs. At the same time, the film emphasizes the immensity of the country, developing a geographical trope of capital importance in recent Brazilian cinema. This trope suggests that the present phase of its imaginary and its reflexion involves the exploration of new frontiers, and a desire to verify *in loco* the actual effects of Third World capitalism in the service of national integration, a preoccupation present not only in *Idade da Terra, Bye Bye Brasil,* and *Iracema* but also in a number of features by non–Cinema Novo directors, as in the case of Ozualdo Candeias's *A Opção ou as Rosas da Estrada* ("The Option; or, the Roses of the Highway," 1980), Raulino's *Noites Paraguaias* ("Paraguayan Nights," 1981), Geraldo Morais's *A Difícil Viagem* ("The Difficult Journey," 1982) and Augusto Seva's *A Caminho das Índias* ("On the Road to the Indies," 1982). This reaching out to the frontiers represents a historic return to one feature of the early Cinema Novo films. When Brazilian cinema wants to speak for Brazil as a whole, when it wants to speak of national identity, it continues to reach beyond the urban centers, where the filmmakers live and work, to the strength and density of the "other Brazil": the Northeast, the Amazon, the vast Brazil far from the wealthy and Europeanized South. When it wishes to speak of modernization as a global process, Brazilian cinema observes that process at its frontier points, at the very edges of the national experience. And even when it immerses itself in the city, it is to encounter the traces of the margins in the center. Thus we reencounter the archaic within the modern, whether in the form of the Northeasterners and obscure religious practices that invade the apartment of *Tudo Bem,* or the immigrant workers who build the subway in *The Fall,* or the hillbilly singers Zé Rico and Milionário who star in Nelson Pereira dos Santos's *Estrada da Vida* ("Road of Life," 1980), or the *caipira* characters of André Klotzel's *Marvada Carne* (1984) standing in awe of a bank of TV monitors in a shop window, or the immigrants, soccer players, and prostitutes that people countless São Paulo films.

The Hillbilly and the monitors: *Marvada Carne* **(1984)**

The Recuperation of the Past

At times the director finds the "other Brazil" in the historic past, as in Carlos Diegues's *Quilombo* (1984). Here Diegues returns to the theme of his first feature *Ganga Zumba* (1963) — black resistance against slavery. Both films celebrate the historical reality of Palmares, the most spectacular and long-lived of the free communities, or *quilombos,* founded by runaway Africans in Brazil. If *Ganga Zumba* brought its characters to the threshold of freedom, *Quilombo* brings them into the promised land itself. The narrative of *Quilombo* sweeps over a historical period from 1650 to 1695, moving through three distinct phases. In the first, a rebel group led by Ganga Zumba flees from a sugar plantation and makes its way to Palmares. In the second phase, Palmares, under Ganga Zumba, has become a prosperous and independent community. In the third phase, another leader, Zumbi, is forced to lead the struggle in an atmosphere dominated by internal tensions and external aggressions. The Palmarinos are ultimately massacred and Zumbi himself is killed, but outbreaks of resistance, as the final intertitles inform us, go on for another century. The overall movement of the film, then, is from spontaneous revolt to the construction of a community, to the violent destruction of that community, and a final coda pointing to ongoing struggle.

Quilombo's gallery of characters includes: Ganga Zumba (Toni Tornado), the African prince who leads the enslaved out of bondage into the promised land of Palmares; Acotirene, a symbolic figure associated with African strength and spirituality; Dandara (Zezé Motta), associated with the African spirit Iansã, whose performance of religious rituals saves Ganga Zumba. The Jewish immigrant Samuel (Jonas Bloch), meanwhile, represents the many Sephardi Jews and *marranos* who fled the Inquisition and took refuge in Brazil; his dialogue in the film brings to the flight of the slaves biblical echoes of the Exodus, the parting of the Red Sea, and the Promised Land. The film valorizes African culture by associating its characters with the *orixás* of *candomblé:* Ganga Zumba is linked to Xangô; Zumbi to Ogum (the *orixá* of metal, agriculture, and war). At one point, a venerable figure refuses last rites in Latin and insists on singing in Yoruba. After his death, Ganga Zumba appears magically with Xangô's ax in hand. (Unfortunately, these allusions to Yoruba culture are historically inaccurate; Palmares was in fact culturally Bantu rather than Yoruba, the latter group being relative latecomers to Brazil). But in any case, Diegues foregrounds the symbolic value of African culture, while also insisting on the need for struggle.

A didactic saga based on fact, legend, and imaginative extrapolation, *Quilombo* is part historical reconstruction and part musical comedy, one partially drawing its style from the carnival pageants of Rio's "samba schools," whose spectacles also involve the fanciful re-creation of historic events. At the same time, the film is self-designated "science fiction" in that it projects a utopian future.[26] Diegues aims at poetic synthesis rather than naturalistic reproduction, constructing a plausible historical hypothesis which is above all *poetically* correct. The challenge of conveying the historical grandeur of Palmares while retaining a sense of magic and surreality is not, unfortunately, always successfully

Zezé Motta as Dandara in *Quilombo* (1984)

425

met. The ritual costumes, the turbans, body paint, and hairstyles, along with the quasi-theatrical lighting, at times suggest a kind of Afro-Brazilian Disneyworld. At its best moments, however, the film, with the help of the Gilberto Gil's pulsing and deliberately anachronistic soundtrack music — electronic Afro-derived samba-rock — not only evokes a historical utopia but also communicates a sense of what that utopia might have felt like.

Quilombo is not the only latter-day Cinema Novo film to bring to fruition a project first conceived in the late 1950s or early 1960s. Such is the case as well of Hirszman's *They Don't Wear Black Tie*, Eduardo Coutinho's *Cabra Marcado para Morrer*, and Nelson Pereira dos Santos's *Memórias do Cárcere* ("Prison Memories," 1984). This last film, based on the prison memoirs of Brazilian novelist Graciliano Ramos, charts Ramos's descent, in the late 1930s, into the hell of the prisons of populist dictator Getúlio Vargas. More specifically, the film chronicles Ramos's imprisonment between March 1936 and January 1937. Arrested without explanation as part of an antileftist sweep, Ramos is subsequently conducted on a forced tour of diverse forms of incarceration: ordinary jail, correctional facility, penal colony. Dos Santos slightly tampers with the actual chronology of events in order to emphasize a downward spiral of degradation, so that Ramos begins as a relatively pampered political prisoner and ends as the abused victim of the aptly-named "colônia," a virtual concentration camp on the Atlantic coast. But simultaneous with this descent, the film displays a very different movement. With each new body blow aimed at systematic dehumanization, Ramos gains character and humanity. Ramos, whom we have seen as a complex, proud, and somewhat solitary man with an intense interior life, turns incarceration into a springboard for liberation. He becomes a more committed human being at the same time that he comes to appreciate his vocation as a writer. Within the abject promiscuity of the prison, he discovers what separated him, the progressive bourgeois intellectual, from the people. The Third World gulag becomes, for him, the scene of a purificatory rite.

Despite the director's claim to have followed the memoirs "quite closely," the film is creatively unfaithful to the source. Apart from reducing the memoirs' some three hundred characters to a manageable one hundred, the film insinuates that Ramos's manuscript is saved for publication by the collective effort of the prisoners. In actual fact, Ramos lost his prison manuscript and his memories only became transformed into writing over a decade later. While the book is dispassionately paratactic in its presentation of events, moreover, the film arranges all the dramatic situations around a central crescendo — the writer's increasing participation in the life of the prison and the prisoners' increasing collaboration in the work of the writer. A whole network of accomplices helps Ramos write, not only by providing anecdotes and information but also by physically protecting the manuscript, now become a group patrimony. But the prisoners also need the writer; an

Nelson Pereira dos Santos filming *Prison Memories*

activist asks him to correct a manifesto, and even the warden requests stylistic advice. The film allegorizes the author's vision of the role of the progressive artist, whose "witness" turns the common experiences into remembered history and thus offers a ringing endorsement of the vocation of literature (and by analogy, the cinema) as a critical register of social existence.

Within the prison, we encounter a varied gallery of characters, all based on real-life prototypes: the seasoned militants (Leninists, Trotskyists), the rebellious soldier, the Jewish doctor, the worker, the Northeasterner. One Jewish woman character is based on Olga Benario Prestes, the communist who was sent to Brazil from training in Moscow in order to collaborate with Luis Carlos Prestes (the leader of the Brazilian Communist Party). Olga was later imprisoned, and under Vargas's orders, given over to the Gestapo to die in a German death camp. In the film, as in life, the other prisoners protest her abduction en masse but are ultimately tricked by the authorities. The police, guards, warden, and military officials, for their part, are treated without dogmatism; Dos Santos, like Ramos, can see the human being behind the uniform.

Prison Memories is allegorical in the sense that it uses one set of events, which transpired in the 1930s, to speak about another set of events. Just as the "joke" in *Vidas Secas* ("Barren Lives," 1963) consists in its being set in the past (yet nothing has changed), so *Prison Memories* has everything to do with the Brazil of *abertura*. The prison's "Freedom Radio" speaks of debts and bankers' agreements, and a soldier tells the writer, in a transparent allusion to two decades of military rule, "It will take you civilians a good while to get rid of us." The eagerness of the prisoners to come to decisions by vote evokes, for the Brazilian, the energetic 1984 campaign for direct presidential elections. The film

Carlos Varela as Graciliano Ramos in *Prison Memories* (1984)

begins and ends with the Brazilian national anthem, at a time when patriotism was back in style in Brazil, precisely because of redemocratization. The anthem marks the film as a microcosmic statement, suggesting that Brazil has the aspect of a prison, yet one whose prisoners will soon be freed.

In other films, the filmic dialogue with Brazilian history takes on an archival and historiographic dimension in the effort to recover material hidden in studio warehouses, government offices, and libraries. A number of films deploy photographs, archival footage, interviews, and off-screen narration in filmic reflexions on the past. Exemplary in this sense are two films by Sílvio Tendler, both of which concern Brazilian presidents. *Os Anos JK* ("The JK Years," 1980) focuses on Juscelino Kubitschek, the president who inaugurated Brasília in the 1950s, while *Jango* (1982) concerns João Goulart, popularly known as "Jango," the duly-elected president deposed by the 1964 coup. Both films demonstrate that even documentaries can be "allegorical," using a coded language which manipulates past events to talk about present policies. Agile exercises in historical apologetics designed to heighten the stature of their subjects, the films use fluent verbal-visual narration to laud Kubitschek's conciliatory liberalism and Goulart's leftist reformism in ways that reinforce the general spirit of *abertura* characteristic of the moment of the film's production.

The Trope of the Highway

Another key trope in the cinema of the past two decades has been the highway. Early 1960s films (*Vidas Secas, Viramundo, Grande Cidade*) were already fascinated by the theme of internal migration from the impoverished interior. Rui Guerra's *The Guns*, as seen earlier, was structured around the opposition between the urban world of weapons and trucks and the rural world of hunger and millennial religion, in a film that counterposed a documentary style for the peasants with a narrative fiction linked to the urban characters, with whom the spectator is made to identify as the "colonizers" of the rural world. Over a decade later, a similar conflict animates Bodansky/Senna's *Iracema* (made in 1975, but released only in 1980 due to censorship); this story of a poor Indian girl (whose name, an anagram of "America," alludes to a romantic nineteenth-century Indianist novel) is also relayed by counterposed cinematic techniques. The authors go beyond reportage to compose a multileveled text which is at once specific and general, documentary and allegorical — a synthetic view of the entire process of "conservative modernization." Given the centrality of documentation to the film's project, the filmmakers carefully authenticate images and sounds registered in situ. An interminable tracking shot records a gigantic man-made forest fire, showing that the fire's dimensions on the screen do not depend on manipulative editing. When shooting the religious festival in Belém, with thousands of the faithful congregating under the watchful eyes of a church official and police, the filmmakers behave like news reporters mingling with the crowd. Here, in contrast to the preceding example, it is the very discontinuity of the editing that points to the fact that the producers of image and sound are limited beings who, far from controlling the event, can capture it only in fragments, exhibiting irregular movement and other "flaws" that lend credibility to the account of the specific here-and-now.

The film's itinerary and the empirical data it generates profile an enormous natural space defiled by "progress." Ecological disaster and social exploitation configure an institutionalized hell. The highway provides a privileged setting for the "free investment" of distant capital (from southern Brazil and abroad) that organizes an intensified exploitation of the labor force, illegal land seizures, contraband in precious hardwoods, and new circulations of goods and human beings. One scene parallels migrant workers, prostitutes, and cattle as "pieces" that are "hauled" in trucks and sold to a foreign-owned plantation. Rather than use collage or discontinuous editing, Bodansky/Senna deploy incongruous documentary strategies derived from the cinema verité tradition, here made strange through the cynical interventions of the lead actor (Paulo César Pereio) in the "real world." (The actor pretends to be a truck driver around people who do not know him to be an actor).

Edna de Cássia in *Iracema* **(1975/1980)**

The confrontation, in this allegory of modernization, crystallizes around the relation between the jingoistic truck driver Tião Brasil Grande (Big Brazil Sebastian) played by Pereio, and Iracema, the Indian girl played by the nonprofessional Edna de Cássia. The alienation effect works within the shot, as Pereio provokes ordinary people to words and action, contaminating brute experience with theatricality. As simultaneously the character Tião Brasil Grande and a cinema verité interviewer, Pereio both plays in and comments on the scenes. And within the asymmetrical couple Tião/Iracema, Tião is active agent,

430

initiator, entrepreneur; Iracema is passive and acted upon, prostitute, commodity. Tião is associated with the pet project of the dictatorship, the Transamazonian Highway, and the modernizing nationalism it represents. He speaks in the jingoistic slogans of the period: "Onward Brazil!"; "There's no stopping this country!"; "Love it or leave it." He embodies the arrogance of the "economic miracle" and the ill-advised Pharaonic ambitions that led to the Third World's largest foreign debt. His grotesquerie forces the "patriotic" spectator to acknowledge his/her complicity in the deplorable invasion of the Amazon. The film develops, then, a structural contrast between two filmic approaches: first, that of cinema reportage with hand-held camera, registering the ecological devastation and human exploitation in the Amazon, and second, that of fictional and allegorical procedures involving the relationship of Tião and Iracema. In a total interpenetration of documentary and fiction, the film understatedly denounces the human toll of frontier "development." And if Iracema in José de Alencar's novel embodied the noble savage, the native woman who responds to colonization by offering her love to a European knight, her contemporary namesake is clearly the victim of a twentieth-century conquistador, ambulatory emblem of imperializing ambition.

Iracema returns to a perennial theme of Brazilian cinema. Ever since the silent period, Brazilian films have turned to the Indian as subject. Oswaldo Caldeira's *Ajuricaba: O Rebelde da Amazônia* ("Ajuricaba: Rebel of the Amazon," 1977), in this same vein, stresses historical continuities by shuttling between Indian resistance in the eighteenth century and resistance to neocolonialism in the present. It tells the story of Ajuricaba, an eighteenth-century chief of the Manau tribe who fought against his people's enslavement by organizing a pan-Indian Confederation against the Portuguese. (The story is well-known in the Amazon region but virtually unknown in the rest of Brazil.) After a four-year struggle, he finally leaped to his death rather than surrender. The film's precredit sequence, set in the present, deploys aerial shots to depict the discovery of an Indian corpse in the river. The media record the event as part of their daily routine of registering sensational violence. Then the narrative backtracks into the past, with another killing of an Indian, this time by eighteenth-century Portuguese adventurers. Ajuricaba (Rinaldo Genes) is already chained and on his way to prison. From this point on, the film shuttles between past and present, between Ajuricaba as heroic rebel and Ajuricaba as present-day Indian, proceeding down the river past the slum housing in which Indians now live. Throughout the film, both as an eighteenth-century and contemporary character, Ajuricaba says almost nothing; the word belongs to the colonizer. The film suggests the historical continuities not only between the diverse incarnations of Ajuricaba, as a transhistorical figure, avatar of indigenous suffering and resistance, but also between the colonizing Portuguese and the contemporary multinational corporations which have turned the *zona franca* of Manaus into a glittering image of neocolonialism. But rather than force the parallels, Caldeira leaves it up to the spectator to make the inference. At the finale, the film has Ajuricaba become a metalworker — the kind of worker who led the revolts in the late 1970s (i.e., perhaps reflecting a classical leftist class-over-race strategy). The film's ending begins the story once again, as the voice-over repeats ". . . once upon a time there was an Indian," as if to say that the legend survives not only thanks to popular memory but also because of the cinema, one of whose functions is to become the repository of myths, renewed again with each projection.

We return to the Indian, and the Amazon, in a much later film, Hector Babenco's *At Play in the Fields of the Lord* (1991). Although American-financed, the film employed a Brazilian producer (Francisco Ramalho, Jr.), a Brazilian director of photography (Lauro Escorel), and a number of well-known Brazilian players (José Dumont, Nelson Xavier). The Babenco film uses hegemonic financing circuits in order to make what at first glance looks like a Hollywood-style superproduction (costing $36 million, i.e., more than scores of Brazilian features put together). But as what Eugênio Bucci calls an "anti-American blockbuster," *At Play in the Fields of the Lord* offers disillusioned subtlety, social contradiction, and spectatorial ambivalence instead of Hollywood's usual Manichean resolutions.[27] Despite the film's high production values, its use of stars (e.g., Daryl Hannah, Tom Berenger), its spectacular scenery, and its source in a best-selling novel by Peter Matthiessen, the film unsettled many First World audiences by its hostile portrait of the role of Europeans in the Amazon.

Wolf (Tom Waits) and Lewis Moon (Tom Berenger) in *At Play in the Fields of the Lord* (1991)

Aeore (S. Yriwana Karaja) in *At Play in the Fields of the Lord*

The film offers an interesting comparison, in this sense, with another film released the same year, Bruce Beresford's *Black Robe,* which treats the same topic — the role of European-brought religions in relation to native peoples — but which, unlike *At Play in the Fields of the Lord,* was immensely successful in the North American market. The different responses to these two films derive, one suspects, from the fact that while *Black Robe* is set in the safely distant past (the sixteenth century), the Babenco film is set in the explosive present. And while *Black Robe* is critical of the Jesuits, it forgives them because they "did it all for love." *At Play,* in contrast, portrays the Protestant missionaries specifically, and Europeans and Euro-Americans generally, as neurotic, arrogant, puritanical, insensitive, and ultimately dangerous to the general well-being. (The missionaries never really succeed, furthermore, in their project of converting Indians to Christianity.) The Brazilian policeman tells the two aviators (played by Tom Waits and Tom Berenger) to bomb the Niaruna village "just to scare them." Contact with whites, even with well-intentioned whites, the film suggests, always means death for the Indians. The pilots and the missionaries are symbolically linked in their mission; as it flies over the Amazon, the plane casts a reflection on the water in the form of a cross. Despite the tensions between them, the missionaries, the pilots, and the gold seeker mutually reinforce one another. Even the empathetic characters can provoke calamity. The genocide of the tribe results from the fact that Lewis Moon, the Berenger character who is supposedly half-Cherokee, kisses both Andy (Daryl Hannah) and his native wife. The missionary Martin

Quarrier (Aidan Quinn) tells Lewis Moon that " as an American he would be proud to have Indian blood," to which Lewis responds sardonically, "And just how much Indian blood would an American be proud to have?" Everyone projects their own ethnocentric vision onto the Indians; even the Jewish character Wolf (Tom Waits) sees them as "the lost tribe of Israel, Jewish just like me." At the same time, the Indians are not noble savages but rather ordinary people faced by a devastating historical juggernaut.

The Cinema of Pleasure

The effort to develop a viable project of national entertainment has mobilized a generation of filmmakers who emerged from Cinema Novo and even from Marginal Cinema. This common project has led not only to a qualified return to the notion of spectatorial pleasure but also to the heightening of technical standards, to more care with scriptwriting, and to a dramaturgy and mise-en-scène closer to the high production values fostered by Brazilian television, which has now largely replaced Hollywood as the technical superego of Brazilian cinema. In these films we find a less rigid approach to themes — seen by some as a relief from the repression of the orthodox left and its "ideological patrols" (in Carlos Diegues's polemical phrase of the late 1970s) — as filmmakers demand the right to express their personal fantasies and utopias, whether in accord with the reigning ideologies or not. Filmmakers refuse the "advice" of those who call for greater sociological realism and political engagement, and assert their (postmodern) right to treat "minor themes" and "local issues," without making grand political statements or allegorical totalizations. At times, therefore, they opt to do nothing more than sensitively register the quotidian, whether the mood be melancholy as in Luiz Fernando Goulart's *Marina* (1976), lyric as in Carlos Diegues's *Chuvas de Verão* ("Summer Showers," 1978) and *Dias Melhores Virão*, comic as in David Neves's *Muito Prazer* ("Glad to Meet You," 1979), or amorous as in Jabor's *Eu Te Amo* ("I Love You," 1980) and *Eu Sei Que Vou Te Amar* ("I Know I'm Going to Love You," 1986). Others combine Brazilian cultural materials with accessible mainstream style as in Fábio Barreto's *O Rei do Rio* ("The King of Rio," 1984) and *Luzia Homem* ("Man Luzia," 1987), or in Murilo Salles's *Faca de Dois Gumes* ("Double-Edged Sword"), a well-conducted thriller starring Paulo José.

We find this move toward pleasure and fantasy in the films of the post–Cinema Novo generation, largely from São Paulo, a generation accustomed to military rule but also initiated into the counterculture of mind-bending drugs, polymorphous sexuality, and anarchistic politics, eager for alternatives in all areas and ready to elaborate a vision of

Carla Camurati as Shirley Shadow in *Cidade Oculta* (1986)

Brazil based on its own experience of history. While not a "school" in the sense of Cinema Novo, the young São Paulo filmmakers — also known as the "Vila Madalena" group after their favorite neighborhood — do share certain traits, notably their link to ECA (the Communications School at the University of São Paulo), and their attempt to break out of isolation by returning to narrative fiction and the skillful construction of audience identification, but without betraying the national culture. The filmmakers follow a middle path between the didacticism of Cinema Novo and the provocations of the Underground. Rather than metacinematic deconstruction, the authors propose what Jean-Claude Bernardet calls a "false naturalism," a pseudorealism that shows it is aware that realism is a lie, a kind of representation that passes itself off as real but constantly "de-realizes" itself.[28] In this postmodernist cinema, the filmmaker eschews grand ambitions in order to avoid grand disappointments and aims instead for a cinema that is at once more modest, more open, and more solicitous of the audience's affection.

A well-realized example of this tendency is Chico Botelho's *Cidade Oculta* ("Hidden City," 1986). As the title suggests, the city (São Paulo) forms the virtual protagonist of the film. The scenario privileges nighttime São Paulo, with its punk-nihilist subcultures, its Karaoke bars and nightspots. A cross, in filmic terms, of *Metropolis* and *Blade Runner*, *Cidade Oculta* portrays São Paulo as a synthesis of the world's cities, at times evoking New York, at times Tokyo (much of the film was shot in the Japanese neighborhood called "Liberdade"), and at times West Berlin. José Roberto Eliezer's cinematography features canted frames and off-kilter *Touch of Evil*–like compositions and a shinily metallic video-game aesthetic. The film's pastiche plot revolves around two-

435

dimensional characters with cartoonish names: the bandits "Angel" (Arrigo Barnabé) and "Jap" (Celo Saiki), and the nightclub performer Shirley Shadow (Carla Camurati), all caught in a life-and-death struggle with a corrupt policeman named "Big Rat" (Cláudio Mamberti). The film plays knowingly with an intertext that includes comic books, cabaret, musical comedy, music video, and *film noir*. *Cidade Oculta* appeals to a younger media-formed generation of Brazilians for whom Cinema Novo–style didacticism has become largely irrelevant. Yet the film does not completely abandon social consciousness, which here takes the form of the satirical portrayal of the policeman, constructed by the official media as a heroic crusader against drugs, but in fact a mafioso drug addict. The sound track is propelled by the avant-gardist music of Arrigo Barnabé, a syncretic music that mingles the influence of samba, rock, and jazz with that of Stockhausen, Schoenberg, Bartók and *musique concrète*, and that forms a perfect musical analogue to the hypermodern feeling of the story and images.

Another São Paulo film, Suzana Amaral's *A Hora de Estrela* ("Hour of the Star," 1985), garnered many international awards as well as enthusiastic reviews after its opening in New York. A rare Brazilian graduate of a North American film school (New York University, where her classmates included Jim Jarmusch and Susan Seidelman), Amaral in some ways fits into the new era of filmmaking, both in the sense of her film's modest subject — the misadventures of an awkward, uneducated, virginal girl from the Northeast in the concrete jungle of São Paulo — and in its pseudonaturalist manner, which melds a documentary flavor with the feeling of fable. The film discards the reflexive structure of the Clarice Lispector source novella — by which a sophisticated upper-class male narrator grapples with the problem of bringing to life a simple-hearted lower-class character — in favor of an unmediated third-person approach to its theme. The result is a kind of updated neorealism, but this time without neorealism's occasional lapses into melodrama.

The film's protagonist, Macabea (Marcélia Cartaxo), can be seen as the latter-day descendant of the unglamorous and barely articulate characters of certain first-phase Cinema Novo films (for example, the peasants Fabiano and Vitória in *Vidas Secas*). Macabea is defined by her pathetic mimicry of those who are slightly more sophisticated than she is, for example Olímpico (José Dumont), another Northeastern migrant with equally gloomy prospects. Her character is constructed by an array of sharply observed details: her modest way of undressing *under* the bedcovers, her way of wiping her nose on her blouse collar, her nibbling on fried chicken as she urinates into a wash basin, her passion for guava and cheese, her vain chewing of aspirins as a cure for an ill-defined malaise. Time flows viscously; the tick-tock of its passage is heard throughout the film. The finale conveys Macabea's dying vision as she is run down by a luxury car; she races in slow motion toward a fair-haired millionaire. Where the film differs from Cinema Novo is in

Marcélia Cartaxo as Macabea in *Hour of the Star* **(1985)**

its relative conventionality of technique (psychologized narration, shot–counter shot for dialogue), its refusal of all social allegory (Macabea exhibits not a trace of class consciousness or incipient rebellion), and in its readiness to grant its central character a fantasy life, even if a truncated one. What the film achieves, finally, is an honest, often humorous lucidity within its self-defined limits.

More recently, Walter Salles Jr.'s *A Grande Arte* ("High Art," but retitled "Exposure" for distribution abroad), an adaptation of a police novel by Rubem Fonseca, won commercial distribution in the United States. On the model of some West German films, *A Grande Arte* (1991) aims at an international market, features an American star, and is shot in English. After 1960s films like *Black God, White Devil,* which could *only* be Brazilian, *A Grande Arte* offers a film that manages not to seem Brazilian. Beginning with its technically dazzling, exhilarating *Frenzy*-like overture shot, which takes us from a close shot of the face of an assassinated woman in a hotel room, through the window and up and out to a high aerial view of Rio — all in sixty-seven seconds and without a single cut — the film succeeds in its ambition of being a well-crafted genre film à la Hollywood, complete with English dialogue and an American actor (Peter Coyote) as protagonist. Unlike other Brazilian directors who play with Hollywood genre conventions (Ivan Cardoso, Rogério Sganzerla, Chico Botelho, Guilherme de Almeida Prato) and unlike American directors who practice genre revisionism (e.g., Martin Scorcese, Robert Altman, Lawrence Kasdan), Walter Salles Jr. treats the conventions with only a modicum of critical distance. The film seems to look at Brazil through alien eyes. But as Eugênio Bucci points out, other features of the film (the kinds of physiognomies, the casting of Brazilian TV actors, and especially "its desire to seem what it is not") betray, almost against the director's wishes, the film's inescapable "Brazilianess."[29]

Coproductions and Magic Realism

One discerns a similar turn away from rigorous political commitment toward a certain kind of pleasure and fantasy in latter-day literary adaptations by Rui Guerra and Nelson Pereira dos Santos. Subsequent to the highly politicized *The Fall* and his pro-Frelimo documentary *Mueda, Massacre e Memória* in 1978, Guerra turns increasingly to literary adaptations, notably of the work of Gabriel García Márquez (*Eréndira*, 1982, and *A Fábula da Bela Palomera*, 1986) and of Antônio Callado (*Kuarup*, 1988). *Eréndira*, a coproduction funded from Brazilian, Mexican, and German sources, was originally written by García Márquez as a screenplay, but when the prospects for a film version began to dim, García Márquez placed a mention of the story in *100 Years of Solitude*, while also refashioning the materials of the screenplay into two works of prose fiction — a novella ("Innocent Erendira and Her Heartless Grandmother") and a short story ("Death Constant Beyond Love"). By the time Guerra was chosen to direct a film version, García Márquez had lost the original screenplay and had to write a new script based on the existing works of fiction and on his memories of the screenplay. Both Guerra and García Márquez come from rich, "polyphonic" cultural backgrounds: the Mozambican-born Guerra studied filmmaking in France but has always been identified with Cinema Novo, while García Márquez is associated with the mestizo culture of the Caribbean coast of Colombia. Like García Márquez, Guerra has always mobilized the fantastic in the service of an underlying realism. His tropicalist *The Gods and the Dead* (1970), for example, combines a realistic portrayal of the historical "Wars of the Colonels" in Brazil with an allegorical style incorporating popular legends and theatrical exaggeration. With its gaudily painted rivers and exuberant artifice, that film might have easily been an adaptation of a García Márquez novel, with the Brazilian Northeast standing in for García Márquez's legendary Macondo.

When *Eréndira* begins, the girl protagonist (Cláudia Ohana) is fourteen and living with her eccentric grandmother (Irene Papas) in a lugubrious mansion, where she serves as maid, cook, and confidante. When she forgets to extinguish the candelabra one night, the mansion catches fire and burns to the ground. "My poor dear," the matriarch tells Eréndira without a trace of hostility, "your entire life will hardly be sufficient to repay me." After informing Eréndira of the exact extent of her debt, she begins to set up the means of repayment — the prostitution of Eréndira. The first customer, the local grocer, weighs Eréndira and pays for her by the kilo. Because of Eréndira's beauty and the grandmother's management skills, Eréndira soon becomes the most sought-after courtesan in the region. As she services interminable lines of smugglers, deserters, and other marginals, the grandmother sits at the entrance, haggling over prices and checking coins with her teeth.

As they progress from region to region in their ambulatory bordello, the matriarch and her ward become the focal point of a host of subsidiary entertainments — snakecharmers, freaks, musicians. At one point, monks abduct Eréndira, cut her hair and force her to work, but she escapes and returns to her guardian. The pair then begin to follow the electoral campaign of Senator Onésimo (Michel Lonsdale), in hopes of a letter of recommendation "certifying their morality." The senator makes populist speeches and sleeps with Eréndira, telling her that they are both alone; their professions, it is implied, have more than a little in common. One day, a golden-haired boy named Ulysses sneaks into Eréndira's tent and introduces her to noncommercial love. He persuades her to escape with him in a truck, but his father and her grandmother catch up with them after a desert chase. From that point on, the lovers conspire to take the matriarch's life. After a number of abortive attempts, they finally manage to kill her, but Eréndira runs away from Ulysses as well, leaving footprints that mysteriously fill with blood.

At times, Guerra comes up with particularly telling equivalents to the magical mango world of García Márquez, where blood flows green and tastes like mint, and where the sun rises at night and sets at dawn. Guerra preserves the García Márquez magic not through expensive Spielbergian effects but rather through minimalist evocation. First of all, Guerra showcases the words themselves by transforming the third-person narration of the story into the direct-voice dialogue of the film. Much of the dialogue evokes a kind of nonchalant surreality. "Waltzes are more expensive," a musician declares, "because they are sadder." The improbable names of the characters — "Amadis" with its reference to Don Quixote's literary exemplar, "Ulysses," with its epic ring — also introduce us to a world where ordinary life participates in grandeur and enchantment. The decor, meanwhile, in which turn-of-the-century cameras, World War II planes, and contemporary trucks commingle in anachronistic abandon, reinforces the feeling of a tropical no-whereland. While absurd on a literal level, the superimposition of epochs speaks on a deeper level of the palimpsestic temporality of the Latin American experience, where the coexistence of different historical periods — of the pre-Columbian, the colonial, and the contemporary — is a fact of life. The more obvious magical touches in the film — snowflakes that change color, love that lights candles, footprints that spring blood — evoke a world where the borders between sleep and wakefulness have become somewhat blurred. It is no accident that the film features two sleepwalkers — Eréndira and her grandmother. The

Irene Papas as the Grandmother in *Eréndira* (1982)

latter sleeps with her eyes open and rants while she dreams, and the dreams themselves, paradoxically, have a realistic element. "What day was it in your dream?" Eréndira asks her grandmother, whose dreams repeat themselves predictably like so many daily routines.

The images in *Eréndira* are carefully crafted, with striking contrasting colors associated with specific characters — royal purple and black for the grandmother, white and blue for Ulysses. The film features perennial Guerra devices such as long, elegant tracking shots which emphasize their own autonomy, along with some novelties such as the deployment of dissolves in which one of the images momentarily freezes. Guerra skillfully exploits sound — the director is also a musician and composer — orchestrating music, animal noises, and sound effects into a polyrhythmic montage. He also plays on diverse generic registers. The attempts to murder the resilient grandmother, for example, are treated in modes ranging from broad farce to tragedy and opera. A poisoned cake lethal enough to kill three elephants provokes nothing more than a self-satisfied belch and a good night's sleep. An explosive device leaves the grandmother only mildly fazed, like those cartoon characters who survive massive quantities of dynamite. Ulysses' interminable knifing of the old woman, meanwhile, evokes the ponderous, stylized agonies of tragic opera.

We feel the near-indestructible grandmother in *Eréndira* as a queenly presence, a mad descendant of the queens of Sophocles and Ionesco, partly because of significant props (chair-throne, regal robes, scepter), but also because of the powerful performance of Irene Papas, who comes to us already wrapped in the aura of Greek tragedy. While hugely villainous, the grandmother is not an unalloyed ogre. She is also an oracle who speaks truths, especially about men and love. In a bizarre way, she wants to protect Eréndira. In her credo, wealth signifies freedom from men. Eréndira, meanwhile, also partakes of the enigmatic. At the beginning, she passively submits to each outrage and humiliation with a mechanically obedient "Yes, Grandmother." In sociological terms, she evokes a reality with which Guerra and García Márquez are doubtless familiar — girls who prostitute themselves to survive. Isolated in her grandmother's mansion, imprisoned within the ambient hypocrisy, Eréndira has no critical distance on her oppression. She evolves from innocence at fourteen — symbolized by her lack of palm lines — to experience at twenty. Ulysses introduces her to love, but she ultimately flees him as well. She remains the matriarch's daughter.

Evocative and suggestive rather than didactic, *Eréndira* is rooted in cultural values rather than in any obvious political agenda. We can discern, however, a realistic subtext. The two central metaphors in the film — debt and prostitution — indirectly call attention to the causal substratum of events. In the present historical conjuncture, Eréndira's situation inevitably calls to mind the "debt trap" currently plaguing Latin America. Eréndira's debt is massive, cruel, and rooted in a past that weighs, as Marx said, like a nightmare on the brains of the living. (A corollary theme in the film has to do with parental violence against children — Eréndira abused by her grandmother, Ulysses whipped by his father, a freakshow woman turned into a spider for "disobeying her parents.") The film also points allegorically to the criminal origins of wealth. The grandmother initially becomes rich through her association with a smuggler. Like the conquistadors, she exploits Indian labor, and renews her wealth by pandering her granddaughter. Childhood prostitution is here is both literal fact and social parable. It is shown not only as pervasive but also as linked to religion, politics, and the media. The Church, for example, abducts Eréndira and exploits her even more brutally than the grandmother had. The politically powerful, meanwhile, give their blessing to the enterprise. The wealthy character Sánchez, as a "person of weight," certifies the pair's morality. The entertainment media, finally, are also linked to prostitution: the bordello stands at the hub of an array of commercialized entertainments. While the events of *Eréndira* seem fantastic, then, they point to real life. García Márquez and Guerra use fantasy to expose the real, deploying the real in order to give fantasy a local habitation and a name, in a style at once historical and fabulous.

More than a decade after *Eréndira*, Nelson Pereira dos Santos also moves toward a version of "magic realism" in his adaptation of Guimarães Rosa's *A Terceira Margem do Rio* ("The Third Bank of the River,"

441

1993). Like *Eréndira, The Third Bank of the River* is a coproduction (French and Brazilian) and, like the Guerra film, it too ingeniously interweaves diverse stories by its source author. Beginning with the story that provides the title for the film — the virtually wordless drama of a man who abandons his family to live on a boat in the middle of the river — Nelson Pereira dos Santos integrates four other stories. Lio-jorge (Ilya São Paulo) the son (in Nelson's re-creation) of the enigmatic boatman of the first story, follows an enchanted cow and thus becomes the protagonist of another story ("Seqüência") in which the cow leads him to the most beautiful woman in the world (Sonja Saurin). From their romance is born the miracle-working saint Nhinhinha (Bárbara Brandt) from still another story ("A Menina de Lá"). But the family is then persecuted by an evil group of brothers evocative of corrupt policemen or "death squads" — the Dagobé brothers — from yet another story, one of whom desires Nhinhinha. To get rid of him, Lio-jorge calls the philosopher-assassin (Jofre Soares) from still another story ("Fatalidade"). Feeling threatened, the family flees to Brasília. The postcard vision of the magnificent buildings of the city — concretizations of official modernity — give way to scenes of squalor reminiscent of the *favelas* of Rio. Apart from mixing different source stories, *The Third Bank of the River* also mixes distinct styles and motifs from Dos Santos's own oeuvre. As long as the film takes place in the interior of the country, the film remains close both to Rosa's mythic-rural literary universe and to the sertão of Dos Santos's own *Vidas Secas*. (The mother is played by Maria Ribeiro, the Vitória of the earlier film.) The communication between the son and the mysterious river-loving father, for example, is delicately evoked as an asymmetrical dialogue; we see that the father's plate has been emptied, but we never see the father. But when the family moves to the periphery of Brasília, the spectator moves with them from rural fantasy into the urban squalor portrayed in *Rio 40 Graus, Rio Zona Norte,* and *Amuleto de Ogum*. Magical effects, not all of them elegantly done, characterize both sections, however. Nhinhinha engenders many García Márquez-style metamorphoses: she conjures up rain and frogs during a drought, candy moves out of the TV into the mouths of waiting spectators, a samba school magically materializes. But the film reveals the limits of magical solutions: a close shot showing Nhinhinha giving out candy to children opens up to reveal an infinite line of more waiting children. As with *Eréndira*, there is a pessimistic undercurrent within the magic realism; no one seems safe anymore, whether in the city or in the sertão.

Return to the Future: *Twenty Years After*

One film from the mid-1980s self-consciously reflects on the history of that cinema and thus recapitulates many of the themes we have been developing. Eduardo Coutinho's reflexive documentary *Cabra Marcado para Morrer* — literally, "Man Marked for Death" but translated into English as "Twenty Years After" — traces the historical trajectory of Brazil, and of Brazilian cinema, from the early 1960s through 1984, the date of the film's release. Coutinho's initial project, conceived in the optimistic left-populist years before the 1964 coup d'état, was to dramatically reconstruct the real-life political assassination, in 1962, of the peasant leader João Pedro Teixeira. The performers were to be João Pedro's comrades in work and struggle, the locale would be the actual site of the crime, and among the "actors" would be the deceased leader's widow. The coup d'état interrupted the filming, however; the filmmakers and peasant participants were dispersed, and the material already shot was hidden. Almost two decades later, encouraged by the political liberalization of the 1980s, the filmmaker sought out the hidden footage and the original "performers." In the present-day film, we watch the participants in the original film watching themselves in the

Elizabete in *Twenty Years After* (1984)

443

1964 film, bearing witness not only to the scars left by dictatorship but also to the continuity of popular struggle.

A key figure in *Twenty Years After* is João Pedro's widow, Elizabete, who carried on her husband's militancy, leading demonstrations and even traveling to Brasília to denounce his assassination. The filmmaker discovers her living in another state, under an assumed name, cut off from former friends and much of her family — all necessary, as she explains, "in order not to be exterminated." After suffering extreme oppression, she is bruised but also resilient and even cautiously militant. With the filmmaker's help she reencounters her family, reassumes her true name, and reaffirms her political convictions. In her capacity for disappearing, surviving, and then reappearing, she resembles, as critic Roberto Schwarz points out, the filmmaker himself. The emotion generated by the film arises from the encounter of a committed filmmaker with an authentic popular heroine who, despite everything, manages to connect the dots of her political trajectory, just as the filmmaker completes his cinematic project. In the renewed confluence of political cinema and popular struggle, both cineaste and peasant leader resume their struggle and mark their solidarity.[30]

Cabra Marcado para Morrer reveals the dispersion and disintegration of the family and the erasing of identity by repression. (Significantly, the only member of the extended family who has succeeded has done so thanks to a grant to study medicine in Cuba.) But the descent into hell is doubled by a reverse journey which leads, if not to paradise, at least to a historical situation where questions can be posed again. Here, the cinema literally intervenes in the life of the oppressed, and the story of the film begun, interrupted, and now completed is mingled with the story of those with whom the filmmaker dialogues. It is owing to the filmic meeting between the filmmaker and Elizabete that she emerges from the underground and recomposes her identity.

Between *Cabra* 1964 and *Cabra* 1984, the issues — repression, squatter's rights, agrarian reform, unionization — have not changed, but their filmic treatment has. The 1960s meeting with the widow is paralleled by the highly didactic cinema of the period — a mélange of *Salt of the Earth*-style realism, with hortatory dialogue and idealizing low-angles, and the heroicized image of "the People" promoted by the leftist Center of Popular Culture, which sponsored the original film. The 1980s meeting with the widow takes place in the era of network television and the evolving experience of the Brazilian documentary. The filmic language is more dialogical, less inclined to discourse omnisciently *about* the other, and more inclined to listen *to* and learn *from* the other. The film incorporates into its own process and editing the recuperation of identity. It adroitly articulates the procedures of the traditional documentary (especially offscreen commentary) with more contemporary direct-cinema techniques, and here we glimpse the presence of the television professional, Eduardo Coutinho, from the well-known Brazilian network series "Globo Reporter." We see his crew

Images from *Cabra* 1964

working within the frame, making us acutely aware of a film-in-the process-of-being-made before our eyes. We have here, then, a summa of themes: documentary report, metacinema, the voice of the other, intertextuality (here in the most literal sense), and the impact of history, in a synthesis at once political, social, anthropological, and filmic.

Tizuka Yamasaki's *Patriamada,* made in the same period as *Cabra Marcado,* registers the mass movement for direct elections in 1984, embroidered together with the story of a love triangle between three fictitious characters: a middle-aged industrialist (Walmor Chagas), a struggling documentary filmmaker (Buza Ferraz), and an energetic reporter (Débora Bloch). As Julianne Burton points out, the three characters all have allegorical resonances, each representing different social milieus: the post–Cinema Novo filmmaker, the bourgeois industrialist, and the young woman who grew up under the dictatorship. The film is doubly reflexive in featuring a filmmaker, a TV news reporter, and a film-within-the-film (also called "Patriamada"). The film language throughout is inflected by television in its diverse modalities: reportage, music video, and, in the fiction story, the *telenovela.* The media are also used as a way to "bind" diverse spaces, especially in the Candelaria sequence which records a gigantic carnival-style rally in favor of direct elections, but where TV's monitoring the events are used to link the demonstration itself with the hugely diverse audience watching it on television,[31] while Milton Nascimento's "Bailes da Vida," one of the anthems of the direct elections movement, plays on the soundtrack.

Crisis and Response: The Short Film

After the euphoric interlude of *"abertura,"* the indirect election of Tancredo Neves/José Sarney, the direct election of Fernando Collor de Mello in 1989 (followed by his impeachment in 1993), and the election of Fernando Henrique Cardoso in 1994, we find a present situation characterized by a complex reorientation. One response to the industrial crisis has been a proliferation of shorter films, and later, videos. Indeed, over one thousand short films were produced during the 1980s, not only in Rio and São Paulo but also in Rio Grande do Sul and Minas Gerais; and this efflorescence of short works is rooted in a longer history; since the middle of the 1980s, especially, it has been the short film and video that have energized Brazilian media-makers. Fueled by laws that obliged movie theaters to exhibit Brazilian shorts before the almost invariably foreign features, and by laws that withheld a small percentage of box-office revenues for financing small-scale production, the short film enjoyed a period of rich experimentation. At the same time, the official pro-short policy had some perverse repercussions in that exhibitors favored industrial short films (e.g., those of Primo Carbonari) to more auteurist or experimental films. At times, exhibitors would deliberately juxtapose a technically rudimentary short film — for example, a scratchy black-and-white Brazilian animation film such as Stil's *A Mão* ("The Hand") — with a high-tech blockbuster — for example, a gorgeously colored 70 mm print of *E.T.* — precisely in order to "embarrass" the short. When audiences did respond well to short films, as was the case with Jorge Furtado's *Ilha das Flores* ("Isle of Flowers," 1989), where spectators showed more interest in the short than in the feature, exhibitors would withdraw the short. At times there occurred a provocative dialogue between the two formats, as when a Clint Eastwood *Dirty Harry*-style film was accompanied by Arthur Omar's *O Inspetor* ("The Inspector"), a deconstructive parody of the same genre.

The Brazilian short films that began to flourish in the 1980s tended to be full of fantasy, media consciousness, and intertextual allusion. Ivone Margulies, Márcio Doctors, and Sílvia Roesler's *Pão ou Pães* (1980) offers a pastiche of the kinds of images typical of Brazilian television. Vivian Ostrovsky's "beach symphony" film, *Copacabana Beach* (1982), orchestrates an impressionist collage of images taken from Copacabana Beach between sunrise and dusk, in an ironic take on the Malibu-like body culture that flourished in the 1980s. Wilson Barros's *Diversões Solitárias* ("Solitary Diversions," 1983) describes an urban world in which human relations are constantly mediated by machines: answering machines, pinball machines, computer screens, video monitors. Maria Rita Kehl and Nelson Villas Boas's *Ecos Urbanos* ("Urban Echoes," 1983) treats the avant-garde musicians of São Paulo, examining the city itself as a polyphony of musical noises. Cao Hamburger's *A*

Arthur Omar's *The Inspector* **(1988)**

Garota das Telas ("Silver Screen Girl," 1988) is an animated stylistic exercise that plays with multiple genres: science fiction, noir, western, musical). Indeed, the cinema is a theme in many of the shorts, as is evident even in their titles: Eliana Fonseca's *Frankenstein Punk* (1986), Antônio Cecílio Neto's *Três Moedas na Fonte* ("Three Coins in the Fountain," 1988), and Carla Camurati's *A Mulher Fatal Encontra o Homem Ideal* ("The Femme Fatale Meets the Ideal Man," 1987). Isaac Weinfeld and Márcio Kogan's *Idos com o Vento* ("Gone with the Wind," 1983) offers a "biography" of Margaret Mitchell (drawn from the jacket of the novel) and features transvestite Patrício Bisso as Scarlett O'Hara. Nelson Nadotti's *No Escurinho do Cinema* ("In the Darkness of the Movie Theater," 1989) shows a couple at the movies becoming involved, à la Woody Allen's *Purple Rose of Cairo,* in the cinematic affairs of Burt Lancaster and Deborah Kerr in *From Here to Eternity,* Charlie Chaplin and Virginia Cherrill in *City Lights,* and Kim Bassinger and Mickey Rourke in *9 1/2 Weeks.* Roberto Henkin's black-humored documentary *Memória* ("Memory," 1990) reveals the sad destiny of films which, no longer being exhibited, are picked apart and transformed into brooms. Michael Ruman's *20 Minutos* ("20 Minutes") parodically offers the ensemble of elements — preview, newsreel, short film — which usually precede feature films in commercial cinemas. Among the most prolific and inventive of the directors of shorts has been Arthur Omar. His *Música Barroca Mineira* ("Baroque Music from Minas," 1981) mixes documentary, fiction, and cybernetic invention in its discussion of the work of the black classical composers from eighteenth-century Minas Gerais. *O Som ou o Tratado de Harmonia* ("Sound or Treatise on Har-

Arthur Omar

mony," 1984) analyzes the role of sound in the cinema. *The Inspector* (1989) plays with the conventions of the police thriller by confronting the spectator with the corpses left by Rio's death squads. Here the fiction-documentary relation is scrambled, questioned from within. We accompany a real detective in his actual work environment, yet the detective uses highly unconventional methods — for example, dressing up as a woman or priest — in order to accomplish his goals. He himself fictionalizes the real, in the manner of popular detective novels (which he reads at police headquarters), of "photo-*novelas*" (in which he participates as a model), and of TV police serials like *Barreta*.

The short film also benefited from foreign support in the form of coproductions with Channel 4, 2DF, and Spanish Television, or with the provision of grants to filmmakers exploring specific topics relevant to North American–South American dialogue (for example, the Rockefeller Foundation's Media Arts Program for Latin America). In 1991 the Goethe Institute's Experimental Film Workshop in Rio, conducted by German filmmaker Christoph Janetzko, generated ten short films by student filmmakers from the Federal University in Niterói. Heterogeneous in form, the films, all budgeted at under three thousand dollars, try to reconcile the apparently contradictory mandates of compelling storytelling and formal experimentation. While telling stories, they tend to avoid conventional continuity editing. In Suzana Silva's *Primeiro Movimento* ("First Movement"), the violence suffered by Rio's street children is filtered through the consciousness of a young middle-class woman in a nightmarelike narrative. A beautifully composed shot of the woman descending a hill (which is actually her own body treated as an imaginary landscape) offers a stark contrast to the nervous hand-held documentary camera moving around the bodies of the street population. In the same series, *Bahia* ("Bay") is a stenographic "city symphony" film about Rio de Janeiro. The film deploys sound to juxtapose a daily routine of the city (the ferry crossing the Rio bay over to Niterói) with the war in the Persian Gulf (another bay). Using reversible stock, the film presents delicate emulsion scratches on its surface, making the viewer aware of the bidimensionality of the filmic space, despite the contrasting depth of the Rio-Niterói Bridge and the Bay as compositional objects. The image is also flattened through opposing movements of direction which create a contradictory dynamic, contrasting the slow movement of the ferry, on the left, with the rapid speed of the cars on the bridge, to the right. Pablo Lacal's *Gostosa* ("Sexy") offers a study in nude cinematography in a rapid montage of close-up images of fragmented bodies in an imagined beach paradise, where they are momentarily seen as united during sexual intercourse. Body and landscape are fused in a utopian gesture, as highly texturized color moves from the plenitude of the deep blue and shiny sea to the rough texture of golden wet sand brushing against skin. At the same time, the soundtrack's complex fabric of plural voices undermines the unity of the self, calling attention to shifting identities and even gender roles. The male voice-over slyly turns into a female one. The whole film supposedly "represents" a sexual scene, but in fact we might be dealing only with a fantasy or a telephone conversation. Marcello Augusto Teixeira's *Morte por Água* ("Death by Water"), finally, deploys a complex array of quotations and allusions (e.g., Peter Greenaway's *Prospero's Books*, the films of Derek Jarman and Manoel de Oliveira, the poetry of T. S. Eliot). Using "The Wasteland" as its voice-over narrative text, *Morte por Água* creates a dense and allusive atmosphere which catalyzes a plurality of possible interpretations.

Jorge Furtado's *Isle of Flowers* (1989) vividly exemplifies the spirit of social and formal renovation within the short film, bringing the 1960s' "garbage aesthetic" into the postmodern era. Described by its author as a "letter to a Martian who knows nothing of the earth and its social systems," Furtado's fifteen-minute short uses Monty Python–style animation, archival footage, and parodic-reflexive documentary techniques to indict the distribution of wealth and food around the world. The "isle of flowers" of the title is a Brazilian garbage dump where famished women and children are gathered in groups of ten and are given five minutes to scrounge for food. But before we get to the garbage dump, we are given the itinerary of a tomato from farm to supermarket to bourgeois kitchen to garbage can to the "Isle of Flowers." At the same time, Furtado's collage is structured as a social lexicon or glossary: "Human beings are biped animals with highly developed telencephalon and opposable thumbs," whereas pigs "do not even have a thumb." And the definitions are interconnected. In order to follow the trajectory of the tomato, we need to know the origin of money: "Money was created in the seventh century before Christ. Christ was a Jew, and Jews are human beings." We then move swiftly to the Holocaust, where Jews, garbagelike, are thrown into death camp piles. Throughout, the film moves back and forth between minimalist definitions of the human — those bipeds with telencephalon and opposable thumbs — to the ideal of freedom evoked by the film's final citation from Cecília Meireles's *Romanceiro da Inconfidência:* "Freedom is a word the human dream feeds on, that no one can explain or fail to understand."

But this summary gives little sense of the experience of the film, of its play with documentary forms and expectations. First, the film's visuals — old TV commercials, newspaper advertisements, health care manuals — themselves constitute a kind of visual garbage. Second, the film, whose preamble states that "this is not a fiction film," mocks the positivist mania for factual detail by offering useless precision: "We are

Jorge Furtado's *Isle of Flowers* (1989)

450

in Belém Novo, city of Porto Alegre, state of Rio Grande do Sul. More precisely, at thirty degrees, twelve minutes and thirty seconds latitude south, and fifty-one degrees eleven minutes and twenty-three seconds longitude west." The film also parodies the conventions of the educational film, with its authoritative voice-over and quizlike questions ("What is a history quiz?"). Humor becomes a kind of trap; the spectator who begins by laughing ends up, if not crying, at least reflecting very seriously. Opposable thumbs and highly developed telencephalon, we are told, have given "human beings the possibility of making many improvements in their planet"; a shot of a nuclear explosion serves as illustration. Furtado invokes the old carnival motif of pigs and sausage, but with a political twist; here the pigs, given inequitable distribution down the food chain, eat better than people. We are given a social examination of garbage; the truth of a society is in its detritus. Rather than having the margins invade the center as in carnival, here the center creates the margins, or better, there are no margins; the urban bourgeois family is linked to the rural poor via the sausage and the tomato within a web of global relationality.[32]

The title of another Brazilian "garbage" video, Eduardo Coutinho's documentary *Boca de Lixo* ("The Scavengers," 1992), is triply allusive: literally, "mouth of garbage," the phrase also evokes "red-light district" and "garbage cinema." The film centers on poor Brazilians who live and survive thanks to a garbage dump outside of Rio. Here too garbage defines and illuminates the world; the garbage can, to paraphrase Trotsky, is history. Along with rotten food and discarded consumer products, we find a classroom globe, reminding us of the globe-logo which opens *Isle of Flowers*. But rather than take a miserabilist approach, Coutinho shows us people who are inventive, ironic, and critical, who tell the director what not to film and what interpretative mistakes to

Eduardo Coutinho's *The Scavengers* **(1992)**

Eduardo Coutinho's *The Scavengers* (1992)

avoid. Rather than outcasts or pathetic people, the film's subjects exist on a continuum with Brazilian workers in general. In fact, they encapsulate the country as a whole; they have held other jobs, they have worked in other cities. While for Coutinho the stealing of others' images for sensationalist purposes is the "original sin" of the documentary and TV-reportage genres,[33] the garbage-dwellers repeatedly insist that "Here nobody steals," as if responding to the accusations of imaginary middle-class interlocutors. Instead of the suspect pleasures of a condescending "sympathy," the middle-class spectator is obliged to confront vibrant people who dare to dream and to talk back.

Another short documentary, Francisco César Filho's *Rota ABC* (1991) explores the lives of people living in the industrial periphery of São Paulo. The film begins with a citation of Luis Sérgio Person's *São Paulo S.A.* (1965), a classic film about industrialization, and specifically the automobile industry. *Rota ABC* contrasts the optimistic pronouncements of characters in the earlier film with a description of the mentality and style of life of young people, many of them with little hope for jobs, now living in the same area. The film features hip-hop groups like the "Garotos Podres" (The Rotten Boys) and the "Mulheres Negras" (Black Women) who articulate critique and disillusionment. One song, "Suburban Worker," goes as follows: "I was born in a working-class suburb / in an underdeveloped country / just to be part of the mass / of a bankrupt society / without hope / for a better life / since the parasites / are sucking our blood." (The director had already explored the social role of music, specifically of rap and punk music, in *Hip Hop São Paulo*, 1990.) Another hip-hop short, Tatá Amaral's *Viver a Vida* ("Just Livin'," 1992), offers a Brazilian reaccentuation of American popular culture. The film chronicles the life of young black, office boy during a day in São Paulo. Proud of his new sneakers, he moves from overcrowded

Rota ABC (1991)

buses to long lines in banks and has encounters with nonworking phones and other urban frustrations, all presented as if in illustration of the lyrics of a rap song. In the end his sneakers are stolen, while a coda has him dancing in front of a graffiti-covered wall reminiscent of the opening and closing shots of Spike Lee's *Do the Right Thing*.

Other short videos display a bracing irreverence and humor. Sérgio Goldemberg's *Sem Camisinha Não Dá* ("No Rubber, No Way," 1992) deploys a kind of rap-video aesthetic in a public-service video, about AIDS, made for street kids and using the language of street kids. Unlike much official AIDS-related media, the video is radically prosexual and uses direct humor and plain talk instead of moralism and grandiloquence to combat prejudices and ignorance. Carlos Nader's *Beijoqueiro* (wittily translated into English as "Portrait of a Serial Kisser," 1992), meanwhile, paints an ironically sympathetic portrait of a real-life character at once endearing and frightening, João Alves de Mora, known as "the kisser," a man whose passionate avocation is to kiss the famous and the infamous alike. His self-confessed anthropophagic desire is to "devour a piece of his idols." With a crowded schedule of celebrities on his hit list, the kisser spends all his energies plotting how to get past police and security people to plant aggressive kisses on the likes of Frank Sinatra, the Pope, and George Bush. The filmmaker becomes his accomplice as the kisser begins to plan his "attacks" with camera angles in mind. The film ends with an extraordinary sequence in which an entire soccer stadium hails the kisser in rhythmic chants.

The "Artificial Paradises" Production Company in São Paulo, meanwhile, has specialized in mean, aggressive, discomfiting films. Paulo Sacramento's *Ave* ("The Bird," 1993) revolves around a weird encounter in an attic, where a young man injects himself with chicken blood and then becomes possessed by the chicken's spirit. The film plays on diverse cultural anxieties — phobias about hypodermic needles, the fear of AIDS-contaminated blood transfusions, the transmutations brought about by "trance" religions, and so forth. In another film from the same company, Deborah Waldman's *Noite Final* ("Final Night," 1993), a young woman on the verge of committing suicide goes to the movies, where she fantasizes about massacring the audience. She then drives to meet a young man, whom she runs over. The film ends with files of cars moving menacingly toward the spectator. Such films reflect a kind of *Reservoir Dogs* sensibility — violent, cynical, and self-referential — translating the pessimism of a young generation fatigued by perpetual economic crisis and repeated political defeats.

The existence of low-cost video recorders, along with computer graphics and technologies, has to some extent democratized audiovisual production, generating the works of video-makers such as Luis Carlos Lacerda (*Trilhos Urbanos*), Artur Matuck (*Maurício Prisioneiro*), Nelson Motta (*Compacto Noites Cariocas*), Aurélio Michiles (*Via Lactea Dialética*), Daisy Schmidt (*TV-Arte Tecnologia*), Roberto Sandoval (*Aleatório*), Sandra Kogut (*Parabolic People*), Eder Santos (*Uakti*), Ricardo Neuenberg (*Stress Beat*), Nelson Villas Boas a.k.a. "Big" (*Malditas Calmarias*), Regina Váter (*Sobrevídeo*), Rita Moreira (*Walking Around, She Has a Beard*), Walter Salles Jr. (*Outras Palavras*), and many others. The new computer and video technologies also facilitate a break with orthodox cinematic aesthetics. Rather than the 1960s "aesthetic of hunger," video-makers can now deploy a kind of cybernetic minimalism, achieving maximum beauty and effect for minimum expense. Video switchers allow the screen to be split, divided horizontally or vertically, with wipes and inserts. Keys, chroma-keys, mattes and fader bars, along with computer

Hip Hop São Paulo (1990)

graphics, multiply audiovisual possibilities for fracture, rupture, polyphony. An electronic "quilting" can weave together sounds and images in ways that break with linear character-centered narrative. The conventional decorum of dominant cinema (eyeline matches, the 30° rule, cutaway shots) can be superseded by proliferating polysemy. The capacity for palimpsestic overlays of images and sounds facilitated by electronics and cybernetics opens the doors to a renovated, multichannel, and polyphonic aesthetic. The electronic image, some critics argue, is more susceptible to reflexivity; it reveals itself as a mediated production rather than as certified fact. Video can "de-realize" the visible world. With video, postproduction becomes as important as the shoot — indeed, often there is no shoot. Thus the electronic media are less canonical and "normative," less constructed by hidebound institutional and aesthetic traditions.[34] With electronic media, it is possible to mix technologies, to mingle the photographic with the electronic, as filmmakers like Júlio Bressane, Arthur Omar, and Andrea Tonacci habitually do, making possible what Arlindo Machado calls the "hybridization of alternatives." Within "cinevídeo," filmic material is reworked in video postproduction.[35] While the costs of film production have kept going up, furthermore, the cost of video equipment keeps going down. And given the elaborate electronic resources available for postproduction, all sorts of experiments become possible.

Film and Social Movements

Since the authoritarian regime in Brazil severely constricted the official space for social activism, the 1970s and 1980s witnessed a veritable explosion of new social movements in the alternative public sphere: human rights groups, militant labor unions, "Church Base Communities" (popular church-based organizations), squatter associations, environmental organizations, Indian groups, and so on. At the same time, the countercultural attitudes of the 1960s become socialized and disseminated despite the political eclipse of the left. Speaking of Latin America generally, Jorge Castañeda sums up the process:

Changes in life-styles, customs, forms of political engagement, and attitudes toward the "other," and a major upheaval of cultural mores and production, took place across the continent. The young attempted to incorporate political opinions into their everyday life; the cultural realm became politicized and transformed by the alterations around it. In literature, the arts, the theatre and music, in sexuality and dress codes, through growing up and giving birth, the urban, intellectualized middle classes were undergoing a major transformation. In highly conservative societies, this represented a monumental shakeup.[36]

455

To the extent to which larger social movements grow in strength, the production of film and video documentaries echoes, mediates, and even advances this process. The 1980s and 1990s bring, as a consequence, a strong harvest of pro-indigenous, black-liberationist, ecological, gay and lesbian, leftist and feminist films and videos (the categories are obviously not mutually exclusive). To mention just a small sample, Júlio Azcarate's *O Povo de Veneno* ("The Poison People," 1991), reveals the genocide of the Zuruaha Indians due to their contact with white invaders at the end of the last century. Lise Torok and Helena de Rocha's *Pantanal: Vida ou Morte* ("Pantanal: Dead or Alive," 1984) and *Pantanal: Equilíbrio Ameaçado* ("Pantanal: The Balance Threatened," 1886) deal with the ecological threat to the Pantanal region in Mato Grosso. Eduardo Coutinho's *The Debt Game: Who Owes Who?* (1991) documents the role of international agencies in creating the "debt trap" that impoverishes Brazil. Rita Moreira's *A Dama de Pacaembu* ("The Lady from Pacaembu," 1983) treats a related subject, this time from below, in its eloquent portrayal of a homeless woman, daft but weirdly lucid, who claims to have been married to one of the Rockefellers.

The question of racism and black consciousness, meanwhile, apart from emerging into the "light" of prestige productions like *Quilombo* and *Chico Rei,* and after being touched on by black filmmakers like Antônio Pitanga and Waldyr Onofre in their 1970s features, is also treated in the films of Zózimo Bulbul (*Dia de Alforria,* "Day of Liberation," 1981; and *Abolição,* 1988), Juana Elbein dos Santos (*Arte Sacra Negra I: Orixá Ninu Ilé,* 1978; and *Arte Negra Sacra II: Metamorfose das Mães Nagô,* "Metamorphosis of Nagô Priestesses," 1979), Roberto Moura (*Sai Dessa, Exu,* "Cut It Out, Exu," 1973), Raquel Gerber (*Ylé Xoroque,* 1981), and Carlos Blajsblat (*Egungun,* 1981). Silvana Afram's

A Kiss on the Mouth (1987)

Mulheres Negras ("Black Women of Brazil," 1986) discusses the multiple oppressions suffered by Afro-Brazilian women, emphasizing Afro-Brazilian religion as a place of spiritual refuge and solidarity among women. Eunice Guttman's *Benedita da Silva* (1991) profiles the first black woman, in this case from the *favelas,* to be elected a member of the Brazilian parliament (and almost elected Mayor of Rio de Janeiro).

The women's movement in Brazil has been intimately linked to these other social movements, as feminist groups formed to combine consciousness-raising with political activism.[37] In the cinema, a feminist perspective had already marked such features as Tizuka Yamasaki's *Patriamada* and *Paraíba Mulher Macho* (1984), the story of Anayde Beiriz, feminist poet and bohemian from the 1930s; Norma Benguel's *Eternamente Pagu* ("Eternally Pagu," 1987), the life story of the modernist "muse" Patrícia Galvão; and Teresa Trautman's *Sonho de Menina Moça* ("Dream of a Young Girl," 1987). The same feminist and social activist spirit animates scores of documentaries, notably: Inês Castilho's *Mulheres da Boca* ("Woman from the Red-Light District," 1981), a sympathetic study of the sex workers from the Boca de Lixo, and *Hystérias* (1983), a feminist analysis of the whole question of hysteria, as here expressed in the possession dance of Juliana Carneiro da Cunha. Marilha de Andrade and Eliana Bandeira's *É Menino ou Menina?* ("Is It a Boy or a Girl?" 1978) denounces the gender stereotypes that imprison girls especially, while *A Terceira Idade* ("The Third Age," 1982), not unlike Yvonne Rainer's *Privilege,* offers a feminist analysis of menopause. One of the more prolific makers of feminist shorts is Eunice Guttman. Her *Só no Carnaval* ("Only During Carnival," 1982) analyses the Carioca phenomenon of carnival cross-dressing. *Vida de Mãe é Assim Mesmo* ("That's How a Mother's Life Always Is," 1983) exposes the "double day" lived by low-income women who work outside and have nowhere to leave their children. Lúcia Murat's *Que Bom te Ver Vivo* ("How Nice to See You Alive!" 1989), offers a hybrid fiction-documentary rendering of the experiences of women prisoners under the dictatorship, while the Lilith Video Collective's *Beijo na Boca* ("A Kiss on the Mouth," 1987) gives a sympathetic portrayal of prostitution in São Paulo.

Gay and lesbian issues, already treated in feature films such as Bruno Barreto's *Beijo no Asfalto* ("Kiss on the Asphalt," 1985), Sérgio Amon's *Aqueles Dois* ("Those Two," 1985), Sérgio Toledo's *Vera* (1987), and Sérgio Bianchi's *Romance* (1988), have also been examined in short films and videos. Tânia Cipriani's *Que Viva Eu* ("Long Live Myself," 1988), portrays a Brazilian artist in Lisbon dying, with tremendous flair, of AIDS. *No Mirror* (1991), features gay artist Hunter Reynolds in his drag character Patins du Prey. Karim Ainouz's *Seams* (1993) constitutes an experimental gay memoir, while Rita Moreira's *Temporada de Caça* ("Hunting Season," 1989), examines the assassination of gays in Brazil. Flávia Moraes's short *O Brinco* ("The Earring," 1989) subverts spectatorial assumptions that romance is always heterosexual. Flavio

How Nice to See You Alive! (1989)

Ribeiro's *Nature Knows No Shame* (1990) uses fiction/documentary/auto-biography to analyze the discourses around male homosexuality, while his *Fuck the Pope* (1994) lampoons a religious leader who prefers a "dead Catholic to a used condom." Tânia Cipriani, finally, is making a film about AIDS in the *candomblé* community.

In this same activist and experimental vein, it is important to mention the work of independent TV producers like Olhar Eletrônico in São Paulo (for example, the tongue-in-cheek news reports in the 1980s of Ernesto Varela) and TV Viva and SOS Corpo (a women's health group that makes videos about feminist and human rights issues) in Recife. TV Viva's *Axé de Fala* ("Talking Strong Vibes"), for example, features the African-Brazilian music of Waldir Afonja, while *Alafim Oyo* (1989) shows the *afoxé* Alafim Oyo in the streets of Olinda during carnival. *A Sangue Frio* ("In Cold Blood," 1992) documents the life of street kids in Brazil. SOS Corpo productions, meanwhile, has produced videos such as *O Que Faço com Esse Tesão* ("What Do I Do with This Sexual Desire?" 1985), *Diafragma* ("Diaphragm," 1986), *Camisinha* ("Rubber," 1986), *Planejamento Familiar* ("Family Planning," 1986), and *Sexo na Classe* ("Sex in the Classroom," 1986). The election of a Worker's Party mayor and administration in São Paulo in 1989 also led to the founding of TV Anhembi, whose aim it was to empower community politics through alternative television. The group's primary production project was a series of closed-circuit, site-specific live video events entitled "Talk São Paulo." One episode, entitled "Women of São Paulo" (produced by TV Anhembi and featuring popular *telenovela* star Acora Raimundo), begins with a vignette that plays out a gender reversal whereby the woman protagonist complains that her husband has been very slow in

Vera (1987)

preparing her coffee and ironing her clothes. In a documentary on the episode, this vignette is then projected on the video wall of Anhembi's mobile projection unit, where passersby react to the vignette, leading to a full-scale debate about the sexual politics of domestic relationships, punctuated by clips from other videos on topics of gender or racial oppression.[38]

Indigenous Media

The most remarkable recent development has been the emergence of "indigenous media" (i.e., the use of audiovisual technology such as camcorders and VCRs) for the cultural and political purposes of the indigenous peoples of Brazil. The phrase itself, as Faye Ginsburg points out, is oxymoronic, evoking both the self-understanding of aboriginal groups and the vast institutional structures of TV and cinema.[39] Within "indigenous media," the producers are themselves the receivers, along with neighboring communities and, occasionally, distant cultural institutions or festivals such as the Native American film festivals held in New York and San Francisco. Indigenous media is an empowering vehicle for communities struggling against geographical displacement, ecological and economic deterioration, and cultural annihilation.[40] Indigenous film and video-makers confront what Ginsburg calls a "Faustian dilemma": on the one hand, they use new technologies for cultural

459

self-assertion; on the other, they spread a technology that might ultimately only foster their own disintegration. The leading analysts of indigenous media, such as Ginsburg and Terence Turner, see such work not as locked into a bound traditional world but rather as concerned with "mediating across boundaries, mediating ruptures of time and history," and advancing the process of identity construction by negotiating "powerful relationships to land, myth, and ritual."[41] At times, the work goes beyond merely asserting an existing identity to become "a means of cultural invention that refracts and recombines elements from both the dominant and minority societies."[42] Indigenous media thus bypass the usual anthropological hierarchy between scientist/anthropologist/filmmaker, on the one hand, and object of study and spectacle on the other. At the same time, "indigenous media" should not be seen as a magical panacea for the concrete problems faced by indigenous peoples or for the aporias of anthropology. Such work can provoke factional divisions within indigenous communities and can be appropriated by international media as facile symbols of the ironies of the postmodern age (see note 43).

In São Paulo, the *Centro de Trabalho Indigenista* (Center for Work with Indigenous Peoples) has been working in collaboration with indigenous groups since 1979, teaching video-making and editing, and offering technologies and facilities in order to protect indigenous land and consolidate resistance. While "indigenous media" is meant largely for the Indian peoples themselves, non-Indians also make films about their collaboration with indigenous people. *Taking Aim* (1993), by Mônica Frota, documents the director's work with the Kayapo to develop the project *Mekaron Opoi Djoi* ("Those Who Create Images"), drawing on archival footage, stills, and computer animation to create an ironic documentary that juxtaposes pro-Indian perspectives with grandiloquent government documentaries about the Amazon.[43] In Vincent Carelli and Dominique Gallois's *The Spirit of TV* (1990), the members of the Waiapi tribe, newly introduced to TV, reflect on ways that video can be used to make contact with other tribes and defend themselves against the encroachments of federal agents, goldminers, and loggers. "It's good to know other people thanks to TV," they say upon seeing the first images. "While we never had images of our parents," they add, "now young people can see the old who have died." Taking an eminently pragmatic approach, the Waiapi ask the filmmakers to hide the tribe's weakness to the outside world: "Exaggerate our strength," they say, "so they won't occupy our land." In a playfully ironic reference to the myth of the cannibal savage, the Waiapi say: "Show them that when we get drunk we tear off the arms of white people and eat them — very delicious!"

In *Arco de Zo'e* ("Meeting Ancestors," 1993), Chief Wai-Wai recounts his visit to the Zo'e, a recently contacted group whom the Waiapi had known only through video images. The two groups compare hunting and weaving techniques, food, religious rituals, body decorations,

The Spirit of TV (1990)

myths, and history: "They have the same language, the same skin, but their lips are different." The film communicates the diversity of indigenous cultures; for example,. Chief Wai-Wai has difficulty adjusting to the nudity of his hosts. *Like Brothers* (1993), finally, recounts the cultural exchange between the Parakateje of Para and their relatives the Kraho of Tocantins. The two groups exchange information and strategies for maintaining their language and identity and for resisting Euro-Brazilian domination. In all the films, the "outside" spectator is no longer the privileged interlocutor; video is primarily a facilitator for exchange between indigenous groups. On a secondary level, "outsiders" are welcome to view these exchanges and even support the cause

Meeting Ancestors (1993)

in financial or other ways, but there is no romantic narrative of redemption whereby the raising of spectatorial consciousness will somehow "save the world." In these videos the non-Indian spectator must become accustomed to "Indians" who laugh, who are ironical, and who are quite prepared to speak of the absolute necessity of killing non-Indian invaders.

Among the most media-savvy of the indigenous groups are the Kayapo, a Go-speaking people of central Brazil who live in fourteen communities scattered over an area roughly the size of Great Britain. When a documentary crew from Granada Television went to Brazil to film the Kayapo in 1987, the Kayapo demanded video cameras, a VCR, a monitor, and videotapes as the quid pro quo for their cooperation. They have subsequently used video to record their own traditional ceremonies, demonstrations, and encounters with whites (so as to have the equivalent of a legal transcript). They have documented their traditional knowledge of the forest environment and plan to record the transmission of myths and oral history. For the Kayapo, as Turner puts it, video media have become "not merely a means of representing culture . . . but themselves the ends of social action and objectification in consciousness."[44] The Kayapo not only sent a delegation to the Brazilian Constitutional Convention to lobby delegates debating indigenous rights but also videotaped themselves in the process, winning international attention for their cause. Widely disseminated images of the Kayapo wielding video cameras, appearing in *Time* and the *New York Times Magazine,* derive their power to shock from the premise that "natives" must be quaint and allochronic, as if existing in another time — "real" Indians don't carry camcorders.

Meeting Ancestors (1993)

In the Granada Television documentary *Kayapo: Out of the Forest* (1989), the Kayapo and other native peoples stage a mass ritual performance to protest the planned construction of a hydroelectric dam. One of the leaders, Chief Pombo, points out that the dam's name (Kararao) is taken from a Kayapo war-cry. Another, Chief Raoni, appears with the rock star Sting in a successful attempt to capture international media attention. At one point, a woman presses a machete against the company spokesman's face as she scolds him in Kayapo. Another woman, in a remarkable reversal of colonialist *écriture*, tells the spokesman to write down her name, reminding him that she is one of those who will die because of the dam. The spectator enamored of "modernity" comes to question the reflex association of hydroelectric dams with an axiomatically good "progress."

The National Revisited

The profusion of films and videos relating to issues of race, ethnicity, gender, and sexuality give expression to the progressive side of a "postmodern" moment when the old nationalist and Third World-ist discourse no longer reigns in the same way. But if these films translate a progressive, activist impulse, they also go against the grain of another discourse. In the middle of the deep economic crisis of the early 1990s, we now encounter, in some quarters, a fatigue with the very idea of the national, a disenchantment with the nationalist project (or at least with

463

the hope that it could be realized) along with a loss of faith in its relevance for the cultural debate. In the wake of the collapse of Communism and the worldwide self-questioning of the left, nationalist discourse has lost much of its charismatic power and political persuasiveness. To many, and especially to a denationalized elite, it has come to seem "empty," lacking in historical substance and cultural specificity. Here Brazil accompanies and is inflected by a more general disenchantment, in the "peripheral" countries, with the old liberationist discourse, as well as by novel political and philosophical currents in the "metropolitan" countries. Simultaneous with national disenchantment, an ahistorical "postmodern" internationalist discourse has emerged, a discourse which argues that the category of nation has become obsolescent. Within the global village of transnational capitalism, a certain postmodernism argues, all cultures are caught up in the meaningless whirl of mass-mediated simulacra and the consequent standardization of human existences. In many cases, we find a retreat from collective projects in favor of absorption into an atomized society broken up into an infinity of self-seeking monads. Current neoliberal orthodoxies, meanwhile, reject the national in the name of "globalization" and "competitiveness." The old metanarrative of inevitable progressive change leading to an ever more egalitarian society now gives way to the "new" metanarrative of the "end of history" and the inevitable movement of all societies toward Western-style formal democracy in politics and the benevolent reign of the market in economics. (What is forgotten in this new metanarrative is the fact that free-market radicalism will necessarily exacerbate the already glaring inequities of Brazilian society.) At the same time, an altered philosophical conjuncture, and specifically the poststructuralist attack on the "centered subject," also subtly undermines the idea of the national. While on one level seeming to promise a reformulation of old hierarchies, on another poststructuralism casts doubt, by extension, on the nation as the noble protagonist of a collective epic, as a transindividual cogito or Sartrean "self-writ-large." The deconstructive assault on the "originary," meanwhile, also calls into question the idea of an "originary" nation. The old utopia of "authentic" national culture, under all these onslaughts, comes to seem a hopelessly nostalgic chimera.

But theory is lived differently depending on whether one is "centered" in Paris or São Paulo, and political struggle has not come to an end just because a few theorists have declared the "end of history." The Brazilian internationalists, those whom we might call the "antinationalist internationalists," do not by their mere wish magically cease living a national situation they would desperately like to transcend; the pathos of their internationalism derives precisely from their status as cultural consumers on the periphery. A conscious option for internationalism does not short-circuit the mechanisms that effectively disappropriate peoples of their culture or nations of their power. If postmodernism has spread the feel of First World consumerist culture around the globe, it has hardly deconstructed the relations of power between the metropolitan and the marginalized countries. Those nostalgic for the glory days of Third World nationalism, on the other hand, cannot through an act of will of the nation-subject annihilate an internationalism built into a society inevitably molded by the planetary spread of Euro-American culture, the international media, and transnational capitalism. But the question of the national will not simply disappear, even if it comes to be formulated with more modesty and nuance. But since Latin-American nation-building, as Jorge Castañeda points out, is incomplete, and since the cause of social change is inseparable from redeeming the nation for "the people," the left has no choice but to remain nationalistic.[45]

Throughout this century, Brazil has received, translated, and critically revised any number of First World intellectual and artistic movements, reformulating the dominant culture so as to subtly undermine its claims to universal authority. One finds the zenith of such creative-critical reformulations in Brazilian popular music, in the ways that composer-singers like Caetano Veloso or Gilberto Gil anthropophagically absorb all of the world's musics — soul, rock, reggae, pop, calypso, and so on — in order, paradoxically, to crystallize their evolving and open-ended conception of "Brazilianness." In such cases, we find a progressive matching between the international movements and the vital necessities of the national culture, a "matching" in which Brazilian cinema has so far been less successful. The various international "post" trends have yet to find a liberatory "translation" in Brazil. Certain forms of internationalism, in this sense, can become a cover for hegemony, and the postmodern rejection of the national a figleaf masking an ongoing process of peripheralization.

Looking to the Future

We may end on a note of cautious optimism. After the impeachment of Collor and the election of Fernando Henrique Cardoso, we find a few promising signs. In 1993 the new government of Itamar Franco freed up $40 million for national film production, not as a charitable gesture but rather as a fulfillment of the government's legal obligation to hand over the money collected in the previous four years owing to a small levy on tickets sold — money destined for the development of Brazilian cinema. At this writing, in 1995, we find a substantial resumption of feature production because of the return of some federal financing, the framing of a nationalist "Audiovisual Law," and the sponsorship of film production by a number of states, municipalities, and banks (e.g., Banco Nacional, Banespa). We also find the emergence of high-tech video production companies such as Marcello Dantas's

Magnetoscopio in Rio, and municipal collectives like RioFilme. The recent (1994–95) improvements in the economy generated by the "plano real" — the reduction in inflation, the stabilization of the currency, the return of capital to Brazil — will also, hopefully, improve the situation of the cinema.

A number of recent feature films, interestingly, have addressed the situation of cinema itself. Suzana Moraes's *Mil e Uma* ("A Thousand and One," 1993) — the title alludes both to *Arabian Nights* and to Fellini — focuses on a filmmaker's desperate attempts to complete a film. Mauro Farias's *Não Quero Falar Sobre Isso Agora* ("I Don't Want to Talk About That Now," 1991) also reflexively evokes the crisis in Brazilian cinema. The story revolves around a young Carioca, Daniel O'Neill (Evandro Mesquita), who tries to survive as a screenwriter, but whose scripts are rejected and who therefore tries his hand at other arts such as pop music and photography, only to become, ultimately, a drug dealer. The protagonist's trajectory, as José Geraldo Couto points out, parallels that of many talented Brazilian filmmakers (e.g., Arnaldo Jabor) forced to abandon (if only temporarily) their profession. But in O'Neill's case the author himself is more convinced of his talent than other people are. While he protests his fate as "misunderstood genius," the spectator sees little more than charm combined with a certain self-centeredness and irresponsibility.

Carlos Reichenbach's *Alma Corsário* (1993), for its part, also speaks of the friendships of artists. The film traces the lives of two friends from their adolescence in the 1950s through the political agitation (and drug experimentation) of the 1960s and continues into the 1990s when the two old friends are celebrating the publication of *Continente Ocidental* (Occidental Continent), a book of their poetry. Everything is told in flashbacks with constant returns to the celebration in the present. Sprinkled with references to other films such as Truffaut's *400 Blows* and Godard's *La Chinoise*, the film's emphasis throughout is on the ultimate coherence and authenticity of the poet-protagonist who is always marginalized but who never relinquishes his left-anarchist vision. In one sequence, the protagonist takes off a series of politicized T-shirts; the last reads: "Anarchism." (The title of André Klotzel's *Capitalismo Selvagem* ["Savage Capitalism," 1993] also evokes a return to politics.) More specifically, the film returns to the issues raised both by *Macunaíma* and by *Avaeté*, in that the film's protagonist, played by José Mayer, is an Indian who is brought to the city as a child, the survivor of a massacre perpetrated by the owners of a mine in the Amazon region. (The protagonist's name — Hugo Victor de Assis — with its play on Victor Hugo and Assis de Chateaubriand — evokes the romantic movement and its primitivist idealizations.) In the present, the protagonist appears as the rich heir of the company. Unaware of his ancestry, he orders the destruction of a tribe in order to exploit the tribe's land. In this sense, he would seem to embody the proposition advanced by Paulo Emílio Salles Gomes — that Brazilians are both "occupier" and

Paulo Betti in *Lamarca* (1994)

"occupied."[46] A love affair with the journalist Elisa Medeiros (Fernanda Torres), who interviews him, leads to the discovery of his identity as a "savage." Although he oscillates, he ultimately rejects the journalist who, in the middle of the jungle, acts exactly like *Macunaíma*'s "Uiara," the water-sprite who devours the protagonist who lovingly swims after her. In fact, the very scene from *Macunaíma* in which Uiara devours the hero is cited by the Klotzel film.

Carlos Diegues's *Veja Esta Canção* ("Rio's Love Songs," 1994), meanwhile, features well-known players like Fernando Montenegro and Débora Bloch in four different stories, each inspired by the lyrics of popular songs by Gilberto Gil, Chico Buarque, Caetano Veloso, and Jorge Benjor. Rogério Sganzerla's *Tudo é Brasil* (1995) returns to the director's obsessive theme — Orson Welles in Brazil — this time using archival material from the Department of Press and Propaganda to denounce the role of the Brazilian government in the Welles debacle. Carla Camurati's low-budget costume drama *Carlota Joaquina, Princesa do Brasil* (1995), a portrait of the period when the Portuguese Court moved to Rio de Janeiro, has been very successful at the box office. Among the other recently completed works are: Guilherme de Almeida Prado's *Perfume de Gardênia;* Walter Hugo Khoury's intimist drama *Forever* (the title and dialogue are in English); Sérgio Bianchi's *A Causa Secreta* ("The Secret Cause," 1994); André Luiz Oliveira's *Louco por Cinema* ("Crazy for Cinema"); Ugo Giorgetti's *Sábado* ("Saturday"); Helvecio Ratton's *Menino Maloquinho* ("Crazy Kid"); Ricardo Dias's *No Rio das Amazonas* ("On the Amazon"); José Antonio Garcia's *O Corpo* ("The Body"); Pedro Jorge de Castro's *O Calor da Pele* ("Skin Heat"); and Sérgio Rezende's *Lamarca*, the story of a 1960s leftist guerrilla

467

assassinated by the military regime. (Rezende was the director in 1985 of *O Homem da Capa Preta* "[Man in the Black Cape]", one of the rare box-office successes in the 1980s.) Many of these most recent films, interestingly, return to the supposedly obsolete questions of politics and the national. José Joffily's *Quem Matou Pixote* ("Who Killed Pixote?") will investigate the death, at police hands, of the actor who played the title role in the Babenco film. The title of Lui Farias's *Rota 66: A Policia que Mata* ("Route 66: Police Who Kill") already speaks for itself. Tizuka Yamasaki's *Gritos de Amor* ("Love Screams"), finally, will fictionalize the lives of street children. Brazil now also has, like all civilized countries, its own sequels: *Vai Trabalhar Vagabundo II* ("Go to Work, Bum II," directed once again by Hugo Carvana) and *Matou a Família e Foi ao Cinema II* ("Killed the Family and Went to the Movies II"), this time directed not by Júlio Bressane but by Neville d'Almeida.

The short fiction film also maintains its strength in this same period. José Roberto Torero's *Amor* (1994) uses black-and-white still photos to portray the trajectory of a provincial couple, Apollo and Diana, from their first relationship as childhood friends, through adolescent romance, to a nightmarish marriage, professional decline, physical decadence, and ultimately, mutual, reciprocal murder. This central narrative, recounted in voice-over by the ironically intimist voice of actor Paulo José, is counterpointed by other didactic vignettes, narrated by the famously cynical voice of actor Paulo César Pereio. These vignettes present a conjugal combinatory of weirdoes as carnivalesque echoes of the core story of the film.

Jorge Furtado's *Matadeira* ("The Machine Gun," 1994) returns to the scene of Canudos, site of the governmental massacre, at the end of the nineteenth century, of millenary rebels led by Antônio Conselheiro, an historical episode memorialized by Euclides da Cunha's *Rebellion in the Backlands* (and by Vargas Lhosa's *War of the End of the World*), and invoked in many Brazilian films (notably, *Black God, White Devil, The Guns*, and *Antônio das Mortes*). Furtado tells the story of this battle in an unconventional way, combining the orchestrated movements of children's dolls with a sophisticated narration about the British selling arms to Brazil to facilitate the massacre of poor Northeasterners left unemployed due precisely to Britain's "hostile takeover" of the Brazilian textile industry. With its collage structure and its constant shifting of modes of narration, using animation, miniatures, period photographs, staged episodes, and docu-data, *A Matadeira* extends and amplifies the stylistic research deployed in Furtado's earlier *Isle of Flowers*. Laís Bodanski's *Cartão Vermelho* ("Red Card," 1994) treats the subject of the sexuality of children. The film's protagonist, the only girl on a soccer team, dreams of becoming a female Pelé. She kicks the ball with unfailing accuracy, but instead of aiming at the goal she aims at the other players' scrotums. The boys become angry with her, force her up against the wall, and strip her in order to see what she has between her legs. Shifting into didactic mode, the film has one of the boys design a vagina on a wall and explain its functions, after which they all return to the game. Bruno Viana's black-and-white short *Geraldo Voador* ("Geraldo the Flyer," 1994) offers a filmic x-ray of the social situation of Brazil. The film's protagonist, a street child in Rio's *favelas*, dreams of flying, but he has to survive by selling drugs. Ultimately, he is killed by the leader of a rival drug gang; he flies toward his death, while a vulture flies over him.

Finally, Helena Solberg (with David Mayer) is completing her feature-length tribute to Carmen Miranda — *Bananas Is My Business*, mixing archival material with staged scenes in which a transvestite enacts the Carmen Miranda role. We also find surprising collaborations in the realm of television, specifically the collaboration between *chanchada* veteran Carlos Manga and video-generation filmmaker Jorge Furtado on a prestigious miniseries (*Maria Moura*) based on a socially conscious novel by Rachel de Queiroz. Television has now largely taken over the role of adapting Brazilian literary classics. Jorge Amado, Graciliano Ramos, Érico Veríssimo, Guimarães Rosa, Machado de Assis, Lima Barreto, Rubem Fonseca, and Dias Gomes are among those whose work has passed through the electronic adaptation machine. Among the literary adaptations now under way in the cinema are Paulo Thiago's version of Lima Barreto's *Triste Fim do Policarpo Quaresma* ("The Sad End of Policarpo Quaresma"), Walter Lima Jr.'s version of *Memórias de um Sargento de Milícias*, Bruno Barreto's version of Fernando Gabeira's *O Que É Isto, Companheiro* ("What's This, Comrade!"), Suzana Amaral's version of Rubem Fonseca's *Caso Morel* ("The Morel Case"), Guilherme de Almeida Prado's version of Júlio Cortázar's *A Hora Mágica* ("The Magic Hour"), Norma Benguel's version of *O Guarani*, Carlos Diegues's version of Jorge Amado's *Tieta do Agreste* (with Sonia Braga in the title role), Leilany Fernandes Leites's version of Rachel de Queiroz's *Memorial de Maria Moura*, Bruno Barreto's version of *O Que É Isso Companheiro* ("What Kind of Behavior Is This, Comrade?"), Hugo Carvana's version of Fernando Sabino's *O Homen Nu* ("The Naked Man"), and Emiliano Ribeiro's version of Lygia Fagundes Telles's *As Meninas* ("The Girls").

Brazilian cinema, as José Inácio de Melo Souza has pointed out, has suffered many "deaths." It first died after the "bela época (1907–1911)," when foreign distributors came to dominate the market. It died again after the advent of sound (1929–1934), when it seemed that Brazil could not keep up with new sound technologies, and production declined precipitously. It died again with the end of Vera Cruz only to give way to the veritable renaissance called Cinema Novo.[47] If Brazilian cinema will probably never return to the glory days of the 1950s, 1960s, and 1970s, it still will not die. Rather, it will probably maintain a minimal autonomous existence as national feature film and coproduction, while also "disappearing" into the larger universe of the audiovisual — into television, into video, into cable, the short film, music video, and into the work generated by video computer technologies. The most recent pronouncements of the death of Brazilian cinema, one hopes, will come to be seen as decidedly premature.

Notes

1. Parts of this final section are based on an essay which first appeared in *Film Quarterly* 41, no. 3 (Spring 1988) as an article by Robert Stam and Ismail Xavier entitled "Recent Brazilian Cinema: Allegory/Metacinema/Carnival." That essay was subsequently revised and supplemented by materials written by Robert Stam, João Luiz Vieira and Ismail Xavier. Some of the longer discussions of films (*Bye Bye Brasil, Eréndira, They Don't Wear Black Tie,* and *Quilombo*) first appeared as review-essays by Robert Stam in *Cineaste.* We would also like to express our gratitude to *Jump Cut,* where some of the materials in the original book first appeared as part of a special section on Brazilian cinema: *Jump Cut,* nos. 21 (1979) and 22 (1980).

Gary Crowdus, Fabiano Canosa, Richard Peña, Jeff O'Conner, Faye Ginsberg, Alissa Powers, and José Carlos Avellar were especially helpful in locating stills. We would also like to call attention here to the various U.S. distributors and institutions which handle some of the films and videos mentioned here, and who also provided us with stills: Cinema Guild, Cine-World, First Run Features, International Film Circuit, the International Media Resource Exchange, Kino International, Miramax, New Yorker Films, New Line Cinema, Samuel Goldwyn, Video Data Bank, Videoteca del Sur, and Women Make Movies. Video stores in major cities (for example, Kim's in New York City) are also beginning to carry tapes of Brazilian films. The Latin American Curriculum Resource Center at Tulane University also distributes Brazilian videotapes for classroom use.

2. Renato Ortiz, *A Moderna Tradição Brasileira: Cultura Brasileira e Indústria Cultural* (São Paulo: Brasiliense, 1988).

3. Data included in Livia Antola and Everett Rogers, "Television Flows in Latin America," *Communications Research* 2, no. 2 (April 1984); and Tapio Varis, "The International Flow of Television Programs," *Journal of Communication* 34, no. 1 (1984).

4. There is now emerging a significant body of work, in Portuguese and in English, on Brazilian television. See, for example, C. R. Avila Avemdola, *A Teleinvasão: A Participação Estrangeira na Televisão do Brasil* (São Paulo: Cortez, 1982); Sérgio Caparelli, *Televisão e Capitalismo no Brasil* (Porto Alegre: L&PM, 1982); M. E. Bonavita Federico, *História da Comunicação: Rádio e TV no Brasil* (Petrópolis: Vozes, 1982); Randal Johnson, "Deus e o Diabo na Terra do Globo: *Roque Santeiro* and Brazil's 'New Republic'," in *Studies in Latin American Popular Culture* 7 (1988); Maria Rita Kehl, *Reflexão para uma História da TV Globo* (Rio: Funarte, 1982, mimeo); Ortiz, *A Moderna Tradição Brasileira*; Carlos Alberto M. Pereira and Ricardo Miranda, *Televisão* (São Paulo: Brasiliense, 1983); and Joseph Straubhaar, "The Transformation of Cultural Dependence: The Decline of American Influence on the Brazilian Television Industry," Ph.D. diss., Fletcher School of Law and Diplomacy, University of Wisconsin, 1982.

5. See Fredric Jameson, "Third World Literature in the Era of Multinational Capitalism," *Social Text* 15 (Fall 1986).

6. See, for example, Roberto Schwarz, "Cultura e Política 1964–1969," written in 1970 and anthologized in *Pai de Família e Outros Ensaios* (Rio: Paz e Terra, 1977); O. C. Louzado Filho, "O Contexto Tropicalista," in *Aparte,* no. 2 (1968); Gilberto Vasconcelos, *De Olho na Fresta* (Rio: Graal, 1977); Celso Favametto, *Tropicália, Alegoria, Alegria* (São Paulo: Kairós, 1979); and Ismail Xavier, "Alegoria, Modernidade, Nacionalismo," (São Paulo: Editora Funarte, 1985).

7. These concepts are debated in Ismail Xavier, "Allegories of Underdevelopment: From the Aesthetics of Hunger to the Aesthetics of Garbage" (Ph.D. diss., New York University, 1982), available through University Microfilms.

8. See Roberto Schwarz, "Nacional por Subtração," in *Que Horas São* (São Paulo: Companhia das Letras, 1987).

9. See Benedict Anderson, *Imagined Communities: Reflexions on the Origins and Spread of Nationalism* (London: Verso, 1983), and E. J. Hobsbawm and Terence Rogers, eds., *The Invention of Tradition* (Cambridge: Cambridge University Press, 1983).

10. For an overview of cinematic and literary reflexivity, see Robert Stam, *Reflexivity in Film and Literature: From Don Quixote to Jean-Luc Godard* (New York: Columbia University Press, 1992).

11. See João Luiz Vieira, "Hegemony and Resistance: Parody and Carnival in Brazilian Cinema" (Ph.D. diss., New York University, 1984).

12. This material became the basis for a feature-length reconstruction on *It's All True* (1993) by

Richard Wilson, Bill Krohn, Myon Meisel, and Catherine Benamou, and shown at the 1993 New York Film Festival.

13. For more on Welles and *It's All True*, see Robert Stam "Orson Welles, Brazil, and the Power of Blackness," a special issue on Welles from *Persistence of Vision*, no. 7. (1989). We would also like to thank Heloísa de Buarque de Halanda for sharing her documentation on Welles in Brazil.

14. "Carlos Reichenbach: A Conversation," *Framework*, no. 28 (1989).

15. For an overview of Reichenbach's work, see João Luiz Vieira, "Rebel with a Cause: The Films of Carlos Reichenbach, Jr," *Studies in Latin American Popular Culture* 7 (1988).

16. See essay 27, Paulo Emílio Salles Gomes, "Cinema: A Trajectory Within Underdevelopment," in this volume.

17. See João Luiz Vieira, "As Sete Vampiras: Transilvania Follies," *Caderno de Crítica*, no. 2, Rio de Janeiro (November 1986).

18. The path leading from Rui Guerra's *Os Fuzis* ("The Guns," 1964) to *Malandro* exemplifies the trajectory of a number of Cinema Novo from anti-Hollywood aggressivity to a qualified return to the notion of spectatorial pleasure. While *Os Fuzis* features an austere sound track with virtually no diegetic or commentative music, *Malandro* features a lush musical comedy score. While the earlier film was shot verité-style *in loco*, the latter film was shot within stylized studio decors. And while the earlier film showed hostility to the dominant model, *Malandro* reveals a kind of affection for the Hollywood film.

19. Quoted in Luiz F. A. Miranda, *Dicionário de Cineastas Brasileiras* (São Paulo: Arte Editora, 1990), p. 26.

20. On the situation of homeless children in Brazil, see Gilberto Dimerstein, *Brésil: La Guerre des Enfants* (Paris: Fayard, 1991), pp. 25–26.

21. For a more detailed discussion of *Pixote*, see Robert Stam, "Pixote" in *Cineaste* 12, no. 3 (1983).

22. Cinema Novo's elision of the working class was first pointed out by Jean-Claude Bernardet in his *Brasil em Tempo de Cinema* (Rio de Janeiro: Paz e Terra, 1977).

23. For an interview with Leon Hirszman about *Black Tie*, see "Recovering Popular Emotion: An Interview with Leon Hirszman," in *Cineaste* 12, no. 2 (1984).

24. To give just one example of unequal exchange, the Brazilian composers who wrote the songs for *Black Orpheus* (1958), some of the most popular ever written, made almost no money while the French producer, Sacha Gordine, purportedly enriched himself on the royalties (*source:* Ruy Castro, *Chega de Savdade* [São Paulo: Companhia das Letras, 1991]).

25. For a more detailed analysis of *Bye Bye Brasil*, see Randal Johnson, *Cinema Novo x 5* (Austin: University of Texas Press, 1984), pp. 83–90, and Robert Stam, *"Bye Bye Brazil,"* *Cineaste* 11, no. 1 (Winter 1980–81).

26. Carlos Diegues described *Quilombo* as a "kind of science fiction film, in the sense that I was not just interested in recounting what had happened in my country, but in projecting the future." See Carlos Diegues, "Choosing Between Legend and History: An Interview," *Cineaste* 15, no. 1 (1986): 12.

27. See Eugênio Bucci, "Do Filme Brasileiro que Parece Americano (E do Americano que Parece Brasileiro)," *Revista USP*, no.19 (September–October–November 1993). See also Lúcia Nagib, "Nota em Favor de um Filme Internacional," in the same issue.

28. See Jean-Claude Bernardet, "Os Jovens Paulistas," in Ismail Xavier, Jean-Claude Bernardet, and Miguel Pereira, eds., *O Desafio do Cinema* (Rio de Janeiro: Zahar, 1985).

29. See Bucci, "Do Filme Brasileiro que Parece Americano," p. 84. Bucci contrasts the Salles Jr. film with *At PLay in the Fields of the Lord* as a film with American financing but which looks profoundly Brazilian.

30. See Roberto Schwarz, "O Fio da Meada," in *Que Horas São*.

31. For a detailed textual analysis of both *Cabra Marcado para Morrer* and *Patriamada*, see Julianne Burton, "Transitional States: Creative Complicities with the Real in *Cabra Marcado Para Morrer* ('Man Marked to Die: Twenty Years Later') and *Patriamada* ('Sing the Beloved Country')," in *Studies in Latin American Popular Culture* 7 (1988).

32. Jorge Furtado's *Esta não É a sua Vida* ("This Is Not Your Life," 1992) prolongs the director's reflexions on the nature of documentary, posing such questions as: How does the documentarist find a topic? What does it mean to "know" about someone's life? How much has the spectator learned about someone's life by seeing a documentary? How do you film your subject?

33. Coutinho, quoted in *Revista USP*, no. 19 (September–October–November 1993): 148.

34. See Arlindo Machado, "O Diálogo entre Cinema e Vídeo," in *Revista USP*, no. 19 (September–October–November 1993).

35. See Machado, "O Diálogo entre Cinema e Vídeo."

36. Jorge G. Castañeda, *Utopia Unarmed: The Latin American Left After the Cold War* (New York: Random House, 1993), p. 199.

471

37. On feminist movements in Brazil, see Sônia E. Alvarez's *Engendering Democracy in Brazil* (Princeton: Princeton University Press, 1990); Daphne Patai, *Brazilian Women Speak* (New Brunswick, N.J.: Rutgers University Press, 1988); and June E. Hahner, *A Mulher No Brasil* (Rio de Janeiro: Civilização Brasileira, 1976).

38. We are indebted to Brian Goldfarb's unpublished article: "Public Television Culture and Community Media Politics: TV Anhembi, São Paulo, Brazil 1989–1992."

39. See Faye Ginsburg, "Aboriginal Media and the Australian Imaginary," *Public Culture* 5, no. 3 (Spring 1993).

40. Indigenous media have remained largely invisible to the First World public except for occasional festivals (for example, the Native American Film and Video Festivals held regularly in San Francisco and New York City, or the Latin American Film Festival of Indigenous Peoples held in Mexico City and Rio de Janeiro).

41. Faye Ginsburg, "Indigenous Media: Faustian Contract or Global Village?" *Cultural Anthropology* 6, no. 1 (1991): 94.

42. Ginsburg, "Indigenous Media," p. 94.

43. For a critical view of the Kayapo project, see Rachel Moore, "Marketing Alterity," *Visual Anthropology Review* 8, no. 2 (Fall 1992), and James C. Faris, "Anthropological Transparency: Film, Representation, and Politics," in Peter Ian Crawford and David Turton, eds., *Film as Ethnography* (Manchester: Manchester University Press, 1992). For an answer by Turner to Faris, see "Defiant Images: The Kayapo Appropriation of Video" (Forman Lecture, RAI Festival of Film and Video in Manchester 1992), forthcoming in *Anthropology Today*.

44. See Terence Turner's account of his long-standing collaboration with the Kayapo in "Visual Media, Cultural Politics, and Anthropological Practice," *The Independent* 14, no. 1 (January–February 1991).

45. Castañeda, *Utopia Unarmed*, p. 298.

46. See Paulo Emílio Salles Gomes's "Cinema: A Trajectory within Underdevelopment," in this volume.

47. See José Inácio de Melo Souza, "A Morte e as Mortes do Cinema Brasileiro e Outras Histórias de Arrepiar," in *Revista USP*, no. 19 (September–October–November 1993).

The Contributors

JOAQUIM PEDRO DE ANDRADE (1932–1988) was one of the original participants in the Cinema Novo movement. His filmography includes *O Padre e a Moça* ("The Priest and the Girl," 1965), *Macunaíma* (1969), *Guerra Conjugal* ("Conjugal War," 1974), and *O Homem do Pau-Brasil* ("The Brazil-Wood Man," 1981).

SÉRGIO AUGUSTO has written film criticism for a wide variety of publications, most recently as a regular columnist for *A Folha de São Paulo*. He is the author of a book on the *chanchadas* (*Este Mundo É um Pandeiro*, 1989).

JOSÉ CARLOS AVELLAR is the author of *Imagem e Som/Imagem e Ação/Imaginação* (1982) and the editor of the film journal *Cadernos de Crítica*. He has written on the political aesthetics of Latin American cinema, and is currently cultural director of RioFilme.

JEAN-CLAUDE BERNARDET teaches in the School of Communications at the University of São Paulo. He is the author of many books on Brazilian cinema, including *Brasil em Tempo de Cinema* (1967), *Trajetória Crítica* (1978), *Cinema Brasileiro: Propostas para uma História* (1979), *Vôo dos Anjos* (1992), and *O Autor no Cinema* (1994).

GRAHAM BRUCE, a film professor in his native Australia, is the author of *Bernard Herrmann: Film Music and Narrative* (1985).

TERRY CARLSON did his graduate work in cinema studies at New York University.

GUSTAVO DAHL's filmography includes *O Bravo Guerreiro* (1968), *Uirá, Um Indio em Busca de Deus* (1972), and *Tensão no Rio* (1982). From 1974 to 1979 he was head of the distribution section of Embrafilme.

CARLOS DIEGUES, an original participant in the Cinema Novo movement, is the director of, among others, *Ganga Zumba* (1963), *A Grande Cidade* (1965), *Os Herdeiros* (1968), *Xica da Silva* (1976), *Bye Bye Brasil* (1979), *Quilombo* (1983), *Dias Melhores Virão* (1988), and *Veja Esta Canção* (1994).

CARLOS ESTEVAM was executive director of the Popular Centers of Culture of the National Students' Union in the early 1960s. He has been Secretary of Education for the State of São Paulo.

ROBERTO FARIAS has long worked as a producer and director. Among his films are *Assalto ao Trem Pagador* (1962), *Selva Trágica* (1964), and *Para Frente Brasil* (1981). In 1974 he became director of Embrafilme.

MARIA RITA GALVÃO teaches film history in the School of Communications of the University of São Paulo. The author of *Cinema Paulistano* (1975), she has done research on the life and work of Alberto Cavalcánti.

PAULO EMÍLIO SALLES GOMES was a leading Brazilian intellectual from the 1940s until his death in 1977. The author of a seminal critical biography of Jean Vigo, Paulo Emílio helped found the Film Department of the University of Brasília and later the Cinema sector of the School of Communications of the University of São Paulo. Among his other books are *Panorama do Cinema Brasileiro* (coauthored with Adhemar Gonzaga) and *Humberto Mauro, Cataguases, Cinearte* (1974).

The filmography of Mozambican-born Cinema Novo participant RUI GUERRA includes *Os Cafajestes* (1962), *Os Fuzis* (1963), *Os Deuses e os Mortos* (1970), *A Queda* (1976), *Eréndira* (1982), *Malandro* (1985), and *Kuarup* (1988).

ARNALDO JABOR directed *Opinião Pública* (1967), *Pindorama* (1970), *Toda Nudez Será Castigada* (1973), *Tudo Bem* (1978), *Eu Te Amo* (1980), and *Eu Sei que Vou te Amar* (1984). Along with making films, he writes a regular column for *A Folha de São Paulo*.

MARSHA KINDER teaches film at the University of Southern California. Among her books are *Self and Cinema: A Transformationalist Approach* (coauthored with Beverle Houston, 1979), *Playing with Power in Movies, Television, and Video Games* (1991), and *Blood Cinema: The Reconstruction of National Identity in Spain* (1993).

ELIZABETH MERENA, who did her graduate work in Cinema Studies at New York University, is currently an administrator with the New York State Council on the Arts.

ELICE MUNERATO is a journalist from Rio de Janeiro.

MARIA HELENA DARCY DE OLIVEIRA teaches film in Rio de Janeiro.

RICHARD PEÑA is Director of the New York Film Festival and of the Walter Reade Theatre. He has published widely on international cinema and teaches regularly at Columbia University and New York University.

The filmography of GLAUBER ROCHA (1939–1981) includes *Barravento* (1962), *Deus e Diabo na Terra do Sol* (1963), *Terra em Transe* (1966), *Antônio das Mortes* (1968), *O Leão das Sete Cabezas* (1969), *Cabezas Cortadas* (1970), and *Idade da Terra* (1980).

ROBERTO SCHWARZ is the author of a number of books on Brazilian literature and literary theory, such as *Ao Vencedor as Batatas* (1978), *Pai de Família* (1979), and *Que Horas São* (1987). *Misplaced Ideas*, a collection of his essays, was published by Verso in 1992.

The filmography of ROGÉRIO SGANZERLA includes *O Bandido da Luz Vermelha* (1968), *A Mulher de Todos* (1969), *O Abismo* (1978), *Nem Tudo É Verdade* (1985), and *Tudo É Brasil.*

ALEX VIANY was the author of *Introdução ao Cinema Brasileiro* and director of *Agulha no Palheiro* (1952), *Rua Sem Sol* (1953), *Sol Sobre a Lama* (1963), and *A Noiva da Cidade* (1978).

JOÃO LUIZ VIEIRA, Ph.D. from New York University (1984), is Professor of Cinema Studies at Federal University of Rio de Janeiro (Niterói). Former Curator of the Rio Cinemateque, he is the author of *Espaços de Sonho,* a book about the architecture of movie palaces, and one of the authors of *D. W. Griffith and the Biograph Company.* In 1996 he will be teaching on a Fulbright at the University of New Mexico in Albuquerque.

ISMAIL XAVIER is Professor of Cinema in the School of Communications at the University of São Paulo. With a Ph.D. from New York University (1982), his books include *Discurso Cinematográfico* (1977), *Sétima Arte: Um Culto Moderno* (1978), *Sertão/Mar* (1983), and *Alegorias do Desenvolvimento* (1992). A revised version of *Allegories of Underdevelopment* is forthcoming from University of Minnesota Press.

Mixed Herbs

(Makes about 1/3 cup)

3 tablespoons dried sweet basil
1 tablespoon dried marjoram
1 teaspoon dried thyme
1 teaspoon dried oregano

★   ★   ★

Mixed Hot Spices

3 tablespoons chili powder
1-1/2 teaspoons cumin
3/4 teaspoon cayenne pepper
1/4 teaspoon turmeric

★   ★   ★

Mixed Sweet Spices

3 tablespoons cinnamon
1-1/2 teaspoons allspice
1-1/2 teaspoons ground cloves
3/4 teaspoon ground ginger
3/4 teaspoon ground nutmeg
3/4 teaspoon mace

Section One

RECIPES

Beef

§ One-Pot Pot Roast §
(Serves 2, with leftovers)

Hearty beef and vegetable goodness prepared in a single pot. You can add more vegetables, too—fresh or frozen peas, green beans, or other favorites. Save the leftovers for tomorrow's meal.

2 pound boneless beef chuck roast
2 teaspoons beef bouillon granules or 2 bouillon cubes, mixed with 1/2 cup water
2 tablespoons lemon juice
1/2 cup wine, red or white (optional)
1 small onion, sliced
1 carrot, sliced
1 potato, sliced (peel if you prefer)
1 clove garlic, pressed or minced
1 teaspoon Mixed Herbs
Bay leaf
1/4 teaspoon pepper

Preheat oven to 350°.
Place beef in baking dish.
Pour bouillon, lemon juice and wine over meat.
Sprinkle with herbs and pepper.
Add vegetables and cover
Bake 1-1/2 hours, until tender.

Tempt Your Appetite
When food and eating seem a bore, there are several ways to perk up your appetite. Suggestions:
—Take a walk. Even a short walk outside will stimulate your circulation and appetite.
—Set a special table. A pretty placement, a candle, a cloth napkin and "company" china can make a meal seem more appealing, whether you dine alone or with others.

§ Meat and Potatoes §
(Serves 1)

For those who love a stick-to-the-ribs standby.

1/2 cup cooked, diced beef roast
1/2 cup beef gravy (packaged or left over)
1/4 cup cooked, mashed potatoes (instant packaged
  potatoes allow trouble-free preparation, but are higher in
  sodium)
2 tablespoons milk
1 teaspoon butter or margarine
1/2 cup cooked carrots or peas
1/2 teaspoon Mixed Herbs

Preheat oven to 350°.
Mix beef with gravy in baking dish.
Add all other ingredients.
Stir and bake 15 minutes.

§ "Yoganoff" with Zucchini §
(Serves 2)

Enid Byron shares this taste-pleaser with her neighbors and gets
rave reviews. The stroganoff-like sauce is based on lower-calorie
yogurt. (For authentic stroganoff, Enid uses sour cream instead of
yogurt.)

1/2 pound sirloin or filet of beef, cut in strips
1 tablespoon vegetable oil
1 clove garlic, minced
1/2 cup fresh mushrooms, sliced
1 tablespoon butter or margarine
1 tablespoon flour
3/4 cup beef bouillon

2 tablespoons white wine (optional)
1 teaspoon catsup
1/2 cup sliced zucchini
1/4 teaspoon dill
1/4 cup plain yogurt

Sauté beef in oil in skillet, browning all sides.
Add garlic and mushrooms and sauté lightly.
Remove beef, garlic and mushrooms from pan and set aside.
Melt butter and add flour and catsup, stirring until smooth.
Add bouillon and simmer, stirring until thickened.
Add wine, beef and mushrooms, cover and simmer 45-60 minutes, until tender.
Add zucchini and cook another 5 minutes.
Stir in dill and yogurt and heat. Do not boil.

§ "No-Peek" Stew §
(Serves 2)

From a superb cook who enjoys an occasional no-trouble meal comes this unusual dish. Edith Owenbey puts it in the oven at lunchtime and its ready by evening. "The result is like something from a crockpot," she says.

1/2 pound lean stew beef, cut in bite-sized pieces
1 potato
1 carrot
Other vegetables, as desired.
1 can tomato soup, undiluted

Mix all ingredients and place in baking dish.
Cover and place in cold oven.
Turn oven to 250° and leave for 5 hours. If more liquid is desired add water.

§ Raisin Beef §
(Serves 2)

1 tablespoon vegetable oil
3/4 pound lean beef, cut in cubes
2 cloves garlic, minced
1 teaspoon Mixed Herbs
4 tablespoons liquid from canned tomatoes, or water
1 potato, peeled and sliced
1 carrot, sliced
Pinch nutmeg
1/4 cup raisins
1/2 cup canned tomatoes, drained (or fresh, chopped)

Sauté beef cubes in skillet until browned on all sides.
Add garlic, Mixed Herbs and liquid.
Cover tightly and simmer 30 minutes. Add more liquid if desired.
Add potato and carrot slices, cover and simmer 20 minutes, until
meat and vegetables are tender.
Stir in tomatoes, raisins and nutmeg. Simmer, uncovered, until sauce
thickens.

§ Snappy Ginger Beef §
(Serves 2)

2 slices bacon
1/2 onion, chopped
1/2 cup beef broth or bouillon
1/4 cup crushed ginger snap cookies
2 tablespoons brown sugar
1 tablespoon vinegar
3/4 cup cooked beef, cut in cubes

Sauté bacon in skillet until crisp. Remove bacon and crumble.
Place all other ingredients except beef in skillet.
Add bacon and simmer 10 minutes.
Add beef cubes and simmer until heated through.

§ Moon's Minestrone Soup §
(Serves 6-8)

A university professor, "Moon" often shares this favorite recipe with
his students. He advises cooking "lots of soup; it's good the next
day and easy to freeze for later."

    4 cups water
    1-1/2 pounds beef with bone (or stew meat)
    1/4 cup kidney beans
    1/2 teaspoon salt
    2 bay leaves
    1/4 cup chopped celery
    1 onion, sliced
    1/2 teaspoon hot pepper sauce
    1 16-ounce can tomatoes
    1 cup shredded cabbage
    3 carrots, sliced
    1/2 cup vermicelli pasta
    1 cup frozen peas
    1 zucchini, sliced
    Parmesan cheese, grated

Combine water, beef, beans, salt and bay leaves in kettle.
Heat to boiling and skim foam.
Cover and simmer 2 hours.
Add celery, onion, hot sauce, cabbage, tomatoes and carrots and
    simmer 30 minutes.
Add vermicelli, peas, and zucchini and simmer 15 minutes.
Remove bay leaves and serve, topped with Parmesan cheese.

§ Swiss Steak Special §
(Serves 2 generously)

Vegetables and meat cook together in a tomato-garlic sauce, combining flavors to create a superb meal in a single pot.

    1/2 pound round steak or flank steak
    1 tablespoon flour
    1/4 teaspoon pepper
    1/2 onion, sliced
    2 garlic cloves, pressed or minced
    2 tablespoons vegetable oil
    1 bay leaf
    1/2 teaspoon Mixed Herbs
    1 potato, chopped
    1 carrot, chopped
    2/3 cup tomato juice (or combined tomato sauce and
        water)
    1/2 teaspoon vinegar

Rub flour and pepper on steak.
Lightly brown onion and garlic in 1 tablespoon hot oil in skillet.
Remove from pan and set aside.
Brown steak on both sides in 1 tablespoon oil in skillet.
Add onion, seasonings, tomato juice and vinegar.
Cover and simmer 1 hour, adding more liquid if needed.
Arrange potatoes and carrots around meat.
Cover and simmer 30 minutes.

Buy Double, Save Trouble

When a recipe calls for one-half pound of ground beef, buy a full pound and make hamburger patties with the other half. Separate the patties with waxed paper and freeze for another meal.

§ Oriental Beef §
(Serves 2)

Crisp vegetables, tender beef, and the tang of ginger combine to create the flavor of the Orient. Substitute other vegetables according to taste: green beans, broccoli, water chestnuts and asparagus are good choices.

> 1 tablespoon vegetable oil
> 10-12 strips lean beef
> 2 tablespoons sliced onions
> 1 carrot, cut diagonally
> 1 celery stalk, cut diagonally
> 1/4 cup green pepper chunks
> 1 teaspoon chopped fresh ginger
> 1 garlic clove, chopped or pressed
> 1 cup beef broth or bouillon
> 1 tablespoon cornstarch
> 1 tablespoon soy sauce

Heat oil in skillet or wok.
Sauté beef strips until brown. Remove beef from pan.
Add vegetables and saute until tender but still crisp.
Stir in ginger and garlic.
Add broth or bouillon and beef, cover and simmer 5 minutes.
Mix cornstarch with soy sauce and add to beef mixture,
    stirring until thickened.

§ Meat Loaf §
(Serves 2, with leftovers)

A rich, beefy loaf with bread crumbs—easy to make by grating frozen French bread.

> 1 egg
> 1/2 pound lean ground beef

1/4 cup tomato sauce or stewed tomatoes
3 tablespoons bread crumbs
1 teaspoon soy sauce (optional)
2 tablespoons grated carrot
1 teaspoon lemon rind, grated or minced
1 clove garlic, pressed or minced
Dash pepper

Preheat oven to 375°.
Beat egg.
Add all other ingredients and mix with hands.
Place mixture in loaf pan.
Bake 45 minutes.

§ Beef 'N Beans §
(Serves 2)

1/2 pound lean ground beef
1 cup (9-ounce can) baked beans
1/2 cup crushed pineapple with juice
2 tablespoons brown sugar
1/4 cup catsup

Preheat oven to 350°.
Sauté ground beef in skillet until browned. Drain fat.
Add all other ingredients.
Pour into baking dish.
Bake 40 minutes.

Conserve Energy
On days when you have more energy, cook enough for more than one meal. Save the extras for the next day, or freeze to keep them for a day when you don't feel like cooking—or even thinking about it.

§ E-Z Ground Beef Casserole §
(Serves 2)

Esther MacLaren's one-dish meal is delicious and quick to fix-a good hot dinner after an afternoon with her book club.

1/2 pound lean ground beef
1/2 onion, chopped
1/4 cup white rice
1-1/2 cups water or beef bouillon
1 potato, peeled and cubed
1 carrot, sliced
1/4 teaspon salt
Dash pepper
2 teaspoons soy sauce

Preheat oven to 350°.
Brown beef and onion in skillet. Drain fat.
Mix all other ingredients, pour into baking dish.
Bake 30 minutes. (Dish may also be cooked on top of stove.)

§ Chili Hash §
(Serves 2)

Not too hot, not too mild— a beef chili dish that has a just-right touch of spice.

1/2 onion, chopped
1/2 green bell pepper, chopped
1/2 pound ground beef
1 tablespoon vegetable oil
1 cup tomato sauce
1/2 cup water
1/4 cup uncooked brown or white rice
1/2 teaspoon chili powder

1/4 teaspoon oregano
Dash cumin
Dash pepper

Preheat oven to 350°.
Heat oil in skillet and sauté onion, green pepper and beef until
  lightly browned. Drain fat.
Stir in all other ingredients.
Pour into oiled baking dish.
Cover and bake one hour, until rice is tender.

§ Goulash §
(Serves 2 generously)

Vera Porter contributes this recipe for a hearty, flavorful one-dish
meal.

1/2 pound lean ground beef
1/2 cup cooked macaroni
2 tablespoons chopped green bell pepper
1 tablespoon steak sauce
1 cup (1 small can) cream-style corn
1/2 can tomato soup
Dash salt and pepper
1/2 cup grated cheddar cheese

Preheat oven to 350°.
Brown ground beef in skillet. Drain fat.
Add all other ingredients except cheese and stir.
Place in baking dish and sprinkle with cheese.
Bake 45 minutes.

§ Deep-Dish Spaghetti Bake §
(Serves 2, with leftovers)

4 ounces spaghetti, cooked
1/2 pound lean ground beef
1/2 onion, chopped
1/2 teaspoon salt
1 clove garlic, pressed or minced
1/4 teaspoon oregano
1 teaspoon sweet basil
Dash hot pepper sauce
1 16-ounce can stewed tomatoes
1/3 cup chopped mushrooms, canned or fresh
1/2 cup grated Parmesan or Romano cheese (or other
  favorite cheese)

Preheat oven to 375°.
Sauté ground beef in skillet until browned.
Add onion and sauté until tender. Drain fat.
Stir in remaining ingredients except spaghetti and cheese and bring
  to a simmer.
Stir in spaghetti.
Pour mixture into greased casserole and place in oven.
Bake 20 minutes.
Sprinkle with grated cheese and bake 5 more minutes.

Exercise
Healthful eating is an important part of maintaining physical fitness. Another part is regular exercise. Scientists say that you may reduce the risk of coronary heart disease by exercising enough to burn 2000 calories per week. You'll feel better, too. Walking, bicycling and swimming are ideal and pleasant forms of exercise. If you walk briskly for 30 minutes, you will expend 150 calories. A leisurely swim will burn 200 calories in 30 minutes, and half and hour of golf takes 125 calories. If you are not accustomed to exercise, start slowly. Ask you doctor which exercise or sports are best for you; then get out and enjoy yourself!

§ Spaghetti With Meat Sauce §
(Serves 2)

1/2 pound lean ground beef
1 tablespoon vegetable oil
1/2 onion, chopped
1/2 green pepper, chopped
1 8 ounce can stewed tomatoes or 1 can tomato paste
    with 3 cans water
2 cloves garlic, minced
1 teaspoon Mixed Herbs
1/2 teaspoon sugar (optional)
4 ounces spaghetti

Sauté ground beef and onions in oil in skillet until meat is browned.
  Drain fat.
Add all other ingredients except spaghetti.
Cover and simmer 2 hours, stirring occasionally. Add water if more
  liquid is needed.
Cook spaghetti in boiling water in kettle just until tender. Drain.
Serve sauce over spaghetti and sprinkle with Parmesan cheese, if
desired.

§ Stuffed Green Peppers §
(Serves 2)

2 green bell peppers
2 tablespoons chopped onion
1 tablespoon vegetable oil
1/2 pound lean ground beef
1/2 cup dry bread crumbs
2 tablespoons grated cheddar cheese
1 teaspoon Mixed Hot Spices

1/2 cup tomato sauce
2 tablespoons water

Preheat oven to 375°.
Slice top off peppers. Discard stem and chop trimmings. Remove
  seeds and membranes from peppers.
Blanch peppers (about 4 minutes in boiling water).
Heat oil in skillet. Sauté onion and pepper trimmings.
Add beef and sauté until browned. Remove from heat. Drain fat.
Mix crumbs, cheese and seasonings and add to beef mixture.
Spoon into peppers.
Place peppers in buttered baking dish.
Mix tomato sauce and water and pour over and around peppers.
Bake 30 minutes.

Stretching
Our bodies were made to move. When we don't stretch and
move, we become less flexible and more prone to injury. Slow,
easy stretching of our major muscle groups relieves tension and
promotes agility.

You can stretch almost any time, anywhere. While watching
television, for example, take regular breaks in which you consciously reach and stretch your arms and legs. Gently rotate
your head; slowly raise and lower your shoulders; breathe deeply. You will feel a lovely sense of relaxation and well-being.

§ Hamburger Stew §
(Serves 2)

1/2 pound lean ground beef.
1 tablespoon vegetable oil
1/2 onion, chopped
1 celery stalk with leaves, chopped
1 patato, cubed, (peel if your prefer; it's not necessary)
1 garlic clove, sliced
1/4 teaspoon salt
Dash pepper
1 bay leaf
1 beef bouillon cube
2 cups water

Heat oil in saucepan.
Saute' ground beef in oil until browned. Drain fat.
Add all other ingredients.
Bring to a boil, then simmer for one-half hour, adding water
  if needed.

§ Prime Time Pizza §
(Serves 1)

Just right for a no-muss, no-fuss supper while you watch a favorite
TV program.

  4 biscuits from refrigerated package. (There are usually 10
    to a package—bake them all and save the extras for
    future meals).
  1/2 cup lean ground beef or pork sausage
  1 tablespoon vegetable oil
  3 tablespoons tomato sauce

Grated cheese
2 tablespoons chopped onion
1 tablespoon Mixed Herbs

Preheat oven to 400°.
Place biscuits on ungreased baking sheet. With water glass, press
    biscuits into flat circles.
Sauté ground beef and onion until lightly browned. Add herbs.
Top each biscuit with a spoonful each of tomato sauce, meat
mixture and grated cheese.
Bake 10-12 minutes.

Chewing Solutions
When chewing is a problem or dentures give you trouble:
eat a variety of softer foods (mashed potatoes, eggs, cottage
cheese, oatmeal, cream of wheat, applesauce, gelatin, banana).
Use tools for the work your teeth can't do. Grind or chop fruits,
vegetables and meats in a grinder, blender or food processor.
Your kitchen knife can help, too. Use it to chop raw foods finely
instead of serving them whole or sliced.

PORK & HAM

§ Midwest Pork Chops §
(Serves 2)

Good old-fashioned midwestern cooking makes use of regional foods, as in this succulent recipe from Fred Johnson, born and raised in Illinois farm country.

2 pork chops
1 tablespoon vegetable oil
2 teaspoons chopped onion
1/4 teaspoon sweet basil
1/4 teaspoon thyme
1/2 cup creamed corn
2 tablespoons chopped green bell pepper
1 tablespoon yogurt or cream
2 tablespoons flour
Dash pepper

Preheat oven to 350°.
Brown chops on both sides in oil in skillet.
Place chops in baking dish.
Mix all other ingredients and spread over chops.
Cover and bake 45 minutes.

Liquids are Important
Most people know the value of fiber in the diet, but many are not aware that with increased fiber, we need more liquids. Drink water at mealtimes and during the day—8 to 10 cups. Serve more than coffee with meals: bouillon, vegetable juice, fruit juice and soup are good choices. Plenty of non-alcoholic liquid intake will help prevent dehydration, constipation and illness.

§ Pineapple Pork Chops §
(Serves 2)

2 lean pork chops or shoulder steaks
1 tablespoon vegetable oil
1 tablespoon flour
1/2 cup canned crushed pineapple
1/4 teaspoon curry powder
1 teaspoon cornstarch
2 teaspoons brown sugar
2 teaspoons prepared mustard
1/2 cup wine or pineapple juice or water
Dash pepper

Preheat oven to 350°.
Sprinkle chops with flour, salt and pepper.
Brown chops in oil in skillet.
Place chops in baking dish.
Stir all other ingredients into skillet and simmer until slightly
    thickened.
Pour sauce over chops, cover and bake 30 minutes.

§ Cranberry Pork Steaks §
(Serves 2)

Combine meaty pork with the tartness of cranberries for the best
flavors of both. Save some pork for tomorrow's dinner, or cook
an extra steak.

2 lean pork steaks
Dash pepper
2 tablespoons jellied or whole cranberry sauce, fresh or
    canned
2 slices orange peel (or 1 teaspoon grated peel)

Place steaks in baking pan and sprinkle with pepper.
Top each steak with cranberry sauce and orange peel.
Bake uncovered for 45 minutes.

§ Pineapple Sweet and Sour Pork §
(Serves 2)

1/2 pound lean pork, cut into cubes
1 tablespoon vegetable oil
1/2 cup beef bouillon
Dash pepper
2 tablespoons chopped green pepper
2 tablespoons chopped green onion (scallion)
1/2 cup crushed or chunk canned pineapple
1 tablespoon sugar
1/4 cup juice from pineapple
2 tablespoons vinegar
1 tablespoon cornstarch
1 teaspoon soy sauce

Brown pork cubes in oil in skillet.
Add pepper and bouillon and simmer 30 minutes.
Add vegetables and pineapple.
Mix all other ingredients together, stir and add to pork dish.
Simmer 10 minutes, stirring.

Seek Variety
To maintain a balanced diet and fend off mealtime boredom, eat a variety of foods. Be adventurous and try a new flavor or dish or spice occasionally. Once you may have disliked cayenne pepper or yogurt or broccoli; but tastes change, and you may find new enjoyment that surprises you.

§ Sausage Pepper Sauté §
(Serves 2)

1/4 pound sliced pork sausage
2 tablespoons chopped onion
2 tablespoons chopped bell pepper
2 tablespoons chopped mushrooms
1 garlic clove, minced
1 tablespoon sherry (optional)
1 teaspoon Mixed Herbs
Chopped parsley

Sauté sausage pieces in skillet.
Add onions and peppers and sauté until golden brown.
Add garlic, herbs and sherry and simmer 5 minutes.
Sprinkle with parsley.

§ Curried Ham with Fruit §
(Serves 1)

Spicy and fruity, but not too sweet.
1 slice cooked ham
1/4 cup crushed pineapple with juice (or chopped peaches)
1 teaspoon lemon juice
1 teaspoon brown sugar
1/2 teaspoon curry powder

Heat oven to 350°.
Mix all ingredients except ham.
Place ham slice in baking dish or on piece of aluminum foil with
   sides turned up to form edges.
Pour sauce over ham.
Bake 15 minutes.

§ Succotash Ham §
(Serves 2)

1/2 onion, chopped
1 tablespoon butter or margarine
1/4 cup water
1/2 cup fresh or frozen lima beans
1/2 teaspoon Mixed Herbs
1 cup corn, fresh or frozen
1/2 cup diced, cooked lean ham

Saute' onions in butter in saucepan until yellow.
Add water, beans and seasonings and simmer, covered, 15 minutes.
Add corn and simmer, uncovered, 3 minutes.
Add ham cubes and heat.

§ Sugar-and-Spice Ham Loaf §
(1 small loaf)

Serve this lightly spiced ham dish hot or cold; leftovers make excellent sandwich fillings, spread with mustard or mayonnaise.

1/2 cup dry bread crumbs
1/3 cup milk
1 egg, lightly beaten
1 cup cooked ham, ground or chopped fine
1 teaspoon brown sugar
Pinch cloves
1/4 teaspoon dry mustard

Preheat oven to 350°.
Mix bread crumbs, milk and egg.
Add all other ingredients and stir gently.
Place in oiled loaf pan and bake 40 minutes.

§ Ham-Stuffed Squash §
(Serves 2)

1 acorn squash
2 tablespoons cooked lean chopped ham
2 tablespoons crushed pineapple *or* cranberry sauce
1 tablespoon brown sugar *or* 1 tablespoon orange juice

Preheat oven to 350°.
Split squash and remove seeds.
Place cut sides down on baking sheet and bake 30 minutes.
Mix all other ingredients.
Remove squash halves from oven, turn cut sides up and fill each
   with ham mixture.
Bake 30 minutes, until tender.

§ Supper Salad §
(serves 1)

1/2 cooked potato, cut in cubes
1 stalk celery, chopped
1 green onion (scallion), chopped
1/3 cup cooked, diced ham
3 tablespoons mayonnaise
1/4 teaspoon dill
1/2 teaspoon prepared mustard
1 teaspoon vinegar
Parsley

Combine potato, celery, onion, and ham.
Mix mayonnaise with dill, mustard, and vinegar.
Combine both mixtures and chill.
Garnish with parsley.

POULTRY

§ Chicken Curry §
(Serves 2)

1/2 cup cubed cooked chicken
3 tablespoons onion, chopped
3 tablespoons vegetable oil, butter or margarine
1 clove garlic, pressed or minced
3 tablespoons flour
1-1/2 cups chicken broth or bouillon
1 tablespoon curry powder
1/4 teaspoon tumeric
Dash cayenne pepper
3 tablespoons chopped apple
3 tablespoons raisins

Sauté onion in butter or oil in saucepan until golden.
Add garlic and apple, stir and remove with onion from pan. Set aside.
Stir flour and seasonings into hot oil and cook until bubbly.
Add broth, stirring until thick.
Add chicken, cooked onion mixture and raisins, and heat.
Serve with condiments such as coconut, chopped banana, peanuts
   and chutney.

Almost-Free Soup
Save the bones of poultry, meat or fish in a plastic bag in the refrigerator (or freezer, if saving longer than 2 days). When you've collected a few odds and ends of vegetables—half an onion here, a zucchini there—throw them together with 3 cups of water, parsley sprigs, a bay leaf, a squeeze of lemon, a garlic clove, and a dash of salt and pepper. Simmer for a couple of hours, discard the bones, and you'll have a nutritious, delicious meal that costs next to nothing.

§ Mustard Cream Chicken §
(Serves 2)

Dale Welton retired engineer, likes the tangy touch of mustard in this chicken dish, his kitchen specialty. "It not only tastes great, it's low in fat," he says.

3 - 4 chicken pieces, skin removed.
3 tablespoons Dijon-style mustard
1/4 teaspoon pepper
1/2 cup chicken broth or bouillon
1/3 cup yogurt

Spread mustard over chicken pieces and refrigerate 3 or more hours.
Preheat oven to 350°.
Place chicken pieces in baking dish and sprinkle with pepper.
Add chicken broth.
Bake 40 minutes, basting occasionally.
Remove from oven and stir in yogurt.
Return to oven and heat for 5 minutes.

§ Chicken Cacciatore §
(Serves 1-2)

2 -3 pieces chicken, skin removed
1 tablespoon vegetable oil
1 clove garlic, pressed or minced
1/2 teaspoon rosemary
2 tablespoons vinegar
1/2 cup red wine
1/4 teaspoon pepper
2 tablespoons tomato paste
3 tablespoons chicken broth or bouillon

Saute' chicken pieces in oil in skillet until lightly browned.
Add garlic and stir.
Add rosemary, vinegar, pepper and wine. Simmer, uncovered, to
   reduce liquid.
Add tomato paste and broth, or tomato sauce, and simmer 30
   minutes, turning chicken pieces occasionally.

§ Chicken Salad §
(Serves 2)

1/2 cup cubed cooked chicken
1 celery stalk, chopped
1 teaspoon lemon juice
3 tablespoons mayonnaise
1/4 teaspoon tarragon
Dash salt and pepper
1 hardcooked egg, cut in chunks
2 tablespoons chopped almonds or other nuts
Lettuce

Toss together all ingredients except egg, nuts and lettuce.
Fold in eggs and chill.
Arrange on lettuce leaves and sprinkle with nuts.

Spices versus Digestion
When you're trying to lower salt intake but find certain herbs
and spices upsetting, it's hard to avoid a bland, flavorless diet.
One answer: Experiment. If you can't tolerate one spice, try
another or try smaller quantities. Keep experimenting until you find what suits you and your digestion.

§ Chicken a' la King §
(Serves 2)

1 tablespoon butter or margarine
1/4 cup chopped celery
1 tablespoon chopped green pepper
1 tablespoon flour
1/2 teaspoon Mixed Herbs
1 cup chicken broth or bouillon
1/2 cup cooked cubed chicken
1/4 cup evaporated milk

Sauté celery and green pepper in butter in saucepan.
Stir in flour and herbs.
Add chicken broth and stir until thickened.
Add chicken and milk and heat to simmer.

§ Baked Chicken §
(Serves 1)

Versatile chicken is here popped into the oven and left to turn brown and tender. Save the bones for delicious homemade soup.

2 pieces chicken, with skin removed.
1 tablespoon vegetable oil
1 teaspoon butter or margarine
1/4 teaspoon Mixed Herbs
Dash pepper
1 garlic clove, pressed or minced
2 tablespoons lemon juice
1 tablespoon honey

Preheat oven to 350°.
Heat butter and oil in baking pan in oven until butter melts.
Sprinkle chicken pieces with herbs and pepper.
Dip each chicken piece in melted butter and oil and turn.
Bake 40 minutes.
Mix garlic, lemon juice, and honey in bowl.
Pour over chicken and return dish to oven for 10-15 minutes.

§ Ginger-Coconut Chicken §
(Serves 1-2)

2 pieces chicken with skin removed
1 tablespoon vegetable oil
2 tablespoons plain yogurt
1 tablespoon prepared mustard
2 tablespoons chopped or flaked coconut
1/2 teaspoon chopped fresh ginger
Dash salt

Heat oil in skillet.
Sauté chicken pieces until golden brown.
Pour off excess fat, cover, and cook over low heat 20 minutes.
Mix yogurt, mustard, ginger and salt and pour over chicken.
Continue cooking, uncovered, 5 minutes.
Sprinkle with coconut before serving.

Drugs and Alcohol

If you're on medication, avoid alcohol. It can be dangerous to your health to mix tranquilizers, painkillers, antibiotics, antihistamines or other drugs with alcohol. Don't drink while you're taking drugs without your doctor's specific approval.

§ Chicken With Greens and Tomato §
(Serves 2)

3 - 4 pieces chicken
2 tablespoons butter or vegetable oil
1 clove garlic, minced or pressed
1 green onion (scallion), chopped
1/2 green bell pepper, chopped
2 tablespoons chopped parsley
1/2 teaspoon Mixed Herbs
1/2 cup fresh or canned tomatoes, chopped

Preheat oven to 350°.
Sauté chicken in butter or oil in skillet until browned.
Place chicken in baking dish.
Add all other ingredients.
Cover and bake 40 minutes. If sauce is too thin, thicken with flour.

§ Chicken Liver Special §
(Serves 2)

1/4 pound chicken livers
1/2 onion, chopped
1 tablespoon vegetable oil
1/4 cup chicken broth or bouillon
1/4 teaspoon fresh chopped ginger
1/4 teaspoon sugar
1/4 teaspoon lemon juice

Sauté onion in hot oil until yellow.
Add livers and sauté 5 minutes.
Add all other ingredients and simmer 5 minutes. If sauce is too
  thin, thicken with 1 teaspoon cornstarch dissolved in water.

§ Stir-Fried Chicken §
(Serves 2)

1/2 cup chopped broccoli
2 tablespoons vegetable oil
1 garlic clove, minced
1/2 teaspoon fresh ginger, minced
2 tablespoons bean sprouts, fresh or canned
2 tablespoons water chestnut, sliced
1/4 cup snow peas (optional)
1/2 cup chicken broth or water
1 tablespoon soy sauce
1 cup cooked chicken, cut in strips

Heat vegetable oil in skillet or wok.
Add broccoli and cook, stirring, until bright green—about 3
   minutes.
Stir in garlic and ginger.
Add all other ingredients and cook, stirring, until heated through.

Vinegar, The Kitchen Helper
Lowly, inexpensive vinegar can be used in many ways other
than cooking. Use it (2 or 3 tablespoons) when washing dishes,
along with your regular detergent, to make dishes shine. Rinse
jars for food storage with a mixture of water and vinegar, to
eliminate odor. Clean appliances and countertops with full-
strength vinegar to cut through grease and grime. Wipe the
rubber tubing on the refrigerator door, as well as the refrigerator
interior, with vinegar; this helps prevent mildew. Freshen your
coffeemaker by running it through a cycle with vinegar and
water—then rinse. Use full-strength vinegar to remove fruit and
vegetable stains from fingers and dishes.

§ Stuffed Cornish Game Hen §
(Serves 2)

1 game hen (thaw if frozen)
1/2 onion cut in small chunks
1/2 celery stalk in chunks
Juice of 1/4 lemon
1/2 teaspoon Mixed Herbs
2 tablespoons melted butter

Preheat oven to 350°.
Place hen in small roasting pan.
Pour lemon juice into hen.
Stuff hen with onion, celery, herbs and squeezed lemon section.
Drizzle with melted butter.
Roast one hour, basting occasionally with pan juices.

§ Sweet and Sour Chicken §
(Serves 1-2)

2 pieces chicken, skin removed
2 tablespoons prepared mustard
2 tablespoons honey
2 tablespoons lemon juice
1 teaspoon soy sauce
1 teaspoon vinegar

Combine all ingredients in bowl.
Marinate in refrigerator for 1-2 hours.
Place chicken pieces on broiling pan.
Broil 10 minutes, basting with sauce occasionally.
Turn pieces and broil another 10 minutes.

§ Chicken Milano §
(Serves 2)

1 cup cooked chicken, cubed
1 tablespoon vegetable oil, butter or margarine
2 tablespoons chopped onion
1 tablespoon flour
Dash pepper
1 clove garlic, minced or pressed
1/4 teaspoon salt
1 cup chicken broth or bouillon
2 tablespoons peas, fresh or frozen
1 tablespoon sherry (optional)
2 tablespoons grated Parmesan cheese
1 cup cooked brown rice

Melt butter in saucepan.
Sauté onion and garlic in butter until golden (do not brown).
Add salt, pepper and flour and stir until bubbly.
Add broth and simmer, stirring, until mixture thickens.
Add peas, cover and simmer 5 minutes.
Add chicken and sherry and heat.
Spoon over rice and sprinkle with cheese.

Enjoy Every Mouthful
Eating well involves more than providing fuel for your body. It's a sensory experience meant to be savored. Eat slowly, taking the time to appreciate and enjoy your meal.

§ Salad Dressing Chicken §
(Serves 1-2)

2 pieces chicken, skinned
2 tablespoons oil-and-vinegar salad dressing
1 tablespoon vegetable oil

Coat chicken pieces with dressing.
Place in refrigerator 3-6 hours.
Sauté chicken in oil in skillet until browned.
Cover and continue cooking over low heat 30 minutes.

§ Tarragon Chicken §
(Serves 2)

4 pieces chicken
2 tablespoons butter, margarine, or vegetable oil
2 tablespoons flour
1/4 teaspoon salt
1/8 teaspoon pepper
1/8 teaspoon paprika
1/4 teaspoon tarragon

Preheat oven to 400°.
Melt butter or oil in baking pan in oven.
Mix flour and herbs in bowl.
Dip chicken pieces in flour mixture, covering all sides.
Place chicken in single layer in baking pan.
Bake 30 minutes. Turn chicken pieces and continue baking 20
   minutes, until tender. For crisp skin, broil 3-4 minutes after
   chicken is cooked.

§ Chicken Parmesan §
(Serves 1-2)

2 pieces chicken, skin removed
1/2 cup soft bread crumbs
1/4 cup grated Parmesan cheese
1 clove garlic, pressed or minced
1/4 teaspoon salt (1/2 teaspoon garlic salt may be
    substituted and garlic omitted)
Dash pepper
2 tablespoons vegetable oil or melted butter

Preheat oven to 350°.
Mix all ingredients except chicken and oil or butter in bowl.
Dip chicken pieces in oil or butter, then in crumb mixture, coating
    well
Place chicken in single layer in baking pan.
Pour any remaining butter or oil over chicken.
Bake 1 hour.

§ Fruit Juice Chicken §
(Serves 2)

As the chicken bakes, the fruit juices bubble around it, creating
a sauce that is tangy, with a hint of sweetness—a perfect complement to tender, moist chicken.

2 chicken breast halves, with skin removed
1 tablespoon melted butter or margarine
1/4 teaspoon salt
1/8 teaspoon pepper
1/2 teaspoon fresh chopped ginger (optional)
1/2 cup grapefruit juice
1/2 cup pineapple juice

Preheat oven to 350°.
Place chicken breasts in baking pan.
Pour butter over and sprinkle with salt and pepper.
Pour juices over chicken.
Add ginger.
Bake 45 minutes.

§ Jambalaya Chicken §
(Serves 2 with leftovers)

1 tablespoon vegetable oil
1 stalk celery, chopped
1/4 cup chopped onion
1/4 cup chopped green pepper
1/2 cup uncooked white rice
1 cup chicken broth or bouillon
1 clove garlic, chopped or pressed
Dash cayenne pepper
1 cup cooked chicken, cut in cubes

Sauté celery, onion and green pepper in oil in skillet until lightly
  browned.
Add all other ingredients except chicken.
Cover and simmer 20 minutes, until rice is tender.
Stir in chicken and simmer 5 minutes.

Be Sociable
Mealtime is a social time. You'll enjoy eating far more if you
have company. Invite a neighbor or friend to join you for dinner. Share a potluck with a neighbor. Cultivate new and old
acquaintances and keep your zest for food and friends alive.

§ Chicken-Stuffed Tomato §
(Serves 1)

1/3 cup diced, cooked chicken
2 teaspoons mayonnaise
1 teaspoon lemon juice
1 teaspoon chopped parsley
1/2 celery stalk, chopped
1 tablespoon chopped water chestnuts (optional)
1 fresh tomato
Lettuce

Combine all ingredients except tomato and lettuce.
Slice top from tomato and scoop out seeds and flesh, leaving thick
    shell.
Chop tomato flesh and add to chicken mixture.
Spoon into tomato shell and serve on lettuce.

§ Chicken Cobbler §
(Serves 1)

1/3 cup cooked, diced chicken
1 cup chicken broth or bouillon
1 tablespoon flour mixed smooth in 1/4 cup water
2 tablespoons frozen peas
1/4 teaspoon salt
1/4 teaspoon Mixed Herbs
2 biscuits, uncooked (packaged refrigerated or homemade)

Preheat oven to 400°.
Mix all ingredients except biscuits.
Pour into baking dish or pie pan.
Flatten biscuits slightly and place on chicken mixture.
Bake 15 minutes, until biscuits are golden brown.

§ Penny's Thousand-Year Chicken Soup §

Penny Avila, a gifted and well-known poet, says she has been cooking this delicious soup for "a thousand years." Her family and guests still love it. Refrigerate or freeze the unused portion for another meal.

Back and neck of chicken or turkey
2 whole onions, cut in chunks
2 stalks celery, cut in chunks
1 parsnip, chopped
1 turnip, chopped
2 carrots, sliced
1/2 teaspoon salt
Water

Pull and discard fat and skin from poultry.
Place chicken pieces in kettle and cover completely with water.
Bring to a boil and skim off foam.
Add all other ingredients.
Simmer 3 hours.
Discard bones before serving.

Freezer and Microwave: If You've Got Them, Use Them
Two conveniences that make life in the kitchen easier are the freezer and microwave oven. If you have either or both of these appliances, take advantage of them. Buy ground beef or chops in volume and freeze serving-size quantities. When you make soup, double the quantity and freeze half of it. Frozen foods thaw swiftly and cooking time is cut drastically with a microwave oven.

§ Turkey Parmesan §
(Serves 2)

1/2 pound ground turkey or 1 cup finely-chopped, cooked
   turkey
1 egg, lightly beaten
1/4 cup dry bread or cracker crumbs
1 tablespoon Italian-style salad dressing (or other favorite
   style)
Dash pepper
1 tablespoon vegetable oil
2 tablespoons tomato sauce
1/4 teaspoon sweet basil
2 tablespoons grated Parmesan cheese

Mix turkey with egg, crumbs, salad dressing and pepper and form
   patties.
Heat oil in skillet and brown patties on both sides.
Sprinkle tomato sauce on patties.
Sprinkle each patty with sweet basil and cheese.
Serve or broil 1 minute to melt cheese.

§ Turkey Tetrazzini §
(Serves 2)

4 ounces spaghetti, cooked
1/2 cup cooked, diced turkey
1/4 cup fresh mushrooms, chopped
2 tablespoons butter or margarine
1 tablespoon flour
1/2 cup turkey or chicken broth or bouillon
1/3 cup milk
1 tablespoon sherry (optional)

1/4 teaspoon sage
Dash salt and pepper
2 tablespoons grated Parmesan cheese

Preheat oven to 325°.
Melt butter in saucepan.
Sauté mushrooms and remove from butter
Stir flour into butter and heat until mixture bubbles.
Add broth and stir over low heat until thickened.
Add milk, sherry and seasonings.
Stir in turkey, mushrooms and cooked spaghetti.
Place mixture in baking dish and top with cheese.
Bake uncovered 15 minutes, until golden brown.

§ Turkey Patties §
(Serves 2)

1/2 pound ground turkey
1/2 teaspoon sage
1 tablespoon chopped onion
Dash salt and pepper
1 tablespoon vegetable oil

Mix all ingredients except oil.
Form patties.
Sauté oil in skillet 8 minutes on each side.

Buy Small

Buy only what you need, to avoid needless waste and expense. Unless you plan to use that extra cup of canned corn within a day or two, it's better to buy the smaller sized can. Otherwise it will probably sit in your refrigerator until it's too old to use.

---

§ Lo-Cal Turkey Breast §
(Serves 2, with leftovers)

Crisp on the outside, moist inside—without skin or salt.

Turkey breast (thaw if frozen)
1 cup water
1 clove garlic, minced
1 tablespoon chopped onion
1/4 teaspoon nutmeg
1/2 teaspoon Mixed Herbs
1/8 teaspoon sage
1/8 teaspoon pepper
1/8 teaspoon paprika

Heat oven to 350°.
Remove turkey skin.
Place turkey breast on rack in baking dish or roasting pan.
Pour water into pan (pan should be half-filled with water).
Sprinkle turkey with all other ingredients.
Bake 20 minutes per pound of turkey.

§ Turkey with Broccoli and Almonds §
(Serves 2)

Rosemary Webster finds this a flavorsome way to make use of left-over turkey. It's quick to fix and goes well with potatoes or yams. Serve it with a crisp green salad, and you have a fine meal.

1 cup cut-up cooked turkey or 3/4 cup ground cooked
    turkey
1/2 can (11-1/2 ounce size) cream of mushroom soup
1/4 cup water or chicken or turkey broth

1 tablespoon sherry (optional)
1/2 cup cut-up fresh or frozen broccoli pieces
2 tablespoons chopped almonds

Preheat oven to 400°.
Mix all ingredients except almonds.
Place in baking dish and bake 20 minutes.
Sprinkle with almonds.

Losing Weight

If you are heavier than your ideal weight, consult your doctor or dietitian and plan a weight-loss diet. If you exercise, eat wisely, and cut down on fats and sugar, the extra pounds will melt away. A few tips for losing weight:

—Don't skip meals. Eat three small meals a day and snack on low-calorie foods such as carrots, celery and fruits.

—Eat fish and poultry more frequently than red meat.

—Keep busy; don't eat out of boredom.

—Don't deprive yourself. With your doctor or dietitian work out a diet that includes your favorite foods.

—Avoid alcohol; drink plenty of water and fruit juices.

SEAFOO D

§ Fish Fillet Vinaigrette §
(Serves 2)

A low-sodium, low-cholesterol dish that gives a tangy boost to nutritious seafood. The sauce does double-duty: any leftover vinaigrette not cooked with the fish may be used as salad dressing!

2 fish fillets, fresh or frozen and thawed
1 tablespoon vinegar
2 tablespoons vegetable oil
1/4 teaspoon crumbled dry tarragon or 1/2 teaspoon fresh tarragon
1/8 teaspoon black pepper
Pinch paprika
2 tablespoons grated Parmesan or Swiss cheese (optional)

Heat oven to 400°.
Mix vinegar, oil tarragon, pepper and paprika to make vinaigrette.
Place 1 tablespoon vinaigrette in baking dish.
Place fillets in baking dish.
Spoon sauce over fillets until coated.
Bake 12 minutes, until fish is tender and flakes easily.
Sprinkle with grated cheese; return to oven to melt cheese.

Fish Oil

Remember the old-fashioned tonic, cod-liver oil? Scientists are finding the Grandma was right: Oil from fish may not have nutritional value, but supply substances that reduce blood pressure, lower cholesterol, and protect against some diseases. To get the benefits of "omega-3" fatty acids, many nutritionists recommend eating fish two or three times a week. Large quantities, such as those found in fish-oil capsules, are not necessary.

§ Fish Special §
(Serves 2)

1/2 pound white fish (halibut, snapper, cod, perch)
1/2 cup chopped onion
1 clove garlic, minced
2 tablespoons chopped mushrooms
1 tablespoon butter
1/2 cup spinach, fresh or frozen and thawed
1/2 teaspoon salt
Dash pepper
1 egg
1 tablespoon grated Parmesan cheese

Place fish in skillet of simmering water with slice of onion and
  lemon.
Cover and simmer 5-7 minutes.
Drain, remove fish from pan and flake with fork, discarding skin
  and bones.
Sauté onion, garlic and mushrooms in butter in skillet.
Add fish, spinach and seasoning and simmer 4 minutes.
Add egg and stir.
When egg is set, sprinkle with cheese.

§ Fish With Herbs §
(Serves 2)

1/2 pound fish fillets
1 tablespoon butter or margarine
2 tablespoons chopped onion
Dash salt
1 teaspoon Mixed Herbs
2 teaspoons lemon juice

1 teaspoon cornstarch
1/4 cup white wine or chicken or fish broth
1 egg yolk
1 tablespoon chopped nuts (optional)

Preheat oven to 400°.
Sauté fish fillets and onion in butter for 3 minutes, turning fish once.
Mix together lemon juice, cornstarch, wine and egg in saucepan and cook until thickened. Add herbs.
Place fish in baking dish and pour sauce over.
Bake until sauce bubbles, about 10 minutes.
Garnish with minced parsely.

§ Fish in Mushroom Cream Sauce §
(Serves 2)

1/2 pound fish fillets (any firm, white fish)
2 tablespoons butter or margarine
1/2 onion, chopped
1/2 cup chopped mushrooms
1 tablespoon lemon juice
1/2 teaspoon teriyaki or Worcestershire sauce
1/2 teaspoon prepared mustard
1/2 cup plain yogurt

Sauté onions and mushrooms in butter in skillet until lightly browned, and remove from pan. Set aside.
Cut fish into bite-sized pieces.
Sauté fish pieces in butter until golden brown.
Add onions, mushrooms and all other ingredients.
Stir and heat until mixture bubbles.

§ Dilly Yogurt Fish §
(Serves 2)

1/2 pound frozen fish fillets
1/4 cup dry white wine
1/2 chicken bouillon cube with 2 tablespoons water
  or 2 tablespoons chicken broth
1/4 teaspoon dill
Dash pepper
2 tablespoons plain yogurt

Place fillets in baking dish.
Pour all ingredients except yogurt over fillets.
Cover and leave to thaw at room temperature.
Preheat oven to 350°.
When fish fillets are thawed, bake 20 minutes, basting occasionally.
Drain liquid from cooked fish into saucepan and simmer until it
  reduces to about 1/3 cup. (For additional flavor, add a spoonful
  of chopped mushrooms and onions.)
Stir in yogurt and heat. Serve sauce over fish.

Accessorize

Just as a touch of jewelry adds interest to clothing, so "accessories" add interest to food. The possibilities are endless.
Try these, for example:
—chopped nuts on cooked broccoli
—cinnamon on yogurt
—dash of hot pepper sauce in tomato juice
—chopped chives over scrambled eggs
—mint leaves in cucumber salad
—chili powder in split-pea soup
—crushed ginger snap cookies on fruit

§ Spicy Red Snapper §
(Serves 2)

1/2 pound red snapper
2 tablespoons Worcestershire or steak sauce
1 tablespoon catsup
1 tablespoon vegetable oil
1 teaspoon vinegar
1/4 teaspoon curry

Cut fish into bite-sized pieces and place in greased baking pan.
Combine all other ingredients and pour over fish.
Broil 3 inches from heat for 4 minutes.
Turn and brush with sauce.
Broil 4 minutes longer, until fish is tender.

§ Ginger Snapper §
(Serves 2)

Not the cookie variety, but a well-seasoned, gingery red snapper,
its sauce an excellent complement to the nutritious fish.

1/2 pound red snapper fillet
1/4 teaspoon pepper
1 tablespoon vegetable oil
2 tablespoons chopped onion
1 clove garlic, chopped or pressed
1 teaspoon chopped fresh ginger
2 tablespoons sherry or white wine

Cut fish into strips or bite-sized pieces and sprinkle with pepper.
Sauté onion in oil in skillet until lightly browned.
Remove onion and set aside.

Sauté fish until golden brown.
Stir in ginger and garlic.
Add wine and simmer 5-8 minutes, until fish flakes easily with
   fork.

§ Baked Fish With Mushrooms and Tomato §
(Serves 2)

1/2 pound white fish fillets
2 tablespoons lemon juice
1 sliced tomato
1/2 cup sliced mushrooms, fresh or canned, and drained
1/2 teaspoon Mixed Herbs
1/2 onion, chopped
1 tablespoon vegetable oil or butter

Preheat oven to 350°.
Place fish fillets in baking dish and pour lemon juice over.
Add tomato slices, mushrooms, herbs and onion.
Drizzle with oil or butter.
Cover and bake 10 minutes.
Uncover and bake 10 more minutes.

Lemon, the Great Flavorizer
Many good cooks say their secret lies in that package of tangy
flavor, the lemon. Its juice and grated rind can enhance almost
any dish, from meat loaf to oatmeal cookies. To make a lemon
easier to squeeze, simmer the whole fruit in water for 5 minutes.

§ Foil Fish §
(Serves 1)

1 fillet of firm-fleshed white fish
1/2 lemon, sliced
1 tablespoon melted butter
1 tablespoon white wine, sherry or chicken broth
Dash salt and pepper

Preheat oven to 375°.
Place fish on sheet of aluminum foil.
Place lemon slices over.
Add other ingredients and fold edges of foil tightly over.
Bake 15 minutes.

§ Spicy Fish Stew §
(Serves 2)

1 cup (one 8 ounce can) stewed tomatoes with liquid
   (Cajun-style is best)
1/4 cup water
1 small potato, chopped
1/2 cup chopped celery
1/2 cup chopped onion
1/2 pound firm-fleshed white fish, cut in bite-sized pieces
1/4 teaspoon Mixed Hot Spices

Place tomatoes, liquid and water in saucepan and bring to boil.
Add potatoes, cover and cook until nearly tender (about 8 minutes).
Add all other ingredients, cover and simmer 10 minutes.

§ Curried Fish Bites §
(Serves 2)

1/2 pound white fish fillet, cut in bite-sized pieces
2 tablespoons flour
1 tablespoon wheat germ
1 teaspoon curry
Dash cayenne
2 tablespoons vegetable oil
1 tablespoon butter or margarine
1/4 cup chopped nuts
Parsley

Mix flour with seasonings.
Coat fish pieces with flour mixture.
Heat oil and butter in skillet.
Sauté fish until lightly browned on all sides, about 10 minutes.
Sprinkle nuts on fish and garnish with parsley.

§ Fish On Spinach §
(Serves 2)

1/2 pound white fish fillets
1 tablespoon lemon juice
1 cup chopped spinach, fresh or frozen and thawed
1 tablespoon vegetable oil
Dash salt and pepper
1/4 teaspoon nutmeg
2 tablespoons grated Swiss cheese

Preheat oven to 350°.
Sauté fish in oil in skillet until lightly browned.
Place spinach in buttered baking dish.

Place fish on spinach bed.
Sprinkle with seasonings and cheese.
Bake 15 minutes.

§ Fish-Stuffed Peppers §
(Serves 2)

2 green bell peppers
1/2 cup cooked fish, flaked
1/4 cup chopped onion
1/4 cup bread crumbs
1 tablespoon lemon juice
1/4 teaspoon salt
Dash pepper
1/4 cup tomato sauce
1/4 teaspoon dill

Preheat oven to 350°.
Cut tops from peppers and remove seeds and membranes.
Blanch peppers for 3 minutes in simmering water in saucepan.
Mix fish, onion, crumbs, lemon juice, salt and pepper.
Add dill to tomato sauce.
Stuff peppers with fish mixture and place in baking dish.
Pour sauce over.
Bake 20 minutes.

Grow and Snip Your Own
Fresh herbs add sparkle and verve to your meals, and the best way to get them is to grow your own. If you don't have out-door space, grow chives, marjoram and thyme in pots on your kitchen windowsill. (Don't overwater, or they'll be spindly.) When you want a spoonful, all you do is snip!

§ Salmon With Cheese §
(Serves 2)

Good as a casserole or spread, hot or cold, on crackers or toast.

1 tablespoon butter or margarine
1 tablespoon flour
1/2 cup canned salmon
Liquid from salmon and water to equal 1/2 cup
1/4 teaspoon dill
2 tablespoons bread crumbs, buttered
2 tablespoons grated cheese

Preheat oven to 400°.
Melt butter in saucepan.
Stir in flour, salt and pepper, and heat until bubbly.
Add liquid and stir until thick.
Add salmon.
Place mixture in baking dish or custard cups.
Top with bread crumbs and cheese.
Bake 15 minutes.

§ Salmon Steaks Superb §
(Serves 2)

2 fresh salmon steaks
1/4 cup sliced fresh mushrooms
1 tablespoon butter or margarine
1/4 cup white wine
Dash salt and pepper
Hollandaise Sauce (page 85)

Sauté mushrooms in butter in skillet. Remove mushrooms from pan and set aside.
Sauté salmon lightly (add more butter if necessary).
Add wine, seasonings and mushrooms and simmer 10 minutes.
Serve with warm Hollandaise Sauce.

§ Tasty Tuna §
(Serves 1)

Simple to prepare, yet packed with protein, vitamins, and flavor.

1/2 cup canned tuna fish
1/3 cup cracker crumbs
1 tablespoon chopped onion
2 tablespoons chopped celery
1 tablespoon mayonnaise, sour cream, or yogurt
1/8 teaspoon pepper
Slice of cheddar or Swiss cheese

Preheat oven to 325°.
Mix all ingredients except cheese in baking dish.
Top with cheese.
Bake 20 minutes.

§ Tuna Chowder §
(Serves 2)

2 tablespoons dry onion soup mix
2 cups water
Dash pepper
Dash cayenne
2 stalks celery, chopped
1/2 cup noodles

1 6-1/4 ounce can water-packed tuna
2 tablespoons frozen peas
1 egg yolk
1/2 cup light cream or milk

Combine soup mix and water and bring to boil in saucepan.
Add seasonings, celery, and noodles.
Cook uncovered 10 minutes.
Stir in tuna and peas and simmer 15 minutes.
Beat egg yolk with cream or milk and stir mixture into chowder.
Heat and serve.

§ Tuna-Vegie Dish §
(Serves 2, with leftovers)

1 celery stalk, sliced
1/2 tablespoon chopped onion
1/2 cup water
1/2 teaspoon Mixed Herbs
1 cup canned tomatoes
1/2 cup uncooked brown or white rice
1 can tuna fish, drained

Mix celery, onion, water, herbs and tomato liquid in skillet and
   bring to boil.
Add rice and bring to boil.
Cover and simmer 20 minutes for white rice, 45 minutes for brown.
Add tomatoes and tuna and heat.

§ Tuna Loaf §
(Serves 2)

Protein-rich, low in fat, and inexpensive, this loaf recipe was developed by Jacquelyn Bee, an energetic 82-year-old. She serves it with lemon wedges, green beans, and a mixed-fruit salad.

1/2 cup water-packed tuna fish, drained
2 tablespoons dry bread crumbs
1 egg, slightly beaten
1 tablespoon oats
2 tablespoons skim milk
1 tablespoon lemon juice
1 tablespoon chopped parsley
1 tablespoon chopped green onion (scallion)
1/4 teaspoon salt
Dash pepper
3 tablespoons soft bread crumbs

Preheat oven to 400°.
Mix all ingredients except soft bread crumbs.
Spoon into oiled loaf pan.
Bake for 20 minutes.
Sprinkle soft crumbs over loaf and return to oven for five minutes to brown, or brown under broiler.

§ Tuna on a Muffin §
(Serves 2)

1/2 can tuna fish, drained
2 tablespoons chopped celery
2 tablespoons chopped green or dry onion
1 tablespoon chopped dill pickle or 1/4 teaspoon dill
2 teaspoons prepared mustard

2 tablespoons mayonnaise
Dash salt and pepper
3 tablespoons grated cheddar cheese

Mix all ingredients except cheese.
Spoon on English muffins and sprinkle with cheese.
Broil until cheese melts.

§ Tuna au Gratin §
(Serves 2)

1 7-ounce can tuna fish, drained
4 tablespoons chopped onion
2 tablespoons chopped green pepper
1/4 cup mayonnaise
2 tablespoons dry bread or cracker crumbs
2 tablespoons grated Parmesan or other cheese

Preheat oven to 350°.
Mix all ingredients except crumbs and cheese.
Spoon into baking dish.
Top with crumbs and cheese.
Bake 20 minutes.

§ Shrimp-Corn Curry §
(Serves 2)

1/2 cup small cooked shrimp, canned or fresh
1 cup cooked corn
1/2 cup chopped celery
1/2 teaspoon curry powder
2 tablespoons mayonnaise

Dash salt and pepper
Lettuce

Mix all ingredients.
Place in refrigerator to chill.
Serve on bed of chopped lettuce.

Drugs and Food

When you have to take medication, be aware of how drugs interact with foods. What you eat has an effect on the way drugs behave in your body, and some drugs may promote dietary deficiencies. Three popular drugs, antacids, aspirin and laxatives, are examples. The aluminum hydroxide in antacids can contribute to phosphate deficiency. Aspirin can cause bleeding in the gastrointestinal tract. Laxatives can affect the absorption of vitamin D or deplete bone phosphorus. If you take lots of aspirin to ease arthritis pain, for example, you may need a diet higher in iron and should consult your doctor about it.

Eggs & Cheese

★ ★ ★ ★ ★

NOTE: Most physicians recommend limiting the consumption of eggs to 2 or 3 per week. Consult your doctor if you need to restrict your dietary intake of fats and/or cholesterol.

★ ★ ★ ★ ★

§ Pineapple Eggnog §
(Serves 1)

A chilled, fruit-sweetened eggnog is a winning choice for a quick dose of flavor and nutrition. Vary the fruit juices for an occasional change.

- 1 cup cold milk
- 1 egg
- **1 teaspoon sugar**
- 1 teaspoon vanilla
- 2 tablespoons frozen concentrated pineapple or other fruit juice
- Nutmeg

Place all ingredients except nutmeg in blender or food processor and blend until smooth.
Pour into glass and sprinkle with nutmeg.

Calcium in Your Diet

Dairy products are the best source of calcium, but they may not give all you need.If your doctor suggests calcium supplements, ask about the best quantity for you. Megadoses of calcium can increase the risk of kidney stones. (A man over the age of 51 should have 1000 milligrams of calcium a day; a woman needs 1500 milligrams a day.)

§ Macaroni and Cheese §
(Serves 2)

A rich, creamy, cheesy version of an old favorite. To add even more protein, stir in cubes of cooked chicken, turkey or ham or sliced frankfurters. For lower sodium content, use chicken or turkey, low-sodium cheese, and no additional salt.

> 1 cup cooked macaroni noodles
> 1 tablespoon butter or margarine
> 1 tablespoon flour
> 1 teaspoon dry mustard
> Dash hot pepper sauce
> 1/4 teaspoon salt
> 1 cup milk
> 1 cup grated cheddar cheese

Preheat oven to 375°.
Melt butter in saucepan.
Stir in flour, mustard and salt and heat until bubbly.
Stir in milk and cook, stirring, until slightly thickened.
Remove from heat and stir in 3/4 cup cheese and hot pepper sauce.
Add macaroni and mix.
Spoon into greased baking dish and sprinkle with remaining cheese.
Bake 20 minutes.

§ Onion-Pepper Omelet §
(Serves 1)

> 1/4 onion, sliced thin
> 1/4 green bell pepper, sliced thin
> 1 tablespoon vegetable oil
> 2 eggs
> 1/8 teaspoon nutmeg
> 1/8 teaspoon sweet basil
> Dash dill, salt and pepper

Heat oil in skillet.
Sauté onion and pepper slices until onion is golden brown.
Beat eggs lightly with fork or whisk and add seasonings.
Pour into skillet and cook over medium heat until eggs are set.
Lift edges occasionally to allow uncooked portion to pour into
  bottom of pan.
With spatula, fold omelet in half. Garnish with parsley.

§ Swiss Eggs §
(Serves 1)

1 hardcooked egg, sliced
1 tablespoon butter or margarine
2 teaspoons flour
3/4 cup milk
1/4 cup grated Swiss cheese
1/4 teaspoon dry mustard
1 tablespoon sherry (optional)
1 slice toast

Preheat oven to 350°.
Melt butter in saucepan.
Stir in flour and heat until bubbly.
Slowly add milk, stirring until smooth.
Add mustard and 2 tablespoons cheese.
Add sherry.
Tear toast into bite-sized pieces and place in buttered baking dish.
Place egg slices on toast, pour sauce over and sprinkle with remaining
  cheese.
Bake 10 minutes.

§ Tomato-Egg Bake §
(Serves 1)

1 large, fresh tomato
1 egg
1/4 teaspoon dill
1 teaspoon chopped onion
1 tablespoon grated cheese (any kind)

Preheat oven to 350°.
Slice top off tomato and scoop out pulp, leaving a thick shell.
Mix tomato pulp with egg and all other ingredients.
Stuff tomato shell with mixture.
Place in buttered baking dish and bake 15 minutes.
Top with additional grated cheese and return to oven to allow cheese to melt.

§ Broccoli and Egg §
(Serves 1)

1 tablespoon vegetable oil
1/2 cup chopped fresh broccoli
1/4 cup water
1 egg
Dash salt and pepper
1/4 teaspoon sweet basil
Pinch marjoram
2 tablespoons milk

Heat oil in skillet.
Add broccoli and stir for 1 minute.
Add water, cover and simmer for 5 minutes. Remove pan from heat.

Mix egg with all other ingredients.
Pour egg mixture over broccoli and cook over low heat until egg
is set—about 4 minutes.

§ Corn Pudding §
(Serves 2)

2 eggs, beaten
1 cup cooked or canned corn, drained
1 cup milk
Dash salt
Dash hot pepper sauce
2 tablespoons chopped green onion
1 celery stalk, chopped
1 tablespoon chopped green pepper

Preheat oven to 350°.
Mix corn, eggs and milk.
Add remaining ingredients and mix.
Pour into buttered baking dish.
Set dish in hot water in shallow pan.
Bake 40 minutes, until knife inserted in center comes out clean.
Let stand 5 minutes to set before serving.

Freeze Extra Eggs
If you have more fresh eggs than you will use within ten days
or so, break them into a glass or plastic container and place
them in the freezer. They will keep for weeks. (Don't try to
freeze eggs in the shell.)

§ Mushroom-Zucchini Frittata §
(Serves 2)

1/4 cup chopped fresh or canned mushrooms
2 tablespoons chopped onion
1/4 cup chopped zucchini
2 tablespoons vegetable oil
1 clove garlic, pressed or minced
3 eggs
1/4 cup milk or cream
Dash salt and pepper
1/2 cup soft bread crumbs
1/2 cup grated cheddar cheese

Preheat oven to 350°.
Sauté mushrooms, onion and zucchini in oil in skillet until golden
  brown.
Add garlic and stir.
Beat eggs with milk or cream, salt and pepper.
Add mushroom mixture, bread crumbs and cheese.
Pour into baking dish or oven-proof skillet.
Bake 30 minutes, until set in center and lightly browned.

§ Cheese Soubise §
(Serves 2)

A delicious version of a French country dish.

1/2 onion, sliced
3 slices green bell pepper
2 tablespoons butter or margarine
1 cup cooked rice (leftover or prepared from instant
  package)
1/2 cup chicken broth or bouillon
Dash pepper
2 tablespoons grated cheese

Preheat oven to 325°.
Saute' onion and pepper in butter in skillet until lightly browned.
Stir in rice, pepper and broth.
Spoon into buttered baking dish and cover.
Bake 40 minutes.
Add cheese and stir to melt.

§ Eggs Benedict §
(Serves 1)

This gourmet treat is as easy as stacking a sandwich.

English muffin, toasted
Bacon slice, cooked and crumbled
Egg poached in milk
Hollandaise sauce, canned or homemade (see below)

Place bacon and egg on muffin
Pour sauce over and serve.

§Easy Hollandaise Sauce §

1 egg yolk
1/2 teaspoon lemon juice
Pinch salt
2 tablespoons butter or margarine

Place yolk, lemon juice and salt in blender and blend until smooth,
   or use electric mixer.
Melt butter until bubbly.
Slowly pour hot butter into egg and lemon mixture while blending.

§ Easy Quiche §
(Serves 1)

It's easier to prepare than traditional quiche, but it's full of the same rich goodness.

    1 slice toast, broken into bite-sized pieces
    1 tomato, peeled and sliced
    2 slices bacon, cooked and crumbled (optional)
    1/2 cup grated cheese (Swiss or cheddar)
    1/2 cup milk
    1 egg
    Pinch salt and pepper
    Dash hot pepper sauce
    1/4 teaspoon prepared mustard

Preheat oven to 350°.
Place toast pieces in small pie pan or baking dish.
Add tomato slices and bacon.
Sprinkle with grated cheese.
Mix eggs, milk and seasonings and pour over other
   ingredients.
Bake 30 minutes.

No-Fat Cooking

To avoid using fats in cooking, spray the skillet or baking dish with a non-stick commercial spray when your recipe calls for a greased pan. Another way to avoid fats is by cooking with pans that have been treated with non-stick coating.

§ Egg-in-a-Nest §
(Serves 1)

Margaret Hoffman serves this, along with sliced oranges topped with powdered sugar, to her grandchildren when they come for a visit. "I eat it, too, without the salt," she says. "It's a good breakfast for any age."

> 1 tablespoon butter or margarine
> 1 slice whole wheat bread
> 1 egg
> Dash salt and pepper
> Pinch sweet basil or dill

With knife or cookie cutter, cut hole in bread.
Melt butter in skillet.
Place bread in skillet.
Break egg into hole in bread.
Sauté until light brown and turn.
Continue cooking to taste.
Sprinkle with salt, pepper and herbs.

§ Double Cheese Pudding §
(Serves 1)

Soft, cheesy, rich and tasty.

> 1 egg
> 1 green onion, chopped
> Dash salt and pepper
> 1/4 cup creamed small-curd cottage cheese
> 2 tablespoons grated cheddar cheese

Preheat oven to 350°.
Mix all ingredients.
Pour into buttered baking dish.
Bake 20 minutes.

§ Eggs with Corn and Bacon §
(Serves 2)

2 slices bacon
1/2 onion, chopped
1/2 green bell pepper, chopped
1/2 cup creamed corn
Dash salt and pepper
Dash hot pepper sauce
2 eggs, beaten

Fry bacon until crisp, remove from skillet and crumble.
Pour off bacon fat, leaving about 1 tablespoon in skillet.
Sauté onion and green pepper in bacon fat until tender.
Add all other ingredients and cook over medium heat until eggs
    are set.
Sprinkle crumbled bacon over eggs.

Think Zinc

A mineral that is often inadequate in our diet is zinc, which
is essential for many metabolic processes. It helps us resist
disease and infection. Meat, seafood and eggs are good sources
of zinc.

§ Chili Cheese §
(Serves 2)

This is a down-home favorite among those who like a spicy touch of Texas in their chili.

1 slice bacon
3 tablespoons chopped onion
3 tablespoons chopped green or red bell pepper
1/2 cup cooked kidney beans
1/3 cup grated cheddar cheese
1 fresh tomato, chopped, or 1/4 cup tomato sauce
1/4 teaspoon chili powder or Mixed Hot Spices

Fry bacon until crisp, remove from skillet and crumble.
Sauté onion and pepper in bacon fat.
Add all other ingredients and bacon.
Cook, stirring, 5 minutes.

§ ElRose's Bacon and Eggs §
(Serves 1)

ElRose Groves, hospitable hostess, serves this quick and tasty dish often to her Bed-and-Breakfast guests.

1 slice bacon, cooked until almost crisp
1 egg
2 tablespoons cottage cheese

Preheat oven to 350°.
Line custard cup or other small baking dish with bacon; place in circle around edge of dish.
Break egg into dish.
Spoon cottage cheese over egg.
Place in oven and bake 10 minutes or until egg is done as desired.
Serve with dash of paprika and parsley sprig for color.

§ Egg Foo Yung §
(Serves 2)

1 tablespoon vegetable oil
1/4 cup chopped onion
2 tablespoons chopped celery
1 clove garlic, chopped or pressed
1/2 cup chopped cooked shrimp, pork or chicken
2 tablespoons bean sprouts
3 eggs, lightly beaten
1 teaspoon soy sauce

Sauté onion and celery in oil in skillet until tender but crisp.
Add garlic, shrimp and sprouts and stir.
Mix eggs and soy sauce and pour over.
When eggs are set, fold in half, omelet-style.

§ Bacon and Potato Eggs §
(Serves 2)

1 potato, cooked and sliced
2 slices bacon
2 eggs
1 tablespoon milk
1/4 teaspoon Mixed Herbs
1/4 cup chopped tomatoes

Fry bacon in skillet until crisp.
Add potato slices and fry until lightly browned.
Mix eggs, milk, herbs and tomatoes.
Pour over potatoes and bacon.
Cook over low heat until eggs are set.

§ Yogurt and Egg Dressing §
(About 2/3 cup)

A combination of flavors that adds zest to any crunchy green salad. It's low in fat and sodium, too.

1/2 cup plain, low-fat yogurt
1 hardcooked egg, chopped
1 teaspoon curry powder
1 green onion, chopped
Dash pepper

Mix all ingredients and chill.

§ Cheese Puffs §
(Serves 1)

2 slices bread
2 slices Swiss cheese
1/2 cup milk
1 egg

Preheat oven to 350°.
Place cheese between bread slices, sandwich-style.
Place in buttered baking dish.
Combine milk and egg and beat lightly.
Pour milk and egg over bread.
Bake 20 minutes, until puffy.

Substitute Ingredients
Substitutes may be used for many ingredients in our recipes. Instead of egg, use frozen egg substitute; instead of yogurt, sour cream or sour cream substitute.

BREAD

§ Super-Muffins §
(12-15 muffins)

One bowl, one fork and a muffin tin—that's all you need to make these easy treats. They pack a lot of nutrition and fiber into a small space, and they freeze well.

    1 egg
    1 cup milk
    1/3 cup vegetable oil
    1 cup white flour
    1/2 cup whole wheat flour
    1/2 cup wheat germ
    2 tablespoons bran (wheat or oat)
    1/4 cup brown sugar
    1/4 cup molasses
    1/2 cup raisins
    1/2 cup grated apple
    1 tablespoon baking powder
    1/2 teaspoon salt

Preheat oven to 375°.
Mix egg, milk and oil in bowl.
Stir in all other ingredients, using a fork. Mixture will be lumpy.
Spoon batter into muffin tins, greased or lined with cupcake papers.
Fill 2/3 full.
Bake 20 minutes.

Bake Small
Keep a supply of small containers, saucepans and baking pans on hand, to make it easy to cook for one or two. Many dishes can be baked in custard cups, for example, which will also cut the baking time.

§ Bed-and-Breakfast Bran Muffins §

ElRose Groves and her retired minister husband, Everett, serve delightful breakfasts at their charming Bed-and-Breakfast cottage on Puget Island, Washington. One of ElRose's special treats is this bran muffin, easy to make because "the batter keeps for two to three weeks in the refrigerator. So I can serve fresh-baked muffins to our guests every morning."

> 1 cup boiling water
> 2-1/2 teaspoons baking soda
> 1/2 cup shortening or vegetable oil
> 1 cup sugar
> 2 eggs, beaten
> 2 cups buttermilk
> 2-1/2 cups flour
> 1 teapspoon salt
> 2 cups all-bran cereal
> 1 cup bran flake cereal
> 1 cup chopped dates or raisins

Add soda to boiling water and allow to cool.
Cream shortening with sugar (or mix oil and sugar).
Add eggs and stir in buttermilk.
Add flour and salt alternately with water and soda mixture.
Stir in cereals and dates or raisins.
Cover batter and store in airtight container in refrigerator. May be stored 2-3 weeks.
When ready to bake, preheat oven to 375°.
Spoon batter into greased muffin tins.
Bake 15-20 minutes.

Appetite Pepper-Uppers

Eat your meal in a different spot from your usual dining area. Move to a comfortable chair in the living room or sit near a window for a change.

§ Wheat Sticks §

Chewy and satisfying: a good substitute for bread or crackers.

1 tablespoon honey
1/4 cup vegetable oil
1/2 cup milk
1 cup whole wheat flour
1 cup wheat germ
1/2 teaspoon salt

Preheat oven to 325°.
Blend honey, oil and milk.
Add other ingredients and mix.
Knead lightly on floured board.
Roll dough into strips, 1 inch wide and 3 inches long.
Bake 25 minutes. (For crisp sticks, roll thin and bake 20 minutes.)

§ Cornmeal Biscuits §

Piping hot from the oven, Esther MacLaren's cornmeal biscuits go well with almost any meal. For a touch of the South, serve them with ham and honey.

1-1/4 cups flour
3/4 cup cornmeal
4 teaspoons baking powder
1/2 teaspoon salt
1 tablespoon sugar
4 tablespoons shortening or margarine
3/4 cup milk

Preheat oven to 450°.
Sift dry ingredients.
Blend in shortening or margarine.

Add milk.
Knead dough lightly.
Roll to 1/2-inch thickness and cut with 2-inch cookie
    cutter.
Place on baking sheet and bake 15 minutes.

§ Hazel's Quick Coffee Cake §
(8-inch-square baking pan)

Hazel Jensen first tried this recipe fifty years ago. It's been a breakfast
standby for her family, and an afternoon treat for many visitors,
ever since.

    2 cups flour
    2 teaspoons baking powder
    1/2 teaspoon salt
    1/2 cup sugar
    1/4 teaspoon mace
    1 egg, beaten
    1 cup milk
    2 tablespoons melted butter

Preheat oven to 425°.
Mix dry ingredients.
Add egg, milk and butter and mix.
Pour into buttered baking dish and sprinkle with topping.
Bake 20 minutes.

Topping

    2 tablespoons flour
    1/2 teaspoon cinnamon
    2 tablespoons brown sugar
    1 tablespoon soft butter

Mix all ingredients until crumbly.

§ Pineapple Danish §
(Serves 1)

1 slice whole wheat toast
2 tablespoons cream cheese or small-curd cottage cheese
1 slice canned pineapple or 2 tablespoons crushed
    pineapple
1/2 teaspoon cinnamon
Dash nutmeg

Preheat broiler.
Spread toast with cheese.
Top with pineapple and sprinkle with spices.
Broil until heated, about 3 minutes.

§ Oatcakes §
(6 pancakes)

A hearty, nutty version of the usual breakfast pancake, this one full of nutritious oats.

1/2 cup white flour
1/3 cup uncooked oats
1 tablespoon oat bran (optional)
2 teaspoons baking powder
1/4 teaspoon cinnamon
1/2 cup low-fat or skim milk
1 egg, beaten
1 tablespoon vegetable oil or melted butter

Heat griddle or skillet and oil lightly.
Combine all ingredients, stirring just until mixed.
Spoon batter on hot griddle to size of cake desired. Turn once, when
  edges are lightly browned.
Serve with jam, syrup, or puréed fruit topping.

Battle Cholesterol With Oat Bran

When you add a spoonful of oats or oat bran to a meat loaf, casserole, batch or cookies, or other food, you may be lowering your risk of cardiovascular disease—the disease which causes more than half of all deaths in the United States. Studies over the past several years show that water-soluble fibers, such as those contained in oats and the more concentrated oat bran, can help to lower blood cholesterol. And that means healthier arteries.

§ Orange-Honey Loaf §
(One 5x9-inch loaf pan)

An orange-flavored, cake-like bread that keeps well. Soaked with a marmalade glaze, it's delicious for breakfast, afternoon tea, or dessert at dinner.

> 1/2 cup (1 cube) butter or margarine
> 1/2 cup honey
> 2 eggs, beaten
> 3 tablespoons orange marmalade (low-sugar, if possible)
> 1-1/2 cups white flour
> 2 tablespoons baking powder
> 1/4 teaspoon salt
> 1/4 teaspoon baking soda
> 1 tablespoon grated orange or lemon peel
> 1/4 cup chopped nuts

Preheat oven to 325°.
Mix butter and honey.
Add eggs and marmalade and beat well.
Add flour, baking powder, salt and soda, and mix.
Stir in orange or lemon peel and nuts.
Pour into buttered loaf pan (5x9-inch).
Bake 1 hour.
Pierce top with fork at 1-inch intervals, and pour glaze over.

Glaze

> 2 tablespoons butter or margarine
> 2 tablespoons orange marmalade
> 2 tablespoons powdered confectioner's sugar

Melt butter in saucepan.
Stir in marmalade and heat.
Add sugar, stir and heat.

§ Blueberry Sweet Bread §
(One 9x5-inch loaf pan)

With blueberries available year-round, you can make this delicious bread any time. Esther MacLaren, who contributes the recipe, cautions that it's best to use frozen, unthawed berries.

2 cups white flour
1/2 cup sugar
2 teaspoons baking powder
1/2 teaspoon salt
1/2 teaspoon baking soda
2 teaspoons grated orange peel
2 cups *frozen* blueberries
1 egg, lightly beaten
3/4 cup orange juice
2 tablespoons vegetable oil

Topping

3 tablespoons sugar
1 tablespoon cinnamon
2 tablespoons melted butter or margarine

Preheat oven to 350°.
With fork or wooden spoon, mix flour, sugar, salt, soda, baking powder and orange peel.
Fold in blueberries.
Add eggs, orange juice, and oil, stirring carefully.
Pour batter into greased 9x5-inch loaf pan.
Mix topping ingredients and sprinkle on bread batter.
Bake 50-60 minutes or until toothpick inserted in center comes out clean.

§ Best-Yet Walnut Bread §
(One 8x4-inch loaf pan)

Beth Donaldson perfected this recipe. She says, "It's festive enough for teatime, but don't let it fool you. This bread is hearty food and grand for lunchbox sandwiches." It's lower in fat than many sweet breads because it contains no butter or oil.

1 egg
1 cup sugar
3 cups sifted flour
2 tablespoons wheat germ
1 teaspoon salt
4 teaspoons baking powder
1 cup milk
1 cup coarsely chopped walnuts

Preheat oven to 350°.
Combine egg and sugar and beat well.
Mix in all other ingredients except nuts.
Stir in nuts.
Spoon into greased loaf pan and bake 1 hour.

Vitamin and Mineral Supplements: Do you need them?
The best source of advice on dietary supplements is your doctor or dietitian. Your balanced diet may be enough, or your individual needs may call for additional vitamins or minerals. Don't waste your money on unnecessary supplements, and don't endanger your health with megadoses. Get professional advice.

§ Granny's Baking Powder Biscuits §

1 cup flour
2 tablespoons wheat germ
1 tablespoon baking powder
1/2 teaspoon salt
2 tablespoons vegetable oil
5 tablespoons milk

Preheat oven to 400°.
Combine dry ingredients.
Mix oil and milk and stir into flour mixture.
Place between two sheets waxed paper and knead lightly.
Roll out 1/2-inch thick, and cut with biscuit cutter.
Place on baking sheet and bake 12 minutes, until browned.

§ Blueberry Oatmeal Muffins §
(Makes about 12)

Esther MacLaren, always noted for her efficiency, keeps the dry ingredients for this recipe in a quart jar in the cupboard. When she's ready to bake, all she has to do is add the liquids. The result is a flavorful, nutritious muffin that is good any time of day.

1-1/4 cups oats
1 cup whole wheat flour
1 tablespoon baking powder
1/3 cup sugar
1/2 teaspoon salt
1 cup milk
1 egg, lightly beaten
1/4 cup vegetable oil
3/4 cup blueberries, fresh or forzen

Preheat oven to 425°.
Combine dry ingredients.
Add egg, milk, oil and stir just until blended.
Stir in berries.
Spoon into greased muffin tins or tins lined with cupcake papers.
Bake 20-25 minutes.

§ Spicy Baked Pancake §
(Serves 1)

This light pancake puffs to a golden brown as it bakes. Philip Shaw, who contributed the recipe, doubles it to serve two generously when he's making a weekend brunch. Served with an assortment of jams, hot coffee, and a dish of fresh fruit on the side, it makes a toothsome meal that is easy to prepare.

1 egg, lightly beaten
1/4 cup flour
1/4 cup milk
1/8 teaspoon Mixed Sweet Spices
1 tablespoon butter or margarine
1 tablespoon confectioner's powdered sugar
Lemon wedge

Preheat oven to 400°.
Combine egg, milk, flour, and spices and mix to lumpy batter.
Melt butter or margarine in oven-proof skillet.
Pour in batter.
Bake 15 minutes, until pancake is golden brown.
Sprinkle with sugar and lemon juice.

Avoid Spoilage

As our senses dim with age, we run a greater risk of eating foods that have lost their freshness. Watch the dates on milk and yogurt cartons, and don't keep opened foods longer than a few days in the refrigerator. Fresh meat should not be kept longer than one or, at the most, two days before cooking. If in doubt, throw it out. Saving a few cents is not worth the risk to your health.

VEGETABLES & FRUITS

§ Mashed Potatoes Plus §
(Serves 2)

A soufflé-like dish that's full of dairy goodness. With a crisp green vegetable or salad, it makes a meal.

> 1/2 cup hot mashed potatoes (1 cooked potato or 1/3 cup instant packaged potato buds)
> 1/4 cup milk
> 1/4 teaspoon salt
> 1 tablespoon butter, melted
> 1 egg, separated
> 1 tablespoon lemon juice
> 2 tablespoons grated cheddar or Swiss cheese

Preheat oven to 375°.
Mix milk, salt, butter and egg yolks with mashed potatoes.
Beat egg whites until stiff peaks form.
Fold whites into potato mixture.
Stir in lemon juice.
Place in buttered baking dish and top with cheese.
Bake 20 minutes.

Contrast Aids Appetites
When you serve soft foods, such as mashed potatoes and gelatin salad, contrast them with crunchy dishes like cucumbers and broccoli. Contrast colors, too, so your plate will seem appealing. Foods come in so many colors, you can make your plate as colorful as an artist's palette—and that will please your palate.

§ Mildred's Tomato-Cheese Soup §
(Serves 1)

Mildred Waters, an active 90-year-old artist from Laguna Beach, California, often prepares this nutritious soup for a light supper.

    1/2 cup stewed tomatoes
    2 tablespoons Swiss or cheddar cheese, grated
    1 egg

Place tomatoes in saucepan, bring to boil and simmer to reduce liquid.
Add cheese.
Beat egg slightly and stir into tomato-cheese mixture.
Serve hot with buttered toast.

§ Ginger Carrots §
(Serves 1)

The gentle bite of ginger and garlic combine with the natural sweetness of vitamin-rich carrots for a taste-pleasing vegetable dish.

    1/2 carrot, cut in slivers
    1 tablespoon butter or margarine
    1/4 teaspoon chopped fresh ginger
    1 clove garlic, chopped or pressed
    1/4 cup white wine or water

Sauté carrot slivers in butter or margarine in skillet.
Add ginger and garlic and stir (do not brown).
Add wine or water, cover and simmer 5-8 minutes.
Remove cover and simmer until liquid evaporates.

§ Potato Nachos §
(Serves 1)

When you're in the mood for a quick, hot snack, try this nutritious version of nachos, the popular cheese-covered chips.

1 potato, cut in 1/4-inch slices (peel if desired)
1/4 cup cheddar cheese

Preheat oven to 375°.
Place potato slices in single layer on buttered baking sheet.
Bake 15 minutes.
Turn potatoes and sprinkle with cheese.
Bake 10 minutes.

§ Onions au Gratin §
(Serves 2)

Rich in flavor and distinctively spicy.

1/2 onion, chopped
2 tablespoons butter or margarine
2 tablespoons flour
Dash salt and pepper
Few drops hot pepper sauce
1/4 teaspoon cumin
1/2 cup grated cheddar cheese

Preheat oven to 350°.
Sauté onions in butter in skillet until tender and remove from heat.
Add all other ingredients, reserving 2 tablespoons cheese.
Place mixture in greased baking dish or custard cups and sprinkle
    with reserved cheese.
Bake uncovered 20 minutes.

§ Pineapple Beets §
(Serves 2)

1/3 canned pineapple chunks, drained
3 tablespoons liquid from drained pineapple
1 tablespoon vinegar
1/2 teaspoon cornstarch
1/4 teaspoon Mixed Sweet Spices
1 cup (1 small can) sliced beets, drained

Place all ingredients except pineapple chunks and beets in saucepan
and mix well.
Simmer, stirring, until thickened.
Add beets and pineapple and heat.

§ Vegetable-Rice §
(Serves 2)

1/4 cup uncooked rice, brown or white
1 tablespoon vegetable oil
1/2 potato, diced (peel if preferred)
1/2 carrot, diced (peel if preferred)
1/3 cup fresh chopped green beans (or 4 tablespoons
    frozen)
1/2 teaspoon Mixed Hot Spices
1 clove garlic, minced or pressed
1/8 teaspoon minced fresh ginger
1 cup chicken broth or bouillon

Heat oil in saucepan.
Add potato, carrot and beans and sauté, stirring, 1 minute.
Add all other ingredients except broth and cook 2 minutes.
Add broth and bring to boil.
Cover and simmer 20 minutes for white rice, 45 minutes for brown
    rice.

§ Quick-Stuffed Baked Potato §
(Serves 1)

1 medium potato, washed, unpeeled
1/4 cup cooked chili, with or without meat
3 tablespoons grated cheddar cheese

Preheat oven to 400°.
Bake potato 50 minutes.
Heat chili in saucepan.
Split potato; pour chili over.
Top with cheese.
Place potato on aluminum foil under broiler; broil until cheese melts.

§ Potatoes and Green Beans §
(Serves 1)

1/2 potato, sliced
1/4 cup fresh green beans, chopped
1 teaspoon butter or margarine
1/2 teaspoon dill
Dash salt
1 tablespoon grated cheddar cheese

Place potato slices in saucepan.
Place beans on potatoes.
Add water to cover (about 1/3 cup).
Cover, bring to boil and simmer 10 minutes.
Drain and add all other ingredients.
Cover and remove from heat.
Serve when cheese has melted.

§ French Onion Soup §
(Serves 1)

4 tablespoons dried onion soup mix
1/4 onion, sliced
1 tablespoon vegetable oil
Thick slice French bread
2 tablespoons grated Parmesan cheese

Prepare soup according to package directions, using 1 cup water.
Sauté onion slices in oil in skillet.
Add soup to skillet and simmer.
Place French bread in soup bowl and ladle soup over it.
Sprinkle with cheese.
Place under broiler a few seconds to melt cheese.

§ Summer Soup §
(Serves 2)

A chilled vegetable soup, perfect for a hot summer evening.

1 cup chopped broccoli
2 cups chicken broth or bouillon
1/2 onion, chopped
1 tablespoon butter or margarine or vegetable oil
1/4 teaspoon salt
Dash pepper
Dash nutmeg
1/4 teaspoon curry powder
1 teaspoon chopped parsley
1 tablespoon lemon juice

Sauté onion in butter or oil in skillet until tender.
Add all other ingredients except lemon juice.
Simmer 10 minutes.
Cool, then purée in blender or food processor.
Add lemon juice and chill in refrigerator 4 hours or more.

§ Creamy Tomato Soup §
(Serves 2)

A low-sodium special that costs little and is simple to prepare and home-made delicious.

> 1 tablespoon butter or margarine (unsalted if possible)
> 1 tablespoon flour
> Dash pepper
> 1/4 teaspoon dill
> 1/4 teaspoon marjoram
> 1 cup milk
> 1/2 cup tomato sauce
> Few drops hot pepper sauce

Melt butter in saucepan.
Add flour and pepper, stirring until flour bubbles.
Add milk and cook until thick, stirring constantly.
Add all other ingredients and stir until smooth. Heat but do not
   boil.

Emergency Planning
Be prepared for bad weather or days when you're unable to get to the grocery store. Stock an emergency shelf with nonfat instant powdered milk, peanut butter, canned soups and fruits, canned fish and stews. If you have a freezer, keep a week's supply of meat, bread and vegetables on hand. Cheese and milk may also be frozen.

§ Potato-Onion Soup §
(Serves 2)

Easy and quick to make with dried, packaged potatoes.

1/2 cup water
1/2 onion, chopped
1 chicken bouillon cube
1 cup low-fat or skim milk
1/2 cup instant packaged mashed potatoes
Chopped parsley

Combine water, onion and bouillon in saucepan and heat to
  boiling.
Stir in milk and instant potatoes and heat. Thin with more milk,
if desired.
Sprinkle with parsley and serve.

§ Pineapple-Carrots §
(Serves 1)

1/2 carrot, minced
2 tablespoons crushed pineapple, drained
1 teaspoon butter or margarine
Dash salt
1 tablespoon rum (optional)
1/4 teaspoon Mixed Sweet Spices

Preheat oven to 350°.
Steam carrots in saucepan with 1/4 cup water 10 minutes.
Place carrots and all other ingredients in buttered baking dish.
Bake 10 minutes.

§ Green Beans Parmesan §
(Serves 2)

Parmesan cheese dresses up an ordinary green vegetable and turns it into a party fare.

1 tablespoon chopped onion
1 tablespoon butter or margarine
1/2 cup green beans, fresh or frozen
3 tablespoons water
Pinch salt
1/4 teaspoon sweet basil, fresh or dried
3 tablespoons grated Parmesan cheese

Sauté onion in butter in saucepan until lightly browned.
Add all other ingredients except cheese.
Cover and simmer until tender, about 12 minutes.
Sprinkle with cheese.

§ Garden Stew §
(Serves 2, with leftovers)

This meal-in-a-dish is a favorite of Eudora Benson, a retired book-keeper who loves to eat but is much too busy planning her next travel adventure to spend much time in the kitchen. "Just remember, it's a quarter cup of everything," she says.

1/4 cup *each:*
  chopped broccoli, fresh or frozen
  grated cheddar cheese
  chopped mushrooms, fresh or canned
  evaporated milk
  bacon, fried crisp and crumbled (2 slices)
  chopped onion

Preheat oven to 350°.
Place broccoli in buttered baking dish.
Cover with cheese.
Add bacon and mushrooms.
Pour milk over all.
Bake uncovered 20 minutes.
Remove from oven, place onions on top, and bake 10 minutes more.

§ Fried Rice §
(Serves 2)

1 tablespoon vegetable oil
1 tablespoon chopped onion
1 tablespoon chopped green bell pepper
1/2 cup cooked rice, white or brown
2 tablespoons chopped, canned water chestnuts (optional)
3 mushrooms, sliced
2 teaspoons soy sauce
1 egg, lightly beaten

Sauté onion, green pepper and mushrooms in vegetable oil until
    tender but crisp.
Add rice, water chestnuts and soy sauce.
Cook 5 minutes, stirring often.
Add egg.
Cook 3 minutes, stirring constantly.

Appetite Pepper-Uppers

—Pay attention to how food looks, just as you do with guests.
A parsley garnish or a curl of orange peel add to the attractive
appearance of your meal. It will taste better if it looks good
to eat.

---

§ Carolyn's Ratatouille §
(Serves 8)

Our consulting dietitian makes a big batch of this tasty vegetable stew and freezes part of it. After a busy day, all she has to do is heat it for a nutritious supper. It has only 50 calories per cup.

1 eggplant, peeled and cut in 1/2-inch cubes
6 medium zucchini, peeled and sliced thickly
2 green or red bell peppers, seeded and cut in chunks
2 stalks celery, cut in diagonal slices
2 cloves garlic, minced
2-3 tablespoons chopped parsley
1/4 teaspoon pepper
1 teaspoon oregano
2 tablespoon vinegar
Dash hot pepper sauce
6 cups diced, canned tomatoes
2 cups chopped fresh mushrooms

In soup kettle, combine all ingredients except mushrooms.
Cover, bring to a boil, and simmer over low heat 20 minutes.
Remove cover and cook over moderate heat 15 more minutes,
   stirring to prevent scorching.
Add mushrooms, heat, and serve.

More Flavor, Not Less
Contrary to popular belief, older people do not usually need bland diets with fewer seasonings. The opposite is true; as our tastebuds become less sensitive with age, we need more flavor-enhancing, not less. Experiment with herbs and spices to find combinations that lend zest to the foods you eat.

§ Spanish Rice §
(Serves 1)

1 tablespoon vegetable oil
2 tablespoons chopped green bell pepper
2 tablespoons chopped onion
1 clove garlic, minced
1/4 teaspoon sweet basil
1/4 cup uncooked white or brown rice
1/4 cup chopped tomato, fresh or canned
1/8 teaspoon salt
1/8 teaspoon oregano
Dash pepper
1/2 cup water

Saute' green pepper and onion in oil in skillet until tender.
Add garlic and basil and stir.
Add all other ingredients and cover.
Simmer 20 minutes for white rice and 45 minutes for brown rice.

§ Corn Chowder §
(Serves 2, with leftovers)

Creamy and delicious with old-fashioned corn flavor.

2 tablespoons vegetable oil
1 tablespoon chopped onion
1 celery stalk
2 tablespoons flour
Dash pepper
1 chicken bouillon cube
1/4 cup water
1 cup milk
1 medium cooked potato, chopped

1 small can creamed corn
Chopped parsley

Sauté onion and celery in oil in saucepan.
Stir in flour and pepper and heat until bubbly.
Dissolve bouillon cube in water and stir into flour mixture.
Add milk and stir until thickened.
Add potato and creamed corn and simmer 2-3 minutes. Do not boil.
If chowder is too thick, add milk to thin.
Sprinkle each serving with parsley.

§ Lentils and Rice §

1/4 cup chopped onion
1/2 cup cooked brown rice
1/2 cup cooked lentils
1 egg, slightly beaten
1/4 teaspoon salt
1 clove garlic, minced
1/2 cup dry bread cubes
1/2 cup canned tomatoes
1/2 teaspoon Mixed Hot Spices

Preheat oven to 350°.
Mix all ingredients and pour into oiled baking dish.
Bake 30 minutes. Serve with catsup or heated, canned cream soup.

Chewing Solutions

Prepare soups, stews or casserole dishes instead of chops and steaks.

§ Lentil Soup §
(Serves 2 generously)

A soup with hearty, robust goodness—perfect for a cold winter's night.

  1/2 cup uncooked lentils
  4 cups water
  1 pork or ham bone
  1/4 cup chopped celery
  1/4 cup chopped carrots
  2 tablespoons chopped onion
  Dash pepper

Place all ingredients in large saucepan.
Bring to boil, turn down heat and simmer about 2 hours.
Remove ham or pork bone, cut any meat from bone and place in soup.
Season to taste.

§ Carrot-Raisin Salad §
(Serves 1)

  1 small carrot, grated
  1/4 cup raisins
  1/4 teaspoon fresh ginger, chopped
  1 teaspoon plain, low-fat yogurt
  Dash nutmeg
  Lettuce

To plump raisins, cover with water in saucepan and bring to boil.
Remove from heat and set aside 5 minutes, then drain.
Mix all ingredients and chill.
Serve on bed of chopped lettuce.

§ Apple-Carrot Slaw §
(Serves 2)

1/2 cup shredded cabbage
2 tablespoons grated carrots
1/4 cup nuts, chopped
1/2 apple, chopped
2 tablespoons raisins

Dressing

2 tablespoons yogurt
1/4 cup cottage cheese
2 tablespoons apple juice

Mix all ingredients except dressing.
Place Dressing ingredients in blender or food processor and mix
  until smooth.
Pour Dressing over mixed salad.

§ Waldorf Delight §
(Serves 1)

1/2 medium apple, chopped
1 teaspoon lemon juice
1 celery stalk, chopped
2 tablespoons mayonnaise
1 tablespoon yogurt
1 teaspoon honey
Lettuce

Sprinkle apple slices with lemon juice and drizzle with honey.
Add all other ingredients and mix well.
Serve on bed of chopped lettuce.

§ Chilled Bean Salad §
(Serves 2)

1/2 cup canned green beans
1/4 red onion, sliced thin
1/4 cup sliced mushrooms, fresh or canned
2 tablespoons vegetable oil
2 tablespoons vinegar

Dressing

2 tablespoons plain yogurt
1 tablespoon mayonnaise
1 clove garlic, pressed or minced
1/4 teaspoon dill weed
1/4 teaspoon lemon juice
1/8 teaspoon dry mustard

Mix all ingredients except Dressing.
Cover and marinate overnight.
Mix Dressing ingredients and chill.
Drain marinated salad, pour Dressing over and serve on lettuce.

Vitamin A: Good and Bad

Vitamin A is necessary to good health—but don't overdo it. An excess of vitamin A can cause headaches, nausea, diarrhea and even liver and bone damage. Ask your doctor or dietitian about vitamin A supplements. Daily servings of yellow and leafy green vegetables may supply all the vitamin A your body needs.

§ Golden Salad §
(Serves 1)

1/2 carrot, grated
1/2 orange, cut in sections
1/2 teaspoon grated orange rind
Chopped lettuce

Dressing

1 teaspoon honey
2 teaspoons vinegar
1/2 teaspoon soy sauce
2 teaspoons vegetable oil

Place carrot, orange and rind on lettuce.
Mix dressing ingredients and pour over.

§ Coleslaw with Pineapple and Carrots §
(Serves 2)

1/2 cup grated cabbage
1/4 cup grated carrot
1/4 cup canned crushed pineapple or chunk pineapple
1 tablespoon mayonnaise
1 teaspoon lemon juice
1 tablespoon liquid from canned pineapple

Mix all ingredients.
Chill and serve.

§ Classic Macaroni Salad §
(Serves 2 generously)

From Vera Porter's recipe file come this old favorite, a salad both smooth and crunchy, ideal for a summer supper.

1/3 cup mayonnaise
1 tablespoon vinegar
2 teaspoons prepared mustard
1/2 teaspoon sugar
1/2 teaspoon salt
1/8 teaspoon pepper
4 ounces elbow macaroni, cooked and drained
1/2 cup chopped celery
1/2 cup chopped green or red bell pepper
2 tablespoons chopped onion

Mix together mayonnaise, vinegar, and seasonings.
Add remaining ingredients and toss to coat well.
Cover and chill.

Freeze Chopped Onion
To avoid tedious chopping every time you need a tablespoon of chopped onion, cut up several at a time (a food processor is a big help with this) and place them in a container in the freezer. Or freeze small quantities in plastic bags so you'll have just the right amount for your recipes quickly available.

§ Grated Carrot Salad §
(Serves 1)

1/2 carrot, grated
1/4 cup grated zucchini
2 tablespoons walnuts or cashews (optional)
1 teaspoon honey
2 teaspoons vinegar
1/2 teaspoon soy sauce
2 teaspoons vegetable oil

Combine all ingredients and mix well.

§ Minty Fruit Salad §
(Serves 1)

Banana, orange, grapefruit, pear, melon, or other fruits (fresh, frozen or canned)

3 or 4 mint leaves, fresh or dried
1 tablespoon lemon juice
2 tablespoons plain yogurt

Chop fruit to equal 1 cup.
Mix fruit with mint and lemon juice.
Allow to stand 15 minutes.
Top with yogurt and garnish with mint leaf.

---

4 Food Groups
Every day eat at least one item from each of the 4 main food groups: (1) Milk and milk products; (2) Breads and cereals; (3) Vegetables and fruits; (4) Meat, fish, eggs and beans.

§ Baked Apple §
(Serves 1)

1 apple
1 tablespoon brown sugar
1 teaspoon butter or margarine
1/4 teaspoon cinnamon
1 teaspoon raisins

Preheat oven to 400°.
Core apple. (Or cut in half and scoop out core from each half.)
Place apple in baking dish and fill with sugar, butter, cinnamon
  and raisins.
Cover bottom of pan with water (1/4-inch deep).
Bake 30 minutes or until tender when pierced with fork.

§ Cranberry Pears §
(Serves 1)

1 fresh whole pear
1/4 cup cranberry sauce
1 tablespoon lemon juice
Dash allspice

Preheat oven to 350°.
Stand pear in baking dish.
Mix lemon, cranberry sauce and allspice and spoon over pear.
Bake 30 minutes.

Chewing Solutions
Avoid sweets, berries, nuts and other foods that stick easily
in teeth. When nuts are called for in the recipes in this book,
they are almost always optional.

§ Peachy Banana Shake §
(Serves 1)

1/2 cup chopped fresh peach (or 1 jar chopped or puréed
  baby food peaches)
1/2 cup milk, whole or skim
1/2 banana
2 tablespoons lemon juice
1/2 teaspoon minced lemon rind
Dash cloves

Mix all ingredients in blender or food processor until smooth.
Serve as drink or freeze as dessert.

§ Frozen Banana §
(Serves 1)

A treat any time of day. Freezing creates a special texture and brings
out the natural sweetness of the fruit.

1 ripe banana
Plastic wrap

Peel banana and cut in fourths.
Wrap in plastic and place in freezer.

Chewing Solutions
—Have your teeth and gums checked regularly by your dentist. If you have dentures, they may need to be replaced. Our gums and facial muscles change as we age, and dentures may not fit as well.

DESSERTS

§ Betty's Lemon Cake Pudding §
(Serves 3)

Betty Parkhurst says this tangy dessert has been a favorite with her family in Illinois for 40 years.

1/2 cup sugar
3 tablespoons flour
Dash salt
1 egg, separated
1/2 cup milk
2-1/2 tablespoons lemon juice
1 teaspoon grated lemon rind

Preheat oven to 350°.
Beat egg white until stiff peaks form.
In another bowl, mix sugar, salt, flour and lemon rind.
Add yolk and milk and mix well.
Fold in egg whites. Mixture will be lumpy.
Pour into buttered baking dish.
Set in pan of hot water and bake 50-60 minutes.

Convenience Foods?

Everytime we go to the supermarket, we see new products on the shelves, many of them "instant" packaged foods. Some offer a great saving in time and effort and are well worth the extra expense. Others are not only expensive, they may be high in sodium, fat and preservatives. Protect yourself by using fresh foods where possible, with the occasional addition of a favorite package.

§ Pineapple Betty §
(Serves 2)

Bread pudding texture, with a dash of fruity, spicy pineapple. Delicious when served warm with milk or ice cream.

1 slice stale bread
1/2 cup crushed pineapple
1 tablespoon brown sugar
2 teaspoons butter or margarine
1/2 teaspoon Mixed Sweet Spices

Preheat oven to 350°.
Cut bread into cubes and sprinkle in buttered baking dish.
Cover with pineapple and sugar.
Dot with butter and sprinkle with spices.
Bake 30 minutes.

§ Blueberry Flummery §
(Serves 2)

1 tablespoon cornstarch
1/4 cup sugar
3/4 cup water
1 cup blueberries, fresh or frozen
Juice and grated rind of 1 lemon
1/4 teaspoon Mixed Sweet Spices

Mix cornstarch and sugar in saucepan.
Add all other ingredients.
Cook, stirring, until slightly thickened.
Chill and serve alone or as a sauce on coffee cake, Vyra's Prune Cake
   (page 142) or Orange-Honey Loaf (page 101).

§ Caramel Custard §
(Serves 2)

2 tablespoons brown sugar
1 egg
1/2 cup evaporated milk (skim or regular)
1/3 cup water
2 tablespoons sugar
1 teaspoon vanilla
1 tablespoon rum (optional)

Preheat oven to 350°.
Press 1 spoonful of brown sugar into each of 2 custard cups.
Beat egg.
Add all other ingredients and mix until smooth.
Pour slowly into custard cups, over brown sugar.
Set cups in shallow baking pan and pour hot water in pan, around
  cups (about 1 inch water).
Bake 45 minutes.
Cool, loosen edges with knife, and unmold onto serving dishes.

Dishpan Hands?

Many of our recipes call for very few utensils and pans. To make clean-up even easier, line your baking pan with aluminum foil. For some firm-textured dishes, such as meat loaf and bar cookies, simply fold heavy-duty aluminum foil to create edges, and you have an instant, disposable pan.

§ Apple-Cran Crisp §
(Serves 3)

2 cups cooking apples, peeled and sliced
1 tablespoon lemon juice
3 tablespoons cranberry sauce, fresh or canned
3 tablespoons flour
3 tablespoons oats
1/4 cup brown sugar
1/4 cup butter or margarine
1 teaspoon Mixed Sweet Spices

Preheat oven to 375°.
Place apples and cranberry sauce in buttered baking dish.
Sprinkle with lemon juice.
Mix all other ingredients with fork or fingers and spoon over
   apple mixture.
Bake 30 minutes. Serve warm, plain or with milk or cream.

§ Apple Spice Cake §
(One 8-inch-square pan)

1/4 cup flour
1-1/2 teaspoons baking soda
1/2 teaspoon salt
1 teaspoon Mixed Sweet Spices
1 tablespoon cocoa
1/2 cup sugar
1/3 cup vegetable oil
1 cup unsweetened applesauce
1/4 cup raisins
1/4 cup chopped nuts (optional)

Preheat oven to 375°.
Mix flour, soda, salt, sugar, spices and cocoa.
In another bowl, combine oil and applesauce.
Add flour mixture and beat until smooth.
Stir in nuts and raisins.
Pour batter into greased 8-inch-square baking pan.
Bake 40 minutes.
Serve topped with applesauce.

§ Dessert Topping §
(Serves 2)

2 tablespoons ice water
2 tablespoons instant non-fat powdered milk
2 tablespoons sugar
2 tablespoon lemon juice

Slowly add powdered milk to ice water, beating until stiff peaks form
(about 10 minutes).
Add sugar and lemon juice.
Chill.

§ Macaroon Torte §
(One 8-inch-square pan)

Esther McLeod contributes this sweet and chewy, easy-to-make treat.

2 egg whites
1/4 cup sugar
1/2 teaspoon baking powder
7 saltines (soda crackers), rolled to make fine crumbs
1/4 cup chopped dates
1/4 cup chopped nuts

Preheat oven to 300°.
Beat egg whites until foamy.
Slowly add sugar and baking powder, continuing to beat until soft
  peaks form.
Fold in cracker crumbs, dates and nuts.
Spoon into buttered 8-inch square baking pan.
Bake 40 minutes. Serve plain or with ice cream or whipped
  topping, sprinkled with chopped dates or nuts.

§ Aunt Esther's Wacky Cake §
(One 8-inch square pan)

A chocolatey-good dessert in great demand for 3 generations of
Esther MacLaren's family reunions. Esther comments: "When I
first tried this recipe, I didn't believe it would work. But it does!"

  1-1/2 cups white flour
  1 cup sugar
  1 teaspoon baking soda
  3 tablespoons baking cocoa
  1 teaspoon salt
  1 teaspoon vanilla
  1 tablespoon vinegar
  5 tablespoons vegetable oil
  1 cup cold water
  1/2 cup chopped nuts (optional)

Preheat oven to 325°.
Sift flour, sugar, baking soda, cocoa and salt directly into 8-inch
  square baking pan.
Make 3 hollows in mixture.
In one dent, pour vanilla. In another dent, pour vinegar. In the
third dent, pour oil.

Pour water over all and stir until smooth.
If nuts are used, sprinkle over batter.
Bake 25 minutes.

§ Pudding Mix §

Make your own mix of dry ingredients and keep it on hand for almost-instant dessert preparation.

> 2/3 cup powdered milk
> 3 tablespoons cornstarch
> 1/3 cup sugar
> 2 cups water
> Dash salt
> Vanilla Pudding: 1 tablespoon vanilla flavoring
> Chocolate Pudding: 1/4 cup baking cocoa
> Caramel Pudding: 1/4 cup brown sugar instead of white

Mix all ingredients in saucepan and heat, stirring until thickened.
Chill and serve.

Vitamin D
A well-balanced diet and regular outdoor activity give most of us the vitamin D we require; high dosage supplements can be dangerous, for they may lead to kidney damage. Consult your doctor or dietitian before taking extra vitamin D.

§ Prune Whip §
(Serves 2)

1/2 cup cooked, drained, chopped prunes
2 egg whites
2 tablespoons sugar
Dash salt
1 teaspoon lemon juice
1/4 teaspoon chopped lemon rind
1/2 teaspoon cinnamon

Beat egg whites until foamy.
Add prunes, sugar, salt and cinnamon and beat until stiff peaks
  form.
Add lemon juice and rind.
Spoon into parfait or sherbet glasses and chill.

§ Oat Wheat Cookies §

1/2 cup shortening
1/4 cup butter or margarine
1/4 cup white sugar
3/4 cup brown sugar
2 eggs
1 teaspoon vanilla
1 teaspoon lemon rind, grated or minced
2 tablespoons molasses
1-1/2 cups white flour
2 tablespoons wheat germ
2 tablespoons oat bran
2 cups oats
1 teaspoon baking soda
1/2 teaspoon salt
1/2 teaspoon Mixed Sweet Spices

Preheat oven to 375°.
Mix shortening, butter and sugar and beat until creamy.
Add eggs, vanilla, and lemon rind.
Add all other ingredients and mix well.
Place walnut-sized pieces of dough on baking sheet.
Bake 12 minutes. (1 cup raisins, coconut, nuts or dates may be added
   to dough, if desired.)

§ Bernice's Oatmeal Cookies §
(About 75 small cookies)

Bernice Peck knows the value of oats to good health; she also knows
the importance of good taste. This cookie recipe is one of her
favorites.

   1 cup shortening
   3/4 cup sugar
   2 eggs
   2 cups oatmeal
   1 cup flour
   1/2 teaspoon baking soda
   1/3 cup milk (skim, low-fat, or whole)
   1 teaspoon cinnamon
   1 teaspoon vanilla
   1/2 teaspoon salt
   1/2 cup raisins, chopped nuts, or chopped dates (optional)

Preheat oven to 350°.
Beat shortening, sugar and eggs until creamy.
Mix in all other ingredients except nuts, raisins or dates.
Stir in nuts, raisins or dates.
Place spoonfuls of dough on baking sheet.
Bake 8-10 minutes.

§ Lemon or Orange Sherbet §
(Serves 2 generously)

A low-sodium, low-fat treat that tastes as good as the best iced desserts.

    1 egg, separated
    3 tablespoons sugar
    3 tablespoons lemon or orange juice
    1/2 teaspoon lemon or orange rind, grated or minced
    3 tablespoons water
    3 tablespoons instant non-fat powdered milk

Add water and powdered milk to egg white and beat until
  mixture forms stiff peaks.
In another bowl, combine egg yolk, sugar, lemon or
  orange juice and rind.
Fold yolk mixture into egg white mixture.
Spoon into shallow pan (or ice cube tray) and freeze.

§ Vyra's Prune Cake §
(One 8-inch-square pan)

A fruit-filled goodie that Vyra Hamilton often serves with tea and coffee to afternoon visitors.

    1/2 cup sugar
    2 tablespoons butter or margarine
    2 eggs
    1/2 cup cooked, chopped prunes
    1 teaspoon baking soda dissolved in 1 tablespoon prune
      juice
    1 cup white or whole wheat flour
    1 teaspoon Mixed Sweet Spices
    1 teaspoon baking powder

Preheat oven to 350°.
Beat sugar, butter and eggs until creamy.
Add prunes and juice with baking soda.
Add flour, spices and baking powder.
Spoon into greased 8-inch-square baking pan.
Bake 30 minutes.

§ Coconut Squares §
(One 8-inch-square pan)

1-1/4 cups white flour
1/2 cup (1 cube) butter or margarine
2 teaspoons brown sugar

Preheat oven to 350°.
Mix ingredients and press into baking pan.
Pour filling over.

Filling

3/4 cup brown sugar
2 eggs, lightly beaten
1 cup flaked coconut
1/2 cup chopped walnuts
1 teaspoon vanilla

Mix all ingredients and pour over first mixture in baking pan.
Bake 35 minutes.

§ Peanut Butter Squares §
(One 8-inch-square pan)

Chewy desserts with peanut protein, perfected by Hilda Janowski, 78 years young and still a peanut butter lover.

1/3 cup peanut butter, creamy or chunky style
1/3 cup butter or margarine
1/2 teaspoon vanilla
3/4 cup brown sugar
1/4 teaspoon salt
1 egg (or 1/4 cup frozen egg substitute)
2/3 cup white flour
1 tablespoon wheat germ
1/4 cup chopped peanuts (optional)

Preheat oven to 350°.
Mix peanut butter and butter.
Add vanilla, sugar, salt and egg and blend well.
Add flour and wheat germ and beat until smooth.
Stir in nuts.
Spread in buttered baking pan.
Bake 30 minutes.

§ Prune-Apple Bars §
(One 8-inch-square baking pan)

Natural sweetness sandwiched between nutritious grains.

1/2 cup brown sugar
2/3 cup white flour
1/2 teaspoon salt
1/4 teaspoon baking soda
1 cup rolled oats, regular or quick-cooking
2 tablespoons oat bran

1 teaspoon Mixed Sweet Spices
6 tablespoons butter or margarine, melted
1 cup applesauce, fresh or canned
1/2 cup cooked chopped prunes

Preheat oven to 375°.
Combine all dry ingredients.
Add melted butter and mix.
Spoon half of mixture into greased 8-inch-square baking pan and
   press with hand or spatula.
Mix applesauce and chopped prunes and spread over flour mixture.
Top with remaining flour mixture.
Bake 20 minutes, until golden brown.

§ Frozen Strawberry Pie §
(One 10-inch pie)

Vera Porter shares two of her favorite strawberry pie recipes. This
one calls for frozen berries, the next for fresh—each is delicious.

2 egg whites
1 teaspoon lemon juice
2/3 cup sugar (or 1/4 cup if berries are sweetened)
Dash salt
2 cups frozen strawberries, thawed
1/2 cup whipping cream
1 teaspoon vanilla
1 baked pie shell

Beat egg white until foamy.
Add lemon juice, sugar and salt and beat until stiff peaks form.
Whip cream and add vanilla.
Fold cream into strawberry mixture.

Spoon into pie shell. (Or spoon into dessert dishes and serve as
   pudding.)
Chill or freeze.
Serve garnished with strawberries and fresh mint leaves, if available.

§ **Vera's Fresh Strawberry Pie** §
(One 9-inch pie)

1 baked pie shell
1 cup fresh strawberries
2 cups vanilla pudding (packaged, or see recipe, page 139)
Whipped topping (page 137)

Stir berries into prepared pudding.
Spoon into pie shell (or serving dishes), top with whipped
   topping and chill.

§ **Star Cookies** §

Another of Vera Porter's specialties, these rich cookies are easy to
make and festive for holidays.

1 cup butter or margarine
2 cups white flour
1/2 cup sugar
1/2 cup finely chopped nuts
Chocolate candy "stars"

Mix all ingredients except chocolate.
Chill dough several hours or overnight.
Preheat oven to 350°.
Shape dough into walnut-sized balls and place on baking sheet.

Bake 10 minutes.
Remove from oven and press a chocolate star firmly into each cookie.
Return to oven for 5 minutes.

§ Cherry Crumb Crunch §
(One 8-inch-square pan)

Esther MacLaren's afternoon and after-dinner visitors give this unusual dessert a top rating. It gets compliments every time it is served.

1/4 cup butter or margarine
3/4 cup white flour
1/2 cup brown sugar
1/2 cup oats
1/2 cup chopped nuts (optional)
1/4 teaspoon baking soda
1/4 teaspoon salt
1/4 teaspoon cloves
1 can (16-ounce) pitted pie cherries, drained

Preheat oven to 350°.
Combine all ingredients except cherries. Mix with fingers until
 crumbly.
Spread 1/2 mixture in 8-inch-square pan.
Spoon cherries over.
Top with remaining crumb mixture.
Bake 30-35 minutes.

Food Storage
Use your refrigerator to store items often kept in the cupboard. Raisins, nuts, bread, coffee, jams and jellies, shortening and peanut butter will all keep longer if chilled.

§ Chocolate Applesauce Cake §
(One 8-inch-square pan)

Edith Owenbey says this recipe came from a pioneer family in Utah. Moist and spicy, the cake is as popular as ever. It keeps well, refrigerated.

    1/2 cup sugar
    1 cup white flour
    1/2 teaspoon cinnamon
    1/2 teaspoon nutmeg
    1/2 teaspoon cloves
    1-1/2 teaspoons cornstarch
    2 tablespoons unsweetened cocoa
    1/2 cup melted butter or margarine or vegetable oil
    3/4 cup unsweetened applesauce
    1 teaspoon baking soda

Preheat oven to 350°.
Mix sugar, flour, spices, cornstarch and cocoa.
Stir in butter or oil.
Add baking soda to applesauce and mix with batter.
Pour into 8-inch-square baking pan.
Bake 1 hour. (1 cup nuts, raisins or candied fruit may be added before baking, if desired).

§ Edith's Oatmeal Cookies §

Another of Edith Owenbey's contributions, these delectable morsels will help add all-important oats to your diet.

    1/2 cup white sugar
    1/2 cup brown sugar
    1/2 cup shortening
    1 egg